Follow the Roar

Follow the Roar

Tailing Tiger for All 604 Holes
of His Most Spectacular Season

Bob Smiley

An Imprint of HarperCollinsPublishers

HarperCollins books may be purchased for educational, business, or sales promotional use. For information please write: Special Markets Department, HarperCollins Publishers, 10 East 53rd Street, New York, NY 10022.

Portions of "Chez Tiger" reprinted courtesy of ESPN/Starwave Partners d/b/a ESPN Internet Venture, 2008.

FIRST HARPERLUXE EDITION

HarperLuxe™ is a trademark of HarperCollins Publishers

Library of Congress Cataloging-in-Publication Data is available upon request.

ISBN: 978-0-06-176397-7

08 09 10 11 12 ID/RRD 10 9 8 7 6 5 4 3 2 1

For Bruce Jenner.
You were right.

"Before starting out, however, I'd like to observe that experienced spectators realize that the least satisfactory way of watching a medal play tournament is to trek around the course with one particular pair of players. It's an accepted fact that walking 18 holes is more tiring than playing them."

—BOBBY JONES,
Augusta National Golf Club
Spectator Guide, 1949

Contents

Preface

February 24, 2008
11:20 am
Marana, Arizona

Stewart Cink lines up an uphill, five-foot putt for par. His opponent, Tiger Woods, is already in the hole with a bogey. Tiger's 4 up on Stewart, halfway through the 36-hole final of the Accenture Match Play. But it's not over. In fact, if Cink makes this, he can stall Tiger's momentum and cut into the lead, starting the last 18 holes a very catchable 3 down. A big putt, to say the least. He takes a practice stroke with his belly putter, then carefully rests it behind the ball. I look around to see if everyone else shares my suspense and notice I'm the only person actually watching Stewart Cink. I follow the gallery's eyes to the far side of the green to see what's so distracting.

Tiger Woods is putting on his watch.

Lonely at the Top

S omewhere just west of Orlando he was improving on perfection. On the driving range just steps
from one of his many houses, he was shaping shots
in the cool December afternoon. Left . . . right . . .
high . . . low . . . The finishing touches in his preparation for yet another season as the undisputed best
player in golf. And on his shoulders he seems happily
to carry the weight of a million fans, of billion-dollar
corporations, and of his own late father's expectations
not just to be the greatest golfer ever, but to do more
for humanity than any man before him.

On that same day, I'd been on the roof of our rented
single-story house in the bowels of L.A.'s San Fernando
Valley for forty-five minutes after having failed to fix
the air conditioner, the poorly balanced aluminum

ladder rocking back and forth in the breeze just out of reach of my right foot, while my wife, my two kids, and the collective universe were completely indifferent to the fact that I was both nowhere to be found and, in more ways than one, completely stuck. If you're ever feeling fragile about your life, I suggest you don't start by comparing yourself to Tiger Woods.

Yet I did. All the time. I couldn't help it. I'd been doing it since long before he ever showed up at the Greater Milwaukee Open in 1996 to utter his famous opening line, "I guess . . . hello, world." Tiger and I both played high school golf in Southern California—he in the city of Cypress, just south of L.A., and I in Ventura, just north of it. He was a grade older, and I specifically remember my sophomore year when my Buena High Bulldogs made it past the first round of regional playoffs. The question before our next tournament was not what the toughest team would be, but whether Tiger Woods would be there. Even then we knew he was special. And since we were high school boys, we hated him for it.

Tiger was a threat to everything all of us had decided went hand in hand with being a teenager—namely the overarching tenet to blend in with the crowd, a commitment threatened only by acne and grounded at all times in a general lack of self-confidence. When he made it to the U.S. Amateur in 1994, we followed him in the paper and on TV as he picked apart his opponents, famously saving the killing blow for the last few holes, when, at the precise moment that the little voice in his challengers' heads started to say, "You know, I could win this thing . . . ," Tiger would effectively tear out their souls with putts no kid is supposed to make, punctuating them with a fist pump that we read as pure aggression. And if you think those defeats don't leave scars, don't talk to Trip Kuehne, Tiger's victim in the finals in 1994. He never turned pro, and fourteen years after the loss, he still hasn't watched the highlights of the match. "I don't want to," he has said, with the same seriousness that someone who survived a plane crash might turn down the opportunity to listen to the last sounds from the cockpit voice recorder. Tiger wasn't just winning golf tournaments; he was crushing spirits.

So when Tiger's fame exploded two years later, a twelve-month span in which he won his third straight U.S. Amateur and sixth straight USGA title, dropped out of Stanford at the age of twenty, signed $60 million worth of endorsement deals, then proceeded to win the Masters by 12 shots, I had already staked out my lonely position as a golf fan who had no interest in watching Tiger Woods succeed. He was talented, but his path to greatness was so merciless and calculated—nothing resembling the country club gentility that typified the way I had been taught to play the game—that to me there would be nothing sweeter than spending my Sundays watching more amicable players challenge him shot for shot and then finish him off, leaving the great Tiger Woods to face the reality that even he can be beaten.

There was just one problem—in the eleven years of my golf watching since Tiger had turned pro, I'd never seen it happen. Never. I mean, I knew it *had* happened. In 1996, a journeyman named Ed Fiori had kept Tiger from winning his first PGA event at the Quad Cities Open. And at the Nissan Open in 1998, Billy Mayfair became (and remains) the only person to beat Tiger in a playoff. Just my luck, somehow I'd missed those Sundays. But I would never miss a major. Thirteen different times Tiger had entered the final round in the lead or tied for the lead, and do you know how many times he had won? Thirteen. Rooting against Tiger on Sunday was the equivalent of watching skeet shooting and rooting for the clay pigeons. Yet, inevitably as the sun set, there I'd be, watching Tiger once again raise a trophy in that obnoxious red shirt and flash that golf-ball white smile, a grin that translated in my head to three simple words: "Bob, you suck."

And so, as I sat on the roof of my house—unemployed, uninspired, out of shape, a once-dependable single-digit golf game in ruins—I finally had to embrace the idea that every person who'd ever taken on the number one player in the world (yes, even Ed Fiori and Billy Mayfair) had long ago reached: maybe Tiger Woods could teach me something.

Tiger himself has said that there's no better way to learn who someone is than by spending quality time in that person's presence. But considering his yacht is named *Privacy* and I didn't have much in the way of a journalistic pedigree (that is to say, I didn't have one), I felt fairly certain that I'd have to track Tiger the old-fashioned way, on foot, from the gallery.

When he arrived in Southern California later that month for his off-season invitational, the Target World Challenge, I was there—from the moment he stepped out of his courtesy car till the second he disappeared into the press tent. Tiger shot the lowest score I'd ever witnessed in person, a 62 and a tournament record. And what took place outside the ropes was just as entertaining. I was lectured by former Olympic Gold Medalist Bruce Jenner, who responded to one of my self-deprecating jokes with a stern, "Never underestimate yourself!" I overheard hysterical conversations, my favorite being the middle-aged guy who told anyone willing to listen that Tiger's ascent to stardom was a lot like Hannah Montana's and "you probably don't know this, but his real name is actually Elrod." By the end I found myself high-fiving grown men I'd never met and would never see again. I wasn't a Tiger fan, but I was struck by the impact he made on everyone else.

I wrote an article about the experience for ESPN.com, a minute-by-minute account of the day. Once it was posted on the site, e-mails flowed in. They ranged from jealous Tiger lovers who wished they had been there to righteous ones who thought I didn't realize that his real name is El*drick*, not Elrod. Mixed in was an e-mail from someone who posed a sincere and absurd question: "Are you going to be doing this all season?" *Yeah, right*, I thought. But over the next few weeks I couldn't shake the idea.

An entire season.

Every tournament.

Every round.

Every hole.

The proposition was intriguing because (1) I wasn't sure it was physically possible; (2) the 62 at the Target World Challenge had me wondering whether this was Tiger's year; and (3) I had no other marketable job skills. I'd spent the last four years writing sitcoms. I'd even had a little success, but every year there were fewer comedies on the air, and on December 14, 2005, the one for which I worked was canceled. I know the date because it was two days after my first child, Danny, was born. So every time someone asked me, "And how old is your son?" I wanted to answer, "Look, there just aren't any jobs right now!"

Coupled with this was the onset of the Hollywood writers' strike, which meant I wasn't allowed to work even if there were a job. When it wasn't resolved within the first few weeks, both sides agreed it was going to last months and possibly all the way to June. Danny would be two and a half.

The idea to follow Tiger for a year wasn't without its obstacles. My friend Andy, a corporate accountant with an admitted obsession with spreadsheets, ran the numbers in Excel and helped me see that even with some help, between traveling and supporting my family, we would run out of money sometime before the British Open in July. But I was convinced I could pull it off if I booked the cheapest flights, rented the smallest cars, and, whenever possible, stayed with friends, family, even strangers along the way.

Another problem was that despite having written a handful of golf pieces for ESPN.com, I had no special access, which meant that everything from getting into the events to keeping up with Tiger from the gallery was solely up to me. Success would require planning, self-discipline, and endurance. None of those was an adjective friends would ever insert in an acrostic of my name.

In the end I decided this was an adventure that needed to be taken. Not just for me, but for anyone who stood to gain something from following greatness. After all, how often does one have the chance to see a person do something better than perhaps it has ever been done before or will ever be done again?

At least that was how I pitched it to my wife.

And so, in the last week of January, I unearthed my work bag from the recesses of my trunk, bought a pedometer and a notebook, kissed my wife and kids, and hit the road. Tiger would tee off in less than twenty-four hours. I couldn't be late.

Follow the Roar

The Machine

The Buick Invitational

Torrey Pines Golf Course
La Jolla, California
January 24–27, 2008

When Torrey Pines Golf Course was refurbished back in 1999, workers discovered that rubble and pieces of old toilets had been used to build up the tees and greens, evidence to all that no matter how pretty the cameras make it look on TV, the home of the Buick Invitational and this year's U.S. Open is at its core a city-owned muni. My old boss Alan wasn't even that kind. "It's a dump," he had pronounced after a weekend trip to play it a few years back. I'd been to the Buick Invitational once before, back when my high school friend A.J. was in college just down the street at UC San Diego. At the time I hadn't been to a professional golf tournament in years, and A.J. had never been to one, a dangerous combination that led to me stupidly telling him that sure, he could go ahead and bring his camera. When A.J. tried to take a picture of Jeff Sluman (why he chose Jeff Sluman of all people remains a mystery) the marshals were all over him, forcing him to hand over his film as if he had just snapped a shot of Area 51.

Tiger Woods' memories of Torrey Pines were likely quite a bit fonder. For one thing, he'd won the Buick a total of five times, including the last three years. But his history there goes back a lot further than that. Every July when Tiger was growing up, his parents, Earl and Kultida, would pack Tiger in their car and head down the 405 freeway, eventually funneling into Interstate 5 in Orange County, then south past the double-boob-shaped nuclear power plant at San Onofre, through the coastal military expanse of Camp Pendleton, passing the bright yellow signs that warned them to watch out for illegal aliens crossing the highway, then finally west to Torrey Pines and the home of the Junior World Golf Championships, one of *the* premier events in junior golf. How premier? In 1984, David Toms won the 15- to 17-year-old division, a South African named "Ernest" Els won the 13- to 14-year-old division, and

Eldrick Woods won the 9- to 10-year-old division. He was only eight. A few years later, he was old enough to play the big course and made the adjustment, winning his age group in 1988, '89, '90, and '91. It was safe to say that Tiger Woods had plenty of positive memories to keep him coming back to San Diego.

Despite the city being just two and a half hours south of L.A., I couldn't remember the last time I'd made the drive. With two little kids, any trip longer than about an hour means trouble. My friend A.J., on the other hand, had never left. Nine years removed from college, he'd risen in the ranks as a mechanical engineer and was working on defense projects that he claimed he couldn't discuss with anyone, including his wife. As a result, any visit with him would inevitably involve some version of this conversation:

"Does your work involve missiles?"

"I can't really talk about it."

"So it *does* involve missiles."

"Stop it."

Our friendship went back to the fourth grade but was cemented a few years later when his parents bought the house next door. He was the smallest kid in the class, and I wasn't much bigger. Nevertheless, that didn't stop us from spending almost every summer afternoon between eighth and ninth grade shooting hoops in my driveway, determined to make the freshman basketball team in the fall. On most afternoons, the sound of one of us bouncing the ball on the cement was enough to draw the other out of his room. We played one-on-one, HORSE, even ran drills we'd learned in basketball camp, anything to improve our game. In early September, the coach's decision was taped to his classroom door. Neither of us made the cut. For two smart kids who had worked hard, it was the first time in our lives that we learned the grown-up lesson that sometimes you can't accomplish everything you want just by trying.

There's not much worse than failing alone, so the fact that both of us fell short made the disappointment manageable, and we instead retreated to the athletic skills we already had. I tried out for and made the golf team in the spring, and A.J. did the same in tennis. After high school, I went east to college and he went south. And after graduation, the real world took over. I met my wife, Hillary, got married, had two kids. He had one dog, then two, then married a pharmacist with a dog of her own. We'd spent the last few years talking more about getting together than actually doing it, and you can keep that up for only so long before friends morph into acquaintances or eventually disappear altogether. So when I called A.J. a few days before the

Buick Invitational to say I might need a place to stay, it was comforting to hear his answer: "Stay as long as you want." Theoretically, I could be going home Friday night if Tiger were to miss the cut. But Tiger doesn't miss cuts. Especially at Torrey Pines.

FIRST ROUND

It's 6:30 in the morning. Not many fans feel the need to arrive at Torrey Pines two and a half hours before Tiger's tee time. As I walk onto the property, the volunteer-to-spectator ratio is two to one, and workers compete over who can hand me the day's pairing sheet. On a grassy island in the parking lot, I sit and enjoy the quiet morning and the comings and goings of less famous golfers. Stewart Cink, six top tens last year but no wins, passes by in a pair of workout shorts carrying his own bag. Boo Weekley, a charmer from the Deep South, walks through security and has to show his ID, the camouflage shirt draped over his shoulder not doing much to scream PGA professional.

Tiger Woods, on the other hand, is nowhere to be found. An hour before his tee time, I move to the driving range where the photographers are antsy, so desperate for his whereabouts that one of them repeats the unhelpful rumor that his caddy had been seen going into the Lodge at Torrey Pines, but that he never came out, like one of the victims in Willy Wonka's Chocolate Factory.

Tiger reenters our lives on a golf cart, edging around the outside of the players' parking lot at top speed, buffeted on one side by his swing coach Hank Haney and in front by Steve "Stevie" Williams, his forty-four-year-old camera-crunching caddy, who, thanks to Tiger, is one of the wealthiest men in his native New Zealand. Secured between his legs is the gray-and-blue Buick golf bag belonging to his boss. Tiger sits stoically, hands on his knees, staring straight ahead. I'd hoped to draw some great insight from his entrance, about the beginning of the new season, but he goes by so quickly that all I can write down is: "Thursday: black shirt."

"Team Tiger" doesn't stop at the public bleacher end of the driving range, but continues up the cart path to the far end, behind security lines. It isn't just at tournaments that Tiger eschews the crowd's eyes. During practice rounds, Tiger always schedules his tee times at first light, knowing that he will be off the course before most fans have even found a parking spot. A marshal told me that they were out so early one day this week that Stevie spent the first few holes wearing an LED headlamp so he could read his yardage book. When fans eventually found Tiger, he didn't walk along the ropes and sign autographs like other players; he walked down the middle of the fairway, head down. I don't get it. Wouldn't the guy who had been trained to play through his own father's nutty intentional distractions (jingling change, toppling golf bags) benefit from playing under the microscope? And didn't he owe his loyal fans a lot more love than he gave? By comparison, the man of the people Phil Mickelson is with me on the close side of the range. When one father and son ask for an autograph, Phil turns and addresses them personally, saying, "I won't sign any right now, but I will after the round." Phil leaves people with hope. Tiger just leaves.

I can't lose him this quickly, not this early in the year. There are only two ways to get closer. One is to exit the tournament grounds altogether and watch Tiger from Torrey Pines Road, the main artery just east of the range that connects the northern town of Del Mar with La Jolla to the south. When I drove down it at 6:25 this morning, the lure of watching pro golfers beat balls for free had already attracted the attention of a handful of bicyclists and joggers who had decided that was a lot more fun than actual exercise. The other option is to somehow bypass security, find a back way to the far side of the range, and see Tiger up close. Chalk it up to early-season bravado, but I choose the latter. I stride down the empty 18th hole on Torrey Pines' North Course, keeping the range on my right up the hill. Near the tee box I cut back across, through the low-rent dirt lot where the caddies are forced to park, then up the embankment to the range. A second red-jacketed security guard is positioned directly in my way. Thankfully, he wants to see Tiger too and is facing the other direction. Head down, I steam right by.

I'm not the only one who has made it through. Two other random guys are there, standing between a couple of parked cars. I want to hear their story, how they got here, but their look says one thing: "Don't talk to us, and we won't talk to you." It's the same look guys exchange when they're shopping by themselves at Victoria's Secret. Thirty feet in front of us, Hank Haney is standing with his arms folded on his chest as Tiger hits majestic middle-iron after majestic middle-iron. No need for last-minute fixes here. If his coach has any critique, I can't imagine what it is. I mean, seriously, if you're Tiger Woods' coach, what could you say? "Good one." *Smack.* "Good one." *Smack.* "*Really* good one." His star student's swing is powerful but controlled, a big-block V8 cruising in third gear. The three of us are mesmerized, but not for long. We have been silent but not invisible, and another guard marches over to deliver the bad news: "No spectators." The other two guys skitter off, but I hold my ground and decide to ask a fair question: "What about press?" In my defense, I don't actually say I *am* press. If he wants to jump to that conclusion and allow me to stay, so be it. But all this question does is pull the string in his back. "No spectators," he repeats in the same tone. I nod and make the long walk back, knowing Tiger is indeed hitting the ball well, and that eventually he will have no choice but to come to us.

Tiger's arrival at Torrey Pines' putting green is completely different from his entrance at the range. Here, he is loose, carefree, all smiles. Even a great warm-up session with Haney would not have left Tiger this giddy. As he works his way around the putting green, more interested in chatting with other players than following the trail of his custom-made Nike Ones, the dynamic is obvious—it's Tiger's first day of school. He goes from the Swede Fredrik Jacobson to the Australian Rod Pampling, getting caught up on the last four months since he has crossed paths with most of them. No one goes to Tiger, of course; he comes to them. No one except George McNeill. And why not? Two years ago he was a club pro in Florida, having failed to find much success on the pro circuits. Deciding to give it one more shot, he not only made it to the final stage of the PGA Tour's qualifying school at the end of 2006, he won it. Before last year ended, he'd won the Frys. com Open and a two-year exemption on the Tour. And now today he arrives at the course knowing he will not only be seeing Tiger for the first time this season, he will also be playing with him, a fact that makes the moment all the more painful when McNeill stretches out his hand toward Tiger and it is obvious that Tiger has no idea who he is. To McNeill's credit, he stands his ground and keeps talking. Eventually, he fills in the blanks, reminding Tiger that they played against each other in college, and Tiger shakes back. After a few more words, McNeill wanders off, and the Big Man on Campus resumes his reunion tour around the putting green.

8:59 AM ▪ The first hole at Torrey Pines South heads due west, away from the clubhouse and toward the Pacific. A 452-yard slight dogleg right par 4 with bunkers on both sides of the fairway, it doesn't ease a player into his round; it pushes him. Standing off to the right side of the tee is the 9 a.m. pairing of Tiger, McNeill, and, rounding out the group, the loopy-swinging Jim Furyk. They swap scorecards, grab their drivers, and then stand, in silence, waiting for the official starter's watch to strike nine. Punctuating the moment, a pair of fighter jets roars out of Miramar Marine Corps Air Station five miles to the east. Three tournaments have already been played this season, and I watched all three of them. But most golf fans aren't like me—they have hobbies, a job, a life. And until they pop their heads out of their cubicles and see Tiger Woods, frankly, they'd rather just be left alone. As the clock strikes nine, the talking stops and a dozen photographers focus their cameras. The real season starts now.

"From Windermere, Florida, five-time defending champ . . . Tiger Woods." *Five-time defending champ.* If that number doesn't cause someone to pause, it should. To put that into perspective, the English golfer Luke Donald is ranked in the top 25 in the sport, and he has won four times. Worldwide. In his entire career.

Over the past few hours, I've been joined by a solid four hundred committed fans whose applause is mixed with a handful of hoots and whistles for good measure. Most people seem to be holding back, wanting to conserve their full range of emotions for the five hours in front of them.

Tiger tees up the ball, his left leg extended behind him as he leans down. Even the most grotesque of golfers does this, but Tiger makes it appear artistic. He stands behind the ball and stares down the fairway, visualizing his shot. At last Tiger is doing something I actually do. When I do it, I see everything. First the fairway. Then the rough. The traps. The trees. Eventually my eyes float way right to some fancy house with new windows that if I were to really block a shot, I just might reach. It's safe to assume that Tiger's visualization skills far exceed mine.

Tiger returns from the trance, addresses the ball, and gives one final look down the fairway. That glance is his trigger, and when it's over, he immediately draws his arms back, his yellow-soled driver orbiting around him before stopping just short of parallel above his head. The unique element of Tiger's swing is what happens next. As the club reverses direction, he appears to almost sit down, using his own weight along with his strength to pull the club face back to the ball with as much speed as possible. From this point comes The Great Unraveling—his wrists, his hips, his back, his shoulders . . . everything uncoiling through impact and turning toward his target in unison. For as squatty as he was at the beginning on his downswing, by the end of it he is tall and light.

Tiger has hit the drive hard, like he always does, but it catches the left fairway bunker, 290 yards away. As he retrieves his tee and heads down the fairway, his fans set off with him. Up ahead, another few hundred are waiting around the green. It's Thursday, round one, hole 1. Everything is possible.

9:47 AM ▪ Tiger stands on the 4th green, sizing up a ten-foot birdie putt. You'd never pick the 488-yard, ocean-hugging 4th as the place Tiger might make his first birdie of the year. But he couldn't make his twenty-foot birdie putt on number 1, missed a twelve-footer on number 2, and was happy with par on number 3 after pulling his approach way left. Yet, here Tiger is, just ten feet away from a tricky left hole position after ripping a drive down the middle and sticking a long-iron just inside Jim Furyk's ball. Furyk makes his, which in turns shows Tiger the exact line for his putt. He can't possibly miss now. He doesn't. Tiger Woods makes his first birdie of 2008 and is into red numbers.

9:55 AM ▪ I catch up with XM radio announcer Mark Carnevale, who is inside the ropes and describing the par-4 5th hole to his invisible audience. ". . . 314 yards to clear the fairway bunkers," he says. This quickly becomes irrelevant when Tiger pulls his drive into some thick grass at the base of a crooked Torrey pine. It's Tiger's first foray outside the ropes this year, and I can't miss it. The problem is, I'm on the opposite side of the fairway. And so, for the first time this year—I'm running—on a golf course, of all places. The only way to get there is to traverse the 275 yards back to the tee box and then around the other side. Along the way I sprint past Tiger's twenty-eight-year-old Swedish wife, Elin, who without ever swinging a club attracts plenty of attention of her own. I arrive at my destination just ahead of her husband and join the seventy-five other people who happened to be in the right place at the right time.

The ball sits nestled on the grassy upslope with the pine looming above it. Tiger walks, takes one look, and pronounces it, in his best deadpan, "perfect." Without any options, he grabs a wedge, puts one leg on top of the grass mound, and bunts the ball down the fairway about eighty yards. He's walking before the divot hits the ground. And what a divot. A squirrel could have been buried alive by the thing. Fans gather around the crater he has left behind and stare down in awe. Mind you, this wasn't even a shot that made it to the green, just a pitch out. One lanky teenager decides to step into Tiger's stance and see what it feels like, then smiles and nods. It feels good. Golf has a deserved reputation of being a rich man's sport, but for a fan it is anything but that. The cheapest ticket you can buy just put us within two feet of the game's biggest star.

10:30 AM ▪ Tiger arrives at the par-3 8th, an uphill 175-yard par 3 that is defended by a three-leaf clover of a bunker short of the green if you don't play enough club. Tiger avoids that mistake but misses left, hole high. It's his first chip of the round. He finished his warm-up this morning with a few just like it. He made the last one, so that positive image has to be bouncing around his brain somewhere.

And just as he did about an hour and a half earlier, he casually chips it in for a birdie. The cheer of eight hundred people is delayed by a split second as our collective brains are jolted out of the malaise into which we'd slipped after three straight pars. I try to move out of the crowd to get to the next hole, but I'm boxed in by those who feel compelled to stand around and discuss what just happened. "How demoralizing is that when you're playing with him?" one man asks. A woman adds, "It doesn't matter where he hits the ball, he always comes out all right." This is another reason that I've rooted against him for so long. When Tiger Woods is playing well, he makes the world's hardest game appear easy. It's unfair.

11:01 AM ▪ There can't be a stranger dichotomy in golf than the west and east borders of Torrey Pines South. On one side there is the coast—unobstructed,

180-degree vistas of the Pacific, a backdrop that is usually filled by hang gliders and catamarans. To the east are business parks, research facilities, and, here at the 9th, the Scripps Green Hospital. As Tiger arrives, dozens of employees in green and blue scrubs line the hospital's chain link fence for a closer look. I close my eyes, listen, and can almost hear abandoned patients calling out, "Nurse? Nurse? . . ." Tiger doesn't make his four but still makes the turn in 34, a good start on the South Course.

11:25 AM ▪ After adding another birdie on the 10th, Tiger passes through a gauntlet of fans as he walks to the 11th tee. There's no one type of person following Tiger Woods. The gallery has the same diversity as the pictures on Girl Scout cookie boxes. It's no wonder every corporation would love a piece of him.

Halfway through the shoot, a shaggy-haired kid sticks out his hand to get a low-five. He's clearly delusional. But as Tiger walks by, he gives it to him. Tiger doesn't smile, doesn't even make eye contact, but he puts out his hand to slap the youngster's before pulling it safely back to his side. The kid's eyes go wide, but not as wide as mine. What I just witnessed was basically the equivalent of Phil Mickelson taking off his shirt and spinning it over his head like a pinwheel. Up to this point I was pretty sure Tiger was a robot built in Earl Woods' basement using secret Army technology. I'm officially upgrading him to Darth Vader—part machine, part man.

The 11th at the south course is the second-longest par 3 on the course, 221 yards played all the way back. Tiger hits a solid shot to twenty feet. As he walks to the green, a group of thirty-something women on the balcony of a nearby office building scream out in unison, "Go, Tiger!" It's so loud that we all, Tiger included, reflexively turn and look. And again Tiger lifts his mask to return the call with a wave. His season is only two hours old, and it's starting to feel like a coronation. That feeling only grows when Tiger makes his putt and gets to 4 under.

11:49 AM ▪ Tiger could only be thinking birdie on 13. A 541-yard par 5, it's the easiest hole on the back nine. *Thinking birdie.* Even when I was a good golfer, I don't think I ever thought birdie. I sometimes didn't even think par. One time I set the bar even lower.

A few years ago, I stumbled into the chance to play in some corporate golf event where Annika Sorenstam was making an appearance. As we piled into our carts, they made the announcement that Annika herself would be playing three holes with every group.

Most of the guys applauded. My mind went in another direction.

Oh, crap.

With every passing year, my ability to play golf or do much of anything else under pressure has crumbled. When I was fifteen, a senior Tour event was coming to town, and to promote it, the tournament held "closest to the pin" contests at courses all over town. I beat out everyone at my dad's course and earned the chance to go to the resort and compete in a second contest against the other qualifiers in town. We met on the 18th fairway. It was a one-shot deal. 160 yards, a little uphill. A 5-iron. I remember being nervous, but had no reason to think those nerves would actually affect the shot, and they didn't. I stuck it to ten feet, won a hundred dollars to spend in the pro shop, and free tickets to the tournament for the week.

Back to Annika. The corporate tournament was a shotgun start, and my group was set to begin on the 10th. As we stepped to the tee, she pulled up in her cart, and waved. I wouldn't just be playing any three holes with Annika, I'd be playing my *first* three holes with Annika. The cocky guy in our group had already hit one down the middle. I was next. With the best female golfer in the game standing off to the side, a content smile on her face, I went through my normal preshot routine. As I set the club behind the ball, I had one goal: don't whiff. I made contact and off it flew. Long. And right. Like seventy yards right. I think I said something like "Ahhh . . . ," but that was just to cover the fact I was so relieved it had gone anywhere. Somewhere between the ages of fifteen and thirty, I hadn't lost just my mental fortitude; I'd lowered my own definition of excellence. As Annika stepped in behind me to tee it up, she waited until my ball had come to a rest on the 12th hole and said, "Well, it's in *a* fairway."

Tiger is in a fairway, too. The correct one. His iron to the green safely clears the five bunkers leading up to the green and he has a chip for eagle. The chip is a good eighty feet long and matches the topography of the hole he just traversed. It starts out flat, then goes steeply downhill before turning back uphill at the end, all the while drifting right. It rolls out to eight feet away. He makes the birdie putt. Five under. And after finally finding a leaderboard, it's official. For the first time in 2008, Tiger Woods is tied for the lead.

12:53 PM ▪ Tiger doesn't slow down, draining a long putt on 15 to get to 6 under. While Tiger and the rest of his group walk the short distance to the next tee, the guy next to me turns and asks: "Furyk—black hat? Tiger—white hat?" I don't know how to respond. It's forgivable not to be sure whether a hole is a long par 4 or a short par 5, but not to be able to differentiate between Jim Furyk and Tiger Woods is something that should get a spectator banned from all professional golf tournaments for life.

I bury what I want to say and confirm that yes, the person in the white hat is Tiger Woods, and move down 16, a 220-yard par 3 with a canyon both left and long of the hole. Down at the green I find myself standing next to Hank Haney. In golf, coaches aren't allowed to give advice once a round starts, but with his student all the way to 6 under, he at least wants to enjoy his work. Maybe Tiger feels Haney watching: after missing the green short, he hits his worst shot of the day, chunking a simple uphill chip that stops ten feet short of the hole. He shakes his head as he goes to mark. How can a guy be 6 under and then do that? Haney winces, and some idiot leans over to him and says, "You need to give him a chipping lesson," then laughs despite the deafening silence. Haney gives the man a sympathy smile, which is generous. Tiger misses his par putt, his first bogey of the year. Furyk and McNeill aren't done yet, but Haney walks away and I do the same.

1:20 PM ▪ Tiger pars 17 and arrives at the 18th 5 under. The 18th hole at the South course plays to 572 yards when the tees are all the way back. More than the other holes, the 18th demands a drive in the fairway, because in front of the green is the course's only water hazard, a broad round lake out of which Bruce Devlin once tried to hit his ball in 1975. He didn't "once" try to do it. He tried seven times and ultimately made a 10. Torrey Pines would later rename it Devlin's Billabong and place a plaque at the bottom of it, a piece of golf history covered most of the year by a layer of muck and forgotten golf balls.

Tiger misses his drive left and it jumps into a bunker. He'll have no choice but to lay up. He walks to the side of the tee box and slams his driver to the ground, then mutters to himself, "Come on . . ." I have seen this enough times to know how it will play out from here. Tiger will par the hole instead of birdie but still post one of the low rounds of the day. Then he will get in front of the cameras and complain about all the shots he left on the course. A reporter will ask him specifically what he needs to work on, and he'll probably say something absurd like, "Everything." And because reporters are professionals, they will nod rather than roll their eyes. Bobby Jones once said, "It would seem that if a person has hit a golf ball correctly a thousand times, he should be able to duplicate the performance at will." Tiger Woods believes this to be true more than anyone else in the history of the sport.

He indeed makes par, an opening-round 67 to put him one shot off the lead. As I shuffle along with the thousand people who are following him by the end of the day, not a single one seems disappointed.

FLAG HUNTING ▪ Beyond the massive bleachers of the 18th green, a thick line of fans armed with Sharpies awaits the players as they leave the scoring trailer and head for the exit. Tiger has a different route in mind. He finishes his postround interviews and slips through a hole underneath the bleachers. He emerges a few seconds later through another hole on the far side, skips across a cart path, and disappears into the Torrey Pines Lodge without ever facing the mob.

Back in the line, my new acquaintance Margaret has just heard the bad news. "He's gone . . ." she says, sounding like a bride who's been left at the altar. Margaret and Tiger would make an interesting couple. Somewhere between fifty and seventy, Margaret's actual age is hidden beneath an enormous pair of Jackie O. sunglasses and an odd brown wig. Beehive on top and long in back. I wasn't alive in the 1960s, but I don't think it's a hairdo that was ever actually in style.

She's the most unlikely of Tiger fans I've come across today, so of course I have to ask her why she likes him so much. "His dad told him to shoot for the stars," she says. "He hit the stars and the sun and the moon." Margaret's been here every day since Tuesday but rarely ventures onto the course, preferring to stay near the clubhouse and get as many autographs for her souvenir flag as possible.

I ask her who some of her prized signatures are. "Oh, I don't know," she says. "I don't like golf." I laugh, but she's not joking. For Margaret, all the other names on that flag are just there to fill in the empty space around the sacred spot she has reserved right in the middle for Tiger.

I notice Jim Furyk pass behind her and tell her she's missing her chance to grab some more window dressing. She can't catch Jim, but she does snag McNeill, who actually held his own today, shooting an even par 72. She turns back around with a smile, "I don't know who that was, but I got him!" In not knowing McNeill, she and Tiger are not that different after all. I tell her who he is, and then, to my horror, I see that McNeill has signed right in the very middle—Tiger's spot. "Oh no. Margaret?" I say, slowly pointing to it. She's quiet for a moment and then reassigns the still empty top-left corner as Tiger's new spot, vowing to get him to sign it before the week is through.

SECOND ROUND

4:45 AM ▪ I just had a dream about him. I mean, honestly, this is sad. Sure, I'm devoting a year to tailing Tiger, but to have him enter my dreams after just one day is a little creepy. I wonder if this is how seemingly healthy people become stalkers. It starts with a general interest. Then slowly over time it morphs into an obsession that consumes their conscious thoughts and eventually takes over their subconscious. I assume that normally takes months or years. Apparently not.

In the dream, Tiger has invited me to a postround dinner with some of his close friends. On my way, I meet my wife, Hillary, and her parents, who attempt to take me to Pinkberry, a trendy yogurt place that I've never been to and whose allure completely baffles me. Its main draw is that the stuff is made with *real* yogurt that is then frozen, versus "frozen yogurt," which—who knew?—is frozen but not real. People line up outside the store for it, then readily admit it's not as good as the fake stuff. All of which has nothing to do with Tiger.

So in my dream I show up at Tiger's restaurant. I'm in a collared shirt, a casual brown jacket, dress shoes, and no pants. I walk up to him and say hello. His greeting is warmer than the one he gave George McNeill but only slightly. "Hey," he says with a slight head nod. After a few awkward seconds, I have nothing more to say and tell him I should probably take off. He thanks me for coming and then calls out to his wife, Elin, whom he calls "Ulna." Tiger asks her when they're going to come to church with me. She hems and haws about it. Before they can decide, I wake up. It's not even worth trying to interpret. It's insane.

5:00 AM ▪ I can't go back to sleep, but that's okay. Perhaps even more pathetic than having a dream about Tiger Woods is the fact that I've got a doctor's appointment at Torrey Pines this morning. You see, since my family lost our Writers' Guild health insurance at the end of the year, we've been under a Blue Cross plan that has an almost unreachable deductible in exchange for a semireasonable monthly premium. It's pretty much scared us off from getting regular checkups and has us, instead, saving our money for when the kids get sick. So when I spotted an RV offering spectators free skin exams from a real dermatologist near the 9th fairway on Thursday, it was as if they were giving away hundred-dollar bills.

9:52 AM ▪ As Vijay Singh, the mighty Fijian, leaves the tee box, vacating it for Tiger's group, a fan leans in to his buddy and says, "Hell, yeah. Here we go." I want to feel the same way, but I'm still thinking about that appointment I just had. As a fair-skinned blond guy who loves golf, I'm a dermatologist's dream patient. But that's only half of it. I also have a red birthmark on one side of my neck and a brown one on my right arm. The last time I went to a new dermatologist, she called in one of her medical interns, who looked at my different marks and exclaimed gleefully, "I've read about these in class!" The doctor tried to make me feel less like a freak by mentioning that Richard Gere actually has the same thing on his arm that I do. But then she called in a nurse who circled my spots with a pen and took Polaroids of them. "For our records," she insisted.

Today's appointment was awkward from the very beginning. The nurse led me into the exam room/ converted RV bedroom and asked, "Do you want upper body only, or would you like a gown?" I went with only upper body. Just because I'm willing to see a doctor practicing out of a motor home on a golf course doesn't mean I've lost all dignity. Even just the top half of me left the female doctor reeling. "You have a lot of moles," she said, as if I'd flown in from some country without mirrors. In the past, doctors would follow that statement by reassuring me that nothing really looked serious. Instead, she picked up a carbon-copy outline of a body and started to note everything that looked suspicious, eventually having to draw arrows to spots when she ran out of space inside the lines. The RV was hot and was listing at a twenty-degree angle, but what really made me uncomfortable was that while watching her scribble, I was reminded of the fact that had been hammering me more and more over the last few years: I'm not a kid anymore. When you hit your thirties, checkups don't end with a pat on the head and a lollipop. They end with warnings. "You promise you'll go see a doctor in Los Angeles?" she said as I put my shirt on. "I promise," I said, grabbing a handful of free sunscreen samples and making for the tee.

11:20 AM ▪ Tiger played his first five holes on the North 1 under par. Not bad but not exactly lighting it up. The North is by far the easier course of the two, and players tend to go low here and hang on for dear life on the South. It looks as if Tiger is doing the opposite.

His group started on the back nine, and his one problem, as it was yesterday, is his driver. He missed left on 10 and right on 11, the dreaded two-way miss off the tee that has always appeared to frustrate Tiger more than any other part of his game. The "two-way miss" is a good golfer's way of describing a bad golfer's problem, that essentially he has no idea which way his ball's going. Walking down the 15th, a simple, down-hill 394-yard par 4, I don't know which way it's going either, but I guess right. Give me five spins on the roulette wheel and I'll be wrong five times, but this call is perfect. Tiger's drive isn't as far right as my first shot with Annika, but it's bad. And since the 15th green is about the farthest point away from civilization on the already vacant North Course, only thirty or forty fans are gathered around his ball. As expected, Tiger is in no mood to socialize.

When Tiger arrives, he's still holding his driver and fuming, his jawbones jutting out beneath his cheeks. He takes one look at his ball and the eucalyptus tree that is blocking his next shot and says, loud enough for us to hear, "Stupid f*****."

Tiger's propensity for swearing on the course is not something of which he is proud and may be the only flaw he routinely fails to keep under wraps. This can mean only that bad language is either the one thing in life Tiger Woods can't beat or he's not really trying to control it at all. His dad, Earl, said that early on he tried to teach Tiger to bottle up his emotions on the course, but in time Tiger proved that his outbursts could spur him on to better results. It's a theory that completely goes against the conventional wisdom of most every sports psychologist. Bob Rotella, golf's most famous guru, goes so far as to make *not* getting angry one of his ten commandments of mental golf, drilling home the mantra that "nothing will bother or upset you on the golf course, and you will be in a great state of mind on every shot." I've read a few of his books myself and have always admired the idea of peace at all costs on the golf course, mostly because as a teenager it was the easiest place to find it.

My father moved out near the end of my freshman year in high school, a public rift in a small town. During that following summer, I was at the course six days a week. If it had been open on Mondays, it would have been seven. My mom dropped me off in the morning, and my dad joined me in the late afternoon for a few holes, a Cherry Coke, and a ride home. His exit hurt everything except my golf game, and by the time school started again in September my handicap was down to 4. During those early-evening drives with Dad, the reasons why he did it never came up. He believed, as a judge and the son of a lawyer, that conflict was best handled calmly, with reason, behind closed doors. Or even better, not at all.

My wife, on the other hand, was raised completely the opposite. As a teenager, Hillary's parents went so far as to remove her bedroom door so she couldn't slam it in their faces. Five years into our marriage, she often said there was nothing so frustrating as when she would have a meltdown and I would just sit in silence, digesting the problem and eventually talking through a solution with only slightly more emotion than a mannequin. From my point of view, there wasn't much to be gained by getting upset. I mean, I had; it just never ended very well. As a kid, I remember being so hacked off that I threw a club fifteen yards down the fairway, walked to get it, and then threw it another fifteen yards. I did this the entire length of a par 5. That night my dad received a call from the man I'd been paired with, who told him he'd never play golf with me again. Another time, I was so angry about a muffed shot that I stepped on the cart's gas pedal before my dad had finished sitting down. The movement slammed him into his seat and wrenched his back for the rest of the round. I had learned my lesson.

Back in the 15th fairway, Tiger is still swinging his driver, another big Rotella no-no—"the only shot you think about is the one at hand!" He finally stuffs it back in the bag, but he doesn't pull out another club yet; rather, he stands behind the ball and places his hands behind his back. And then he closes his eyes. Call it meditating, exorcising demons, I don't know. But the séance lasts a good five or six seconds as some of us in the crowd shoot one another a quick glance to ask,

"Um, what's going on?" When Tiger opens his eyes, his mood is different. Lighter. He shakes out both hands and says, "Okay." Stevie has been waiting patiently, as if this happens a lot, and is ready when Tiger casually asks, "How far?" "Eighty-seven hole, eighty-two front," he shoots back. Tiger nods, then grabs a wedge and punches it under the tree. It comes hotter than he expected, hops the green, and then disappears back down the other side. Tiger doesn't swear about this one but reacts as if it went exactly where he wanted it to and starts walking.

I run the 87-plus-10 yards to the ball, wondering if perhaps he had painted such a positive mental picture of the shot that he was physically unable to see what really happened. Before he was in trouble, but now he's in jail. His third shot has to go under some pine trees, then up a steep bank of thick rough, then back downhill to a pin that is cut close to the back of the green. Tiger looks at the shot, unconcerned and clearly still feeling residual warm fuzzies from his astral planing, pitches the ball up the hill. It appears perfect from our point of view, but once on top we see it never made it to the green, getting snagged by the rough. A bogey would be a gift at this point. Meanwhile, McNeill and Furyk just stand there, putters under their arms, for once waiting for a hack named Tiger Woods.

Tiger gets up to the ball, takes a brief look at the hole, and then, calmly, chips it in for par. Perhaps feeling liberated enough to express real emotion, I open my mouth and out come two words I almost never use: "Holy s★★★." Tiger picks the ball out of the cup and moves off to the side of the green, where he coolly starts to reapply some lip balm. He's a monster. Or at least a monster with lips that dry out easily. We're still cheering, but he doesn't appear to hear us. Stevie's laughing, but Tiger doesn't notice him. He's still somewhere else. Furyk putts out for a conventional par, then sidles over to Tiger, shaking his head and smirking. Finally, Tiger snaps awake and laughs. It is the deepest and scariest focus I've ever seen.

1:09 PM ▪ After that mystical par on 15, Tiger Woods steps on the gas. He promptly birdies the 16th, an uphill 336-yard par 4, using a 3-wood off the tee for one of the first times all week. *Seven under.* He birdies the 18th, the boring 520-yard par 5 that I sneaked across the day before to get to the range. *Eight under.* On the par-5 1st, he blocks one into the right trees, and when the marshal asked us all to take ten steps back, Tiger tells us to stay put, adding "I'm not playing that badly, am I?" Up and down for birdie. *Nine under.* On the short 326-yard 2nd, Tiger short-sides himself but makes the putt for three anyway. *Ten under.* And for good measure, he birdies the 4th. *Eleven under.* I add them up as I walk. Five birdies in seven holes?!

I go out of my way to catch a glimpse of the only leaderboard on the North Course. At 11 under par, Tiger Woods is in the lead. By four. A fan next to me notices Furyk's total and says, "Four under, that's good," then thinks for a second and adds, "unless you're Tiger, in which case that's crap." In a matter of less than two hours on a Friday morning, and ignited by something that on paper will look like a "nothing special" par, Tiger Woods has put away a tournament that won't officially be over for two more days.

PHOTO OP ▪ Who knew that all this week I'd been trying to get close to Tiger and all I needed to do was head to the Buick Clubhouse along the 18th fairway. You may remember the commercial in which Tiger opens the front door in a nice sweater and says some version of "Hi. Welcome to the Buick Clubhouse. Come on in . . ." What doesn't quite come through in that ad is that the actual Buick Clubhouse isn't a clubhouse at all but an enormous big-rig trailer with fake wood paneling. To get in, all I have to do is fill out a form, which "just takes a second," yet I assume will mean I'll be receiving e-mails from Buick for the next ten years. The cool thing about the "clubhouse" is that after posing for a photo in front of a greenscreen, a computer lays in a picture of Tiger, so it looks as if he and I really had our picture taken together. The finished product is pretty impressive. Oliver Stone would peg it for a fake right away, but most of my golfing buddies would never suspect a thing. It's marketing genius. By only having to smile once, Tiger has found a way of appeasing hundreds of thousands of fans.

THIRD ROUND

Tiger has a four-shot lead entering Saturday and is paired with Stewart Cink and Kevin Streelman, the world's 1,354th-ranked player. Streelman is the perfect example of the no-name pro I would love to see topple Tiger. He has spent the last seven years bouncing around minitours, the low point coming a few years back when he was deserted by a group of disillusioned investors who had promised to pay his tournament entrance fees. This week he was only an alternate into the field and found out just five minutes before his tee time that a spot had opened up. Now, after two solid rounds, he has his chance to take on Tiger and see if he can keep things close.

But I know he probably won't. For years the cake-walk has always been my least favorite of the Tiger wins, because after spending all week looking forward to seeing a gripping tournament, I'd make a sandwich, turn on the TV right at twelve o'clock on Saturday, and discover it was already over. At least with the nail-biters I could get through the majority of a weekend before Tiger ruined it. Hillary could always tell what had happened by the droll look on my face.

"Tiger's winning?"

I'd nod.

"Is it close?"

I'd shake my head. "I'm sorry," she would always say, secretly happy that Tiger's dominance had won her another six hours of quality time with me before I returned to work on Monday morning.

The only person who is refusing to admit this week's event is over is Tiger himself. And ironically, it is that refusal that makes his winning all the more inevitable. "They're not handing out the trophy today," he said yesterday to the press. "Anything can happen." It's a nice thought, but no, anything can't. Tiger doesn't lose tournaments when he has a four-shot lead. All his comment does is safeguard himself against some catastrophic, one-in-a-billion scenario—that either a La Jolla hang glider wipes him out on the 12th hole or he incorrectly signs his scorecard and is disquali-fied, but even in the case of the latter, I have to imag-ine that the official in the scorer's trailer would look at Tiger's card, then slowly slide it back to the biggest name in sports and say, "Are you *sure* you want to turn this in?"

10:54 AM ▪ Tiger has cruised through the first three holes as expected, par-par-par, then adds a birdie on the hard 4th for the second time in two tries this week. Streelman actually had a chance to make himself known on the first hole after knocking it inside Tiger to just five feet, but he missed. Now evidence of a blowout is everywhere. Back at the tee, I passed two twenty-something girls having what they surely considered their first deep discussion about Tiger.

"It's amazing how good you can get at golf so quickly."

"Didn't he start when he was three?"

"I guess that is kind of a long time when you think about it."

Further down the fairway, a dad watches only half-interestedly as Tiger passes by, instead helping his sons collect pinecones to take home. Even I can't keep my focus and start talking to a fellow spectator, Dwayne, and his wife, who are sporting the most high-tech periscopes I've ever seen. About an inch thick and made of hard metal, they put the '80s cardboard ones to shame. They not only extend, they focus and even zoom. "It's even got a hook for your pants," Dwayne's wife boasts. Turns out the devices are for sale in the Torrey Pines pro shop. But what's really odd is that they are made and distributed by none other than Phil Mickelson's father. "Don't you feel guilty about watching Tiger and not Phil?" I ask. "We watch enough of him too," Dwayne says, slightly insulted at the insinuation, then quickly turns back to Tiger. At eighty bucks a pop, his wife warns me not to buy one unless I'm planning on seeing more than one golf tournament this year. I laugh and know I have just found my strangest tax write-off for 2008.

11:01 AM ▪ There haven't been as many sportswriters tracking Tiger from inside the ropes as I'd imagined. The only one I have seen walking a few holes every day is a writer I've nicknamed Luau Larry. I don't know his real name or for whom he writes, but he is always wearing a Hawaiian shirt tucked into shorts, a look that exposes a pair of tan legs of which he seems rather proud. It has been downright cold some mornings this week and pants are never an option. I've also never seen him actually write anything down. He just tromps along inside the ropes, occasionally using his collapsible metal monopod seat to time and again nab the best seat in golf. I'll admit it, I'm jealous.

11:10 AM ▪ Matt Kuchar has experience playing around Tiger's gallery, just not like this. While Tiger is busy nearly holing his approach into number 5, up on number 2 Kuchar has just blown his approach long and left, a bad miss that hits the cart path and then careens an extra twenty yards down the hill and right into the middle of Tiger's throng. Faced with a ridiculous flop shot over a camera tower and a couple of pine trees, the always grinning 1998 U.S. Amateur champ can only laugh at the fact that his gallery has instantly gone from literally seven people to about a thousand. And since Tiger is on the verge of going to 14 under, the crowd is delighted to turn its attention to a player whose round is actually in jeopardy. Matt surveys the shot, then opens up his lob wedge as much as he can and swings. Somehow, the shot clears the trees and lands short of the flag, leaving him just eight feet for par. He receives a Tiger-size cheer as he strides up the hill, high-fiving fans the entire way. Within thirty seconds, his gallery is back to seven.

12:25 PM ▪ I don't know how the San Diego Police Department decided which cop should walk along with

Tiger Woods' group this week, but clearly height was a factor. Officer Brian Freymueller is big. Six-feet-five and solid. He doesn't need a billy club; he looks as if he could do just as much damage with a paper towel roll. And for the first two days, he's been a tough guy to crack. On Thursday, I mustered the courage to ask him if he's allowed to enjoy this. He wouldn't answer. On Friday, he laid into a college kid who ran under a marshal's ropes, nearly melting him with his Ray-Bans. But as I lean around the corner of 10 to see where Tiger's approach has landed, Freymueller is suddenly next to me giving color commentary, "He's about fifteen feet hole high. Probably not going to be happy with that." Glad to see he's loosening up, I tell him I guess this beats waiting for someone to roll through a stop sign. As he thinks of a reason to arrest me, I slink back into the crowd.

12:34 PM ▪ Tiger hits his best shot of the day on the downhill, 220-yard 11th. I'm positioned perfectly behind the ball as he zones in on the back-left pin. It's a high laser that starts one yard left of the flag, then corrects its course about halfway to the hole. It looks as if it might go in and ends up just six feet past the cup. Kevin Streelman's caddy can only shake his head in silence. When Tiger makes the putt, which at this point I can only assume he will, he'll be at 15 under par. For perspective, 15 under par was Tiger's winning score last year and he still has twenty-five holes left. Streelman, of course, is going the other way. With a double on 9 and a bogey here, he's nine shots back.

2:36 PM ▪ Tiger adds two more birdies before he is done, one at 15 and the other a tap-in at 18 for a round of 66. In five hours, he has doubled his lead from four shots to eight. Streelman could muster only a 75. *Another crushed spirit*, I think. But for some reason Streelman is beaming as he shakes Tiger's hand. He's acting as if he just received a medal from the president.

Back at my buddy A.J.'s house, I go online and find the transcript of Streelman's postround interview. "What was it like?" he was asked. "Man, that was one of the coolest things ever, no doubt about it. [Tiger] was fun to watch but just kind of fun to compare myself against him, as well. It's inspiring and very educational." Huh. Tiger apparently wasn't going to be the star in any of Kevin Streelman's recurring nightmares.

When Tiger came on the Tour in the mid-1990s, his approach to the sport was thoroughly different from the status quo and therefore totally offensive. During his first week back in 1996, Tiger said his goal was not to finish second or third but to win. His interviewer, two-time U.S. Open champ Curtis Strange, chuckled and said, "You'll learn." Actually, Strange learned. Tiger won his first Tour event five weeks after that and his second just two weeks later.

Twelve years later, there's a new generation of players arriving on Tour who, like Streelman, has never questioned Tiger's superiority. Getting whooped by him doesn't make them dry heave, it makes them want to improve. At thirty-two years old, Tiger has become a mentor—whether he wants to be one or not.

FINAL ROUND

For most of Saturday night, it looked as if there might not be any tournament taking place today. Southern California typically only has one stretch of bad weather every year, and it happens to be when the Tour schedules its annual West Coast swing. Back in 2005, the rain farther north was so heavy that it shortened the Nissan Open in Los Angeles to just 36 holes. At the same event a year later, rain caught Tiger and Stevie without umbrellas, and Tiger would later withdraw with the flu, the first time in his professional career he had ever withdrawn. None of that sounds as bad as the weather forecast that I caught Saturday night. It wasn't "heavy rains" that caught my attention but "cyclones and tornadoes." When the rain and wind start to beat against A.J.'s house early this morning, I figure that's it: despite having a giant lead, Tiger will have no choice but to hang out in La Jolla for one more day until Mother Nature lets him make it official.

Nevertheless, by 8 a.m., the storm of the century has slowed a bit, so I put on my rain pants and head for the course.

10:40 AM ▪ A real golf fan has to be ready for anything, and at nine o'clock this morning, my outfit makes a lot of sense. Wool socks, jeans, rain pants, a thermal shirt, a sweater, a rain jacket, a beanie, and an umbrella. No storm is going to slow me down, not this early in the year. There's just one problem. It is a problem that has been developing for the last hour and has come to fruition just as Tiger stripes his drive down the middle of the first fairway. The last remaining cloud in Southern California has just blown past Torrey Pines. The only thing for which I'm not prepared is the sun.

The jacket can be wrapped around my waist along with the sweater. The beanie would probably fit in my pocket, and the umbrella might go through a belt loop. None of this really matters, of course, since the end result is that I look like a complete fool. Until I meet Nelson, a fit-looking fifty-three-year-old who is somehow wearing even more layers than I. "How'd you place in the Iditarod?" I want to ask. Instead I just go with the safer "Beautiful day." He rolls his eyes, and for the first time this season, I've found a kindred spirit. Nelson woke up early, drove an hour, and over-reacted to the weather for one reason—to follow Tiger Woods. He didn't bring a friend or his wife, just him-self, knowing that no matter how bad the tempest was, he would see something amazing. He receives that gift early when Tiger drains a 35-foot putt on the 1st for birdie. Nineteen under. Tiger waves as he walks to the cup. "He's been like this all week," I say, as if I were describing a great-uncle who hasn't taken his medicine. When Nelson finds out how I'm spending my year, he asks the question I've started to get a lot: "Do you know him?" "Yeah, right," I say.

When two random guys meet on a golf course, the information about each other usually trickles out slowly, and only just between tee shots and approaches. One of my favorite lines is from *Golf Digest*'s David Owen, who joked that after years of playing golf with his friends, he knew most of their spouses' names and even what some of them did for a living. Nelson oper-ates a little faster. And so had his parents. When his dad turned eighteen, he asked Nelson's mom to marry him. She was fourteen. So why should I be surprised that within two holes, I have heard most of Nelson's life story? His job, his wife, his kids.

One of his stories is about his oldest son, Jesse, who four years ago was a Major League Baseball prospect at just seventeen, throwing 95 mph, batting .605, and running a 5.0 to first base as a freshman in high school. One day Jesse came home complaining of soreness in his throwing arm. It took a year of tests before doctors finally discovered cancer. With specialists unable to tell how much of the cancer was in the soft tissue and how much was in the bone, he started chemotherapy the very next day. After six months, they took a break to do a month of radiation, then gave the humerus two to three weeks to rest before they removed it altogether, saving his life but ending his dream of playing in the pros.

Nelson's faith is no great secret. You don't name your kids Jesse, Samuel, Hannah, and Gabriel unless you've taken a few spins through the Bible. And no doubt seeing your son go through so much pain and loss is either going to push you away from God or draw you closer. For Nelson, it was the latter. "It's sometimes hard to see how God orchestrates things in life, but you have to believe he is, even if you don't understand it," he says as we charge up the hill from 5 to 6, having seen Tiger make pars on the last four holes. There's not a bit of resentment in his voice and certainly no looking back, just a peace about life's dead ends that can only be supernatural.

12:15 PM ▪ Walking down number 6, I predict that Tiger will birdie it. "You think so?" Nelson asks. First off, I tell him I'm insulted that he'd even question me, considering I've watched all fifty-nine of the holes Tiger has played this season. I explain that the 6th is one of the only holes out here that Tiger has not played well this week. He's parred it twice, but since it's a downwind, 560-yard par 5, that's bad. This time around, Tiger puts his third shot to four feet, sinks the putt for a birdie 4, and Nelson promises never to doubt me again. Twenty under par. And a ten-shot lead.

1:45 PM ▪ After his first bogey in forty-five holes at the 7th, Tiger cruises till he reaches the 11th, where he leaves his shot on the par 3 in the back-right corner. Unfortunately, the pin is in the front left, leaving him a terror of a putt, a good fifty feet long. Tiger isn't reading it all at once. He's reading it in sections, dissecting it from beginning to end, then piecing it back together little by little to decide exactly what his line should be. This is the longest he has taken reading any putt all week. He walks to the side of the putt, judging its steepness. He reads it from behind the cup, looking back to his ball. He spends so much time on it that I start to think maybe it's not even his turn. But his fellow players Stewart Cink and Joe Durant are watching Tiger, too. To have any chance, he has to putt across the side of the tier the first forty feet, then get the ball to die a good ten feet above the hole, where it will take a seventy-degree turn back toward the front of the green and pick up speed. The only thing that can stop it at that point is the hole itself.

Believing he has the putt decoded, he hits it, then straightens up to see how he did. The ball rides the tier like a surfer, then slows and cuts left down the hill. It's racing now, nearing the cup. As impossible as it seemed, it falls in the right side for birdie. Tiger is the only real show in town today and five thousand eyes are there to scream an "Ohhhhh!" when it drops. Even I have to join in this time.

When a football team calls a play, you don't know which one it has chosen until the ball has been hiked and the players go into motion. But here at the 11th we were able to watch Tiger at work and knew exactly what he was attempting to do before he ever drew the putter back. But that still doesn't mean anyone believed he could make it.

With the ball safely in the cup, Tiger raises the grip end of his putter above his head and pumps his right arm. Stevie picks it out and tosses the ball back, where he casually slips it into his pocket and heads to the 12th tee.

2:50 PM ▪ Nelson returns, having disappeared for a few holes to buy one of the Mickelson periscopes. And now that he has an unobstructed view on the 14th, he suddenly believes he can see things no one else can see.

"Tiger looks tired," he says, pulling away from the eyepiece.

"You're nuts."

"Here, look." I begrudgingly put it up to my eye.

"He's not tired," I say. "Besides, he's drinking Tigerade. He'll be fine."

Nelson's not buying it and takes the periscope back. "I don't know. I think he's struggling. I can see his slumped shoulders. I'm worried about him." I tell him those aren't slumps; those are muscles. But Tiger indeed bogeys the 14th, 15th, and 16th, dropping to 17 under. "Something's wrong," Nelson says, in case I'd forgotten his earlier pronouncement. "Fine," I say, "he's tired. *I'm* tired!"

I had e-mailed my old boss Alan earlier in the week to tell him the pedometer I'm wearing says I'm walking close to six miles a day, to which he responded that I was the only member of the striking Writers Guild of America whose walking distance went up once I stopped picketing.

As a member in good standing with the Writers Guild ("good standing" meaning I don't currently owe the union any money), I am expected to picket four hours a day, five days a week. Best I could see, the only immediate benefit of this strike was that rather than referring to myself as an unemployed writer, I could now tell people I was a *striking* writer, which makes me sound much more important.

I wasn't able to picket the first day of the strike. I will neither confirm nor deny that I may or may not have been playing golf with a friend. Driving home from the place I may or may not have been, I called an old coworker to tell him what I had shot and to see how the picketing was going. He said it was so painful that after just one day on the lines, he had already called the Guild and asked if there was anything he could do instead. *Way to be tough, Norma Rae,* I thought.

The next day, I showed up to picket at CBS along with a couple hundred other energized writers. As a car drove by and honked, a friend raised his fist and yelled, optimistically, "We're winning!" A little later two eighty-something writers who probably hadn't worked in thirty years anyway began smashing their signs against a teamster's truck and then attempted to open his passenger door to challenge him to fisticuffs. The whole thing was actually a lot of fun. For about forty-five minutes. I spent the next hour realizing what a waste of life this was. Then, at the two-hour mark, I decided I was ready to give in to the studios' demands. You don't want to pay us for running shows on the Internet? Fine. You want to get rid of residuals altogether? I'm listening. Just please don't make me walk in circles while pretending to talk on the phone with my agent again. So much for not wanting to walk.

3:10 PM ▪ Tiger rights the ship on the 17th with a par and plays down the 18th hole with a seven-shot lead. The smiles he has buried all week are coming easily now, the finish line in sight. The crowd cheers as Tiger hits his third shot in close to the back-right pin. Nelson says good-bye as he heads for the merchandise tent, and I find myself enjoying the walk up 18. I understand why Tiger enjoys winning so much. It's hard to feel bad about yourself when a few thousand people are on their feet applauding you. I know I never took one swing this week, but as I reach the 72nd green, I secretly pretend that some of the accolades are for me.

Tiger makes the twelve-footer at the last hole for a round of 71, a four-day total of 19 under and the largest margin of victory in the history of the tournament. It's the sixth time he has started the year with a victory and his 62nd win on the PGA Tour, tying him with Arnold Palmer.

It's impossible to walk away from this first tournament and not appreciate the things Tiger can do that no one else can. Even the most hardened golf fan couldn't deny that. But I understand even less why so many people consider him beloved. He's too good. Too intimidating. At least to me—and the other 153 players in the field.

After picking up my new periscope, I make for my car and spot Margaret (with the beehive wig) waiting at the city bus stop on Torrey Pines Road. "Margaret!" I say. "Did you ever get Tiger's autograph?" "Yes!" she says, then pulls it out to show me. He wouldn't sign the flag, but he signed her Buick Clubhouse picture with faux Tiger that she'd had taken earlier in the week. "He signed it and then he gave me this little smile." She does her best Tiger half smile to help me visualize the moment. As for the flag, Margaret says she'll bring it back next year. Forget next year. He'll be back in June for the U.S. Open.

Eldrick of Arabia

The Dubai Desert Classic

The Majlis Course—Emirates Golf Club
Dubai, United Arab Emirates
January 31–February 2, 2008

I f you pick up a globe, put your finger on Los Angeles, then run it up to the North Pole and back down the other side of the planet, you will hit Dubai, the biggest city in the United Arab Emirates. In other words, after going to the tournament that couldn't be closer to home, I am now traveling as far as I possibly can. I stumble upon this fact during my one full day between Tiger's tournaments when I look at the itinerary Hillary is printing out and ask, "Where is Dubai, anyway?" Most Americans who travel there undoubtedly ask that question, but they probably don't ask it twenty-four hours before they board the plane.

The whole adventure of this year had caught me a little off guard. Until the Writers Guild went on strike, I was busy trying to sell a TV pilot I had written called *Viva Doug*. It was about an American loser who at the low point of his life discovers that his childhood pen pal has risen to power as a dictator in a South American country and is giving Doug all the credit for making him the ruthless monster he has become. In total honesty, I started writing it as a movie but couldn't get past the first thirty pages, so I chopped off the end and told people it was meant to be a TV pilot the whole time. I had gone in to pitch it to Fox, a meeting that I thought went well, until the end of the meeting when the V.P. to whom I was pitching thanked me and then asked if I had opened the Fiji Water she had given me.

"Yeah, actually I did."

"Oh. That's okay. If you hadn't, I was just going to ask if I could have it back."

Writing and trying to sell that script was one of the two moments of levity in an otherwise dim two-year career stretch. The other was a brief stint writing for *The ½ Hour News Hour*, a sort of a Republican version of *The Daily Show* for the Fox News Channel. As with most new shows, some elements really worked, some didn't. But the concept was a home run, enough to make me announce during my second week there, "This show will run forever!" Two days later we were canceled.

Dubai is certainly not the first place one thinks of going when running low on money, but since Tiger's going, I have no choice. I will fly on Delta from L.A. to Atlanta, then take a direct flight from Atlanta all the way into Dubai. Tiger will travel on his private jet, of course, and said earlier in the week that to pass time on the plane he usually spends the whole flight eating. I don't have that luxury. Despite the second leg of my flight clocking in at just under fourteen hours, the reservation states that my flight includes dinner only.

Leaving the family for the Buick was easy. This one's tough. Hillary inadvertently lightens the mood at the curb when she tells me to make sure I drink a lot of water and walk around a lot during the flight so I don't have a stroke. "How old do you think I am?" I ask before giving her a hug. I lean in and kiss my daughter, Katie, who is still too young to know how far away I'm really going, and then do the same to my son, Danny. As I wheel my bag away, I turn back one last time, and through the tinted glass I can make out his little hand, waving good-bye.

L.A. TO ATLANTA ▪ Thankfully the woman with the forty pounds of frozen raw meat at her feet is near me for only the three-and-a-half-hour leg of my journey. "They don't have Trader Joe's in Myrtle Beach," she explains to the poor couple sitting next to her. Every seat on the flight has its own mini-TV, but until further notice this lady is the in-flight entertainment. Within twenty minutes of takeoff, she is watching *Just Shoot Me* on her TV and the first *Lord of the Rings* movie on her portable DVD player, a strange combination that has her snickering one second and completely entranced the next. When *Just Shoot Me* ends, I notice that an episode of the sitcom *Yes, Dear* comes on. An episode I wrote. Writing for TV, it is always hard to get an accurate idea of what people really think of your work. Family and friends reflexively say they loved it. The next day the ratings come in and tell you a few million people were watching, but you never know if they actually enjoyed it. Frozen Meat Girl is temporarily distracted by Gandalf and Frodo, so I wait. After a few minutes she looks back up at the TV, scrunches up her nose, realizes what she's watching (or, perhaps even worse, isn't), and, for the first time in the flight, turns the TV off.

Tiger Woods never rests on past accomplishments. He makes new goals, looks ahead. I'm not that secure, which explains why I put down my book, flip on my episode, and begin laughing out loud at jokes I wrote three years ago. I watch the whole thing, then turn it off, but only after my name flashes in the credits, almost too small to see on the four-by-six-inch screen. When I wrote that episode, I thought I knew exactly how life was going to play out; the new house by twenty-eight, the country club membership by thirty-five, the flying car by forty. I might even have achieved some of it if I had actually made any effort to put the plan into motion. Instead, I did nothing. And now I'm on a flight to the other side of the Earth, playing catch-up with the help of the world's greatest athlete.

ATLANTA TO DUBAI ▪ I am curious to see what kind of people actually travel to Dubai. Our gate is about the farthest one from the center of the terminal, and the collection of people scattered about is comprised of some of the most intimidating men I've ever seen. Most of them are wearing khaki cargo pants and work boots. They're middle-aged, leathery, tattooed. Mixed in with them is a smattering of women who aren't scary at all, just scared. Once on the flight I find out that for most of them, the final destination isn't Dubai; it's Iraq. They've signed on for a tour of duty, so to speak, with KBR, a former subsidiary of Halliburton and the largest nonunion construction company in America.

Sitting next to me on the flight is Mary, a small, curly-haired former FedEx driver who pretends she's excited about the year ahead, but doesn't act like it. The lure of working in Iraq is simple: the pay is good, and as long as you stay out of the United States for 330 days, it's tax-free. "329 left," Mary says. She didn't even know she was going to Iraq until Friday and did her required weeklong training just this past week, the worst part of which was wearing "the banana suit," a claustrophobic yellow outfit that will protect her from chemical attacks. The man on the aisle, Bill, is just finishing his second year in Iraq and tells her not to worry about the suit. "I don't even know where mine is."

Bill is the poster boy for KBR, a beefy, sixty-year-old former concrete pourer from Illinois who cannot resist the lure of $1,800 a week. On his most recent trip home he was able to pay cash for a $30,000 truck. Next time he's buying a modular home. Mary knows what she'll do with the money, too. She recently bought a spot in an RV park near the water in Galveston. Her motor home is waiting for her to come back and fix it up.

I tune in to an episode of *Megastructures* about Dubai's famous palm-shaped island. The show gladly spits out over-the-top facts, figures that you just accept because you have no way of proving or disproving any of them. The nuttiest is that so much earth was moved to build the island, it's "enough sand and rock to build a twenty-five meter wall . . . around the entire world." Really? This is how Dubai operates and survives—hype.

I wake up from a long stretch of sleep and tune my TV to the map that shows our progress. A few hours ago, we were off the coast of Ireland. Now I see we're about to fly right over Iraq. On cue, the plane banks smoothly to the right, then straightens course. I pull up my shade and see miles and miles of fog. When my eyes adjust, I see it's not fog at all but sand. We're flying down the east coast of Saudi Arabia. After an hour the plane banks back to the left, Iraq no longer below us, and descends over the Persian Gulf and into the bright lights of Dubai.

As the plane taxis to the runway, the interior lights come on and so does the welcome music. It takes me a second to place the song, but then it's unmistakable— "The Little Drummer Boy." Not the musical accompaniment I would have guessed for my first moments in a Muslim country. The song is shut off abruptly, and we roll the rest of the way in silence.

I collect my bag and jump into a taxi whose cabbie, Mahmut from India, asks where I'm staying. Dubai is home to the world's most lavish hotels, none more famous than the sail-shaped Burj Al Arab, Tiger's home for the week and the tallest hotel in the world.

I'm staying on the first floor of the Golden Sands Hotel Apartments, a low-price option that is still costing me $200 a night. But when I say "Golden Sands," Mahmut asks me a debilitating question:

"Which one?"

Apparently saying Golden Sands is the equivalent of arriving in Chicago and saying you're staying at the Best Western. Mahmut decides to take me to the closest Golden Sands, where they can look up my reservation on their computer. While driving, he asks me why I'm in Dubai. "To see Tiger Woods," I say.

"Who?"

I had to fly halfway around the world, but I've done it. I've met the first person who doesn't know who Tiger Woods is.

"Tiger Woods?"

No response.

"The golfer?" I mimic a golf swing as Mahmut looks in the rearview mirror. "Oh yes," Mahmut says, now clearly knowing exactly the man in question.

FIRST ROUND

Though I have no real pull in the world of sportswriting, one night while I was in San Diego, I went to the Dubai Desert Classic Web site to see how much tickets cost and found a tab marked "Media Accreditation." I clicked, and it opened to an online form to apply for official credentials for the week. *It can't be this easy*, I thought. I filled in my name, e-mail address, and phone number. The only question that tripped me up was "media type." Not liking any of the choices they gave me, I put in "other," then hit send. Some part of me wondered whether it was wise to mess with the system in an Arab country, but two seconds later an e-mail popped up in my inbox: "Your application was successful and you have been approved to receive media accreditation for the 2008 Dubai Desert Classic."

This morning I take a cab across town to the Emirates Golf Course, passing minivan after minivan packed with workers heading to construction sites, and climb the steps to the white media tent. Behind the main desk is a well-dressed employee of Pakistani descent speaking perfect English. "Good morning," she says as I tentatively slide the e-mail across the desk. She picks it up, looks at it briefly, and then hands me my pass. The credential won't get in me inside the ropes, but it will get me closer to Tiger than I will probably get all year.

The Dubai Desert Classic is officially a European Tour event, but looking at where it has been playing, you'd never know it. Last week the Euro Tour was in

Qatar. Three weeks ago it was in South Africa, and next week it is headed to India. At least it's not fighting the fact that no one really wants to play golf in Europe until spring. Tiger first played in the Dubai Desert Classic in 2001, took a few years off, and has now played every year since 2004. He finally won in 2006, defeating South Africa's Ernie Els in a playoff when Els dunked his ball in the water on the first extra hole. For someone who won't even show up for all the PGA events in his home state, there must be another reason Tiger's here, and it's not because he's doing some work on the side for KBR. The European Tour allows its sponsors to give players undisclosed appearance fee money in order to lure them to events. If the rumors are true, Tiger has already made $2–3 million by the time his jet touches the ground.

7:25 AM ▪ Seven days and 8,338 miles from La Jolla, Tiger Woods and I are back on the range. I feel sorry for the chump warming up next to him. He doesn't even have a Tour bag; he has one of those walking bags with a stand. And not even a nice walking bag with a stand. As Tiger crushes a 3-wood, the player next to him duck-hooks his shot, and quickly looks away in shame. When Tiger enters the field, it's remarkable how many players automatically have no chance of winning. I'm sure this guy is a good golfer. He may have even won a tournament or two in his life. But never before have I seen such a stark contrast between a very good golfer and a great one.

8:15 AM ▪ Tiger is starting this morning on the 10th tee and is paired with Scotland's Colin Montgomerie and Sweden's Niclas Fasth. Around me are only a hundred fans or so. The peppy British announcer kindly asks the gallery to put away cell phones and cameras, saying that there are plain-clothed officials in the crowd who will be monitoring us. This can't possibly be true, since the man next to me is using his videocamera and still camera at the same time. He's obviously a tourist, and a look around makes me think everyone else is, too: Brits, Germans, Africans, Indians, and most of them openly taking pictures.

With the empty warning out of the way, the announcer shifts gears to what really matters. "And now on the tee, the 2006 winner of the Dubai Desert Classic. . . . From the United States . . . Tiger Woods." There's no jet lag on his swing as his drive on the 550-yard 10th splits the fairway. While Monty and Fasth can't get any closer to the green in two shots than eighty-five yards, Tiger carries his second all the way to the rough just short of the green. His chip rolls out just short of the hole. A tap-in birdie to start his day.

8:30 AM ▪ There are a lot of things you aren't allowed to do in Dubai, but exaggerating is certainly not one of them. According to the tournament Web site, the Emirates Golf Club was built when "His Highness General Sheik Mohammed bin Rashid Al Maktoum, Vice-President, Prime Minister of the UAE, Ruler of Dubai and Minister of Defense gave his approval for the innovative concept of developing a grass golf course in the desert." Tacking five different titles onto just one man is pretty bold, but pretending to be the first golf course ever built in a desert is over the line. It's certainly pretty, with lush green fairways separated occasionally by dark brown bunkers and bright blue lakes. There are no pastels here. Everything's bold. Even more striking are the skyscrapers of various shapes and sizes that surround us. Some are finished, others are still being built, but there's no real organization to their layout, as if the city planners don't really know which way they're going to expand next.

Tiger's iron to the straightforward 169-yard 11th starts right and stays right. He yells to himself in the third person, "Tiger!" then adds an expletive. Down at the green the Indian man next to me sees Tiger's ball just twenty feet from the hole and says, "That's a *bad* shot for Tiger?"

9:06 AM ▪ Compared to the Buick, the crowds here are sparse. It would make following Tiger relatively easy except for the marshals. They may not care about cameras, but they are passionate about there being absolutely no movement while a player hits a shot. It doesn't matter if Niclas Fasth has his back to us and is a hundred yards away; the marshals hold up their hands, yell "Stand, please!" and we all resign ourselves to the fact that we've just signed on for a four-and-a-half-hour game of Red Light/Green Light.

With Tiger going for the green in two on the 13th, I get a chance to catch up to him. He and Stevie lean against the bag and look around, pointing out the buildings that have sprouted up since they were here last February. The green clears, and Tiger pushes his 3-wood so far right that he drops his club on the follow-through. As I walk ahead, it's clear why he's upset—there's a lake to the right of the green, and he is in it. It's his first penalty stroke this year.

"In England, that's called 'taking a piss.'" That was my introduction to Ali, a hip, Kangol-wearing British expatriate who has spent the last twelve years working for one of the thousands of sheiks who essentially own and run the emirate. It doesn't make Ali a local, but almost. I ask him why I haven't seen any actual Arabs on the course. It's an easy answer. "Arabs hate golf," he says. Ali, on the other hand, loves it. He even credits Tiger's book *How I Play Golf* for his seven-handicap and *five* holes in one. I've never had a hole in one, and I've been playing since I was eight, but what makes me more jealous is that before the season started, Ali was able to find 33-1 odds on Tiger winning the Grand Slam and was smart enough to put a hundred pounds on it. In the United Kingdom. One of the few Muslim laws Dubai hasn't discarded is a ban on gambling. "It's just a matter of time," Ali insists, pointing out that it's hard to bill yourself as the Vegas of the Middle East without it.

Tiger takes a drop out of the water, then nestles his fourth shot to three feet to save par.

9:30 AM • The 14th at the Emirates is a downhill, dogleg left par 4 with desert on both sides. Even without wind, the safest shot for Tiger is a low stinger with his 3-wood to the center of the fairway. Without much fanfare, he hits his second shot to eight feet and makes the birdie to go to 2 under. Walking down 15, I spot a man in the traditional white *dishdasha* robe and Arab headdress, the first real local I've seen all day, and point him out to Ali. Ali notices the way the headdress is spun around his head and corrects me. "He's from Saudi Arabia."

11:41 AM ▪ Tiger is breezing through this round. He's birdied the 18th and the 1st, stuck it close on the par-3 4th to grab another shot, and arrives at the par-4 6th already 5 under par. The 6th is without a doubt the hardest hole on the course. It's uphill, 485 yards, with a waste bunker all down the left, a traditional bunker on the right, and deep rough everywhere else. You must hit driver, and even if you find the fairway, you're faced with a narrow, elevated green and another trap waiting to swallow any shots that come up short. He addresses the ball and, when he needs to most, hits his best drive of the day. It draws about three yards before landing and rolling out, 315 yards away. Colin Montgomerie, who is next to play, turns and says to the crowd, "This kid's got potential." The crowd laughs, and Tiger smirks.

Monty is always happiest on the European Tour, a place where he has won the Order of Merit (the Tour's top money earner) a record eight times. Yet he has never won a major championship. Even more remarkable is that he has never won *any* tournament on American soil. At age forty-four, the chances of either are starting to fade.

Monty's chummy relationship with Tiger has come a long way since they were paired together on Saturday at the 1997 Masters. Down by three shots, Monty said he considered himself the favorite. Eighteen holes later, and after shooting a not entirely embarrassing 74, Monty was down by nine. Asked if there were a chance Tiger could still lose, Monty snapped, "Have you just come in? Have you been away? Have you been on holiday? There is no chance. We're all human beings here. There's no chance humanly possible." That Saturday round was so dizzying for Monty that he went out the next day and shot an 81, finishing an unbelievable 24 shots behind Tiger. He's just one back of Tiger today, but after his joke he goes on to double-bogey the 6th, slipping out of contention.

12:11 PM ▪ Dubai's hottest months are obviously during the summer, when 110 degrees and up isn't considered outrageous. But even in January the temp has climbed to the mid-80s. If I can just hold on for forty-five more minutes, there are free bottles of water in the media tent. And unlike in Hollywood, no one will be asking for them back.

But first Tiger has to negotiate the 8th. The par-4 6th is a tough hole, but the par-4 8th is a great hole. The tee shot is elevated and looks down on a fairway a good forty feet below it. In the distance, dozens of skyscrapers rise above the palm trees. From the landing area, the hole turns uphill and right, tempting players to cut off some of the corner from the tee. But missing right may lead you to the most penal place on the course, an open expanse covered in scrub brush where a ball will almost never be found. Tiger avoids all the potential mess, arrives at his ball in the fairway, and yawns. That would be the only evidence that he's tired. He knocks his second shot into birdie range and drops the putt, making a simple 3 on a hole that will humble most players before the week is through.

By the end of the day, eleven players shoot 67. None shoots 66. Tiger shoots 65. And after watching him walk away with a par on the last, I was about to experience my first Tiger Woods press conference.

12:51 PM ▪ "Tiger Woods in the interview room," Michael Gibbons, the moderator, calls out quickly as he tries to keep pace with Tiger as he strides through the media tent. I grab a seat, assuming a stampede, but many of the reporters hang back by the entrance, anxious to get back to the stories they've already started writing.

The moment Tiger is seated, Gibbons begins by asking him to take us through his birdies and bogeys.

Tiger didn't have any bogeys, but he's not rattled by the insult. Instead, he proceeds to fly through his round in a display of memory that is as impressive to me as the 65 he just shot:

"Started on ten. I hit driver and a five-wood just short. Chipped up to about an inch and made that. Fourteen, I hit a five-wood and a five-iron to about eight feet and made that. Eighteen, I hit three-wood and a three-wood and two-putted from about thirty-five feet. On number one, I hit a driver and a seven-iron to about twenty feet. Four, I hit a seven-iron to about two feet. Seven, I hit a six-iron to about eight feet and made that. Eight, I hit a driver and a seven-iron to again about eight feet and made that."

He can remember all that, and I'm not even sure which hat I am currently wearing on my own head. With the floor now open to questions, he is asked how his play today compared to last week. "Oh, definitely better. I had two good days of practice the last couple days and started to hit the ball a lot better than I did last week." A lot better than a week in which he won by eight? I stifle my amusement. This guy is unreal. A few more questions, and the reporters are already out of ammo. Tiger Woods is difficult to interview. In general, if a player is in the lead, he'll follow his round with a visit to the press tent. Because Tiger is in the lead so often, there aren't many golf-related questions he hasn't been asked after more than a decade. Outside of lobbing softball questions about the rewards of fatherhood, personal questions are typically off limits. Even what seems like the most banal of inquiries can be shot down without warning. After winning the 2006 British Open and talking candidly about the emotions of winning his first major since his father's death, Tiger was asked the seemingly less personal question of what he might put in the Claret Jug trophy to celebrate. "Beverage of my choice, and not just once." The press room laughed and a reporter naturally followed by saying, "May I ask what the beverage of your choice is?" "Yes, you can," Tiger answered. "You just asked. Will I answer? No."

What remains are the questions that are neither personal nor about golf, which are my favorite because of how tortured Tiger becomes when they're asked. During yesterday's press conference, while I was still at 30,000 feet, Tiger was asked what he thought about Barack Obama. "Oh God, here we go," Tiger said. His angst goes back to an understandable lack of trust with the press. In 1997, when he was only twenty-one, he famously told some inappropriate jokes to a *GQ* reporter and was dismayed when the writer put them into print. Since then, he says in public only what he wouldn't mind reading on the front page the next day.

And because he says so little, that's usually where his comments land.

Which leads back to his Obama answer. "Well, I've seen him speak. He's extremely articulate, very thoughtful." Then, perhaps recognizing he was coming too close to an endorsement, he changes course. "I'm just impressed at how well, basically all politicians really do, how well they think on their feet." Ironically, it's exactly what Tiger just did.

Some writers have critiqued Tiger's press conferences as bland. I don't see that at all. I see calculation, the upshot of which is that he remains in complete control. In a room of thirty writers all hoping to convince their editors that sending them to Dubai was a worthwhile expense, shutting them up is pretty fun to watch.

After we sit in silence for a few beats, Tiger says, "Is that *it*?" After one more question, it is. Tiger says thanks and stands up, and I, thinking it appropriate after his round of 65, start to applaud. When no one else in the press tent follows my lead, I feel like an idiot. Only after the fact do I remember the famous maxim: no cheering in the press box. My cover nearly blown, I slip out the door and head for the taxis.

THE TIGER WOODS ▪ It doesn't seem like such an outrageous idea. All I want to do is drive to Al Ruwaya, the golf course Tiger is designing, and see what it looks like. The announcement that Tiger's first foray into golf course architecture would be in Dubai came at the end of 2006. On Wednesday, Tiger told the press he hadn't made it out to the site yet this trip, but that they have two holes shaped and are working on a third. Two and a half holes in fourteen months? What are they using, Tonka trucks? Everything in Dubai happens quickly, except, for some reason, this. The course's Web site isn't much more helpful and provides no photos of the progress, just some rough sketches of what the holes will look like when they're completed. I want to see for myself and figure that when I find it, I will be one of the first.

Outside the Golden Sands I flag down a taxi and meet Rashid, a thirty-five-year-old Pakistani driver with a half-beard who has been circling the area for forty minutes looking for a customer. He's more dressed up than the other taxi drivers I've had. Wearing brown slacks, a long-sleeved cream-collared shirt, and a bright orange tie with matching orange epaulettes on his shoulders, Rashid sports a pseudomilitary look that inspires my confidence.

"Okay, Rashid, do you know where the golf course is that Tiger Woods is building?"

"Golf course, yes!" He peels out and we head south.

Within ten minutes, we've left the city and are driving through the desert. That's one of the many strange things about Dubai. It's massive and over the top, yet if you drive five miles inland from the Persian Gulf, there's nothing to see but sand. Especially today. "What's wrong with this weather?" "Yes, not good," Rashid says. It was cold and windy this morning, but I didn't think much of it. But now, as we drive deeper into the desert, visibility drops to a few hundred feet and the world around us turns brown. Rashid flips on his lights as blown sand starts to pile up on the highway. "What's going on?" I ask. *"Shmal,"* Rashid says. A *shmal* is the rarest of Dubai weather—a winter sandstorm. Twenty minutes outside town, Rashid makes a right at a sign for the Dubai Sports Complex. We follow the road until it comes to an end at an outdoor race track where, even in this weather, a fleet of Porsches is zipping around corners.

"Okay!" Rashid turns and says with a smile.

"Okay, what?"

"Race track!"

"No, *golf course*," I say. Like I did the night before with Mahmut, I show him my best golf swing.

"Oh, *golf.* . . ." He shakes his head, embarrassed.

I give him the rest of the information I have, which isn't much. "It's a golf course supposedly inside Dubailand." He lights up. "Dubailand!" He wheels the car around with the same speed as the Porsches next to us, and off we go again.

Dubailand is the Arab world's answer to Disneyland but, not surprisingly, a few hundred times bigger. Covering three billion square feet (another Dubai "fact"), the megacomplex will include theme parks, sports stadiums, apartments, hotels, and shopping. Between residents, tourists, and workers, Dubailand claims that it will boast a population of two and a half million people, an estimate that becomes even more absurd when I realize that's bigger than the entire current population of Dubai itself.

Rashid finds the main entrance. On the outside wall I see the black, round Arabic symbol I recognize as the logo for Tiger's golf course and housing development and underneath it, "The Tiger Woods." I love the "the." If you needed an original name but still wanted to capitalize on Tiger's involvement, I suppose that's the most obvious way to do it. We drive through a thirty-foot-high wooden gate, clearly mimicking the front gate of Jurassic Park, and continue on toward the Dubailand welcome center. Looping over and around the yellow building is a roller coaster with people in it. Not a real roller coaster, of course, and not real people. Dummies hang upside down in the cars with their hands up, having a fantastic time. Next to the roller coaster is a one-third scale model of the space shuttle, ready to blast off. And flying over the roof is a giant downhill skier. None of these is a working attraction, just things to whet your appetite until the actual Dubailand is built. Best I can tell, this welcome center *is* the only part of Dubailand that is built. And judging by the empty parking lot, the population hasn't quite hit two and a half million.

I hop out of the cab and experience the *shmal* for the first time. In the three seconds it takes to run to the double doors, sand is coating every exposed inch of me. When the automatic doors won't open, I force them apart with my hands and duck inside.

On the other side are three Pakistani workers, surprised to see anyone. Official current Dubailand population: five (I'm padding the numbers by counting Rashid, too).

No time for small talk.

"I'm looking for *The* Tiger Woods."

They stop and turn to each other, discussing the question in Urdu; then the head guy says in English, "Take him upstairs."

The lackey takes me to an elevator, and we climb to the second floor. Maybe those weren't dummies in that roller coaster. Maybe that's how Dubailand disposes of anyone who dares to look for The Tiger Woods before it's finished. The doors open, and I'm led down the hall to a giant map of Dubailand. Not what Dubailand looks like now, of course, but what it will look like two hundred years from now when it's completed. He points out the golf course and housing community on the map.

"There. The Tiger Woods," he says.

"How do I get there?"

"Al-Ain Road, then . . . right on *this*." He points to another street.

"And what's the name of that street?" I ask, hopeful.

"Hmm . . . I don't know."

Back in the cab, my fare has topped 90 dirhams (about thirty bucks), and I'm carrying only 120. "It's off Al-Ain Road, Rashid. Let's try again tomorrow." I slump back into my seat. "Al-Ain Road, tomorrow!" Rashid exclaims and begins the trip back toward the city. In the world of taxi drivers, there is no sweeter ride than a foreigner trying to find an oasis in the desert.

SECOND ROUND

12:25 PM ▪ As Tiger sets to begin his round, I already know the mistake I've made. Five days ago in San

Diego, I was stuck in the sun wearing rain gear. Today I'm stuck in the cold wearing shorts and no jacket. Tiger, of course, is thoroughly prepared for the conditions. Beneath his white Nike shirt he is wearing a black skintight undershirt made of space-age material and looks thoroughly comfortable. The high winds are whipping sand onto the golf course and have forced Tiger to wear sunglasses, a rare sight. He sports the black shades only between shots, but the additional piece of equipment is a real distraction since he never really knows where to put them. Throughout the first hole, the glasses travel from his face to the top of his hat to resting on the golf bag to the pocket on Stevie's bib. Along the way Tiger misses the fairway, misses the green, hits a poor chip, and makes a poor putt to start with a bogey.

12:50 PM ▪ The 2nd hole at the Emirates Golf Club is a short, 351-yard par 4 with a lake along the right side. The water is usually only a semi-concern, but today's wind is blowing hard left to right, meaning a well-struck shot down the middle might still end up wet. I move ahead of the crowds and down the left side, figuring that's where Tiger will go to avoid the big mistake. He does, and his drive flies over our heads and through the rough before trickling into the desert. A British marshal scampers over and drops his hat on top of the ball to mark it.

As Tiger arrives, the marshal picks it up like a waiter revealing a gourmet meal. Instead, Tiger's treated to a fried egg, his ball sitting smack in the middle of a footprint. Tiger studies the shot, worried about whether he can even get a club on it from that lie. As he mulls it over, I feel something foreign on my shoulder. I slowly turn to find that a wee tourist has decided that the best way to see is to go on his tiptoes and rest his chin on me. Now, how can I not respect someone willing to do that? Besides, as the temperature continues to drop, I actually appreciate all the body heat I can get, even if some of it's not mine. Tiger indeed has trouble getting much club on it and advances it only thirty yards toward the hole. He scrambles for par, fortunate not to start with back-to-back bogeys.

1:13 PM ▪ Despite the weather, the crowd has doubled from only a few hundred yesterday to a thousand today. The rush to get to number 3 leads to anarchy as fans duck under ropes and run toward the tee box to beat Tiger there. Watching people from every race and religion running, I realize this is like the Olympics for out-of-shape people. The 3rd, a straight, slightly uphill par 5, is playing dead downwind, and Tiger takes advantage of it, launching a drive high into the air, carrying sixty yards past Monty's drive. He makes a 4 to get back to 7 under for the week.

1:57 PM ▪ As Tiger surveys a thirty-foot putt for birdie on the 7th, I am easily the most uncomfortable that I've ever been on a golf course. It's a little hard for me to explain. I mean, it's cold, maybe in the mid-50s, but every winter in college I was one of the last people on campus still wearing shorts to class. These chills may be more than just because of the storm. Last night I ate at Kentucky Fried Chicken's Dubai location, maybe not the smartest decision. I try to take notes but find my hands won't stop shaking, so I stuff them inside my short-sleeved shirt. When Tiger makes his long birdie putt, I'm compelled to pull them back out and clap.

3:53 PM ▪ On the range yesterday morning, Tiger finished his warm-up by hitting a handful of massive forty-yard hooks. I figured he was either having a stroke or there was a hole out here where that was the ideal shot to play. There are actually two. The first is here at the 13th, a 550-yard, dogleg left par 5. Like the 3rd hole earlier in the day, this too is playing downwind, and Tiger smokes it. Over the fairway, over the rough, past a set of palm trees, over all of us, finally touching down between two bushes in the desert. Three more feet in any direction, and he has no shot at all. When he and Stevie finally arrive after the long journey from the tee, Tiger shakes his head and says, "Best swing I made all day." Blocked by the bushes, Tiger hits a wedge into the fairway and, for the second straight day, leaves the birdie hole with just a par.

4:05 PM ▪ Even though he didn't make a bogey and remains near the top of the leaderboard at 7 under, Tiger feels the need to regroup. He walks to the side of the tee and drops his head to think, then takes a few practice swings in slow motion, as if he's retraining his arms to do what has always been second nature. Dubai loves exaggeration, but the extra focus it takes to play quality golf in bad weather can't be overstated. Wind has a way of turning good shots into bad ones a lot more than it seems to make bad ones good. And for a self-described "control freak" like Tiger, I imagine nothing is more unnerving than believing he has factored in everything on a shot, only to have the wind switch directions or gust or stop altogether. Tiger breaks from his one-man huddle and drills a 3-wood stinger into the teeth of the wind, over the bunker, and onto the fairway.

The pep talk that I thought was unnecessary ends up helping him to play the last five holes 1 under par after playing the first thirteen at just even. His *shmal*-filled round of 71 is just enough to hold the lead by a shot heading into the weekend.

Back at the hotel, the first thing I do is take the hottest shower possible. After twenty minutes, the chills I've picked up during the day are still there. I bundle up in all the layers I should have been wearing at the course and order a pizza from room service. It is a creepy-looking pizza. It is round and there is cheese on top, but that is where the similarities to an actual pizza end. The dough is spiked with some curry-like spice, and the inclusion of butter and ketchup packets don't exactly bespeak the kitchen's confidence that they know what they're doing. But having not eaten anything since breakfast, I force down three pieces and fall asleep around nine.

Two hours later, I wake up and know at least one of my streaks is coming to an end. The last time I threw up was February 2000. There was nothing noteworthy about it. But after a few years had passed, I started to think, "Huh, I haven't been sick in a while." Eventually, it became something I boasted about at dinner parties. But now, in Dubai of all places, the streak comes to an end. Afterward, I am expecting that immediate relief, for my body to say that the worst has passed. It doesn't happen. And so I just lie there in the middle of the bathroom, picturing what a Dubai hospital is like. I haven't seen one, but it is safe to assume it is the biggest in the world. Or maybe it is built in the shape of a giant thermometer. Either way, I had a good run with Tiger. A hundred and eight holes. Six rounds. To borrow the line Gary Koch used when calling Tiger's snaking birdie putt at the 17th hole of the 2001 Players Championship, I am "better than most."

I never do call a doctor, figuring whatever they charge for house calls in Dubai is an expense no father of two with bad health insurance can afford. And in the morning I feel better. Not much, like 2 percent, but it is enough to give me hope that maybe I can survive six more miles around the course. Tiger isn't off till one, so I stay in bed till ten, then find Rashid's card and give him a ring. "Al-Ain Road!" he says when I tell him who it is. He'll be downstairs in ten minutes.

THE TIGER WOODS, TAKE 2 ▪ Rashid is already outside, using the extra time to wipe the last of the sand off his Corolla. There are no signs of yesterday's storm, despite the fact the English-language paper outside my door led with the headline "Winds Shred Life in UAE." As we head back to the desert, I ask Rashid about his family. Turns out he has a wife and one child, neither of whom he's seen in two years. His story is pretty much the standard one in Dubai. He'll stay away from home for another five to seven years, then return with enough money to buy a house and support his family. He's not sad about it. If anything, he's proud. "In Pakistan, no money for taxi driver." His time in Dubai will be long but not without end, and when he returns home, he'll be a hero.

When we reach Al-Ain Road, our task becomes a question of which empty desert cross street to turn down. There are no street signs, no 7-Elevens, nothing. We take our first right and hope. After a few miles, a structure comes into view. We drive a little bit closer, and I see some sort of tower. Off on the right side of the cab, we pass a sign in the desert that read, "Military compound. No cameras allowed."

"I don't think this is it, Rashid."

"It's okay."

"Turn around, Rashid."

He doesn't listen and keeps heading toward the yellow security gate, walled in on every side. I stuff my camera under my jacket as we pull up to the guard window. There's no one there. In fact the whole place appears abandoned. On the other side of the gate, the empty desert road continues in a straight line. More of Dubai's smoke and mirrors.

"This isn't it."

"Yes." Rashid finally agrees.

We pass through the gates and make a U-turn as another car comes our way. Rashid waits and flags him down. As the burly man walks over us, Rashid rolls down my window. Thanks, Rashid.

"Do you know *The* Tiger Woods?" I ask.

He thinks for a moment then nods. "Al-Hibab Road."

Rashid repeats it, "Al-Hibab Road?!"

"Yes."

"Al-Hibab Road! *Salam Maleka!*"

This is as excited as I've seen Rashid in two days.

"You know where Al-Hibab Road is?" I ask.

"No."

Even if he did know where it was, we couldn't leave anyway. A pack of camels has appeared out of the desert and crosses through the unguarded gate and into the base. It's such a perfect Arabian moment that despite the signs, I pull out my camera and take some pictures. "They're going to Jumeirah Beach!" Rashid says, making a pretty good joke for someone with limited English.

We try every road within ten miles. Eventually, Rashid turns off the meter. "Too much money," he says. We stop at a junkyard and ask some workers. Nothing. We find an isolated model home development and ask the guard. "I don't know," he says. And so, after another hour and with Tiger's tee time approaching, I quit. "It doesn't exist, Rashid." If nothing else, that would certainly explain why Tiger hadn't been out to see it yet. There isn't anything to see. The Tiger Woods is buried underneath the sand like all the other things on my Dubai map, existing on paper but not in reality. In silence, Rashid drives me back toward the Emirates Golf Club, still sick and now also defeated.

THIRD ROUND

As he did last Saturday, Tiger starts the weekend in the lead and paired with a relative unknown chasing him. Last week, Kevin Streelman, this week a roly-poly former club professional from Ireland named Damien McGrane. But McGrane's reaction to playing with Tiger doesn't exactly have him bouncing off the walls when he met with reporters yesterday.

"Has it been a big ambition to play with him?"

"No, I wouldn't say it's my lifelong dream."

"Do you think you'll be nervous?"

"I hope not."

The sense is that McGrane is just one of the sixty-eight remaining European Tour regulars who doesn't particularly want to let Tiger show up at one of his own events, scoop up a giant appearance fee, and take home the trophy as well.

1:40 PM ▪ Tiger is even par through his first three holes when I run into Asif. He is the tenth person who has stopped me and asked to test-drive my periscope. Dubai claims to have everything a person could want, but no one has one of these. Asif is an East Indian Kenyan who was born in Canada but now lives in Dubai. For Asif, as for most of the people I've met here, Dubai is just a lily pad on which he'll float until life takes him somewhere else.

Still waiting for Tiger to turn on his magic, I ask Asif for any places in Dubai I have to see before I leave. "Forget about the tourist spots. You need to see the *real* Dubai." He tells me about the northern part of the city, where vendors sell gold and jewelry, and beat-up water taxis float along Dubai Creek. It sounds refreshingly different from the controlled glitz Dubai pushes on tourists. "And watch out for the whores," he adds. Maybe not so refreshing.

2:30 PM ▪ By the time Tiger sprays his drive into the desert on the 8th, he has lost his lead. At 1 over par for the day, he is now two shots behind Sweden's Henrik Stenson. And the hard-to-scare McGrane is still where he was, just one shot back. Most of Tiger's game is solid, but his driver is a disaster. The crowds have shrunk, too, with just a few hundred people outside the ropes. As big a draw as he is, European fans seem more willing to ditch even the world's best to track a player who is actually posting a good number.

The exodus puts me in the front row as Tiger looks at the trouble shot he has left himself. The ball is well below his feet, a downhill sidehill lie off the sand to an elevated green. Further complicating things is a row of palm trees right in front of him. Tiger stands behind the ball and runs the odds of pulling off different shots through his swoosh-covered supercomputer. I finally grasp just how hard it really is for even Tiger to win a golf tournament. Every part of his game is firing except one, and he's suddenly playing catch-up. Last week's blowout at the Buick Invitational isn't really the norm, it's an anomaly. In 2007, Tiger won seven times, but in six of those events his margin of victory was only two shots.

All of which makes a shot from the desert on Saturday's front nine just as critical as a shot on the back nine Sunday. He grabs a 5-iron and takes a few practice swings, exaggerating the motion of rolling his wrists over at impact. He's going low with a draw. Right between the trees. As he steadies himself over the ball, a marshal reminds us to "Stand, please!" in case we've somehow forgotten by the five hundredth time. A fan slowly lifts her camera phone and takes a silent picture. Tiger's shot splits the ten-yard gap in the palms and turns up the hill. It hits in the fairway and rolls, climbing the slope as best it can. When it stops, it's only seven or eight yards short of the green. A chip and a putt later, Tiger saves his par.

3:52 PM ▪ But on a perfect day in Dubai, pars aren't good enough. Everyone is surging up the leaderboard, and Tiger is being left behind. Ernie Els is now 10 under after starting his back nine eagle-birdie-par-birdie. Tiger is still stuck at 8 under with two surging Swedes, Peter Hedblom and Henrik Stenson. I wish Nelson from Torrey Pines were here to look through his periscope and diagnose exactly what's wrong.

Tiger has appeared patient all day, but when he airmails the 13th fairway for the second day in a row, he's fried. He has to take a one-stroke penalty out of the bush and is not in that happy swami place he found on the 15th at Torrey Pines North last week. He stands behind his ball, notices the shadow of a fan's head near it, then lifts his foot and stomps on it, ordering it to move. He's acting as if the fan was making shadow puppets or something. He can take out his anger on his golf bag, but to do it on one of us seems like a dangerous precedent. It doesn't take him long to realize this, and when the head ducks away, Tiger immediately says, "Thank you." Then for good measure, "Thank you. I appreciate it." To succeed in golf, players are often encouraged by their sports psychologists to be themselves. The problem for Tiger is that he's an intense guy in love with a gentleman's game.

4:41 PM ▪ Tiger lumbers through the back nine still at 8 under. When he arrives at the last hole, Ernie has finished with a 7-under 65 and a score of 11 under. Last year's champ, Stenson, is in the clubhouse at 10 under. Lee Westwood and Graeme McDowell have caught up and are both in at 8 under as well. Tiger is just 1 under since his brilliant opening round on Thursday. But he still has the 18th.

The 18th at the Emirates is the other hole where Tiger wants to hit his big sweeping hook. A 564-yard par 5, it looks a little as if someone took the 18th at Torrey Pines and bent it ninety degrees left, right down to the lake that fronts the entire green. Average-length hitters can't reach, but Tiger's drive is bombed and settles slightly into the rough, 230 yards from the hole.

Tiger knows he's behind. Some players get nervous by looking at leaderboards, believing that ignorance is bliss. I've noticed that Tiger can't stop looking. The more knowledge he has, the better. With Ernie at 11 under, he is going for the green. From up near the green, I look back and see Tiger take out his 3-wood. It seems like a lot of club from 230 yards until I see it start off high, a soft cut shot that he wants to land gently on the green. It moves a little right, then a little more. Even from two hundred yards back I hear Tiger start yelling at it, "Go . . . Go!" Halfway over the lake, the ball stops dead, like a harpoon without enough rope. It falls to the water and disappears with a splash.

The gallery is confused. I'm not confused, I'm miffed. *I sacrificed my eight-year throw-up streak just so I could witness a Saturday afternoon tank job?* There is no club tossing from Tiger, no bag kicking, no shadow stomping, either, just resignation that he's made his task tomorrow that much harder. He putts out for a bogey to some polite applause. He'll start the final round four shots behind Els.

THE REAL DUBAI ▪ Feeling unimpressed by Tiger's play and still nauseous, I leave my hotel looking for the "real Dubai," as Asif called it. The worker at the front desk says I can walk to the Creek more easily than taking a cab. He obviously doesn't realize what I've been doing the last two weeks. But at this point, what's another couple of miles? Being a pedestrian here is tricky, though. There is so much construction going on that as I make the hike I'm constantly butting up against closed-off sidewalks or open trenches that force me into traffic, where I face a whole other set of dangers.

Within a few blocks of the hotel, everything changes. No cranes or malls or McDonald's; they have been replaced by hole-in-the-wall restaurants, Indian barbers cutting hair, and eight-story apartment buildings that go on as far as I can see. As I walk, I look in the windows and see some people watching TV; others are outside retrieving clothes from the balcony. It's funny, but the real Dubai isn't particularly Arab at all. It's Pakistani and Indian and Asian. And almost completely devoid of women. It makes sense considering that Rashid and so many others left their wives at home when they came here, but it is bizarre to spend even a little bit of time in a place where the men seem to outnumber the women a hundred to one. Which explains Asif's warnings about the prostitutes. I arrive at the "Creek," a dredged inlet from the gulf spreading 350 yards from one side to the other. Lighting both sides of the waterway are orange lamps to help guide boats across. One of them pulls up and offers to take me to the other side, but I wave him off and head for bed.

FINAL ROUND

After Rashid's and my failure in the desert, I call him one last time to show me two things I felt confident we could find: the Persian Gulf and the Burj Al Arab hotel. As far as the gulf goes, my ignorant American mind was picturing waves of oil lapping the shore. It's actually beautiful and blue, but don't call it the Persian Gulf. It's the Arabian Gulf, a reminder of the U.A.E.'s long-standing cultural tension between itself and its neighbor a hundred miles to the north in Iran. From there it's off to the tallest hotel in the world, where Tiger has spent his week. Only hotel guests are permitted inside the gates of the Burj Al Arab, which sits three hundred feet offshore, so Rashid and I make do with the view from afar. I feel as if I've become a skeptic on this trip, but it just doesn't look that big. This seems like a fact they couldn't get away with inventing, so I ask someone else on the outside looking in if it's true. She clarifies it for me—the Burj Al Arab is the tallest *single-purpose* hotel in the world. You've got to love Dubai. I take out my Burj Al Arab postcard and draw a little asterisk on its giant heliport.

12:10 PM ▪ Tiger arrives at the 1st tee, going with the red mock T over the collared shirt this week, a look I'm confident in saying no other golfer in the world can pull off. Really, he could show up to play in a red tank top with a black bicycle helmet on his head and I'm convinced someone would nod and say, "Now, that is cool."

Tiger can pull it off because he plays like this: his drive on the first hole is straight down the middle, forty yards ahead of the Irishman McGrane, who is still playing with Tiger after hanging tough with a 72 yesterday. From there Tiger stuffs his second shot to three feet. He doesn't waste a second on the birdie, tapping it in and getting himself back to 8 under.

1:21 PM ▪ Tiger is waiting at the 7th tee, in the midst of making a run at the leaders who are just teeing off. He's played the first six holes 2 under par and has pulled back to within a few shots of Ernie Els. But it's all on hold for a moment, as the group on the green is taking forever to putt. Tiger leans against a cooler and says to no one in particular, "How slow are these guys playing?" For a control freak, he does a good job disconnecting. He just swings his legs and checks out the scenery, noticing everything except the hundreds of people staring at him.

While he waits, England's Lee Westwood crosses by. Westwood is two years older than Tiger but until recently has been wrapped in an ever-present layer of baby fat. Working with trainers, he has lost six inches on his waist, picked up fifteen yards off the tee, and rediscovered the winning ways he had early in his career.

As he passes by, he sees Tiger's dropping score and smirks at him, a look I take as Westwood saying, "You're going to win every damn tournament this year, aren't you?" As if reading his mind, Tiger shrugs his shoulders and smiles back.

1:45 PM ▪ The smiles come to an abrupt stop at the 9th green when, after two solid shots, Tiger three-putts. He birdied three out of his first four holes on the front but plays his last five in 2 over. The walk between nines takes me past a leaderboard, and I take a look to see where Tiger stands.

Tiger often speaks of a score he secretly has in his head during the final round that he believes he needs to shoot in order to win the tournament. Last night while walking back from the Creek, I did the same and came up with a round of 65. Fourteen under par.

But with nine holes left, the leaderboard reads like this:

Els	−12
Stenson	−11
Oosthuizen	−10
Kaymer	−10
McDowell	−9

And tacked on at the very bottom, almost just to be nice:

Woods	−8

Tiger is just as far behind as he was when he started his round. I don't know what Tiger's number is, but he can't get to mine.

2:31 PM ▪ Tiger makes a routine birdie on the par-5 10th and is facing a difficult pitch shot behind the green on the long par-4 12th. The lie is downhill and half buried, but the grass still looks wispy, a combination that makes how hard to hit it a total guess. It's the kind of lie that Judge Smails from *Caddyshack* might kick and say, "Don't count that, I was interfered with," but Tiger doesn't have that luxury.

From that weird downhill lie, with no more than twenty-five feet to the hole, Tiger takes a half swing with the face of his wedge wide open. It pops right out, lands softly on the green, and he watches as it rolls into the right side of the cup for a birdie. The fans let out their loudest cheer of the week, while a Brit next to me waves his cap and says, "Good show!" I didn't know people actually did that. The renewed smiles on everyone's faces tell me they think he can still pull this off.

2:46 PM ▪ He'll have to keep it going on the par-5 13th. The hole has bullied him this week—in the water Thursday, the desert Friday, and yesterday, a bush. Today he avoids all the trouble and casually knocks in a three-footer for his third birdie in four holes. *Eleven under.*

3:01 PM ▪ An hour ago, Tiger was completely out of this tournament. Now, as I make for the 14th green, I start to do the math in my head. If he birdies the short par-4 17th and the par-5 18th, he can get to 13 under. But something else would have to fall.

From 170 yards, Tiger drops his second shot to ten feet, just short of the hole. He tears off his glove aggressively as he strides to the green, wanting to get in as many holes as possible before the magic runs out. Watching him circle his putt, I sense that I am actually anxious. I'm legitimately worried that he will miss this and squander a chance to pull even closer. Maybe my nerves can be explained away as a spike in nationalism because we are both so far from home, but I think some part of me is beginning to care about whether or not Tiger Woods wins. His birdie putt starts just left of the hole, bends back toward the cup, and drops in the front. *Twelve under!* I join the crowd and cheer, outclapping most of those around me. He's birdied four of his five holes on the back nine. Tiger does a very subtle fist pump, like you might do to get Heinz ketchup out of a bottle. He grabs the ball out of the cup, hops over the hole, and keeps on going, off the green and up to the 15th tee.

As I head up the hill, I look to my right and see that Tiger and I are within a foot of each other. For the first time, I feel a need to say something to him. His resolve over these five holes has been too amazing to ignore. Without giving it any thought, I blurt out "Good putt, Tiger!" He doesn't stop. He doesn't look. He ignores me.

3:12 PM ▪ Ernie Els may be four groups behind Tiger, but when Tiger steps to the 15th tee, Ernie is putting on the 11th green, no more than fifty feet away. During yesterday's press conference, Els said he likes to see what other players are doing. "And especially Tiger . . . he could get red hot at any time and you'd like to see what's going on." He might want to rethink that strategy. After hearing the cheer at fourteen and now seeing him in the flesh, the man nicknamed "The Big Easy" promptly yanks his four-foot par putt. It never even touches the cup, and he slips back to only 12 under. I don't believe what I'm seeing. In a mere five holes, Tiger has gone from having no chance of winning to being tied for the lead.

When Tiger is playing well, he's in everybody's head. But no big-name player has lost to Tiger as often as Ernie. At the 1998 Johnnie Walker Classic in Thailand, Els was up eight shots heading into the final round and lost to a surging Tiger on the second hole of sudden death. Two years later, at the Mercedes Championship, they dueled again into extra holes before Tiger drained a forty-foot putt to beat him again. And then there was two years ago, right here at the Desert Classic. Tiger and Ernie were tied after 72 holes when Ernie's 4-iron into the 18th green came up short in the lake, handing Tiger yet another victory. A win here would begin to heal a few of the South African's wounds.

3:39 PM ▪ With pars on 15 and 16, Tiger has to finish with back-to-back birdies to have a chance. The scorecard for the 17th hole at the Emirates says it's 359 yards long. But if Tiger can convince himself that the entire right side of the hole isn't a golf ball graveyard filled with stumpy palm trees, bushes, sand, and rocks, it's merely a 320-yard blind shot to the green. Needing birdie, there's no doubt he will be cutting the corner.

I run for the green, anxious to see where his drive comes down. It's harder to find a good spot ever since Els and Tiger crossed paths. In a moment that couldn't have done much for Ernie's fragile confidence, many of his fans peeled off and have decided to follow Tiger instead. From the green we can't see Tiger and he can't see us; our only clue is watching those fans positioned halfway to the tee.

We see their heads turn in unison, and our murmurs build as everyone braces for the thud. It lands on the front left part of the green, safe, and we cheer Tiger's gutsy play. He has a perfect angle to the back-right pin. This back nine has showcased almost every facet of Tiger's game. Chipping—12. Irons—14. And now, on 17, his incredible length and accuracy off the tee when he must have it. Tiger's bump and run for eagle looks good, but Tiger is begging it to turn a little more right. It skims the left edge and doesn't stop rolling until it is a missable eight feet away. As he walks to mark it, he turns and reads the leaderboard.

Els	−12	through	13
Oosthuizen	−12		F
Woods	−12	through	16

I narrow my focus onto the small circle of white-painted dirt around the inside of the cup. That's all that matters now. The putt slips over the front edge. Tiger steps toward the hole and punches the air. The crowd cheers again, silently chastising itself for ever wasting its time watching Ernie Els. Tiger is at 13 under and has the lead all to himself.

3:49 PM ▪ But he still hasn't reached my number. Fourteen under. The high hook off the 18th tee is step one. He clobbers it, wrapping it around the desert forest and stopping it just before it hits the rough on the far side of the fairway. How important is that hook he was working on Thursday morning? By pulling it off, he is fifty yards closer to the hole than McGrane, who, despite playing well yesterday, has become only a footnote at this point. He and Tiger were tied when they started the round. Tiger now leads him by ten.

Tiger is almost close enough to power a 3-iron all the way to the front pin, but the last thing he wants to do is flirt with the water and give the tournament away. At least I'm hoping that's what he's thinking. Just to make sure, I find myself starting to give Tiger advice under my breath:

Don't be stupid, don't be stupid . . .

He grabs his 5-wood, then Stevie's towel, and rubs down the grip, needing every bit of tackiness for a shot with this much at stake.

The moment he hits it, there's no chance it's wet. Any of the wind that knocked down his 3-wood yesterday can't touch his 5-wood today as the ball flies the green, bounces, and then gets hung up in the deep rough in front of the back bunker. Tiger drops his club in frustration. To the chagrin of the European tourists next to me who are just down for a relaxing holiday, I restart my one-way dialogue:

Up and down, up and down, up and down! . . .

4:00 PM ▪ At most PGA events, ringing the 18th green is a series of grandstands. Here there is only one large bleacher to the left of the green while behind it are three separate, glassed-in "corporate chalets" used by the sponsors and the sheiks themselves, many of whom are practically pressing their noses against the glass and staring down at Tiger playing his shot from the rough beneath them.

Because the ball is in the grass but his feet are in the bunker, he tries all sorts of stance/swing combinations before he finds one he likes. Besides that, he also has to factor in the thing he thought he was done worrying about—the lake. The green slopes severely back to front, and he just watched Damien McGrane hit not one but two balls into the water. If his pitch jumps out of the grass, it won't stop. He finds the spot on the green where he wants it to land, and returns to the ball, where he takes, I count, *seven* more practice swings. I've never seen anything done with such decisiveness.

For all of Tiger's hard work, he finally hits it, only to have it pop straight up and dribble onto the green, twenty feet short of the hole. Tiger fumes, tossing his wedge toward his bag in disgust. It clangs against his clubs and falls to the ground as Stevie hands him his putter.

And so it ends. After all his effort to pull close, he's just going to fizzle out with a par. He doesn't need to spend much time on the putt. It's going to do what he was hoping his chip would do, downhill and a couple of feet left to right. In the chalet behind the green, the sheiks are still watching, but not as intently. For eight holes at least, there was nothing boring about golf.

4:01 PM ▪ I never considered that he might actually make it. The first ten feet of the putt, I'm thinking about how I will kill time between the end of the tournament and my flight. But then I notice Tiger is beginning to backpedal as it gets close. Wait, I've seen this kind of thing on television. But it can't actually happen now. While I'm standing here. Suddenly, the putt disappears from view and Tiger turns and fires a huge right hook as the sheiks behind the glass rejoice. I throw my hands in the air and start to laugh. Fourteen under! The number. *My* number!

I pull out my notebook and start scribbling down his score and his stats. He has just delivered a 6-under-par 31 on the back nine on a Sunday. After three-putting the 9th, he only needed ten putts total to play the next nine holes. The crowd cheers, but either they're Els fans or they don't truly appreciate what just happened. Only a few dozen people in the grandstands are actually on their feet. Perhaps the rest are thinking the way I did until nine holes ago: that Tiger's style is, frankly, unbecoming. Or it might just be Dubai. If there's a place in the world that can numb your senses and distort your definition of the word *unbelievable*, this is it.

The only matter left to be decided is whether Tiger can be caught. Everyone else has already folded, but Els remains at 13 under and still has the 18th to play. His drive is solid, to the first cut of rough on the right side, close to where Tiger was. Chances are he will be on or near the green, looking at an eagle to win or a birdie to tie. Instead, his ball is swatted down by the same mysterious wind that grabbed Tiger's the day before, and it lands in the water at least twenty yards short of the green. Ernie passes by me, head down, once again on the losing end of a Tiger miracle. His body language matches that of the man next to me, who is muttering to himself, "Astounding . . . astounding . . . They handed it to him, didn't they? *Didn't they?*" No, Tiger handed it to *them* on Saturday. And on the back nine Sunday, he took it back.

I wheel my suitcase down the steps of the press tent and out to the long taxi line. Two Arab men, both in headdresses, one with a baseball cap perched on top, are directing the cabs and the people, matching up fans who are going to the same parts of town to speed up the queue. The two African men ahead of me are headed to Deira, and I join them, knowing from there it is only a short ride to the airport. One of them can't stop smiling and saying "That was amazing." The other won't stop shaking his head. Most of the fans this week had seemed to watch the action in a daze, almost impossible to impress. Njaaga and Jonathan are a couple of fantastic exceptions.

Njaaga is small, wiry, full of energy, while Jonathan is bigger and calmer, saving his thoughts for the brief moments when Njaaga isn't talking. Forty-something friends from Kenya, the two of them made the four-and-a-half-hour flight solely to see Tiger Woods. It wasn't just because they wanted to do it; Njaaga felt he had to. "In the Muslim religion, I read how in life you have to go to Mecca before you die. That is how this was." The closest he came to Tiger before this was in Milwaukee, of all places. When business took him there a few years back, he went out of his way to visit Brown Deer Golf Club, the place where Tiger made his professional debut back in 1996. "I just wanted to connect with him," he says. When the head pro realized how far Njaaga had come, he went into the back of his shop and dug up an old Greater Milwaukee Open hat for him. He points to it on his head, "And now I wore it to Dubai and he *won!*" I look at Jonathan. He's still shaking his head.

As we drive north on Sheik Zayed Road, we go back through Tiger's round, shot by shot, none of us having seen anything the other didn't but still needing to describe what happened just to make sure it really did. In a week where at times I wondered why I had come at all, in the end my only regret is that I didn't run into these guys until the taxi home.

At this point I realize Tiger can do things no one else ever can or will. That was my justification to

Hillary at the beginning of the year, but now I actually believe it. That said, I still have my hang-ups. As
our cab crosses the Creek into Deira, I know Njaaga is
just the Tiger fan to ask about one of them. "Doesn't
it bother you that he ignores us? That he's just this
cold, calculated killer?" I am still wincing from my
"Good putt, Tiger" that went unappreciated back on
14. Njaaga doesn't answer right away. He thinks about
it and nods, affirming my point of view as a legitimate
gripe. Finally, he speaks. "The way I look at it . . ." he
pauses, picking his words carefully, "that's his work."
He thinks for another moment, and then repeats it,
"That's his *work*." I'm starting to realize that Tiger
Woods works best with his head down.

Fist Pumps of Fury

The WGC-Accenture Match Play Championship

The Gallery Golf Club at Dove Mountain
Marana, Arizona
February 20–24, 2008

There is a good chance my car might not make it across the Arizona desert once, let alone twice. A two-door Ford Explorer, it is the first new car that I bought and paid for all by myself. For years, I have protected and cared for it, never trusting anyone but myself to wash it. Two recent events told me things had changed. When I was home from Dubai, I put my son, Danny, in the back to go on an errand and, while I was strapping him into his car seat, he pointed at something on the floor.

"Dada, what is that?"

"That is called an air freshener. It makes Daddy's car smell good."

He looked at me for a second and then said, "But your car doesn't smell good."

The other incident was back in January, when I drove it into the side of our house. I was backing out of our narrow driveway, lost track of where I was, and heard a loud scraping noise. I got out and saw that the stucco wall was basically sanding down the back right quarter panel of my car. Theoretically, this should have been devastating. But I just shrugged, straightened it out, and drove away. My car has been exacting its revenge ever since by having random accessories break without warning. First was the handle that hung down from the inside of the passenger door to help passengers climb out. I was driving down the freeway when it just dropped off like a bat dying in its sleep. Next was the dashboard light that tells me how much gas I have in my tank. Was that important? The latest thing to go was the power on my driver's-side window. The car probably had another five thousand miles in it, but the eight-hour drive to the Accenture Match Play would be our last road trip together. And if Tiger were to lose in the first round on Wednesday, I'd be back home in thirty-six hours.

L.A. TO TUCSON ▪ I have never gone on a trip in my life without knowing where I'd be staying. When my family took a month-long cross-country vacation together in the late 1980s, my parents had every hotel reserved before we left. I grew up convinced that if we hadn't booked that Flagstaff Days Inn two months ahead of time, we would have been forced to sleep in our car. Still smarting from my Dubai tab, I cautiously dove into the underground economy of Craigslist to see what my other options were. On the cheap end was a thirty-five-dollar-a-night room in an apartment downtown, but the three people renting it seemed a little too interested in finding out my sexuality first. On the expensive end was a Bates Motel–looking one-bedroom, one-bath overlooking the Saguaro National Park for seventy-five dollars a night, the perfect place to stay if you want to be killed in your sleep and have your body easily disposed of before sunrise. The best option was a guest house in North Tucson for sixty dollars a night. I had left a message with Cheryl, the owner, but by the time I left home, I'd yet to hear back.

Since the most distracting things along the five-hundred-mile route are prisons, there is plenty of time to think about life. And for me that means Tiger. Two tournaments, two wins. I shake my head. He just *had* to be thoroughly impressive from the very beginning. His

Sunday comeback had sucked me into his vortex, and I am excited to see how in the world it can be topped.

In between prisons, I hear from Cheryl. The guest house is all mine. I arrive over an hour late, mostly due to the fact that I don't realize there is an hour time difference between the two cities, but also because of the layout of Tucson itself. Ninety percent of the city sits east of Interstate 10, its only freeway. When I exit Prince Road, I naively start to organize my things at stoplights, thinking I'm almost there. Fifteen minutes later, I'm still driving, passing through mile upon mile of liquor stores, check-cashing places, and a dumpy-looking bar called the Elbow Room. They hold a top-tier golf tournament in this town? It seems like a chamber of commerce's worst nightmare. Eventually the seedy Tucson gives way to middle-class Tucson and I'm driving through the tract homes of Cheryl's neighborhood.

Cheryl has an Earth Woman sort of feel to her, her hair curly and graying with a peaceful face frozen in a consistent half-smile. The winter is her busy season as far as guests go, the big rush being the first two weeks of February, when Tucson holds its annual gem show. I'm sure Tiger came into town early to hit that. With her sons grown up and moved on, she figured if she could pick up some extra cash throughout the year, why not? The guest house is a few hundred square feet, and she diligently explains all the nuances of it, right down to making sure I know how to use a TV remote and work a plug-in fan. She even shows me how to stop the shower drain in case I feel like taking a bath.

Next, I have to sign Cheryl's meticulous checklist of every item that is currently in the guest house to prevent getting away with theft. Apparently that gem show crowd is filled with a lot of kleptomaniacs. The only glitch in the whole system is Cheryl's minimum four-night policy, meaning if Tiger can't hang on until the quarterfinals, I'll ultimately spend more money here than if I had spent three nights in an actual hotel where everything anyone would want to steal is already bolted to the floor.

I pay her the money and a deposit and say good night, but she insists that before going to bed I take any and all valuables out of my car, then whispers, "This *is* Tucson." I don't know what the town's official motto is, but I'm hoping that Cheryl's sticks.

FIRST ROUND: J. B. HOLMES

I have seen only one kung fu movie in my life, and staring at the sixty-four-man bracket for the Accenture Match Play, it is the best parallel I can draw to what Tiger Woods will face this week. In *Fist of Fury*, Bruce Lee plays Chen Zhen, a Chinese martial artist who goes to a Japanese school to avenge the murder of his teacher. When he enters, one of the students walks toward him and stretches out his arms to give Zhen a hug. Zhen promptly elbows him in the face, then tosses him against the wall. Another student with an exceptionally bad wig steps forward and starts to swing. Zhen blocks his punch, spins around, and then flips the guy like a baton, at which point the remaining forty students have seen enough and circle around him, ready to pounce. One by one, they rush at Zhen and then watch in horror as he chops, kicks, and generally humiliates each of them in unique and creative ways before he gives one final sneer and walks away victorious.

That would be Tiger's best-case scenario. He hadn't won the Tour's only regular season match play event in four years and had won it twice in only eight tries. For most of that eight-year stretch, he used the fairly legitimate excuse that the greens at the La Costa Resort where it was played were so bumpy and slow that plenty of perfectly stroked putts could never find the bottom of the cup. But last year, no doubt in response to his and others' complaints, the event was moved to Arizona's Gallery Golf Club at Dove Mountain, a private 36-hole club twenty miles north of Tucson. Out here the only bumps on the green are man-made. And in a moment that, at the time, was thoroughly enjoyable for me, it was just such a man-made bump, a ball mark that Tiger never saw, that kicked his par putt offline on the 19th hole and cost him last year's third-round match against Australia's Nick O'Hern.

Over the course of 72 holes, Tiger could make mistakes and still win. Dubai had proven that. But in match play, a stretch of only a few bad holes could end his week and his win streak. "It's a sprint," Tiger had told reporters yesterday. And if your opponent makes more birdies than you do, it's over.

Tiger's first experience with match play came at the age of thirteen. He made it to the quarterfinals of the Southern California Junior Match Play, shot 69, and lost. He came home and told his dad, "I shot a better score than he did, but he won the match. That doesn't seem right." Nearly twenty years after the loss, when a reporter asked if he remembered who beat him that day, he fired back, "James Mohan."

I am a little worried that this year's James Mohan might be J. B. Holmes, a stocky, goateed twenty-six-year-old from Kentucky who doesn't seem to scare easily. Similar to the NCAA tournament, the four brackets for the Match Play are decided by ranking, so whoever ends up facing Tiger Woods in the first round is near the bottom of that list. But J.B. is coming to the Match Play having just won the FBR Open up the freeway in Phoenix three days ago—by way of a one-hole play-off against Phil Mickelson. Under the pressure of sudden death, J.B. hit his opening drive 359 yards. If he is intimidated by top players, that is a weird way of showing it.

11:46 AM ▪ From the top row of the Dove Mountain driving range, it's hard not to be distracted by the view. The lush green course lined with dormant brown rough sits in the shadow of Arizona's Catalina Mountains, the tallest of which is snowcapped. Looking west isn't so bad either: a thirty-mile vista where the desert is broken up by endless cacti, jagged brown peaks, and, far off to the north, an airline graveyard for planes that haven't been used since 9/11.

The bleachers are standing-room-only for one reason: Tiger is on the range. The first sound when Tiger hits a golf shot on the driving range is the thwack of steel colliding with the cover of a golf ball. The second is a few hundred people saying, "Umm!" as they watch it fly out of sight.

12:02 PM ▪ I wedge myself into the right side of the tee on the 1st, a downhill 588-yard par 5. "Stroke Play

Tiger" was pretty impressive the last two tournaments, and I am anxious to see how he compares to "Match Play Tiger." J.B.'s problem is that either way he will still be playing some version of Tiger. After the compulsory introductions and the subtle doff of his white TW-logoed hat, Match Play Tiger Woods hits his opening tee shot off the world right. It's not easy to silence the bleachers on the first tee of a golf tournament. These are fans who have sacrificed a few hours of watching more exciting shots in exchange for being able to tell their friends they saw Tiger Woods hit his first shot of the day. Yet the swing and resulting ball flight bring such an uncomfortable reaction you'd think Tiger had kicked a puppy.

I slink away to find out what exactly happened and find Tiger's ball resting in the side yard of the adobe house between the 1st and the 18th holes. Out of bounds. No one up at the tee knows this, so Tiger makes it halfway down the fairway when a rules official meets him and breaks the news. He's steamed and never does retrieve the ball. He just grabs his driver, hops into the cart, and makes the drive of shame back to the tee.

After his second drive (and third stroke), Tiger still hasn't caught up to J.B.'s first, a dead-straight high bomb that showed no sign of nerves. This first-hole disaster reminds me of a high school golf match where my team played Hueneme High, the worst team in our league. Theirs was a squad filled with players who had started playing the sport the day after they signed up to be on the team. The kid with whom I was playing hacked his way down the first hole, and by the time he arrived at the first green, he was exhausted, covered in sweat, his shirt already untucked, and laying ten. He stood on the fringe huffing, then tried to summon the strength to somehow take off his golf bag. He couldn't do it, spinning around two times before ultimately collapsing next to the green, refusing to get up.

This is going to be a long day, I remember thinking. The good news for Tiger is that he's only 1 down.

12:39 PM ▪ After matching pars on the 2nd, J.B. has a downhill birdie putt on the 3rd hole that no one expects him to make. From my position below the hole, I can't even see the cup. So when he putts it and I hear the gallery higher up on the green gasp, I assume J.B. missed it—until he reaches into the cup and pulls it out. The crowd has shown its cards early in this match, and none of us wants to believe that the world's hottest golfer is 2 down through three holes.

1:07 PM ▪ It's not getting any better. On the 635-yard par-5 5th, Tiger is busy fumbling around, his third shot having been mercifully saved from sliding into a grassy collection area when it drops inside a sprinkler hole. Before he takes his free drop, he reminds Stevie not to touch his ball until it has rolled at least two club lengths, a breach in the rules that would cost him the hole. When J.B. knocks his third shot to eight feet and makes the putt for birdie, it doesn't matter. Just like that, Tiger is 3 down through five.

1:15 PM ▪ The only thing more out of whack than Tiger's game is the XM radio strapped to my arm. Some XM employees were lending them to fans for the day so we could hear the play-by-play of all the other action around the course. It was a great idea, but somehow I have lost XM's PGA Tour station, and the radio is permanently locked on the painful 1980s Gary Numan song, "Cars." I don't know how it happened. After the fourth time through, I take off my headphones and slip them around my neck.

Tiger lightens the mood at the 450-yard 6th when he drops his second shot hole high as J.B. misses left. J.B. makes a solid up and down for par, but Tiger has a real shot at three. A freshly-permed woman near me watches and says, "I'd like to see him do a pump!" Tiger makes the birdie, but no pump. Not when he's still 2 down.

1:29 PM ▪ The 7th at Dove Mountain is normally the kind of hole Tiger can't lose. At 314 yards with no bunkers protecting the front of the green, Tiger can take a driver and knock it on. But J. B. Holmes can do the same thing with a 3-wood. It's a very rare thing to see Tiger outdistanced with every club in his bag. Perhaps feeling the pressure, he takes a big swing off the tee and is late getting his hands through the ball, missing right as he did on the 1st. I tune back in to XM to try to forget about the match and find Gary Numan on his last verse again, one line now sounding far too ominous:

*I know I've started to think about leaving
tonight . . .*

I can't take it anymore and remove the battery. Mercifully, J.B. only makes par to halve the hole. Tiger must be concerned, but one would never know it by looking at him. When he first came on Tour, he was twenty years old. Back then, his facial expressions during a round would run the gamut from goofy to fiery. At thirty-two, he seems to have settled in at sober. Even when he's being threatened by the lowest guy in the bracket, what used to be his poker face now *is* his face.

1:33 PM ▪ Traditionally, "the turn" refers to the midway point where the golf course turns back to the clubhouse for the inward nine holes. Out here the turn comes between the 7th and 8th holes, where after miles and miles of heading directly downhill and away from the Catalina Mountains, we flip around and begin the long climb back toward the clubhouse. Calling this place "The Gallery" is very ironic. I can't imagine a worse golf course at which to be a spectator. The course and the view are beautiful, but never have 18 holes been spread farther apart from one another. Combine that with the number of snowbirds out here for the winter, and the abnormal number of first aid stations along our route makes sense. There is simply no way all of these fans are going to make it back to 18 on their own steam. And if Tiger doesn't start playing better, he might not make it there either.

2:23 PM ▪ The par-5 10th is the first hole all day that both Tiger and J.B. play well, with each of them looking at eagle putts. After J.B. misses, Tiger concedes the birdie and focuses on his chance to claw back to 1 down. He runs it five feet by. It's an impossible stat to know, but I've got to believe Tiger's opponents concede a higher percentage of putts to him than they do to other players out of sheer respect for how clutch he is. Tiger slowly walks to the ball, talking to himself but still keeping an ear open in case J.B. says the three best words in match play: "Pick it up." J.B. seems torn about it but makes him putt it. It catches the edge and drops in. There's no cheer for this birdie, only a collective "Whew . . ."

2:55 PM ▪ The two arrive at the 13th with Tiger still 2 down and only six holes left. After putting my battery back in, my XM radio is finally working and I catch the on-course announcer suggesting that J.B. is "starting to realize what is happening here." I think he's a long way past realization. If he were a pitcher throwing a no-hitter, this is like the sixth inning. Not close enough to start counting outs but not so far away that he hasn't briefly considered what it will feel like to be lifted on his team's shoulders.

The elevated back tee on 13 is the highest spot on the course. From on top, the tee shot sends players barreling downhill to the green 479 yards away. J.B. still has the honors and coolly hits his drive into play and out of reach for Tiger. J.B.'s length probably wouldn't bother Tiger so much if he weren't also hitting it so dang straight. Tiger again misses right. I'm surrounded by a dense pack of Tucson retirees, and we watch together in disbelief as the ball disappears into the desert. Tiger is down 3 with just five to play.

This is a true disaster. If Tiger had tossed down some birdies on the front as he did in Dubai, I'd feel more hopeful, but he has been flat from the beginning. Almost mortal.

Before I left home yesterday, I called my friend Ralph to see if he wanted to come with me. Ralph is the most passionate Tiger Woods fan I know, and for years we spent entire rounds of golf debating his true greatness. He had almost agreed to join me for this leg of the journey, until he remembered he had a cat. All I can think about now is how angry he would be if he were standing here, five hundred miles from home, his cat meowing helplessly in some kennel.

3:07 PM ▪ Three down with five to play. After Tiger's 1994 victory in the finals of the U.S. Amateur, *Sports Illustrated*'s Rick Reilly called it "the greatest comeback in the tournament's 99-year history." On that day Tiger was 3 down with 9 to play. If Tiger wins this, I might just use that bathtub Cheryl taught me how to work.

Tiger and J.B. cut in front of me and across the cart path that connects 13 with 14. I grip the thin rope in my hands as they pass. Tiger's poker face is even more furrowed. No one feels like cheering. The only sounds are Tiger's metal spikes clicking along the cement ground.

The 14th is a 192-yard par 3 without many tricks to it. As J.B. studies the yardage book, an older man leans across the ropes and says in complete calm, "Tiger. Let the legend grow." It was the same thing Earl had told him in the middle of that historic '94 U.S. Amateur when he found himself way down. I don't think Tiger hears him, but he immediately lowers his head. I had stood four feet from him when he did this on the 15th hole at Torrey Pines North. Tiger is willing himself to slip into The Zone.

He refuses to watch J.B.'s shot. Once it's airborne, Tiger steps forward and tees up his ball. What J.B. does has no effect on his strategy: hit the green, make a birdie, keep going. Tiger looks calmer than he has the rest of the round. His shot lands in the flattest spot, the dead middle of the green, no more than fifteen feet away from the left-center pin. He has a chance. Before it stops rolling, I start running, across forty yards of groomed desert sand that looks like a Zen garden and past the corporate boxes, to a small gap between the grandstands and the TV tower where I can watch the most important putt of the match.

It couldn't break much, maybe dying a little to the right. Three feet from the cup, Tiger takes a step toward the hole with his left leg, and as the putt falls into the cup, he whips his putter back toward him with two hands as if he's snagged a fish on the end of it. He has to go a long way back, but he is in a position with which he's familiar. Two down with four to go. It's the same deficit he had at the 1996 U.S. Amateur. When he came back and won that one, *Sports Illustrated* merely dubbed it the most "dramatic" Amateur ever.

3:18 PM ▪ With the scent of a Tiger comeback in the air, the number of photographers following Match 29 starts to swell. After Tiger puts his second shot to seventeen feet, they walk single file line up the 15th hole, weighed down by equipment and probably cursing this course even more than I am.

Next to the green I see J. B. Holmes's wife. Golfers' wives have become easy for me to spot on the course. With no exception, they're attractive, have enormous diamond rings on their left hands, and are unnaturally interested in golf. I first noticed her on one of the early holes, where, to her credit, she was weaving her way through the crowds without missing a shot. Even though J.B. hasn't displayed any emotion today, she has become a good barometer for me of what is probably going on inside her husband's head. Early on, she was full of smiles and cheers. When J.B. went 3 up on 13, she was standing on a chair with a perfect view of Tiger's bogey, and all was right in the world. But as I see her now, she's nervous, looking as if she just ate something she's violently allergic to and is waiting for the symptoms to kick in.

J.B. sends his birdie putt down the hill. It rolls so far past that when it stops, he is still away. His par putt coming back doesn't fall either. It's his only mistake of the day and couldn't have come at a better time for Tiger. A two-putt par will draw within one. From our angle, no one can see the cup. Tiger putts it but then quickly straightens and walks toward the hole as if he has just stroked the worst putt of his professional career. We all groan, thinking he might not win the hole after all, only to have the ball disappear for a birdie. Tiger doesn't react. Why should he? The message he sends by holing a putt he doesn't need to make is enough of an exclamation point.

3:33 PM ▪ The 178-yard 16th is the last par 3 on the course, and the pin is in a nasty spot, back of center and pushed to the very left edge. Anyone who misses the green on that side will likely be playing his second shot from the desert scrub. After putting his last two approaches to about fifteen feet, he leaves this one to a safer twenty, right of the pin and below the hole. Tiger could take these last three holes and use them to teach an investment seminar on calculated risk.

Every fan in attendance seems to have abandoned the other matches in favor of this one. The only way I can see anything is by squatting down and peering through a small gap underneath the electronic scoreboard. It's the only thing making any noise, humming like an industrial fridge as Tiger tries for back-to-back-to-*back* birdies. As J.B. watches, doing his best to convince himself that this is exactly how he envisioned the match proceeding, Tiger's putt rolls uphill, slides left, and slams into the cup. He pedals toward the desert and fires a right-handed haymaker toward Phoenix. When J.B. misses, the match is all square with two to play.

3:42 PM ▪ To all of Tiger's real fans, his victory is no longer in doubt at this point. They're running and laughing and slapping one another's backs as they head up the 17th hole. If the 17th had been a par 3 or par 4, I could understand their optimism. But it's an uphill, 601-yard par 5 that gives J.B. just enough of an advantage off the tee to plant some doubt. After Tiger finds the right rough with his drive, J.B. flies his thirty yards past Tiger's and straight down the middle. It is terrifying to look down a hole that is a third of a mile long and realize that both of these golfers are fully planning on reaching it in just two shots.

From the rough, Tiger still has 270 yards left. Uphill. I couldn't cover that distance with a teed-up driver and a rubber bouncy ball. Tiger thinks he can do it with a 5-wood. He unleashes it dead on line. It carries the last fairway bunker and keeps rolling, finally reappearing when it climbs onto the green, forty feet from the right-hand flag. J.B. reaches with an iron that ends up outside Tiger's ball.

From that far away in an all-square match, Tiger isn't trying to make an eagle. Then again, he wasn't trying to make his birdie on 15 either. On the hillside behind the 17th green, five hundred fans are on their feet before the putt is ever hit. With J.B. still a knee-knocker away for birdie, Tiger strikes the ball with authority, keeping his head down long after the putt is gone. We track it for him and watch as it waves to J.B.'s mark on the way by and falls in. An eagle 3! Tiger lifts his putter straight up with his left hand, then clenches his right fist and roars after it drops. The scream from the crowd overwhelms Tiger's as fans throw their own fist pumps into the air. He has just won his fourth straight hole to go 1 up, playing them in an unthinkable 5 under par. J.B. can only chuckle. Before turning and running up 18, I spot his wife. She has her hands over her face. I think she's crying.

4:15 PM ▪ J.B. has a good look at birdie on the last hole but doesn't make it. It's over. J.B. shakes Tiger's hand and walks off, no doubt in search of a suitable cactus on which to impale himself. Tiger crosses through the line of fans and spots Lee Westwood up ahead on the putting green. Just like two Sundays ago in Dubai, Westwood doesn't speak to Tiger, only smiles. Tiger shrugs back, perhaps thinking *maybe I am going to win every damn tournament this year.*

The ESPN columnist Bill Simmons has said that he doesn't know how anyone can come up with more things to say about Tiger Woods at this point. To some degree he's right. How many times can I say "unbelievable" before it stops *being* unbelievable? Maybe I should swear off the word for the rest of the year. What feels more natural is to replace it with a different word. Until further notice, Tiger Woods is ridiculous.

Back at Cheryl's, I knock on her door to tell her the news. When she opens it, I see a set of bongo drums on the ground.

"How was your game?" she asks.

"Tiger won!"

"Yeeeeaaay!" she says, clapping her hands and joining in the celebration.

SECOND ROUND: ARRON OBERHOLSER

In high school, my best friends and I developed an unhealthy obsession with Pink Floyd. We started by buying their most famous albums, first *The Wall* and then *Dark Side of the Moon*, but it soon grew to the point that having every song they recorded wasn't enough. I started tracking down solo albums by the less successful members of the band. My friend James pounced on the movies they had made in their early years that included such must-have moments as the drummer Nick Mason standing in a buffet line ordering pie. "No crust!" he barked as the poor worker cut him a piece.

The peak of our obsession arrived on April 16, 1994, when Pink Floyd came to the Rose Bowl in Pasadena. The concert was the culminating event of years of undeterred adoration. We were only sixteen, but for each of us, that night was the greatest of our entire lives.

And the next day was the worst. We woke up in our separate houses and faced the reality that whatever happened that day or any day after could in no way be as significant as April 16.

That's how it feels as I sit in the bus driving up the long straight road from the parking lot to see Tiger play Arron Oberholser on day two of the Accenture Match Play. Arron's always seemed like a likable player, straightforward and well spoken. He had risen into the top fifty in the world after a strong 2006, but for months he's been trying to recover from bursitis in his shoulder, and with the inflammation finally subsiding, he's making the Match Play his first start of the year. It's hard to imagine much of a fight from someone who has played even fewer events than Tiger.

As Tiger did the day before, Arron hits it into the desert on the first hole to fall 1 down. Tiger never relinquishes the lead, making five routine birdies and zero bogeys to win 3 up on the 16th hole.

Given no choice but to accept how unbelievable, excuse me, ridiculous, Tiger is, I feel a burden to share it with people who might have never seen it for themselves. Plus, I can't stand the thought of trudging all alone to number 7 and back for three more days. So before Tiger's third-round match against Aaron Baddeley, I think of the perfect solution. I place my first ad on Craigslist.

THURSDAY NIGHT ▪ "FREE TICKET for Friday," the posting begins. That should get their attention, I think. But it is only fair to tell people what I am expecting: "You've got to walk with me and you've got to be able to keep up—we're watching Tiger and Tiger only once he tees off." I wonder if I am being too harsh. What am I talking about? This is a *free* ticket. In fact, I'm not being specific enough, so I keep going. "No bathroom breaks, no long beer lines, no 'my feet hurt.' Tiger doesn't complain, you can't either."

The only reason I have any extra tickets at all is due to my college roommate, Rob. His dad is an Oklahoma State grad who had made a few runs at the Senior Tour before settling into retirement. He remains close to a number of pros, especially the ones who went to OSU. One of them is Scott Verplank, who is in the field this week. Even though I've never met Verplank, he agreed to set aside some tickets. Early on Wednesday I went to the will-call window to pick them up and saw he had set aside not just one set but two.

My Craigslist post went up around six o'clock. The first response came within a half hour, but none is funnier than one from a guy named David, who replies, "I'll take it." Before I can answer, he has sent me a second e-mail, "I will take it," as if the drill sergeant tone of my post made him fear I would punish him for using a contraction. But I had said, "First come, first serve," and that means Mike, a sixth-grade teacher who is off for rodeo break, is the person pretending to be my friend tomorrow. A few hours later I hear from George, Mike's brother, who gives me the bad news that Mike's wife isn't letting him go. Not even during rodeo break? But George has never seen Tiger either and is wondering if I might take him instead. I'm not sure what to do until George says he drives a Town Car for a living and that he would be glad to pick me up and drive me to the course. Just like that, I've gone from going alone to going in style.

THIRD ROUND: AARON BADDELEY

"So what is rodeo week anyway?"

"Stupid-ass Tucson s***," George explains as we head up Oracle Road, a shortcut to Dove Mountain. At least I hope it is a shortcut. George is thirty-three, stocky, and has a gun in his glove compartment. He's already shown it to me. Even though his car is technically a Town Car, its best years are behind it, and most of his rides involve taking kids under Child Protection Services to see their deadbeat parents in the middle of the desert. For him, this is just the latest in a series of tough Arizona jobs.

George used to steam clean jet engines for Honeywell. However, when the summer heat would hit 120 degrees on the tarmac, he would pass out. He'd wake up to find his grittier coworkers staring down at him, angry that he was once again slowing them down. Another time he worked for a telemarketing company, selling people computers over the phone. After being there a few weeks, he looked around and realized,

"Hey, where are the computers anyway?" A few days after he quit, the place was raided by the feds.

All this to say, he wasn't so intimidated by a long walk on a cool, cloudy day.

12:17 PM ▪ Tiger makes his strongest start of the week, with birdies on 1 and 2 to immediately go 2 up. The only person looking stronger is George. So far he has been a model student. He used the port-o-potty in the parking lot, he kept up with me on the walk to the driving range, and even though he bought a bottle of water, he did it before Tiger teed off. On the course, he's even outpacing me a little bit. When he realizes that we are stuck in the mob trying to walk from the 1st to the 2nd, he does what until this point I was afraid to do: he ventures off the cart path and starts bounding through the flora and fauna, long-jumping cacti two at a time.

12:34 PM ▪ The par-4 4th hole at the Gallery is a total beast, 495 yards and the only hole where water comes into play. A long, dark lake protects the entire right side, even for the big hitters. Down the left side are more cacti, the cart path, George, and I. It's a drive that must scare Tiger. If he misses right, the hole's over. If he misses left, it's probably over, too. But at least left he might get lucky and bank it off my head and back into the fairway. "Incoming!" a marshal yells before running for cover. Tiger misses both George and me, but his ball comes to rest at the base of a prickly pear cactus.

Mark Rolfing, NBC's on-course commentator, comes over to inspect the lie. "What do you think, Mark?" someone asks. "Could hurt," he says. I'm about to be closer to Tiger than I've been all week. George is blending in nicely, wearing his XM radio and looking starry-eyed as Tiger approaches. But Tiger has a problem. He has no shot. The line to the green is blocked by the cactus, and he can't just punch it out without goring himself. He stares at it for a minute before grabbing an iron and then flipping it over. He's going to play the shot left-handed.

I'm actually left-handed, though I play golf right-handed. At one point I lost so much confidence in my putting that I thought perhaps I would do better from the other side of the ball and demo'd a left-handed putter from a pro shop. As it turns out, I'm equally bad.

Tiger's left-handed swing is depressingly good. But it's not perfect, lacking that confident release of the club through impact, as if his brain is resisting doing something imperfectly. After a few awkward practice swings, his real shot misses the middle of the club face, and the ball squirts off to the left. It looks as if it might reach the fairway until it hits one of the metal poles holding up the gallery rope and stops dead.

It took two and a half tournaments, but I have finally witnessed Tiger Woods make a mental mistake. He should have moved it. He purses his lips and closes his eyes, but he's not thinking those mysterious peaceful thoughts that led him to go 5 under on J.B. two days ago. This is unadulterated self-loathing at its finest. He flips the club back around to his good side and draws it back to take a giant whack at the cactus. I scan the gallery and see that no one looks worried about this. They are all like George, still beaming, unaware that if Tiger follows through on this, we will all be covered in needles. And, after the ensuing lawsuit, rich. But Tiger stops short, believing he has left the cactus sufficiently scared, and walks away.

1:00 PM ▪ Both players are putting for birdie on the 6th. Tiger is thirty feet, Baddeley fifteen. Tiger misses and "Badds," as Tiger and other players call him, makes it. The one thing Tiger hasn't faced this year is a hot putter, and Badds is always one of the best, ranking 4th last year in putts per round. His game has been a little off this morning; he has just dirtied his perfect white pants trying to escape the desert on the 5th. But Badds does have a history of being a giant killer.

Eight and a half years ago, when he was still an eighteen-year-old amateur, Badds pulled off one of the most forgotten upsets in golf when he toppled then number three in the world Colin Montgomerie to win the Australian Open. Gary Player called him "a better player at eighteen than Jack Nicklaus was at the same age." No pressure, though. Badds would turn pro, win the event again the next year, and then completely lose his swing.

He nearly quit the game but kept working and eventually met Mike Bennett and Andy Plummer, golf coaches who were trying to sell touring pros on a radically different swing style that they dubbed the "Stack & Tilt," the basic tenet of which is to do the exact opposite of everything you've ever been taught about the golf swing. This was intriguing to me since I already do just that. Basically, instead of swinging his weight to his right side on the backswing, Badds bends his left knee toward the ball, keeping his head directly over it. Coming down, he snaps the leg back and stands up, a simpler move that theoretically enables the club to make more consistent contact.

I tried it a few times and nearly broke my wrist from hitting the ball so fat. "Less tilt!" I remember yelling. But with Badds, it may be one of golf's prettiest swings, devoid of many moving parts. Within a year of overhauling his swing, Badds won his first Tour event at the Verizon Heritage in 2006.

1:16 PM ▪ Tiger arrives at the par-4 7th tee, sits down on a cooler, and takes off his shoe. He shakes it, and a rock falls out. I begin to realize my increasing level of obsession when I point it out to George as if it's a note-worthy event. The rock must have been the problem, I think to myself, because he flies his 3-wood all the way to the green and has just twenty-five feet for eagle.

As George leads the way, I notice Luau Larry again, the Hawaiian-shirted sportswriter. He hadn't traveled with me to Dubai, but he's back on the Tiger beat this week. Right now he's lying on the ground holding one of his tan legs. Without having to negotiate hundreds of fans outside the ropes, he has somehow managed to walk into a cactus. I look at it as a cautionary tale, and I focus back on the desert in front of me.

1:46 PM ▪ Two days ago Tiger brought us the come-back. Yesterday was the stress-free win. After a slow start for Badds, today is shaping up to be the duel. They both make 3's on 7. On 8, Badds rolls in a long putt for another birdie, and then on 9, he nearly chips it in. Tiger responds with a birdie of his own. He points coolly at the ball as it drops in. I count up the circles on my scorecard and see there have been eight birdies between them.

2:17 PM ▪ Eight birdies was nothing, I'm realizing. Tiger and Aaron both birdie the par-5 10th, both birdie the par-4 11th, and both birdie the par-4 12th! Fourteen birdies in twelve holes? George points out that this is suddenly feeling like video-game golf.

2:25 PM ▪ And what good video game these days doesn't have violence? After not missing a shot all day, Tiger's drive on the 13th hits an old marshal right on top of the head. The ball bounces twenty feet back into the air and disappears into the desert. The marshal bends over in pain, and blood starts to run off his white hair. There are worse ways to die than from being hit by Tiger Woods. Like being hit by Retief Goosen, for example. Medics rush to make sure he's okay, but when Tiger walks up, the marshal is all smiles. Tiger gives him an autographed glove and a handshake. As the man is happily carted off the battlefield, Tiger goes to look for his ball. He finds it but loses the hole, and is back to all square.

2:40 PM ▪ The birdie barrage was fun when Tiger was hanging tough at 1 up, but all square is a different matter. Badds stuffs it in close on 14 and again makes birdie. If I give Badds credit for a birdie on the conceded 13th, which wasn't that unrealistic, he has now birdied 6, 7, 8, 10, 11, 12, 13 and 14! That's eight of the last nine holes!

Tiger has had enough and sticks an 8-iron on the 16th to just four feet from the hole. Badds three-putts and concedes. Back to all square. At this point there's no walking. We are all running through the desert, with George leading the charge, cigarette in hand. The carnage inside the ropes has spread to the gallery outside. On the way to 17, we pass a beefy guy with blood dribbling down his leg. It's like D-Day out here; some people are getting dragged down by cacti, others are just giving up, either too tired to go on or too afraid they'll spill their beers.

3:14 PM ▪ Badds hits first into 17, the uphill 600-yarder, and puts it twelve feet right behind the front-center pin. Tiger answers with an iron, just outside Badds's shot and left of the hole. Coming off Badds's three-putt on the last, I'm nervous about a hot putter zeroing back in, but he can't get his to drop and neither can Tiger. All square with one to go.

3:30 PM ▪ Racing up the 18th fairway, I appreciate just how unreal George has been. Here's a guy whose only exercise involves flipping his meter on and off for twelve hours a day and he's somehow surviving seven miles, most of it running, some of it while downing a half pack of cigarettes. But on the final climb, he starts to fade. I turn and see the crush of fans steaming behind us. We can't stop. "We're almost there," I say. He doesn't answer, just puts his head down and keeps going. I pull ahead and run the last stretch, up and around to the far right side of the green. I make it, but my legs are shaking. I put my hands on my knees, turn around, and see there's no sign of George. I don't even consider going back. George would want me to go on. A minute later he cruises up and hands me an ice-cold bottle of water.

"We might need this if it goes extra holes." The student has become the mentor.

3:30 PM ▪ The green on 18 slopes severely back to front, and the pin is cut in the middle toward the left side. The only easy putt is from below the cup. We can't see the players, but we know from their drives that Badds is hitting first.

3:31 PM ▪ Slam. Baddeley's ball drops six feet right of the flag.

3:32 PM ▪ Slam. Tiger's drops nine feet past it.

3:34 PM ▪ The players receive applause as they walk to the green. The fans in the bleachers know only that the match is tied; they can't possibly appreciate the level of play it took to keep it like that. But those of us who have been hoofing it from the beginning cheer most loudly.

Tiger stands over his putt and has to be playing for birdie with Badds so close. "Oh, God . . ." The lady in the front row looks away before Tiger putts. Here she maneuvered to claim the best spot against the ropes, and she can't bear to watch.

Tiger misses. It's the first must-make putt I've seen him miss this year. Proof that he was only thinking 3, the ball rolls five feet past the hole.

Now one of golf's best putters has a slick right-to-left breaker to end it all. The woman in front can't watch this one either. Tiger glares at the cup as if ordering it to make sure this putt doesn't go in. Badds gently plays it a good two feet out to the right. I can't believe it will break that much, but it breaks even more and misses low. Like Tiger's, it keeps rolling and ends up three feet past the hole. Here we thought birdie would win, and now neither of them even has par.

In my head I flash to the way Tiger lost to Nick O'Hern in the third round last year. All Tiger had to do that day was make a straight, four-foot putt to win on the first extra hole. He hit it straight, but the ball lurched when it rolled across an old mark, and it missed the cup on the right side. The hole was tied, and Tiger lost outright on the next one. Tiger said afterward that he had been "so enthralled with the line" that he never saw the tiny crater.

Tiger won't make the same mistake. He inspects every inch of this one before pulling the trigger. It's in for a 4. "Yesss!!" George and I scream in celebration/relief. Badds makes his, too. We're going extra holes.

Because I knew to run to the far side of the 18th green, we can now head straight down number 1, while the other fans are blocked at the crossing near the first tee. George is impressed by my navigating, a compliment that means a lot more coming from a professional driver.

3:43 PM ▪ Not everyone is happy that this has gone extra holes. Down in the fairway a father is having an argument with his son, who must be seven or eight. I don't need to hear the beginning of the fight to pick right up in the middle:

Dad: "It might be an *eighteen*-hole playoff, so get used to it!"

The kid whines.

Dad: "People are running. What are you doing? You're moping!"

Kid: "I don't *want* a playoff . . ."

Dad: "Then go home. Walk!"

I tell George to slip the boy and the dad his card. In a few weeks, they might be new customers.

3:43 PM ▪ Badds is in the fairway on the 1st, with an iron in to a back pin on the par 5. He's about to take the club back when another kid, one who actually wants to be here, sneezes. It forces Badds to back off and start again. Then, impressively, Badds hits it to ten feet. For eagle. As Tiger steps into his second shot, the kid's father leans over. *"Don't sneeze,"* he says.

3:54 PM ▪ Tiger puts it on the green as well but can only two-putt. For the second straight hole, Badds has a putt to win. This one is much easier than on the 18th, slightly downhill and nearly straight. He draws his buttery stroke back and releases the putter toward the hole. Tiger watches it, prepared to accept defeat, but right at the end it slips off to the left and misses the cup. Badds falls to his knees. Tiger quickly turns with Stevie already clomping ahead of him. There's no ruminating Tiger's fortune; we instinctively bolt for number 2, the 20th hole of the match. George and

I pass a group of middle-aged men who are laughing as they go, saying, "I'm running at a golf tournament!"

4:04 PM ▪ Tiger's play reflects a man energized by not one but two brushes with death. He hits his approach on the par-4 2nd to fifteen feet and continues striding toward the green. Badds is on the right side of the fairway with a better angle to the pin but leaves it out to the right, thirty feet away. A lot of the crowd has decided not to venture this far away for a second time, so seeing the action is not a problem, but George insists on running anyway. "I thought you were beat?" I say in between my gasps for air. He confesses that he downed a Snickers bar behind 18.

Badds's birdie doesn't fall, and for once today it is Tiger who faces a putt to win. It's almost completely straight, a little uphill, and heads away from the gallery and out toward the desert. I look back at George and see that for some reason he has taken one of his shoes off. He turns it over and shakes it, even though there are no rocks in it. "This is for Tiger," he says.

Tiger hits it, watches it for a moment, and while the putt is still rolling, he turns to Badds and removes his cap to shake his hand. The ball isn't even in the hole yet! With Tiger not even watching, it drops in. "Ohhhhh!!!" the crowd roars. George and I join the chorus. Tiger doesn't just win, he wins with flair. Up at the green, Stevie takes the ball out of the cup and heaves it into the crowd. Rain starts to fall for the first time all day, as if God had been holding back the weather till Tiger's work on Earth was done. As we turn around and make the mile walk back up to the buses, Tiger hops into a Lexus and disappears into the desert.

Yesterday I couldn't understand the fans who seemed convinced that Tiger would beat J.B. when their match was all square. Too many weird things can happen in golf. But having seen him walk away a winner time after time, I get it. In fact, I feel that same comfort. Tiger Woods is more than good. He's dependable.

I'm not a fair-weather fan. When I was in sixth grade, my Los Angeles Dodgers won the World Series. In the twenty years since then, they have won one play-off game, but I keep rooting. Between 2004 and 2006, I attended eleven different games. They lost all eleven. I even began trying different cities, going to games in San Diego and San Francisco to break my streak. No luck. A friend who is a Padres fan started inviting me when his team was in town just to increase their chances of victory.

I won't abandon the Dodgers, but I'm ready to root for someone who knows how to get the job done. The tournament deftly routes the line for the buses through the inside of the official souvenir shop. When George and I get back into line, he's wearing a neon yellow windbreaker, and I've swapped out my beat-up old hat for a new one. It's dark red with the Match Play logo on the side and a "TW" logo on the front.

QUARTERFINALS: K. J. CHOI

Come Saturday morning, only eight players are still standing out of the original sixty-four. Except for Vijay Singh and Tiger, most of the big names are long gone. Phil Mickelson and Adam Scott were out after the second round. Ernie Els, still reeling from the loss in Dubai, decided only at the last minute to come play, then promptly lost on day one.

Match Play is the rare tournament where the longer one survives, the earlier the tee time becomes. In order to whittle down the eight in time for tomorrow's final, today includes both the quarter and semifinal matches. Tiger's match begins at 7:45 a.m. and means I am back on the bus up the hill at 6:30.

Tiger's quarterfinal match pairs him against "The Tank," South Korea's K. J. Choi. A short and stout former power lifter who sings hymns on the golf course to relax, he manages to be intimidating and disarming at the same time. His swing plane resembles the way he used to lift weights, straight up and straight down, making for a consistent and boring fade with every single swing.

The Choi match is compelling only in that for so long nothing happens. From numbers 3 through 9, K.J. and Tiger par every hole. With Badds and J.B., the tournament had that Sunday energy to it. With Choi, all of a sudden it feels as if we are back to Thursday morning. At one point I begin to wonder if they have forgotten that the whole premise of match play is for one player to beat the other. Tiger eventually ends the stalemate with a chip-in eagle at the par-5 10th. He tosses in three more birdies over the next six holes and wins 3 up on the 16th green.

The victory puts Tiger into the final four, meaning that even if he loses in the semifinals, he will still have a spot in Sunday's consolation match for third place, which, of course, he would hate with every fiber of his *first place or nothing* mind-set. Either way, I need to find a courtesy phone. I've made it through my four-night minimum and need Cheryl's guest house for one more day. "I'm holding the room contingent on positive outcomes," she says. Groovy.

SEMIFINALS: HENRIK STENSON

Of all Tiger's opponents this week, Sweden's Henrik Stenson is the one I most fear. Part of that is because he wears wraparound Oakley sunglasses. But the logical part is that Stenson is quietly becoming one of the game's best players. And he has done it by stealing a page from Tiger's playbook. When his game bottomed out in 2001, Stenson's mental coach decided to put him through a spin-off of the Earl Woods finishing school. Believing his student needed to toughen up, he made Stenson hit balls while wearing a blindfold. When the blindfold came off, he finally trusted his swing and has since won four times on the European Tour, not to mention last year's Accenture Match Play right here at Dove Mountain.

Tiger never admits to being intimidated by anyone. Or even any*thing.* Last year Jason Sobel from ESPN.com asked him to name his greatest fear.

"Greatest fear?" His brain couldn't even comprehend the idea. "I don't really have any."

Sobel pressed. "No fears at all?"

"No, not really. I can't think of any."

I half expected Sobel to dump a box of poisonous snakes at his feet, but it didn't happen. The response was another example of Tiger's macho determination never to expose weakness. Nothing positive could happen if he were honest with his answer. If, for example, he confessed to a fear of people with muttonchop sideburns, chances are good they would suddenly be

FIST PUMPS OF FURY · 147

all the rage on the PGA Tour. But if Tiger were to be intimidated by another player, it certainly wouldn't be Henrik Stenson. Not only is Stenson one of the players Tiger flew past on Sunday in Dubai, he is also the player who was paired with Tiger that day back in December at the Target World Challenge when Tiger shot 62. Stenson? 72.

1:13 PM ▪ Neither Tiger nor Stenson plays well the first five holes. As a result, they're spending most of their time throwing clubs and kicking their bags. I barely notice these fits of rage anymore, but they're completely shocking to Bryan, the forty-six-year-old mechanic with slicked-back hair who claimed my extra ticket today. When Tiger uses an especially colorful turn of phrase after pulling his second shot on the par-5 5th, Bryan's eyes go wide, and he asks, "Boy, have you ever seen him mad like that?" Uh, yeah.

Even though Bryan says "boy" and "gosh" and "golly" a lot, he is probably one of the toughest men I've met. He receives a cortisone shot once a year because of shooting pain up and down his left arm, the result of three decades of working with wrenches. The shot doesn't always help, and sometimes it doesn't take at all. For years he taught auto repair for the state, teaching kids in the juvenile prison how to fix cars. And really, when you're working closely with prisoners, what safer place is there to be than surrounded by blunt metal objects?

After building up a pretty good pension, a Tucson vocational school offered Bryan the chance to run its auto repair department. He said yes, throwing away his state retirement for the chance to be in charge of something for the first time in his life. Six weeks after making the move, he was informed that the program wasn't actually accredited and the Department of Labor was going to shut it down. Rather than give up, the guy who had no experience dealing with bureaucracy found a way to bypass months of red tape and convince the local community college to come on board and make the program legit. So when I notice Bryan limping down number 7, I don't push him to keep going. I figure he will probably push himself.

2:15 PM ▪ I have seen Tiger this mad; I just haven't seen him mad this often. On the 9th, he slams his club back into the bag as Stevie happily escapes to go rake the fairway bunker. At 10, he slashes his club through the rough after missing the green in two. He's struggling but still 1 up.

Meanwhile, Bryan has officially hurt himself. He's not sure what's wrong, it might just be a cramp, but the limp is getting worse and we have three miles of uphill walking to go. This is Bryan's first golf tournament. His real passion is NASCAR, where if a driver were to win five straight events like Tiger, he would be reviled, not beloved. Part of that is because of the flare with which Tiger wins, but it's also because of how he loses. He doesn't whine like Jeff Gordon, or punch people, like Tony Stewart (although the thought of Tiger using one of his spinout fist pumps to drop Rory Sabbatini would only increase his fan base). Looking back on last year's British Open, an event where Tiger finished a disappointing 12th place, his post-round interview is heavy-laden with self-effacement. "I couldn't" . . . "I didn't" . . . "I wasn't." His failures are his fault. The flip side is that when he wins, he can take ownership for it all the more.

3:27 PM ■ Stenson hits the green on the par-3 16th and makes a fifteen-footer for 2. The putt makes Tiger pay for six straight pars, and the match is suddenly all square. It's Stenson who blinks on the next hole, only managing a par whereas Tiger makes a sandy birdie to take the 1-up lead into 18.

3:45 PM ■ Walking toward the final green, I tell Bryan that, as George and I did yesterday, we should keep going to the far side in case it goes extra holes. I feel bad because Bryan has already gone the 16 holes with me this morning for the K.J. match, and now this one is going at least 18. We've logged well over ten miles at this point, and Bryan has admitted that he thinks he has a groin pull. When I give him the news, he just throws up his hands. "Why stop now? Why does it matter now?"

The pin on 18 is cut in the front-left corner, and Tiger is already safely on the green. With Tiger looking at no worse than par, Stenson's only hope is to make a birdie and hope Tiger misses. His approach shot is a little greedy and comes up just short of the flag, a mistake that sends his ball zipping back another ten yards and off the green. Now he must chip it in to keep playing. Stenson's steely look remains as he stares down his third shot. He pitches it up, and, like his second shot, it hits on the upslope and starts rolling back toward him. He could force Tiger to two-putt, but while his ball is still moving, Stenson walks up to it and slaps it into the gallery with his wedge as he takes off his hat. The crowd had given Tiger a winner's cheer when he reached the green, but now it's official. He is into the finals. And now that I look at them, Stenson's sunglasses aren't that scary after all.

CHAMPIONSHIP MATCH: STEWART CINK

In 1884, Thomas Potter, the secretary of the Royal Liverpool Golf Club and founder of what became the British Amateur, decided a 36-hole match play final was the ultimate way to decide a champion. This was back when the options of what to do with your day was a choice between hanging out with the sheep and watching golf.

On the other side of the bracket from Tiger is Stewart Cink, a lanky thirty-four-year-old from Georgia with a long, gentle swing that makes me feel as though the best way to watch him hit balls is from the comfort of a rocking chair. He and Tiger have already played together this year, during the third and fourth rounds of the Buick Invitational, where he started the weekend eight strokes back. He had no chance. Today he will be starting all square . . . and still has no chance. It's not his fault; it's just that with every match over the course of the long week, Tiger has made fewer and fewer mistakes.

7:45 AM ▪ Next to the first tee sits the powder blue Walter Hagen Cup, the official trophy of the Accenture Match Play. It's made from Wedgewood china, making it the most fragile trophy in golf. Before the final match begins, the two girls in charge of seeing it's not broken spin it around so Tiger and Cink can pose next to it on the first tee. It's considerate of the tournament directors to give Cink his chance to see it up close, just once.

Feeling too drained after yesterday to take on another new fan, I've given my Sunday ticket to George again and tell him to feel no obligation to keep up with me. But he's still with me on the 1st green, so I ask about his Saturday night. Apparently, he drove to Mexico to place a sports bet, then he and his buddies stayed up late drinking, two of them passed out on the ground after fighting about who would drive to the gun show, he fell asleep on the couch, and the last guy was playing online poker until 5 a.m. I waited for him to add, "Isn't that crazy?" He didn't. I had the impression that that wasn't much different from every other Saturday night.

8:08 AM ▪ Tiger birdies the 2nd. One up.

8:50 AM ▪ Tiger birdies the 5th. Two up.

9:14 AM ▪ Tiger birdies the 7th. Three up.

9:22 AM ▪ Cink three-putts the 8th. Four up.

9:55 AM ▪ Tiger sticks it on the 11th. Five up.

9:56 AM ▪ Keep in mind that NBC's coverage doesn't start for *two hours*. Somewhere in the media trailers behind number 12, a producer is frantically trying to figure out how he can fill the last three hours of the network's four-hour broadcast.

11:22 AM ▪ Tiger gives NBC a reprieve, arriving at Dove Mountain's 18th only 4 up. And for once today, he's struggling. He finds the fairway bunker, then the greenside bunker, then chunks his sand shot, and angrily walks away with a bogey.

All Cink has left is a five-foot putt for par. If he makes it, it will stall Tiger's momentum and give him the slimmest of hopes that he can make a run during the afternoon round. As Stewart wiggles his feet before drawing back his belly putter, I look and see that everyone is certainly interested, but not in Cink. In fact I'm the only person watching Stewart. I follow the crowd's eyes to the far fringe of the green, where Tiger Woods is doing the riveting activity of putting on his watch.

If only Cink knew that no one was watching him. He might not have missed it.

It's his last chance to derail Tiger. After a one-hour break for lunch, Tiger returns, removes his watch, and stretches his lead all the way to 8 up, closing the match with a soaring wedge over a dry desert wash to two feet. When they get to the green, Cink doesn't make Tiger putt it. They remove their hats and expose their distinctive horizontal tan lines across their foreheads, a product of 117 holes in the Arizona desert.

As officials gingerly place the trophy on its wooden pedestal and photographers swarm the green, off to the side a middle-aged sound technician named Bob is panicking. He's already been told that NBC is going live to Jimmy Roberts in two minutes to interview Tiger, and he can't get any power to the mike. He flips the switches on and off. Nothing. He pulls out the extension cord and tries again. Nothing. "Thirty seconds, Bob . . ." His entire day is built around this one event, and he is on the verge of total fail-ure. The fans who have had 29 holes to get plastered start laying into him, too. "Come on, Bob!" Twenty seconds. Bob pulls the extension cord and runs it through another outlet in the corporate tent next door. Five seconds. The dials light up. "We're good." As NBC goes to Jimmy and Tiger, Bob nearly collapses from the stress. The same drunk fans applaud his save. "We love you, Bob!"

The win is Tiger's third straight win in 2008 and sixth straight win going back to last season. Because Jimmy's mike is working, I hear him recite the stunning fact that Tiger is now only ten PGA Tour wins away from Jack Nicklaus, whose seventy-three victories is second on the all-time list. It reminds me of one of the popular complaints I've picked up from other Tiger skeptics over the year: the notion that Tiger appears to be a better golfer than he actually is; that if Tiger had to face the same Hall of Fame players as Nicklaus, fields that included Arnold Palmer and Gary Player and Lee Trevino and Tom Watson, he wouldn't be such a dominant force in golf.

After this week, I don't buy it. At the Match Play, I saw a golfer who seamlessly adapts to any level of competition. When Oberholser could manage only three birdies in round two, Tiger needed only five. When J. B. Holmes threw down six, Tiger responded with seven. And when Baddeley somehow made ten birdies over twenty holes, Tiger was able to make eleven. After witnessing every hole of Tiger's season, the more compelling question to consider is which professional golfers playing today will never see the Hall of Fame because they had the misfortune of being born within ten years of Tiger Woods.

MATCH PLAY FALLOUT ▪ My car survives a windy trip across the desert and pulls up to our house just after 1 a.m. late Sunday night. Everyone is asleep. Our house has cheap, creaky wooden floors, and over the course of the five months we've been here, I have learned the circuitous route I need to take between any two points to keep from making noise. I don't even have to think about it anymore. Open the door, take one small step to the left, then a big one forward and onto the rug. From there it is two paces toward our stereo followed by a hard right turn and then two giant steps into the hallway. The rest is easy: hug the right side of the hallway without knocking the frames off the wall, find the door to our bedroom, and I'm in. But after making it there, I decide I should go see Danny. I rub his back, "Hey, buddy . . ." I can't see him, but I can hear him roll over and look up through the dark. "Dada, you came back!"

It's weird, but by physically disappearing for these short stretches of time, I see that I'm not as invisible as I thought I was on my roof a few months before. When I'm gone, I'm missed. After every round of the Match Play, I would call home and tell Hillary the good news. She was excited on Wednesday and Thursday, but by Saturday she was one of the only people actively following Tiger's season who was wishing his unbeaten streak would mercifully end.

In coming home, I am the prodigal dad. "Come, family, sit at my feet and I will tell you about my adventures in the desert . . ." The next night I take everyone out to dinner at our favorite hot dog stand. Danny and I go and order while Hillary takes Katie to find a table. As I walk to get into line, she asks me to order a side of chips. I remember, but only when they deliver the food. "Oops, I forgot the chips." Hillary looks at me, disappointed, and says, "It's fine," in that tone that obviously means it *isn't* fine. Trying to be a Tiger-like man of action, I flag down a server and ask what it would take to have a side of chips. "Fifty-five cents." Fifty-five cents to be a hero? I can do that. I give him a dollar, tell him to keep the change, and do everything but stand up and take a giant bow. Hillary sees the whole thing differently, saying "I just said *'It's fine,'* we don't need chips. You're not listening to me!" It's not exactly the fist pump moment I imagined. But in fairness, I have only been following Tiger since January; I can't expect to have all my problems solved already. For now I can only conclude that the answer is not as simple as going to golf tournaments a couple times a month.

Hats Off for the King

The Arnold Palmer Invitational

Bay Hill Club
Orlando, Florida
March 13–16, 2008

When Tiger won the Buick Invitational in January, he was merely accomplishing the expected. The comeback at Dubai was spectacular, except that it happened while most people in the United States were asleep. But with the Match Play, Tiger could not be ignored, and the sports world is responding accordingly. On the Golf Channel, former player turned analyst Frank Nobilo feels no shame in declaring Tiger "the greatest player that will ever play the game." On ESPN, *Pardon the Interruption*'s Michael Wilbon goes further, saying the question is no longer whether Tiger is the most dominant golfer of all time but whether he is the most dominant *athlete* of all time.

In January, Tiger had caused a lot of eye-rolling when he said on his Web site that winning the professional Grand Slam (all four major championships in one calendar year) was "easily within reason." Attaching the word "easily" to something that had never been achieved seemed a little . . . bold. By the time the Arnold Palmer Invitational at Bay Hill is in sight, the question of whether Tiger could win the Grand Slam has been pushed aside by an even wilder idea—could he have golf's first undefeated season? Turns out that Tiger has already done that, too. When he was eleven, he won all thirty-six junior events he entered.

Since Tiger actually lives in Isleworth, a gated community only a mile west of Bay Hill, this will be my one chance to stay at his place, but even after adding 117 holes to the tally in Tucson, he still doesn't know I exist. At some point I figured that he would hit a wayward shot, we would make eye contact, and there would be a moment of recognition where his nose would scrunch up and he would say, "Don't I know you from somewhere?" I would then run through all the adventures he and I have shared, whereupon Stevie would reach into his bag and serve me with one of

Tiger's standard-issue restraining orders. And as long as I only had to stay a hundred yards away, I could probably still see most of his shots.

Thankfully, I have a backup plan, but it's dependent on someone I haven't spoken to in more than a year. My first job after college was as a production assistant on the sitcom *Sabrina, the Teenage Witch*. I'm still not sure why they hired me. I sat down for the interview, my first one since graduation, and the production coordinator who was interviewing me said, "First off, what's with your name? 'Robert.' That's a little different." He was serious.

"Uh, it's . . . just a family name . . . pretty common actually."

"Huh. Just never heard it before, I guess."

He flipped through a giant stack of résumés and found mine, setting it on top. From across the desk I could see the confusion. At the top where it said my name, I had inadvertently added a small "b" in front of the capital "R" in Robert, making my name read "bRobert." Here I was, an English major out of Princeton, and I'd misspelled my own name. "You know what, actually that's a typo," I said. "It's supposed to just be Robert. Or Bob." Four minutes later, I was walking back to my car. The interview was over. I drove away, assuming they would go with someone who could spell, but waiting at home was a message asking if I could start Monday.

Kelly was the assistant to the head writer and one of the people who couldn't believe they had hired me. Her boss didn't give her much to do, so she filled her days with involving herself in everyone else's lives, and when I went out on a date with another assistant in the office, she went around my back to find out if the girl had fun and whether she would go out with me again if I asked her. I was livid. Kelly said my point was irrelevant since the girl said she had a great time and would love to go out again. Four years later, Hillary and I were married.

Kelly eventually moved home to Florida and started working for the Golf Channel. I decide to go ahead and send her an e-mail. A week before I head to Bay Hill, she calls to say I can stay with her and her husband and casually throws in, "Oh, by the way, you want to be interviewed by the Golf Channel?" I'm on my way.

KING OF THE HILL ▪ The first time Arnold Palmer saw Bay Hill was in 1965, four years after the plot of land was developed by a group of investors from Tennessee. He was invited down along with Jack Nicklaus and two other players to play in an exhibition match and proceeded to beat Nicklaus by seven shots. He decided he liked the place and made it his winter home before buying it outright in 1970.

Behind Torrey Pines, no other Tour venue has such a long relationship with Tiger Woods. At fifteen, Tiger came to Bay Hill and won the 1991 U.S. Junior Amateur, going extra holes for the first of his six straight USGA titles. When he unlocked the secret to winning at Bay Hill as a pro, he was unstoppable, winning Arnie's tournament four years in a row between 2000 and 2003, the last victory more impressive than any other. The night before the final round in '03, his then girlfriend, Elin, made a pasta dinner, and within a half hour he was violently ill in every possible way. They considered checking him into a hospital, but Tiger was worried that doctors wouldn't let him check out. He warmed up with only a handful of balls and headed to the 1st tee. In between running to the bushes, he shot the day's low round and won by 11 shots.

But since 2003, mysteriously, he hasn't won again. He hasn't even come close, finishing no better than 20th. The best explanation involves Bay Hill's rough, which has been grown longer in recent years to defend the course from longer hitters who tend to miss fairways. During his Wednesday press conference, Tiger was more than happy to offer his own nuanced theory for the dry spell: "I just haven't played well." If there were going to be an obvious tournament to derail his perfect season, this was it.

FIRST ROUND

7:31 AM ▪ Eighteen days ago I pulled out of a dirt field in the middle of the desert and headed home. This morning I pass beneath the twisting water slides of Wet'n Wild and into the mammoth cement parking lot at Universal Studios Orlando. The tourist attractions are the lifeblood of this city sitting in the center of Florida. With my silver Rav4 rental car locked, I ride up an escalator, step onto a moving walkway, then hop onto a waiting bus headed for Bay Hill. If only there were four Egyptian women willing to fan me with palm fronds, it would be the perfect morning commute.

7:42 AM ▪ Our bus winds two miles through the police-lined neighborhood surrounding Bay Hill, a collection of houses ranging from modest to monstrous, and drops us off at the entrance to the "Arnold Palmer Priceless Moments Pavilion Presented by Master-Card." The tent is huge, which may have been the only way to squeeze its name on a wall. Inside are displays covering Arnie's personal life and professional life. Heading through this first time, I'm shocked to read that all seven of the King's major championships came within only a seven-year period. A young Jack Nicklaus ended his reign earlier than anyone expected, and when Arnie won his last, the 1964 Masters, he was only thirty-four.

There's no guarantee on how long we'll be able to see Tiger Woods play golf at its highest level. After he won the Wachovia Championship last year, he talked about how fickle a sport it can be. "This game," he said, "you have it for a little bit and it goes away, then you've got to get it back again." Someday he won't get it back again. And when that happens, he's already said he's not going to stick around. As he told Ed Bradley on *60 Minutes*, "When my best isn't good enough to win anymore, I'm gone. I'm racking the cue and I'm going home." For as special as Tiger is, it may be naive to think that just because his dominance hasn't been challenged by age 32, it never will be.

8:13 AM ▪ The crowds are impressive early on this cool and clear Thursday morning, a solid two deep around the driving range. They also seem to be the least diverse, a sea of sixty-something Caucasian men. I ask Ken, who just so happens to be a sixty-something Caucasian man, to explain. He says they're all retired, and when you wake up at 4 a.m., this isn't early.

Tiger is nearing the end of his range session, sporting a cool blue shirt with subtle white stripes. I'm pretty sure his hat and pants are black, but they might be navy blue. I lean over to Ken again: "Do his pants look black or navy blue to you?" He doesn't answer. Since buying that Tiger Woods hat, I've turned a dark corner from observation to obsession.

All week in Arizona, Tiger had warmed up by making an exaggerated head turn through the ball, similar to what Annika Sorenstam does during her actual swing. He never did it during the tournament, but the move seemed to be a clue that he was struggling with rotating through the ball, a mistake that can lead to some big blocks to the right. Today his head isn't chasing the ball at all. He's just piping 5-wood after 5-wood down the center of the range.

8:50 AM ▪ Tiger starts on the 10th hole this morning. Directly behind the tee is a single grandstand with a few hundred people filling its eight rows. A few fans sneak photos, their contraband phones popping up like a whack-a-mole game as Tiger looks down the fairway. The 10th at Bay Hill is exactly 400 yards, a slightly uphill dogleg right where the ideal shot is a 3-wood that cuts the corner and scares the people in the beer garden along the right side before drawing back into the fairway. Tiger has no problem with the tee shot, or his second, putting it onto the back tier and just eight feet from the hole. He reads the putt from both sides, then fixes a mark between his ball and the cup. He makes it. Tiger is under par before Universal Studios has even opened.

10:12 AM ▪ Tiger cruises along, missing a birdie opportunity at 13 and parring 14 before we cross over residential Bay Hill Boulevard to the 15th tee. The final four holes at Bay Hill are one of the year's great closing tests. It starts here, a tight, 425-yarder lined with out of bounds and a group of magnolia trees so dark that their leaves appear almost black from the tee box. If you can make it through, the fairway cuts hard to the right to a green with bunkers in front, to the right, and in back. It's a nice, short par 4 that eases you into the homestretch.

Tiger lands safely between the magnolias but misses the green to the right with a pitching wedge. With a wedge? It's a rare mistake, and it costs him his first bogey of the week when he can't knock it close from the deep rough. He's back to even par.

10:20 AM ▪ There's nothing short about the 16th, sixty yards longer than 15 and even more penal.

Until last year it had always played as a par 5, but to bring winning scores closer to par, Arnie agreed to move the tees up and make it a long par 4, a change that forces players to hit a long iron or hybrid club into the green rather than lay up. If they pull their approach left, they'll for sure be in one of Bay Hill's seven lakes. If they're short, they'll find the tributary that runs in front of the green and connects to another lake on 17.

Tiger avoids every body of water and makes a nice up and down for par.

10:47 AM ▪ Bay Hill does not ease up for its last two holes. The 17th is a 219-yard par 3 over water. Tiger gives himself a good look at birdie, but it doesn't fall. He grimaces at the missed opportunity and walks the twenty yards to the 18th tee.

10:57 AM ▪ My dad once went to Florida, and on his return he declared it "the flattest place on Earth." Which is why I stand at the 18th tee shocked to discover that Bay Hill's most famous hole is a blind tee shot. From the 441-yard back tee, Tiger can't see the flag or the green and definitely not the lake, the course's most famous water hazard. Pros dislike blind tee shots because they have no specific target toward which they can aim. I prefer blind tee shots, figuring the less I know the better.

Tiger finds the fairway, and we walk uphill where all the hole's awful mysteries are revealed. If global warming ever does make water levels rise significantly, the narrow banana-shaped 18th green at Bay Hill may be planet Earth's first casualty. Everything about the hole, from the grandstands to the jagged rocks to the raised traps, forces a player to doubt whether the putting surface is really there at all.

Should Tiger need any further reminders on how easily this hole can ruin his round, he receives one courtesy of his playing partner, Mark Wilson. Wilson's second shot to the left-center pin hits the rocks and careens back into the lake. He walks forward until he finds a distance that doesn't make him sweat, drops a ball, and puts it in the water again. The workers on the big manual scoreboard facing the green were just finishing posting Wilson's name and scores after a solid 2-under start, but his quadruple-bogey 8 drops him out of contention.

Wilson's demise has no effect on Tiger, who makes a routine 4 and heads to the 1st tee still hanging on at even par.

11:35 AM ▪ On the bus ride I had met Dave, a sixty-something fitness buff who is visiting family in central

Florida for the week. He had confessed to being a big Phil Mickelson fan but had never seen Tiger in person. I invited him along so he can see what all the fuss is about.

Outside of Tiger's opening birdie, Dave hasn't seen much, and I'm worried about losing a possible convert. Now, after his third tough pitch out of the deep rough today, Tiger still has twenty feet left for par on the 2nd. As Tiger looks over his putt, I explain to Dave how Tiger's focus seems to spike when facing long par saves. Birdie putts are opportunities to move ahead. But clutch par putts keep him from losing ground. Tiger waits until I'm done with my explanation, then drains the twenty-footer to stay at even par, and Dave looks at me as if I am Tiger Woods' svengali.

12:32 PM ▪ If the 6th at Bay Hill weren't buried in the front nine, it might be the course's most famous hole: 558 yards, every bit of which is played around Bay Hill's largest lake, a near-perfect circle of water that appears large enough to sink the *Titanic* without anyone knowing.

The question for any golfer standing on the tee is "What's my line?" Tiger and Stevie spend a good minute checking the yardage book, making sure they're doing the math right. If Tiger isn't aggressive enough, he'll end up in one of the traps along the right. If he's too aggressive, well, the problem is obvious. In 1998, John Daly hit six balls into the water and left the hole having made an 18.

Tiger picks his target and hits it so completely straight, there's no need for him to watch it. He bends down and salvages his tee. Because the hole continues to curve around the lake, the second shot isn't as long, but is just as dangerous for players who want to reach it in two. Tiger calmly puts his ball on the green and lags his eagle putt to four feet for birdie—no need for Match Play–type miracles quite yet.

After the birdie at 6, Tiger pars out for an even round of 70. I can find no reason for the tepid play other than Tiger's explanation from yesterday—he just needs to play better. He missed a few drives into the trees on the right, on two occasions he missed the green with a wedge in his hands, and when he did find the greens, he couldn't make a putt. I was not surprised when Dave apologized and left me on number 7 to follow golf's human highlight reel, Fred Couples. At age forty-eight, the 1992 Bay Hill champion had rolled out six birdies and a much more exciting round of 65. Tiger will start tomorrow 5 shots behind him and will need to fix something at the Isleworth range tonight.

SECOND ROUND

As the season has worn on, I have become more and more savvy about how to smuggle my cell phone. The first morning at the Buick Invitational, I took it with me and had it in my pocket. I walked past a smiling security guard who said, "Is your cell phone turned off, sir?" I smiled back, "It sure is," and kept going, only for him to change tones and snap, "You *can't* have cell phones on the course. You'll need to hand it over." It was a trap and, frankly, a good one. For the rest of the week I simply denied I had it. At the Dubai Desert Classic, I could have duct-taped it to my ear and security wouldn't have said anything. The Match Play stepped it up with metal detectors and wands, but George said if I stuffed it inside my pants, they wouldn't find it.

Friday at the Arnold Palmer Invitational I not only bring my cell phone, but I also need to use it, which is a much riskier proposition. While Tiger is on the putting green, I see a text message saying the producer of Golf Channel's nightly news show would like to interview me tonight about my adventures but that he has a few questions in advance.

I slip behind a fence near what turns out to be the club's laundry facilities. Workers scurry in and out with sheets, towels, tablecloths, and napkins. Judging by that, these fans must be the messiest on Tour. As I wait to be connected, I feel a breeze that smells like cold cuts intermittently blowing on my neck. I turn and see a round security guard with a bushy orange mustache standing one foot from me, his hands on his hips. He's wearing a black guard outfit and a matching hat with the word SECURITY on it in yellow letters in case there is still any doubt.

I decide to turn away slowly, hoping he'll be called off to a real emergency or maybe just lunch. He doesn't budge, so once the producer comes on the line, I start inserting inane, showbiz-sounding questions into our conversation to make me sound important, like "What time we on camera tonight?" and at least three or four times wedge in the phrase "Tiger and I." When the phone call ends, he's still there. "Hi." I say, figuring my phone is goners, but hopefully not me with it. He pushes the button on his walkie-talkie. "Security to base." We stand in silence. There's no answer. "Got a few minutes?" he asks, facetiously, I presume. We walk to his nearby golf cart, and he tells me to have a seat. We take off around the ninth green as incoming fans stare at me as if I've done something wrong. Which, okay, I have. I try to act cool, put my feet up on the cart, and make small talk.

"What's your name, man?"

"Lynn."

"*Lynn*?" I'm so convinced I have heard wrong that I start to spell it. "L-Y—"

"N-N," he finishes, sternly. I change the subject.

"So have you seen Tiger this week?"

"Yesterday on eighteen," he tells me. "He's almost as big as I am." For clarity's sake, Tiger is roughly 190 pounds. Lynn is pushing 300 if not already there. Even if he is just comparing their heights, it's the best example yet of how much everyone wants to look at Tiger and find some way to believe "I *am* like him."

We arrive at Lynn's destination, the main security office, where Sandy sits behind a desk. I already met Sandy yesterday. She is the petite but gruff woman who responded to my question of whether I could bring my periscope this week by scoffing and saying no.

The moment of reckoning has come. Sandy looks to her burly guard, wondering what awful thing I have done. I put my head down. He speaks. "This guy is writing a golf book, setting up interviews, that sort of thing. He *needs* to be able to use his cell phone on the course." Lynn's a softie! He asks Sandy if she has any more stickers for security-approved cell phones, the ones reserved for doctors with patients who might die if they aren't reachable. Sandy begins looking around her desk, a workspace covered in security hats, volunteer badges, and old newspapers. After a few seconds, she gives up and with that same curt manner as yesterday says, "Is your phone on vibrate?"

"Silent."

She shrugs. "So just don't make any phone calls. And if it goes off, you better believe Tiger Woods will toss your phone as far as he can throw it."

3:20 PM ▪ Tiger's second round officially started two hours ago on the 1st hole, when his ball came to rest and the marshal looked down and joked, "Hey, how come Tiger's playing a Pinnacle?" From there he would finish his first eight in only 1 under par. It's not too thrilling, considering Vijay Singh is already in the clubhouse having shot 66-65 to post 9 under heading into Saturday. Tiger's in trouble. And as he stares down a twelve-foot birdie putt on the 9th green, I finally understand why. The green is patchy, dying, and, in some places, dead. I don't know how anyone can make any putts except by sheer luck.

Tiger's win streak has been the big news at Bay Hill this week, but close behind it is the tale of something even more unstoppable: nematodes—parasitic worms that have been feasting on the roots of Bay Hill's TifEagle greens since last summer. The greenskeepers knew something was wrong, but after being unable to cure it, they sent a sample to a professor of plant pathology at Clemson, where the Ph.D. discovered the worms. At that point, it was too late; the worms had caused too much damage. Because so many of Bay Hill's greens are elevated, I hadn't seen the destruction until now. Jim Furyk told reporters that the greens were "fine." Tiger called them "not very good." They were both being generous. This 9th green is so bad that large sections of it have clearly been painted with green fertilizer to cover the damage.

Supposedly these worms are barely a few millimeters in length, but I have found articles saying nematodes as long as twenty-seven feet have been discovered inside the carcasses of dead sperm whales, and some part of me is waiting for a big one to burst through the brown turf as in Frank Herbert's *Dune* and swallow a player, preferably Vijay.

I focus back in on Tiger, who, on second glance, has left himself a birdie putt that avoids any bad spots. He makes it, but it's now apparent that for Tiger to make a serious run, he must find a way to putt well on unpredictable greens.

3:56 PM ▪ The par-4 11th at Bay Hill, like the 3rd and the 6th holes, wraps around the right side of a big round lake, 438 yards from tee to green. Tiger takes an aggressive line off the tee with a fairway wood, his ball stopping so close to the water that when he hits his second shot, his divot lands in it, leaving Stevie with a little less work to do. The line for his approach is even gutsier than his tee shot, landing ten feet left of the back left pin and only a few feet right of being wet. He misses the putt.

4:28 PM ▪ On the 13th hole, Tiger again knocks it into birdie range. And again misses. I'm standing with Darnell, a Tiger fan who came all the way from Bermuda to watch him this week and is just shaking his head. "It's one thing to be respectful, but somebody has got to say the truth. These greens are *bad.*" It's true, but at the same time, other players are posting low scores on these same greens. They are making some adjustment that Tiger isn't.

5:03 PM ▪ On the long par-4 16th, Tiger misses right off the tee and finds himself completely blocked by the bleachers facing the 17th green. Most marshals tend to overreact upon seeing Tiger's ball and force the gallery back three times farther than we need to go. The marshal at the 16th seems intimidated by the enormity of moving three hundred people and lets us stay where we are, within a yard of the ball. Stevie shows up, sees the lack of room he's been given, rolls his eyes, and asks the marshal to take charge.

We're moved just in time for the arrival of Tiger, who strolls up, takes one look at his ball, and immediately asks for a rules official. He waits. So we wait. It has been a frustrating two days, and he stands still with no emotion. But when the rules official arrives and tells Tiger that he has the option of playing the shot as it lies, Tiger smiles and laughs. "No, I do not want to play it *as is.*" The only other time I have seen his genuinely friendly personality break through like this was late in the finals of the Match Play when he bounced a drive off a woman's leg. He walked up with a toothy smile and said, "I'm sorry. I am *so* sorry. I wasn't trying to hit it over here. I was trying to hit it over *there.*" Both examples make it obvious that the space between his game face and his smile is a lot thinner than he would like his opponents to believe.

5:10 PM ▪ Tiger ultimately takes a free drop off the cart path, then an additional drop away from the bleachers. His second shot shoots through the trees and winds up in that terrible fifteen- to twenty-foot range. No surprise, he misses. The longest putt he has made all week remains his Thursday par putt on number 2.

5:32 PM ▪ On the 18th Tiger hits it *again* to fifteen feet. He has hit nearly every green on the back nine and has eight straight pars to show for it. Vijay remains the leader at 9 under, while Tiger sits stalled at 2 under. He needs this. He is above the middle-front hole position, a putt that should have some good speed to it. He leaves it dead on line but a few inches short. That makes him 0 for 6 on the back nine with makeable birdie putts. He makes his par, reaches into the cup, and, revealing his true sentiments, flips the ball behind his back and into the lake. A 70-68 start for Tiger. He makes the cut by only four shots and will begin the weekend farther out of the lead than when he teed off this morning.

THE GOLF CHANNEL ▪ This isn't my first time in front of the camera. Between my junior and senior years of college, I worked as an extra for the summer. For three months I bounced from show to show, literally being used to fill empty space. I had a recurring role on the teen show *Boy Meets World*, where I routinely played the mute, out-of-focus high school student. In the short-lived drama *Vengeance Unlimited*, I played a pivotal role as the out-of-focus guy who walks past the same window four or five times.

Thanks to that summer, I'm not particularly nervous about being interviewed by the Golf Channel's

Todd Lewis, the cheery former sports anchor at the CBS affiliate in Orlando who joined the network at the beginning of the year. Besides, I have plenty to talk about—my adventures with Rashid, running six miles with George, and, of course, Tiger. If I do completely blank once the red light goes on, Todd assures me I can go back and do another take. While the makeup artist goes to work on me, the different on-air personalities stick their heads in to say hello. They don't need to introduce themselves but they do anyway—"Hi, I'm Brandel," "Hi, Rich Lerner . . ." "Hey there, Kraig Kann . . ." It's not false modesty. They come off like a group of guys that doesn't tolerate ego. It's refreshing, and it makes sense.

After all, the Golf Channel is a long way from Hollywood, just a one-story building wedged in the middle of a nondescript Orlando business park. The channel may be available in 75 million households worldwide, but if it were ever to grab even 1 percent of that number, everyone at the network would party long into the night at the local Bennigan's.

The stage is completely dark but for the lights on the set. With the exception of Todd, the cameraman, and me, everyone else hangs back in the control room, watching the feed from the stage floor. Todd preps me with a few of the questions he will ask,

I nod, and off we go. We finish the first take, and I'm excited to go again to see if I can make myself sound interesting this time. Todd listens as I explain how I'm going to improve on my second take. He puts his finger to his earpiece, smiles, and says, "They're telling me we're done." Driving to dinner, I console myself with the thought that, if nothing else, I was finally in focus.

THIRD ROUND

There is irony in the fact that my first experience following Tiger was in the Sherwood Country Club parking lot last December. It's the exact same place I had stood as a thirteen-year-old when my dad took me to my very first golf tournament, Greg Norman's Shark Shootout. He and I walked up from the dirt lot and caught sight of the clubhouse, an all-brick mansion that was the most beautiful building we'd ever seen in our lives. We just stood there in silence, gawking. Someone walked behind us and said, "That's the *tennis* clubhouse." We kept going up the road and came to the main clubhouse, something so massive and over the top it was hard to believe that no war-ending treaties had ever been signed behind its white pillars. We wandered past the front and down through the empty parking lot when a car pulled up. Out stepped Arnold Palmer.

My dad had grown up in Pittsburgh and cemented his love for Palmer from the gallery at the 1962 U.S. Open at Oakmont. The tournament built to a Monday playoff between western Pennsylvania's favorite son and a young, pudgy kid named Jack Nicklaus. The whole way around, my dad remembers the hometown crowd not just rooting against Nicklaus but actually booing him. It was bad enough that he was from Ohio, but to be from Ohio *and* beating Arnie was sacrilege. In the end, Nicklaus held off Palmer—and the crowds—and won by three shots. It was the first major of his career.

Seeing Arnie in person at age thirteen was immobilizing. I didn't know how a human being was supposed to handle a moment of such significance. My dad told me to run and find a golf pencil. I did and was back in time to catch the King walking by. I remember my dad said, "Morning, Arnie," as if he were part of his regular foursome. Arnie smiled and said, "Hello." I said nothing, just held out the pencil, and my ticket. He signed it, then headed into the clubhouse, a cashmere sweater stuffed under his arm. I remember thinking how normal he was. That he *could* be one of the guys in my dad's foursome. That he would rib him after a bad shot and applaud the good ones and wouldn't think about heading home after the round without having a drink and a sandwich in the bar. Even back then, I knew that was what made Arnold Palmer special. He was one of us.

11:27 AM ▪ When the seventy-eight-year-old Arnie appears on the range at Bay Hill, he receives the welcome he deserves, a standing ovation from the bleachers. He's wearing a soft orange shirt, gray slacks, and half-hidden beneath his slight paunch, a green belt from Augusta National, one of the *ninety* clubs to which he belongs. He stops to talk to Fred Couples, and picks up Fred's 3-wood to waggle it, still appreciating the feel of a shaft he is too old to hit. He moves from Couples to Tiger, who pats him on the back. When the season started, Tiger was one PGA win behind Arnie. Less than two months later, he has already passed him.

11:51 AM ▪ I move down the number 1 fairway a few minutes ahead of Tiger and read in the daily pairing sheet about Vijay's second-round 65. At first he seems to be playing at a level he can't sustain, having chipped in not once but twice yesterday. Then I read that Vijay is still recovering from a bout of food poisoning he picked up in India last month, as a result of which he claims to have lost eighteen pounds. Tiger was onto something back in 2003—apparently the secret to winning here is to become violently ill.

11:57 AM ▪ Tiger starts his round by missing right and leaving himself a downhill lie from the deep rough to the green. Tiger peers down at his lie, almost afraid to look, then shakes his head. He goes with a short iron, opens the face and his stance, and takes a giant rip at the ball, the club almost flying out of his hands from the speed of the swing. The crowd loves it. It ends up twelve feet away. After yesterday, I know he can two-putt from there, but he actually makes it. Three under. Exactly the start he needs. From this far behind, he needs to post a low number on the front nine and scare as many of the two dozen players teeing off after him as possible.

12:22 PM ▪ The afternoon wind is picking up as Tiger reaches number 3, a mini version of number 11, just under 400 yards around the lake. It's downwind, and Tiger plays aggressively along the left side of the fairway near the water. He leaves his second shot ten feet away, downhill. *Again* he makes it! Four under. He said to reporters yesterday that more than the line, the bad greens are messing with his speed; that he just needs to adjust to hitting them harder than he is used to doing here. Consider the adjustment made.

Another adjustment he has made today is to manually fix as many defects in his line as he can. Before his birdie putt on the long par-4 4th, I decide to count. One . . . two . . . three . . . four . . . five . . . six. Most of us don't fix that many marks in a month. But it pays off as he drops it in for his third birdie in his opening four holes. "That's the Tiger we know and love," a fan says. At 5 under, he's pulled within four of Vijay, who hasn't even teed off yet.

1:05 PM ▪ Back on the 6th, the massive par 5 around the lake, Tiger's drive leaks right and jumps just a yard into the rough. The first one on the scene is Luau Larry. It's the first I've seen him this week. His leg reveals no sign of the Tucson cactus incident, and he walks up to Tiger's ball to take a look at the lie. A fellow sportswriter jokingly asks, "What do you see, Feherty?" Larry always appears humorless, but I'm hoping he'll see the rare opportunity to try out his best Irish lilt. To my disappointment, all Larry says is a flat and accent-free "It's okay."

1:43 PM ▪ An okay lie isn't good enough for a birdie, and Tiger plays the rest of the front nine 1 over to make the turn at 4 under par for the week. Vijay remains at 9 under. No one else is lower than 6 under, meaning that Tiger's 33 on the front nine has put him within striking distance.

2:15 PM ▪ On the 11th, the wheels have come off for Ben Crane, Tiger's fair-skinned playing partner, whose face has been recently coated with a thick layer of white sunblock. Tiger made the hole look easy with a two-putt par, but Crane pulled his second into the lake, dropped, played his fourth onto the green, then rolled his bogey putt well past the hole.

Anyone plays slowly en route to a triple-bogey seven, but even when he's playing well, Crane remains one of the Tour's slowest members. As Crane looks over his double-bogey putt, Tiger walks to the back of the green and stands next to Dottie Pepper, NBC's on-course commentator fitted with headset, mike, and a battery-packed belt. They start whispering and laughing about something as Tiger crosses his arms, then puts them on his hips, then crosses them again in an exaggerated fashion. I'm not sure what's going on until I look back down the 11th fairway and see Pat Perez, the Tour's most impatient player, going nuts waiting for Crane. On cue, Pat crosses his arms, then puts them on his hips. Tiger and Dottie laugh at Tiger's dead-on impression.

Once again, Tiger is using other players' weaknesses to his own advantage, never once letting Crane or Perez do anything but make him smile.

3:09 PM ▪ By the time Tiger arrives at the fairway on the 15th, Vijay has dropped a shot and Tiger's down only four. The wind has been growing stronger all afternoon, and on the tree-lined 425-yard hole, it begins to gust straight into the players' faces. Tiger faces a tough second shot from the right side of the fairway, an approach that he will have to somehow get around the hole's trademark magnolia trees.

Golf purists criticize the modern player for his inability to shape shots, and as usual, Tiger is the exception to the rule. Where other players hunger for control, Tiger's Nike balls are custom-designed with an extra-soft cover so he can turn the ball even more. He aims his stance to the left and the face of his forged Nike blade to the right, and slashes across the ball from out to in, sending it left of the magnolias and then cutting back hard to the right and straight at the pin. It's not amazing, it's not unbelievable. I don't even think it's ridiculous. It's beautiful. It drops out of the wind and stops three feet from the hole. No nematodes can stop this putt from going in the cup. Tiger is within three.

3:26 PM ▪ Tiger pipes it down the middle on the 16th, the scariest par 4 at Bay Hill. The pin is cut only four or five paces off the front edge near the water, and the wind continues to gust in his face. Showing his range of shots, he chokes down this time and hits one low, with less fade than before. While the ball is in midair, the fan in front of me, Kevin, declares that it will be close. I trust him. He's a key performance analyst at Boeing and has an Indiana Jones–style hat with the chin strap pulled tight, a pair of binoculars, and a range finder to determine exactly how far away each player is. The ball skids to a stop no more than four feet away. "A lot of these guys on Tour are golfers," Kevin says. "Tiger's an athlete." Tiger makes another three. Six under.

3:44 PM ▪ As long as none of the leaders pulls much farther away from him than 10 under, he will have a chance tomorrow. After a par on 17, I make my way down the left side of 18 and see that the leaders have gotten closer to Tiger, not further. The wide-eyed Nick Watney had it to 9 under, but bogeyed the 13th to fall to 8. The Swedish-born/Southern-raised Carl Pettersson fell back to 8 after a bogey on the 9th. And Vijay has just played the 5th through 8th holes 5 *over* par and slipped two shots *behind*

Tiger. The traditional Sunday-afternoon crumble at the feet of Tiger is happening, but it's happening on a Saturday.

3:55 PM ▪ Tiger pars the 18th, signs his scorecard for a 66, and moves to the outdoor media area, where he is quickly surrounded by reporters and cameramen. A crowd of a few hundred of us gathers on the other side of the metal barricade to eavesdrop, but we can't hear a thing. Still, none of us leaves. An old man next to me brings out the digital camera he has hidden in his pants and is trying to take a picture, but he's too short. I take it from him, hold it up high over the mob, and snag a good one. I try to zoom in and make it even better when I look up in the grandstands and see a group of marshals pointing me out to, of course, Lynn the security guard. As he lumbers down the stairs to nab me, I slip between the crowds and escape for the bus.

THE BAD DOG ▪ When Tiger leaves Bay Hill, he drives home to Isleworth to work out and watch the leaders finish. As Kevin, the Bay Hill superfan, had said, Tiger is an athlete, and after years of keeping his workout regiment under wraps, he finally revealed it to *Men's Fitness* last year. He typically goes to the gym six days a week, sometimes up to three hours at a time. I don't know why this should surprise me. When Tiger was a kid, he overcame a debilitating stutter by talking to his dog. Sometimes, he would talk so long that his dog fell asleep.

The first thirty minutes of Tiger's workout is purely stretching, from the obvious body parts like his back, all the way to his toes. Weightwise, Tiger generally does high-rep sets versus power lifting and bench pressing. At 190 pounds, he already has plenty of bulk. The big concern for his trainer is keeping Tiger's body symmetrical, not wanting any part of him to be out of balance with the rest, a flaw that could upend everything else. The rest of his routine is rounded out with cardio and core training, which leads to the most disturbing quote of the article: "I like doing sit-ups, thoroughly enjoy them. I think they're fun." If a man can convince his mind that sit-ups are fun, there is no limit to what he can achieve.

I also decide to strengthen my core and go to Steak n Shake. It's my fifth time to this hamburger joint in three days. Even though the service and food are growing progressively worse, I can't resist going back again and again. The combination of meat, fries, and shake gives me all the things my body needs after five hours on the course.

If I had known what was taking place back at Bay Hill, I never would have left. The leaders who had shown some cracks as Tiger made his late charge completely collapsed once his 6-under total was officially posted. Bart Bryant was a few shots ahead and found the water on 16 to fall back into a tie with Tiger. Nick Watney, who had already slipped to 8 under when I left, pulled his drive on 16 out of bounds, then hit his fourth shot into the water left of the green. He'd make a quadruplebogey and finish at 4 under. Carl Pettersson double-bogeyed the 10th and bogeyed the 15th, falling past Watney to only 3 under. And while Vijay recovered from a front-nine 40, he couldn't pull ahead of Tiger, joining the party at 6 under. By the time I return to Kelly's house and check the scores, Tiger is tied for the lead with four other players and has landed in the final group.

After thoroughly enjoying the highlights of the field's collective demise, I need to hit some balls. Considering I have dragged my clubs with me across the country, I might as well use them. The only lit driving range nearby is the Bad Dog Driving Range. There are four sizes of buckets from which to choose: "Runt," "Lap Dog," "Pick of the Litter," and . . . "The Bad Dog," 180 balls guaranteed to make all ten fingers bleed. I go with Lap Dog. Rather than hit balls without a purpose, as I usually do, I try to maximize the pressure and pretend I'm actually playing alongside Tiger. After a few dozen swings, he stops me. "Wait," imaginary Tiger says. "One shot. Closest to the hole. You get inside my ball, you can write about our round. If not . . . we never met."

I take a breath, focus on the red flag 105 yards away, factor in the left-to-right breeze, and swing. It bounces once, kicks right, and, best I can tell, settles up next to the eight-inch-wide red-painted flagpole. I win, Tiger. I imagine his reaction, silent and cold, then saying "Two out of three?" I refuse the temptation to end on anything but a good one and leave the rest of the balls behind.

FINAL ROUND

Last night Tiger went from in the mix to in the lead, and as a result, Tiger mania is sweeping central Florida. A few thousand fans are already with me lining the 1st fairway, anxious to be part of his win streak. The spectrum of the fans officially falls between two extremes. Next to me is a guy in his early twenties, dressed like Tiger Woods. Red Tiger Woods Nike shirt, black pants, black hat. He's completely humorless. There's no smiling, his arms are crossed.

For him, this is war. He needs to concentrate on Tiger and will not be distracted by any of my dumb questions. When I ask him if he's a big Vijay fan, he turns, gives me an eerie Tiger-like scowl, eyes barely visible beneath his hat, then turns back to face the fairway.

The other extreme is partying behind me. Even though Tiger hasn't teed off, Daryl and his rowdy friends have just arrived from their preround victory celebration at the beer garden. Daryl flew in from Seattle, but the rest of the group is local. He introduces me to the rest of his buddies. There's Jessie, then Joe. "Yo, Francis!" I meet Francis. I think that's it until Daryl asks, "Anybody seen Cedric?" I count five. Daryl says there's eleven of them total, and if I want to have fun, I need to stick with them.

"If you can keep up with me, I'll walk with you guys for a few holes," I say. Daryl's insulted.

"If *you* can keep up with *us*." Oh, it is on.

"All I know is I'm one beer more sober than you are."

Joe pipes in. "One? Try two or three."

These guys are sort of interested in golf and very interested in women. When Suzann Pettersen, an athletic blonde who happens to be the number three female golfer in the world, walks by, Daryl turns around and takes notice. "I have *got* to go visit Sweden!" he says, loud enough for her to hear. Neither of us tells him she's from Norway.

It's not the first time Pettersen has been here this week. She came to watch Tiger yesterday, too. After Tiger smashed his drive on the 12th hole, she turned to her parents and started laughing. Walking down the fairway, I asked her what the biggest difference is between his game and hers. "He just hits it so much harder than I do," she said. When top-tier athletes from the same sport start showing up at events, something special is happening.

2:06 PM ▪ I troop along with Daryl and company as Tiger makes a solid par on the first. On the 218-yard par-3 2nd, Tiger knocks his shot about eighteen feet short of the cup, a definite birdie chance. Before Tiger has even gotten to the green, Daryl and the group start walking to number 3.

"Where are you guys going?" Daryl turns around and keeps walking backward while talking to me.

"Oh, we don't stay for putts."

"What are you talking about?"

"If we stay for putts, we'll fall behind. Francis knows *all* the tricks." My time with them lasts only one and a half holes. But I get over it quickly when Tiger makes the birdie they missed and takes the outright lead at 7 under.

3:51 PM ▪ Throughout the rest of Tiger's front nine, Daryl and I are repeatedly leapfrogging each other. After raising his putter to celebrate a ten-foot par save on the 4th, the rest of Tiger's front nine is precision. He hits every green and defies the nematodes again on the pockmarked 9th for a twenty-foot birdie putt from off the fringe that puts him at two shots clear of the pack at the turn. The only thing he can't do is make a stupid mistake.

4:00 PM ▪ And then he makes a stupid mistake. After laying back off the 10th tee with just an iron, he plants his second shot no more than seven feet from the hole, then three-putts. The birdie try never touches the hole. The par putt lips out. One minute earlier, I was wondering whether the Tour's trophy engraver has ever tried carving Tiger's name with his eyes closed. Now I'm realizing what one small bogey has done. It has given the other players the worst possible thing in the world—hope.

When Tiger's mom, Tida, was interviewed in 2006 for the *60 Minutes* piece on Tiger, she explained the mind-set she had passed on to her son about competition. "You have to, no matter how close friends you are . . . you must kill that person." The bogey at 10 is the equivalent of Tiger lifting his foot off the field's collective throat and asking "Everyone all right down there?" He is suddenly tied at 8 under with Bart Bryant, who had birdied the 10th when he passed through five minutes earlier. Other players are suddenly energized to make moves, too. Cliff Kresge climbs the leaderboard to –7. So does Hunter Mahan. The relaxing back nine I had envisioned is over before it starts.

4:35 PM ▪ Tiger scraps around for pars on the next two holes and comes to the 364-yard 13th, a short par 4 with water in front. It's short enough that Tiger can hit a long iron off the tee and still only have a sand wedge into the green. He has to reapply the pressure, and stuffs a sand wedge just over the pond and within twelve feet of the tucked front pin. I scan his line for dead spots, but it's only Tiger's fault if he misses this one. He raps it hard uphill and into the grain, and it falls in on the front side. Any birdie is a big birdie right now, but his timing forces his chasers to take some risks on those tough final four holes.

4:45 PM ▪ With Tiger still putting for a par on 14, I steal Daryl's "trick" and jump ahead. The crowds have swelled this afternoon to five deep, the thickest Sunday crowds of the year. Down at 15, I catch up with Bart Bryant in the group ahead in time to see him make a four-footer for a birdie of his own and back into a tie for the lead.

Watching Bart Bryant, I can't help but think of Ed Fiori, the forty-three-year-old journeyman who knocked off Tiger at the Quad Cities Open in 1996 to deny the rookie his first Tour victory. As Fiori was then, Bryant is in his mid-forties and is built more like a high school gym coach than a finely tuned athlete. There is something unnerving about that age, a window of time when a golfer's body will sometimes let him play well, but the world won't think any less of him if he doesn't. If a twenty-eight-year-old loses down the stretch to Tiger, it's a choke. If a forty-five-year-old loses, it's a valiant effort. It isn't that Bryant doesn't have anything to lose. A win would earn him an invitation to the Masters next month and the CA Championship next week. But for now he must be relishing a position where the expectations couldn't be lower.

4:51 PM ▪ At 9 under, Tiger and Bryant are two shots clear of anyone else. They aren't in the same twosome, but they're close enough to keep tabs on each other, giving the tournament a match play feel. Tiger plays conservatively off the tee on the par-4 15th, hitting only a 5-wood to make sure he stays between the magnolias. Of course, it helps that his 5-wood still goes 250 yards. He two-putts for par to keep pace.

5:09 PM ▪ Tiger lays back off the 16th as well, taking a 3-wood on a par 4 that is 485 yards long. For a player who early in his career had the reputation of swinging out of his spikes and then dealing with the consequences, he has displayed a tremendous amount of patience throughout this win streak. He has never once looked harried. When he was down four strokes at the turn in Dubai, he told Stevie he needed to shoot 30 to win, then meticulously picked off birdies one by one, playing for the safe side of each green rather than firing at every pin. The mature Tiger Woods may not always be as flashy from tee to green, but his restraint only makes him even more dangerous.

The result of Tiger's safe drive is a 200-yard approach. He still manages to leave it hole high in the middle of the green. As his birdie putt falls off to the left, Tiger bends over his putter as if he's falling on his sword.

5:28 PM ▪ Just as Bryant did a few minutes earlier, Tiger has a birdie look at the par-3 17th, but can't make it. He angrily pounds down a bump he has deemed the cause of the miss. Even though he came alive on

Saturday to slide into first place, the longest putt I have seen him make all week remains his par save on number 2 way back on Thursday.

After three days, I've learned that to get from the right side of 17 to the left side of 18, I will have to sprint past the tee box and make it to the crosswalk before the marshals close the ropes. When Tiger's birdie effort doesn't drop, I take off full speed, which is a few steps faster than it was back at the Buick, and arrive at the crosswalk right as the marshal places the white rope back on the pole. He flashes me a fake smile and turns around. I can either wait until Tiger has teed off and then try to find a spot down the bleacher-lined left-hand side or keep going down the right, where I will only get as close as the front edge of the lake before reaching a dead end. The crowds down the entire left side are at least ten deep, and no one is leaving.

I run down the right side. On my way, Tiger's tee ball passes me, a low 3-wood placed perfectly to the left side of the fairway. It's my first view of Bay Hill's 18th green with its traditional Sunday pin placement, three quarters of the way to the green's right edge and only a few yards from the water. The trouble short is obvious. The trouble long is hard to miss as well, three bright white bunkers curving like a boomerang around the green's back side.

5:35 PM ▪ Up ahead, Bryant rolls his thirty-five-foot birdie putt toward the hole. From two hundred yards away, a fan near me says "Miss," under his breath. "Miss. Miss it." He's like D'Annunzio in *Caddyshack* trying to spook Danny Noonan. Bryant indeed misses and taps in nonchalantly for an impressive 67, safely in the clubhouse at 9 under. We cheer, having to give the guy credit for not buckling under the pressure. Tiger needs a par to tie or a birdie to win. As always, he has done it before. In 2001, he faced a fifteen-footer to beat Phil Mickelson and made it. First he must hit the green.

As Tiger and Stevie start to discuss the shot, the wind begins to gust differently than it has all day. It switches direction 180 degrees and begins to blow in our faces, as if a special-effects team just flipped a switch to make Tiger's second shot to the 18th that much harder to judge.

He has 170 yards. With the wind, it's at least another ten, maybe more. He chooses a club and backs away as the wind gusts again. A siren blares in the distance, then fades. Tiger steadies himself one more time and hits a hard cut toward the middle of the green. It clears the water and lands safely on the other side, twenty-five feet above the hole to the left. He hands Stevie his club with his right hand as Stevie gives him an open-palm low-five with the other.

The low-five is a much safer option than the forever awkward celebration they shared after Tiger chipped in for birdie on the 16th at the 2005 Masters. Stevie followed one of the greatest shots in golf history by trying to christen the moment with a high-five. He managed to make contact with no more than one of Tiger's five fingers, then stood there waffling between a fist pump and a forearm bash to make up for it. It exemplified why Tiger Woods was never meant to play a team sport. Someone else was always bound to make him look worse than he was.

His Ryder Cup stats prove it. In his singles matches, he hasn't lost since 1997. But in team play, the greatest player in the world has a losing record—seven wins, twelve losses.

5:45 PM ▪ From my spot on the corner of the lake, I'm looking straight across the water as Tiger walks the length of the putt, down to the hole and then back again. There are so many things to distract a lesser life form. An NBC crew guy shuffles down the grassy bank behind him, gripping his boom mike. From under the bleachers, Arnie emerges and stands watch in his navy blue Bay Hill blazer.

Tiger's head is on a pivot, but it's only in order to keep the line of the putt always centered between his eyes. He walks slowly; nothing is rushed. He actually appears to relish the pressure of the moment. I met a clinical psychologist one day at the Match Play and asked him for a professional opinion on Tiger's ability to perform under duress. He chalked it up to Tiger having an overdeveloped cognitive and neuromotor reserve, and when the other parts of his brain are stimulated by stress, he can access a "storeroom" of calm. Everyone always wonders how he or she can perform under pressure like Tiger. The Ph.D. I met said it's irrelevant—what Tiger does is something most people couldn't physically do even if they knew how.

5:47 PM ▪ He takes two last strokes before stepping into the ball. As he draws the silver putter back, I notice a bird on the lake dive beneath the water. Dogs can sense earthquakes. Maybe loons can, too. The moment he hits it, the crowd starts to cheer, sounding like a distant wave that won't stop breaking. With the ball having traveled only two feet from Tiger's putter, someone in the back row of the bleachers stands and put his hands up as if he already knows it's in. That is trust. The rest of the grandstands are on their feet when it's halfway to the hole and still on line. As the putt banks to the right, the cheers from those with better views continue to swell and we take our cues from them, screaming the ball down toward the cup. I stop tracking the actual putt when I see Tiger take a few steps backward. *He's done it again.* When it drops, Tiger turns and, in one glorious motion, slams his black TW hat to the ground. Taking my cue from him, I toss my own hat into the air and roar in delight. If there were only a way to harness the energy released around that green, it would power the city of Orlando for a week.

Without waiting for permission, the still-screaming fans around me duck under the ropes and begin racing toward the green. I grab my hat off the ground and do the same. To spend exactly 333 holes roped in and then be running free is thrilling. I know we're heading toward Tiger, but I don't think anyone has thought through what we'll do if we reach him.

Twenty yards from the green, a handful of old marshals bolts across with some rope and stretches it from the lake to the grandstands, bracing itself for the stampede that might very well roll on past them without giving it another thought. I hit the rope. It stretches tight around my waist under the crush of the thousand fans behind me, but the line holds. On the other side of the rope is Larry Johnson, a wiry marshal who finds himself with the most memorable job of the day. "Did they prepare you for this?" I ask. "Not enough!" he says, both laughing and terrified at the same time.

Four tournaments. *Four wins.* Each one more thrilling than the one before. His 64th PGA Tour win ties him with Ben Hogan on the all-time victory list and puts him two ahead of Palmer. As workers scurry to the green to set up microphones and place all the blue-blazered tournament officials in a straight line, I remember an interview David Feherty did on CBS with Tiger during the Buick. He asked Tiger whether twelve wins in a row was possible—twelve being the number it would take to beat Byron Nelson's record of eleven straight victories in 1945. Tiger paused but never took his eyes off Feherty as he casually said, "Uh-huh." When I heard it, I blew it off as another example of Tiger's out-of-control ego. How could he consider breaking a record that ranks as golf's most untouchable achievement. But going back to last year, his win streak stands at seven. If Phil Mickelson hadn't held him off at the Deutsche Bank Championship last September, this would be win number ten.

Eight minutes later, Tiger is back on the green, now wearing a blue blazer of his own and standing in front of Arnie. As Tiger accepts the silver trophy, the man whose statue rests on top of it elbows him in the side and sarcastically calls him a "jerk." Tiger steps to the microphone and tries to sound modest about his finish. "I just happened to get lucky and make a putt."

Someone behind me yells back, "It's not luck!" If it happens once, it's luck. If you do it in Dubai and at the Match Play and again at Bay Hill, it's otherworldly. Supernatural. After that putt, there's no way I can wait two or three weeks to see him play again. And for the first time this season, I won't have to.

Drive for Show,
Putt for . . . D'oh!

The WGC-CA Championship

**The Blue Monster—Doral Golf Resort & Spa
Miami, Florida
March 20–24, 2008**

There are three online reviews on TripAdvisor for the Econo Lodge in North Fort Myers, Florida. They are titled "Very Disappointed," "Don't stay here!!," and "Never stay here, no matter what." Unfortunately, I don't read them until after I am very disappointed and staying there. I had driven down the west coast of Florida from Orlando Tuesday night until I couldn't stay awake any longer when the Econo Lodge appeared majestically in front of me.

The problem is that I am sharing a wall with Moe, a belligerent alcoholic I have heard but not seen who, between his drinking and related carousing, has broken everything in his room by sunrise. At 7 a.m., I abandon the notion of sleep, check out, and head for the Rav4. Outside, Moe is standing in front of his room, dressed but unshaven, tattooed, brown curly hair in knots, preparing the manager for what he's about to see. The manager courageously steps inside as Moe shakes his head, as if even he can't believe what he's done. Driving away, I see a gangly woman slip out Moe's door, followed by a poor maid walking to the Dumpster with a handful of used limes.

My accommodations for the CA Championship in Miami can't possibly be this bad. I'll be staying with Craig—a writer himself who has read about my adventures on ESPN.com and received permission from his fiancée to let me crash on their couch for the week. "We're not creepy," he promises, something that's hard to disprove just by saying it.

To get from Fort Myers to Craig's home in Fort Lauderdale, I drive in a straight line for a hundred miles, across the width of South Florida, on a stretch of highway called Alligator Alley. There are no cities along it, and Kelly had promised that I would see actual gators while I was driving. It seems hard to believe, equivalent to tourists who eat on Rodeo Drive thinking they'll be sharing a bread stick with Angelina Jolie. But sure enough, after only a few miles there is a clearing, and a healthy seven-footer is sitting on the side of the swamp, waiting for a tourist's Rav4 to run out of gas. I check my gauge and keep driving.

In 1959, the New York real estate magnate Alfred Kaskel bought 2,400 acres west of Miami. But saying "acres" makes it sound too civilized. It was swampland, and people thought he had lost his mind. Three years later, the first PGA Tour event was held at Doral—a name Kaskel created by smushing his wife's first name, Doris, together with his own. During the third round that year, Doral's water-flanked 18th hole averaged more than a stroke over par and the head pro dubbed it "a monster . . . a blue monster." The name stuck for both the hole and the course.

For a venue to stay on the Tour schedule for nearly fifty years, it's either hallowed ground (Augusta National, Colonial Country Club) or a little lucky. Doral survived a scare in the mid-'80s when Eastern Airlines, its sponsor of seventeen years, went bankrupt. It was given new life again last year when the PGA Tour took the Ford Championship at Doral and rebranded it the CA Championship. Ironically, "CA" is the rebranded name of Computer Associates, the IT management firm that has taken on sponsorship in the hope that people will forget their chairman is currently serving a twelve-year prison sentence for securities fraud.

But Doral's safe spot on the schedule isn't because of CA, it's because it's also the second of the year's four World Golf Championships (the first being last month's Accenture Match Play). The major pro circuits concocted the WGCs in the late 1990s as a way to bring together the best players on Earth more often than just for the year's four majors . . . and make some healthy TV revenue in the process. In addition to the top fifty players in the world, this week's exclusive seventy-nine-man field includes the top three from the Japan Golf Tour, the Australasian Golf Tour, the Asian Tour, and the South African Sunshine Tour. They're lured by a big purse and the fact that there's not a two-day cut. As long as they finish all 72 holes, they're guaranteed at least a last-place $35,000 paycheck. Who knew that dominating the Sunshine Tour could bring such perks?

All any of this meant for Tiger Woods was that he would be receiving a $360,000 raise. After winning the Ford Championship in 2005 and 2006, he went right ahead and won the CA Championship in 2007 and the bloated first-place check of $1.35 million. It was more prize money than he took home for winning the PGA Championship that same year.

Unlike Bay Hill, the conventional wisdom heading into Doral is that Tiger can't lose. The rough is shorter than last week, its greens are worm-free, and even though he won't be staying at home, Tiger will probably be able to make do with the sleeping quarters on board his 155-foot yacht, brought down from central Florida for the week.

FIRST ROUND

11:15 AM ▪ Just four hours from Orlando, and the weather is completely different. The air is heavy, and elephant gray clouds drag themselves west to east across the South Florida sky. Tiger is on Doral's putting green, surrounded by more than twenty international flags and lagging putts from fifty feet away. The first putt is terrible, stopping twelve feet short. The next two are within four feet. The last ball is tracking toward the cup when K. J. Choi walks up and stops it with the end of his putter. Tiger is shaken out of his focus, sees the offender, and smiles. Direct interference may be the only way for the field to stop him at this point.

12:26 PM ▪ There's nothing monstrous about the first hole at Doral. It's a 529-yard par 5 with only a few scattered palm trees to the right and left. Tiger booms his drive down the middle, so far in fact that he only has a mid-iron left. He lands it on the green and two-putts.

One hole, one birdie. It's hard to know what a winning score is going to be this week. Last year, Tiger finished at 10 under and won by two shots. In 2006, he doubled that number, shot 20 under, but won by only one shot. I suggest that he just birdie the remaining 71 holes to take the guesswork out of things.

1:00 PM ▪ The 2nd hole is even easier than the first—a 376-yard par 4 where Tiger's meticulously planned strategy is apparently to swing out of his shoes. I know it's early in the round, but so far I don't get this course. It's flat, boring, and easy. If that were the criteria to host a World Golf Championship, I should invite someone from the Tour to play Woodley Lakes Golf Course near a muni near my house that is often coated in a thin layer of goose excrement.

1:07 PM ▪ The Blue Monster shows itself on number 3. It's the first water hole on the course and a mirror image of the 3rd at Bay Hill, a long par 4 turning around the left side of a lake. Last year this hole had the fourth-highest stroke average of any hole played on Tour. Today's wind must not be blowing the typical direction, because all Tiger needs is a fairway wood and a wedge to have ten feet for birdie. After missing the birdie on 2, he makes one here. Two under.

2:07 PM ▪ Tiger pars his way to the 7th, a par 4 that reminds me of all the least interesting holes at Torrey Pines and Bay Hill. Long. Straight. Bunkers on both sides of the fairway. There are no choices, no risk/reward. Just hit it between the sand traps and onto the green. It's almost as though when a golf course architect doesn't know what else to do, he hits the "F7" key on his keyboard and out pops a hole like this.

4:15 PM ▪ After a bogey on the 7th, Tiger picks up two more birdies on the par-5 8th and the par-5 10th. But 3 under is only a so-so score today. As he waits his turn on the 14th green, he looks at the leaderboard and sees that Australia's Geoff Ogilvy is done with a 7-under 65 and Phil Mickelson is in with a 5-under 67.

Mickelson long ago decided that his best tack as world number two is to gush about how much more talented Tiger is, then rise to the occasion and beat him just often enough to keep some people wondering. Of the three times Tiger has lost a fifty-four-hole lead on the PGA Tour, one came at the feet of Phil, who stole the 2001 Tour Championship away from him. And last year they dueled in the final pairing at the Deutsche Bank Championship with Phil holding Tiger off to win by two. Their relationship can be summed up by the fact that the only off-course activity they ever share is Ping-Pong between Ryder Cup and Presidents Cup matches. It's civil, but unless there's a win or loss at stake, the sport's two most talented players have nothing in common.

Seeing Phil ahead of him may be the motivation Tiger needs. He rolls in his birdie at 14 and gets to 4 under. With the players having crossed to the next tee, the marshal lowers the ropes and we funnel down 15. But the marshal doesn't see that Craig Connelly, Paul Casey's caddy, is still running the gauntlet. After zigzagging through the crowds, Connelly arrives on the tee and tells the marshal, "You forgot a guy!" The marshal looks toward 14 to see whom. He clarifies: *"Me!"* Connelly has an excuse for being on edge. In the first thirteen holes, Casey has six birdies, four bogeys, and only three pars.

Meanwhile, Tiger seems to have found a groove. His shot on the 175-yard 15th is within ten feet. He makes it to get to 5 under and is tied with Phil.

5:00 PM ▪ If Tiger ever hits a longer tee shot this year than the one he hits on the 17th, I'll be shocked. After yells of "fore right!" from the tee, his drive smacks the cart path along the right side and bounds forward toward the hole. I pace it off and then triple-check the yardage—385 yards. And his angle to the hole could not be better, allowing him to play straight up the skinny neck of the green. He pitches it toward the hole; it jumps onto the green, curves toward the stick, and almost falls in for eagle. His third birdie in four holes puts him at 6 under, ahead of Mickelson and within one of Ogilvy.

5:12 PM ▪ The Blue Monster has a few too many "F7s" for my taste, but Dick Wilson, the post–World War II architect who designed both this course and Bay Hill, certainly knows how to design a hard finishing hole. Unlike the par 4 he shaped at Bay Hill, there are no secrets here. 467 yards. Slightly elevated green. *Don't go left.* The lake that runs down that entire side of the hole is so terrifying to players that I've seen twice as many play from the trees on the right than ever actually hit the water. It's not all nightmares, however. The greatest finish at Doral came back in 2004 in a playoff between the penguin-shaped Craig Parry and my own ticket benefactor, Scott Verplank. Parry found the skinny strip of fairway, which was impressive in itself, then took a 6-iron and knocked it into the hole for an eagle and the win. It was such an impossible feat that the typically intense Verplank never went through the five stages of grief. He went straight to acceptance and started laughing. Last year Tiger came to the 18th with a three-shot lead and took the opposite approach. Rather than test the water, he laid up with his second shot, then two-putted for bogey and the win.

With the afternoon wind replaced by black clouds, Tiger blasts his drive and misses right, into one of the traps and 140 yards from the flag. He takes his pitching wedge from Stevie and burrows his feet into the sand. *Just make a par and get out of here.* His shot lands on, but the green is no less subtle than the water next to it. Tiger has left himself a good seventy feet up and over a ridge to the hole.

As Tiger walks to his ball on the front of the green, the threatening clouds have started to sprinkle, the third time this year that rain has held off until Tiger's nearly done with his round. He keeps his head down, nearly making the birdie but running it up the ridge and five feet by. In the time it takes him to walk to his ball, the sky unloads. It's just what the 18th at Doral needs, more water. Tiger acts as if he doesn't even feel it, which is possible considering his focus. With the rain cascading off the brim of his hat, he looks down at the ball, and then misses the par putt wide. It's the first time he has bogeyed an 18th hole since Dubai and only the 2nd time all year. It drops him back to 5 under and into a tie with Mickelson. If he wasn't planning on coming out firing on Friday, he is now.

FLORIDA CRAIG ▪ My home for the week is only a few blocks from the beach in Fort Lauderdale, a yellow two-bedroom bungalow surrounded by heavy tropical trees and plants. Craig sits at the kitchen table reading *The Wall Street Journal* and wrapped in a blue bathrobe and a three-day old salt-and-pepper beard. On Friday morning, I haven't been awake for thirty seconds when he asks his first question of the day.

"What do you think Tiger is going to shoot today?"

I have no idea. "Sixty-nine."

"What makes you think that?"

Craig's life is an obsession with finding answers. Three and a half years ago he was an NYU law student working as an intern in the office of then attorney general Eliot Spitzer. His responsibilities were simple. Every day he would walk into an office lined from floor to ceiling with boxes of subpoenaed files and pick one, often at random. For the next eight hours, he would pull out every single page, examine it, then slip it back into place. The goal was to find evidence that Marsh & McLennan, one of the nation's largest insurance brokers, was at the center of a multicompany price-fixing scheme. Not even Spitzer knew exactly what that evidence would look like. And somehow Craig found it. On a single 8½-by-11-inch piece of paper. Within a few months, the CEO had resigned and Marsh & McLennan agreed to return $850 million to its policyholders.

A few years removed from sniffing out the smoking gun, Craig is trying to finish a book about corporate fraud in the Eliot Spitzer era, a topic that became a little more complicated when his former boss resigned as governor of New York seven days ago. At this point, Craig is slowly being driven mad by the frenzy of it, alternating between chewing tobacco to stay awake and Tylenol PM to sleep. After downing his morning coffee, he decides to push away from the keyboard and see Tiger Woods in person for the first time in his life.

SECOND ROUND

10:31 AM ▪ Craig and I find a spot in the bleachers as Tiger begins his morning warm-up. Seeing his favorite athlete in the flesh has left Craig silent for a few minutes, but the questions are now flowing again.

"Who was the best man at Tiger's wedding?"

"Some childhood friend, I think."

"So it wasn't Stevie?"

"No, uh-uh."

"What do you think that says about their relationship that he was Stevie's best man but Tiger didn't ask Stevie to be his?"

"Huh. Never really thought about it." It isn't that Craig's questions aren't good. They are fantastic, actually. But my mind is somewhere else. I am stuck on the woman behind us who is embarrassing herself by asking her husband whether Zach Johnson will receive an invitation to the Masters this year since he won it last year.

Tiger's relationship with Steve Williams, like all of Tiger's relationships, remains hard to pin down. But unlike his marriage, this one exists almost exclusively in the public eye. It began here at Doral back in 1999. Stevie was on the bag of four-time major winner Ray Floyd when he received a call from Tiger, who floated the idea of Stevie coming on board. In a telling moment, Stevie hung up on him, believing it was a prank. Stevie doesn't put up with a lot of, well, crap. At the 2002 Skins Game, three years into their partnership, a fan snapped Tiger's picture while he was hitting out of a bunker on the 18th hole. Stevie took the camera and dropped it into a lake. In the second round of the 2004 U.S. Open, he kicked the lens of a New York *Daily News* cameraman, then snatched another camera away from a fan two days later. Stevie is aggressively loyal.

There is no quality Tiger demands more from his entourage than that, but then to ask Stevie to stand in his shadow during a day off at his wedding may have just seemed too cruel. As for why Stevie asked Tiger to be his best man, that one's easy: if you have one chance to make the biggest control freak in sports history play second fiddle to you, you do it.

11:12 AM ▪ Tiger tees off on the 10th hole in three minutes, and we're not there. Craig and I are at the putting green waiting for his dad, Ray, who was supposed to join us but hasn't shown up yet. While Ray isn't Craig's birth father, he raised him from age five. Craig has called him "Dad" for as long as he can remember, and when he turned twenty, he officially took Ray's last name. It's a strong bond, but when it looks as if Ray might make us miss Tiger's tee time, Craig says, "Screw him," and we run to the tee.

11:29 AM ▪ The 10th hole at Doral is a 551-yard par 5 that takes a seventy-degree turn left halfway down the fairway. The entire left side is protected by water, with no traps to save you. All three players in Tiger's group wisely miss right with their second shots into the greenside bunkers.

Tiger tries to spin his third out of the trap, but it hits short and keeps rolling, almost off the back and into the water. With Tiger preparing for his fourth, I ask Craig if his dad has any distinctive features that might make him easy for me to spot. "He has a Van Dyke mustache." That shouldn't be hard. Within twenty seconds I see a skinny sixty-something guy in shorts walk by with a mop of brown hair and a matching Van Dyke mustache. "That him?" Craig turns around. "Dad!" Craig makes room for Ray, who arrives in time to see Tiger tap in for par.

12:06 PM ▪ The par-5 12th hole at Doral doesn't seem hard, but the obscure stats say otherwise. Last year on Tour, it was the par 5 that had the fewest players attempting to reach it in two. It's long, for sure, 603 yards and uphill. But it should really receive some sort of Audubon Society award—to make it tighter off the tee, hundreds of new trees have been planted on the right side over the last few years. It also features a green completely surrounded by bunkers.

None of that scares Tiger from piping his drive and then going for it with his 3-wood anyway, from 265 yards. His second shot splashes down almost hole high in the left greenside trap. Craig, Ray, and I charge ahead and position ourselves behind the green for his third. The electronic scoreboard says he has thirty-eight feet to the pin. He smacks the sand and the ball pops up, bounces twice, and rolls toward the hole. Tiger raises his wedge above his head, signaling anyone who was only half paying attention what is about to happen. It rolls into the hole for eagle. Craig lets out a therapeutic "Whoooooooa!" as Tiger casually kicks the sand off his spikes. As he retrieves the ball from the hole, they update the leaderboard. Tiger is on top.

12:57 PM ▪ The cheers from his eagle echo across Doral, especially as the other scoreboards are updated, but it doesn't scare Ogilvy, who has again pulled ahead of Tiger as we reach the par-4 16th. The 16th is a 372-yard dogleg left par 4. That isn't how Tiger would describe it. In a straight line from tee to green, it is more like 325 yards. Craig, Ray, and I take a short-cut down the left side and pass another lake. There's so much water on this course that this one isn't even in play on any holes. Tiger's smashed drive comes down in the rough twenty yards short of the green. He pitches to ten feet, where his birdie putt thinks about lipping out before falling into the left side of the cup to tie Ogilvy again, this time at 8 under.

1:50 PM ▪ Tiger returns to the 529-yard 1st. Holes like this must be what it was like for Tiger back in 2000 before his power caused every par 5 in the world to be lengthened seventy-five yards. Driver, 7-iron, six feet for eagle. He makes it for his second eagle of the day and is all the way to 10 under.

2:21 PM ▪ Even though he had made birdie look easy on the tough 3rd hole yesterday, today he pulls it left and Craig and Ray have their first outside-the-ropes adventure with Tiger. With trees in front and water right, Tiger decides to just pitch back into the fairway. Once they're gone, Craig is still shocked that hundreds of people just ran full speed to crowd around a golf ball as if it were the last source of heat in a Siberian prison.

3:21 PM ▪ A few holes later, Craig and his dad are on their own when I run into Chris, a tattooed fan who is wearing a red shirt covered in Tiger-related statistics:

> 1 Sam Alexis
> 86 worldwide wins
> 64 PGA Wins
> 13 Majors
> 9 Player of the Years
> 1 FedEx Cup

He says he ironed on every letter himself. I marvel at his work. "How did you get everything so straight?" I ask. "Used my eyes," he explains.

Up at the green on the par-5 8th, I reconnect with Craig and Ray in time to see Tiger make his best putt of the week, a fast, downhill ten-footer for birdie. Ray is a college professor at the University of Miami and limits his response to the putt with applause and a grin. Craig is a ball of energy. When Tiger crosses through to the 9th tee, Craig presses himself against the ropes and screams "TIGER!!!!" into the left ear of Louis Oosthuizen's wife, who has been putting up with the day's (typical) madness to support her Sunshine Tour–playing husband. She takes a deep breath, knowing there is just one hole left. The way Tiger is playing, I want to keep going.

3:46 PM ▪ Tiger's last hole of the day, the par-3 9th, requires a 169-yard carry over water to a middle pin. The line is great, but the club is wrong, and it blows twenty feet past the hole.

It's not a realistic birdie putt by any means. It's speedy and has at least two different breaks in it. And yes, Craig has witnessed a pretty solid round—two eagles and two birdies—but I feel as if it hasn't quite been enough, so I call upon my Tigerpowers and contact the Man for the first time this week. "Come on, Tiger. How about a little more magic . . ." I whisper. Tiger starts his putt three feet right. It can't possibly break that much. But it hits the slope, just like the long bomb he made at the Buick in January, gains speed, cuts back to the left, and straightens out toward the cup. Tiger raises his putter straight above his head and walks the putt in the last foot. Most people give him a warm Friday cheer as he waves not once but twice as our roar gives way to sustained applause. Craig's reaction has more of a *Sunday-I've-lost-my-mind* feel to it. He screams as he jumps up and down, never once thinking about Eliot Spitzer.

The round of 66 puts Tiger one off the lead and into the final group on Saturday. We head for the car, rehashing the day as we walk. There are a few seconds of silence before Craig fills the void.

"So what do you think Tiger will shoot tomorrow?"

THE BIG WINNER ▪ Once again, my spam folder has hit triple digits. It is one of the unforeseen consequences of filling out entry form for every single prize that is being given away on the PGA Tour this season. At the CA Championship alone, I have turned in close to thirty completed stubs to win a trip for two to the World Golf Hall of Fame. They are attached to the bottom of every ticket for the week, and when it poured on Thursday, the whole way back to the car was littered with opportunity. I'm sure it's exactly the vacation my wife has in mind for the end of the season.

She also won't be too excited about the his-and-her Jet-Skis that might be coming our way when my name is pulled from the raffle box at Bay Hill. But I had to. It was right next to the booth that was giving away tickets to see the Orlando Magic in a few weeks, and even though I won't be in Florida to use them, I am still keeping my fingers crossed.

Winning a prize would make up for the harassing e-mails I keep getting from the bamboo furniture factory in northern China that is anxiously wanting to do business with me. It will also help me forget the other e-mail that was apparently sent just to insult me. I never opened it, but the subject was "what a stupidface you have here bobsmiley."

Not all the e-mails in my spam folder are rude, however. The ones from my "Buick Concierge" are so personal I'm worried Hillary will read them and become concerned about the health of our marriage. "Hello Bob," she coyly begins. I know it is a she because next to the text is a photo of a woman standing in a gray pantsuit. After a slow intro, she turns up the heat. "Something piqued your interest. Perhaps it was a sleek, smooth exterior or the thought of spending time in a tranquil, peaceful cabin." *What is she talking about?* "Whether you desire the sheer beauty of Enclave, the sophisticated elegance of Lucerne, or the distinctive style of LaCrosse, you are interested in a wonderful vehicle." *Actually, I was interested in the free golf balls.* "I look forward to taking this journey with you. I'll e-mail again soon. Sincerely yours, The Buick Concierge." I've made Valentine's Day cards for my wife that are less suggestive than that. But all will be forgiven when we're sitting poolside at that new resort northeast of San Diego. We just have to sit through one little time-share presentation first.

THIRD ROUND

After Thursday, Tiger was at 5 under and the 2006 U.S. Open winner Geoff Ogilvy was at 6 under. After Friday, Tiger was at 11 under and Ogilvy was at 12 under. Ogilvy told reporters heading into the weekend that if he could just stay one shot ahead of Tiger every day, he'd be happy. For the thirty-year-old Ogilvy, the Open at Winged Foot was his last victory, and I understand why. In the twenty-one months since, he and his wife, Juli, have had two kids. While at Doral, Juli is sleeping in one room with two-month-old Jasper and Ogilvy is next door with year-and-a-half-year-old, Phoebe. He is having all-nighters, just not the ones that typically derail a young athlete's career.

9:35 AM ▪ Joining Tiger and Ogilvy is another Australian, Adam Scott, who is three shots back of the lead at 9 under. I had figured the pairing of such big-name players would make today a zoo and have brought the periscope, but there's no one here. The locals must know something that I don't.

I head down the first fairway to meet Miller, my first acolyte. A six-foot-four University of Iowa freshman, he had read my original ESPN article about the Target World Challenge and decided to spend his spring break following Tiger for every hole of the CA Championship. It was quite a journey. First, his dad drove from their home in Kansas City to pick him up at school. Next, he flew to Texas to meet his sister and her boyfriend, Robert. From there the three of them drove twenty hours from Dallas to Miami. While his sister has stayed back at the pool, he and Robert have been here every day since Tuesday.

The big highlight? Tiger's bunker shot for eagle yesterday.

It wasn't the shot itself they cherish but the joy of the sand blowing into their eyes after he swung. It isn't the first time I've seen fans revel in bizarre moments. Last week at Bay Hill, Tiger hacked a shot out of the trees and sent grass flying. As Tiger walked away, a fan lit up and turned to his friend to say, "I tasted his divot!"

Fans long to feel connected to Tiger, but since he provides such little personal interaction, we often find ourselves grasping for whatever scraps he leaves behind.

10:10 AM ▪ The three players in the group could not have three more different starts. Tiger misses his opening drive well left, then finds a hole between trees and puts his second shot on the back of the green, leaving himself a long putt for eagle. Ogilvy misses right off the tee, hits a palm tree with his second, then drops his third into the greenside trap. Scott has no problems with anything and hits his second shot within ten feet for eagle.

Miller points out that even though they started at −12, −11, and −9, all three of them could be at −11 when the hole is finished. Can I call him my acolyte if he's more perceptive than I am? Ogilvy saves par from the trap to stay at 12 under, while Adam indeed makes eagle to get to −11. Tiger has a simple six-footer left for his birdie but, strangely, lips it out.

10:30 AM ▪ Tiger is changing his strategy on number 2. After two days of hitting driver within forty yards and not making birdie, he lays back to a hundred. That doesn't work either. He rolls his birdie putt five feet by. Most of the season, I haven't been watching Tiger's short-par putts. He simply doesn't miss them. Yesterday he was ten for ten on all putts inside ten feet. But the missed birdie on the 1st has everyone sticking around, making sure that was just a temporary glitch in Tiger's flawless mechanics.

Unfortunately, it isn't. His par putt, like the last hole, lips out. After three-putting 18 on Thursday, he told reporters yesterday that he fumed about it all the way back to his boat. Now he has three-putted both of his first two holes.

10:36 AM ▪ No one is more bothered by this two-hole start than Dave, a middle-aged Tiger fan in a Cuban guayabera shirt with a rich calypso accent. "Come on, Tiga . . . don't let dem do dat to you . . . ," he says as he heads toward number 3. Since I spotted him behind the first hole, he has been giving color commentary on the action, but not to get attention. He doesn't even seem aware that anyone hears him; he just can't contain it. After Tiger misses another makeable putt on the 3rd, Dave verbalizes what we're all fearing: "Oh, Jesus, 'av mercy. We are in deep sh★★."

Calypso Dave has been here every day. Thursday wore him out, but he went home afterward, took a hot shower, rubbed lotion on his feet, and was back on Friday. "You're following *only* Tiga?" he asks. "Who else would I follow?" I say. He nods in approval, then starts to hum and keeps walking.

11:31 AM ▪ On the 5th green, Scott makes another birdie putt to wrestle the lead away from Ogilvy. Tiger is in position to keep pace with a twelve-foot birdie of his own. "Tiga, I'm going home if you don't make dis," Dave says. A third lip out. Dave curses but doesn't follow through on his threat.

I'm glad I've found Dave because now that I've become a fan myself, I need someone who has my same level of expectations. I've been appalled over the last two weeks to realize how many people in Tiger's gallery have no interest in what he actually shoots. These aren't fans, per se, just people drawn here by the phenomenon; and if Tiger does something spectacular while they're watching, even better. They take many forms. There are the frat boys who bring their girlfriends in high heels. There are the soccer moms whose first reaction to Tiger is usually "Isn't he adorable?" The most irritating to me are the easily impressed spectators—the ones who are so ready to gush that they compliment Tiger on a "good shot!" that has already disappeared with a poof into a sand trap.

Calypso Dave would never do this, and in this moment he knows the only appropriate response to Tiger's putting is anxiety. As for Tiger, he just stretches his neck from side to side and walks to the next hole.

12:24 PM ▪ Tiger makes his first birdie of the day on the 7th and is in position to erase more mistakes at the par-5 8th, where he has given himself another good chance. This time I notice his stroke. His typically smooth artist-like rhythm with the putter is gone. He merely swipes at the putt and misses. Something is wrong.

12:28 PM ▪ On the 9th tee, Tiger separates himself from Scott and Ogilvy and walks to the side of the tee box to talk to himself as he had in San Diego, Dubai, and Tucson. This has become a predictable part of his routine when he is struggling and never fails to spark a return to form. I wait for him to lower his head, but his focus is broken as he looks across the lake and sees Mark Calcavecchia, the heavyset forty-seven-year-old, who is huffing and puffing in the humidity as he walks down the 10th fairway. Last year, Calcavecchia joked with reporters that after playing a lot of golf, he "couldn't run out of a burning house." Tiger never does refocus. He looks at the proudly out-of-shape Calc and laughs, then hits a mediocre shot to the green.

1:05 PM ▪ At the beginning of the day, I didn't understand why there were so few people here. Now I know.

After the cameraman on the 10th films Tiger making an ugly par, he pulls out his plastic rain cover and secures it around his equipment. I look up to the sky and see some dark clouds, but, even more alarming, I see the MetLife blimp heading north as fast as it's two eighty-horsepower engines can fly.

1:11 PM ▪ The first drops of water start to fall as Tiger plays down the 11th. His thirty-foot birdie putt burns the edge as the drips turn to rain. I'm halfway to the 12th tee when a single blast of air horns rings out around the golf course, signaling the immediate suspension of play.

Within fifteen seconds, Tiger has his watch on, the physical manifestation of his return to reality. I turn around, and a fleet of Cadillac SUVs is suddenly idling behind the green. The caddies throw the bags in the back and hop in, with Ogilvy, the leader by three, brazenly taking shotgun over Tiger. The Escalades slip out an exit used by maintenance workers, and two minutes after the horns blow, every player on the entire course is gone.

We spectators, of course, are afforded no such luxuries. Having long ago lost track of Miller and Calypso Dave, I move under a tree to wait it out and notice that I am the only golf fan at Doral who isn't leaving. One man even pulls a giant palm frond off a tree and covers his head as he flees. The locals seem convinced that this will get worse before it gets better. I give in and head back.

4:40 PM ▪ Three and a half hours later, it is still raining. If it weren't for my streak of never missing a hole, I would be long gone. But I can't risk the chance that the storm will pass, the course will dry out, and they'll try to play a few holes before dark.

Over that stretch of time, I have huddled under leaky grandstands, I have stood inside a concession stand, I have received a complimentary massage from some women who work at the Doral Spa, and I have collected another dozen entry forms for that dream trip to the Golf Hall of Fame. I have even been so bored that I stood and watched as Stevie sat by himself and ate a sandwich.

But finally, after doing all that and with the electronic scoreboard giving no more information than "Weather delay," I am out of things to do. I spot a man with a name tag and ask how I can find out if play has been canceled for the day. "Play *has* been canceled for the day," he says. That was easy.

The deluge could not have come at a better time for Tiger. He can return to his yacht, go back to bed, and pretend that today never happened.

ISLEWORTH RED ▪ This has been my longest stretch away from home since either of my kids was born. Eleven nights and counting. Back in L.A., going that long without a father figure was having its effect on Danny. Apparently he had spent most of Saturday walking around the house carrying a bag and declaring "I have a purse just like Mama!" Hillary tried to counteract it by teaching him how to shoot baskets into a trash can. I have never seen her shoot a basket in my life and suspect that this might be just as damaging to his eventual manhood. I need to get home, but it turns out I will be staying in Florida even longer than I thought. And the reason has nothing to do with the weather.

During the first round back at Bay Hill, I was talking with a guy from Tampa who asked me if I were going to the Tavistock Cup. The Tavistock Cup is the annual two-day event between Tiger's Isleworth Golf Club and the rival golf club in Orlando, Lake Nona. It's not an official event on the Tour schedule, but every year it trades off locations and this year it just happens to be at Isleworth. I knew all about it. I just didn't know it started on Monday.

When I told Hillary I was adding a third tournament to my Florida trip, her reaction was the same as my mechanic friend Bryan's when I made him keep walking with me to the far side of the 18th at the

Match Play with a pulled groin: "At this point, what does it matter?" Once I tracked down someone willing to part with one of the hard-to-get passes for the event, the only thing I needed was a collared red shirt. "*Isleworth* red," the member told me. Apparently, if anyone in the gallery shows up without wearing one of the two team colors, he will be denied entrance.

So after Saturday's shortened round at Doral, I go where surely no other person at the über-wealthy Tavistock Cup will be going to procure a red shirt: the Salvation Army. It has a great selection, actually. I almost get to the register with the first one I find, but notice it has the name "Glenda" stitched onto the front. Another one is the shirt from someone's old Target uniform. A third one has a big crawfish on the lapel. At last I find a plain, logo-free collared red shirt. It is only $2.99, which leaves me enough for a new (old) pair of khaki shorts. If I am really going to see Tiger's neighborhood after all, I need to look presentable.

THIRD ROUND, SUNDAY

8:45 AM ▪ About forty serious Tiger fans have beaten me to the 12th tee, where round three will pick up again. I look toward the driving range and see Tiger slowly walking with Stevie down the 10th fairway.

Tiger sizes up what will be yet another birdie on the 4th hole at Torrey Pines South at the Buick Invitational on Saturday, January 26, 2008. *(Robert Beck/ Sports Illustrated/Getty Images)*

Tiger makes his way through a blur of fans. Flanking him is the terrifying Officer Brian Freymueller of the San Diego Police Department, a man so large that small planes have been known to make emergency landings on his shoulders. *(Donald Miralle/Getty Images)*

Tiger reacts to sinking his deconstructed birdie putt on the 12th hole during the final round of the Buick Invitational. *(Jeff Gross/Getty Images)*

Tiger and the gallery dress warmly during Dubai's freak winter sandstorm—except for me (wearing the striped white shirt in the front row four fans to the left of Tiger). Tiger shot 1-under while I picked up hypothermia in the Arabian desert. *(Ross Kinnaird/Getty Images)*

My quest to find The Tiger Woods is delayed by a pack of camels. Rashid: "They're going to Jumeirah Beach!" *(Courtesy of the author)*

After losing his lead, Tiger pulls his drive into the desert on the 8th hole on Saturday in Dubai. *(Karim Sahib/AFP/Getty Images)*

Fourteen-under! Tiger hits my number to complete his Sunday comeback at the Dubai Desert Classic. *(David Cannon/Getty Images)*

Tiger drains his eagle putt on the 17th hole to take a 1-up lead on J. B. Holmes during the first round of the Accenture Match Play, February 20, 2008. *(Scott Halleran/Getty Images)*

Despite Aaron Baddeley making 10 birdies, Tiger still manages to win his third-round match. The win erased any last doubts about Tiger's 2008 form. *(Scott Halleran/Getty Images)*

In the early morning north of Tucson, Tiger pitches from off the green against K. J. Choi in the quarterfinals of the Match Play. *(Robert Beck/Sports Illustrated/Getty Images)*

Tiger waits on the 1st green during the Sunday finals of the Accenture Match Play. Twenty-eight holes later, he would close out Stewart Cink 8 up. *(Scott Halleran/Getty Images)*

Tiger celebrates his winning putt at the Arnold Palmer Invitational on Sunday, March 16, 2008. He would later say he had no recollection of slamming his hat to the ground and only learned of it when he saw his caddy Stevie holding it. He asked, "Why do you have my hat?" *(Andy Lyons/Getty Images)*

Tiger and the tournament's eponymous Arnold Palmer. When Tiger stroked the final putt, Arnie nodded and grinned, knowing Tiger would make it. With the victory at Bay Hill, Tiger moves two in front of The King on the all-time PGA Tour win list. *(Andy Lyons/Getty Images)*

Tiger tees off on the 18th hole during round one of the CA Championship at Doral on March 20, 2008. *Don't. Go. Left. (David Cannon/Getty Images)*

Above left: Tiger raises his sand wedge after making an eagle three from the greenside bunker on the par-5 12th on Friday at Doral. Through two rounds, the Blue Monster was no match for him. *(Warren Little/Getty Images)*

Above right: Putting woes and a pink shirt end Tiger's undefeated streak on the final day of the CA Championship. *(David Cannon/Getty Images)*

Right: But March 24 isn't all bad. After speeding from Miami back to Orlando, I arrive at Isleworth, Tiger's home course, where I enjoy the freedom of no ropes at the Tavistock Cup. *(David Cannon/Getty Images)*

Above: Practicing by himself, Tiger hits to a flagless 12th green prior to the Masters on Tuesday, April 8, 2008. *(Harry How/Getty Images)*

On the final day of the Masters, Tiger reacts in disbelief to yet another missed putt and the end of any hope for a Grand Slam season. Two months earlier, Vegas bookies set the odds of him pulling it off at an astounding 11-2. *(David Cannon/Getty Images)*

Tiger appears to be back in perfect shape as he works on the putting green with coach Hank Haney on Wednesday, June 11, 2008, the day before the U.S. Open. *(Courtesy of the author)*

On the second day of the Open, Tiger plays off the cart path on number 1 and tweaks his knee. He birdies the hole for the first of five straight "3's" and a front nine 30 to move into contention. *(Donald Miralle/Getty Images)*

Tiger makes a 60-foot putt for eagle on the par-5 13th on Saturday at the U.S. Open. The roar that follows will reach outlying planets in seventy to eighty years. *(Harry How/Getty Images)*

Four holes later, Tiger receives a hand from Stevie after he chips in for birdie on the 17th to pull within one of the clubhouse lead. *(Fred Vuich/Sports Illustrated/Getty Images)*

Tiger joins his fans in celebrating the 40-foot eagle putt on the 18th hole that gave him sole possession of the 54-hole lead heading into Sunday. *(Ross Kinnaird/Getty Images)*

Facing page: At 5:52 p.m. on June 15, 2008, Tiger makes a 12-foot birdie putt to force a Monday playoff against journeyman Rocco Mediate. What would have been his most devastating loss became the most clutch moment of his career and perhaps the most electrifying putt in golf history. *(Robert Beck/Sports Illustrated/Getty Images)*

Tiger grabs his knee after a painful drive on number 2 during the final round of the U.S. Open. Quitting was never an option. *(Ross Kinnaird/ Getty Images)*

Tiger plays out of a bunker on the 9th hole to the 15th green during Monday's playoff. He salvages a par but heads to the 16th hole one stroke behind Rocco Mediate. *(Robyn Beck/AFP/Getty Images)*

Tiger and Stevie celebrate after winning the U.S. Open in 91 holes. *(Travis Lindquist/Getty Images)*

Tiger kisses daughter Sam after the landmark victory. Critics said fatherhood might drag down his performance; since her birth, he has won 10 out of 15 tournaments. *(Travis Lindquist/Getty Images)*

While waiting for the trophy ceremony on the 18th green, Tiger and Rocco share their first laugh since walking off number 1 tee earlier that day. In between, Rocco admitted to NBC's Mark Rolfing, "I think I had him a little scared." *(Doug Pensinger/Getty Images)*

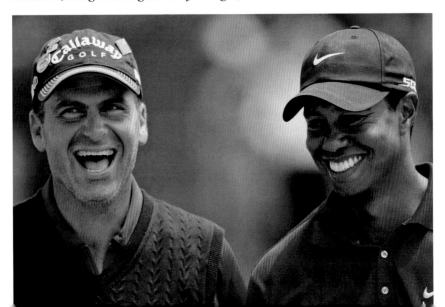

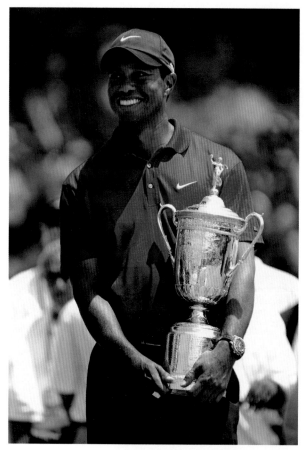

Tiger Woods, winner of the 108th U.S. Open. He would later call it his greatest victory ever. *(Robyn Beck/AFP/ Getty Images)*

The closest I ever came to meeting the man: my Buick Clubhouse picture with virtual Tiger Woods. *(Courtesy of the author)*

Even though it's round three, Tiger is already sporting his Sunday red shirt. Except it is really a Sunday pink, which isn't the powerful statement he really needs to be making at this point.

Keeping pace with him are a few dozen other fans. It's exactly like that *SportsCenter* commercial where Tiger is walking by himself through the quiet ESPN offices, only to reveal that he still has a gallery trailing behind him. Though the fans have to walk around the 11th green, Tiger and Stevie walk in a straight line, under the ropes, across 11, back under the ropes, and up onto 12.

Tiger is all smiles. When Adam Scott arrives, Tiger shakes his hand and says, "Good luck, man." When Geoff Ogilvy walks up, Tiger shakes his hand and says, "Good luck today, buddy." *Buddy?* This is the guy who is now leading by three! What happened to Mom's "You must kill that person"?

Ogilvy is already standing behind his ball when the horns blow. Without looking back at Tiger or Adam, he says, "Good luck, boys," and stripes his drive right down the fairway.

9:30 AM ▪ Tiger misses a twelve-foot putt for birdie on the 12th, but the real sign that he still isn't comfortable with his putter comes on the 13th. While Ogilvy and Scott are busy chipping, Tiger stands off to the side and works on his stroke. Back and through. Over and over. This is something most golfers and many pros do all the time between shots, but never Tiger. He can no longer afford to hide the fact that something is faulty with his mechanics. Ogilvy and Scott have both played, and it's Tiger's turn to putt, whether he wants to or not. He misses again.

10:08 AM ▪ After two more pars, Tiger hits a solid approach on the par-4 16th, past the far right pin within twelve feet. Ogilvy is a few feet outside Tiger and casually makes the quick downhiller. Tiger had to learn something about the speed by watching it, but that's not his problem. His putt wobbles off to the right. Another unhelpful par. As Ogilvy walks to the next tee, Tiger just stands in place and stares at his ball in frustration.

10:44 AM ▪ One more incredible lip-out on 17 and a final missed birdie putt on the last, and Tiger is finished. At least with the third round. One bogey, one birdie, sixteen pars. Seventy-two. Still stuck at 11 under par, his awful putting has put him 5 back of Ogilvy. He's been passed by plenty of others, too, and they aren't a bunch of nobodies: Adam Scott, Vijay Singh,

Jim Furyk, and Retief Goosen. He could expect one or two of them to slip, but all of them? Not likely.

Tiger said in his Wednesday press conference that one area where he has seen the most improvement is his ability to fix things in the middle of his round, saying it has allowed him to take a round that should be a 73 or 74 and turn it into a 64. So either he failed to fix his game today or he did fix it and his 72 was really an 82 in disguise. I fear he's stumped. After signing his scorecard, he walks past security, ignores the autograph seekers, and disappears into the resort. He has three hours to figure things out.

FINAL ROUND

Before I went to bed last night, Craig asked me what I thought the chances were that Tiger would still win this week. I said 60 percent. After the closing seven holes of round three, I'm down to 20 percent. As easy as Tiger has made clutch putts appear this year, the ability to stroke the putter on the correct line is so much more feel than any other aspect of the game of golf. When a player is putting well, there's nothing technical about it. And when a player is putting *really* well, it's almost mystical.

In the best round of golf I ever played, I was 3 over par on the front, which was good but not unbelievable.

As I stood on the 10th hole, looking at my thirty-five-foot birdie putt, I suddenly felt I would make it. And I did. And then I birdied the 12th. And the 14th. And the 16th. Short, long, uphill, downhill, it was irrelevant. The ball was going to go in. This wasn't happening on any course; this was my home course—the same place where as an eight-year-old I would purposefully hit it into the bunkers so I could play in the sand. Even more special, I was playing with my dad, who was so nervous for me that he hadn't spoken in two hours. I came to the 18th green facing a twisting downhill putt for a par and a back-nine 33. I didn't stand over the putt and say, "Okay, now make sure you open the blade exactly five degrees when you take it back . . ." I looked at where I wanted the ball to go and then hit it there. And I made it.

Right now Tiger is looking where he wants it to go and it simply isn't going there. The longest putt he has made in the last two days: six and a half feet. Even if he knows what he is technically doing wrong, I'm not convinced that even Tiger Woods can master the feel he needs to execute it in time.

2:01 PM ▪ Of course, I never considered that his solution would be to just knock it inside six and a half feet. He makes a four-footer on the 1st hole for a quick birdie. Twelve under par. On the short 2nd, the easy hole he has managed to play 1 over for the week, he rolls in a birdie from fifteen feet. Twenty percent chance of winning? Shame on me.

2:19 PM ▪ He finds himself with an eight-foot par putt on the 3rd to keep the momentum going. If it were to go in, I would consider him cured. But for the fifth time in two rounds, Tiger lips out a putt. Golf is not a game of inches. It's a game of millimeters, and that fractional loss of alignment with Tiger's stroke is enough to jeopardize a streak that goes back to last September.

As Tiger walks to the 4th tee with his head down, the air horns blow and Tiger is once again ushered toward a waiting Escalade. Even more frustrating, it's not even raining. There are some dark clouds to the south, but not here. No fans leave this time except for Miller from Iowa, who has a twenty-hour drive to Texas ahead of him tonight. I feel bad because he came all this way and caught Tiger's worst tournament of the year. He feels bad because he never once heard Tiger curse. If he keeps putting like this, it's only a matter of time.

3:25 PM ▪ After a baffling hour of suspended play that saw a total of seven or eight raindrops and zero lightning, many of the fans have decided that God is punishing us for missing church on Easter and have headed home. I take an empty spot in the front row next to the 4th tee. The 4th hole at Doral is the last place any player wants to restart his round. It's the most difficult par-3 on the course, 236 yards over water. Earlier in the week it was playing into the wind and Tiger had to hit a 5-wood. He was still short of the green.

Finally, I see the fleet of Escalades off in the distance. It starts in a single line and then begins splintering off in various directions around the course. Tiger's Cadillac doesn't pull any closer than the 14th tee, leaving him and Stevie to walk the rest of the way on foot. Tiger is not on the tee for more than thirty seconds when a Tour official with an earpiece walks up to the players with a smirk and whispers something. Stevie eavesdrops and immediately picks up Tiger's bag and starts walking away. Tiger follows him and does a half turn toward us and waves. "See ya, guys." And then he's gone.

Huh?

It's another delay.

In the seven hours since he teed off on the 12th hole, Tiger has played only ten holes. I've never been more exhausted and seen less golf in my life. And again, no rain. It's fishy. I'll blame the Australasians. Here's my thinking. Clearly they see that one of their own, Ogilvy, is in the lead and notice that Tiger is desperately trying to make a Sunday charge. It's golf's version of icing the kicker. Satisfied at my increasing ability to blame anyone but Tiger, I stretch out on the grass and wait for the imaginary storm to pass.

4:45 PM ▪ I have never fallen asleep on a golf course before. It is incredible. A cool Miami breeze, the smell of fresh cut grass, no rain . . . Unfortunately, when I awaken, Tiger is still 5 shots back.

The caddies come into view first. Tiger is trailing behind. He has to be tired of this ritual. It's been two and a half hours since the original delay. At some point in the blur of this endless afternoon, I have run into Craig's dad, Ray with the Van Dyke mustache, who came back today with Craig's mom and some family from Minnesota. I tell Craig's teenage nephew Stephen that if he starts to applaud when Tiger arrives at the tee, I'll join in. Stephen leads the way, I follow, and the other thirty fans who have stuck around add to the warm welcome. On a day like this, even Tiger needs some extra motivation. He nods, appreciative. If he somehow pulls this off, I can definitively say I played a role in his comeback.

Despite our support, Tiger takes a long iron off the tee and hits it terribly. I put my hands on my head as

I watch it start dead right. The ball should be wet, but the wind that has come up in the last two hours holds it back and it stays on the bank right of the green.

After so many rain delays, there are fewer fans here than in Dubai, no more than a hundred, so I have an unobstructed view of Tiger's five-foot putt to save par. He starts it two inches outside to the left, and it never moves. It's dead straight. He either misread it or made a poor stroke. Or both. Back-to-back bogeys on 3 and 4, and he is right back where he was four hours ago. Heck, he's right back where he was twenty-nine hours ago! The Australasians have gotten their wish. They have killed Tiger's momentum.

7:03 PM ▪ The next six holes are an exercise in futility. Tiger makes an easy birdie on 6, then puts himself behind a palm tree and has to scramble for a par on 7. He plays like a tactician on the par-5 8th, hitting the fairway, then the green and two-putting for another birdie. But on the par-3 9th, just when he seemed to be finding a way to scrape out a good round, a photographer snaps a shot right in his backswing. "Not in my swing!" he yells the second the ball is airborne. The ball is yanked way left and nearly slips into the lake. He walks to the far side of the tee box as Stevie turns around and looks for the culprit.

Every player deals with photographers. But only Tiger has to do so on every single shot he plays. I want Stevie to go after the guy and swallow his memory card whole. I want him to take his telephoto lens, place it on a tee, and have Tiger Sasquatch it all the way back to the media tent. But he doesn't know who it was. Neither do I. The photographers, of course, all do the collective "Not me!" look and stare up and down their line as if whoever did do it is really going to raise his hand and own up.

Then, adding insult to injury, Tiger's par putt lips out.

And so does his birdie putt on 10. *Seven* lip-outs in twenty-eight holes. I have friends who would melt their putters in a furnace if that happened. The reality of Tiger's failure is finally setting in. When he walks off the green, most of the fans don't say anything. They just watch him go in confused silence. The only cheer anyone tries is one of consolation. "It's okay, Tiger . . ."

7:15 PM ▪ Play is called for darkness as he makes another uninspired par on 11. His day will end in the exact same place it started—next to the tee at number 12—meaning it just took Tiger ten hours to play 18 holes of golf. As he walks to a waiting golf cart, one delusional fan still has life in him and yells out, "Plenty of golf left, Tiger!" Well, he's five shots out of the lead with seven holes to play, and almost every player in front of him has won at least one major. If he pulls a victory off, it will be the greatest comeback of his career.

Tiger's streak isn't the only one in jeopardy on Sunday night. When play is suspended for darkness, I figure that means the first round of Monday's Tavistock Cup will simply be pushed back until Tuesday. But a lot of the Tavistock players are committed to being at next week's regular PGA Tour event on Wednesday, so the best they can do is push the tee times back a few hours until Monday afternoon. So? Well, my guesstimate is that Tiger will finish his fourth round in Miami around 10:20 a.m. He is now scheduled to tee off at the Tavistock Cup in Orlando at 1:42 p.m. Taking a private jet, the three-hour-and-twenty-two minute window is no problem for him. But all I have is my Rav4 and a Google Maps printout that says the drive will take three hours and *forty-nine* minutes. I have quite a day ahead of me.

FINAL ROUND, MONDAY

Even a World Golf Championship becomes a ghost town on a Monday finish. Gone are the Cadillac salesmen and their brochures. Gone are the chipper volunteers handing out CA visors to every person walking through the gates. In fact, gone is anyone at the gate. I just waltz on in. In the big WGC merchandise tent, all that is left is fifteen brown CA Championship T-shirts. Yesterday they were marked down to $10. Today they're $5. The concession stand near the 18th green isn't even being manned by volunteers anymore. A Miami rehab center has agreed to work the registers and sell what's left of the food in exchange for 8 percent of the receipts.

But Tiger is still here. And he is still wearing the same worthless pink shirt from yesterday.

8:20 AM ▪ If there were ever a day this year where Tiger might recognize my face, it is this morning. Back out at the 12th tee, there are no more than twenty of us lined up single file along the left side of the tee box. There isn't even any press, with Luau Larry nowhere to be seen. It's such a small group that it feels awkward when Tiger shows up and we stand in silence. It seems almost rude of us to not say something. So a brave man with his hands in his pockets does.

"Good luck today."

Tiger turns and faces him. "Thank you," he says. It's the first fan Tiger has looked in the eye this season

246 • FOLLOW THE ROAR

whom he hasn't hit in the head with a ball first. Another fan sees the rareness of the opportunity.

"So can you do it today?"

Tiger thinks about it as he bounces the end of his driver lightly on the wet grass with his left hand.

"It'll be tough."

"Six birdies?" another man asks.

"I don't know. Might not be enough. Might need seven." The conversation comes to a casual and natural end. It is such a random, intimate moment in a year that has been everything but. He is a real person, briefly. And the fact that he has a number in his head gives me hope. Because it shows that even though so many things have gone wrong in the last two rounds, he hasn't given up. He has clearly spent at least a minute thinking about what specifically he will have to do to pull this off.

Seven birdies in seven holes. His best run in stroke play this year remains the back nine at Dubai, where he had six birdies in nine holes. But if his putter catches fire, anything is possible. My confidence renewed, I map out the game plan in my head:

Hole 12: par 5 = 3
Hole 13: par 3 = 3
Hole 14: par 4 = 3
Hole 15: par 3 = 2

Hole 16: par 4 = 2
Hole 17: par 4 = 3
Hole 18: par 4 = 4

As long as he eagles the par-5 12th and the drivable par-4 16th, he could get to 19 under and have to par only the tough 13th and nasty 18th. And if the wheels fall off Ogilvy as they did for Els back in February, well, who knows what might happen?

8:30 AM ▪ As we wait for the horn to blow, Tiger's ball is already sitting on the tee. Which is good. I need everyone in this group to play as quickly as possible. I've got a 1:42 tee time back in Orlando.

The horns sound, and Tiger hits it down the left side, in line with the bunker. A fan calls out, "Come back!" There are so few of us that Tiger finishes his thought: "A little! A little!" The shot misses the bunker and stays in the left rough.

Playing with Tiger is Denmark's Anders Hansen and South Africa's Tim Clark, neither of whom can remember who has the honors from yesterday. They clearly don't know this is costing me precious seconds.

8:46 AM ▪ Tiger has a twenty-foot putt for birdie on 12. He makes it! It's jolting to see a putt of any length drop after his clumsy putting over the last forty-eight hours. Thirteen under . . . you just never know . . .

9:06 AM ▪ Tiger misses his birdie putt on the 13th, which is understandable on a 245-yard par 3, but when he misses only a *nine*-footer on 14, that hurts. We all groan in agony. These fans get it. You don't come out early on a Monday morning to watch Tiger play only seven holes when he's down by 5 unless you truly believe he is amazing enough to find a way to win.

9:17 AM ▪ The whole year has seen far too many people scream "Get in the hole!" but when I see Tiger's shot into the 175-yard 15th, I reflexively yell it because, well, the ball looks as if it might go in. It is dead on line with the flag on the right side. The cup itself is blocked from view by the fronting bunker, but after it disappears behind the trap, I see the dozen fans up at the green start jumping up and down as they cheer. I run up to find Tiger's ball is literally two inches left of the cup. I didn't factor an ace into my preround equations. It's his best shot of the week, and if he loses, no one except the twenty of us will remember. The birdie drops him to 14 under. Ogilvy hasn't moved and is still at –17. Tiger is only three back with three to play.

9:26 AM ▪ Tiger is back on the almost drivable 372-yard 16th. He grabs his driver, sees that the group ahead is still on the green, and tells Tim Clark, "I'll wait." I love it. When the green has cleared, Tiger tees up his ball and asks all of us on the left side of the tee to please move back. He sets up and gives one last look around the corner, and I smile. I know Tiger Woods is about to swing as hard as he physically can. When his club face explodes into the ball, I imagine that just over the fence to our right, inside the Miami police shooting range, fifty cops just hit the deck. It goes a long way, but is too high and balloons into the air. "Damn it!" he yells. I start running, somehow thinking that my personal speed has some correlation with how fast Tiger will play.

Tiger's ball comes to rest on the front edge of the bunker short of the green, but it's not totally in the sand. It's a bad break. From there he could be aggressive, but he might flop it into the sand if it comes out too soft. The best he can do is to pitch it twenty feet past the hole and hope to make the putt coming back. The putt is close, but he misses. Still three shots back.

9:55 AM ▪ Tiger still isn't quitting. He sticks his second shot into the 17th only four feet from the hole. He makes it to get to 15 under. Ogilvy hasn't done a thing and remains stuck at 17 under. Neither has anyone else. If Tiger can summon whatever juju Craig Parry used to eagle the 18th four years ago, he can actually still win.

10:06 AM ▪ His drive on the last hole is a bomb, over 320 yards, down the right side of the fairway and the absolute best possible angle for Doral's traditional Sunday pin position—back left. He arrives at his ball dead serious. His heroics this morning have given him a chance, albeit small. Had he made that birdie on 14 and the ace on 15, a par here might have been enough for a playoff. The shot is a little downwind, and at the last second he swaps out his pitching wedge for a 9-iron.

Stevie backs away, and a thought crosses my mind. Am I about to witness the greatest shot in Tiger's career? After all, every tournament so far has yielded a mind-boggling shot that has made the previous tournament's mind-boggling shot less . . . boggling. Tiger gives a last look at his target (the bottom of the cup) and swings. It's right on line, but it looks a little short. "Go! Go!" I yell. It hits ten feet short on the upslope to the back tier. "Bounce!" I scream. It bounces once, then stops and spins back down the hill, twenty feet from the hole.

On Saturday, I couldn't have conceived of a way in which I would be applauding a Tiger loss, but as he shakes his head and walks to the green, we cheer. The last time Tiger lost, one of my children wasn't even born yet.

If there were ever a day for him to phone in the rest of his round, it would have been today. He never even gave it a thought. Before he hits his birdie putt, I bend down and retie my shoes. This is the *easy* part of my day. Tiger's putt glides up the hill, breaks left, and stops a foot away. His streak is dead, but mine is still alive. The moment the ball stops rolling, I take off like a madman past the clubhouse and make for the Rav4.

Chez Tiger

The Tavistock Cup

Isleworth Country Club
Windermere, Florida
March 24–25, 2008

I have three and a half hours to make what should be a four-hour trip. Once I leave the Blue Monster and turn left on Doral Boulevard, it's another half-mile sprint to my car. Well aware of the challenge I am facing today, I didn't risk general parking and the likely wait for the shuttle bus. I'm parked illegally at a bank, facing out, with the gas tank topped off. On the passenger seat, directions that say I'm 243 miles from Isleworth.

As I turn on the Palmetto Expressway, I get the sinking feeling that maybe Tiger's 15 under par finish could get him into a playoff and I'm a complete fool for leaving. I call Craig, who is at home watching the coverage. He gives me the play-by-play down the stretch. When Jim Furyk makes his six-footer to post 16 under, I lay into the accelerator and head north. Ten minutes later, Ogilvy wins with a 17-under finish. Tiger putted like Frankenstein and lost by only two.

I've calculated I need to average eighty miles an hour to pull this off, which means I also need to avoid slow toll lines, road construction, and, most costly, Florida state troopers. The one thing I forget to factor is my own stupidity, which comes into play when I miss the turnoff for the turnpike. The mistake costs me a precious five minutes.

California doesn't have turnpikes, and I'm not sure I understand the concept. Apparently I'm paying Florida for a highway that is just two lanes. It gives me no choice but to become the kind of driver I normally can't stand as I weave between traffic, tailgate the fast drivers, and flash my lights at the slow ones. At one point, the passenger in one of the cars I'm trying to pass leans out his window and says, "Take it easy! It's only Monday!"

By noon, I assume Tiger is leap-frogging me in his private jet, traveling 700 percent faster than I am with his seat fully reclined. He's too high to catch a whiff of the mile-long dump that parallels the turnpike just west of Palm Beach. I fumble to shut down my air-conditioning, but it's too late. The car reeks.

254 • FOLLOW THE ROAR

The road heads north past Jupiter Island, where Tiger owns close to twelve acres stretching from the Intracoastal Waterway to the Atlantic. He bought the first ten acres in late 2005 for $38 million, a local record. He demolished the preexisting property, but the last report is that Tiger's not sure when he'll finish the proposed 10,000-square-foot home and move the family from Isleworth. I wonder if his Realtor mentioned he's only seven minutes up the turnpike from that landfill.

I reach my halfway mark, 122 miles from the course. Tiger will be on the driving range in thirty minutes. For the first time since I was sixteen, my speedometer climbs to ninety. In doing so, I pass a guy in a black Mercedes convertible and do a double-take. As he drives along with the top down, he's steering with one hand and playing a miniature trumpet with the other. I can't decide which of us is more reckless.

Only an hour left, and I'm still 79 miles from Orlando. I don't even know if I'll cut it close at this point. I spot a trooper lurking behind an overpass and shift from drive down to third so he doesn't see any brake lights. The Rav responds, dropping to a respectful seventy-one miles per hour.

With six minutes to go, I'm off the highway and onto the main drag of Tiger's hometown of Windermere, a sleepy hamlet where I'm learning that drivers obey the twenty-five miles per hour speed limit. After going ninety, it feels like slow motion.

It's 1:42 p.m. Tiger is on the 1st tee, and I am still looking for a parking spot. My streak is dead, too. Four hundred and five consecutive holes until now. If I had just caught that first turnpike turnoff or picked some faster toll lanes, things might have been different. I want to be bitter and sulk, but I remember the lesson Tiger taught me this morning at the CA Championship: keep fighting, all the way, no matter what. So once inside the gates of Isleworth, I start to run.

Every year, a few days after the Los Angeles Marathon has ended, there is inevitably a local news story about someone who is still on the course, someone who has severely injured himself along the way but won't quit and is willing himself (now through rush-hour traffic) toward the finish line (which doesn't even exist anymore). I'm that guy. And after a good mile of running past mansions, each one more amazing than the one before, I have nothing left. My legs are heavy from the long drive, my feet are still wet from walking Doral, and all I've eaten today is a free granola bar I grabbed at Bay Hill. So when I hear a golf cart coming up behind me, I do something that probably doesn't happen much around here—I stick out my thumb. The middle-aged Isleworth member behind the wheel slows down, I hop on the back, and my new friend John takes me the last half mile.

On the tee at number 3, I once again find Tiger. It's been three hours and fifty-eight minutes since I left him at Doral. As I catch my breath and relish what may be the most beautiful place I've ever seen, a new streak begins.

THE BUZ AT ISLEWORTH ▪ The best player at my home course growing up was a guy about my dad's age named Buz. Another member once bet Buz that he couldn't make a 4 on eighteen straight holes. He went out and made seventeen 4s in a row before coming to the last hole, a par 5, where he accidentally made an eagle 3 and lost the bet. Twenty years later, Buz claims it never happened, but my friends and I remember the story clearly. I was in awe of Buz from that day forward, believing that making eagles when you are actively trying not to is playing the game of golf at a level bordering on the paranormal. I couldn't imagine how the kids at Isleworth handle the fact that their club's best player is Tiger Woods.

Tiger might not be here if it weren't for Tour veteran Mark O'Meara. Like Arnold Palmer, the first time O'Meara saw Tiger was at the 1991 U.S. Junior Amateur at Bay Hill. After watching the fifteen-year-old kill a drive on the 9th hole, O'Meara said, "Okay,

I've seen enough." He knew then that Tiger was the next big thing. They developed a friendship, and when Tiger left Stanford in 1996, O'Meara opened his home to the Tour rookie, even trying to set him up on dates with his own kids' babysitters. In return, Tiger pushed O'Meara during early-morning practice rounds and encouraged the declining pro not to settle for less in his golf game. Two years later, at the age of forty-one, O'Meara won the Masters. Three months after that, he won the British Open. When Tiger's eight-figure endorsement check from Nike cleared, he could afford to live, well, anywhere. He bought a house in O'Meara's Isleworth neighborhood.

Isleworth isn't old by golf standards. Twenty-five years ago it was a sprawling piece of land southwest of Orlando covered in orchards and surrounded by lakes and cypress trees. A group of investors headed by Arnold Palmer bought the land, built the course, and developed the high-end community before selling it to the Tavistock Group in 1993. When Tiger Woods moved in a few years later, a number of young stars followed suit. The roster of Tour players at Isleworth quickly rivaled that of Orlando's other Tavistock-owned club, Lake Nona, and the neighborhoods began debating the question of who might win in a match between their best players.

The Tavistock Cup is now in its fifth year, and while it isn't an official event, it has a $3.8 million purse and is broadcast to more than eighty countries. If nothing else, it's beautiful to see that in such a crazy, mixed-up world, rich people of different gated communities have found a way to peacefully coexist.

FIRST ROUND

The only thing that reveals how long a day this has been for Tiger is his pants, which after seven holes of golf and a plane ride, lack their usual crispness. Gone, finally, is that pink shirt, replaced by his personal Team Isleworth mock T. The shirt is red, the sleeves are black, and on his left arm is his name and the Nike swoosh, lest anyone forgot.

The Tavistock Cup is comprised of two eleven-man teams competing to earn points toward a team total. Today's matches consist of two-man better-ball medal match play, a format whose name alone ensures that no one can understand what is happening. Essentially, Tiger and his partner (a senior tour player and friend of Tiger, John Cook) will each play a ball and take the lower score between them to build an eighteen-hole total. Their two Lake Nona opponents (Henrik Stenson and Northern Ireland's Graeme McDowell) will do the same. The low score after the round earns two points and a tie wins one, a loss zero. Tomorrow's format is four-ball singles, with each player competing against both of the two opponents in their foursome in an eighteen-hole stroke play match. Making it stroke play rather than match play guarantees that every match, even the blowouts, go the full eighteen holes.

2:15 PM ▪ The teams hit their drives, and I head down number 3 fairway. And I mean fairway. To my delight, the Tavistock Cup doesn't set up any ropes along the holes, thus allowing the privileged two hundred of us who are here to walk wherever we would like, including right behind and next to the players. Heading toward the green on the expansive par-5 3rd, I am literally walking in Tiger Woods' footsteps.

It's such a different perspective on a golf tournament. The entire hole is laid out in front of me, not to the side. Unlike trudging through the rough or the desert, the spongy fairway beneath my feet is comforting, safe. Tiger and I are nearly one.

"Please allow room for the players, sir."

"Sorry."

Okay, so there are limits to how close I can get.

2:24 PM ▪ Well, I have tried for two holes to pretend that I actually care about who wins, but I don't. And as much as they build up this rivalry between the two clubs and claim to keep the trophy secured in a four-inch-thick vault, I don't think anyone else cares that much either.

When I was at Doral, someone referred to the Tavistock Cup as "the biggest cocktail party in golf." That seems to be about right. Residents in blue and red shirts stroll the fairways with their Top-Siders and their Bloody Marys, at times too burdened by their unwieldy celery sticks to applaud. So, for once, I begin tuning out exactly what is at stake and enjoy the scenery and the scene.

Standing out from the sweater-around-the-neck crowd is Stevie, who is wolfing down a Styrofoam container of French fries. I don't think the Tavistock Cup is his favorite assignment. Throughout the season I have noticed that he puts on his caddie bib at the last possible second and always takes it off before Tiger putts out on the 18th. Someone noticed he wasn't wearing it when Tiger made his birdie to win at Bay Hill. Stevie's explanation: "I wasn't thinking playoff." Today he's not wearing it at all. For someone doing an intrinsically subservient job, I see it as his subtle form of rebellion. As for the fancy Tavistock Cup golf bags the players have been given, he has no choice. He drags Tiger's about ten yards before begrudgingly picking it up and heading down the fairway with his fries.

2:38 PM ▪ On the 4th hole at Isleworth, a 479-yard dogleg left, Tiger cuts too much off the corner and finds a fairway bunker. I walk right up to the edge and look down at him. He eyes the flag cut way right, then notices that a couple of photographers have positioned themselves exactly in his line at the front edge of the bunker. "Uh . . . yeah," he says, "that's not a good spot." They move, and he casually hits one of his most impressive shots of the year. From 161 yards (I'm standing on the marked sprinkler head), his iron from the sand starts out high and at the middle of the green. A safe shot. Then it suddenly bends hard to the right and lands within twenty feet of the hole. A brilliant shot.

3:35 PM ▪ As we approach the clubhouse, the crowds have swelled from a few hundred to maybe a thousand, which is still not enough to prohibit me from walking in a straight line wherever I want to go.

"Sir, you need to give the players more space."

"Sorry."

4:15 pm ▪ Between the 1st and 10th tees at Isleworth sits a replica of Arturo Di Modica's famous sculpture of the Wall Street bull. The head of the Tavistock Group is the British tycoon Joe Lewis, an investor who, a week and a half ago, lost more than a billion dollars when Bear Stearns was bought by JP Morgan. The bull is supposedly not for sale. Not yet.

Tiger cuts the corner off the tee on the 409-yard 10th, hitting it ninety yards past the other players in his group. His eighty-eight-yard pitch into the hole sucks off the front, and he has to chip his third. After a quick look at the line, he hits it and watches as it lips out, his eighth one in three days. He smiles and turns to Stevie. "Looks familiar, doesn't it?" It's slightly reassuring that he is still not on his game this afternoon. If he had shown up and made everything in sight, I might have ordered a stiff drink of my own.

5:17 PM ▪ Isleworth is set in and around a series of enormous lakes, the largest more than a mile and a half wide. In the summer, the club sometimes brings in professional water-skiers to coach the neighborhood kids. It explains the over-the-top prizes on the par-3 11th, where five brand-new ski boats are floating in a pond to reward any player who makes a hole in one. Even wilder are the eleven brand-new black Cadillac Escalades lining both sides of the 223-yard 15th. To win one, a player doesn't need to ace the hole. He only needs to win the closest-to-the-pin contest. If he does make a hole in one, every member of the team wins an SUV. When a dealer is willing to line a hole with almost a million dollars worth of cars, it's safe to assume the tournament doesn't include a pro-am.

6:20 PM ▪ Tiger and John Cook arrive at Isleworth's 18th green with their match all square. While I don't care who wins the cup, I don't particularly want to see Tiger lose twice in one day.

Tiger has already made par, but Lake Nona's McDowell and Isleworth's Cook still have birdie putts. In a showing of team solidarity, Tiger goes over and helps Cook with the line. And he doesn't do it half-heartedly. He walks halfway to the hole and does the same routine as if he were putting, feeling the line by swinging one-handed. He gives Cook his read. Cook likes it, but the putt doesn't fall. Now it's all in the hands of McDowell, whose putt is on line, but too hard. It hits the cup, lips out, and actually catches air before stopping a foot away. The match is halved and both clubs earn a point. It's nice to see a lip-out actually help Tiger Woods for a change.

IMG-FREE ▪ I sit down for dinner at nearby Jersey Mike's sub shop and start to flip through the complimentary Tavistock program. The paper they used to print it is of such high quality, the binding so thick, that when I try to hold open the pages with my soda, the cover flies back at me in rebellion. Given the ads inside, it's apparent its producers are well aware of their readers' taste. One realty listing is for a $12 million "French farmhouse" that boasts of having its own massage room and "apothecary theatre lobby." I know what a theatre lobby is, and I know that an apothecary is a pharmacy. How in the world those combine into something enticing is beyond me, but then again, I'm not the Tavistock Cup's target audience.

What I am anxious to read are the profiles on the players. They are all asked a variety of banal questions, such as "Name something you do that's 'green.'" Who knew that England's Justin Rose and his wife make their own compost? I turn to Tiger's Q and A, expecting to read answers filtered through his management team at IMG. What I find are the same seemingly ridiculous questions but, in response, a collection of answers that read as more honest and devoid of calculation than anything he's said in years.

What does he hope someone invents before he dies? "Teleporting." This is a guy who hates to waste time. His favorite childhood cartoon character? Optimus Prime from *Transformers*—the leader of the Autobots who battled without end. If NASA ever okays a trip to outer space, will Tiger go? "Damn right!" The possibility of what is to be gained from a challenge excites him more than the risks. I keep reading. What reality show would he like to be on? "I hate reality shows and would never be on one." As a sitcom writer, no answer could endear him to me more. But my favorite answer is his last. "What disease do you want to see cured in your lifetime?" Most players give the obligatory sad response, naming some illness and then presumably hanging their heads and asking for a tissue. The disease Tiger would like to see cured? "The yips!" My soda almost falls over again, this time from my knocking the table while laughing. It is clear that Tiger is more interesting in private than he believes he can afford to be in public. Would the shoot-from-the-hip Tiger make his sponsors a little nervous? Absolutely. And in doing so, he would attract a mass of golf fans who desperately want to like him, but remain unsure of who he really is.

ROUND TWO

I arrive at the course for day 2 by 8:30 a.m. The players aren't teeing off for almost three hours, but I want to see Tiger's home course as he sees it, early in the morning, so I decide to take a walk. A worker is mowing the 12th fairway. Another is on the green. When they stop, there are no other sounds to be heard. A swan is swimming across Hourglass Lake. A pelican circles above, then dives beak first into the water in search of breakfast. It is almost too perfect, as if behind a hedge I might find a worker with different joysticks to control the various wildlife for maximum serenity.

Between holes, Isleworth's massive open spaces are occupied by eclectic works of art. The current display includes twenty-five different steel sculptures by Bernar Venet, a French artist who claims on the club's Web site that his goal with the collection is "to take the principles of minimalist art and push it to the limits." That seems sort of contradictory to me.

I turn right and walk down Payne Stewart Drive, past the 89,000-square-foot Mediterranean-style clubhouse (almost 70 percent bigger than the White House), and start the long walk to the driving range. The range sits on the far south finger of the property and is surrounded on all sides by water. It's easily fifteen degrees colder down at this end, dipping into the forties and windy. Except for the two people polishing yet another black Escalade, I'm the only one here.

11:00 AM ▪ In a completely surreal moment, an hour and five minutes before his tee time, I watch Tiger open his front door with Stevie and make the walk across the street to the driving range. It's Tiger's shortest commute of the year.

There are many opulent pieces of property around Isleworth. Some estates stretch for a hundred yards. By comparison, Tiger's house is modest: a two-story stucco home that backs up to the water. He could have bought the one that looked like Monticello, but he didn't. Yes, there are the twelve acres on Jupiter Island, but he's in no rush to move there. If he never does, it will be the most expensive case of buyer's remorse in real estate history. But Earl was the same way. When Tiger purchased his mom a new house in the Orange County suburb of Tustin, his dad chose to stay behind in the family's longtime Cypress home. Success, not stuff, is Tiger's definition of greatness.

11:03 AM ▪ On the range, Tiger is chatty, sharing stories with teammate Craig Parry about all sorts of memories from tournaments over the years. Parry laughs when Tiger tells him of a caddy he once had overseas who didn't refer to pin positions as "front" and "back" but "near" and "far." It's another peek into the true gameface-free Tiger.

He is so detached from the event that he calls across to teammate Charles Howell III and asks, "Hey, Chuck, who we playing today?" They'll be facing off in their singles matches against that compost lover Justin Rose and South Africa's Retief Goosen.

12:00 PM ▪ Gary McCord, CBS's handlebar-mustached announcer, stands on the first tee with a microphone, introducing the groups. Since I missed the first two holes yesterday, this is my first look at the opener, a 399-yard par 4 that ducks right. I glance down and see that the yardage markers for these back tees are called the "Tiger" tees. At more than 7,500 yards from the tips, it's the rare place that can push Tiger's limits in preparation for some of the long setups he'll see at majors throughout the year. Still, he could probably play this course in the dark. In fact, he probably has.

12:32 PM ▪ After four pars on the 1st, we move to the 2nd, a 228-yard par 3 over Lake Chase and through a shoot of cypress trees. There's no wind at the tee, but when Charles Howell III's ball clears the trees, a gust pushes the ball hard right and into the big bunker near the lake. Tiger sees what happened and makes an adjustment, flighting his iron even lower. His ball hits the same breeze and gets thrown into the trap anyway. No one else gets any closer. Under these circumstances from these tees, this may be the most difficult par 3 I have ever seen.

1:23 PM ▪ While Tiger waits to play on the 4th green, he and Stevie (again sans bib) notice that the group in front of them is still waiting to hit on the 5th tee. "This is going to be a six-hour day," he says, worried. But he's lucky; he only has to walk down the street when this is over. I wasn't able to change my departure city and have to drive all the way back to Miami tonight.

2:06 PM ▪ With plenty of time to kill, Tiger, Justin Rose, and Chuck Howell stand around and talk about Isleworth's newest team member, J. B. Holmes, who hit a drive nearly 400 yards yesterday on the 18th hole. Tiger takes his driver and mimics J.B.'s abbreviated backswing, taking the club only three quarters of the way to the top, then asks, "How does a guy who only takes it to *there* hit it 350?" They all seem equally bewildered at the thought. Tiger may have beaten him in the first round at the Match Play, but a little bit of J.B. is still in Tiger's head.

4:19 PM ▪ Tiger successfully keeps Lake Nona's Goosen and Rose a few shots back for most of the round, making the day feel all the more mellow. But on 13, his eagle putt from the front of the green to the back pin climbs only halfway up the tier, then turns around and rolls down and off the green altogether. It keeps going another thirty feet to the bottom of a collection area. The Bloody Mary crowd stops stirring long enough to gasp at the miscue. When it's all over, Tiger makes a bogey, Goosen makes par, and Rose makes a birdie. He seems not to want to care about what's going on this afternoon, but suddenly he has no choice.

He responds by hitting a 375-yard drive down the right center of the 14th fairway. When his easy wedge shot sucks back off the green, he helps break in his Tavistock bag by chucking his club at it. He saves par to stay in control of the match.

5:01 PM ▪ Both of the matches are now Tiger's to lose, and he nearly does just that on the 16th, a short par 4 of just 349 yards. Tiger is hitting last and pushes his drive way right. Before even watching it land, he asks Stevie for another ball, thinking the first one is out of bounds. But the seventy-five fans down in the fairway assume that everyone has played and start crossing as Tiger unloads on drive number two. This one is straight down the middle and tracking on one unsuspecting gallery member holding a homemade cocktail. It looks as if it will take out the man, which will then create a domino effect, sending a dozen different fans to the ground in a straight line toward the hole. Instead, the ball whizzes right behind him and rolls up in front of the green. Tiger is too angry about the first drive to notice how close he was to killing one of his neighbors.

5:57 PM ▪ His first drive on 16 ends up being in bounds after all, and his lead is never in jeopardy again. With the end in sight, the speed of play accelerates with every shot. The format is a drag at this point, just delaying the inevitable. Tiger seems ready to be done. For his second shot into 18, he doesn't take any practice swings or try to figure the wind. He hears the yardage, grabs a club, and hits it. It lands on the middle of the green anyway. From there it's a mindless par and a round of 2 under at a track that has been ranked as the hardest course in Florida.

Tiger's two points finishes off the Isleworth rout, with Mark O'Meara's team handing Ernie Els's Lake Nona squad a 191/2-111/2 smackdown. Tiger's cut of the purse is $210,000, just $75,000 less than he won at Doral with his fifth-place finish. He sticks around long enough for the trophy ceremony, but within fifteen minutes, he slips off the green and I lose him in a sea of red and blue shirts. The next time we meet will be inside the gates of the most exclusive golf tournament in the world. The Masters.

First, I just need to figure out how to get in.

A National Travesty

The Masters

Augusta National Golf Club
Augusta, Georgia
April 10–13, 2008

In the mid-1980s, there was rarely any change to my father's Sunday routine. He would play golf in the morning, then return home, change into a pair of beat-up shorts and a T-shirt, and get to work. My parents had bought a new house in 1984, and every weekend for the following two years, Dad was sanding, digging, or mixing something.

First, he cordoned off our side yard with railroad ties and planted alder trees. One of his summer jobs in college was with Davey Tree Expert Company, and as his alders started getting bigger, my thirty-nine-year-old white-collar father would shimmy up to the top and prune them as if he were still nineteen. From there he moved on to the backyard, where he was laying a brick patio all by himself, obsessively cutting hundreds of bricks into an intricate pattern. My sister and I started to wonder if the three hundred pounds of loose sand piled in front of our house was a permanent part of the landscape.

Then, one Sunday afternoon in April, I walked into the living room and found my father sitting five feet from the television.

"What are you watching?"

"The Masters."

That was all he said. I sat down next to him and watched as a plaid-trousered Jack Nicklaus made every single putt he saw. When it was over, my dad stood up calmly and ejected a videotape from the VCR. I had never seen him record a sporting event before. He carefully applied a white label and wrote with a red Sharpie, "1986 Masters." He then snapped off the little plastic tab on the front of the tape, ensuring that no one could ever accidentally record over it. I knew then, at age eight, that the first major of the year was not just another golf tournament.

I have been working on finding a way into Augusta National since February, and I have learned only one thing: I am starting a little late. Tournament badges are made available only to those on the official patron list. And that list has been closed since 1972, before either Tiger or I was even born.

But this is America, and if you can't get it for free, you can always buy it, right? Technically, yes. When I first looked into purchasing a black-market badge back in February, most of the ticket brokers were asking for well over $3,000 for all four days. So I revisited my connections. I talked to friends at the Golf Channel, CBS, ESPN, *Sports Illustrated* . . . nothing. One friend said he knew of a way in: "Parachute." The most creative solution came from a buddy who said I should tape pink flowers to my body and sneak in as an azalea bush.

And now that I am back home from Florida, with Tiger having won four of his first five events and the Vegas line on him winning the Grand Slam holding steady at nine-to-one, the ticket broker price has climbed to more than $5,000, twice what I spent on my honeymoon and equivalent to what I've paid for all my previous trips this season—combined.

But again, it isn't an ordinary golf tournament. It's the Masters. Two weeks after returning home from Florida, I leave for Augusta with a few leads, but only one confirmed ticket. For a Tuesday practice round. I have a thousand dollars stuffed in my wallet and the understanding that I will probably need a lot more.

MONDAY NIGHT ▪ My last leg of the three-part journey is a commuter flight out of Charlotte. I expect it to be sold out and full of golf fans. But there are only a few of us scattered about, easily identifiable by our child-like giddiness. Two such fans sit behind me and work closely together on a crossword puzzle.

"Five down could be wrong," the first one says.

"Well, I'm not real comfortable with this whole area!" They give each other a pep talk and refocus. It's amazing the things men will do on a golf trip that they rarely do with their own wives. They're still working as the plane touches down. Rolling to Augusta's colonial-style terminal, I see thirty to forty private jets parked in the dark near some distant hangars, each of their owners hoping they won't be needed again until late Sunday night.

Outside of the actual Masters badges, the most expensive thing about a trip to Augusta is the hotel room. The Days Inn has a normal rack rate of only $69 a night. This week it's charging $305, and it's been sold out for months. Frankly, it could afford to spend a few dollars and buy an *S* for the sign out front, which currently reads, "We welcome our new and returning guest."

Though I do not have a badge, I am very fortunate to have a free place to stay. A stranger named Joe read a piece I wrote for ESPN about driving to the Tavistock Cup and e-mailed me to offer his couch in Augusta if I wanted it. For the money I would save, I didn't even ask him if he was creepy. I call him around ten o'clock at night when my plane lands. He's a few beers into his evening and tells me to "hurry up and get here—we're watching the coverage!" I follow my GPS through the empty Georgia freeways and exit at Washington Road. Even though it is now pushing eleven, some scalpers sit in lawn chairs near the end of the off-ramp with signs offering to buy any and all badges. Joe had told me to "just turn left at the Hooters" to get to his place, but I can't. I have to keep driving.

I've never been here before, but when I pass Berckmans Road, my heart rate picks up, as if my golf-centric soul instinctively knows where I'm taking it. On my right, a twenty-foot hedge blocks any views from the street. I drive along slowly in the right lane as cars pass me on the left. With no warning, the hedge gives way to a modest white guard shack. Beyond it is a long dark road and, at the very end, lit up in soft yellow light, the unmistakable clubhouse of the Augusta National Golf Club. I react as any mature fan of the game of golf would and should. "Holy crap."

TUESDAY ▪ By 7:30 a.m., I have already passed through security and am standing at the front of the low wooden fence that is separating Masters patrons from the course itself. In front of us is an expanse of perfect grass. The only people on the course are a few volunteers, security guards, and—who else—Luau Larry, using his press credential for an early-morning hula around the sacred grounds.

In 1934, one year after Augusta National formally opened, its cofounder Clifford Roberts suggested calling his new club's tournament "the Masters." The other cofounder, retired golf legend Bobby Jones, thought it was too pompous, especially in the midst of the Great Depression. Instead they named it the Augusta National Invitational Tournament. Five years later, Jones gave in to the (eventually) well-deserved title by which it's been known ever since.

Tiger is one of only three golfers, along with Nicklaus and Palmer, to have won here four times (1997, 2001, 2002, 2005). It's a course that rewards power, strategy, and fearless putting, and Tiger can deftly move among all three. In 2006, he finished third. Last year, he finished second. I'm hoping the trend continues.

All the fans around me already know where they're headed. Some will make for the first tee. Others are going to the bleachers at 16. The gate swings open exactly at eight, and they spread out like kids at Disneyland heading to their favorite ride. I have no plan. Anywhere is a good choice. I follow the slope down and across number 1 fairway, past number 9, then into a large stretch that isn't a hole at all. It turns out that Augusta's original design called for not only a practice area right here but, even stranger, a 19th hole that would be used to settle any outstanding bets. When it was discovered that the hole would obstruct the view of the clubhouse from the 18th green, the idea was scrapped.

I continue in the same direction, in an increasing daze, passing number 8, 7 green, across 15, then 14, and I start to realize that I'm walking, without having really known it, right into the intersection of three of the most famous holes in American golf: Amen Corner. I wander through a grove of pine trees, still slipping downhill, and come to a clearing. There in front of me is the 12th. I can almost hear the voice of Jim Nantz softly purring the hole's botanical name in my ears . . . *Golden Bell* . . . If there was only a flag on the green, I might actually think it were a painting. The hundred fans in front of me start to rumble, and I turn my head to see why. It wasn't Amen Corner that was pulling me. Walking onto the tee from number 11, in black slacks and a black sweater is, of course, Tiger Woods.

Tiger teed off on the back nine before the gates opened and managed to finish only two holes before being discovered. He plays one ball to the left side of the par 3, then changes clubs and plays a second ball to the right. He and Stevie head down to the green and across the Hogan Bridge. It's strange to see them all alone. No other players. No security guards. No cameramen. As Tiger putts in different directions, an Augusta National worker appears from behind us with a yellow flag and speedwalks down the fairway and over the bridge to replace the pin for the four-time champion.

I could follow Tiger, but for once I let him go on without me. Instead I find a spot in the bleachers behind the 12th tee and soak in the view. The three holes that make up Amen Corner flow like Rae's Creek from left to right. The par-4 11th sweeps down through a grove of pines to a subtle, flat green. In the center is the 155-yard 12th, a hole so picturesque that when India's Jeev Milkha Singh comes through, he stops and has his caddy take a picture of him. Tucked behind the 12th green is the tee at the par-5 13th, the most secluded spot on the course. The only people within two hundred yards of it are a couple of officials, intentionally camouflaged by flowers and bushes so as not to spoil golf's perfect panorama.

WEDNESDAY ▪ Already out of tickets, I had walked down Washington Road after Tuesday's practice round and taken down some scalpers' phone numbers. When I wake up this morning, I call them at random to see what the day will cost. The low price is Tony, asking $350. Yesterday, he was working the curb near Arby's. Today, he's set up on the south end of town, just off the Bobby Jones Expressway, and claims to have only one left. I am obviously losing a sense of what is too much to pay for a ticket and set out in my red Pontiac to find him.

On the way, I pass another scalper who offers me the same ticket for only $300. I call Tony to see if he can match the price. "What?!" He's angry. "You're killing me! I could have just sold your ticket to someone for *four* hundred!" He hems and haws as if he's getting ripped off on a ticket that has a face value of $36. His tough Boston accent is intimidating, but it's the first time I've had any leverage, and I let him wriggle. He finally agrees to match it, so I keep driving.

Tony is on the sidewalk with another scalper, working the long line of traffic headed to the course. I pull over, and he comes to the window, but he wants to make small talk first. I'm not sure why I mentioned that I was a TV writer, but he gets excited and decides to pitch me his life story, which he thinks would make a great movie. "It'd be called *Death Row to Front Row*," he says. "You were on death row?" I ask, quietly slipping the car from park into reverse. Tony explains that yes, technically he killed a guy, but eventually they proved it was self-defense and now he's free. "Awesome," I say. His buddy interjects that he thinks *his* life would make a great movie, too, but says it would have to be an adult film.

The conversation thankfully returns to my ticket. Tony's still not convinced that I actually found someone selling "a Wednesday" for $300. He turns to his pal and says, "Should we take a ride?" This is just what I want—to be driving around Augusta with these guys. The other scalper, the sixty-something leader of the gang, cools him off. "You got it for two seventy-five. You made twenty-five. Good." I give Tony the cash, he gives me the ticket. Never having taken the Pontiac out of reverse, I make a quick escape.

At the course I discover that Tiger isn't even going to play a practice round today, which means I just paid three hundred bucks to watch Tiger on the putting green. I can't conceive of being able to play Augusta National and choosing not to do so. But statistically, recent history points to the putting green as the place where Tiger needs to be. He hit more greens at Doral than he had hit any other week since the Buick

Invitational. But the thirty-two putts he had in his third round was his worst number of the entire season. He is still easily the favorite, but the question in my mind is whether he has arrived in Georgia having fixed whatever was wrong in Florida. Based on a story I heard a few months earlier, I can only assume he had.

It was back in February, and my old boss Alan invited me to play Lakeside, a gorgeous, Hollywood-friendly club across the cement-bottomed Los Angeles River from Universal Studios. After our round he introduced me to Ernie, one of Lakeside's starters who had been there for thirty years. "You want a Tiger story? I got one." He told me about a time years ago when Earl Woods was in L.A. having bypass surgery. That day Ernie got a call from Kevin Costner, who told him "Tiger needs a place to hide out." Ernie said no problem, and later that day Tiger showed up. "I tell him, 'What do you want to do? You want to play, you want to hit balls?'" Tiger just held up his hands. In one hand was his putter and in the other were three golf balls. "This is the worst part of my game," Tiger explained.

He walked to Lakeside's putting green, dropped the three balls, and started putting around to the different flags. "An hour and forty minutes later—I timed it—and he's still putting," Ernie says. Finally, Tiger stopped going in circles and found the toughest putt on the green. Ernie stepped out from behind the starter window to show me. It was about twenty-five feet, broke four feet left to right, and was dead downhill. It was Tiger's winning Bay Hill putt on steroids. After another hour and fifty minutes, Ernie realized what the game was. Tiger wouldn't let himself leave until he had made the hardest putt on the putting green three times in a row. Tiger came back the next day and did the same thing. By Ernie's estimation, Tiger spent eight hours on the putting green those two days at Lakeside. It was early 1997. A few months later, Tiger won his first Masters by twelve shots.

FIRST ROUND

Wednesday night I hear from a sportswriter I had met in February. He has found me a badge that I can use for Thursday and Friday. For $1,800. I have prepared myself for this worst-case scenario and have already taken a $4,000 cash advance on my credit card. Amazingly, no one at the Augusta branch of Bank of America seemed thrown by the request. The manager said that for months people had come in and pulled out a few hundred dollars at a time so they would have enough for their black-market badge come April. I asked for so much cash the teller didn't even count it. She just slapped down two prewrapped bundles, each holding $2,000 apiece.

Surrounded by fog, I meet the writer early Thursday morning. I slip him the cash, and he hands me the most sought-after piece of plastic in sports. It is square and white, with a photo of the 12th hole and a hologram that says "Masters 2008." The back side is filled with small print from top to bottom, detailing all the rules I am breaking. The state of Georgia legalized ticket scalping a few years ago, but Augusta National still holds to the policy that the use of a resold badge is prohibited and subjects the user (and the original patron who sold it) to permanent loss of the credential. I pass through the metal detectors and arrive at the ticket scanner. The volunteer scans my badge. It beeps. She looks me in the eye for a moment, then smiles. "Enjoy your day."

11:06 AM ▪ Tiger, wearing khaki slacks and a pink, white, and brown striped shirt, is nearing the end of his warm-up session. The range heads away from the clubhouse and dead-ends at the edge of Washington Road. From outside the gates pedestrians can hear the occasional clang as players hit the fourteen green poles that rise a hundred feet into the air and support the giant net. Yesterday, the short-hitting Tim Clark was having trouble reaching it. Tiger's drives are hitting about halfway up, then falling back to Earth.

This may be a major, but Tiger's routine is the same, and when he finishes on the range, he heads to the chipping green where Stevie has already left handfuls of balls in different places for Tiger to find. The all-white jumpsuit that Augusta makes caddies wear only adds to the Easter Bunny imagery. And of the roughly fifteen times I have watched Tiger practice these shots before a round, I have never *not* seen him make at least one. Today he starts with some soft, high pitch shots. His second effort bounces twice and rolls into the cup. After a few bump and runs, he moves to the sand. His first ball—*in*. After a couple more, he aims toward a different flag. *In*. He aims to the third flag, twenty-five yards away. It stops three inches from the cup. He is ready.

11:40 AM ▪ There's nothing more quaint than the number 1 tee at Augusta National. A round patio umbrella and table sit near the back. Resting on the table is a wooden box filled with tees, Sharpies, and some extra copies of the day's hole positions. Other official paperwork is held in place by a couple of loose rocks. Two Augusta members in their trademark green jackets stand near the table as a pair of young men in blue blazers step onto a split log bench and slide Tiger's name into the metal green sign to the left of the tee. In one of the Masters programs, there is a picture of the first tee from the 1950s. Nothing has changed.

11:45 AM ▪ The comforting southern accent of the starter rings out from the tee: "Fore, please. Tiger Woods driving." We applaud as Tiger touches the brim of his cap and begins his quest for the first single-season professional Grand Slam in the history of golf.

The 455-yard 1st at Augusta National is a hole I have seen on TV and considered flat—which it is, as long as a player carries his drive 290 yards over a deep valley to the top of the fairway where it levels off. Tiger tees up his ball the way I've learned he always does: Nike swoosh on the inside, face up. And pointing toward the hole, the word *Tiger* stamped on the other side. He mashes his drive, and we try to follow it, but it's lost against the gray sky. I figure that when it comes down, the fans near the fairway will clarify. Nothing. Silence. The lady in front of me gives her best guess, "To infinity . . . and beyond." He finds his ball just off the fairway and starts the 2008 Masters with a par.

12:15 PM ▪ The fact that I have never heard anyone mention the beauty of the view from the 2nd tee is a testament to how spectacular the rest of the course is. A 575-yard par 5, it plays slightly downhill through the pines toward one massive, blindingly white bunker on the right side, just over three hundred yards away. From there players hit from what feels like a plateau toward a well-guarded shallow green.

Tiger lays short of the trap off the tee and then lays up again with a long iron. There's no question he could have reached it, but Augusta rewards intelligence more than might, and Tiger knows that the best chance for birdie will come from below the hole, not above.

Even so, he pitches eight feet long and has a downhill putt. His first birdie putt of the day is a poor effort from the moment he strokes it.

12:35 PM ▪ The 3rd is another missed opportunity for Tiger. On this short, uphill par 4, the big decision for Tiger is always whether to hit driver near the base of the elevated green or lay up with an iron. In the final round of the 2003 Masters, Tiger came to the hole down by 3 shots. He wanted to hit an iron. Stevie convinced him to go with the driver. Tiger blocked the drive into some bushes, had to play out left-handed, and eventually made a double en route to a disappointing 75. The duo was overheard cursing at each other throughout the day, and Tiger would later have to release a statement saying that their relationship remained intact despite the public fight.

Feeling more confident about his game now than he was five years ago, Tiger hits driver again and flies it all the way to the upslope of the green but can only put his ball twenty feet away, settling for another par.

1:39 PM ▪ In the pine straw to the right of seven, two camera assistants stay busy rebundling the extra cable into a perfect coil every time the cameraman adjusts his position. I'm sure this isn't done out of boredom. To say that Augusta National prefers things neat is like saying fish prefer being wet.

On Tuesday a number of workers walked through the fairways, whisking the dew off the early-morning grass. Others did the same around the greens, removing any sand that had been blown out of the traps. Neither of those sights shocked me more than when I grabbed a napkin from a dispenser and a worker promptly tucked the next one back inside so it wouldn't have that repulsive loose-napkin look to it. I actually admire the ambitiousness. If the goal of Augusta National is to present the world's greatest golf tournament on one of the world's greatest courses, why strive for anything less than obsessive perfection?

1:49 PM ▪ Tiger leaves the 7th having made seven straight pars. The volunteers working the leaderboards are running low on zeros. The 570-yard 8th hole plays back up the hill that number 2 played down. Tiger pummels a drive 320 yards past the hole's only sand trap and will face 225 yards up the hill.

I want to run around to the back of the green, but I can't. Running is another Masters no-no. The intent is to provide a relaxed environment for all. It's a hard adjustment for me, but I put my head down and speed-walk up the steep hill instead.

The second shot into the long, skinny, bunkerless 8th green is a blind shot. We can't see Tiger down below, but we can only assume it's his ball that we see sailing long and left of the green. It ricochets off the grandstands and kicks hard right, back over to the other side of the green. It's closer to the flag than he would have been, but it's left him an impossible chip that runs uphill to the fringe and then downhill to the flag. He makes only par and wanders away, still unsure about how his second shot ended up where it did. He mutters to the blond-headed Aussie, Stuart Appleby, "I thought it was long left . . ." Appleby might not be able to handle anyone else's problems at this point. While Tiger has parred eight in a row, Appleby has one par, three birdies, three bogeys, and a triple.

3:00 PM ▪ The Masters isn't supposed to be boring. But here, as I watch Tiger miss a birdie putt on number 12, the heart of Amen Corner, I yawn. That makes twelve straight pars. But something is bound to change, since I just joined up with my college roommate, Rob. He has never been to the Masters either and, unlike me, actually has enough power and influence to find himself a free badge for the day.

The only reason we ended up roommates our freshman year was that someone in our school's housing department had a sense of humor. There were eight guys on our wing, two to a room. Their names: Mike and Ryan, Mark and Brian, Rob and Bob, and for good measure, Andrew and Tyler. That one didn't fit the mold until we discovered their last names were Fisher and Crabtree and they went by the nicknames Fish and Crab.

Rob had been recruited by Princeton to play golf, and convinced me to try out for the team sophomore year. I made it. During a team meeting that winter, the coach called me "the definition of dedication." The next day I quit. I just wasn't good enough to make the traveling team, and knew my time was better spent focusing on writing. But I did leave an indelible mark. That spring, the upperclassmen created a one-day team event called the Tiger Cup, named after our school's mascot. The team captain even bought a fancy glass with the Princeton crest on it from the university store and wrote on it in black Sharpie, "Tiger Cup." I was no longer on the team, but I was invited back to even out the numbers. I don't even remember the format, but the trophy was ceremoniously placed next to the first tee. While I watched another player hit, I was swinging my Ping putter around in my hand and heard a clink. I knew exactly what I had done without having to look down. "Smiley broke the Tiger Cup!" the captain screamed in disbelief. The hope was that it would be an annual event, but the tradition began and ended there.

3:30 PM ▪ Rob and I walk down the 13th fairway and look back toward the tee, a shot that demands that a player hit a sweeping draw around the trees to have a clear view of the green. A perfect drive will leave a sidehill lie to a rippling putting surface. Go short of the green, and the ball is in Rae's Creek. Go long, it's in a trap. Go really long, it's in a sea of azaleas. Tiger misses just over the green, and his ball settles into a swale. He decides to chip his third rather than putt it, but he misplays it and the ball rolls back off the green again. His fourth rolls past the hole, and he misses the par putt coming back. I was hoping Rob would change our luck for the better, not worse.

3:45 PM ▪ Unlike the unoriginal holes at Doral, there are no F7s at Augusta National. No two holes could ever be confused with each other. The 14th, for example, has no bunkers. Anywhere. Yet historically, it ranks as one of the course's hardest. It's 440 yards and tight between the pines, with a green that slopes severely left to right. Tiger pulls his drive left just inside the ropes. It's behind a tree and sitting on pine straw, still 200 yards to the hole. Rob and I speedwalk to the spot like a couple of senior citizens doing laps on a cruise ship and are rewarded with a second-row view.

Tiger sees what faces him and wants to go left of the tree. Stevie doesn't mince his words. I'm starting to realize that he never does. "Definitely can't get there." Tiger listens and decides to go low and hook it around the tree instead. He tries to get as stable a footing as he can on the pine needles and swings hard. And tops it. It is a full on, thin, ugly, piece of junk shot that bounces only ninety yards down the fairway. Tiger makes just enough blunders to never let anyone forget just how hard the game of golf truly is. It leads to his second straight bogey. Tiger is now 2-over par, and all since Rob joined me. But I don't need to point it out to him. "Do you want me to leave?" he asks earnestly.

"That's ridiculous," I tell him. "Not yet."

4:05 PM ▪ Every hole at Augusta is named after a species of plant that was discovered on the land in the days before it was a golf course, when it was a rolling, 365-acre property called Fruitland Nurseries. The 530-yard 15th has the toughest-sounding name (Firethorn) but historically ranks as Augusta's easiest hole. A downhill, reachable par 5, it can yield low scores (Gene Sarazen made a double-eagle 2 in 1935), but the dark blue pond in front of the green and another pond behind it make it look like trying to land a plane on a grass-covered aircraft carrier.

Tiger finds himself in trouble again when his second shot misses over the green in two. From Rob's and my perspective, it's a nearly impossible pitch shot. The pin is cut near the back-right edge, and Tiger can only pop it up and hope it doesn't roll all the way to the front.

Tiger stalls before hitting the shot, perhaps in order to allow the grass on Augusta's slick greens to grow infinitesimally longer. While waiting, I try to figure out what I've done today that I haven't done any other. Right as Tiger brings his wedge back, it dawns on me that, this morning, I replaced my stained and faded red TW hat with a bright-green Masters cap. My hat! In one fluid motion, as Tiger's wedge returns to his ball, I pull off the green one, rip my old hat from my belt loop, and place it on my head just as Tiger makes contact.

The ball hops up, lands on the edge of the green, and rolls into the cup for eagle.

The crowd roars for Tiger as Rob and I high-five. After the chip-in eagle, Tiger pars out to salvage a round of 72. It puts him 4 behind Justin Rose and South Africa's Trevor Immelman. I will never change hats again.

LANE'S TOUR ■ I never thought I'd like a couple of self-described "good ol' boys" as much as Joe and Lane, the two guys who have donated their couch for the week. Joe is a twenty-seven-year-old who works for a pest control company, and Lane is a twenty-nine-year-old motor repairman. While they've been friends for years, they have grown closer over the last few months since Lane started dating Joe's cousin. It's a relationship that provides endless opportunities for jokes depending on who is trying to insult whom.

Thursday night, I ask Lane if he'd be willing to give me a tour of his hometown. As we start to drive down Washington Road in his enormous black Ford pickup, I tell him I haven't seen a lot of Priuses here. "What's a Prius?" He isn't joking. I figure a couple of blue-collar guys would roll their eyes about the Masters and all its snobbery. But "the National," as they call it, is their pride and joy. Lane hasn't even been inside the gates for more than a decade, but says without a hint of sarcasm that being there felt like he was "touching God."

I can't disagree with the quasi-spiritual reason to love the Masters, but there's an economic reason to love it, too. The millions of dollars brought in over this one week help to sustain the city for the other fifty-one. And the hotels and restaurants aren't the only ones making out. Lane's girlfriend/Joe's cousin is spending the week working for a catering company. Joe is driving a hospitality van, shuttling businessmen from place to place. If the tips are decent, he'll clear $2,000 by Sunday night. Hundreds of other Augustans, even kids, are working the tournament itself. The school district doesn't try to fight the allure anymore. After years of dealing with students and teachers not showing up for class, now it's easy to know when spring break falls—Masters Week.

Lane has never been west of the Mississippi or north of the Mason-Dixon Line ("When they start playing bowl games up north, then we'll talk"), but he gladly takes me over the Savannah River and into South Carolina. Even though Augusta is only a 3-wood away, he and Joe consider anyone from the neighboring state to be a lower life form. He wheels the truck around and points out the Butt Bridge, named after Major Archibald Willingham Butt, an early-twentieth-century Augusta war hero who died on the *Titanic*.

We pass through Augusta's half-seedy/half-gentrified downtown and head into the hills where the streets are lined with mansions built by Willis Irvin, the same 1930s architect who designed the clubhouse at the National.

Lane's whole tour builds to his final stop: Forest Hills Golf Course. It's too dark to see anything, but in front is a historical marker, and Lane, a true history buff, proudly rolls down my window so that I can read it. Forest Hills is the course where Bobby Jones won the first tournament of his season back in 1930, the year he won golf's only Grand Slam. The fact that few Masters fans will ever see this place is a reminder that winning tournaments like the Dubai Desert Classic is nice, but the legacy of Tiger and his 2008 rests squarely on how he performs in the year's four majors.

SECOND ROUND

Before Friday's round, I go shopping. Augusta National has a permanent gift shop on its property, a massive, forest-green warehouse of all things Masters. The items range from the obligatory shirts and hats to the obscure and the plain odd. I didn't know the Masters has a mascot, but it does. He looks like Mr. Met, the goofy ball-headed New York baseball icon, but wears a green hat instead of a blue one. Throwing a fancy dinner party? No problem. There is a variety of Masters stemware, including martini glasses and even crystal. Want to think about the Masters while you're transferring files? Pick up a logoed USB flash drive. Need something romantic for the wife you abandoned to follow Tiger Woods all year? How about a lovely set of Masters candles? Or maybe some soap imprinted with the Augusta National logo?

The National doesn't release any figures on how much it makes from its merchandise, but I spend $130 without even trying. Most people are walking out having spent not hundreds but thousands. As I see an endless line of credit cards being swiped, it's obvious that Augusta National could use its power to snuff out the secondary ticket market overnight. But it's never, ever going to do so. Without new people coming from different corners of the world to be here, who would buy a Masters mouse pad? Or Masters barbecue tools? Its best ploy is to do what it's been doing—tell people not to buy resold tickets and then make examples of the handful who are dumb enough to get caught. The net result is that the club has increased the allure of being inside its gates all the more.

1:52 PM ▪ By the time Tiger starts his second round, first-round leader Trevor Immelman has already shot a second straight 68 and Tiger is starting round two a daunting 8 shots behind. He acts quickly, making a birdie on the 1st, and is under par for the first time this week.

But no one has much of a chance to enjoy that red "1" on the white scoreboards. On the par-5 2nd, Tiger tries to play a big flop shot to the tucked left pin and dumps it into the trap short of the green from only thirty yards out. He fails to get up and down, and stumbles right back to even par.

3:40 PM ▪ This is starting to feel eerily similar to Doral. Tiger misses a short birdie putt on 3, pars the difficult 4th and 5th, and misses a par putt from five feet on the 6th. He's now *over* par and 9 shots back. I refuse to believe that he hasn't fixed his stroke, so I flash back to a comment he made to reporters early in the week, when he said there was more grass on these greens than he has ever seen. In theory, the thicker and healthier the grass, the more the natural grain will play a role, which could make the greens harder to read. I guess. I have arrived at the point where my tortured justifications for Tiger's poor play no longer make sense even to me.

4:21 PM ▪ He has a chance to bounce back at the 8th, the uphill par 5 where he ricocheted his ball off the grandstands yesterday. Today his long second shot bounces off one of the big anthill-shaped mounds along the left side of the hole and kicks down toward the cup. He has just ten feet for eagle.

While waiting for Tiger to make the long walk, I meet Richard, a friendly-looking bloke in his early forties who speaks in an Australian accent and asks me, "Are you a golf tragic?" I'm not sure what that means, though the term might perfectly describe Tiger's last two rounds. He sees my confusion and translates—"a golf nut." Oh. Yes. Slightly.

Richard is a member of the Australian Parliament and is making his first trip to Augusta as an advocate for Golf Australia, his country's equivalent of the United States Golf Association or Great Britain's Royal & Ancient. The pairings for the first two days were a godsend for him. He receives credit for watching his friend Stuart Appleby while getting to see his hero, Tiger Woods. He's been following Tiger all day and knows that putts like this makeable eagle need to start falling. The ball only burns the edge, and he taps in for a disappointing birdie.

5:05 PM · It's a good thing Richard is here, because enduring this by myself at a cost of $900 a day might make me punch a tree. And I assume that punching anything at Augusta National is grounds for removal and confiscation of my badge. Leaving the course yesterday, two men pushed by me, dragging their friend who had decided the Masters was the ideal place to get completely sloshed. These sorts of indiscretions could be expensive mistakes. Ticket brokers threaten customers with the promise to charge their credit card an additional $10,000 if they don't return their badges at the end of the day—the fear being that if the buyer doesn't have the badge, the National may have taken it and the original owner will have his name forever erased from the patron list.

I already received a warning myself yesterday. While sitting on the hillside near number 6, I stretched out on my elbows, then briefly lay on my back to take some notes. Within fifteen seconds, a uniformed security guard approached and said that elbows were okay, but lying on my back was not allowed. Then for good measure, he added, "And you have to leave your shoes on." My shoes *were* on. The Masters is stunning me with its beauty and perfection, while leaving me completely on edge and uncomfortable at the same time.

Richard and I arrive on the hillside near number 10 green. Tiger's thirty-foot putt for birdie starts six feet right of the cup but breaks only six inches. Tiger has played here every year since 1995, and he just misread a putt by five and a half feet. Even worse, he misses the putt for par and is again 1 over for the week.

5:17 PM ▪ Rather than confront the misery in front of us, Richard and I head down number 11 and talk about past misery, specifically his countryman Greg Norman's sudden-death loss to Larry Mize in the 1987 Masters. Norman's inability to win a green jacket is a national travesty in Australia, none of his losses more painful than when Mize, a local Augustan, chipped in from forty-five yards on the very hole Richard and I are traversing. The shot was so scarring to an entire nation that everyone in Richard's Golf Australia group made a pilgrimage earlier in the week to the very spot just right of the green, where they each stood in silence and considered not what could have been but, in their minds, what should have been.

Despite Greg Norman being the number one player in the world for 331 weeks between the late 1980s and early '90s, the Shark's record when holding a fifty-four-hole lead in majors is a nightmarish one for six. Tiger, on the other hand, is thirteen for thirteen. Australia loves him for just that reason. Where Norman left his countrymen heart-broken time after time, Tiger reminds them that greatness is still possible. Or, as the forever wounded Richard says, Tiger "handles your emotions with care."

5:43 PM ▪ Tiger pars the 11th and 12th. He is the only one on the ten-man leaderboard who is not under par for the tournament. On 13 green, he's so unsure of himself he actually asks Stevie for a read—something he hasn't done more than three times all season. The advice leads to a tap-in birdie and a return to even par. If this were June at the U.S. Open, bouncing around par like this might be just fine, but not when a half-dozen players are cruising between 4 and 8 under.

6:47 PM ▪ Tiger's birdie effort at the 15th is so mediocre that it doesn't garner a single clap. After another ho-hum par on the 16th, my energy is starting to flat-line. So is Tiger's, who until now hasn't given any clue that he is playing below his expectations. But as he arrives at the log bench next to the tee, he lets his driver fall with a clunk and drops his head.

7:06 PM ▪ Tiger senses my growing ire and promptly birdies number 17 after sticking his second shot within a foot of the hole. That didn't seem so hard. If he can just finish at 1 under, his name will stay at the bottom of the leaderboard and provide some much-needed pressure on the twelve players ahead of him. I join the invigorated crowd and move to 18. "No running," a security guard reminds me.

7:10 PM ▪ There are few golf fans who can't close their eyes and picture the 18th hole at Augusta National— the tee box pulled back like the end of a slingshot between two rows of pines, the dual fairway bunkers straight ahead as the hole turns right and uphill to the final sloping green. Tiger just needs to hit something short of the traps, play a midiron to the front of the green, and be happy with a 4.

I'm sure that was his plan, but as I watch his ball sail into the trees way right, a 4 looks unrealistic. There are no crosswalks on the 18th, so getting to the right side requires going all the way back to the tee and around, a distance that is impossible to cover no matter how fast a speedwalker I am becoming.

I watch from the left side as Tiger looks at his ball on the pine straw and then walks toward the adjoining 10th fairway. He's not pitching out. He's actually attempting to advance the ball up the wrong hole.

7:19 PM ▪ I speedwalk up the left side of 18 like a wind-up toy, then back down the right side of number 10 where Tiger's ball has come to rest after weaving 170 yards through the forests of Georgia. Stevie is pacing the distance from the hole by foot since for some reason the shot from 10 fairway to 18 green isn't one they worked on during their practice rounds this week.

To save par, Tiger must hit a lob wedge high and soft, carrying the right bunker but only by a few feet or else it will roll right off the other side. After hitting so many mediocre shots from around the green this week, his most difficult one of all is perfect. It lands just on the green and turns left, heading down toward the hole in the front-right corner. It picks up speed and looks as if it might even go in before hitting Stuart Appleby's unmarked ball, seven feet above the hole.

No front-runner should be experiencing the stress of a par putt on Friday, but there is the definite sense that if he makes this, it could alter the momentum of his entire week. His custom Scotty Cameron putter only moves backward an inch before nudging the ball forward, rolling it past Appleby's mark and into the hole.

It was torture from beginning to end, but Tiger has somehow squeaked out a 71 and should feel blessed to be only 7 back of Trevor Immelman.

THIRD ROUND

I was hoping that the writer who sold me the badge for Thursday and Friday would have heard about what a model patron I was and allow me to use it for the rest of the tournament for free. No such luck. The cost of a scalped weekend badge is even more—$2,000. Outside gate 3A, I pass a man holding a sign with flames around the edge that reads, "Ask me why you deserve hell." I don't need to ask. I just spent $4,100 to attend a golf tournament.

1:00 PM ▪ The weather has been different every day. Thursday the fog was so heavy it delayed play for forty minutes. Friday was windy. Today, rain. Tiger is on the putting green in waterproof pants and a jacket. He's working on his long putts, trying to adjust to the slower speed of the wet greens in this weather. He rolls a forty-footer right at me. It's tracking toward the hole. If he makes it, it will be the longest putt I've seen him make since the 18th at Bay Hill. Right as it falls into the cup, the horns sound.

Tiger's coach, Hank Haney, steps out from the side of the green and Tiger slips under his umbrella. They walk off the putting green and into the clubhouse, where, for a brief moment as the door hangs open, I see members and guests laughing and sharing drinks around the fireplace. But $4,100 did not include a clubhouse pass. I met a ticket broker who dangled one in front of me, but he wanted a cool $10,000 for it. That was almost as much as Arnold Palmer took home in prize money when he won his first Masters in 1958.

1:51 PM ▪ After a half-hour delay, Tiger is on the tee with Andrés Romero, the twenty-six-year-old Argentinean who finished third at last year's British Open. After he and Tiger shake hands, Tiger shows him his ball. "I'm playing Nike Ones," he tells him, information that is news to no one. Tiger hits his opening drive so perfectly that we give it two sets of applause, one when it's in the air and another when it stops at the top of the hill, three hundred yards away.

The crowd at the Masters is not as homogeneous as I'd expected. Young, old, black, white, each one feeling blessed to be here. All have their Masters story on how they came upon their badges. I meet a woman from the Midwest named Paula who came to a Masters practice round back in 1963. She asked how one procures a badge for the actual tournament and was told to just write and ask. So she did. *Thirty-one years later,* she received a letter from the National saying her name had reached the top of the waiting list. She hasn't missed a year since.

Not everyone is as aboveboard as Paula. While new badge holders are limited to two passes a year, the oldest patrons have many more, some as many as eight. Upon their death, they can will them, but again, no more than two. The result is that some families haven't told the National that great-grandpa has actually been dead for years.

2:15 PM ▪ After a par on 1, Tiger hits his standard drive on the par-5 2nd to the edge of the plateau. The pin today is all the way on the green's left side. Tiger knows that if he can get something near the middle, he'll have a real chance at eagle. He takes his 5-wood and draws it around the pine trees. He jogs to the right for a better look (the "no running" rule is apparently limited to patrons). His ball lands softly between the bunkers and on the green, twenty feet away. As his eagle putt rolls toward the hole, Tiger tries to will it in by bending his knees, but it doesn't fall. The tap-in birdie takes him to 2 under.

3:29 PM ▪ Tiger's third-round putter is no warmer than it was on Friday. After the encouraging start, he misses the following chances to move up the leaderboard:

> Hole 3, 20 feet
> Hole 5, 12 feet
> Hole 6, 20 feet
> Hole 7, 12 feet
> Hole 8, 8 feet

Expecting him to make all of them is greedy, but two? At least. The only thing that helps is that I again run into Richard from Australia. When he sees me, he says somberly, "Hi, Bob." "Hello," I answer, as if we're attending the same funeral. As we did yesterday, we walk along and talk about anything except how Tiger is playing.

I was surprised that a proper Aussie would actually want to hang around an American golf fan who had slipped someone a wad of cash to be here. But Richard's personality matches the golf world he has described back home. Australia is not a place dominated with stuffy country club types. At its core, the golf scene is blue-collar. Sometimes too blue-collar. He tells me the story of when Peter Dawson, the secretary of the prestigious R&A, came from Scotland to see the country and was taken to play Inverleigh, a track Richard calls the "the worst course in Australia." Its greens aren't even grass; they're "sand scrape"—a mixture of oil and sand where a player must rake his line before he putts. When Richard heard that the head of golf's oldest governing body had played there, he was mortified. But in the eyes of Dawson's hosts, Inverleigh was real Aussie golf.

3:50 PM ▪ Of all the famous holes at Augusta National, the 10th looks more different in person than any other. First is how steep it is from the tee to the low point in the fairway. It fills in the blanks of my early Masters memories of watching players hit drives that seemed to roll for a hundred yards. With the lengthening of the National over the last ten years, most of those shots have, sadly, disappeared. The 10th is the exception, insulated from most of the change by the putting green, which sits just thirty feet behind it. Most drives still can't make it to the bottom, leaving players to face a downhill lie to an elevated green, a mean combination that causes even pros to hook and even shank their approach shots.

The other sight that is lost between the camera and the TV, no matter how hi-def it may be, is the sheer scale of the hole. The 10th is the home of Augusta National's oldest and tallest pines, and they loom over the green, casting shadows on it the entire day.

As he has been doing all week, Tiger finds the fairway and hits his second to the middle of the green, fifteen feet away. He finally makes one. When he is confident, his putts drop right in the middle of the cup. This one slips in the right side. Still, it's progress. He's down to 3 under.

4:45 PM ▪ After pars on 11 and 12, Tiger draws an iron onto 13 green and two-putts for another birdie. Amazingly, he is within 4 shots of the lead without having solved his putting woes.

5:45 PM ▪ The mini-charge slows as Tiger manages only to par the 14th, 15th, and 16th, leaving him 5 down on 18 tee. Just as he had the day before, he overcuts his drive into the pine trees. Yesterday, his only shot was up number 10. I don't even think he can do that today. He's between tree trunks. Big tree trunks. The Georgia pines down the right side of 18 are a good thirty to forty feet high, and he has at least 175 yards to the flag. Tiger looks up through the grove in front of him and is convinced that he sees a gap no one else does.

As he whips his hips through the shot, he purposefully falls backwards, sending the ball high and out of sight. We hear it clip some needles on the way out and wait for a response from the crowd. After a quiet second, the distant gallery roars. Tiger slams his iron back into the pine straw in celebration.

He has managed to hit the front of the green from nowhere. He lags the birdie short and makes a nervy five-footer for par and a 4-under 68. Although it's hard to believe considering how poorly he putted, it's Tiger's best round at the Masters since 2005. Still leading are Immelman, the shaggy-haired Brandt Snedeker, Steve Flesch, and Paul Casey. The only hope now is that the posting of Tiger's 5-under total will create a Saturday meltdown that rivals the collective collapse at Bay Hill.

6:12 PM ▪ Tiger signs his scorecard and tells CBS's Bill Macatee that he has put himself right back into the tournament. But his problem remains the same. He returns to the practice green and putts by himself as Hank Haney and Stevie whisper on the far side of the green. After a few minutes, Tiger calls out, "Haney!" His coach crosses to him and watches as he strokes one straight eight-footer after another. Haney is watching only one thing—the blade of his student's putter. With each stroke, he tells Tiger exactly how open the face is. "Half a degree," Haney says after a stroke that looks just fine to me. I chuckle at the notion that such a precise calculation can be eyeballed. Even crazier is the idea that Tiger can take that information and translate it into a physical correction.

Haney's style is reserved; he serves mostly as an extra set of highly trained eyes. On the range, he rarely speaks unless Tiger looks to him for an explanation of what he did wrong. He's much closer to my original assessment of him than I thought: "Good one." *Smack.* "Good one." *Smack.* "*Really* good one." At thirty-two, Tiger is beyond hand-holding. Six years ago, Tiger left his longtime coach Butch Harmon in order to fix a swing that no one, especially Butch, thought needed fixing. After all, Tiger had just won six majors over the previous three seasons. But Tiger was adamant his swing was not as consistent as he felt it could be. Following the split, Tiger failed to win in his next ten majors. He endured plenty of media criticism and even Harmon's own well-publicized comments that his longtime student was "in denial" about his game. Tiger stood his ground. After he connected with Haney in the spring of 2004, the pair quickly silenced the critics. Over the last three years, Tiger has tacked on five more majors.

Back on the Augusta practice green, Tiger is still putting and Haney is still watching. He putts two more that roll dead center. "Perfect," Hank says. After eight more minutes in which he makes almost every one, Tiger looks back up at his coach. Hank just nods. "Good," Tiger says. He picks up the balls, and they head for the clubhouse.

FINAL ROUND

Tiger's 68 didn't have the effect on everyone else that I had hoped. By sundown on Saturday, he had actually fallen from 4 strokes behind to 6—two more than Nicklaus overcame to win the '86 Masters. After skipping church on Easter Sunday for the CA Championship, I decide not to make the same mistake twice.

National Hills Baptist sits kitty-corner from Augusta National, right on Washington Road. Thirty-seven-year-old Pastor Kevin Steele stands at the front in a perfectly pressed mint green shirt, a tie, and, on top, a navy blue sleeveless sweater with the Masters logo on the front. "Happy Masters Sunday to all of you," he begins, "but *every* Sunday is the Master's Sunday."

I grew up going to church every week, even while on vacation, and was expecting the usual stares from locals who knew that I didn't belong. But these folks don't do that. They go out of their way to shake my hand and wish me a good morning. What I really need is a good afternoon, and I take the second song as a sign that today I might just witness a miracle.

> *God will make a way,*
> *Where there seems to be no way.*
> *He works in ways we cannot see,*
> *He will make a way . . . for Tiger.*

Fine, the Baptists didn't tweak the lyrics like that. But if God has followed any part of this season, how could He not resist bestowing a little divine help on Tiger? As I cross Washington Road, the hymns mix in my head with another hopeful refrain golf fans hear every year on this day—that the Masters doesn't really start until the back nine on Sunday.

2:05 PM ▪ When I grab the pairing sheet and see that Tiger is playing with Stewart Cink, I let out a little yelp. Not a big yelp—I'm not sure where Augusta National stands on those. If there's one player Tiger has pummeled with regularity this season, it's Cink. Between the Buick and the Match Play, they've spent 75 holes together, and Tiger has a fourteen-shot advantage.

Adding to the positive vibe, I've reconnected with Mark, a Masters patron whom I met in line for the taxis in Dubai, of all places. Now I just need some nematodes from Bay Hill and I'll have Tiger surrounded with something from all four of his previous wins.

2:59 PM ▪ Three holes in, there's no sign of a miracle. Tiger pars 1, is unable to get up and down for birdie on 2, and, for the fourth consecutive day, doesn't make birdie on 3 despite being just short of the green with his drive. To play that hole in even par for the week is nothing less than dreadful.

With Tiger still sputtering, I tell Mark one of my favorite Augusta National stories of the week. Each of the gallery guards (or marshals, as they're called everywhere else) is issued a bright yellow hard hat for the week. The helmets have the Masters logo on the front, and on both sides in red is the number of the hole to which the marshal has been assigned. When I asked one of the guards if he was allowed to keep the hat when the week is over, he said, "Oh no . . ." On the contrary, every night before he leaves, he has to check the hat back in. "And if you don't?" He smirks and tells me about a dentist from Atlanta who decided one year to quit on a Wednesday and just go home. With his hard hat. That night, there was a knock on his door. It was a sheriff from Augusta, 150 miles to the east.

"Are you Dr. White?"

"Yes."

"Sir, I believe you have some property that belongs to Augusta National."

"I don't know what you're talking about."

"Sir, you can either give it to me now, or at seven a.m. tomorrow I will return with a warrant for your arrest." The dentist excused himself and came back thirty seconds later with the hat. I didn't need to ask the gallery guard if Dr. White was ever invited back. Besides losing his inside the ropes access, he lost the best perk in golf—every May, the National says thank you to the gallery guards by inviting them back for a round of golf and lunch in the clubhouse.

3:19 PM ▪ Up at the 5th, Tiger faces a forty-foot putt from the front of the green to the back. It's so steep that as Stevie tends the flag, his feet appear even with Tiger's head. The putt starts left and climbs, then nearly stops at the top before picking up speed and rolling right to the hole. It looks as if he has made his first extreme putt of the week, when it stops only a half inch short. Tiger drops his putter and throws his hat down with both hands in frustration. He stands there for a while, unable to bring himself to tap it in. When he does, he uses the toe of his putter, not giving the blade side the satisfaction of finishing the job.

5:15 PM ▪ With Tiger standing on the 11th green, now six strokes back, he is about to butt up against the Wall. Art Wall, the 1959 Masters Champion. Forty-nine years ago, Wall arrived at the 12th tee five shots behind and caught fire. He birdied five of his last six holes, passed twelve players along the way (including defending champ Arnold Palmer), and won by a stroke. No one since has come back from as many shots in as few holes. If Tiger doesn't pick up a shot here, his only route to victory will be by breaking Wall's record.

It starts with this putt. It doesn't have any of the elevation change like the putt on 5, but it's at least twice as long, roughly eighty feet from beginning to end. In front of me is a member of the golf course staff who has sneaked away to watch a bit of the action. He knows the course as well as anyone and tells me that this is a putt that Tiger can make. Who knows, perhaps Tiger's money range is inside three feet and outside seventy-five.

The putt starts out five feet right, then slowly makes its way to the back of the green, eventually sliding left and dropping into the heart of the cup. The worker next to me turns and shakes my hand while we cheer. The back of the Masters badge has a message from Augusta National cofounder Bobby Jones that reads, "It is appropriate for spectators to applaud successful strokes in proportion to difficulty, but excessive demonstrations by a player or his partisans are not proper because of the possible effect on other competitors." But seeing as Tiger hadn't given the crowd anything to roar about since his chip-in eagle on Thursday, I think Bobby would forgive us for the applause that carries Tiger all the way from the 11th green to the 12th tee. Just like Art Wall, Tiger is down 5 with 7 to go.

5:44 PM ▪ Tiger wants to keep the momentum but can't, straining as his birdie effort on the 12th just misses. He follows it by missing the fairway on the 13th for the first time all week. It's a crucial error. From a crummy pine straw lie, he can only pitch out to about a hundred yards, meaning eagle is out of the question when he needs it most. Back behind us, in the middle of Amen Corner, Immelman has just bogeyed the 12th. A birdie here would pull Tiger within only three. His wedge to the back-right pin along Rae's Creek shows that he is not interested in second place. It hits and stops six feet from the hole.

This is his last chance. Church hasn't worked. Mark from Dubai hasn't worked. Stewart Cink has been completely worthless. All that is left is gritting my teeth and talking to Tiger under my breath. I sound like a high-strung parent at a T-ball game, but I don't care. *Come on, Tiger. You're better than this. Forget technical stuff. Forget Hank saying "Half a degree . . ." You're eleven years old again. You're playing with Pops. If you make this, you beat him for the first time. Just make it.*

When Tiger's putt skirts the hole, I don't gasp. And neither does anyone else. His misses have stopped being surprising. Somewhere between Thursday and Sunday, the exception to the rule has in fact become the rule. And as Tiger and I leave the 14th tee, the crowds that have followed him all week stay behind.

I don't understand. At the beginning of the season, I thought Tiger was ridiculous for thinking that he liked his chances of winning the Grand Slam. But after winning his first four events, I truly believed he could make a legitimate run at history. Yet at no point this week did Tiger even come close to the lead. By the time he made the turn on Thursday, his victory was already dependent on his ability to make a birdie run on a course that doesn't surrender them with the ease it did in 1997. If I could talk to him, I'm not even sure what I would say. "What's wrong with you?" seems like a good place to start.

6:54 PM ▪ The only thing that would ease the pain would be if Trevor Immelman wins by a lot. Like 7 or 8. If he eagles in, that will be perfect. Then I could spend my flight home telling myself and the disinterested people around me that Tiger couldn't have caught him even if he wanted to. But Tiger birdies 18 to finish at 5 under. When his putt falls in, he rolls his eyes and dismisses the ball with a wave of his hand. While he's in the scorer's hut checking his card, the leaderboard flashes the update that Immelman has double-bogeyed 16 to fall back to 8 under. And that's where Immelman finishes, only 3 measly shots ahead of second-place finisher Tiger Woods.

It's the second straight year he's been the runner-up at the Masters, but last season he didn't start the year by saying that winning the Grand Slam was "easily within reason." The press doesn't let him pass without bringing up his statement from January. "I learned my lesson," Tiger admits. "I'm not going to say anything." At least he didn't backpedal on the notion that he still believes it's possible. As for the putting: "I wasn't releasing it, wasn't getting the overspin like I normally do." Despite his Saturday-afternoon putting session with Haney, he never could close his putter blade that last "half a degree." That's all it took to lose the major he seemed most due to win.

AUGUSTA TO CHARLOTTE ▪ CHARLOTTE TO LAS VEGAS ▪ LAS VEGAS TO L.A. ▪ Every summer my hometown of Ventura has a fair. Ventura is a beach town sixty miles north of L.A., and as much as we try to be cosmopolitan, the fair always reveals our true country soul. There is the Arts and Crafts tent, the rodeo, and plenty of 4-H kids displaying their prized sows. Over the years, the fair has been sanitized, but when I was really young, there was still a circus freak element to it. The carny that always intrigued me most was the one advertised as "The Wild Woman." Her greasy assistant stood next to the concealed viewing area and talked about just how wild she was. She came straight from the Amazon and hadn't adjusted to contemporary society. She was raised by reptiles. She was dangerous. She was seductive. And in case we missed it, she was "wiiiiild"! My parents' judgment was so impaired by deep-fried food that they gave in to my nine-year-old curiosity and ripped off two tickets for me to see for myself exactly what a Wild Woman looked like.

I steadied myself with a breath, then climbed the five steps of the metal staircase and arrived at the platform and the window into her world. She sat on the floor, barefoot. Her hair was dark and tousled, and the only thing she wore was a tattered top and a flimsy loincloth. Around her neck was a snake whose tongue flapped in and out. She had spotted me by this point, and when I looked her in the eyes, she snarled. She was everything I hoped for and more in a Wild Woman. Since I felt fairly protected by the glass, I took another minute to take in her surroundings, the cruel pen into which she had been thrown when she was pulled from the jungle just weeks ago. There were leaves and vines and even more snakes. Big ones, little ones, some coiled, some stretched out. But none of them was moving. I pressed my nose against the glass to confirm my suspicions. All of them were completely fake.

My dad met me at the bottom of the stairs. "How was it, pal?" I shook my head, having finally put the pieces together. "She wasn't real." He put his arm around me, and we headed for the giant carpet slide. I was too young to know the word "disillusionment," but I had just experienced it for the first time. It's safe to say that Tiger Woods has never been compared to a trashy woman in a loincloth, but after what I witnessed over the last six days, I feel similarly duped.

Periscope Down

Rehab

April 15–June 11, 2008

When I arrive home from Augusta on Monday, I have no desire to visit tigerwoods.com to see how he has spun the defeat. No need to restock my supply of Tigerade. Might as well delete the Sunday coverage off TiVo. My irrational behavior lasts just over twenty-four hours. Before dinner on Tuesday I receive an e-mail with some breaking news. There is no burying the lead: "Woods Has Knee Surgery, Will Miss a Month."

Tiger's first surgery on his left knee was in 1994, while he was still at Stanford. A benign tumor was discovered and removed. Eight years later, in December 2002, doctors revisited the knee to drain a cyst that was found on the surface of his anterior cruciate ligament (ACL), the main ligament that connects the femur to the tibia. He was out for two months. After pain returned in his knee last summer, the same doctor who performed the '02 procedure went back in, discovered damaged meniscus cartilage, and repaired it.

Meniscus cartilage is the spongy tissue attached to the inside of the knee joint and acts as a shock absorber between the two bones. When it's torn, it means the bone is now rubbing against bone, which is as painful as it sounds. Once repaired, the tissue remains swollen and takes a month or two to shrink to its normal size and allow the joint to flex and accept the full weight of the body without discomfort.

Within a minute I'm back to tigerwoods.com to confirm that this is not a joke. From there I salvage Sunday's final round from our Recently Deleted folder on TiVo. Hillary pops her head out of the kitchen.

"What are you watching?"

"The Masters." Unlike me with my dad back in 1986, she does not join me in front of the television. She groans and returns to the laundry.

I'm looking for evidence. I'm not convinced that Tiger had to do this now. It seems more likely that once he had blown the Grand Slam, he decided to go under the knife and try again next year. And if so, what a jerk. That would far more disappointing than the Wild Woman. That would be as if I had bought two tickets for the Wild Woman, climbed up the stairs, and found Margaret Thatcher drinking tea. I grow angrier until Tiger reaches the 4th hole. Then I see it. After hitting his bunker shot, the cameras cut to him stepping out of the trap. He plants his left leg and tries to climb out. He can't do it. He stops, pulls his left leg back, and steps out with his right instead, using his sand wedge to support himself. David Feherty notices it and says that Tiger looks "weary."

He wasn't weary. He was injured.

Suddenly I'm the detective at the end of *The Usual Suspects* who starts piecing all the clues together long after Kevin Spacey has limped out of the precinct. I remember the shots that Tiger seemed to like, but landed short. I flash to the pitches on 2 and 3 that Tiger couldn't put any closer than twenty feet. I think about the drives at the 18th on Friday and Saturday that he wanted to cut and ended up flaring into the pine straw. And most obvious to me now is the fact that he played only nine holes on Tuesday and no holes on Wednesday.

He wasn't playing like Tiger Woods because he *wasn't* Tiger Woods. He was Lance Armstrong with a flat. He was Michael Jordan with a baseball glove.

A banged-up knee doesn't account for poor putting, but if the injury had affected just three full shots over the course of the week, that could be the difference. It had taken 72 holes to push me away and just one failed attempt to step out of a sand trap to bring me back. Shoot, we really are out of Tigerade.

Four weeks. A month wouldn't be enough time for Tiger to make it back for the Players Championship in early May. Fine. He hadn't won there since 2001 anyway. So that would put him on target for the next event he typically plays, the Memorial, six weeks out. What in the world do I do for six weeks?

The desire to follow Tiger had started with the idea of wanting to see what I could learn along the way. But the painful reality is that most of what Tiger has displayed aren't things anyone can just wake up and do. They aren't even things he could always do. In Tom Callahan's book *In Search of Tiger*, he tells a story about a Tour event Tiger played while still an amateur where he looked up and realized that he was hitting balls between Greg Norman and Zimbabwe's Nick Price, two of the game's top players at the time. He turned to his coach Butch Harmon and quietly asked, "How far away am I, Butchie? When will I be that good?"

There are few quick fixes. But with six weeks, I have a window. It's not much, but if Tiger is going to use that time to rehab and return to normal, maybe I should use it to *stop* being normal and finally try to improve.

42 DAYS UNTIL THE MEMORIAL ▪ Over the last ten years, I have transitioned from a scrappy-looking kid who ate anything he wanted without recourse into a man who continues to eat anything he wants but looks worse and worse every day. Three months of following Tiger up and down hills, and my health is comparable to that of a first-century shepherd. Cardiowise, I am pretty solid, but my body is wasting away on a diet consisting of stale granola bars and bottled water. Since I didn't like paying five bucks for a hot dog, most days on the course I would eat almost nothing; then, when Tiger was done, I'd stop and have one gigantic meal before going to bed. As it now stands, my face is tan and full but everything else is gaunt and pasty.

So, just two days after Tiger's surgery, I buy a used workout bench. It even comes with a bar and some weights. I demote my truck from the garage to the street and set up the bench in its place. I'm not using it today, though; I'm sore just from unloading it.

40 DAYS UNTIL THE MEMORIAL ▪ I've got to believe I have a little head start on Tiger. Tonight he is at Tiger

Jam XI, his foundation's annual fundraiser in Las Vegas. The pictures show him hobbling around on crutches. I, on the other hand, have just benchpressed *forty-five pounds*. Or at least that is what someone told me the empty bar weighs. I'm well aware of how pathetic that is. The maximum weight one can lift should not be the minimum weight possible.

37 DAYS UNTIL THE MEMORIAL ▪ Apparently I wasn't pushing myself enough with the forty-five-pound bar. Three days after I began, I am maxing out at 130 pounds. Most trainers would say that's too soon to see any results, but between sets I take off my shirt right as our fifty-year-old neighbor Sandy walks past our garage. She stops, then backs up to wave and say hello. Hey, if you've got it, flaunt it.

35 DAYS UNTIL THE MEMORIAL ▪ I play a round of golf with John Ziegler, talk radio host and "Pastor of the First Church of Tiger Woods." The house of worship is his Web site, tigerwoodsisgod.com, where Ziegler chronicles everything Tiger does that can be interpreted as divine. The premise makes me laugh and I assume the whole thing is a joke, but after meeting Ziegler, I'm not so sure. "If it wasn't for Tiger Woods, I probably wouldn't be here," he says. He didn't mean playing golf with me, he meant alive. After a rocky 1995 in which he broke up with his girlfriend, lost his job and then his mom, it was his interest in seeing what the nineteen-year-old defending U.S. Amateur champ would do that kept him from taking his own life.

As a professional talker, Ziegler happily fills the void caused by my uncomfortable silence. And, eventually, he admits that he's an agnostic who is having a little fun with the idea that Tiger is God. It doesn't change the fact that his best reason for living was to watch Tiger. "What are you going to do when he retires?" I ask him. "What will you have to fall back on?" I don't know if it's a question that Ziegler has considered, but his response is distressing. "Nothing," he says. Maybe I'm wrong, but I don't think that keeping John Ziegler alive is a pressure that even Tiger Woods wants to bear.

30 DAYS UNTIL THE MEMORIAL ▪ Even though I taped my Golf Channel interview back in March, it is airing for the first time only tonight. With Tiger having been out of action for more than two weeks now, I assume some producer went into the Tiger Vault and I was all that was left. The piece actually turned out pretty well, but I am aware as I watch it that I look chunky.

I keep this to myself and then receive an e-mail from someone I met at Doral who says, "Man, you looked fat!" I was going to skip a day with the weights, but feel compelled to return to the garage.

28 DAYS UNTIL THE MEMORIAL ▪ Tiger has his two-week checkup today and reports to GolfDigest.com that he is "right on schedule" to play again in four to six weeks but gives no further details. It convicts me of the fact that I have set no specific goal as to what I'm trying to achieve during my "rehab." I set two goals. (1) To bench press my body weight (160 pounds) before I leave for the Memorial in Ohio. For some reason, lifting one's own weight is the accepted measurement of masculinity, but I will have to push myself a little more if I am to have any chance at reaching it. (2) To play golf and break 80 before Tiger's return. I used to do this about half the time I played. But I look up my handicap and see that I haven't shot in the 70s in almost a year.

26 DAYS UNTIL THE MEMORIAL ▪ Having goals is definitely making a difference. I am consistently working out every other day, plus I have been to the driving range three days in a row. I don't think this was the "new Bob" my wife was envisioning when I told her she was going to see some real changes over the next six weeks.

I decide to play golf with my dad, believing my daily practice sessions have finally revealed what is wrong with my swing. I shoot a 39 on the front to confirm everything I have been working on and a 49 on the back to make me question all I've ever known.

22 DAYS UNTIL THE MEMORIAL ▪ With my own analysis worthless, it is time to call Keith. Keith is the pro who gave me the last golf lesson I paid for, three years ago. He fixed my swing then, and now I'm back. I ask him whether he wants me to tell him what I think I'm doing wrong. "Nope." He just wants to watch, like Hank Haney. I start to hit some balls, and he quickly says, "Oh yeah . . . uh-huh." Within five minutes, he has unraveled everything, showing me that I am burying my right elbow in my side on the way down, essentially "getting stuck" with every shot. I can get away with it on my short clubs, but it makes my long irons and driver impossible to start on line.

"That's Tiger's old swing problem."

"Yep," he answers. In my efforts to get better, the only thing I have successfully achieved is the one flaw Tiger has gotten rid of.

20 DAYS UNTIL THE MEMORIAL ▪ It has been more than three weeks since Tiger's operation, and there are no new updates out of Isleworth. I feel desperate to fill the void, so I make a short trip to Stanford University. Outside the varsity golf office is a long wall covered with the plaques of every All-American golfer in Stanford's history. I don't think it's a coincidence that the two hanging directly over the office door belong to Eldrick "Tiger" Woods.

I pop my head in, and one of the assistants is watching the Players Championship on a giant flat-screen TV. The walls are coated with photos, flags, and scorecards. The biggest thing of all is a three-by-four-foot framed photo of Tiger, circa 1995. He is wearing a red Stanford hat, a red Stanford shirt, and shorts. He's squatting down to read a putt, and I notice that the elastic on his socks is shot, making them hang loose around his ankles. In two years, that kid with crummy socks would be the most sought after man in sports. The plaque beneath the picture provides the real evidence of his early greatness:

NCAA Individual Champion—1996
Jack Nicklaus National Player of the Year—1996
1st Team All-American—1995, 1996
Pac-10 Champion—1996

Pac-10 Player of the Year—1995, 1996
71.1 Stroke Average
10 Tournament Victories
22 Top-tens in 27 Tournaments

Ten wins in 27 events. That's a 37 percent winning percentage as only a freshman and sophomore. It makes me wish he had stayed in school, just to see how much higher he could have pushed that number before graduation.

Inspired by Tiger's record and using the swing fix that Keith taught me yesterday, I head out for eighteen holes on the Stanford Golf Course. By number 6, I have already ruined my chances of breaking 80. Late in the back nine, I have to look at my scorecard to make sure I will actually break 100. I shoot a 94. At least I hear some Tiger stories. I'm paired with a local contractor, a Stanford professor of ancient religion, and the professor's forty-year-old son, Andrew. Andrew makes sure that I've heard the tale that has become part of the Tiger/Stanford lore. It was the middle of the night during a torrential downpour, and the football team was returning from an away game. As the bus drove by the driving range, a player noticed that the lights were on and told the driver to pull over. A few of them hopped out and found Tiger, soaking wet, pounding balls into the distance. Knowing him from the gym, they called out, "Tiger! What the heck are you doing?" Tiger looked up and said, "Working on my rain game."

There have been no Tiger sightings at Stanford of late, but the assistant coach tells me that earlier in the year when the team traveled to Florida for a tournament, Tiger invited everyone over to his house in Isleworth for a BBQ. A college dropout flipping burgers is usually a cautionary tale. For the Stanford golf team, it's their most powerful recruiting tool.

17 DAYS UNTIL THE MEMORIAL ▪ Tiger appears via satellite at a press conference for the BMW Championship, an event that isn't played until September. When asked for an update on his rehab, he says he is still only chipping and putting and "just trying to get the leg organized." By saying "the leg" and not "my leg," it's as if he refuses to personally associate with his own body part until it's performing up to his standards.

12 DAYS UNTIL THE MEMORIAL ▪ Since I started trying to salvage my golf game a month ago, I have tried to emulate Tiger's work ethic and willingness to change. The results have not been encouraging. Since the Masters I have played four rounds of golf, and my scores in chronological order have been 83, 85, 88, 94.

Today my buddy Paul invites me out to Encino Municipal for a round. I start off by trying one last time to force my elbow in front of my body like Keith had instructed. After four holes, I'm already 3 over par.

While the other guys in the group tee off on the 5th, I move off to the side and thinking about Captain Jay Brunza. Brunza was the Navy psychologist Earl Woods brought home to meet Tiger at age thirteen. The first night, he taught Tiger a few mind tricks. When they went out the next day to play, Tiger birdied five of his first seven holes. The legend only becomes nuttier. In Tim Rosaforte's 1997 book *Tiger Woods: The Makings of a Champion*, Rosaforte says Brunza could soon hypnotize Tiger in less than a minute and that Tiger would stick out his arm and have Earl hang on it without being able to bend it. Tiger had Brunza caddy for him during the 1991 U.S. Junior Amateur, and together they won five straight USGA titles between 1991 and 1995. Then, just as Tiger left the hands-on Butch, he moved on from Brunza, having acquired all the tools he needed.

I'm not ready to be hypnotized or ask my friend Paul to hang on my arm, but it's becoming clear that if my "getting stuck" on the downswing were just a physical correction, I'd be seeing some progress at least. Even when Tiger was failing to win during 2003–2004, he always said "I'm close" and "It's getting better." I'm not getting better. I'm *mentally* stuck, too.

For the first time in years, I decide to forget about my score and just enjoy the round no matter where I hit it. Something basic that I had lost over the years is that golf, after all, is a game. And why play a game if it's not any fun? When I putt out on 18, I have no idea what I shot. As we walk back to the parking lot, Paul finishes adding up our scores.

"Seventy-eight?" he says.

"What? Are you sure?"

"Yeah." Turns out I played the last fourteen holes just 3 over par. "Nice round," Paul says.

"Wow. Thanks. That was fun." For once, I wasn't lying.

6 DAYS UNTIL THE MEMORIAL ▪ The high of breaking 80 carries me through the final stretch of Tiger's rehab. But there is still one goal left. Today is my big workout. The day I go for that magic number: 160 pounds. I do my first set at 125, then my second at 150, then add the final five pounds on either side. I look at the weights, now using almost everything that came with the bench, and decide I shouldn't be doing this without adult supervision.

Hillary is busy blending baby food. When I ask her if she can spot me, she grimaces and says, "I'm scared," as if she's the one who will be lifting the barbell. I tell her she will have to do something only if I can't, which won't happen.

I lie down on the bench and start to take deep breaths. I have no idea if this helps, but the magician David Blaine did it a lot before he held his breath for seventeen minutes in front of Oprah a few weeks ago, so it must be good for something. I lift the bar off the stand and feel its weight on my hands. I refuse to make eye contact with my wife, since I'm sure her look won't be one brimming with confidence. I drop the bar slowly to my chest, inhaling one last time, then push. To my surprise, it pops up rather easily. I did it! With a little discipline, a goal that was completely unrealistic only five weeks ago is one I have actually achieved. And I've still got a week to spare.

Then, of course, I get greedy. Rather than move the bar to the stand and accept the accolades, I drop it a second time down to my chest. This time it doesn't pop up so easily. Thirty percent of the way up, my muscles revolt. Hillary and I probably should have discussed a signal in case I'm in trouble. Hoping not to scare her, I say as calmly as I can, "Help." She reaches down and pulls up, and together we plop the bar back on the stand.

It's rare in our marriage that I am able to do anything that classifies as particularly macho, but this certainly is. Hillary congratulates me, gives me a kiss, then adds, "Don't ever make me do that again." In the history of human accomplishments, almost everything is more heroic than breaking 80 or lifting 160 pounds. But for me, it's a great start.

Three hours later, I find out that Tiger has decided to skip the Memorial. Which means that after eight weeks off, his first event back will be the hardest tournament of the year: the U.S. Open, June 12 at Torrey Pines.

The Man

The 108th U.S. Open

Torrey Pines Golf Course
La Jolla, California
June 12–16, 2008

When the United States Golf Association staged its first Open in 1895, it was only 36 holes. Horace Rawlins, an Englishman and one of only eleven men in the contest, shot a 91 and an 82. And won. From its beginning, it was the most difficult test in golf.

It will be no different for me. The Open is a golf fan's ultimate challenge. Whereas the Masters limits the number of badges to create an intimate experience among the patrons and the players, the USGA creates a different kind of intimacy by cramming in as many people as possible. Those numbers are sure to swell because of Tiger's return. Plus, the sadists at the USGA have decided to pair him with world number two, Phil Mickelson, and number three, Adam Scott, for Thursday and Friday. The predicted attendance is around 50,000 fans per day. For me to follow this group will be the equivalent of trying to watch a Major League Baseball game where, every half inning, the players and all the fans in the stadium migrate to a different field.

But I've done my homework. I pulled out my notes and the overhead map from the Buick Invitational and have refamiliarized myself with the course. I know where traffic will bunch. I know corners to flat-out avoid. And I know where I will have no choice but to sprint.

One part of this trip that is different than any other is that for the first time this year, I have brought the entire family with me. After two months at home, I didn't want to leave them again. They're not coming to the actual tournament, of course. If either of my kids were to scream in Tiger's backswing and cost him a major, I would feel such guilt that the four of us would move to Iceland and only return after Tiger surpasses Nicklaus's eighteen-major mark. Yesterday the four of us piled into the Camry and drove south. Unfortunately, after a half hour, I realized I had forgotten my periscope, so we drove home again. Going to the U.S. Open without it is like going off to slay Dracula without garlic and a wooden stake.

The U.S. Open is the only major that Tiger hasn't won since he overhauled his swing over the 2003–2004 seasons. But it's unfair to say he has struggled. In 2005 and 2007, he finished second. Last year at Oakmont, he had a curving downhill birdie putt on 18 to tie Angel Cabrera, a cigarette-puffing Argentinean, but couldn't pull off the miracle. In '05 at Pinehurst, he finished two shots behind Michael Campbell, a New Zealand–born player who spent the final round running to and from port-o-potties, where he would calm himself by privately doing eye exercises. As much as that seems like a foolproof formula for long-term success, Campbell hasn't won a tournament since.

In between those two runner-up finishes came the 2006 U.S. Open, which was the last time Tiger chose not to play between the Masters and the U.S. Open. His dad, Earl, had died in early May of that year after a long bout with prostate cancer, and Tiger was so distraught that he couldn't bring himself to touch a club. It was understandable.

When Tiger was only six months old, Earl dragged his high chair out to the garage, where Earl was busy hitting balls into a net, trying to make sense of a game he himself had only started playing a year before. After a few shots, he looked up and saw that his baby son was entranced. As Tiger's passion for the game grew, Earl supported him, found the best local teachers, and taught him the importance of practice and hard work. "This game doesn't owe you anything," he told him. And when Tiger's interest waned as a teenager, Earl didn't fight it. He told him to go hang out with his friends. After a few days of video games, Tiger always returned to the sport he loved. As he began to dominate as an amateur and a pro, it was Earl's voice that Tiger heard, sometimes literally, encouraging him and reminding him of the lessons he'd been taught over the last thirty years.

After a month of mourning, Tiger finally did pick up a club and started to prepare for the 2006 Open at Winged Foot. When he showed up a few weeks later, he claimed he was ready. After shooting back-to-back 76s to miss his only professional cut in a major, he admitted that, indeed, he was not.

Tiger claims he is good to go this week and I believe him, mostly because I'm desperate to believe it's true. Over the last two months, watching tournaments without Tiger was thoroughly unsatisfying. Was Sergio Garcia's 5-under win at the Players Championship impressive? Beats me. If Tiger had been there and finished 10 under, then no. By being the best ever, he's also a gauge that tells every other player just how good they really are.

FIRST ROUND

I felt it was only appropriate to start the U.S. Open at Torrey Pines the same way I had ended the Buick Invitational at Torrey Pines—with Nelson, the periscope-loving father of four whom I met on the first hole back in January. He didn't need much convincing to slip away from his work as a financial planner and relive our past glory. Last time we teamed up, Tiger shot a final-round 71, his highest score of the week. But five months later, with the fairways harder and the greens faster, a 71 at Torrey Pines would be pretty good.

Early Thursday morning, as the seaside dew still blankets the course, I notice the most glaring change of all. The rough just inside the ropes is so long it actually has stalks growing on the ends of it. I didn't even know that grass had stalks. And when I put my foot out and try to drag it through the mixture of Kikuyu, rye, and poa annua grass, I can't do it. It's too thick. This is no dumpy municipal track anymore. It's a legitimate test of championship golf.

6:54 AM ▪ I walk to the brick-walled putting green, and, for the first time since the 18th hole at Augusta, have found him. Blue shirt, gray slacks, white swoosh, no crutches. It's the real Tiger. Two months hasn't changed his routine. He's orbiting the putting green with three balls while Hank Haney and Stevie stand off to the side. Everything is as I hoped it would be—completely normal.

7:06 AM ▪ His speed dialed in, Tiger picks up the two balls and makes for the range. For Open week, the traditional Torrey Pines driving range has been overrun by hospitality tents and the player parking lot. It was a low-rent range anyway, the net around it attached to weathered telephone poles. An expansive, three-tiered practice area has been created by mowing down all the grass on the 9th and 10th holes of what was Torrey Pines North.

If it weren't for Torrey Pines North, the USGA might never have entertained the idea of bringing the Open to Southern California for the first time in sixty years. Besides the range, the press tent is way down on top of number 2. Another set of corporate huts covers number 4. And somewhere beneath the concession stands and the 40,000-square-foot merchandise tent is the dead fairway on the North's 1st hole.

With Tiger on the move, half of the crowd begins running. I'm impressed. These aren't the lightweights I assumed they'd be. Some of them may be faster than I, but here's where my preparation will reap some rewards. As the other fans run to the near side of the range, I know from some advance scouting that so far this week Tiger has hit balls only from the far left side of the range. And he is undoubtedly a creature of habit. So as the lines build up for the grandstand closest to Tiger, I walk to the far one and easily find a seat. Tiger bypasses the first set of bleachers, and the crowds react with a disappointed "Ahhhhhh . . ." The second set of bleachers cheers, "Yaaay!" but I already know their fate. Tiger keeps walking. "Ahhh . . ." He arrives in front of me, and we all applaud his wise choice.

I won't feel truly relaxed until I see his first full swing. He finishes with his wedges and grabs what looks like a 9-iron. As Haney stands behind with arms crossed and Stevie polishes clubs that already look impeccable, Tiger hits a flawless, high draw that travels 150 yards and settles within ten feet of the flag. Perfect.

7:58 AM ▪ Nelson and I have paired up directly behind the first tee, our periscopes already rising above the masses. We have no choice. The crowd around us is twenty deep and growing. To the right of the tee box is a full grandstand, and gathering in front is a formless pack of forty sportswriters. Lined up on both sides down the fairway are fifty photographers, their faces already hidden behind telephoto lenses.

Phil Mickelson arrives first, wearing a black collarless shirt and gray slacks, acknowledging his hometown fans with his favorite gesture, the nod. In this regard, Phil truly is the opposite of Tiger, wooing the crowd with his demeanor first and game second. I followed Phil for a round of the L.A. Open during a Tiger off-week back in February, just to compare the two experiences. After hitting a poor shot to the back fringe, Phil arrived and nodded his appreciation to all of us for the warm welcome. What made the whole thing strange was that not a single person had applauded the shot or his arrival. For better or worse, you don't need to work hard for Phil's love. It comes whether you want it or not.

8:05 AM ▪ Adam's off first, then Phil, and finally Tiger. The driver is the only club he wasn't hitting well on the range. He had hooked a few and then tried to hit some low ones, which he missed right. Haney never said a thing. Twenty minutes before the U.S. Open is not the time to be offering swing tips. But maybe he should have said something. Tiger's drive on the 452-yard par 4 is another hook, clearing the left trap and disappearing into the deep rough. Nelson and I turn to leave, but we can't. Since we had arrived on the 1st tee, another twenty rows of people had packed in behind us. I tell Nelson to head to the right, and we force our way through the jam and down the fairway.

8:15 AM ▪ Tiger hasn't made anything worse than a bogey all season. And the last time he made a double bogey at Torrey Pines South was six and a half *years* ago. So I'm a little numb as we walk to number 2 with Tiger starting his "comeback" with a 6. The only thing that was competent was the pitch out from the rough. Everything else was poor. The drive, obviously. The 75-yard wedge that flew the green. The pitch shot back to the hole that ran eight feet by. The final blow was the bogey putt that didn't even touch the lip.

I start to feel the warm pull of negative thoughts. *He's not ready. He's going to embarrass himself.* Somehow Tiger finds a way to be positive about things without sounding as if he's been programmed by a sports psychologist. When he lost the year's first major in April, he said, "I got three more." When he was 7 back after two rounds at Bay Hill, did he consider himself in striking distance? "Oh, yeah." And when his winning streak ended after the CA Championship, "You've just got to get ready for the next one." So what in the world is he thinking right now?

9:01 AM ▪ He makes his first post-op birdie at the cliff-hugging 4th, the same spot he made his first birdie of 2008 back in January. And why not? It's only a 488-yard tight par 4 with death all down the left side. He's back to 1 over.

"What's your game plan?" Nelson immediately asks me after Tiger taps in from two feet. I may have made a mistake by telling him that he was paired with the most savvy fan at Torrey Pines today. It's the equivalent of announcing that the Grand Slam is easily within reason. I could think it, but I probably shouldn't have said it. I tell him to head to the hillside behind the 5th green. From there we will be ahead of the ten thousand fans who have congregated at this corner of the course, and we can zoom up the hill to the 6th ahead of them all.

When Tiger misses his birdie effort from the fringe on number 5, I turn to go and see that the marshals have already raised the ropes to create a passageway for the players. We've missed our chance, and the mob catches up, pressing us against the rope.

First through the chute come the caddies. Then the players. Next comes Officer Freymueller, the giant cop who took a stab at color commentary while doing crowd control at the Buick. I think he has grown another couple of inches since January. His head darts from side to side, looking for someone to Taser. After the cops come the USGA officials. Then the marshals. Then the photographers and TV crew. In all, the procession must number at least a hundred. Back at the CA Championship, Calypso Dave had dubbed them "da vultures" because of their tendency to stand right between he and Tiger and take away his perfect view.

Last are the sportswriters, led by Luau Larry, his calves resembling a pair of yams after six straight months in the sun. The writers receive the bulk of the fan's abuse since they slowly pull up the rear and are single-handedly keeping us from getting to the next hole. It also doesn't help that they look the least intimidating. Fans pepper them with sarcasm—"Hey, no rush!"—and honesty—"You're kidding, right?" The writers do seem as if they're at a class reunion more than at a major championship. They laugh and chat with friends they haven't seen in months, completely indifferent to the fact that thousands of us are standing two feet away, thinking terrible thoughts about each and every one of them.

By the time the ropes come down, even mild-mannered Nelson is cracking. We start to walk up the hill, and a volunteer tells us that because of all the people, they have blocked off the route and the only way to get to number 6 is by walking all the way down number 2 and back. "That's a real good idea," Nelson says, shaking his head. "It *is* a real good idea," the marshal responds aggressively. The U.S. Open is not where I want to take part in my first real fistfight, and we're already falling behind Tiger, so I take off running down number 2, and Nelson follows.

10:10 AM ▪ Tiger continues to right the ship from his opening double with a five-foot birdie on the 8th and arrives at the 9th tee again even par. By getting back to where he started, he has passed Phil, who has slipped to 3 over. It's too early to look at the leaderboard, but I do anyway. The leader is 3 under, a player named Justin Hicks who has made a grand total of $8,464 this year. A player like Hicks is what makes the U.S. Open special. Any golfer with a handicap near scratch can pay the $150 entry fee and try to qualify. A fan next to me has a smuggled BlackBerry and is looking at the players' scorecards. I check out Hicks's opening nine. He's had six birdies and three bogeys. The U.S. Open is supposed to be about pars, and he hasn't made one yet.

11:45 AM ▪ Five holes later, Tiger is back in contention. He birdied the 9th after bouncing a ball off a spectator

and has made a bunch of clutch par saves to settle in at
1 under. His game is what I should have expected after
a layoff where he couldn't hit balls for a month. His full
swing shots are a little wild, but his putting appears as
strong as it was at the beginning of the year.

After Tiger tees off on the 14th, Nelson and I jog
down the right side. The closer we get to the clubhouse,
the more suffocating the crowds become. The marshals see the wave of people coming behind us, and,
just as they did between 5 and 6, they hold up a rope
and tell us we can't keep going down 14. It's ridiculous. When I mapped out my strategy, it was based on
how they had directed traffic at the Buick. I never considered that the USGA would simply not allow people
to follow the marquee pairing that *they* created in the
first place. Even the Masters wouldn't try something
like this. "It's an infringement on our basic rights as
sports fans!" I pronounce. Nelson has wisely tuned me
out and heads down 15.

12:06 PM ▪ We can't see what Tiger is doing back on
14, but it is taking forever and we haven't heard a single
roar. Nelson walks to the scoreboard operator on 15 and
asks what they know. "Double," they tell him flatly.
"A *double*?" Nelson says, loudly enough to depress the
thousand people gathered around the green. He turns
around and stomps back to me. Tiger was only 2 off

the lead before that. Now he has fallen 4 behind Hicks, who is done with a 68, and 3 behind Rocco Mediate, the cheery journeyman who has posted a 2-under round of 70.

12:51 PM ▪ Tiger doesn't make any more mistakes after the 14th and comes to the par-5 18th 1 over. He still hasn't made any bogeys. He has two doubles, three birdies, and a half-dozen world-class par saves, the biggest being a sixteen-footer on 15 that stopped the bleeding after the mysterious disaster on 14.

Nelson and I have secured a prime spot behind the last tee. The hole can stretch all the way out to 570 yards, but it's not playing that far today. The USGA had considered turning the par 5 into a long par 4 for the Open but decided to keep it as is—a birdie hole. It's nice of them, but after the first 17, I'm not sure how much the players can actually enjoy it. It reminds me of my kids' pediatrician, who thinks that slapping on a Big Bird Band-Aid will take away the pain of the shots he's just given them.

Tiger has driver in hand and looks down the left side of the fairway. He is thinking about playing a cut, away from the two bunkers on the left. When he hits it, we applaud as he launches it high with the intended fade into the middle of the fairway. But when I look at him,

I'm confused; from behind he's acting as though he hates it. Slumped shoulders, no twirling of the driver, no quick pickup of the tee. He is frozen, just standing in his follow-through position as the driver slowly slides through his hands, as if his body just had a power failure. It only takes me a second to diagnose what I'm seeing.

It's the knee.

Tiger turns and slowly walks back to Stevie. Most of the fans start to leave, but I can't pull myself away. I'm sure a lot of people see Tiger's expressionless face and confuse it with his typical on-course demeanor. No way. His normal look is intimidating and focused. This look is empty and—is it possible?—fragile. He doesn't limp, not even a little, but he wants to. It is taking every bit of strength to conceal it from Mickelson and Scott and the fifty different cameramen. Those ten awkward steps from the tee to his bag are the most revealing ten seconds of the entire season.

Nelson has seen his own son go through far worse than arthroscopic knee surgery but he recognizes the same look on Tiger's face.

"He's hurt," he says.

"I know."

Tiger has always moved in a cloud of impressive invincibility with which it is hard to identify. But here he is, right in front of us, looking broken. He's the furthest thing from omnipotent; he's a man with a lowercase *m*.

The crowds are so dense that they won't allow us to get much closer to the 18th green than a hundred yards without a fight. We watch from afar as Tiger summons the focus to clear the water of Devlin's Billabong in only two shots, but he still seems flattened by the painful drive. He leaves his uphill eagle putt fifteen feet short and misses the birdie. A three-putt for a par and a 1-over round of 72. Four shots back. Nelson and I were hoping for a day filled with fireworks, and we got only question marks.

SECOND ROUND

Today is June 13, my wife's birthday. For her, it couldn't have fallen on a worse day. When I tell her I have something planned, I lead with "Well, Tiger tees off around one o'clock . . ." Before I can finish, she says, "Oh, this already sounds so romantic." My plan is to take everyone to the beach in La Jolla for a few hours. But as Danny splashes around in the water, I keep finding myself preoccupied, thinking about yesterday.

The press didn't miss what I saw and asked Tiger about his drive on 18 when he finished his round. "It's a little sore," Tiger responded. I start to imagine the worst possible scenarios . . . that what I witnessed was the repaired cartilage coming loose, fluid pooling, infections, pus . . . Back in reality, the kite I'm supposed to be flying with my daughter crashes into the sand, nearly taking out a German family. I see the MetLife blimp heading north toward the course and check my watch. Both tell me it's time to go.

1:00 PM ▪ Tiger starts his day on the back nine, and the only painful thing I notice for the next three hours is the numbers on his scorecard. Four bogeys mixed in with one spectacular eagle, leaving him at 3 over par through twenty-seven holes.

If Tiger has been grimacing, I haven't seen it. But I'm not exactly standing in the front row either. The crowds are thicker today. Walking from the 11th tee to the green, there is no grass to be seen, just a rippling sea of heads, each of us going only as fast as the person in front of us.

My best looks have come from fans who are renting something called Championship Vision, a tiny hand-held TV feeding NBC's live coverage. But it's not quite live. The three-second tape delay has left many spectators confused, and long after Tiger's shots are already in the air, a fan can often be heard announcing "Okay, he's about to hit . . ."

Yesterday, Rocco Mediate was one of many players in the mix. Right now, his lead on Tiger is seven. No fan in good conscience can hate Rocco. At forty-five years old, the only thing intimidating about him is his name. A native of Greensburg, Pennsylvania, just southeast of Pittsburgh, he wears his pants happily pulled up high like *I Love Lucy*'s Fred Mertz, and his scruffy-faced smile disappears only when he turns his head to spit.

But Rocco's career has been littered with just as many highs as lows. After winning at Doral in 1991 and Greensboro in 1993, a ruptured disk and the surgery that followed knocked him out for most of the 1994 season. He clawed his way back to his former level, won the 1999 Phoenix Open and the 2000 Buick Open, then traveled the following week to the PGA Championship, where he sat in a chair, only to have it collapse. Rocco bonked his head on a railing and injured his shoulder, neck, and wrist, ultimately having to withdraw. His most recent run at a major came at the 2006 Masters, where he was in contention on Sunday when his back problems flared up again. He hit three balls into the water on Augusta's 12th and finished with a round of 80.

He's always had the game to contend in a major, he's just never had the luck.

4:05 PM ▪ Tiger has always had both. But that's not what the smashed guy next to me on number 1 thinks: "Tiger's *done!*" Besides the crowds being denser, they are also decidedly drunker, which I attribute to the fact that it's Friday. Most of these people don't have to work tomorrow. At this rate, this guy won't be able to walk tomorrow. But his assessment of Tiger's situation could be right. Seven shots is a lot of ground to make up, but still within the record Lou Graham set in 1975, when he came from 11 shots back after Friday to win his only U.S. Open.

If Tiger's knee is to blame, and if it's only getting worse, I don't really understand what he's doing here. He's right next to the clubhouse. There would be no shame in removing his cap, shaking hands with Mickelson and Scott, and slipping away. He's scheduled to play the Buick Open in two weeks and the British Open the week after that. To risk making his knee worse and then missing those events just so he can finish in a meaningless tie for 30th here is baffling.

But his hat stays on. He tees up the ball and promptly pushes it way right, over the bunkers and down near the cart path. The crowds have already swarmed the ball, so I raise my periscope as high as it goes and watch from afar. Turns out he's not near the path; he's actually on it, or at least his feet are. Flanking him on all three sides are beer-guzzling spectators. It looks as if he's hitting the shot out of a sports bar.

He takes his swing, and the metal cleats under his left foot slip. He immediately grits his teeth in agony. *This is stupid*, I think. But as usual, he hasn't asked my opinion. He's just watching the shot. The ball clears the greenside bunker and lands hole high, fifteen feet right of the pin. The crowd cheers; Tiger shakes off the pain and starts walking. He makes the birdie putt as Rocco bogeys the 10th. Tiger is back within 5 and never once looks at the clubhouse.

4:23 PM ▪ I would have thought that the pain would make him take a more gentle approach to the course. Instead, he is now trying to overpower it. On the short par-4 2nd, he booms a drive 350 yards, then rams a twenty-five-foot putt into the cup. Stevie saddles over to him and gives him a frat boy, congratulatory shove. The push nearly knocks Tiger over, and he hops away on his right foot before reburying the injury. "What are you doing?!" he says. Despite Stevie's best efforts, Tiger is finding his rhythm. It's his first back-to-back birdies since the Tavistock Cup.

5:07 PM ▪ After a par on the par-3 3rd, Tiger birdies the 4th hole for the second straight day, this one a

twenty-foot putt with the Pacific making a blue backdrop behind his right-armed fist pump. He's still not
done. On the 5th hole he makes *another* birdie. Phil
pours one in on top of him, which the crowd loves, but
there's no question about the story of the day. Tiger's
front-nine scorecard now reads 3-3-3-3-3. He's played
his opening five holes in 4 under par. I pass yet another
drunk guy. "That's *sick*," he says, summing up Tiger's
play. The stretch has taken him from 3 over to 1 under
in just over an hour.

5:59 PM ▪ After Tiger pars 5 and 6, I run down the
downhill, dogleg-right par-4 7th and find a spot fifty
yards up from the green. Tiger has put yet another
approach shot within birdie range, fifteen feet left of
the back-right pin. The combination of summer heat,
heavy drinking, and Tiger's rediscovered game leads
the tubby fan next to me to threaten, "If Tiger makes
this, I might have to run across the hole naked." Considering the six empty beer cups nested in his hand,
I think he's serious.

As Tiger takes his last practice stroke, I've never had
a stranger motivation to want a putt to fall. The chance
to see Officer Freymueller figure out how to arrest a fat
naked man without actually touching him would be the
perfect addition to an amazing nine holes. One person

is definitely rooting *against* Tiger: the man sitting at waist level in front of the potential streaker, who says out loud as Tiger draws back his putter: *"Please* don't make this putt . . ."* Tiger misreads it, and we groan in disappointment. The drunk guy takes another sip and stumbles away, adding, "You guys are soooo lucky."

6:29 PM ▪ After another par at the 8th, Tiger has a five-foot putt on the 9th hole for a final birdie and a closing-nine score of 30. 30. It would be his lowest nine holes in a U.S. Open and only a stroke off the nine-hole U.S. Open record of 29. Stevie has his bib off again, finally free from that burdensome piece of weightless fabric. He circles the putt with Tiger, making sure his boss doesn't miss something obvious, and then steps away as Tiger steadies himself over his ball. He knocks it in the dead center. Five under on his second nine and 2 under for the tournament, just 1 shot off the lead.

Tiger waits next to the green, then shakes hands with Phil Mickelson and Adam Scott, both of whom look like they've seen a ghost. *If we can't beat Tiger this week, when can we?* Before he started his run, Mickelson and Scott were within a stroke of him. Tomorrow they'll be teeing off three hours before he does.

THE BEST SWING IN GOLF ▪ Energized by Tiger's play, I head to the course early on Saturday to do all the various touristy things I haven't done yet. There's no Buick Clubhouse and the RV with the free skin screenings is nowhere to be found, but I do find a white tent called the U.S. Open Experience Presented by American Express. It's a terrible name, but inside is a giant glassed-in case containing what I thought was Iron Byron, the clunky metal machine that golf companies use to test the performance of new clubs. In fact, this is the hi-tech version that has long ago replaced Byron, and its name is even less catchy than the tent's. It's the Golf Laboratories Computer Controlled Robot.

I stand there for a long time just watching it swing back and through. With every swing, the rigid steel arm on the black metal base winds up and then unleashes, each time sending the ball into the same exact spot on the hanging target. The strangest job of the week goes to Justin, a guy in his early twenties who has two pockets full of Titleists. Every time the robot is done, he opens the door and places another one on a tee.

As Justin exits for the thousandth time, I ask him if this is the weirdest job he's ever had.

"I used to transfer bull sperm from place to place, so no." Balls are his thing, I guess.

Gene Parente, the CEO of Golf Laboratories, sits on a stool next to the robot, ready to answer all the questions golf nerds like me can think up. Turns out nearly every major clubmaker owns one of their robots, as well

as the USGA and the R&A. It can duplicate any golfer's specific swing conditions: ball speed, head speed,
launch angle, and spin rate. The advantage in this isn't
just for companies making clubs for average golfers.
Nike engineers can set up their robot to mimic Tiger's
swing so they can tailor clubs for him without asking
him to hit a single ball. The cost? $130,000.

Gene says the only way to improve the robot at this
point is to work on the biomechanics of it, essentially to
make it look more like a real person. "Why don't you
just put a hat on it?" I ask. Thankfully, he has a sense
of humor. Or at least he has found one after sitting on
that stool twelve hours a day since Tuesday. He admits
that he's not sure how much more patience he has and
already has his Sunday afternoon explanation ready:
"It's a robot. It hits golf balls. What more do you want
to know?"

THIRD ROUND

It's colder today and breezy, sweater weather for the
players. I refuse to change any of the clothes I wore
yesterday, just in case the reason Tiger shot a 30 on one
leg was that God was smitten by my teal shirt.

The other players around Tiger on the leaderboard
aren't the ones who make me particularly nervous. In

first by a shot is Stuart Appleby, the Aussie who started the year with five straight top tens, but hasn't done much since. Playing with Tiger is Robert Karlsson, a lanky Swede whom Tiger beat in the 2006 Ryder Cup. The only memorable thing about that match occurred on the 7th hole when Stevie dropped Tiger's 9-iron into a lake and couldn't get it back. The rest of the players with Tiger at 1 under include only one major winner, Davis Love III. But in the time since Love won his only major, the 1997 PGA Championship, Tiger has won twelve. Unless Tiger went break-dancing last night, I can only assume he will soon have his first lead of the week.

2:52 PM ▪ As he did Thursday, Tiger pulls his drive off the first. I'm down in the fairway when the ball bonks against a tree and settles just inside the gallery ropes, almost exactly where I tried to drag my foot through the high grass a few days ago. Tiger hacks his way out, and it runs through the fairway into the rough near the green. From here he plays a full-swing flop shot and catches too much of the ball, sending it long and back into the rough. After a terrible chip and a missed putt, he has once again made an opening-hole double bogey.

When he did that on Thursday, I walked away in a daze. Today I spontaneously start clapping and urging him on. I even yell, "That's all right, Tiger," like a soccer coach when the ball rolls through the klutzy kid's legs. Now I understand the difference between cheering and rooting. I thought they were the same thing, but they're not. For most of the year, I have been merely cheering for Tiger, wanting to see exciting things happen because I enjoy good golf and he is the surest bet to provide some. I was like someone at a monster truck rally, just celebrating the spectacle. How much you cheer is inherently connected to how entertained you feel. And when it's over, there's no emotional attachment to whatever you just witnessed. But after seeing the way an injured Tiger is willing himself not only to compete but actually contend, I've begun rooting for him.

Rooting goes deeper. It doesn't ebb and flow when good things or bad things happen. Wins and losses can't change its strength. It's constant and selfless, and when your guy is hurting, it hurts you, too.

To Tiger's ears, cheering and rooting all probably sound the same: one unending chorus of affirmation. Then again, when he is at his best, he may not even hear us at all.

3:35 PM ▪ On the 4th, Tiger's favorite birdie hole, he hits a 3-wood right and into the rough. The pin today is tucked on the back-left shelf, and even from way over here he'll have to carry the bunker to get to it. Tiger goes through his thoughts with Stevie. "I've got to hit it past that front edge to have any kind of angle." Stevie suggests an 8-iron. "Eight isn't enough. If I'm short, I have no shot." He takes a 7-iron, chokes down on it, and promptly hits it exactly where he was trying not to—short and left and into the trap. He makes a bogey to drop yet another shot.

4:02 PM ▪ Tiger pars the 5th, and I head down the 6th to check on the leaderboard to see the damage from Tiger's poor start. No one is playing well, but no one is playing as poorly as Tiger:

	Total	Day
Rocco Mediate	−2	0
Stuart Appleby	−1	+2
Davis Love III	−1	+1
D. J. Trahan	−1	+1
Lee Westwood	−1	0
Tiger Woods	+1	+3

5:40 PM ▪ After Tiger bogeys the 12th, Rocco's lead grows to 5 shots. I continue to clap and yell no matter what, but I'm exhausted.

The par-5 13th at Torrey Pines South is one of only two holes on the course with any legitimate elevation change. The first 400 yards play slightly downhill before the fairway completely drops away into a deep valley that collects any shots to the green that come up short. It's especially true today with the pin only five paces from the front edge.

I have gone ahead to the fairway and look back to see Tiger standing over his drive, still wearing the black sleeveless sweater he started with almost three hours ago. I'm starting to think he should have stuck with his same shirt from yesterday, too.

The tee is so far back, I never hear the sound when he hits the ball, but his now familiar body language says it's going right. I look into the air and I see it, high against the gray sky, *forty yards* right of the fairway. I take off running long before it lands. Since no one else sees it, I look like a crazy person being attacked by a swarm of invisible bees. The ball thuds on the yellow, trampled rough and rolls to within a few feet of a concession stand. I am almost there when an eleven-year-old kid throws me an elbow and boxes me out to claim the best spot.

As we stop, it creates a pileup behind us for all the fans who were running full speed without knowing where the ball was. For the next five seconds, I can hear people behind me colliding with one another. As one guy pulls up, he spills his beer all down the back of another fan. Gore-Tex has probably never been officially tested for its resistance to Budweiser, but I'm happy to report that it beaded right off the fan's back without his knowing.

5:53 PM ▪ From an iffy lie in the trampled rough, Tiger skies his 5-iron onto the back of 13 green. I "excuse me" and "pardon" my way into the middle of the wide hill that rises behind it. Tiger's ball had landed only a few feet from the front hole position, but released all the way to the back fringe, leaving him a sixty-foot monster putt. This is not even a simple lag. Theoretically, if he misjudges the speed, he could roll the putt not only past the hole, but also off the green and down the sixty-yard slope in front of the green. Like most putts, when he hits it, it's followed by the inevitable "Get in the hole!" screams. But this putt is so long that there is time for all sorts of screams: the generic "Tiger!," "Come on!," and "Do it!" My favorite is the nonsensical "Just . . . Yeah!"

The first clue that the putt has a chance comes from the grandstands. They are a source we can trust. These are fans who have been sitting in one spot all day. They have seen dozens of players come through, and they know this green better than anyone else. About twenty feet out, the most confident ones up there stand and start the slow-building "oohhhhHHH . . ." Everyone joins in, hoping for the impossible. Twelve feet out, the volume grows as the putt slows and swings to the left. *There's no way.* We keep yelling. The putt must be tracking, because Stevie is so mesmerized that he only now takes out the pin he's been tending. *There's no way!* Five feet out, the ball is still rolling and Stevie starts to pump his right fist in the air as if there is a real chance this putt could actually drop. It does. I close my eyes, lean my head back as far as I can, and release a primal scream, raising my arms and my periscope into the sky. Then I just start jumping. And jumping. And jumping. I look down as Tiger appears from the right side of my vantage point for the first time, doing what must be his third or fourth or tenth fist pump at this point. He looks as if he is screaming as loudly as I am, but there are no individual noises to be heard. It is just one sustained blast of complete and utter joy.

Supposedly, villagers three thousand miles across the Indian Ocean heard the blast from Krakatoa hours after it happened in 1883. If that's true, around ten o'clock tonight someone in Hawaii is going to look up from his poi and say, "What the heck was that?" The putt moves Tiger from 1 over par to 1 under and within three of Rocco, who just happens to be standing back in the fairway watching everything that just happened.

6:02 PM ▪ I'm hyperventilating, but I have to move. I take off running up the hill. As I pass 14 tee, I see the sad fallen faces of fans, the look of people who know they were so close to history and missed it. "Thank goodness for DVRs," one of them says to his friends, but it doesn't make them feel any better.

As I continue to run, the looks change from chagrin to confusion as people down 14 don't even know what happened. I feel like Paul Revere riding through town. "Tiger made eagle! Tiger made eagle!"

6:04 PM ▪ Down in the fairway, I reach the third type of fan: the rabid ones. These are the fans who have made peace with their loss but only by committing not to miss one more moment, no matter the cost. So when Tiger pushes his 3-wood right and into the crowd again, the rush to the ball is total chaos. I see husbands ditch their wives. Frat boys simply drop their beers and run. Two cops who have been put on advance crowd-control duties immediately dive into the scrum and start pushing people out of the way. A USGA official is next on the scene and plants one khaki-trousered leg on either side of Tiger's ball, shielding it from further threats.

Someone I can't even see barks an order: "Take ten steps back!" No one moves. As the fragile pocket starts to shrink again, a marshal (who, mind you, *paid* $150 to work here this week) gets nervous that the whole thing might collapse altogether and crawls into the space on all fours, reaches between the official's legs, and plants a tiny fluorescent orange flag next to the ball. Entire countries have been liberated with less fanfare than the frenzy around Tiger's missed drive.

6:50 PM ▪ By stringing together pars on 15 and 16, Tiger has climbed to within two of the leader, but the leader is no longer Rocco. Rocco has suffered a mini-collapse, playing those same two holes in 3 over par. The new leader is England's Lee Westwood, 2 under through 17. Of course it would be Westwood. He has spent his entire year as the entertained but uninvolved observer to Tiger's triumphs. It was Westwood who smirked at Tiger in the midst of the Sunday coup in Dubai. And it was Westwood who got a shrug in Tucson after Tiger dusted the desert with J. B. Holmes. Now it is Westwood standing in front of him.

The strangest stat in his career remains the fact that he has won thirteen majors and they have all come while holding the fifty-four-hole lead. Or the negative translation: he has never come from behind on Sunday to win a major. Tiger chalks it up as coincidence, but talking heads have called it the one flaw in an otherwise perfect record. As Tiger has done time and again, the only way to silence critics is to prove them wrong. As much as I'd love to witness it, I'd much rather see him make up two shots in these next two holes and head into Sunday with a piece of that lead.

6:55 PM ▪ Tiger's second shot into the 17th settles on a tongue of grass near the left bunker, playing to a pin that sits in the dead center of the green. I'm squished on the small hill across the green from the ball and can see the hole only through my periscope. But even then I'm looking through other periscopes. My periscope needs a periscope. The flag is limp. The wind that was around for most of the day is gone. Tiger settles into the shot, his right leg straight and his left leg bent as he stands awkwardly on the slope. He takes a final peek at the hole and then chops at the ball in the rough. It pops up and someone screams, "One time!!!!" I follow it like a cameraman through my scope as it bounces once and then disappears. *Wait. What?* I search for a split second, thinking I've just lost it. When the crowd erupts, I stop looking. He just chipped it in.

The putt at 13 had seven or eight seconds to crescendo. This time, the crowd goes from silent to thunderous instantly. I start spontaneously high-fiving the strangers around me who break out in chants of "Tiger! Tiger! Tiger!" He covers his face with his black Nike hat, then scratches his head—happily embarrassed at the way he just tripped up the leaderboard and closed within 1 shot of Westwood.

6:58 PM ▪ Tiger's knee hasn't been an issue for most of the round. But that quickly changed over the round's closing holes. On 15, Tiger toppled over after his drive and had to grab the ground to keep from falling. He hit a 3-wood off 17, but he couldn't hang with it and lost it right. Here at 18, he fights through the pain two more times, first off the tee and then with his 5-wood over the lake, leaving himself his third eagle putt in ten holes.

This one's easier than the bomb he dropped on 13. Forty feet and with less break. Stevie's bib is off, thank heavens, ridding himself of his polyester yoke. Karlsson has already tapped in for a birdie of his own and fled to the edge of the green, anxious to be outside Tiger's blast circle. Yes, a two-putt would give Tiger a share of the lead for the first time all week. Earlier in the year I thought the notion of *thinking birdie* was absurd. But now that bar seems low. No one is thinking birdie right now. We are all thinking eagle. It doesn't matter that he can barely stand up for the full length of his swing. Or that he has had only a few weeks of practice in the last two months. Over the last six holes, our Pavlovian response to seeing Tiger face something undoable is to believe it will be done. And this putt, like the putt at 13 and the chip at 17, is perfectly missable. So why shouldn't it go in too? No one waits twenty feet to start screaming. We are screaming the second the ball's last dimple separates from the face of his putter. It starts off softly, flowing down the green and sliding right. I can't see the hole from the right side of the green, just Tiger and the ball. He's watching it intently. Either he's not sure it's going in, or he's communicating with it telepathically. His gaze never changes and he never moves a step. Not even when it drops into the hole.

Ten minutes ago, Lee Westwood assumed he would have the Sunday lead all to himself. Now he doesn't even have it at all. For the 14th time, Tiger Woods will be starting the final day of a major championship in first place.

From behind the green at 18, I squeeze through the mob in time to catch Tiger disappearing inside the meshed-in grandstands. He travels up its internal staircase, underneath the still cheering fans who have no idea the object of their adoration is right underneath them. The stairs open to an overhead walkway fifteen feet above the ground. As Tiger walks across it, two fans on the ground literally fall to their knees and bow down in homage. They've completely missed the point. What makes every second of today impressive is that he's *not* a god.

He comes down on the other side and is about to walk right in front of me as he heads to sign his scorecard, a half smile on his face. I haven't attempted to speak to him since Dubai, where I was ignored. He's within a few feet now and moving fast. I don't know what to say, so I just stammer out, "Nice finish, buddy!" He looks down and keeps walking. It was lame, yes, but no regrets. And "buddy"? Man, have I come a long way.

UNDER THE BIG TOP ▪ Even after my awkward compliment, I still don't want to leave. Earlier in the week I bumped into a writer I knew who said he was walking to the media tent and asked if I wanted to join him. When I told him I didn't have credentials, he said, "What? Have you seen how big that place is? They give *anyone* credentials." No, not anyone. During Tiger's rehab, I contacted the Tour about any help they could give me and was told that media passes are reserved for people covering golf for news purposes, not for self-help purposes.

But with Tiger having just produced the most gripping closing six holes in major championship history, I don't care what my badge does or does not say. The main entrance to the media tent is blocked by two uniformed guards, but the back entrance is wide open. The loudest noise inside is the air-conditioning, which whirs as hundreds of reporters from Asia to Europe sit at laptops and try to figure out where the heck to begin. On the far side of the tent is the interview room. I pretend to scribble in my notebook as I pass a cop. The periscope hanging off my belt is a dead giveaway, but nobody stops me.

A camera crew is set up and standing on a riser behind the ten rows of chairs. "He's the greatest long putter I've ever seen," one of them says. The sun is sinking low outside, and when the side door of the interview room opens a few minutes later, it casts a long shadow of someone limping up the stairs. Tiger sticks his head in, not wanting to interrupt someone else's interview, but the floor is his.

Joining Tiger at the head table in a blazer and tie is the bespectacled Rand Jerris, the moderator and director of the USGA Museum. Tiger sits down to total silence. *Where is everyone?* Forget media bias; reporters should have carried Tiger on their shoulders all the way from the 18th green. The writers finally converge, most of them standing near the back while a few dozen take seats.

Tiger hits the highlights first, saying that on 13 he was only trying to put his second shot in the back bunker, but it got lucky and stayed on the back of the green. On 17, he hit the pitch too hard, and it got lucky and went in the hole. As for the knee? "If pain hits, pain hits. So be it. It's just pain." This is no twenty-first-century mind-set. We construct our whole lives around avoiding things that hurt or make us uncomfortable. Let's not fight through something that might make us stronger; let's just be happy now. And then when we're not, we're thoroughly confused.

It's getting dark now, and I know the kids are asleep, so I walk the mile and a half out the back gates of Torrey Pines to the taxi stand. Along the way, I pass the 13th green, where the Golf Channel's Frank Nobilo is trying to make Tiger's eagle putt. He gives it a few shots, then gives up. He can't even get it within seven feet of the hole.

FINAL ROUND

Late into the evening on Saturday, I had not totally abandoned the idea that this entire thing just might be rigged. Tiger's part in it was easy—he only had to pretend his leg was hurt, and a remote-controlled golf ball would do the rest. The NBC brass were obviously in on it, as was the USGA, which was setting up the course according to IMG's strict instructions, allowing for maximum drama. I even had an explanation for why the other hundred and fifty players were going along with it. They know that the more Tiger wins, the more people watch golf. The more people watch golf, the larger the overall purse money and endorsement deals. The thing that ultimately brought me back to reality was the fact that the ornery Colin Montgomerie had missed the cut. I couldn't imagine that he would have agreed to the deal unless he were guaranteed a top-20 finish.

12:31 PM ■ I'm standing beside the range with Gilbert, an off-duty marshal who for years played Torrey Pines every Sunday. At 3 a.m. he would put his bag in line at the starter window and go sleep in his car until six. We watch together as Tiger works through his irons. When he gets to his 5-wood, Gilbert asks, "What brand are those?" I pause before answering, in disbelief that he truly doesn't know the answer. "Nike," I say. "Nike makes metals?" Now he's just embarrassing himself. When Tiger's done with his 5-wood, Gilbert gets excited. "Here it comes!" He thinks Tiger is about to hit driver. "Three-wood," I say, trying to be nice. "Three-wood? With the monkey on it?" This is almost too much for me to handle. "It's a bird," I say. I should just let Gilbert be, but after a few more shots, curiosity compels me to ask:

"You watch much golf, Gilbert?" And then one final, amazing answer.

"A *lot*. If it's on, I'm watching."

1:30 PM ▪ On Saturday morning there were fourteen different players within four shots of the lead. Today there are only four: Lee Westwood (1 back), Rocco Mediate (2 back), Geoff Ogilvy and D. J. Trahan (each 4 back). With the extra breeze that has picked up today and the number of tough pin positions expected for the final round, it's hard to imagine anyone outside these four being able to put any pressure on Tiger.

I move down the 1st hole as the crowd back on the tee applauds Tiger's name. What I would give now for that 8-shot lead he had at the Buick Invitational. How I would love to spend my day picking up pinecones and sketching pictures of holes in my notebook. I don't want drama, I want an easy victory. It's the least I can ask for on Father's Day.

1:35 PM ▪ It is wishful thinking. The calm lasts a grand total of six seconds, the amount of time that Tiger's ball is in the air. As it comes down among us along the left side, chaos ensues. "Out of the tree!" a gritty female cop yells at a fan who's trying for a better view. A giggly girl in a push-up bra barrels past me with her boyfriend, saying "This is so exciting!" while giving him kisses. It's a disaster, actually. It takes Tiger three shots just to get inside the ropes. He doesn't find the fairway until his fourth. Five minutes later, he has made his third double bogey of the week on number 1. Tiger didn't have the lead until the 54th hole of the tournament. By the 55th hole, he has already lost it.

For the third time this week, the new leader is Rocco Mediate. Back on the 9th hole yesterday, a fan saw the leaderboard and said, "Rocco is going to be 72 over par tomorrow. I wouldn't consider him a factor at this point." I didn't peg Rocco for quite that bad a round, but based on his fragile back, I assumed his best golf of the week was behind him.

1:50 PM ▪ Tiger looked weaker on the range today than he did the rest of the week during warm-ups. Out of his thirteen drives, he hit only five of them on line and moved in slow motion after each one. My fear that he may not have the stamina of the past three days is confirmed on the 2nd, when, after hitting his drive long and right, he grabs his left knee. Yesterday he lasted fourteen holes before there were any real signs of pain. Today, he makes it through only one. We all try to root him on and he tries to walk but he stops again and bends all the way over at the waist, closing his eyes. The cheering abruptly stops. Some women even cover their mouths, fearing that that swing, as mighty as it was, may have been his last.

Tiger always cites how important it is for him to draw upon past experiences, believing there are almost no situations in which he can find himself that after twelve years on Tour he hasn't faced. He has never played through so much pain, but his dad did. When Tiger was a kid, he was supposed to play in a golf tournament with Earl when his dog accidentally bit most of the way through his dad's middle finger. Earl cleaned it out the best he could, wrapped a bandage around it, and continued to get ready to go to the course. "How are you going to play?" Tiger asked. "When the going gets tough, the tough get going," Earl answered. He played the whole round holding his middle finger off the club. And when the bandage became too bloody, Tiger would swap out the dressing for him so they could keep going.

Earl taught Tiger countless lessons from the driver's seat of a golf cart, but, today, none is as essential as that one. For the umpteenth time this week, Tiger straightens up, pushes off with his driver—and hobbles toward the fairway. He may lose, but he won't stop trying.

2:08 PM ▪ Tiger struggles through number 2 and follows his 6 at the first with a bogey to fall back to just even par and now 2 shots behind Rocco. I'm having my own less painful but equally debilitating issue: my periscope just broke. I noticed earlier in the week that the center metal tube had become loose from all the abuse it had taken. So yesterday morning I went to see my friend A.J., the mechanical engineer with top secret clearance, and asked him if he could fix it. He carried it into his garage like a zoologist holding a baby condor, at which point he took it apart and dropped one of its screws on the ground. We were never able to find it and he assured me that the device would work the same without it, but as I raise the extendable arm to watch Tiger gimp down number 3, the bracket that he promised wouldn't budge has completely fallen off. I jimmy it back together and start questioning our country's national security.

3:10 PM ▪ Tiger scratches out pars on 3 through 7 to stay at even par. Rocco has slipped back with Tiger, and now they're both behind Westwood, who's at 1 under.

There's nothing fun about today. Of course, there wasn't anything fun about yesterday either until the 13th.

Tiger lifts our spirits with a two-putt birdie on the 9th. He shares the lead for almost thirty whole seconds before Westwood birdies it as well and stays a shot in front. But Westwood falters at the 10th when he skulls a shot into the base of the grandstands, joining Tiger and Rocco at 1 under par. The other onetime contenders have all wilted, and so as Tiger and Westwood move to the 11th, the U.S. Open is down to a three-man race.

3:50 PM ▪ The par-3 11th is a hole Tiger has owned in 2008. He birdied it every round during the Buick, the most memorable being the birdie putt that was so long and complicated he had to read it in sections. The hole is in a similar spot today, on the front-left corner, 217 yards from the tee. I'm against the ropes when Tiger passes by, and I spur him on with an inane "Keep chugging!" He chugs, landing his shot fifteen feet past the hole and then sucking it back off the hill and down within five feet. Tiger goes to 2 under and, despite his nightmare start, once again has the lead all to himself.

He seems to have figured it out again. This has become the routine this week: start off with a disaster, make some adjustment, and carry on. Yesterday in the media room he explained that because his swing was so off, he had intentionally been "overshaping" shots during the round. He didn't feel confident hitting his normal little draws or fades, so instead he played what he referred to as "big hooks or big fades" to at least gain some sense of predictability. Tiger likes to say he's stubborn, but what he's showing this week is the willingness to adapt minute by minute.

4:10 PM ▪ He has an easy par on the week's hardest hole, number 12, and walks to the 13th tee holding a 1-- shot lead over Rocco and 2 over Westwood, who missed the fairway on the 12th and made bogey. Of all the changes to Torrey Pines since January, none is as startling to me as the optional tee box on the 13th hole. During the Buick, the par 5 played a friendly 541 yards. Since then, a patch of land that seems to dangle over the Pacific has been flattened and covered in grass, 614 yards from the center of the green. They used the front part of it on Friday, and Tiger made it in two with a 5-wood. He didn't think he could reach from the full distance, and today we'll find out. The tees are all the way back.

But I'm not going. It's only seventy yards past the normal tees but another eighty to the left. Trekking there and back would be like adding another hole to my day. When I did venture back there on Friday, only a few dozen people were there, and most of them hadn't made it anywhere else. It was like a golf fan outpost. I felt guilty for not bringing them provisions. As I walked up, they all nodded in my direction, as if to congratulate me on a safe journey. It was a shame that most people who come to the Open never make it there. The ocean sits below, and looking north across the deep canyon is the green at the faraway par-3 3rd. It's the prettiest spot on the whole course.

4:15 PM ▪ Instead I arrive early on the hillside behind the green, where fans have packed themselves in, hoping what Tiger does today will match the miracle of his sixty-foot eagle putt from yesterday. His drive from the back tee finds the left edge of the fairway, a perfect angle for the hole cut on the far right side of the green. While we wait for him to make the hike back to civilization, I discover that I am standing next to a Tiger hater.

"He has a lot to learn from Jack and Arnie," he's telling his friends. I insert myself into their conversation.

"Really. Like what?"

"Well, for one thing he doesn't wave enough." He doesn't *wave* enough? That is Tiger's big crime? I couldn't believe it. What sort of an insecure person is upset that he hasn't been waved to? This guy is a complete joke. It takes me a few seconds of rolling my eyes before I remember that that's pretty much how I felt for most of the last twelve years. What I had failed to appreciate during that time was the significance of Tiger's focus. I thought it was a pseudo act allowing him to be rude. In reality that's the only way he can perform at the level he does. A more gallery-friendly version of Tiger would, without a doubt, not be as dominating or effective at pulling off the unbelievable with such regularity. I'm willing to sacrifice a Miss America wave for two eagles in a six-hole span.

Tiger is so far away down 13 fairway that he has to be hitting his 3-wood. The moment the ball is airborne, he immediately hates it and slashes his club back through the grass. It starts left and turns left, vanishing over the far corner of the green and out of sight. It's the same spot where Westwood went just a minute earlier. Since we can't see it, we're not sure how to react. If the two of them missed a little left, they're in the rough. If they went even farther, there are only bushes, canyons, and penalty strokes. The photographers run en masse and disappear below.

A few minutes after Tiger arrives, a ball flies up from the mystery location and lands on the back of the green, thirty feet above the hole. Okay, but not great.

Off in the distance, I hear a roar. Tiger two-putts for par to hang on to his 1-shot lead.

The far-off roar was from the 14th green, where Rocco had made birdie to move to 2 under and into a tie with Tiger. But the standard-bearer for Tiger's group shows something worse. It says Tiger is only 1 under par, not 2. A photographer fills in the blanks. "In the hazard." Out of sight, Tiger had made a bogey and not a par. With only five holes left, his 1-shot cushion has just become a 1-shot deficit.

4:30 PM ▪ Thankfully, the 14th is a definite birdie hole, but only today. Mike Davis, the USGA's senior director of Rules and Competitions, has successfully convinced his bosses to let him do something a little unorthodox for a U.S. Open. He has moved the tees 170 yards closer to the hole and made it a reachable par 4. The switch had been rumored all week and finally happened today. At just 267 yards, it's the shortest par 4 at a U.S. Open since 1955.

It's a fabulous idea, forcing every player who walks up to that tee to think. There will be no automatic club pulling here today. With Tiger and Stevie talking through their options, I squish in closer to hear what they're saying. Tiger asks Stevie what he thinks about trying to get there with a wood. "I wouldn't," Stevie says. They go back and forth, and Stevie just keeps shaking his head. Stevie never says it, but if Tiger hits the same 3-wood that he just hit from the fairway on the last hole, he'll be in the canyon and with it will go any chance of victory.

Tiger takes an iron. There are scattered boos from those who have waited an hour in the hope that Tiger might knock it on and make an eagle. Instead, he lays up to 100 yards and walks away with only a par. Westwood, being 3 back of Rocco, has no choice but to rip a 3-wood straight at the pin. He knocks it on and two-putts for birdie to pull himself right back into contention.

5:03 PM ▪ Tiger doesn't take advantage of a Rocco bogey on 15 when he blows his drive off the planet right and into the crowd, leading to his second bogey in three holes. Westwood makes a routine par. With three holes left, I double-check the leaderboard:

Mediate	−1
Woods	E
Westwood	E

I turn around and walk to the far left tee on 16, where reality begins to set in. *One down with three to go.* Rocco is already through the tough 16th, and I can see him walking toward the green on 17, dressed in all black but the most colorful player on the course. Tiger can't assume that Rocco will finish any worse than 1 under. It means he needs to pick up one stroke somewhere in the next three holes.

I had first seen the pin on the par-3 16th when I walked in this morning from the back gates. I started laughing, thinking maybe it had been put there as an overnight joke. The USGA's pin sheet says the hole is five paces from the back left corner. But from the tee box, the flag looks as if it's dangling off the edge of Torrey Pines State Park. It's the sucker pin to end all sucker pins, and any shots left of it have no chance of staying on the green or even on the property. The smart shot is to the middle of the green, which is where Westwood puts it to guarantee a par. Tiger's shot from 200 yards across the canyon starts right at the flag. *He's cracked.* He has overdone his pain medications and thinks this is the last hole and he has to make birdie. It lands exactly on line but a yard short in the rough and stops dead. Another foot, and it would have been absolutely perfect. Behind me at 17, the crowd lets an out an "Ohhhhh!" which tells me that Rocco had a look at birdie but missed.

Up at the green, Tiger takes the pin out. I guess if he was trying to make it from 200 yards, there is no reason to question whether he thinks he can make it from only eight. His pitch comes out too hard and doesn't check up, sliding six feet past the cup. By going for birdie he may not even make a par.

A friend once rode a roller coaster that had such a sharp turn that it temporarily shrunk his field of vision. It's the same thing that happens to fighter pilots. And it's happening to me a little right now. For Tiger to put his body through this week, to sacrifice who knows how many more events this year only to lose this one, is a crippling thought. If Tiger misses this putt, he can't win. He's just not as strong as he was yesterday to make up 2 shots in two holes. I'm 150 yards away, standing on the cart path, and I have to sit down. I set my scope on the ground and bury my head. I know Tiger has hit the putt when the murmurs build. The fan to my left is watching through binoculars: "He missed it . . ." *No.* ". . . he made it!!!" I peel myself off the pavement. Two holes left and still 1 down.

5:31 PM ▪ Next to the 17th green, a long line of naive fans waits for a spot in the grandstands. The marshal in charge says, "In about five minutes, I can seat you all." Behind me a few hundred other fans are walking down 15 and heading home. *Home.* It's like watching the Moon landing and then turning off the TV right as Neil Armstrong steps out of the capsule. I don't know

390 • FOLLOW THE ROAR

who they are or what good reasons they think they have for leaving, but they should never, ever refer to themselves as golf fans.

Tiger's approach shot from the fairway comes up thirty feet short of the hole. Up ahead are cheers on 18. Par cheers, not birdie cheers. It means that Rocco has finished the day 1 under. Tiger's putt for a three is never close on 17. And why should it be? In a week where he can't escape drama, it only makes sense that the U.S. Open would have to come down to the final hole.

5:36 PM ▪ Tiger walks to 18. He doesn't look beaten, just old. This week has erased whatever remained of that twenty-four-year-old kid who won the 2000 U.S. Open by 15 strokes. He's a grown man pushed to his limits. Tiger and Westwood face the same challenge: a birdie to tie. Westwood has the honors and misses his drive right into the right bunker. Tiger's drive starts down the left side and stays there, one-hopping into the left bunker. They both just took the easy birdie out of the equation. Each will have to lay up and make a putt.

5:41 PM ▪ The farther I move down 18, the less I see. Tiger becomes visible only in flashes as I rush behind rows and rows of fans. His layup from the trap misses the fairway right. It's a tired sort of shot. All day he has been using his clubs to help him into and out of bunkers, but this one he chucks at the side of his golf bag. Tiger needs to get up and down from one hundred yards out of U.S. Open rough to tie Rocco.

5:45 PM ▪ If I wanted a guaranteed view of his putt at 18, I should have arrived six hours ago. As it is, I am twenty-five people back on the right side, parallel with the front of the green, and can see only by using my periscope and standing on my tiptoes. Behind me are another five rows of people. And beyond that is the Lodge, where fans are lined up at every possible balcony. Tiger's wedge hits fifteen feet right of the front right pin and sucks back to twelve. The crowd reacts as if it's a gimme, an instant roar mixed with piercing whistles. I'm not so confident.

Westwood's third lands fifteen feet behind the pin and receives a more tepid response. It's not just that his shot is three feet farther away, it's that every moment of this week feels like an over-the-top sports movie, and I don't think any of us sees how Westwood possibly fits into the plot. He's stuck between the legend and the journeyman. Westwood misses his putt short and right and makes way for the most pressurized moment of Tiger's career.

5:52 PM ▪ My view of the putt is dependent entirely on the man in the third row wearing the floppy hat. I will never meet him or even know what he looks like, but every time he moves his head an inch, it creates a domino effect as the twenty-plus people behind him all adjust their own heads to see. Next to me is a small group of middle-aged friends. Two of them are standing on chairs. The third one is standing on the ground and can't see a thing. From above comes the question "What are the odds he makes this?" "Sixty-forty he makes it," responds the man without a chair. In spite of all I've seen, I don't go as high. "Fifty-fifty," I say.

There are only so many victories in every man's life. At some point, Tiger will miss a putt that he must make, and everyone will instantly realize how we have taken his greatness for granted. Tiger's preshot routine is normal until the moment he usually steps into the putt. Rather than taking one last glance, he stops and stares down the line for what has to be an extra ten seconds. He runs through his mental checklist: line—two inches right to left. Grain—down. Speed—firm. Ten seconds is a long time to make thirty thousand people wait in wretched silence. And it was more than thirty thousand. It's 3:52 a.m. in Kenya. I picture Njaaga kneeling in front of the TV, wearing his hat from the Greater Milwaukee Open. It's almost nine in Fort Lauderdale. Craig could only be pacing back and forth yelling obscenities, falling another day behind on his book. Even Cheryl in Tucson has to know what is happening, watching the coverage while a thin line of incense wafts up from the hearth.

Tiger steps forward and into the putt, now with his back to me. I begin to pray. It's not a complicated prayer. *Please, Lord . . . Please, Lord . . . Please . . .* The stroke is compact and the ball appears from behind Tiger, rolling left toward the hole. Four feet out, he takes one step back. It means he hit it exactly as he wanted to, but then he holds his position. He's not sure if he has made it. His back scrunches down as he tracks it the last ten inches. If this goes in, it won't be in the center. It dives into the right side of the cup. What follows is the sound of thirty thousand prayers being answered at the exact same moment. Our joy collides with the screams from the grandstands and engulfs Tiger in the middle. He could have turned in any direction, but he pivots on his bad knee and faces me with both hands clenched, then roars as he leans back with his face toward the sky. As the communal blast echoes back and forth in waves across the green, I turn and hug the man next to me. Someday Tiger will lose, but not today. Five minutes later, back behind the 18th green,

NBC's on-course commentator Mark Rolfing hurries by. A fan calls out, "Another day, Mark!" Mark stops and smiles. "Why not?"

MONDAY PLAYOFF

7:10 AM ▪ I practically float through the metal detectors. "Have a marvelous day," I say to the lone woman scanning tickets this early in the morning. I can't stop grinning. I just can't believe I'm back again. This must be what it feels like to survive a near-death experience. I'm acting like George Bailey at the end of *It's a Wonderful Life*. Hello, putting green! Hello, cart barn! And look at those grandstands. Have these always been such a beautiful shade of green?

7:55 AM ▪ I take my now traditional spot at the far left side of the driving range but notice that the USGA has decided to set up Tiger and Rocco together on the far *right* side of the range. They even have their name placards waiting for them and their range balls of choice sitting in perfect pyramids.

No, no, no, no . . . *Tiger is not going to like this,* I think. I nervously move to the right grandstands and wait. A few minutes later, Tiger strides in from the putting green and walks right past his USGA-assigned spot, says nothing, and just points the grip of his putter toward his old spot on the far end. I love this guy. Two range workers spring into action, one grabbing the placard and the other trying to pick up the pyramid without all the balls toppling. It doesn't matter. Stevie is already crossing in with his own plastic bucket of balls. This isn't Shell's Wonderful World of Golf. It's the U.S. frickin' Open.

8:01 AM ▪ Rocco makes his appearance, happy to hit balls wherever they want him to. In his hand is what looks to be an iced coffee from McDonald's. Only Rocco would want a beverage that makes him even more jittery. Tiger is the man. Rocco is the *everyman*. He's the player who shows up at my local golf shop every February to sign autographs and give out door prizes. That's not an analogy—Rocco really does that. The only prize I have seen Tiger personally give away was in Dubai, where, in the middle of the trophy ceremony, officials somehow convinced him to stick his hand into a giant drum of raffle tickets and pull out a winning number. But the prize there wasn't a sleeve of Top-Flites, it was an all-expenses-paid trip to South Africa.

Rocco's the perfect foil to Tiger Woods. When Tiger scowls, Rocco smirks. In the press room last night, he was midsentence when Tiger walked in the side entrance. "You better watch yourself tomorrow, pal," Rocco said. Tiger backed off his red Tigerade and grinned.

Rocco appears harmless, but three years ago he put down $10,000 to play in the World Series of Poker and finished 600th out of almost six thousand players. He may do everything with a smile, but nothing is accidental, right down to the fact that out of all the shirts he could have worn today, he chose red, Tiger's patented Sunday (and now Monday) color.

As giddy as I am to be here, I can't get past the feeling in my gut that Rocco might make this closer than anyone probably thinks. Last night, as I received and made the now-daily round of phone calls from the friends I have made along the way, I floated Rocco's real chances to Craig from Florida. He almost hung up on me for even suggesting it. "Rocco is playing out of his mind!" he argued. "There's no way he keeps it up." As I have learned so many times over the years, nice guys don't beat Tiger. Except maybe this one.

8:58 AM ▪ The crowds are still light this morning, and I have no problem stepping right up near the ropes on the 1st tee in time for the players' introductions. "From Naples, Florida, Rocco Mediate." The crowd cheers, and Rocco turns and waves a friendly, flitty wave to the crowd. If only that Tiger hater from yesterday were here, he would feel so affirmed right now. "And from Windermere, Florida, Tiger Woods." The crowd roars its praise as Tiger tugs at the brim of his black cap. "Mr. Mediate has the honor. Play away, please." When Rocco tees up his ball, he doesn't let one leg stretch out behind him gracefully like every other guy on Tour. He straddles the spot where he wants to put the tee and then bends over at the waist like an old man picking a newspaper off his driveway.

It doesn't matter how it looks; he finds the left side of the 1st fairway and in play, which is more than Tiger can say this week. There may be other more memorable shots played today, but none can make Tiger as nervous as his tee shot here. Four tries. No fairways. Three double bogeys. He draws the club back and bends his left knee, then fires it toward the target as his hands drop into the slot and release the club down the line with a blast. His ball is past Rocco's in about three seconds, but the marshal behind the tee is signaling *right* to the volunteers in the fairway. Somehow the ball hits in the rough and takes one giant hop left and back into the fairway. Fifth time's the charm. Tiger hits the green and two-putts, while Rocco misses a six-footer to save par. I wonder if Craig is right. This could be over very quickly.

9:29 AM ▪ After four holes, the 1-shot lead has flip-flopped. Rocco is now a stroke up on Tiger after nearly holing his shot to the par-3 3rd. But out of the fairway bunker on the 5th, Rocco pulls his approach. "Fore left!" I'm above the green as the ball bounces once on the cart path, bounds thirty feet down the hole, and hits the cart path a second time. When it finally stops, it's resting twenty yards left on the steep, burnt-out downslope way left of the green. I look at the shot he has to play and decide there is zero chance he will pull this off. When he walks up, a USGA official reminds us that we need to stand still and be quiet. Rocco shrugs his shoulders and says, "Or you can talk." He nearly saves par, but the bogey brings him back to even with Tiger.

11:14 AM ▪ For the morning's first ten holes, the crowd seems legitimately torn. They can't for the life of them figure out which player is the underdog. At first glance, it's Rocco, the 158th-ranked player in the world, who two weeks ago was in a sectional qualifying tournament just to earn a spot to be here. But then there's Tiger, the fallen hero who has at times looked like he might have to swap out two of his fourteen clubs for crutches just to get through the week. In the middle of the back-and-forth over the front nine, I hear one overwrought fan say that she just wishes *both* players could win.

But after Rocco misses short par putts on the 8th and 9th holes to fall 3 shots behind, they have found their hero. I notice the change right away when Tiger's shot into the par-3 11th disappears into the sand, and the crowd begins to cheer. Not a cheer against Tiger, but a cheer of encouragement for Rocco. He answers the call with an iron to the middle of the green and closes the gap to 2.

11:27 AM ▪ I sprint ahead and all the way down the left side of the 505-yard 12th and see that the grandstands way out here are not actually full, so I sit down like a normal spectator. What a concept. Rocco continues to apply pressure by putting his tee shots in the fairway, while Tiger is starting to get sloppy. Another Rocco par on 12 paired with a Tiger bogey, and the lead is down to just 1.

11:53 AM ▪ With a pair of birdies on the par-5 13th, Tiger and Rocco move to the 14th, which, for the second day in a row, the USGA's Mike Davis has set up at the forward reachable tees. The crowd around the tee greets their man with a cheer: "Let's go, Rocco! *Clap, clap, clap-clap-clap.*" Tiger has completely lost his grip on the fans' affections. I'm worried how falling out of favor affects him, but he is buried in Stevie's yardage book. The advantage of making the crowds invisible is that he doesn't notice them when they're for or against him.

Yesterday, Tiger said the tees were so far forward here that it put him right between hitting a 3-wood and a 5-wood, so he had no choice but to play safe and lay up with an iron. In a move that the poker-playing Rocco must appreciate, the USGA is calling Tiger's bluff because it has moved the tees back an extra five steps. It doesn't change Rocco's plan. He puts his 3-wood right on line and just short of the green. Tiger doesn't hesitate. He reaches for the kiwi bird head cover (or monkey, if you're Gilbert) and uncovers his 3-wood. The crowd cheers his bravado. He hits it down near Rocco and just into the rough. The bad lie hurts him, and he can make only a par while Rocco taps in for his second straight birdie. With eighty-six holes now played in the U.S. Open, Tiger and Rocco are once again tied.

12:10 PM ▪ Out of fourteen holes, Rocco and Tiger have only had the same score three times. They both parred 2, they both parred 4, and they both birdied 13. Other than that, one of them has drawn blood every time. It's an all-out battle. Sprinting from 14 green down 15 fairway, I'm joined by seven other fans as we fly in and out of cross-traffic. The 15th at Torrey Pines is a tight, 478-yard par 4 with a towering line of eucalyptus trees down the left side. Off the tee, Rocco is in the fairway again, and Tiger is so far right that, from my spot near the green, I can't even tell exactly where he is.

"Is his ball on the cart path?"

"He's in the sand," a fan tells me.

"The sand?" I'm confused. One of the other features of the 15th is that it's the only hole at Torrey Pines without a fairway bunker. "There's no trap over there," I say. There isn't one on 15, but there is one on number 9. Tiger is forty yards off line.

Even so, Rocco is *still* farther from the hole and has to play first. He lifts the club over his head with his two hands, a clumsy stretch to just keep everything loose. He addresses the ball in his typical fashion, a series of nervous twitches and false starts before drawing the club back and then flailing at it in a way that no one would copy, but that he can repeat with unbelievable accuracy. The approach hits just past the front pin and stops twenty feet long. There is no choke in this guy today.

Back on number 9, Tiger is finalizing his attack. Besides the fact that he is on the downslope of a bunker on the wrong hole and behind a tree, it's a fairly routine shot. Tiger digs his feet in, takes a last look, and goes with a flailing swing of his own, wrapping his arms around his body and trying to will the ball left around the tree and over the greenside bunker. We all lose sight of it in the air and wait. It lands on the front part of the green, releases, and rolls inside Rocco's ball by at least ten feet—it's the best shot out of trouble that I've ever witnessed.

12:20 PM ▪ Rocco is away. A downhill putt, left to right. It's still accelerating when it flies into the hole. As the crowd erupts, Rocco braces himself with his putter, as if waiting for the cup to cough it back up, having realized the ball is not a Nike One. All I can do is stand in stunned silence. Rocco shrugs and waves, then walks off to the side of the green, where he immediately turns his back on the 15th green and faces 16, already thinking about his next shot and what the wind is doing above the trees.

Unlike Rocco, Tiger's killer instinct is always on the surface, and when Rocco's birdie drops, Tiger's expression never changes. He's only looking at his own birdie putt—a downhiller as well, but ten feet closer. When Tiger knocked his second shot stiff, he must have thought he would be putting to take the lead. Now he needs it just to stay even. His birdie putt starts three inches right, and never comes back. Now everyone is shocked, twelve thousand people all telling one another, "I can't believe this." Rocco's birdie has already deadened my senses. Just like yesterday, Tiger is 1 down with three to go.

The inside-the-ropes mob must be two hundred people at this point, and at the front of the procession headed to 16 is Rocco. Seeing him go, the irony hits me. What I am witnessing is exactly the scenario I have been dreaming of since 1996: the unheralded, likable everyman challenging Tiger shot for shot on the biggest of stages and actually pulling it off. For twelve years it was just this possibility that kept me tuning in even when every bookie in the world said there was no chance Tiger could lose. And now that it's happening, I can't imagine anything less enjoyable.

In 1986, when Tiger was ten, Tiger and Earl came down as they did every summer for the Junior World Golf Championships. Tiger's age division always played at Presidio Hills, a pitch-and-putt course near SeaWorld. But with Tiger having turned ten, Earl told him he was a big boy now, and he would treat Tiger to eighteen holes anywhere he wanted. Tiger said Torrey

Pines South. For him to let the Open slip through his grasp at a course he's cherished for more than twenty years may come as close as anything ever could to crushing his spirit.

12:32 PM ▪ On 16, both Rocco and Tiger try to hole their forty-foot birdie putts from the front of the green. Rocco's misses right. Tiger's heads for the center of the cup and comes up one inch short. He never leaves important putts short. The putter drops from his left hand in disbelief. One stroke down with two to play.

12:46 PM ▪ On 17, Tiger hits his first fairway since the 9th hole. Rocco hits the green and two-putts. So does Tiger, again leaving his birdie effort on line but short. They pass through the ropes from 17 to 18. For the third straight day, Tiger needs to make up a stroke on the last hole. If he can't, it's over. From the middle of the crowd, someone says, "Order your DVD today!" In time I may grow to acknowledge that is a pretty funny line, but not right now.

Rocco uses the big towel on his golf bag to wipe down his face. He's nervous. One more good hole and he will be the oldest winner ever of the U.S. Open. And a legend. After bogeying the 10th, Rocco has played the back nine 3 under par. And hasn't missed a single fairway . . . until now. The second Rocco sees where he's hit his tee shot, he growls, mad at himself. I can't follow the ball, but I don't need to. With his big draw, his only misses are left. Rocco will have to lay up.

Tiger doesn't need any more motivation to hit the fairway. He just has to erase any memories of his blocked drive on the 15th, the last time he used this club. If there's one thing Tiger has done well this week, it's forget. The double bogeys, the lost leads, the pain . . . His driver stops just short of parallel and rockets back down through the ball. It's high, fading, and perfect. He can go for the green.

12:53 PM ▪ It's a Monday afternoon, and there are more people here today than yesterday. By seventy-five yards out, the only open gap through which to move is a single-file line with fans pressing in on both sides. The top speed of this line is roughly one inch every other second. I get into the queue just as Tiger's iron from the fairway clears the lake and lands on the front of the green. He will have a long putt for eagle to a back-right pin. When Rocco's third shot lands on the green, the crowd cheers again. I can't see a thing. My view is blocked by the back side of the scoreboard. I pull up my scope and do the very complicated maneuver of walking while using a periscope. My left eye looks through the sight, waiting for a clear shot. My right eye watches the woman in front of me and tries to keep the number of times I bump into her under a hundred.

I have to use the sounds and my imagination to guess what's happening. From watching 602 holes so far, this comes easily to me. I can still hear some scattered conversations. It means that Tiger has stopped halfway between his ball and the hole, swinging the putter through with only his left hand while looking at the cup. Rocco is moving manically, keeping busy with his towel, drying things that probably aren't even wet. When the chatter stops, it means that Tiger is over the ball, the hand-drawn black line on top aimed right down his line. Stevie is off to the side. Is he wearing his bib? He has to be. This is the rare time when he doesn't want the round to end.

I clear the end of the scoreboard just as Tiger's forty-foot eagle putt leaves the putter. If he makes it, Rocco can't catch him. Right away, the grandstands tell us he's missed it. It's a foot right and slides four feet long. He has avoided the worse sin of not even giving himself a chance, but he's given Rocco Mediate a birdie putt to win the U.S. Open. Tiger walks straight-faced to the ball and marks it, hoping he'll need to make it.

Rocco is in the middle of the green and has less than twenty-five feet to the hole. After working with his caddy on finding the right line, he fidgets one last time and hits it. The moment he does, everyone screams. Some are hoping to will it in, others trying to keep it out. His comes closer than Tiger's but rolls by on the high side and settles three feet away. People hoot and clap, knowing that if they both make their short ones, the most-watched Monday playoff in U.S. Open history will keep going.

Tiger summons Stevie to take a look at the putt. Stevie looks at it from both sides twice and then shrugs. If there's any break in it, he doesn't see it. Tiger is satisfied and starts to pull the trigger on what is usually a gimme when a seagull dive-bombs the green. Even the animal kingdom is making him work for this. He backs off, starts over, and putts it firm, dead center. Stevie was right and it rolls right into the heart of the hole. Rocco makes his par, and both men shoot an even-par 71. They remove their caps and shake hands. Seventy-two holes wasn't enough. And neither is ninety.

1:11 PM ▪ The good news is that it's not 1946. Back then, when Lloyd Mangrum, Byron Nelson, and Victor Ghezzi tied after the first eighteen-hole playoff, the USGA made them play a *second* eighteen holes. In 1954, it changed to "hole by hole," a format that really just means sudden death. With Rocco plopped on the 18th green double-checking his scorecard, an announcement from a speaker informs us the playoff will continue at the 460-yard 7th, then move to the 8th, then back to 18. I've decided that they will do this in perpetuity for thirty to forty years, until either Rocco or Tiger dies.

1:20 PM ▪ Tiger hasn't missed a drive on the 7th all week; it's just one of those holes that sets up well for his eye. He finds the right edge of the fairway. By contrast, it's a terrible hole for Rocco, a left-to-right hole for a right-to-left player. He misses his drive left and into the fairway bunker. It was out of the fairway bunker on 5 this morning where Rocco pulled his approach and bounced it off the cart path twice. He pulls it again, up against the grandstands.

Tiger's ball is only 150 yards from the hole. He and Stevie dissect the wind as they have all week, throwing grass into the air, looking at the tops of the trees and the row of flags behind them on the grandstands at 18. When ESPN.com did a feature on Stevie in April, Tiger joked, "Good luck trying to make him sound intelligent." Stevie does the occasional goony thing, but he has worked his tail off this week. It's hard to quantify who is the best caddy in golf, but he is undoubtedly the best caddy for Tiger—a perfect balance of everything Tiger needs at his side during the course of a round. He can be a jock, a jerk, a cheerleader, and, right now, a meteorologist.

It's only a short iron from this distance. The pin is cut left of the green's one bunker. Tiger swings at it hard, one last brutal twist of the knee as the club compresses the ball for a millisecond before it soars above the pines and lands safely on the front of the green, thirty feet from the hole.

1:24 PM ▪ Rocco takes a free drop away from the bleachers and pitches it long, twenty feet away for par. All weekend Tiger has had putts he needed to make just to stay alive. Now he has one to win. As on 16, it's on line and stops an inch short. Tiger falls onto his knees. He has nothing left. He uses his putter for leverage as he stands back up, then uses it again to tap in for par on the 91st hole. Rocco must make his left-to-righter or it's over. Nothing seems impossible at this point. Way off in the distance, at least two holes away, I hear one last fading chant by a single fan: "Let's go, Rocco . . . Let's go, Rocco . . ."

Tiger and Stevie retreat to the right side of the green. Even now, Tiger is stoic, never flinching, never dropping his guard at the risk of losing. He watches the hole with the same death glare he gave me that first morning at the Buick Invitational. Rocco's putt heads down the hill. The pace is right, the line looks good, but it never breaks. Tiger Woods has just won the 108th U.S. Open.

I've cried three times in my life while watching professional sports. The first was after Kirk Gibson's ninth-inning home run to win Game 1 of the 1988 World Series. I was eleven. It was an L.A. kid's dream— the injured outfielder (oddly enough, also a left knee) coming off the bench to play hero one last time. The second was during the 1999 U.S. Open at Pinehurst: Payne Stewart's winning par putt on the last hole to beat Phil Mickelson. At the time, Phil was waiting for word from his wife, Amy, who was due with their first child any moment. He was crushed by the loss. Payne came over to him, grabbed his somber face with both hands, and said between tears, "There's nothing like being a father." I wouldn't have kids for six years, but I knew then that this was a man with the right priorities. The third time is right now, on number 7 at Torrey Pines after watching a broken Tiger Woods summon the will to win his fourteenth major championship.

His Saturday chip-in on 17 gave us embarrassed delight. The Sunday birdie to stay alive on the 18th triggered a scream toward the heavens. But as Rocco's putt misses on the high side of the hole, for a moment Tiger Woods has no reaction at all. He stands on the fringe of the 7th green with his hands on his hips, his mind focused on only one thing—the 8th tee. He won't relent, even when it's over.

Stevie turns and hugs him, and he's caught off guard. Cautiously, he returns the embrace, coming out of his daze little by little. Eventually, a smile appears. Rocco crosses over, and Tiger removes his cap, his hair matted and thinning. As he extends his right hand, Rocco brushes it aside. For the second time in less than a minute, Tiger's surprised by a hug.

The trophy ceremony is back on the 18th green. Since the bleachers have been full since late this morning, security lets us stream under the ropes and form a line in front of the lake. Tiger beat me to the green and is already there with his mom, Tida, his wife, Elin, and holding his daughter, Sam. She doesn't want him to leave, but he has to. The U.S. Open trophy is waiting to be claimed.

Jim Vernon, the USGA president, tries to introduce himself, but the microphone balks at the idea, sending feedback through every speaker. "How about that?" he says. If he weren't planning on cutting to the chase, he is now. "Please join me in welcoming our 108th U.S. Open Champion . . . Tiger Woods." Tiger takes the silver trophy, kisses it, and raises it high above his head. We all have one more true roar left in us, and now is the perfect time to use it.

48 HOURS LATER ▪ I usually love hearing from Miller, the Iowa student who drove twenty hours from Texas to go to the CA Championship in March. He always seems to know interesting news about Tiger Woods long before I do. Miller is the one who told me Tiger had bought a $65 million estate in the Hamptons. It turned out to be a mistake, but I told him to keep the hearsay coming, because every once in a while, rumors turn out to be true. Unfortunately, the rumor he delivers today has already been confirmed by the Associated Press: Tiger Woods is done for the season.

Tiger tore his ACL, the ligament that connects the bones in the knee. And he didn't do it during the U.S. Open; he did it last July while on a run around Isleworth. In between, he had merely won ten of thirteen events. But the stress of playing on a weakened knee led to the cartilage damage, which in turn led to the surgery after the Masters. The hope was that the knee would be strong enough to carry him through the rest of the season.

When the rehab in April and May proved slower than Tiger expected, he kept working anyway and two weeks before the Open was told that he had fractured his tibia in two places. The fractures would heal as long as he spent three weeks on crutches and three more weeks of rest. According to Hank Haney, Tiger looked at the doctor and said, "I'm playing the U.S. Open, and I'm going to win."

The news explains why I swore I heard Haney's voice crack Monday afternoon in the press tent. At that point, Rocco had already come and gone, defeated but not discouraged. It had to be the first press conference a moderator ended by saying "Congratulations" to someone who had just lost. Rocco left behind his black Callaway hat covered in three collectible Open pins. It would be in Rand Jerris's carry-on the next day and on display at the USGA Museum by Wednesday morning.

Tiger was gone, too, off to film various sit-down interviews on the cliff behind the tent. In his place he left Hank. With the exception of when Hank told Tiger his putter blade was open "half a degree" at Augusta, I had never heard him speak. He was thoughtful and sensitive, the anti-Stevie. Whereas Stevie is happiest behind the wheel of a racecar, Haney appeared perfectly content just standing in the corner, his hands in his pockets. Reporters gathered around him, including Luau Larry. For the first time all year, he and I were getting the scoop at the same time.

There wasn't a flurry of questions. It was mostly just Hank talking. He explained how Tiger had prepared for this week, if one can call it preparing. "It was limp to the balls, hit five, then limp back to the cart." When he had hit fifty, he was done. *For the day.* That wasn't even half the number of balls Tiger had hit Monday morning on the range. When he tried to talk about how much this Open meant to Tiger, that's when I thought I caught him stifling tears. He knew then what I wouldn't know until today—that Tiger had given up the chance to play good golf for the rest of the year in order to play his best golf for just one glorious week.

Afterword

The night that Tiger won his second U.S. Amateur in 1995, Earl Woods made a prediction. "Before he's through, my son will win fourteen major championships." At the time, the crowd around him cheered, but also laughed. Earl was prone to over-the-top statements. Thirteen summers later, I hope that number was a lowball estimate, because now Tiger is there. Fourteen. Four short of Jack Nicklaus's record. And injured.

When the news of his season-ending surgery filtered down to people who don't follow golf, a period of time that took less than three hours, I received a lot of phone calls from friends treating the situation as if there had been a death in the family. "I . . . I just heard," most of the calls began.

But assuming he returns stronger than ever, as doctors predict, there was no need to mourn. In 2008, Tiger Woods played in seven official events worldwide. He won five of them, all with a torn ACL and the last one with two stress fractures. That's not a bad season. In fact, as I write this, two and a half months after the U.S. Open and with all the majors now over, Tiger remains in first place on the 2008 PGA Tour money list with almost $5.8 million earned. Trailing him, by over a half-million, is Vijay Singh, who has now played in fourteen more Tour events this season than Tiger.

This is what my dad finds so amazing about Tiger. He was convinced that Jack Nicklaus would be the last player to ever dominate the sport. By the early 1980s, the talent pool was deeper than it had ever been, and the end result was parity. The top players, almost all of which were country-club bred, blended together in a haze of shaggy hair and polyester pants. The fact that the person who would threaten all of Nicklaus's records was an African-American who grew up playing on a military golf course was mind-boggling. And fantastic.

It was never Tiger's talent I questioned. I was stubborn, but I wasn't dumb. It was his attitude that always left me scratching my head. I couldn't understand how so many fans could happily root for someone who seemed to go to great pains to ignore each and every one of them. It appeared that America was drinking the Kool-Aid, or more appropriately, Tiger Gatorade, and the only reason to adore him was that Buick and Nike and TLC Laser Eye Center told them to do it.

Few of the fans I met felt his coldness. And like Gilbert, the fan I met on the driving range who didn't know Nike made "metals," not everyone even connected Tiger to his various endorsements. Only I was looking at Tiger and seeing an unhealthy obsession with winning. Most people just looked at him and saw a man who was determined to succeed and refused to apologize for it.

It's an out-of-fashion idea. In fact, the kind of man Tiger Woods represents is out of fashion. He's direct and disciplined. He rarely switches his opinion. He holds a grudge like a back-nine lead on Sunday. And the things that he can't control he treats with the same repeated thought: *It is what it is.* Over the course of his interviews and press conferences with reporters in 2008, he used that phrase a total of eighteen times. The noise of fighter jets near Torrey Pines: "It is what it is." The diseased greens at Bay Hill: "It is what it is." The rain delays at the CA Championship: "It is what it is." His troubled knee: "It is what it is."

Our modern-day heroes tend to be conflicted and sensitive, which eventually leads them to be bumbling and then, most deflating, apologetic. Any honest person knows Tiger Woods makes mistakes. He swears too much. He probably shouldn't have skipped his daughter's baptism. And perhaps he should have waited until his ball was actually in the hole before taking off his hat to shake Aaron Baddeley's hand at the Match Play.

But dwelling on Tiger's flaws seems like a misuse of resources. There are plenty of professional athletes who already fill that role quite nicely, doing far worse things with impressive regularity. His strengths are what deserve our attention.

And yet when you mash all those strengths together, the God-given and the learned, there's still no guarantee of greatness. It all hinges on something ultimately quite simple: a passion for improvement. Tiger Woods never did acknowledge me. For all I know, we'll never even meet. But that doesn't mean I don't know him. And with every tournament he wins, he reminds me of what can be achieved when someone does what he loves the best that he possibly can.

MONDAY, U.S. OPEN, 3:30 PM ▪ After Hank Haney's impromptu interview, I take my broken periscope and my notebook and walk back through Torrey Pines.

Workers are already soaking the hard and dry Open greens. Inside the Lodge, there are no signs of Tiger's unforgettable victory ninety minutes earlier. The gift shop is empty, its one worker lost in thought. A few couples are eating a late lunch in the grill. At the bar are plenty of empty seats, where Open highlights play to low volume in the background. The little hint of what has happened comes when I step outside and Tiger Woods walks right past me, gripping the U.S. Open trophy tightly against his chest. After everything that happened this week, he is not about to let it go.

I walk out to Torrey Pines Road and wait at the curb. A few minutes later, a gray Camry pulls up with a wife and two kids inside who are anxious to have me back. "I'll drive," I say. I click my seat belt, and we head home.

Acknowledgments

Above all else, I must thank my wife, Hillary, for (1) encouraging me to follow Tiger Woods at the Target World Challenge and (2) showing great patience when what she thought was a harmless idea overtook our lives.

It's impossible to forget the day in January when David Hirshey at HarperCollins asked what would happen to the book if Tiger became injured—we shared a laugh over the absurdity of the thought. Thanks to David for his faith in Tiger (and me) from the beginning. I'm also indebted to Kate Hamill, my editor at HarperCollins, whose lack of obsession with golf made the finished product far better as a result. Assisting both of them was George Schlesinger, the lone golfer in Harper's office, who undoubtedly spent weeks defending my obscure golf terms without me knowing.

Scott Miller diligently served as my research and stats guru . . . all between his freshman and sophomore years in college. I made it clear that he would be receiving no summer credits from this, but he didn't stop until every last question was answered.

Thanks to my TV agent, Tom Wellington at Endeavor, for introducing me to my book agent, Shawn Coyne. Both made getting something published appear easy. But I would not have even had an idea to pitch if it weren't for Jason Sobel at ESPN.com, and his willingness to let an unemployed TV writer take a crack at golf humor.

Without the wisdom of the following writers and readers, I'd still be agonizing over my introduction: WFB, Grant Nieporte, Alan Kirschenbaum, Greg Garcia, Bob Pease, Bob Sandberg, Jamie Rhonheimer, Sharon Sampson, Jeremy Blachman, James Melcher, Pink Smiley, Mom, and Dad.

Since I couldn't pay them, I have to mention all those who made the adventure just that: Craig Nelson, Jay, Kelly and Dan, Craig and Katie, Joe and Lane, Grant Geckler, Matthew, Howard Wolf, Joe Buti, Doug Austin, Dr. Marc Lederman, Mike Werle, Dan and Mary Pennington, Drew and Jerry Leamon, Rob and Jim Hays, Scott Verplank, Bob Tway, and my kids, Danny and Katie.

And, of course, thanks to the great Tiger Woods himself. Hurry back.

Finally, to all true Tiger fans, who have the highest expectations in sports, I hope this book makes you feel that you were right there alongside me. And based on the size of the crowds I've traveled with this year, maybe you were.

BEFORE *the* STORM

Also by Diane Chamberlain

DIANE CHAMBERLAIN

BEFORE *the* STORM

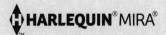

Recycling programs
for this product may
not exist in your area.

ISBN-13: 978-0-7783-1549-0

BEFORE THE STORM

Printed in U.S.A.

First printing: June 2008
10 9 8 7 6 5 4 3 2 1

www.Harlequin.com

For John, both helpmate and muse

Laurel

They took my baby from me when he was only ten hours old.

Jamie named him Andrew after his father, because it seemed fitting. We tried the name out once or twice to see how it felt in our mouths. Andrew. Andy. Then, suddenly, he was gone. I'd forgotten to count his fingers or note the color of his hair. What sort of mother forgets those things?

I fought to get him back, the way a drowning person fights for air.

A full year passed before I held him in my arms again. Finally, I could breathe, and I knew I would never, ever, let him go.

Chapter One

Andy

When I walked back into my friend Emily's church, I saw the pretty girl right away. She'd smiled and said "hey" to me earlier when we were in the youth building, and I'd been looking for her ever since. Somebody'd pushed all the long church seats out of the way so kids could dance, and the girl was in the middle of the floor dancing fast with my friend Keith, who could dance cooler than anybody. I stared at the girl like nobody else was in the church, even when Emily came up to me and said, "Where were you? This is a lock-in. That means you stay right here all night." I saw that her eyebrows were shaped like pale check marks. That meant she was mad.

I pointed to the pretty girl. "Who's that?"

"How should I know?" Emily poked her glasses higher up her nose. "I don't know every single solitary person here."

The girl had on a floaty short skirt and she had long legs that flew over the floor when she danced. Her blond hair was in those cool things America-African people wear that I could never remember the name of. Lots of them all over her head in stripes.

I walked past some kids playing cards on the floor and straight over to the girl. I stopped four shoe lengths away, which Mom always said was close enough. I used to get too close to people and made them squirmy. They need their personal space, Mom said. But even standing that far away, I could see her long eyelashes. They made me think of baby bird feathers. I saw a baby bird close once. It fell out of the nest in our yard and Maggie climbed the ladder to put it back. I wanted to reach over and touch the girl's feather lashes, but knew that was not an appropriate thing.

Keith suddenly stopped dancing with her. He looked right at me. "What d'you want, little rich boy?" he asked.

I looked at the girl. Her eyes were blue beneath the feathers. I felt words come into my mind and then into my throat, and once they got that far, I could never stop them.

"I love you," I said.

Her eyes opened wide and her lips made a pink O. She laughed. I laughed, too. Sometimes people laugh *at* me and sometimes they laugh *with* me, and I hoped this was one of the laughing-with-me times.

The girl didn't say anything, but Keith put his hands on his hips. "You go find somebody else to love, little rich boy." I wondered how come he kept calling me little rich boy instead of Andy.

I shook my head. "I love *her*."

Keith walked between me and the girl. He was so close to me, I felt the squirmies Mom told me about. I had to look up at him which made my neck hurt. "Don't you know about personal space?" I asked.

"Look," he said. "She's sixteen. You're a puny fourteen."

"Fifteen," I said. "I'm just small for my age."

"Why're you acting like you're fourteen then?" He laughed and his teeth reminded me of the big white gum pieces Maggie liked. I hated them because they burned my tongue when I bit them.

"Leave him alone," the pretty girl said. "Just ignore him and he'll go away."

"Don't it creep you out?" Keith asked her. "The way he's staring at you?"

The girl put out an arm and used it like a stick to move Keith away. Then she talked right to me.

"You better go away, honey," she said. "You don't want to get hurt."

How could I get hurt? I wasn't in a dangerous place or doing a dangerous thing, like rock climbing, which I wanted to do but Mom said no.

"What's your name?" I asked her.

"Go home to your fancy-ass house on the water," Keith said.

"If I tell you my name, will you go away?" the girl asked.

"Okay," I said, because I liked that we were making a deal.

"My name's Layla," she said.

Layla. That was a new name. I liked it. "It's pretty," I said. "My name's Andy."

"Nice to meet you, Andy," she said. "So, now you know my name and you can go."

I nodded, because I had to hold up my end of the deal. "Goodbye," I said as I started to turn around.

"Retard." Keith almost whispered it, but I had very good hearing and that word pushed my start button.

I turned back to him, my fists already flying. I punched his stomach and I punched his chin, and he must have punched me too because of all the bruises I found later, but I didn't feel a thing. I kept at him, my head bent low like a bull, forgetting I'm only five feet tall and he was way taller. When I was mad, I got strong like nobody's business. People yelled and clapped and things, but the noise was a buzz in my head. I couldn't tell you the words they said. Just bzzzzzzzzz, getting louder the more I punched.

I punched until somebody grabbed my arms from behind, and a man with glasses grabbed Keith and pulled us apart. I kicked my feet trying to get at him. I wasn't finished.

"What an asshole!" Keith twisted his body away from the man with the glasses, but he didn't come any closer. His face was red like he had sunburn.

"He doesn't know any better," said the man holding me. "You should. Now you get out of here."

"Why me?" Keith jerked his chin toward me. "He started it! Everybody always cuts him slack."

The man spoke quietly in my ear. "If I let go of you, are you going to behave?"

I nodded and then realized I was crying and everybody was watching me except for Keith and Layla and the man with glasses, who were walking toward the back of the church. The man let go of my arms and handed me a white piece of cloth from his pocket. I wiped my eyes. I hoped Layla hadn't seen me crying. The man was in front of me now and I saw that he was old with gray hair in a ponytail. He held my shoulders and looked me over like I was something to buy in a store. "You okay, Andy?"

I didn't know how he knew my name, but I nodded.

"You go back over there with Emily and let the adults handle Keith." He turned me in Emily's direction and made me walk a few steps with his arm around me. "We'll deal with him, okay?" He let go of my shoulders.

I said "okay" and kept walking toward Emily, who was standing by the baptism pool thing.

"I thought you was gonna kill him!" she said.

Me and Emily were in the same special reading and math classes two days a week. I'd known her almost my whole life, and she was my best friend. People said she was funny looking because she had white hair and one of her eyes didn't look at you and she had a scar on her lip from an operation when she was a baby, but I thought she was pretty. Mom said I saw the whole world through the eyes of love. Next to Mom and Maggie, I loved Emily best. But she wasn't my girlfriend. Definitely not.

"What did the girl say?" Emily asked me.

I wiped my eyes again. I didn't care if Emily knew I was crying. She'd seen me cry plenty of times. When I put the cloth in my pocket, I noticed her red T-shirt was on inside out. She used to always wear her clothes inside out because she couldn't stand the way the seam part felt on her skin, but she'd gotten better. She also couldn't stand when people touched her. Our teacher never touched her but once we had a substitute and she put a hand on Emily's shoulder and Emily went ballistic. She cried so much she barfed on her desk.

"Your shirt's inside out," I said.

"I know. What did the girl say?"

"That her name's Layla." I looked over at where Layla was still talking to the man with the glasses. Keith was gone, and I stared at Layla. Just looking at her made my body feel funny. It was like the time I had to take medicine for a cold and couldn't sleep all night long. I felt like bugs were crawling inside my muscles. Mom promised me that was impossible, but it still felt that way.

"Did she say anything else?" Emily asked.

Before I could answer, a really loud, deep, rumbling noise, like thunder, filled my ears. Everyone stopped and looked around like someone had said Freeze! I thought maybe it was a tsunami because we were so close to the beach. I was really afraid of tsunamis. I saw one on TV. They swallowed up people. Sometimes I'd stare out my bedroom window and watch the water in the sound, looking for the big wave that would swallow me up. I wanted to get out of the church and run, but nobody moved.

Like magic, the stained-glass windows lit up. I saw Mary and baby Jesus and angels and a half-bald man in a long dress holding a bird on his hand. The window colors were on everybody's face and Emily's hair looked like a rainbow.

"Fire!" someone yelled from the other end of the church, and then a bunch of people started yelling, "Fire! Fire!" Everyone screamed, running past me and Emily, pushing us all over the place.

I didn't see any fire, so me and Emily just stood there getting pushed around, waiting for an adult to tell us what to do. I was pretty sure then that there wasn't a tsunami. That made me feel better, even though somebody's elbow knocked into my side and somebody else stepped on my toes. Emily backed up against the wall so nobody could touch her as they rushed past. I looked where Layla had been talking with the man, but she was gone.

"The doors are blocked by fire!" someone shouted.

I looked at Emily. "Where's your mom?" I had to yell because it was so noisy. Emily's mother was one of the adults at the lock-in, which was the only reason Mom let me go.

"I don't know." Emily bit the side of her finger the way she did when she was nervous.

"Don't bite yourself." I pulled her hand away from her face and she glared at me with her good eye.

All of a sudden I smelled the fire. It crackled like a bonfire on the beach. Emily pointed to the ceiling where curlicues of smoke swirled around the beams.

"We got to hide!" she said.

I shook my head. Mom told me you can't hide from a fire. You had to escape. I had a special ladder under my bed I could put out the window to climb down, but there were no special ladders in the church that I could see.

Everything was moving very fast. Some boys lifted up one of the long church seats. They counted one two three and ran toward the big window that had the half-bald man on it. The long seat hit the man, breaking the window into a zillion pieces, and then I saw the fire outside. It was a bigger fire than I'd ever seen in my life. Like a monster, it rushed through the window and swallowed the boys and the long seat in one big gulp. The boys screamed, and they ran around with fire coming off them.

I shouted as loud as I could, "Stop! Drop! Roll!"

Emily looked amazed to hear me tell the boys what to do. I didn't think the boys heard me, but then some of them *did* stop, drop and roll, so maybe they did. They were still burning, and the air in the church had filled up with so much smoke, I couldn't see the altar anymore.

Emily started coughing. "Mama!" she croaked.

I was coughing, too, and I knew me and Emily were in trouble. I couldn't see her mother anywhere, and the other adults were screaming their heads off just like the kids. I was thinking, thinking, thinking. Mom always told me, in an emergency, use your head. This was my first real emergency ever.

Emily suddenly grabbed my arm. "We got to hide!" she said again. She had to be really scared because she'd never touched me before on purpose.

I knew she was wrong about hiding, but now the floor was on fire, the flames coming toward us.

"Think!" I said out loud, though I was only talking to myself. I hit the side of my head with my hand. "Brain, you gotta kick in!"

Emily pressed her face against my shoulder, whimpering like a puppy, and the fire rose around us like a forest of golden trees.

Chapter Two

Maggie

My father was killed by a whale.

I hardly ever told people how he died because they'd think I was making it up. Then I'd have to go into the whole story and watch their eyes pop and their skin break out in goose bumps. They'd talk about Ahab and Jonah, and I would know that Daddy's death had morphed into their entertainment. When I was a little girl, he was my whole world—my best friend and protector. He was awesome. He was a minister who built a chapel for his tiny congregation with his own hands. When people turned him into a character in a story, one they'd tell their friends and family over pizza or ice cream, I had to walk away. So, it was easier not to talk about it in the first place. If someone asked me how my father died, I'd just say "heart." That was the truth, anyway.

The night Andy went to the lock-in, I knew I had to visit my father—or at least try to visit him. It didn't always work. Out of my thirty or forty tries, I only made contact with him three times. That made the visits even more meaningful to me. I'd never stop trying.

I called Mom to let her know the lock-in had been moved from Drury Memorial's youth building to the church itself, so she'd know where to pick Andy up in the morning. Then I said I was going over to Amber Donnelly's, which was a total crock. I hadn't hung out with

Amber in months, though we sometimes still studied together. Hanging out with Amber required listening to her talk nonstop about her boyfriend, Travis Hardy. "Me and Travis this," and "me and Travis that," until I wanted to scream. Amber was in AP classes like me, but you wouldn't know it from her grammar. Plus, she was such a poser, totally caught up in her looks and who she hung out with. I never realized it until this year.

So instead of going to Amber's, I drove to the northern end of the island, which, on a midweek night in late March, felt like the end of the universe. In fourteen miles, I saw only two other cars on the road, both heading south, and few of the houses had lights on inside. The moon was so full and bright that weird shadows of shrubs and mailboxes were on the road in front of me. I thought I was seeing dogs or deer in the road and I kept braking for nothing. I was relieved when I spotted the row of cottages on the beach.

That end of the island was always getting chewed up by storms, and the six oceanfront cottages along New River Inlet Road were, every single one of them, condemned. Between the cottages and the street was another row of houses, all waiting for their turn to become oceanfront. I thought that would happen long ago; we had to abandon our house after Hurricane Fran, when I was five. But the condemned houses still stood empty, and I hoped they'd remain that way for the rest of my life.

Our tiny cottage was round, and it leaned ever so slightly to the left on long exposed pilings. The outdoor shower and storage closet that used to make up the ground floor had slipped into the sea along with the septic tank. The wood siding had been bleached so pale by decades under the sun that it looked like frosted glass in the moonlight. The cottage had a name—The Sea Tender—given to it by my

Grandpa Lockwood. Long before I was born, Grandpa burned that name into a board and hung it above the front door, but the sign blew away a couple of years ago and even though I searched for it in the sand, I never found it.

The wind blew my hair across my face as I got out of the car, and the waves sounded like nonstop thunder. Topsail Island was so narrow that we could hear the ocean from our house on Stump Sound, but this was different. My feet vibrated from the pounding of the waves on the beach, and I knew the sea was wild tonight.

I had a flashlight, but I didn't need it as I walked along the skinny boardwalk between two of the front-row houses to reach our old cottage. The bottom step used to sit on the sand, but now it was up to my waist. I moved the cinder block from behind one of the pilings into place below the steps, stood on top of it, then boosted myself onto the bottom step and climbed up to the deck. A long board nailed across the front door read *Condemned,* and I could just manage to squeeze my key beneath it into the lock. Mom was a pack rat, and I found the key in her desk drawer two years earlier, when I first decided to go to the cottage. I ducked below the sign and walked into the living room, my sandals grinding on the gritty floor.

I knew the inside of the cottage as well as I knew our house on Stump Sound. I walked through the dark living room to the kitchen, dodging some of our old furniture, which had been too ratty and disgusting to save even ten years ago. I turned on my flashlight and put it on the counter so the light hit the cabinet above the stove. I opened the cabinet, which was empty except for a plastic bag of marijuana, a few rolled joints and some boxes of matches. My hands shook as I lit one of the joints, breathing the smoke deep into my lungs. I held my breath until the top of my head tingled. I craved that out-of-body feeling tonight.

Opening the back door, I was slammed by the roar of the waves. My hair was long and way too wavy and it sucked moisture from the air like a sponge. It blew all over the place and I tucked it beneath the collar of my jacket as I stepped onto the narrow deck. I used to take a shower when I got home from the cottage, the way some kids showered to wash away the scent of cigarettes. I thought Mom would take one sniff and know where I'd been. I deserved to feel guilty, because it wasn't just the hope of being with Daddy that drew me to the cottage. I wasn't all that innocent.

I sat on the edge of the deck, my legs dangling in the air, and stared out at the long sliver of moonlight on the water. I rested my elbows on the lower rung of the railing. Saltwater mist wet my cheeks, and when I licked my lips, I tasted my childhood.

I took another hit from the joint and tried to still my mind.

When I was fifteen, I got my level-one driver's license and was allowed to drive with an adult in the car. One night I had this crazy urge to go to the cottage. I couldn't say why, but one minute I was studying for a history exam, and the next I was sneaking out the front door while Mom and Andy slept. There was no moon at all that night and I was scared shitless. It was December and dark and I barely knew how to steer, much less use the gas and the brake, but I made it the seven miles to the cottage. I sat on the deck, shivering with the cold. That was the first time I felt Daddy. He was right next to me, rising up from the sea in a cloud of mist, wrapping his arms around me so tightly that I felt warm enough to take off my sweater. I cried from the joy of having him close. I wasn't crazy. I didn't believe in ghosts or premonitions or even in heaven and hell. But I believed Daddy was there in a way I can't explain. I just knew it was true.

I felt like Daddy was with me a couple more times since then, but tonight I had trouble stilling my mind enough to let him in. I read on the internet about making contact with people who'd died. Every website had different advice, but they all said that stilling your mind was the first thing you needed to do. My mind was racing, though, the weed not mellowing me the way it usually did.

"Daddy," I whispered into the wind, "I really need you tonight." Squeezing my eyes more tightly closed, I tried to picture his wavy dark hair. The smile he always wore when he looked at me.

Then I started thinking about telling Mom I wouldn't be valedictorian when I graduated in a couple of months, like she expected. What would she say? I was an honors student all through school until this semester. I hoped she'd say it was no big thing, since I was already accepted at UNC in Wilmington. Which started me thinking about leaving home. How was Mom going to handle Andy without me?

As a mother, Mom was borderline okay. She was smart and she could be cool sometimes, but she loved Andy so much that she suffocated him, and she didn't have a clue. My brother was my biggest worry. Probably ninety-five percent of my time, I thought about him. Even when I thought about other things, he was still in a little corner of my mind, the same way I knew that it was spring or that we lived in North Carolina or that I was female.

I talked Mom into letting Andy go to the lock-in tonight. He was fifteen; she had to let go a little and besides, Emily's mother was one of the chaperones. I hoped he was having a good time and acting normal. His grip on social etiquette was pretty lame. Would they have dancing at the lock-in? It cracked me up to imagine Andy and Emily dancing together.

My cell phone vibrated in my jeans pocket and I pulled it out to look at the display. Mom. I slipped it back in my jeans, hoping she didn't try to reach me at Amber's and discover I wasn't there.

The phone rang again. That was our signal—the call-twice-in-a-row signal that meant *This is serious. Answer now.* So I jumped up and walked into the house. I pulled the door closed to block out the sound of the ocean before hitting the talk button.

"Hi, Mom," I said.

"Oh my God, Maggie!" Mom sounded breathless, as though she'd run up the stairs. "The church is on fire!"

"*What* church?" I froze.

"Drury Memorial. They just cut into the TV to announce it. They showed a picture." She choked on a sob. "It's completely engulfed in flames. People are still inside!"

"No way!" The weed suddenly hit me. I was dizzy, and I leaned over the sink in case I got sick. *Andy.* He wouldn't know what to do.

"I'm going over there now," Mom said. Her car door squeaked open, then slammed shut. "Are you at Amber's?"

"I'm…" I glanced out the door at the dark ocean. "Yes." She was so easy to lie to. Her focus was always on Andy, hardly ever on me. I stubbed out the joint in the sink. "I'll meet you there," I added. "At the church."

"Hurry!" she said. I pictured her pinching the phone between her chin and shoulder as she started the car.

"Stay calm," I said. "Drive carefully."

"You, too. But *hurry!*"

I was already heading toward the front door. Forgetting about the Condemned sign, I ran right into it, yelping as it knocked the air from my lungs. I ducked beneath it, jumped to the sand and ran down the boardwalk to my Jetta. I was miles from the church in Surf City. Miles from my baby brother. I felt so sick. I began crying as I turned the key in the ignition. It was my fault if something happened to him. I started to pray, something I only did when I was desperate. *Dear God,* I thought, as I sped down New River Inlet Road, *don't let anything happen to Andy. Please. Let it happen to me instead. I'm the liar. I'm the bad kid.*

I drove all the way to Surf City, saying that prayer over and over in my mind until I saw the smoke in the sky. Then I started saying it out loud.

Chapter Three

Laurel

THERE IS ONLY ONE STOPLIGHT ON THE TWENTY-SIX MILES OF Topsail Island. It sits two short blocks from the beach in the heart of Surf City, and it glowed red when my car approached it and was still red when I left it behind. If there'd been a dozen red lights, they wouldn't have stopped me. People always told me I was a determined woman and I was never more so than the night of the fire.

Miles before the stoplight, I'd seen the yellow glow in the sky, and now I could smell the fire itself. I pictured the old church. I'd only been inside it a few times for weddings and funerals, but I knew it had pine floors, probably soaked with years of oily cleaner, just tempting someone to toss a match on them. I knew more than I wanted to know about fires. I'd lost my parents to one, plus Jamie had been a volunteer firefighter before he died. He told me about clapboard buildings that were nothing but tinder. Probably one of the kids lit a cigarette, tossed the match on the floor. Why oh why did I listen to Maggie? I never should have let Andy go. Maggie was around him so much, she thought of him as a normal kid. You got that way when you were around him a lot. You got used to his oddities, took his limitations for granted. Then you'd see him out in the world and realize he still didn't fit in, no matter how much you'd tried to make that happen. It was easy to get seduced into thinking he was okay when

the environment around him was so carefully controlled and familiar. Tonight, though, I threw him to the wolves.

The street near Drury Memorial was clotted with fire trucks and
police cars and ambulances and I had to park a block away in front of
Jabeen's Java and The Pony Express. I'd barely come to a stop before
I flew out of my car and started running toward the fire.

A few people stood along the road watching clouds of smoke and
steam gush from the church into the bright night sky. There were
shouts and sirens and a sickening acrid smell in the air as I ran toward the front doors of the church. Huge floodlights illuminated
the building and gave me tunnel vision. All I saw were those gaping
doors, smoke belching from them, and they were my target.

"Grab her!" someone shouted.

Long, wiry arms locked around me from behind.

"Let go of me!" I clawed at the arms with my fingernails, but whoever was holding me had a grip like a steel trap.

"We have a staging area set up, ma'am," he shouted into my ear.
"Most of the children are out and safe."

"What do you mean *most*?" I twisted against the vise of his arms.
"Where's my *son*?"

He dragged me across the sandy lot before loosening his hold on
me. "They've got names of the children on a list," he said as he let go.

"Where?" I spun around to see the face of Reverend Bill, pastor
of Drury Memorial. If there was a person on Topsail Island I didn't
like, it was Reverend Bill. He looked no happier to realize it was me
he'd been holding in his arms.

"One of *your* children was here?" He sounded stunned that I'd let
a child of mine set foot in his church. I never should have.

"Andy," I said. Then I called his name. "Andy!" I shaded my eyes from the floodlights as I surveyed the scene. He'd worn his tan pants, olive green-striped shirt, and new sneakers tonight. I searched for the striped shirt, but the chaos of the scene suddenly overwhelmed my vision. Kids were everywhere, some sprawled on the sand, others sitting up or bent over, coughing. Generators roared as they fueled the lights, and static from police radios crackled in the air. Parents called out the names of their children. *"Tracy!" "Josh!" "Amanda!"* An EMT leaned over a girl, giving her CPR. The nurse in me wanted to help, but the mother in me was stronger.

Above my head, a helicopter thrummed as it rose from the beach.

"Andy!" I shouted to the helicopter, only vaguely aware of how irrational I must have seemed.

Reverend Bill was clutching my arm, tugging me across the street through a maze of fire trucks and police cars to an area lit by another floodlight and cordoned off with yellow police tape. Inside the tape, people stood shoulder to shoulder, shouting and pushing.

"See that girl over there?" Reverend Bill pointed into the crowd of people.

"Who? *Where?*" I stood on my toes trying to see better.

"The one in uniform," he shouted. "She's taking names, hooking parents up with their kids. You go see—"

I pulled away from him before he could finish the sentence. I didn't bother looking for an entrance into the cordoned-off area. Instead, I climbed over the tape and plowed into the clot of people.

Parents crowded around the officer, who I recognized as Patty Shales. Her kids went to the elementary school in Sneads Ferry where I was a part-time nurse.

"Patty!" I shouted from the sea of parents. "Do you know where Andy is?"

She glanced over at me just as a man grabbed the clipboard from her hands. I couldn't see what was happening, but Patty's head disappeared from my view amid flailing arms and angry shouting.

From somewhere behind me, I heard the words "killed" and "dead." I swung around to see two women, red eyed, hands to their mouths.

"*Who's* killed?" I asked. "*Who's* dead?"

One of the women wiped tears from her eyes. "I heard they found a body," she said. "Some kids was trapped inside. My daughter's here somewhere. I just pray to the Lord——" She shook her head, unable to finish her sentence.

I felt suddenly nauseated by the smell of the fire, a tarry chemical smell that burned my nostrils and throat.

"My son's here, too," I said, though I doubted the woman even heard me.

"Laurel!" Sara Weston lifted the yellow tape and ducked under it, running up to me. "Why are you here?" she asked.

"Andy's here. Is Keith?"

She nodded, pressing a trembling hand to her cheek. "I can't find him," she said. "Someone said he got burned, but I——"

She stopped speaking as an ominous creaking sound came from the far side of the church—the sort of sound a massive tree makes as it starts to fall. Everyone froze, staring at the church as the rear of the roof collapsed in one long wave, sending smoke and embers into the air.

"Oh my God, Laurel!" Sara pressed her face against my shoulder and I wrapped my arm around her as we were jostled by people trying to get closer to Patty. Parents stepped on our feet, pushing us one way, then another, and Sara and I pushed back as a unit, bullish and driven. I probably knew many of the people I fought out of my way, but in the heat of the moment, we were all simply desperate parents. *This is what it was like inside,* I thought, panic rising in my throat. *All the kids pushing at once to get out of the church.*

"Patty!" I shouted again, but I was only one voice of many. She heard me, though.

"Laurel!" she yelled. "They took Andy to New Hanover."

"Oh God."

"Not life threatening," Patty called. "Asthma. Some burns."

I let out my breath in a silent prayer. *Thank you, thank you, thank you.*

"You go." Sara tried to push me away, but I held fast to her. "Go, honey," she repeated. "Go see him."

I longed to run back to my car and drive to the hospital in Wilmington, but I couldn't leave Sara. "Not until you've heard about Keith," I said.

"Tracy Kelly's parents here?" Patty called.

"Here!" a man barked from behind me.

"She's at Cape Fear."

"Is Keith Weston on the list?" Sara shouted into the din.

I was afraid Patty hadn't heard her. She was speaking to a man who held a pair of broken glasses up to his eyes.

"Keith Weston was just airlifted to New Hanover," Patty called.

"Oh, no." Sara grabbed my arm so hard I winced. I thought of the helicopter rising into the sky above me.

"Let's go," I said, pulling Sara with me through the sea of people. Tears I'd been holding in spilled down my cheeks as we backed away, letting other parents take our places. "We can drive together."

"We'll go separately," Sara said, already at a run away from me. "In case one of us has to stay longer or——"

"Mom!" Maggie suddenly appeared at my side, winded and shivering. "They told me Uncle Marcus is here somewhere, but I couldn't find out anything about Andy."

"He's at New Hanover." I grabbed her hand. "I'm parked over by Jabeen's. Let's go."

I took one glance back at the smoking church. The ragged siding that still remained standing glowed red against the eerie gray sky. I hadn't thought about my former brother-in-law being there, but of course he was. I pictured Marcus inside the church, moving slowly through the smoke with his air pack on, feeling his way, searching for children who never stood a chance. Could he have been hurt when the roof collapsed? *Please, no.* And for the briefest of moments, I shifted my worry from Andy to him.

Maggie and I barely spoke on the way to Wilmington. She cried nearly the whole time, sniffling softly, shredding a tissue in her lap. My eyes were on the road, my foot pressing the gas pedal nearly to the floor. I imagined Andy trying to make sense out of the chaos of a fire and its aftermath. Simply moving the lock-in from the youth building to the church had probably been more than he could handle.

"Why did you say they moved the lock-in to the church?" I asked when we were halfway there.

"The electricity went out in the youth building." Her voice broke. "I heard some kids *died,*" she said.

"Maybe just rumors."

"I'm so sorry I talked you into letting Andy—"

"Shh." I reached for her hand. "It's not your fault, all right? Don't even think that." But inside I was angry at her, at how cavalierly she'd told me, *Oh, Mother, he'll be fine!*

I tried to pull my hand from hers to make a turn, but she held it tightly, with a need that was rare for Maggie, and I let our hands stay locked together for the rest of the trip.

The crammed waiting area of the emergency room smelled of soot and antiseptic and was nearly as chaotic as the scene at the church. The throng of people in front of the glass reception window was four deep. I tried to push through, carving a space for Maggie and myself with my arms.

"Y'all have to wait your turn," said a large, wide woman as she blocked my progress.

"I need to find out how my son is." I kept pushing.

"We all need to know how our children are," said the woman.

A man in the waiting area let out sudden gut-wrenching sobs. I didn't turn to look. I wanted to plug my ears with my fingers. Maggie leaned against me a little.

"Maybe it was the electrical," she said.

"What?"

"You know, how the electricity was out in the youth building? Maybe that's connected to the fire somehow."

The woman ahead of us left the window and it was finally our turn. "They told me my son was brought here," I said. "Andrew Lockwood."

"All right, ma'am. Have a seat."

"*No!*" I wailed, the sound escaping my mouth like a surprise. "Please!" I started to cry, as though I'd been holding the tears in by force until that moment. "Tell me how he is! Let me go to him. He's…he has special needs."

"Mom…" Maggie tried to pull me away from the window.

The receptionist softened. "I know, honey," she said. "Your boy's okay. You take a seat and someone will come get you right quick."

I nodded, trying to pull myself together, but I felt like fabric frayed too much to be mended. Maggie led me to one of the seats in the waiting area and when I looked at her I realized that she, too, had dissolved in tears once more. I hugged her, unable to tell whether it was her shoulders quaking or my own.

"Laurel?"

I saw a woman heading toward us from the other side of the room. Her face and T-shirt were smeared with soot, her hair coated with so much ash I couldn't have said what color it was. Beneath her eyes, two long, clean trails ran down her cheeks. She'd had a good cry herself. She smiled now, though, as she took both my hands in hers. I recognized the slightly lopsided curve of the lips before I did the woman. Robin Carmichael. Emily's mother.

"Robin!" I said. "Are you all right?"

"Fine," she said. "And Andy's fine, too," she added quickly, knowing those were the words I needed to hear before anything else.

"They won't let me see—"

"What about Emily?" Maggie interrupted.

Robin nodded toward the other side of the waiting area, where I spotted Emily curled up on a chair, hugging her knees and holding a bloodstained cloth to her forehead.

"She's gonna be okay," Robin said, "but we're waiting to get her seen. She cracked her glasses right in two and got a little cut over her eyebrow." Robin still held my hands and now she looked hard into my eyes. "Andy saved Emily's life." Her voice broke and I felt her grip tighten on my fingers. "He saved a load of people tonight, Laurel."

"*Andy?*" Maggie and I said at the same time.

"Yeah, I know." Robin clearly shared our amazement. "But I swear, it's the truth."

"Mrs. Lockwood?" A woman in blue scrubs stood at the entrance to the waiting area.

"Yes!" I stood up quickly.

"Come with me."

We were ushered into one of the treatment areas I remembered from three years earlier when Andy broke his arm at the skating rink. The room had several beds separated by curtains. Someone was screaming behind one of the curtains; someone else cried. But the curtain was not drawn around Andy's bed. He was bare chested and barefooted, but wearing his now-filthy pants. A woman in blue scrubs was bandaging his left forearm, and he wore an oxygen cannula below his nose. Andy spotted us and leaped off the bed, the gauzy dressing dangling from his arm, the cannula snapping off his face.

"Mom!" he shouted. "There was a big fire and I'm a hero!"

"Andy!" the nurse called sharply. "I need to finish your arm."

Maggie and I pulled Andy into a three-way hug, and I breathed in that horrible acrid scent from the fire in great gulps. "Are you okay, sweetie?" I asked, still holding him tight. He fidgeted beneath my arms, and I knew they'd given him something for the asthma. I could tell by the spring-loaded tension in the muscles of his back, that's how well I knew my son. Still, I wouldn't let go of him.

Maggie came to her senses first, pulling away from us. "The nurse still needs you, Panda Bear," she said. She lifted his arm and I saw the angry red swath that ran from his wrist to the bend of his elbow. First degree, I thought with relief. I led him back into the cubicle and looked at the nurse as Andy climbed onto the bed.

"Is that the worst of it?" I asked, pointing to his arm.

She nodded as she fit the cannula to his nostrils again. "Check it tomorrow for blisters. We'll give you a prescription for pain. He'll be okay, though. He's a lucky fella."

"I made a new friend," Andy said. "Layla. I saved her."

"I'm glad, sweetie." I dusted ashes from his hair until its nutmeg color showed through.

The nurse carefully taped the gauze to his arm again. "He doesn't seem to feel pain," she said, looking at me.

"Not when he's wired like this." Maggie boosted herself onto the end of the bed.

"He'll feel it later." I remembered the swim meet last year when he hit his head on the side of the pool. He swam lap after lap, blood trailing behind him, not even aware he was hurt until the adrenaline had worn off.

"Did you *hear* me, Mom?" Andy said. "I saved Layla."

"Emily's mother told us you saved several people." I smoothed the elastic strap of the cannula flat behind his ear. My need to touch him, to feel the life in him, was overpowering. "What happened?"

"Not several," he corrected me. *"Everybody."*

"You need to talk to him?" The nurse was looking over our heads, and I turned to see a man in a police uniform standing a few feet behind us. He looked at Andy.

"You Andy Lockwood?" he asked.

"Yes," I answered for him.

The man took a few steps closer. "You're his mother?"

I nodded. "Laurel Lockwood. And this is my daughter, Maggie."

The nurse patted Andy's bare shoulder. "Give a holler, you need anything," she said, pulling the curtain closed around us as she left.

"I'm ATF Agent Frank Foley," the man said. "How about you tell me what happened tonight, Andy?"

"I was the hero." Andy grinned.

The agent looked uncertain for a moment, then smiled. "Glad to hear it," he said. "We can always use more heroes. Where were you when the fire began?" He flipped open a small notebook.

"With Emily."

"That's his friend," I said. "Emily Carmichael."

"Inside the church?" Agent Foley asked, writing.

"Yes, but she's my friend everywhere."

Maggie laughed. I knew she couldn't help herself.

"He's asking if you and Emily were inside the church when the fire broke out," I translated.

"Yes."

"Where in the church were you? Were you standing or sitting or..."

"One question at a time." I held up a hand to stop him. "Trust me," I said. "It'll be easier that way." I looked at Andy. "Where were you in the church when the fire broke out?"

"I don't remember."

"Try to think," I prodded. "Were you by the front door or closer to the altar?"

"By the baptism pool thing."

"Ah, good." The agent wrote something on his notepad. "Sitting or standing?"

"I stood next to Emily. Her shirt was inside out." He looked at me. "She used to do that all the time, remember?"

I nodded. "So you were standing with Emily near the baptism pool thing," I said, trying to keep him focused. "And then what happened?"

"People yelled fire fire fire!" Andy's dark eyes grew big, his face animated with the memory. "Then they started running past us. Then some boys grabbed a…the long thing and said one two three and broke the window with the bald man."

It was my turn to laugh as the words tumbled out of his mouth. An hour ago, I'd been afraid I'd never hear my precious son speak again.

Agent Foley, though, eyed him with suspicion. "Were there drugs there, Andy?" he asked. "Did you drink or take any substances to-night?"

"No, sir," Andy said. "I'm not allowed."

The agent stopped writing and gnawed his lip. "Do you get it?" he asked me. "The long thing? The bald man?"

I shook my head.

"Are you still talking about being inside the church, Panda?" Maggie asked.

"Yes and the boys caught on fire, but there were no ladders, so I told them to Stop! Drop! Roll! and some of them did. Keith was there." He looked at me. "He was mean to me."

"I'm sorry," I said. Sara was my best friend and I was worried sick about her son, but Keith could be a little shit sometimes. "You mean there were no ladders to escape the fire, like the ladder we have in your room at home?"

"Right. There weren't any," Andy said.

"Okay," Agent Foley said. "So while this was happening, where were you?"

"I *told* you, at the baptism thing." Andy furrowed his forehead at the man's denseness.

The agent flipped a few pages of his notepad. "People told me you got out of the church and—"

"Right," Andy said. "Me and Emily went out the boys' room window, and there was a big metal box on the ground, and we climbed onto it."

"And then what happened?"

"We were outside."

"And what did you see outside? Did you see any person out—"

"One question at a time," I reminded him.

"What did you see outside, Andy?" Agent Foley asked.

"Fire. Everywhere except by the metal box. And Emily was screaming that nobody could get out the front door because fire was there. I saw somebody *did* get out the door and they were on fire. I don't know who it was, though."

"Oh God." Maggie buried her face in her hands, her long dark hair spilling in waves over her arms. I knew she was picturing the scene as I was. Sitting there with Andy, it was easy to forget how devastating the fire had been for so many people. I thought again of Keith. Where was he?

"Did you see anyone else outside beside the person on fire?" the agent asked.

"Emily."

"Okay. So you went back in."

"You went back *in,* Andy?" I repeated, wondering whatever possessed him to reenter the burning church.

Andy nodded. "I climbed on the metal box and got into the boys' room and then called for everyone to follow me."

"And they did?" the agent asked.

"Did they what?"

"Follow you?"

"Not exactly. I let some of them, like my friend Layla, go first."

He pulled the cannula from his nostrils and looked at me. "Do I still have to wear this?"

"A little longer," I said. "Until the nurse comes back and says you can take it off."

"So you let Layla go out the window first?" Agent Foley nudged.

"And some other kids. Then *I* followed *them*. But some were still following me, too." He wrinkled his nose. "It's hard to explain."

"You're doing fine, sweetie," I said.

"How did you know the...metal box was there?" the agent asked.

"I don't remember."

"Try to remember," I said.

"I saw it when I went to the bathroom."

"When was that?" the agent asked.

"When I had to pee."

Agent Foley gave up, closing his notepad with the flick of a wrist.

"Sounds like you *are* a hero, Andy," he said.

"I know."

The agent motioned me to follow him. We walked outside the curtained cubicle. He looked at me curiously.

"What's his, uh, disability?" he asked. "Brain injury?"

"Fetal Alcohol Spectrum Disorder," I said, the words as familiar to me as my own name.

"Really?" He looked surprised, glancing over my shoulder as though he could see through the curtain. "Don't those kids usually...you know, have a look to them?"

"Not always," I said. "Depends on what part of them was developing when the alcohol affected them."

"You're his adoptive mother then?"

The police on Topsail Island know me and they know Andy and

they know our story. An ATF agent in Wilmington, though, was a world away.

"No, I'm his biological mother," I said. "Sober fifteen years."

His smile was small. Tentative. Finally he spoke. "You've got a year on me," he said. "Congratulations."

"You, too." I smiled back.

"So—" he looked down at his closed notepad "—how much of what he says can I believe?"

"All of it," I said with certainty. "Andy's honest to a fault."

"He's an unusual kid." He looked over my shoulder again.

"You don't need to tell *me* that."

"No, I mean, in a fire, seventy-five percent of the people try to get out the front door. That's their first reaction. They're like a flock of sheep. One starts in that direction and they all follow. The other twenty-five percent look for an alternate exit. A back door. Bash open a window. Who's the bald-headed guy he was talking about?"

"I have no idea."

"Anyway, so Andy here goes for the window in the men's room. Strange choice, but turns out to be the right one."

"Well," I said, "kids like Andy don't think like that first seventy-five percent, or even the twenty-five percent. It was sheer luck. He could just as easily have gone for...I don't know, the ladies' room window, let's say, and still be stuck there." I hugged my arms across my chest at the thought. "Do you know if everyone got out okay? I heard rumors that some didn't."

He shook his head. "This was a bad one," he said. "Last report, three dead."

I sucked in my breath, hand to my mouth. "Oh, no." Some parents wouldn't have the luxury of hearing their children tell what happened tonight. "Do you know who?" I thought of Keith. Of Marcus.

"No names yet," he said. "Two of the kids and one adult is all I know. A lot of serious burns and smoke inhalation. This E.R.'s packed tight as a can of sardines."

"What's the metal box?" I asked.

"The AC unit. Whoever laid the fire skipped around it."

"Whoever... You're saying this was *arson?*"

He held up a hand as if to erase his words. "Not for me to say."

"I know there was an electrical problem at the youth building. Could that have affected the church?"

"There'll be a full investigation," he said.

"Is that why you asked Andy if he saw anyone else outside the church?"

"Like I said, there'll be a full investigation," he repeated, and I knew that would now be his answer, no matter what question I asked.

I opened the curtain around Andy's bed once I returned to his cubicle, and noticed a man sitting on the edge of a bed on the other side of the room. His head was bandaged and his T-shirt-clad broad shoulders drooped. When he looked up to say something to his nurse, the movement made him wince. I recognized the dark hair, the thick-lashed brown eyes. He passed a tremulous hand over his face and I saw the sheen of tears on his cheek.

Andy's nurse was listening to his lungs. She asked him to breathe deeply. To cough. I took that moment to whisper to Maggie.

"Ben Trippett's over there," I said. Ben was a volunteer firefighter, twenty-seven or twenty-eight. He was also Andy's swim-team coach and I wasn't sure how Andy would react to seeing him there, injured and upset.

Maggie started as if I'd awakened her from a dream, then followed my gaze to the other side of the room. She knew Ben fairly well, since she coached the younger kids' swim team.

Maggie got up, and before I could stop her, walked across the room toward Ben. He'd be embarrassed that we'd seen him crying, but Maggie was seventeen and I had to let her make her own errors in judgment. Her back was to me as she greeted Ben and I couldn't see his reaction. But then she pulled a rolling stool close to the bed and sat down and they talked, both of them with their heads bowed as though they were sharing a prayer. Ben's shoulders shook, and Maggie reached out and rested her hand on his wrist. She amazed me at times. Had she learned that compassion from me, watching me with Andy? I doubted it. All good things about Maggie had been Jamie's doing. A seventeen-year-old girl finding it in herself to comfort a grown man. I was, for just a moment, in awe of her.

Andy's nurse straightened up. "Let me take your vitals and then I'll see about getting you discharged," she said.

Andy stuck out his left arm for the blood pressure cuff.

"Your other arm, Andy," the nurse said. "Remember? You need to be careful with the burned arm for a few days."

She took his blood pressure and temperature and then left us alone.

"I'm going to write a book about being a hero," Andy said, as I reached beneath the bed for the plastic bag containing his shirt and shoes.

"Maybe someday you will." I considered bringing him down to earth a little, but how often did he get to crow about an accomplishment? Other people would not be so kind, though.

Opening the bag, I recoiled from the pungent scent of his clothes. "Andy, what you did tonight was very brave and smart," I said.

He nodded. "Right."

I thought about letting him leave the hospital without his odorous shirt or shoes, but it was chilly outside. I handed him the striped shirt.

"But the fire was a very serious thing and a lot of people were hurt." I hesitated. It was best that he heard it from me. "Some died."

He shook his head violently. "I saved them."

"You couldn't save everyone, though. That's not your fault. I know you tried. But don't talk to people about how you're a hero. It's bragging. Remember, we don't brag."

"Is it bragging if it's in a book?"

"That would be okay," I said.

Behind me, the glass door plowed open and I turned to see Dawn Reynolds fly through the room toward Ben.

"Oh my God! *Ben!*" She nearly knocked Maggie off the stool as she rushed to pull Ben into her arms. "I was so scared," she said, crying. Tears welled in my own eyes as I watched the love and relief pour from her. She and Ben lived together in a little beach cottage in Surf City, and Dawn worked with Sara at Jabeen's Java.

"I'm okay." Ben rubbed her arms in reassurance. "I'm all right."

Maggie quietly stood up, offering the stool to Dawn, then walked back to us.

"Is he okay?" I nodded toward Ben.

"Not exactly." She bit her lip. "He has a seven-year-old daughter who lives with his ex-wife in Charlotte. He keeps thinking about her being trapped like that. He's upset that people…" She looked at Andy, then me. "You know."

"I explained to Andy that some people died in the fire," I said.

Maggie started to cry again. She reached in her jeans pocket for her shredded tissue. "I just don't understand how this could happen."

"I'm going to write a book about it so it won't be bragging," Andy said as he pulled on one of his shoes.

Maggie stuffed her tissue in her pocket again. She lifted Andy's leg so his foot rested on her hip as she tied his shoelaces. "Ben said a beam landed on his head," she said. "Uncle Marcus was with him."

Marcus. I remembered what the ATF agent had said: *Two kids and one adult.* And for the second time that night, my fear and worry shifted from my son to my brother-in-law.

Chapter Four

Marcus

I DIALED LAUREL'S NUMBER FOR THE THIRD TIME AS I SWERVED onto Market Street. Voice mail. Again. Cute, Laurel. Now's not the time to pretend you don't know me.

"Call me, for Christ's sake!" I shouted into the phone.

I still couldn't picture Laurel letting Andy go to a lock-in, especially one at Drury Memorial.

I'd just come out of that fire pit when Pete ran up to me.

"Lockwood!" He'd only been a few feet away, but he had to shout above the racket of generators and sizzling water and sirens. "Your nephew's at New Hanover. Get out of here!"

It took a second for his words to register. "Andy was *here?*" I shrugged out of the air pack and peeled off my helmet. My hands had been rock steady inside the church. Suddenly, they were shaking.

"Right," Pete called over his shoulder as he raced back to the truck. "Drop your gear and get going. We'll take care of it."

"Does Laurel know?" I shouted as I stripped off my turnout jacket, but he didn't hear me.

I ran the few blocks to the fire station, yanking off my gear along the way until I was down to my uniform. Jumped into my pickup and peeled out of the parking lot. They'd closed the bridge to all traffic other than emergency vehicles, but when the officer guarding the entrance recognized me, she waved me through. I'd tried Laurel at home as well as her cell. Now I called the emergency room at New Hanover. I had to dial the number twice; my hands were shaking that hard. I set the phone to speaker and dropped it in the cup holder.

"E.R.," a woman answered.

"This is Surf City Fire Marshal Marcus Lockwood," I shouted in the direction of the phone. "You have a patient, Andy Lockwood, from Drury Memorial. Can you give me a status on him?"

"Just a moment."

The chaos at the hospital—sirens and shouting—filled the cab of my pickup. Someone screamed words I couldn't make out. Someone else wailed. It was like the frenzied scene at the fire had moved to the hospital.

"Come on, come on." My fists clenched the steering wheel.

"Mr. Lockwood?"

"Yes."

"He's being treated for smoke inhalation and burns."

Shit.

"Hold on a sec…"

I heard her talking to someone. Then she was back on the phone. "First-degree burn, his nurse says. Just his arm. He's stable. His nurse says he's a hero."

She had the wrong boy. The words "Andy" and "hero" didn't go together in the same sentence.

"You sure you're talking about Andy Lockwood?"

"He's your nephew, right?"

"Right."

"His nurse says he led some kids out of the church through the men's room window."

"What?"

"And she says he's going to be fine."

I couldn't speak. I managed to turn off the phone, then struggled to keep control of the pickup as the road blurred in front of me. As nerve-racking as the fire had been, it hadn't scared me half as much as those last couple of minutes on the phone.

Now that I knew Andy was going to be okay, I was royally pissed off. The fire was arson. I had been on the first truck out and done a quick walk around. The fire ring was even on all four sides of the building. That didn't happen by accident.

I understood arson. I'd been the kind of kid who played with matches and I once set our shed on fire. I tried to blame it on Jamie, but my parents knew their saintly older son would never be that stupid. I don't remember my punishment—just the initial thrill of watching Daddy's oily rags explode into flame on his workbench, followed by terror as the fire shot up the wall. So I got it—the thrill, the excitement. But damn it, if some asshole had to start a fire, why a church filled with kids? Why not one of the hundreds of empty summer homes on the island? The building itself was no great loss. Drury Memorial had been on a fund-raising kick for years, trying to get the money to build a bigger church. So, was that just a coincidence? And was it a coincidence that the lock-in was moved from the youth building to the church? Whatever, it felt good to be thinking about the investigation instead of Andy.

Ben Trippett and Dawn Reynolds were coming out of the E.R. as I ran toward the entrance. Now *there* was a guy who could call himself a hero. As much as I wanted to see Andy, I had to stop.

"There's the man!" I said, clapping him on the shoulder.

"Dude," Ben said, with a failed effort at a smile. He leaned against Dawn and in the light from the entrance I saw her eyes were red.

"How's the head?" He'd been crawling in front of me in the church when something—a joist or a statue or who knew what—crashed on top of him, knocking off his helmet. In the beam from my flashlight, I'd seen blood pouring down his cheek.

"Seventeen stitches." Dawn pressed closer to him. "Maybe a concussion."

"You saved at least one life tonight, Trippett," I said. "You can have my back anytime."

Truth was, I hadn't liked going in with him. Ben had been a volunteer for less than a year, and I was sure he wouldn't last. He had the desire, the ambition and the smarts, but he was claustrophobic. He'd put on the SCBA gear, take that first breath through the face piece and freak out. Full-blown panic attack. The guys razzed him about it. Good-natured teasing at first, but when the severity of the problem became clear, the taunting turned ugly, and I couldn't blame them. No one wanted to go into a fire with a guy they couldn't trust. Ben had been ready to quit. Ready to leave the island altogether. But he finally made it through the controlled burn during a training session, and a month or so ago, he told me he was ready to go live.

"You sure?" I'd asked him. "There's a huge difference between a controlled fire and a live burn."

"I'm sure," he'd said. He hadn't been kidding. He was ahead of me tonight, inching on his hands and knees through the burning church, when his low-air alarm sounded. We'd both started out with full tanks, but nerves made you chew up the air faster and he was running on empty.

"Let's go!" I'd shouted to him, the words muddy from behind

my mask. He heard me, though. I knew he did, but he didn't turn around. Instead, he kept moving forward and I thought he was losing it. I heard the dull thud of whatever hit his helmet. Heard his grunt of pain. Saw the streak of red on his cheek. "Ben!" I'd shouted. "Turn around!" But he kept right on going.

I called into my radio. "I've got an injured man with low air," I said, but through the murk, I suddenly saw the screen of his thermal image camera. There was someone in front of us. He was going after one of the kids.

The girl had crawled into her sleeping bag and somehow found an air pocket. Ben grabbed her, and together we dragged her from the church. She was unconscious but alive.

"Your boyfriend's a stubborn SOB," I said now to Dawn. "But there's a girl who's lucky he is."

"I know," Dawn said.

"I heard some kids didn't make it," Ben said. "I should've stayed. Maybe we could have—"

"You couldn't stay, man." I gripped his shoulder. "Your head was split open."

Ben pressed his sooty fingers to his eyes. He was gonna come unglued any second.

"It's okay, buddy," I said. "You did good tonight." The hospital lights fell on his dark hair and all of a sudden, he reminded me of Jamie. That brawny bulk of him that made me feel scrawny by comparison. Big man with a soft heart.

"Do you hear him, Ben?" Dawn turned to Ben, one hand on his chest. "You did all you could, sugar." She looked at me. "Do you know how it started?"

"Arson, most likely."

"Who would do something like that?" Dawn asked.

I shook my head. "Y'all happen to see my nephew inside?" I looked past them through the glass doors of the E.R. "Andy?"

"He's there." Dawn touched my arm. "He's okay."

Andy sat cross-legged on a bed in the E.R., looking like a skinny little Buddha with a bandaged forearm, and my throat closed up. Laurel sat next to the bed, her back to me, black hair falling out of a barrette. Maggie was curled up at the end of the bed, hugging her knees.

Andy spotted me as I opened the glass door.

"Uncle Marcus!" he called.

I reached the bed in a few strides and leaned past Laurel to hug him. His back felt boyish and narrow—a little kid's back, though his muscles were tight from swimming. I inhaled the smoke from his hair, unable to speak. Finally, I got a grip on myself and stood up.

"Good to see you, Andy." My voice felt like sandpaper in my throat.

"I'm a hero," Andy said, then glanced quickly at Laurel. "Can I tell Uncle Marcus that?"

Laurel chuckled. "Yes," she said. "Uncle Marcus is family." She looked at me. "I told Andy that he shouldn't brag."

I put an arm around Maggie and hugged her to me. "How're *you* doin', Mags?"

"Okay," she said. She didn't look okay. Her face was waxy. Beneath her eyes, the skin was purplish and translucent.

"Don't worry," I said, squeezing her shoulders. "He's okay."

"*Who's* okay?" She was definitely out of it.

"Andy, babe," I said.

"Oh, I know." She leaned forward, rubbed her hand over Andy's knee.

"How about you, Marcus?" Laurel asked. "You're a mess. Are you okay?"

"Fine," I said. "But I'd like Andy to tell me why he's a hero."

There was no place to sit, so I leaned against the side of Laurel's chair, hands in my pockets. Andy jumped into the story with a zeal that made me forget my anger at Laurel for not calling me. He was suddenly a storyteller.

Laurel glanced up at me as Andy spun his tale. Our eyes locked for about half a second. She was quick to look away.

Andy was on a roll. "So, I clumb out the—"

"Climbed, sweetie." Laurel stroked her thumb over his hand.

"I climbed out the boy's room window and onto the metal box with Emily and then went back in and got everyone else to follow me out."

"Unreal," I said. "Like the Pied Piper of Hamelin."

"Who's that?" Andy asked.

"The Pied Piper is a man from a fairy tale, Andy," Laurel said. "Children followed him. That's what Uncle Marcus meant. You were like the Pied Piper because the children followed you."

"I thought it was rats that followed him," Maggie said.

I groaned. "Never mind. It was a bad analogy to begin with."

Laurel looked at her watch, then stood up. "Can I talk with you a minute?" she asked.

I leaned toward Andy, my hands on the sides of his head as I planted a kiss on his forehead. Breathed in that stench of fire I never wanted to smell on him again. "See you later, Andy," I said.

I had to run to catch up with Laurel outside the room. She was a jogger—a vitamin-chomping health nut—and she didn't walk as much as dart. Now she turned toward me, arms folded—her customary posture when talking with me. That was the way I usually pictured her in my mind—arms across her chest like a shield.

"Why the hell didn't you call me?" I asked.

"Everything happened so fast," she said. "And look. Keith Weston's here somewhere."

Whoa. "Keith was at the lock-in, too?"

She nodded. "He was airlifted. Sara left the fire about the same time I did, but I haven't seen her."

"Come on." I started walking toward the reception desk.

"An ATF agent was here talking to Andy," Laurel said.

"Good." They were moving fast. That's how I liked it.

"He said three people were killed. Do you know who?"

"No clue." I knew she was scared Keith was one of them. So was I. I touched her back with the flat of my palm. "There were plenty of injuries, I know that much."

We'd reached the desk, but the clerk was too overwhelmed to be bothered. I stopped a guy in blue scrubs heading toward the treatment area.

"Can we find out the condition of one of the fire victims?" I asked after identifying myself. "Keith Weston?"

"Sure," he said, like he had nothing better to do. He disappeared down a hallway.

I looked at Laurel. "Is this for real?" I nodded toward the treatment room. "He led other kids out?"

"Unbelievable, isn't it? But the agent said it was true. I think it was because he didn't think like everyone else—you know, heading for the front doors."

"And he has no fear," I added.

Laurel was slow to nod. Andy had plenty of fears, but she knew what I meant. He had no sense of danger. No real understanding of it. He was impulsive. I thought of the time he dove from the fishing pier to grab a hat that had blown off his head.

The guy in scrubs came back. "He's not here," he said. "They took him straight up to UNC in Chapel Hill."

Laurel covered her mouth with her hand. "The burn center?"

He nodded. "I talked to one of the medics. They induced a medical coma on the beach."

"Is he going to make it?" Laurel's hand shook. I wanted to hang on to my anger at her, but that trembling hand did me in.

"That I don't know," the guy said. "Sorry." His beeper sounded from his waistband, and he spun away from us, taking off at a run.

"Is his mother with—" Laurel called after him, but he was already halfway down the hall.

Laurel pressed those shaky hands to her eyes. "Poor Sara."

"Yeah," I said. "I'm just thankful Andy's okay."

"Oh, Marcus." She looked at me. Right at me. More than a half second this time. "I was so scared," she said.

"Me, too."

I wanted to wrap my arms around her. I needed the comfort as much as I needed to comfort her. I knew better, though. She'd stiffen. Pull away. So I settled for resting my hand on her back again as we headed toward the treatment area and Andy's bed.

Chapter Five

Laurel
1984

JAMIE LOCKWOOD CHANGED ME. FOR ONE THING, I COULD never again look at a man on a motorcycle without wondering what lay deep inside him. The tougher the exterior, the greater the number of tattoos, the thicker the leather, the more I'd speculate about his soul. But Jamie also taught me about love and passion and, without ever meaning to, about guilt and grief. They were lessons I'd never be able to forget.

I was eighteen and starting my freshman year at the University of North Carolina when I met him. I was pulling out of a parking space on a Wilmington street in my three-month-old Honda Civic. The red Civic was a graduation present from my aunt and uncle—technically my adoptive parents—who made up for their emotional parsimony through their generosity in tangible goods. I checked my side mirror—all clear—turned my steering wheel to the left, and gave the car some gas. I felt a sudden *thwack* against my door and a meteor of black leather and blue denim streaked through the air next to my window.

I screamed and screamed, startled by the volume of my own voice but unable to stop. I struggled to open my door without success, because the motorcycle was propped against it. By the time I escaped through the passenger door, the biker was getting to his feet. He was a huge pillar of a man, and if I'd been thinking straight, I might have been afraid to approach him. What if he was a Hells Angel? But all I could think about was that I'd hurt someone. I could have killed him.

"Oh my God!" I ran toward him, moving on sheer adrenaline. The man stood with his side to me, rolling his shoulders and flexing his arms as if checking to see that everything still worked. I stopped a few feet short of him. "I'm so sorry. I didn't see you. Are you all right?"

A few people circled around us, hanging back as if waiting to see what would happen.

"I think I'll live." The Hells Angel unstrapped his white helmet and took it off, and a tumble of dark hair fell to his shoulders. He studied a wide black scrape that ran along the side of the helmet. "Man," he said. "I've got to send a testimonial to this manufacturer. D'you believe this? It's not even dented." He held the helmet in front of me, but all I saw was that the leather on his right sleeve was torn to shreds.

"I checked my mirror, but I was looking for a car," I said. "I'm so sorry. I somehow missed seeing you."

"You need to watch for cyclists!" A woman shouted from the sidewalk. "That could have been my son on his bike!"

"I know! I know!" I hugged my arms. "It was my fault."

The Hells Angel looked at the woman. "You don't need to rag on her," he said. "She won't make the same mistake twice." Then, more quietly, he spoke to me. "Will you?"

I shook my head. I thought I might throw up.

"Let's, uh—" he surveyed the scene "—let me check out my bike, and you back your car up to the curb and we can get each other's insurance info, all right?" His accent was pure Wilmington, unlike mine.

I nodded. "Okay."

He lifted his motorcycle from in front of my door, which was dented and scraped but opened with only a little difficulty, and I got in. I had to concentrate on turning the key in the ignition, shifting to Reverse, giving the car some gas, as if I'd suddenly forgotten how to drive. I felt about fourteen years old by the time I managed to move the car three feet back into its parking space. I fumbled in the glove compartment for my crumpled insurance card and got out.

The Hells Angel parked his motorcycle a couple of spaces up the street from my car.

"Does it run okay?" I asked, hugging my arms again as I approached. It wasn't cold, but my body was trembling all over.

"It's fine," he said. "Your car took the brunt of it."

"No, *you* did." I looked again at the shredded leather on his arm. "I wish you'd...*yell* at me or something. You're way too calm."

He laughed. "Did you cut me off on purpose?"

"No."

"I can tell you already feel like crap about it," he said. "Why should I make you feel worse?" He looked past me to the shops along the street. "Let's get a cup of coffee while we do the insurance bit," he said, pointing to the café down the block. "You're in no shape to drive right now, anyway."

He was right. I was still shivering as I stood next to him in line at the coffee shop. My knees buckled, and I leaned heavily against the counter as we ordered.

"Decaf for you." He grinned. He was a good ten inches taller than me. At least six-three. "Find us a table, why don't you?"

I sat down at a table near the window. My heart still pounded against my rib cage, but I was filled with relief. My car was basically okay, I hadn't killed anyone, and the Hells Angel was the forgiving type. I'd really lucked out. I put my insurance card on the table and smoothed it with my fingers.

I studied the width of the Angel's shoulders beneath the expanse of leather as he picked up our mugs of coffee. His body reminded me of a well-padded football player, but when he took off his jacket, draping it over the spare chair at our table, I saw that his size had nothing to do with padding. He wore a navy-blue T-shirt that read Topsail Island across the front in white, and while he was not fat, he was not particularly toned either. *Burly. Robust.* The words floated through my mind and, although I was a virgin, having miserably plodded my way through high school as a social loser, I wondered what it would be like to have sex with him. Could he hold his weight off me?

"Are you doin' all right?" Curiosity filled his brown eyes, and I wondered if the fantasy was written on my face. I felt my cheeks burn.

"I'm better," I said. "Still a little shaky."

"Your first accident?"

"My last, too, I hope. You've had others?"

"Just a couple. But I've got a few years on you."

"How old are you?" I asked, hoping it wasn't a rude question.

"Twenty-three. And you're about eighteen, I figure."

I nodded.

"Freshman at UNC?"

"Yes." I wrinkled my nose, thinking I must have *frosh* written on my forehead.

He sipped his coffee, then nudged my untouched mug an inch closer to me. "Have a major yet?" he asked.

"Nursing." My mother had been a nurse. I wanted to follow in her footsteps, even though she would never know it. "What about you?" I opened a packet of sugar and stirred it into my coffee. "Are you a Hells Angel?"

"Hell, no!" He laughed. "I'm a carpenter, although I *did* graduate from UNC a few years ago with a completely worthless degree in Religious Studies."

"Why is it worthless?" I asked, though I probably should have changed the subject. I hoped he wasn't going to try to save me, preaching the way some religious people did. I was beholden to him and would have had to listen, at least for a while.

"Well, I thought I'd go to seminary," he said. "Become a minister. But the more I studied theology, the less I liked the idea of being tied to one religion like it's the only way. So I'm still playing with what I want to be when I grow up." He reached toward the seat next to him, his hand diving into the pocket of his leather jacket and coming out with a pen and his insurance card. On his biceps, I saw a tattooed banner, the word *empathy* written inside it. As sexually excited as I'd felt five minutes ago, now I felt his fingertips touch my heart, hold it gently in his hand.

"Listen," he said, his eyes on the card. "Your car runs okay, right? It's mostly cosmetic?"

I nodded.

"Don't go through your insurance company, then. It'll just cost you in the long run. Get an estimate and I'll take care of it for you."

"You can't do that!" I said. "It was my fault."

"It was an easy mistake to make."

"I was careless." I stared at him. "And I don't understand why you're not angry about it. I almost killed you."

"Oh, I was angry at first. I said lots of cuss words while I was flying through the air." He smiled. "Anger's poison, though. I don't want it in me. When I changed the focus from how I was feeling to how *you* were feeling, it went away."

"The tattoo…" I pointed to his arm.

"I put it there to remind me," he said. "It's not always that easy to remember."

He turned the insurance card over and clicked the pen.

"I don't even know your name," he said.

"Laurel Patrick."

"Nice name." He wrote it down, then reached across the table to shake my hand. "I'm Jamie Lockwood."

We started going out together, to events on campus or the movies and once, on a picnic. I felt young with him, but never patronized. I was drawn to his kindness and the warmth of his eyes. He told me that he was initially attracted to my looks, proving that he was not a completely atypical guy after all.

"You were so pretty when you got out of your car that day," he said. "Your cheeks were red and your little pointed chin trembled and your long black hair was kind of messy and sexy." He coiled a lock of my stick-straight hair around his finger. "I thought the accident must have been fate."

Later, he said, it was my sweetness that attracted him. My innocence.

We kissed often during the first couple of weeks we saw one another, but nothing more than that. I experienced my first ever orgasm with him, even though he was not touching me at the time. We were on his bike and he shifted into a gear that suddenly lit a fire between my legs. I barely knew what was happening. It was startling, quick and stunning. I tightened my arms around him as the spasms coursed through my body, and he patted my hands with one of his, as though he thought I might be afraid of how fast we were going. It would be a while before I told him that I would always think of his bike as my first lover.

We talked about our families. I'd lived in North Carolina until I was twelve, when my parents died. Then I went to Ohio to live with my social-climbing aunt and uncle who were ill-prepared to take on a child of any sort, much less a grief-stricken preadolescent. There'd been a "Southerners are dumb" sort of prejudice among my classmates and a couple of my teachers. I fed right into that prejudice in the beginning, unable to focus on my studies and backsliding in every subject. I missed my parents and cried in bed every night until I figured out how to keep from thinking about them as I struggled to fall asleep: I'd count backward from one thousand, picturing the numbers on a hillside, like the *Hollywood* sign. It worked. I started sleeping better, which led to studying better. My teachers had to revise their "dumb Southerner" assessment of me as my grades picked up. Even my aunt and uncle seemed surprised. When it came time to apply to colleges, though, I picked all Southern schools, hungry to return to my roots.

Jamie was struck by the loss of my parents.

"Both your parents died when you were twelve?" he asked, incredulous. "At the same time?"

"Yes, but I don't think about it much."

"Maybe you *should* think about it," he said.

"It's all in the past." I'd healed from that loss and saw no point in revisiting it.

"Things like that can come back to bite you later," he said. "Were they in an accident?"

"You're awfully pushy." I laughed, but he didn't crack a smile.

"Seriously," he said.

I sighed then and told him about the fire on the cruise ship that killed fifty-two people, my parents included.

"Fire on a cruise ship." He shook his head. "Rock and a hard place."

"Some people jumped."

"Your parents?"

"No. I wish they had." Before I'd perfected my counting-backward-from-one-thousand technique, vivid fiery images of my parents had filled my head whenever I tried to go to sleep.

Jamie read my mind. "The smoke got them first, you can bet on it," he said. "They were probably unconscious before the fire reached them."

Although I hadn't wanted to talk about it, I still took comfort from that thought. Jamie knew about fire, since he was a volunteer firefighter in Wilmington. For days after he'd fight a fire, I could smell smoke on him. He'd shower and scrub his long hair and still the smell would linger, seeping out of his pores. It was a smell I began to equate with him, a smell I began to like.

He took me to meet his family after we'd been seeing each other for three weeks. Even though they lived in Wilmington, I was to meet them at their beach cottage on Topsail Island where they spent most weekends. I'd probably been to Topsail as a child, but had no memory of it. Jamie teased me that my mispronunciation of the island—I said *Topsale* instead of *Topsul*—was a dead giveaway.

By that time, he'd bought me my own black leather jacket and white helmet, and I was accustomed to riding with him. My arms were wrapped around him as we started across the high-rise bridge. Far below us, I saw a huge maze of tiny rectangular islands.

"What *is* that down there?" I shouted.

Jamie steered the bike to the side of the bridge, even though ours was the only vehicle on the road. I climbed off and peered over the railing. The grid of little islands ran along the shoreline of the Intracoastal Waterway for as far as I could see. Miniature fir trees and other vegetation grew on the irregular rectangles of land, the afternoon sun lighting the water between them with a golden glow. "It looks like a little village for elves," I said.

Jamie stood next to me, our arms touching through layers of leather. "It's marshland," he said, "but it does have a mystical quality to it, especially this time of day."

We studied the marshland a while longer, then got back on the bike.

I knew Jamie's parents owned a lot of land on the island, especially in the northernmost area called West Onslow Beach. After World War II, his father had worked in a secret missile testing program on Topsail Island called Operation Bumblebee. He'd fallen in love with the area and used what money he had to buy land that mushroomed in value over the decades. As we rode along the beach road, Jamie pointed out property after property belonging to his family. Many parcels had mobile homes parked on them, some of the trailers old and rusting, though the parcels themselves were worth plenty. There were several well-kept houses with rental signs in front of them and even a couple of the old flat-roofed, three-story concrete viewing towers that had been used during Operation Bumblebee. I was staggered to realize the wealth Jamie had grown up with.

"We don't live rich, though," Jamie had said when he told me about his father's smart investments. "Daddy says that the whole point of having a lot of money is to give you the freedom to live like you don't need it."

I admired that. My aunt and uncle were exactly the opposite.

All the Lockwood houses had names burned into signs hanging above their front doors. The Loggerhead and Osprey Oasis and Hurricane Haven. We came to the last row of houses on the island and I began to perspire inside the leather jacket. I knew one of them belonged to his family and that I'd meet them in a few minutes. Jamie drove slowly past the cottages.

"Daddy actually owns these last five houses," he said, turning his head so I could hear him.

"Terrier?" I read the name above one of the doors.

"Right, that's where we're headed, but I'm taking us on a little detour first. The next house is Talos. Terrier and Talos were the names of the first supersonic missiles tested here."

Those two houses were mirror images of each other: tall, narrow two-story cottages sitting high on stilts to protect them from the sea.

"I love *that* one!" I pointed to the last house in the row, next to Talos. The one-story cottage was round. Like all the other houses, it was built on stilts. The sign above its front door read *The Sea Tender*.

"An incredible panoramic view from that one." Jamie turned onto a narrow road away from the houses. "I want to show you my favorite spot," he said over his shoulder. We followed the road a short distance until it turned to sand; then we got off the bike and began walking. I tugged my jacket tighter. The October air wasn't cold, but the wind had a definite nip to it and Jamie put his arm around me.

We walked a short distance onto a spit of white sand nearly surrounded by water. The ocean was on our right, the New River Inlet ahead of us and somewhere to our left, although we couldn't see it from our vantage point, was the Intracoastal Waterway. The falling sun had turned the sky pink. I felt as though we were standing on the edge of an isolated continent.

"My favorite place," Jamie said.

"I can see why."

"It's always changing." He pointed toward the ocean. "The sea eats the sand there, then spits it back over there," he moved his arm to the left of us, "and what's my favorite place today may be completely different next week."

"Does that bother you?" I asked.

"Not at all. Whatever nature does here, it stays beautiful." Neither of us spoke for a moment. Then Jamie broke the silence. "Can I tell you something?" For the first time since we met, he sounded unsure of himself. A little shy.

His arm was still around me and I raised mine until it circled his waist. "Of course," I said.

"I've never told anyone this and you might think I'm crazy."

"Tell me."

"What I'd really like to do one day is create my own church," he said. "A place where people can believe whatever they want but still belong to a community, you know?"

I wasn't sure I understood exactly what he meant, but one thing I'd learned about Jamie was that there was a light inside him most people didn't have. Sometimes I saw it flash in his eyes when he spoke.

"Can you picture it?" he asked. "A little chapel right here, full of windows so you can see the water all around you. People could come and worship however they chose." He looked toward the ocean and let out a sigh. "Pie in the sky, right?"

I did think he was a little crazy, but I opened my mind to the idea and imagined a little white church with a tall steeple standing right where we stood. "Would you be allowed to build something here?" I asked.

"Daddy owns the land. He owns every grain of sand north of those houses. Would *nature* let me build it? That's the thing. Nature's got her own mind when it comes to this spot. She's got her own mind when it comes to the whole island."

The aroma of baking greeted us when we walked into Terrier. Jamie introduced his parents Southern style as Miss Emma and Mr. Andrew, but his father immediately insisted I call him Daddy L. Miss Emma had contributed the gene for Jamie's full head of wavy dark hair, although hers was cut in a short, uncomplicated style. Daddy L was responsible for Jamie's huge, round brown eyes. They each greeted their son with bear hugs as if they hadn't seen him in months instead of a day or so. Miss Emma even gave *me* a hug and a kiss on the cheek, then held my hands and studied me.

"She's just precious!" she said, letting go of my hands. I caught a whiff of alcohol on her breath

"Thank you, ma'am," I said.

"Didn't I tell you?" Jamie said to his mother as he helped me out of my leather jacket.

"I hope you're hungry." Daddy L leaned against the doorjamb. "Mama's cooked up a storm this afternoon."

"It smells wonderful," I said.

"That's the meringue on my banana pudding you're smelling," Miss Emma said.

"Where's Marcus?" Jamie asked.

I hadn't met him yet, but I knew Jamie's fifteen-year-old brother was something of a bad boy. Eight years younger than Jamie, he'd been a surprise to parents who'd adjusted to the idea of an only child.

"Lord only knows." Miss Emma stirred a big bowl of potato salad. "He *was* surfing. Who knows what he's doing now. I told him dinner is at six-thirty, but the day he's on time is the day I'll keel over from the shock."

Jamie gave his mama's shoulders a squeeze. "Well, let's hope he's not on time, then," he said.

An hour later, we settled around a table laden with fried chicken, potato salad and corn bread. Marcus was not with us. We were near one of the broad oceanside windows and I imagined the view was spectacular in the daylight.

"So, tell me about your people, darlin'," Miss Emma said as she handed me the bowl of potato salad for a second helping.

I explained that my mother grew up in Raleigh and my father in Greensboro, but that I lost them on the cruise ship and was raised by my aunt and uncle in Ohio.

"Lord have mercy!" Miss Emma's hand flew to her chest. She looked at Jamie. "No wonder you two found each other."

I wasn't sure what she meant by that. Jamie smiled at me and I figured I could ask him later.

"That explains your accent." Daddy L looked at his wife and she nodded. "We were trying to peg it."

Daddy L helped himself to a crisp chicken thigh. He glanced at his watch, then at the empty chair next to Jamie. "Maybe you could talk to Marcus about his grades, Jamie," he said.

"What about them?"

"We just got his interim report, and he's fixin' to flunk out if he doesn't buckle down," Miss Emma said quietly, as if Marcus could overhear us. "Mostly D's. And it's his junior year. I don't think he knows how important this year is for getting into college." She looked at me. "Jamie's daddy and I never made it to college, and I want my boys to get an education."

"I love going to UNC," I said, although I was really thinking that she and Daddy L had done quite well for themselves without a college degree.

"I'll talk to him," Jamie said.

"He spends all the time he's not in school on that surfboard," Miss Emma said, "and then is off with his friends on the weekends, no matter what we say."

"Boy's out of control," Daddy L added.

I'd been in the house only an hour, but already the primary Lockwood family dynamic was apparent: Jamie, despite the long hair and the tattoo and the motorcycle, was the favored son. Marcus was the black sheep. I hadn't even met him and I already felt sympathy for him.

We were nearly finished when we heard the downstairs door open and close. "I'm home!" a male voice called.

"And your dinner's cold as ice!" Miss Emma called back.

I heard him on the stairs. He came into the dining room bare-footed, wearing a full-length wet suit, the top unzipped nearly to his navel. He had a lanky, slender build that would never fill out to Jamie's bulk, even though Jamie had eight years on him. A gold cross hanging from his neck glittered against the tan that must have been left over from summer, and his hair was a short, curly cap of sun-streaked brown. He had Miss Emma's eyes—blue, shot through with summer sky.

"Hey." He grinned at me, pulling out the chair next to Jamie.

"Go put some clothes on," Daddy L said.

"This is Laurel," Jamie said. "And this is Marcus."

"Hi, Marcus," I said.

"You're a sandy mess," Miss Emma said. "Get dressed and I'll heat you a plate in the microwave."

"Not hungry," Marcus said.

"You still need to change your clothes if you're going to sit here with us," said his father.

"I'm going, I'm going." Marcus got up with a dramatic sigh and padded toward the bedrooms.

In a few minutes, I heard the music of an electric piano. The tune was halting and unfamiliar.

Jamie laughed. "He brought the piano with him?"

"If you can call it that," Miss Emma said.

Daddy L looked at me. "He wants to play in a rock-and-roll band," he explained. "For years, we offered to buy him a piano so he could take proper lessons, but he said you can't play a piano in a band."

"So he bought a used electric piano and is trying to teach himself how to play it," Miss Emma said. "It makes me ill, listening to that thing."

"Ah, Mama," Jamie said. "It keeps him off the streets."

After we'd eaten the most fabulous banana pudding I'd ever tasted, I wandered down the hall to use the bathroom. I could hear Marcus playing a song by The Police. When I left the bathroom, I knocked on his open bedroom door.

"Your mother said you're teaching yourself how to play."

He looked up, his fingers still on the keys. He'd changed into shorts and a navy-blue T-shirt. "By ear," he said. "I can't read music."

"You could learn how to read music." I leaned against the doorjamb.

"I'm dyslexic," he said. "I'd rather have all my teeth pulled."

"Play some more," I said. "It sounded good."

"Could you recognize it?"

"That song by The Police," I said. "'Every Breath You Take'?"

"Awesome!" His grin was cocky and he had the prettiest blue eyes. I bet he was considered a catch by girls his age. "I'm better than I thought," he said. "How about this one?"

He bent over the keys with supreme concentration, the cocky kid gone and in his place a boy unsure of himself. The back of his neck looked slender and vulnerable. He grimaced with every wrong note. I struggled to recognize the song, to let him have that success. It took a few minutes, but then it came to me.

"That Queen song!" I said.

"Right!" He grinned. "'We are the Champions.'"

"I'm impressed," I said sincerely. "I could never play by ear."

"You play?"

"I took lessons for a few years."

He stood up. "Go for it," he said.

I sat down and played a couple of scales to get the feel of the keyboard. Then I launched into one of the few pieces I could remember by heart: *Fur Elise*.

When I finished, I looked up to see Jamie standing in the doorway of the bedroom, a smile on his face I could only describe as *tender*. I knew in that moment that I loved him.

"That was beautiful," he said.

"Yeah, you're good," Marcus agreed. He tipped his head to one side, appraising me. "Are you, like, a sorority chick?"

I laughed. "No. What made you ask that?"

"You're just different from Jamie's other girlfriends."

"Is that good or bad?" I asked.

"Good." Marcus looked up at his brother. "She's cool," he said. "You should keep this one."

I heard the sound of dishes clinking together in the kitchen and left the brothers to help clean up. I found Miss Emma up to her elbows in dishwater.

"Let me dry." I picked up the dish towel hanging from the handle of the refrigerator.

"Why, thank you, darlin'." She handed me a plate. "I heard you playing in there. That was lovely. I didn't know a sound like that could come out of that electric thing."

"Thanks," I said, adding, "Marcus plays really well by ear."

"It's his *choice* of music that makes me ill." I had the feeling nothing Marcus did would be good enough for her.

"It's what everybody listens to, though," I said carefully.

She laughed a little. "I can see why Jamie likes you so much."

I felt my cheeks redden. Had he talked about me to his parents?

"You care about people like he does."

"Oh, no," I said. "I mean, I care about people, but not like Jamie does. He's amazing. Three weeks ago, I almost killed him. I did. Now I feel like…" I shook my head, unable to put into words how I felt. Taken in. By Jamie. By his family. More at home with them than I'd felt in six years with my icy aunt and silent uncle.

"Jamie does have a gift with people, all right," she said. "The way some people are born with musical talent or math skills or what have you. It's genetic."

I must have looked dubious, because she continued.

"I don't have the gift, Lord knows," she said, "but I had a brother who did. He died in his thirties, rest his soul, but he was…it's more than kindness. It's a way of seeing inside a person. To really feel what they're feeling. It's like they can't *help* but feel it."

"Empathy," I said.

"Oh, that stupid tattoo." She squirted more dish soap into the water in the sink. "I about had a conniption when I saw that thing. But he's a grown man, not much his mama can do about it now. He doesn't *need* that tattoo." She scrubbed the pan the corn bread had been baked in. "My aunt had the gift, too, though she said it was more of a curse, because you had to take on somebody else's pain. We were at the movies this one time? A woman and boy sat down in front of us before the lights were shut out. They didn't say one single word, but Aunt Ginny said there was something wrong with the woman. That she felt a whole lot of anguish coming from her. That was the word she used—*anguish*."

"Uh-huh," I said, keeping my expression neutral. Miss Emma was going off the deep end, but I wasn't about to let her see my skepticism.

"I know it sounds crazy," she said. "I thought so too at the time. When the movie was over, Aunt Ginny couldn't stop herself from asking the woman if she was all right. Ginny had a way of talking to people that made them open right up to her. But the woman said everything was fine. As we were walking out of the theater, though, and the little boy was out of earshot, she told us that her mother'd had a stroke just that morning and she was worried sick about her. Ginny'd picked right up on that worry and took it inside herself.

She ended up with a bleeding ulcer from taking on too many other people's worries. That's how Jamie is, too."

I remembered Jamie after the accident, when I wondered why he'd expressed no anger toward me. *You already feel like crap about it,* he'd said. *Why should I make you feel any worse?*

I shivered.

Miss Emma handed me the corn-bread pan to dry. "Here's what happens with people like Jamie or my brother or my aunt," she said. "They feel what the other person feels so strong that it's less painful for them to just…give in. I knew when Jamie was small that he had the gift. He knew when his friends were upset about something and he'd get upset himself, even if he didn't know what had them upset in the first place." She reached into the dirty dishwater and pulled the stopper from the drain. "One time, a boy he barely knew got his dog run over by a car. I found Jamie crying in bed that night—he couldn't have been more than eight or nine. He told me about it. I said, you didn't even know that dog and you barely know that boy. He just kept crying. I thought, oh Lord have mercy on me, please. Here's my brother and Aunt Ginny all over again. It's a scary thing, raising a child like that. Most kids, like Marcus, bless his heart, you have to teach them how other children feel and how you need to be sensitive to them and all." She pulled another dish towel from a drawer and dried her hands on it. "With Jamie, it was the opposite. I had to teach him to take care of himself."

I bit my lip as I set the dry pan on the counter. "Are you trying to…are you warning me about something?" I asked.

She looked surprised. "Hmm," she said. "Maybe I am. He likes you. I can tell. You're a nice girl. Down-to-earth. You got a good head on your shoulders. He's had a few girlfriends who took advantage of his kindness. I guess I'm asking you not to do that. Not to hurt him."

I shook my head. "Never," I said, thinking of how good it felt to have Jamie's arms around me. "I couldn't."

I thought I knew myself so well.

Chapter Six

Laurel

"I GUESS WE'RE SUPPOSED TO SIT UP THERE." MAGGIE POINTED to the front row of seats in the crowded Assembly Building. Trish Delphy's secretary had called us the day before to say the mayor wanted us up front at the memorial service. I was sure our special status had to do with Andy, who was scratching his neck beneath the collar of his blue shirt. I'd had to buy him a new suit for the occasion. He so rarely had need of one that his old suit no longer fit. I let him pick out his own tie—a loud Jerry Garcia with red and blue swirls—but I'd forgotten a shirt and the one he was wearing was too small.

"We'll follow you, sweetie," I said to Maggie, and she led the way down the narrow center aisle. The air hummed with chatter, and the seats were nearly all taken even though there were still fifteen minutes before the start of the service. There'd been school buses in the parking lot across the street, and I noticed that teenagers occupied many of the seats. The lock-in had attracted children from all three towns on the island as well as from a few places on the mainland, cutting across both geographic and economic boundaries, tying us all together. If I'd known how many kids would show up at the lock-in, I never would have let Andy go. Then again, if Andy hadn't been there, more would have died. Incredible to imagine.

I sat between my children. Next to us were Joe and Robin Carmichael, Emily's parents, and in front of us was a podium flanked by two dozen containers of daffodils. Propped up on easels to the left of the podium were three poster-size photographs that I was not ready to look at. To the right of the podium were about twenty-five empty chairs set at a ninety-degree angle to us. A paper banner taped between the chairs read *Reserved for Town of Surf City Fire Department*.

Andy was next to Robin, and she embraced him.

"You beautiful boy," she said, holding on to him three seconds too long for Andy's comfort level. He squirmed and she let go with a laugh, then looked at me. "Good to see you, Laurel." She leaned forward a little to wave to Maggie.

"How's Emily doing?" I asked quietly.

Joe shifted forward in his seat so he could see me. "Not great," he said.

"She's gone backward some," Robin said. "Nightmares. Won't let us touch her. I can hardly get her to let me comb her hair. She's scared to go to school again."

"She had her shirt on inside out," Andy piped in, too loudly.

"Shh," I hushed him.

"You're right, Andy," Robin said. "She was already sliding back a ways before the fire, but now it's got real bad." She raised her gaze to mine. "We're going to have to take her to see that psychologist again."

"I'm so sorry," I said. Emily had suffered brain damage at birth, and I knew how far they'd come with her over the years. How hard it had to be to have a child who hated to be touched! Many FASD kids hated being touched, too, but I'd gotten lucky with Andy; he was a hugger. I needed to rein that hugging in with people outside the family, though, especially now that he was a teenager.

Robin looked behind us. "So many people affected by this…mess," she said.

I didn't turn around. My attention was drawn to the Surf City firefighters who were now filing into the seats reserved for them. In their dress blues and white gloves, a more sober-looking bunch of men—and three women—would be hard to find, and as they sat down, a hush washed over the crowd. I saw Marcus glance at us, and I quickly turned my attention to the pink beribboned program I'd been handed when I entered the building.

Some people had wanted to put the memorial service off for another couple of weeks so the new Surf City Community Center would be open and the event could be held in the gymnasium. But the somber mood of the island couldn't wait that long. In the week since the fire, that's all anyone talked about. The part-time counselor at the elementary school where I worked was so inundated with kids suffering from nightmares about being burned or trapped that she'd had to refer the overflow, those whose fears showed up as stomachaches or headaches, to me. People were not only sad, they were angry. Everyone knew the fire was arson, although those words had not been uttered by anyone in an official capacity, at least not publicly.

Maggie hadn't said a word since we walked into the building. I glanced at her now. Her gaze was on the firefighters and I wondered what she was thinking. I was never sure how much she remembered of her father. She had a framed picture of Jamie in his dress blues on her bureau beside a picture of Andy taken on his twelfth birthday. There was another picture, taken a couple of years ago at a party, of herself with Amber Donnelly and a couple of other girls.

She had no picture of me on the bureau. I realized that just the other day.

Andy started jiggling his leg, making my chair vibrate. I used to rest a hand on his knee to try to stop his jiggling, but I rarely did that anymore. I'd learned that if I stopped the energy from coming out of Andy in one place, it would come out someplace else. Jiggling his legs was preferable to slapping his hands on his thighs or cracking his knuckles. Sometimes I pictured a tightly coiled spring inside my son, ready to burst out of him with the slightest provocation. That's most likely what happened when Keith called him names at the lock-in. It was rare for Andy to react with violence, but calling him names could do it.

"Hey, I know him!" Andy said suddenly.

"Shh," I whispered in his ear. I thought he meant Marcus or Ben Trippett, but he was pointing to the third poster-size photograph at the front of the room. It was Charlie Eggles, a long-time real estate agent in Topsail Beach. Charlie'd had no kids of his own but often volunteered to help with community events. I'd been saddened to learn he was one of the fire victims. I looked at his engaging smile, his gray hair pulled back in his customary ponytail.

"It's Mr. Eggles," I whispered to Andy.

"He held on to me so I couldn't hit Keith again." I watched a crease form between Andy's eyebrows as reality dawned on him. "Is he one of the dead people?"

"I'm afraid he is," I said.

I waited for him to speak again, but he fell silent.

"What are you thinking, love?" I asked quietly.

"Why didn't he follow me when I said to?"

I put my arm around him. "Maybe he didn't hear you, or he was trying to help some of the other children. We'll never know. You did the very best you—"

Somber piano music suddenly filled the room, swallowing my words, and Trish Delphy and Reverend Bill walked up the center aisle together. Reverend Bill stood behind the podium, while the mayor took the last empty seat in our row. Reverend Bill was so tall, skinny and long necked that he reminded me of an egret. Sara told me that he came into Jabeen's Java every afternoon for a large double-fudge-and-caramel-iced coffee with extra whipped cream, yet there was not an ounce of fat on the man. He was all sticks and angles.

Now he craned his long neck forward to speak into the microphone. "Let us pray," he said.

I bowed my head and tried to listen to his words, but I felt Maggie's warm body against my left arm and Andy's against my right. I felt them breathing, and my eyes once more filled with tears. I was so lucky.

When I lifted my head again, Reverend Bill began talking about the two teenagers and one adult killed in the fire. I forced myself to look at the blown-up images to the left of the podium. I didn't know either of the teenagers, both of whom were from Sneads Ferry. The girl, Jordy Matthews, was a smiling, freckle-faced blonde with eyes the powder-blue of the firefighters' shirts. The boy, Henderson Wright, looked about thirteen, sullen and a little scared. A tiny gold hoop hung from one end of his right eyebrow and his hair was in a buzz cut so short it was difficult to tell what color it was.

"...and Henderson Wright lived in his family's old green van for the past three years," Reverend Bill was saying. "We have people in our very own community who are forced to live that way, through no fault of their own." Somewhere to my right, I heard quiet weeping, and it suddenly occurred to me that the families of the victims most likely shared this front row with us. I wondered if it had been necessary for Reverend Bill to mention the Wright boy's poverty. Shrimping had once sustained Sneads Ferry's families, but imported seafood was changing all that. There were many poor people living amidst the wealth in our area.

I thought of Sara. Ever since I'd heard that Keith had referred to Andy as *rich,* apparently with much disdain, I'd been stewing about it. Andy and Keith had known each other since they were babies and the disparity between our financial situations had never been an issue, at least as far as I knew. I wondered now if there was some underlying resentment on Sara's part. God, I hoped not. I loved her like a sister. We were so open with each other—we had one of those friendships where nothing was off-limits. We'd both been single mothers for a decade, but Jamie had left my children and me more than comfortable. We had a handsome, ten-year-old four-bedroom house on the sound, while Sara and Keith lived in an aging double-wide sandwiched in a sea of other mobile homes.

My cheeks burned. How could I have thought that didn't matter to her? Did she say things to Keith behind my back? Had Keith's resentment built up until it spilled out on Andy at the lock-in?

Sara had been at the UNC burn center with Keith since the fire, so we'd had no good chance to talk. Our phone conversations were about Keith's condition; he was still battling for his life. Although the most serious burns were on his arms and one side of his face, his lungs had suffered severe damage, and he was being kept in a medi-cated coma because the pain would otherwise be unbearable.

Neither of us brought up the fight between our sons. Maybe she didn't even know about it. She had one thing on her mind, and that was getting Keith well. I'd offered to help her pay for any care he needed that wouldn't be covered by his father's military health insurance, but she said she'd be fine. Was it my imagination that she'd sounded chilly in her response? Had I insulted her? Maybe she simply resented the fact that Andy was safe and whole while her son could die.

Everyone around me suddenly stood up. Even Andy. I'd been so caught up in my thoughts that I didn't realize we were supposed to be singing a hymn, the words printed on the back of the program. I stood up as well, but didn't bother singing. Neither did Andy or Maggie, and I wondered where *their* thoughts were.

Long ago, Sara helped me turn my life around. When I got Andy out of foster care, he was a year old and I had no idea how to be a mother to the little stranger. After all, Jamie'd been both mother and father to Maggie when she was that age. It was Sara who helped me. Keith was nearly a year older than Andy, and Sara was a goddess in my eyes, the mother I wanted to emulate. Keith was adorable, and our boys were friends. They stayed friends until Andy was about nine. That's when Keith started caring what other kids thought, and my strange little son became an embarrassment to him. Andy never really understood the sudden ostracism. In Andy's eyes, everyone was his friend, from the janitor at school to the stranger who smiled at him on the beach. Over the past few years, though, I was glad Keith and Andy had drifted apart. Keith got picked up for drinking once, for truancy a couple of times, and last summer, for possession of an ounce of marijuana. That was the last sort of influence I needed over Andy. Andy longed to fit in and, given his impulsiveness, I worried how far he'd go to reach that goal.

We were sitting again and I felt ashamed that I'd paid so little attention to the service. Reverend Bill swept his eyes over the crowd as he vowed that "a new Drury Memorial will rise from the ashes of the old," embracing everyone with a look of tenderness, skipping over my children and me. Literally. I saw his eyes light on the man sitting next to Maggie, then instantly slip to the Carmichaels on the other side of Andy. We were the heathens in the crowd, and Reverend Bill carried a grudge for a good long time. I was willing to bet his eyes never lit on Marcus either when he looked in the direction of the firefighters. Still, I felt for the man. Even though his congregation was planning to build a new church, he'd lost this one. I knew some families were talking about suing him for negligence. Others wondered if Reverend Bill himself might have set the fire for the insurance money. I was no fan of the man, but that was ridiculous.

My gaze drifted to Marcus. His face was slack and I could suddenly see the first sign of age in his features. He was young. Thirty-eight. Three years younger than me. For the first time, I could begin to see how he'd look as he got older, something I'd never have the joy of seeing in Jamie, who'd only been thirty-six when he died.

Reverend Bill and Trish Delphy were changing places at the podium. Trish licked her lips as she prepared to speak to the crowd.

"Our community will be forever changed by this terrible tragedy," she said. "We mourn the loss of life and we pray for those still recovering from their injuries. But I'd ask you to look around you and see the strength in this room. We're strong and resilient, and while we'll never forget what happened in Surf City on Saturday, we'll move forward together.

"And now," she continued, "Dawn Reynolds has an announcement she'd like to make."

Ben Trippett's girlfriend looked uncomfortable as she took her place behind the podium.

"Um," she began, "I just wanted to let y'all know that I'm coordinating the fund-raising to help the fire victims." The paper she held in her hand shivered and I admired her for getting up in front of so many people when it obviously made her nervous. "The Shriners have come through like always to help out with medical expenses, but there's still more we need to do. A lot of the families have no insurance. I'm working with Barry Gebhart, who y'all know is an accountant in Hampstead, and we set up a special fund called the Drury Memorial Family Fund. I hope you'll help out with a check you can give me or Barry today, or you can drop by Jabeen's Java anytime I'm working. Barry and I are thinking of some fund-raising activities and we'd like your suggestions in that...um...about that." She looked down at the paper. "We'll make sure the money gets to the families who need it the most."

She sat down again at the end of our row. I saw Ben, his head still bandaged, smile at her.

Trish stood up once more at the podium.

"Thank you, Dawn," she said. "We have a generous community with a generous spirit and I know we'll do all in our power to ease the suffering of the families hurt by the fire.

"Now I'd like to recognize the firefighters and EMS workers who did such an amazing job under grueling circumstances. Not only our Town of Surf City Fire Department, but those firefighters from Topsail Beach, North Topsail Beach and the Surf City Volunteer Fire Department as well."

Applause filled the building, and as it ebbed, I saw Trish drop her gaze to us.

"And I'd like to ask Andy Lockwood to stand, please."

Beside me, I felt Andy start.

"Go ahead, sweetie," I whispered. "Stand up."

He stood up awkwardly.

Before the mayor could say another word, applause broke out again, and people rose to their feet.

"Are they clapping for me?" Andy asked.

"Yes." I bit my lip to hold back my tears.

"Why did they stand up?"

"To honor you and thank you."

"Because I'm a hero?"

I nodded.

He grinned, turning around to wave at the crowd behind us. I heard some subdued laughter.

"Can I sit down now?" Andy asked finally.

"Yes."

He lowered himself to his seat again, his cheeks pink. It took another minute for the applause to die down.

"As most of you know," Trish said, "Andy not only found a safe way out of the church, but he risked his own life to go back in and lead many of the other children to safety. Our loss is devastating, but it would have been much worse without Andy's quick thinking and calm in the face of chaos."

Andy sat up straighter than usual, his chest puffed out a bit, and I knew he was surprised to find himself suddenly the darling of Topsail Island.

Chapter Seven

Andy

MOM PUT HER VITAMINS IN A LINE BY HER PLATE. SHE ATE
breakfast vitamins and dinner vitamins. Maggie and I only ate breakfast ones. Maggie passed me the spinach bowl. Dumb. She knows I
don't eat spinach. I tried to give it to Mom.

"Take some, Andy," Mom said. "While your arm is healing, you
need good nutrition."

"I have lots of nutrition." I lifted my plate to show her my chicken
part and the cut-up sweet potato.

"Okay. Don't spill." She put her fingers on my plate to make it go
on the table again.

I ate a piece of sweet potato. They were my favorite. Mom made
sweet potato pie sometimes, but she never ate any. She didn't eat
dessert because she didn't want to ever be sick. She said too many
sweet things could make you sick. Maggie and I were allowed to eat
dessert because we weren't adults yet.

"Andy," Mom said after she swallowed all her vitamins, "your
arm looks very good, but maybe you should skip the swim meet tomorrow."

"*Why?*" I *had* to swim. "It doesn't hurt!"

"We need to make sure it's completely healed."

"It *is* completely healed!"

"You've been through a lot, though. It might be good just to take a rest."

"I don't *need* a rest!" My voice was too loud for indoors. I couldn't help it. She was pressing my start button.

"If your arm is all better, then you can."

"It's better enough!" I wanted to show her my arm, but I punched it out too hard and hit my glass of milk. The glass flew across the table and crashed to the floor. It broke in a million pieces and milk was all over. Even in the spinach.

Mom and Maggie stared at me with their mouths open. I saw a piece of chewed chicken in Maggie's mouth. I knew I did an inappropriate thing. My arm did.

"I'm sorry!" I stood up real fast. "I'll clean it up!"

Maggie catched me with her hand.

"Sit down, Panda," she said. "I'll do it. You might cut yourself."

"I'll get it." Mom was already at the counter pulling off paper towels.

"I'm sorry," I said again. "My arm went faster than I thought."

"It was an accident," Mom said.

Maggie helped her pick up the pieces of glass. Mom put paper towels all over the milk on the floor.

"My arm did it because it's so strong and healed," I said.

Mom was scrunched on the floor cleaning milk. Sometimes when I talk, she looks like she's going to laugh but doesn't. This was one of those times.

I put my napkin on top of the spinach to clean off the milk.

"Andy," Maggie said, while she got five or maybe six more paper towels. "I know you're upset that you might not be able to swim, but you've *got* to think before you react." She sounded exactly like Mom.

"I *do*," I said. That was sort of a lie. I *try* to think before I act, but sometimes I forget.

Mom stood up. "We'll check your arm again in the morning." She threw away the milky paper towels. "If it still looks good and you feel up to it, you can swim."

"I'll feel up to it, Mom," I said. I *had* to be there. I was the secret weapon, Ben told me. I was the magic bullet.

The pool was the only place where my start button was a very good thing.

Chapter Eight

Maggie

I WAS SPACED-OUT AS I LINED UP MY TEAM OF TEN LITTLE
Pirates at the end of the indoor pool. Aidan Barber pranced around
like he had to pee and I hoped that wasn't the case.

"Stop dancing, Aidan," I called to him, "and find your mark."

He obeyed, but then Lucy Posner actually sat down on the edge
of the pool and started picking at her toenails.

"Lucy! Stand up! The whistle's going to blow any minute."

Lucy looked surprised and jumped to her feet. I usually loved
these kids. I was good with them. Incredibly patient. That's what the
parents always told me. *You're so much more patient with them than I am,
Maggie,* they'd say. Now that I was floating through this meet like I
was in a weird dream, I had no patience at all. I wanted it to be over.

People talked about canceling the meet, since it was only a week
since the fire. It was like Mom had called me to say the church was on
fire minutes ago instead of days; I was still that shaken up. I couldn't
sleep. I kept seeing flames and smoke pouring out of the church and
was afraid of what I'd dream if I shut my eyes.

Since I coached the little kids' team, I had some say about if we
should hold today's meet between our team, the Pirates, and the
Jacksonville team, the Sounders. I voted for canceling. I told Ben,
who coached Andy's team, that it was totally insensitive to hold it,

but mostly I didn't think I could concentrate. Ben wasn't much in the mood for a meet either. He still had a bandage over the gash on his forehead, and he was on pain meds for his headache.

One of the girls who was in the burn center at UNC was on Ben's team, though, and her parents wanted us to have the meet. *The kids need it,* her mother said. *They need the normalcy.* They persuaded Ben, and I didn't have much choice but to go along.

The whistle blew and my kids were off, paddling furiously through the water in a way that usually made the people in the bleachers laugh, but either there was less laughter today or I couldn't hear it through the fog in my head. I shouted encouragement to my kids without really thinking about what I was saying.

I got through their event—they lost every match and that was probably my fault—but they didn't care. I hugged every one of their cold, wet little bodies as they came out of the pool and told them they did great. I was so glad it was over. I pulled my shorts on over my bathing suit and headed for the bleachers. Ben passed me as his team came together at the end of the pool.

"They're getting better," he said.

I almost laughed. "Yeah, sure."

I climbed the bleachers to sit next to my mother. "You're so good with those kids," she said, as usual. "I love watching you."

"Thanks."

I looked for Andy at the end of the pool and found him right away. Even though he was on a team with kids his age, he was a little shrimp and easy to pick out. He was jabbering to a couple of kids who were, most likely, tuning him out. Ben put his hand on Andy's shoulder and steered him to the edge of the pool in front of lane five.

Andy's burn was so much better. I looked at him lined up with the other high schoolers. I would have felt sorry for him if I didn't know his skill. His tininess always faked out the other teams. He was ninety pounds of muscle. He had asthma, but as long as he used his inhaler before a meet, no one would ever guess. I watched him at the edge of the pool, coiled up as tight as a jack-in-the-box. Ben called him his team's secret weapon. I smiled, watching him lean forward, waiting for the whistle. Next to me, my mother tensed. I thought we were both holding our breath.

A whistle lasts maybe a second and a half, but Andy always seemed to hear the very first nanosecond of the sound and he was off. This time was no different. He leaped through the air like he'd been shot from a gun. In the water, he worked his arms and legs like a machine. I used to think his hearing was more sensitive than the other kids', that he could hear the sound of the whistle before they could. Then Mom told me about the startle reflex, how babies have it and outgrow it, but how kids with fetal alcohol syndrome sometimes keep it until their teens. Andy still had it. At home, if I walked around the corner from the living room to the kitchen and surprised him, he'd jump a foot in the air. But in the pool, his startle reflex was a good thing. Ben's secret weapon.

Mom laughed as she watched the race, her hands in fists beneath her chin. I didn't know how she could laugh at anything so soon after the fire. I wasn't sure I'd ever be able to laugh again.

"Hey, Mags." Uncle Marcus suddenly showed up on the bleachers. He squeezed onto the bench between me and the father of one of the kids on Ben's team.

"Hey." I moved closer to Mom to give him room. "I didn't know you were here."

"Just got here," he said. "Sorry I missed your team. How'd they do?"

"The usual," I said.

"Looks like Andy's doing the usual, too." Uncle Marcus looked toward the water, where my brother was a couple of lengths ahead of everyone else. "Hey, Laurel." He leaned past me to look at my mother.

"Hi, Marcus," Mom said, not taking her eyes off Andy, which could just be a mother-not-wanting-to-look-away-from-her-son kind of thing, but I knew it was more than that. My mother was always weird about Uncle Marcus. Cold. Always giving him short answers, the way you'd act with someone you were tired of talking to, hoping they'd get the hint. I asked her about it once and she said it was my imagination, that she didn't treat him differently than anyone else, but that was a total crock. I thought it had to do with the fact that Uncle Marcus survived the whale while Daddy didn't.

Uncle Marcus was always nice to her, pretending he didn't notice how bitchy she acted. A few years ago, I started thinking of how cool it would be if Mom and Uncle Marcus got together, but Mom didn't seem interested in dating anyone, much less her brother-in-law. Sometimes she and Sara went to a movie or to dinner, but that was it for my mother's social life. I thought her memory of my father was so perfect she couldn't picture being with another man.

The older I got, the more I thought she should have something more in her life than her part-time school nurse job, her every single day jogs, and her full-time job—Andy. I said that to her once and she turned the tables on me. "You're a fine one to talk," she said. "Why don't *you* date?" I told her I wanted to focus on studying and coaching, that I had plenty of time to date in college. I shut up then. Less said on that topic, the better. If Mom knew how my grades had tanked this year, she'd realize I wasn't studying at all. That was the good thing about having a mother who only paid attention to one of her kids.

The race was down to the last lap and I stood up along with everyone else on the bleachers. I spotted Dawn Reynolds in the first row near the end of the pool. She had no kids on the swim team; she was there to watch Ben. I followed her gaze to him. Ben had on his yellow jams with the orange palm tree print. His chest was bare, with some dark hair across it. He was tall and a little overweight, but you could see muscles moving beneath the tanned skin of his arms and legs.

"Go, Pirates!" Dawn yelled, her hands a megaphone around her mouth, but she wasn't even looking at the swimmers. She was so obvious that I felt embarrassed watching her. It was like watching someone do something very personal, like inserting a tampon. I imagined climbing down the bleachers when the race was over to sit next to her. I could ask her how the fund was doing. I could ask if there was a way I could help. I wanted to in the worst way. I knew Mom put in three thousand, and I gave five hundred from the money I was saving for extra college expenses, although I told Mom I only gave a hundred. Andy gave thirty from his bank account. Money was not enough. I needed to do more. I watched Dawn cheer on Ben's team, imagining the conversation I'd never have with her.

The race was almost over. Andy was in the lead. Surprise, surprise. "Come on, Andy!" I yelled. Mom raised her fists in the air, waiting for the moment of victory, and Uncle Marcus let out one of his ear-piercing whistles.

Andy slapped the end of the pool, and the applause exploded for him, like it had two days before in the Assembly Building, but he just turned and kept swimming at the same insane pace. Mom laughed and I groaned. He'd never understood about ending a race. At the end of Andy's next lap, Ben leaned over, grabbed him by his arms and lifted him out of the pool. I saw him mouth the words *You won!* to Andy, and something else that looked like *You can stop swimming now.*

We all sat down again. Andy looked at us, grinning and waving as he walked to the bench.

Uncle Marcus leaned forward again. "I've got something for you, Laurel," he said.

My mother had to break down and look at him then. "What?"

Uncle Marcus pulled a small folded newspaper article from his shirt pocket and reached across me to hand it to her.

"One of the guys was up in Maryland and saw this in the *Washington Post.*"

I looked over my mother's shoulder to read the headline: Disabled N.C. Boy Saves Friends.

Mom shook her head with a laugh. "Don't they have enough of their own news up there?" She looked at Uncle Marcus. "I can keep this?"

"It's yours."

"Thanks."

Uncle Marcus took in a long breath, stretching his arms above his head as he let it out. Then he sniffed my shoulder. "You wear chlorine the way other women wear perfume, Mags," he teased.

He was not the first guy to tell me that. I liked that he said "women" and not "girls."

The pool had been my home away from home since it was built when I was eleven. Before that, I could only swim during the summer in the sound or the ocean.

Daddy taught Andy and me how to swim. "Kids who live on the water better be good swimmers," he'd said. He taught me first of course, before Andy even lived with us. One of my earliest memories was of a calm day in the ocean. It was nothing major. Nothing special. We just paddled around. He held me on his knees, tossed me in the air, swung me around until I practically choked on my laughter. Total bliss.

When I was a little older, Andy joined us in the water and he took to it the same as I did. Daddy'd told me that Andy probably wouldn't be able to swim as well as I could, but Andy surprised him.

I couldn't remember ever playing in the water with my mother. In my early memories, Mom was like a shadow. When I pictured anything from when I was a little girl, she was on the edge of the memory, so wispy I couldn't be sure she was there or not. I didn't think she ever held me. It was always Daddy's arms around me that I remembered.

"How's Ben's head?" Uncle Marcus asked.

"Better," I said, "though he's still taking pain meds."

"You know who he reminds me of?"

"Who?"

"Your father." He said this quietly, like he didn't want Mom to hear.

"Really?" I tried to picture Ben and Daddy standing next to each other.

"Not sure why, exactly." Uncle Marcus put his elbows on his knees as he stared at Ben. "His build. His size, maybe. Jamie was about the same height. Brown eyes. Same dark, wavy hair. Face is different, of course. But it's that…brawniness or something. All Ben needs is an empathy tattoo on his arm and…" He shrugged.

I liked when he talked about my father. I liked when anyone, except Reverend Bill, talked about Daddy.

I was probably five or six when I asked Daddy what the word "empathy" meant. We were sitting on the deck of The Sea Tender, our legs dangling over the edge, looking for dolphins. I ran my fingers over the letters in the tattoo.

"It means feeling what other people are feeling," he said. "You know how you kissed the boo-boo on my finger yesterday when I hit it with a hammer?"

"Uh-huh." He'd been repairing the stairs down to the beach and said, "Goddamn it!" I'd never heard him say that before.

"You felt sad for me that I hurt my finger, right?"

I nodded.

"That's empathy. And I had it tattooed on my arm to remind me to think about other people's feelings." He looked at the ocean for a long minute or two and I figured that was the end of the conversation. But then he added, "If you're a person with a lot of empathy, it can hurt more to watch a person you care about suffer than to suffer yourself."

Even at five or six, I knew what he meant. That was how I felt when something happened to Andy. When he fell because his little legs weren't steady enough yet, or the time he pinched his fingers in the screen door. I cried so hard that Mom couldn't figure out which of us was hurt at first.

When I heard that Andy might be trapped by the fire—that *any* of those children might be trapped—the panic I felt might as well have been theirs.

"I was worried about him," Uncle Marcus said.

I dragged my foggy brain back to our conversation. "About who?" I asked. "Daddy or Ben?"

"Ben," Uncle Marcus said. "He had some problems in the department at first and I didn't think he'd last. Claustrophobia. Big guy like that, you wouldn't think he'd be afraid of anything. But after the fire at Drury—" he shook his head "—I realized I'd been wrong about him. He really proved himself. All he needed was the fire."

And right then I knew it wasn't fog messing up my brain. It was smoke.

Chapter Nine

Marcus

EXCELLENT DAY FOR THE WATER, AND THE BOATERS KNEW IT. From the front steps of Laurel's house, I stopped to look at Stump Sound. Sailboats, kayaks, pontoon boats. I was jealous. I had a kayak and a small motorboat. I used the kayak for exercise and fished from the runabout. Or on those rare occasions I had a date, I'd take the boat for a sunset spin on the Intracoastal. I had this fantasy of taking Andy out with me someday. Never happen, I told myself. Give it up.

I rang Laurel's doorbell.

Nearly every Sunday that I wasn't scheduled to work, I did something with Andy. Ball game. Skating rink. Fishing from the pier. Maggie used to come, too, but by the time she reached Andy's age, she had better things to do. I got it. I was fifteen once myself. I liked the time alone with Andy, anyway. He needed a man in his life. Father figure.

My beautiful niece opened the door and gave me a kiss on the cheek. I'd dated a woman a while back who turned out to be too artsy-fartsy for my taste, but I did learn a few things from her. We were standing in the National Gallery in Washington one time, in a room full of paintings of women. Most of the women had thick wavy hair and big, heavy-lidded eyes. They looked like they were made of air. You could lift any one of them up with a finger.

"These paintings remind me of my niece," I told my date.

"Really?" she asked. "She has a Pre-Raphaelite look to her?"

Whatever, I thought.

"I'd like to meet her," my date said.

We broke up before she could meet Maggie, but since then, whenever I saw my niece, the term Pre-Raphaelite popped into my mind even though I didn't know what it meant. I would have given my right arm—*both* my arms—for Jamie to have the chance to see the long-haired, heavy-lidded beauty his daughter had become.

"What are you up to today, Mags?" I asked.

"Studying at Amber's," she said. "I have some exams this week."

I sat down on the stairs that led to the second story. "You can see that ol' light at the end of the tunnel now, huh?"

She nodded. "You better have my graduation on your calendar."

"Can't imagine you gone next year," I said.

"I'll only be in Wilmington."

"It's more than geography, kiddo," I said.

She looked up the stairs, then lowered her voice. "How's Mom gonna manage Andy without me?" she asked.

"Hey," I said, "I'm not going anywhere. All your mom has to do is say the word and I'm here."

"I know."

"You decide on a major yet?"

She shook her head. "Still between psych and business."

I couldn't see a Pre-Raphaelite woman in one of those stiff, pin-striped business suits. Her choice, though. I'd keep my trap shut.

"You've got plenty of time to decide," I said.

Maggie swung her backpack over her shoulder. "Do they know what caused the fire yet?" she asked.

I shrugged. "We're still waiting on results from the lab."

"You're in charge, aren't you?" she asked.

"On the local side, yeah. But once there are fatals…" I shook my head. "The State Bureau of Investigation and ATF are involved now."

"Oh, right. That guy who talked to Andy at the hospital."

"Right." I got to my feet. "Your brother upstairs?"

"Yeah." She smiled. "Wait till you see his room. It looks like a Hallmark store. Oh, and Mom said don't mention anything about him writing a book. She hopes he'll forget about it."

"He's still talking about that?"

"Every once in a while." She clipped her iPod to her low-rise jeans.

"Your mom home?"

"Went for a run." She popped in the earbuds. "Later," she said, pulling open the door.

Maggie wasn't kidding about the Hallmark store, I thought as I walked into Andy's room. Greeting cards were propped up on his desk and dresser and the windowsills. Tacked to the cork wall he used as his bulletin board, clustered around the charts Laurel had made to keep him organized. *What I Do Before Going to Bed on a School Night: 1. Brush teeth 2. Wash face 3. Put completed homework in backpack. 4. Pick out clothes to wear to school.* And on and on and on. Laurel was a very patient woman.

Andy was at his computer and he swiveled his chair around to face me.

"What's with the cards?" I asked.

"They're thank-yous." He stood up and handed me one. The front was a picture of an artificially elongated dachshund. Inside it read, *I want to extend my thanks.* Then a handwritten note: *Andy, you don't know me, but I live in Rocky Mount and heard about what you did at the fire and just want you to know I'd want you around any time I needed help!*

He handed me a few others.

"Some are from people I know," he said as I glanced through them. "And some are from people I don't know. And some girls sent me their pictures." He grinned, handing me a photograph he had propped up next to his computer. "Look at this one."

I did. *Yowks.* She had to be at least twenty. Long blond hair and wispy bangs that hung to her eyelashes. She wore a sultry look and little else. Well, all right, she had on some kind of skimpy top, but it didn't cover much. I looked up at Andy and caught the gleam in his eye. He scared me these days. He used to see girls as friends, like his little skew-eyed pal, Emily. Now, he was getting into *fights* over girls. When did that happen? His voice was starting to change, too, jarring me every once in a while with a sudden drop in pitch. Sometimes standing next to him, I smelled the faint aroma of a man. I bought him a stick of deodorant, but he told me Laurel'd already gotten him one. That was part of the problem. If Laurel would just *talk* to me about Andy, we wouldn't be buying him two sticks of deodorant. It had to scare her, too, the changes in him. The temptations he could fall victim to because he wanted to be one of the guys. By the time I was Andy's age, I'd been having sex for two years and drank booze nearly every day. I didn't have a disability and I still managed to screw myself up. What chance did Andy have of surviving his teens?

"How about we fly your kite on the beach today?" I suggested.

"Cool!" Andy never turned me down.

Laurel suddenly appeared in the doorway. She had on her running shorts and a *Save the Loggerheads* T-shirt. Her cheeks were a bright pink. She leaned against the jamb, arms folded, a white sheet of paper dangling from her hand. "What are y'all going to do today?" she asked.

"We're going to fly my kite," Andy said.

"That'll be fun," she said. "Why don't you go get it? It's in the garage on the workbench."

"I can get it when we leave," Andy said.

"Get it now, sweetie," Laurel said. "We should check it and make sure it's all in one piece. It's been a while since you flew it."

"Okay." Andy walked past her and down the stairs.

So Laurel wanted to talk to me without Andy there. A rarity. I tried to look behind the half smile on her face.

"You won't believe the email I got this morning," she said.

"Try me." I was stoked she wanted to share something with me. Who cared what it was? She looked down at the paper instead of at me. With her head tipped low like that, I could see that the line of her jaw was starting to lose its sharpness. To me, she'd always be that pretty eighteen-year-old girl Jamie brought home so long ago. The girl who played *Fur Elise* on my electric piano and who took me seriously when I said I wanted to play in a band. Who never made me feel second-best.

"It's from a woman at the *Today* show," she said, handing me the paper. "They want Andy and me to fly to New York to be on the show."

"You're kidding." I took the paper from her and read the short email. She was supposed to call the show Monday to make arrangements. Would appearing on TV be good for Andy or not? "Do you want to do it?" I asked.

"I think I'd like to," she said. "It's a chance to educate people. Make them aware they can't drink while they're pregnant. And that kids with FASD aren't all bad and out of control and violent and... you know."

Once you got Laurel started on FASD, it was hard to reel her in.

"Those bits they do are short." I didn't want her to get her hopes up. "They might just want to hear about Andy and the fire and not give you a chance to—"

"I'll get my two cents in," she said. "You know I will."

"Yeah." I smiled. "You will." I looked around the room at the cards. Swept my arm through the air. "It's bound to generate more of this stuff." I picked up the photograph of the blond from Andy's desk. "Did you see this one?"

Her eyes widened. "Lord, no!" she said. "Ugh. I'll keep a better eye on his mail."

"His email, too."

"Marcus." She gave me one of her disdainful looks. "I check *everything.* His email, where he surfs, his MySpace page. You know me."

I heard Andy on the stairs and quickly plucked the picture from her hand and set it back on his desk.

"It's perfect!" Andy blew into the room, the box kite just missing the doorjamb.

"Okay, you two," Laurel said. "Don't forget the sunscreen. It's in the drawer by the refrigerator. You'll grab it, Marcus?"

"I'll do that." I put my hand on the back of Andy's neck. "Let's go, And."

I trotted down the stairs with him, feeling pretty good. It was a step forward, Laurel telling me about the *Today* show, although she was so psyched, she probably would have told the plumber if he'd been the only person available. Still, it was progress.

For a year or so after Jamie died, Laurel didn't let me see the kids at all. My parents were dead. My brother as well. Laurel, Maggie and Andy were all the family I had left, and she cut me out. I'd had some shitty periods in my life but that year was my worst. I'm sure it was Sara who got her to let me back in. It was slow going at first. I could only see the kids with Laurel skulking someplace nearby. Then she finally gave me freer rein. "Just not on the water," she'd said.

I didn't blame her for her caution. How could I? She had good reason not to trust me.

After all, she believed I killed her husband.

Chapter Ten

Laurel
1984-1987

JAMIE COULD INDEED KEEP HIS WEIGHT OFF ME WHEN WE MADE love. I discovered, though, that I didn't want him to. Blanketed beneath him, I took comfort in the protective mass of him. Being with him, whether we were making love or riding his bike or talking on the phone, made me feel loved again, the way I'd felt as a young child. Loved and whole and safe.

We dated my entire freshman year at UNC. When I went home to Ohio for the summer, we kept in touch by phone and mail and made plans for him to come visit for a week in July. I told Aunt Pat and Uncle Guy about him as carefully as I could. They didn't like the fact that he was four years older than me. I could only imagine what they would say if I told them that there were really five years between our ages. They liked his religious studies degree, jumping to the conclusion that he was a Presbyterian like they were—and like they thought I still was. I'd been swayed by Jamie's negativity about organized religion and was gradually coming to understand his own deep, personal and passionate tie to God. They didn't understand why he was a carpenter when he should be using his degree in a "more productive manner." I wanted to tell them he was a carpenter because he liked being a carpenter and that his family had more money than they could ever dream of having. But I didn't want them to like Jamie for his family's wealth. I wanted them to like him for himself.

On the evening Jamie was due to arrive, Aunt Pat and Uncle Guy waited with me on the front porch of their Toledo home. They sat in the big white rocking chairs sipping lemonade, while I squirmed on the porch swing, my nerves as taut as the chains holding the swing to the ceiling. I tried to see my aunt and uncle through Jamie's eyes. They were a handsome couple in their late forties, and they looked as though they'd spent the day playing golf at a country club, although neither was a golfer and they couldn't afford the country club.

Although it was July, Uncle Guy had on a light blue sweater over a blue-and-white-striped shirt, and he didn't appear to be the least bit uncomfortable. He had chiseled good looks accentuated by the fact that he combed his graying hair straight back.

Aunt Pat wore a yellow skirt that fell just below her knees as she rocked. She had on sturdy brown shoes and panty hose. Her yellow floral blouse was neatly tailored, and her light brown hair was chin length, curled under, and held in place with plenty of spray. I tried to see my gentle mother in her face many times over the years, but I never could find her in my aunt's hard-edged features.

As dusk crept in from the west, I suddenly heard Jamie's motorcycle, still at least two blocks away. My heart pounded with both trepidation and desire. It had been a month since I'd seen him and I couldn't wait to wrap my arms around him.

"What's that ungodly sound!" Aunt Pat said.

"What sound?" I asked, hoping she was hearing something I could not hear.

"Sounds like a motorcycle," Uncle Guy said.

"In *this* neighborhood?" Aunt Pat countered. "I don't think so."

I saw him rounding the corner onto our street, and I stood up. "It's Jamie," I said, and I knew the meeting between my relatives and the man I loved was doomed before it even began.

He pulled into the driveway. His bike sounded louder than it ever had before, the noise bouncing off the houses on either side of the street. I walked down the porch steps and across the lawn. I wanted to run, to fling myself into his arms, but I kept my pace slow and even and composed.

I saw him anew as he pulled off his helmet. His hair fell nearly to the middle of his back. He took off his jacket to reveal what I'm sure he considered his best clothes—khaki pants and a plain black T-shirt. I saw how out of place he looked in this starched and tidy Toledo neighborhood.

He opened his arms and I stepped into them, only long enough to whisper, "Oh God, Jamie, they're going to be insufferable. I'm so sorry."

They were worse than insufferable. They were downright rude to him, shunning his attempts at conversation, offering him nothing to eat or drink. After a half hour of the coldest possible welcome, I told Jamie I'd show him to the guest room and we walked inside the house.

Upstairs, I led him into the spare room that I'd dusted and vacuumed that morning and closed the door behind us.

"Jamie, I'm sorry! I knew they'd be difficult but I really had no idea they'd be this...mean. They're not mean people. Just cold. They—"

"Shh." He put his finger to my lips. "They love you," he said.

"I...what do you mean?"

"I mean, they love you. They want the best for you. And here comes this big, hairy, scary-looking guy who probably doesn't smell so good right now and who has a blue-collar job and no car. And all they can see is that the little girl they love might be traveling down a path that can get her hurt."

I pressed my forehead to his shoulder, breathed in the scent of a man who'd been riding for two days to see the woman he loved. I loved him so much at that moment. I envied him, too, for his ability to step outside himself and into my aunt and uncle's shoes. But I wasn't sure he was right.

"I think they just care what the neighbors will think," I said into his shoulder.

He laughed. "Maybe there's some of that, too," he said. "But even if that's true, it's their fear coming out. They're scared, Laurie."

"Laurel?" my aunt called from the bottom of the stairs.

I pulled away from him, kissing him quickly on the lips. "The bathroom's at the end of the hall," I said. "And I'll be back as soon as I can."

I walked downstairs, where Aunt Pat waited for me. Her face was drawn and lined and tired. "Come out on the porch for a minute," she said.

On the porch, I took my seat on the swing again while Aunt Pat returned to the rocker. "He can't stay here," she said.

"*What?*" That was worse than I'd expected.

"We don't know him. We don't trust him. We can't——"

"*I* know him," I said, keeping my voice low only to prevent Jamie from hearing me. I wanted to scream at them. "I wouldn't be in love with someone who wasn't trustworthy."

Uncle Guy leaned forward in the rocking chair, his elbows on his knees. "What in God's name do you see in him?" he asked. "You were raised so much better than that."

"Than *what?*" I asked. "He's the best person I know. He cares about people. He's honest. He...he's very spiritual." I was desperately trying to find a quality in Jamie that would appeal to them.

"What does that mean?" Aunt Pat asked.

"He plans to start his own church some day."

"Ah, jeez." My uncle looked away from me with disgust. "He's one of those cult leaders," he said, as if talking to himself.

"I think your uncle's right," Aunt Pat said. "He has some kind of power over you, or you wouldn't be with someone like him."

She was right that he had power over me, but it was a benevolent sort of power.

"He's a good person," I said. "Please. How am I supposed to tell him he can't stay here when he just rode all the way from North Carolina to see me?"

"I'll pay for him to stay in a hotel for one night," Uncle Guy said.

I stood up. "He doesn't need your money, Uncle Guy," I said. "He has more money than you would know what to do with. What he needed from you was some tolerance and—" I stumbled, hunting for the right word "—some *warmth.* I should have known he wouldn't find it here." I opened the screen door. "He'll go to a hotel, and I'll be going with him."

"Don't...you...dare!" My aunt bit off each word.

I turned my back on them and marched into the house, amazed—and thrilled—by my own audacity.

In the end, Jamie wouldn't let me go with him. He told my aunt and uncle that I was a special girl and he could understand why they'd want to protect me so carefully.

"You talk like a sociopath, Mr. Lockwood," my uncle said, any remaining trace of cordiality gone.

Even Jamie was at a loss for words then. He left, and I sat on the porch steps the entire night, alternating between tears and fury as I imagined Jamie alone in a hotel room, tired and disappointed.

My aunt and uncle tried to coerce me into changing colleges in the fall, but my parents had been very wise. Even though they died in their early forties, they'd left money for my college expenses as well as a legal document stating the money was to be used at "the college, university or other institute of higher learning of Laurel's choice."

When I left Toledo for UNC that fall, I took everything with me. I knew I'd never be coming back.

Jamie proposed to me during the summer of my junior year and we set a wedding date for the following June. I exchanged an occasional letter with my aunt and uncle, but the wedding invitation I sent them went unanswered and, as far as I was concerned, that was it. I was finished with them. I didn't miss them—I was already so much a part of the Lockwood family and knew Miss Emma and Daddy L better than I'd ever known Aunt Pat and Uncle Guy. Daddy L was mostly a benign presence, a quiet man with an uncanny business sense when it came to real estate. Miss Emma couldn't survive without her three or four whiskey sours every afternoon-into-the-evening, but no one ever said a word about her drinking, as far as I knew. She was the sort of drinker who grew more mellow with each swallow. Marcus was cute and sweet but self-destructive, and he knew how to push his parents' buttons—as well as Jamie's. He'd long ago been labeled the difficult child and did his best to live up to expectations.

He landed in the hospital with a dislocated shoulder after wiping out on his surfboard because he was so drunk. He got beaten up by a girl's father for bringing her home late—by twelve hours. And twice before Jamie and I were married, he was arrested for driving under the influence. Daddy L bailed him out once. The second time, Jamie took care of it quietly so their parents wouldn't know. Marcus was a real challenge to Jamie's yearning to be empathic.

But I loved each of the Lockwoods, warts and all. I was so happy and full of excitement in those days that I no longer needed to count backward from a thousand to fall asleep. We were married the week after I received my nursing degree. Daddy L surprised us with the gift of The Sea Tender, the round cottage on the beach, my favorite of his properties. I took a job in a pediatrician's office in Sneads Ferry, where I fell in love with every infant, toddler and child that came through the door. With every baby I held, I longed for one of my own. I felt the pull of motherhood in every way—biological, emotional, psychological. I wanted to carry Jamie's baby. I wanted to nurse it and love it and raise it with the love my parents had showered on me before their deaths. I had no family of my own any longer. I wanted to create a new one with Jamie.

While I worked in the doctor's office, Jamie left carpentry to get his real estate license, manage his father's properties, and join the Surf City Volunteer Fire Department on the mainland. He even cut his hair—a radical change in his looks it took me a while to get used to—and bought a car, although he never did get rid of his motorcycle.

Living on the island in the eighties was extraordinary. I'd commute the easy distance to my job, then drive to the docks in Sneads Ferry to buy fresh shrimp or fish, then drive home to paradise. In the warm weather, I'd open all the windows in the cottage and let the sound of the waves fill the rooms as Jamie and I made dinner together. It was a time that would live in my heart always, even after things changed. I would never forget the peaceful rhythm of those days.

I knew Jamie had never lost his yearning for a church, so I wasn't surprised when he asked his father if he could build a little chapel on the land next to the inlet.

Daddy L laughed.

"It'll wash away in the first storm," he said, but he told Jamie to go ahead. He couldn't deny his favorite son anything.

We'd made friends with a few other year-round people on the island and across the bridge in Sneads Ferry, and three or four of them bought into Jamie's idea of a new kind of church and volunteered to help him build it. Daddy L suggested he build the foundation and walls out of concrete like the Operation Bumblebee towers that seemed able to withstand anything Mother Nature handed out. Jamie built his chapel in the shape of a pentagon with a steeple on top, so that no one would mistake it for anything other than a house of worship. Panoramic windows graced four sides of the building. He made heavy wooden shutters that could be hung over the windows when the weather threatened the island. Over the years, the wind stole the steeple four times, but no window was ever broken until Hurricane Fran in '96. Even then, the concrete shell of the chapel remained, rising out of the earth like a giant sand castle.

There was no altar in the chapel, no place for a minister to stand and preach. That's the way Jamie wanted it. He would be one of the congregation. Marcus, who was still living at home in Wilmington while attending community college, came down to help Jamie build pews out of pine, even though he never really bought into the whole idea of Jamie starting his own church. The pews formed concentric pentagons inside the building. Daddy L burned the words *Free Seekers Chapel* into a huge piece of driftwood, and Jamie hung the sign from a post buried deep in the sand near the front door.

Despite Jamie's desire to be one of the congregation, he did become an ordained minister of sorts. He saw an ad in the back of a magazine, and for thirty dollars, purchased a certificate showing him to be an ordained minister in the Progressive Church of the Spirit. He didn't take it seriously. He thought it was pretty funny, actually, but it enabled the people who loved his vision to call him *Reverend,* and that meant something to them.

Jamie and I agreed to wait to start a family until after the chapel was built, and as soon as the last pew was in place, I stopped my pills. The pediatrician I worked for warned me it would take a while to get pregnant after being on the pill for several years, but I must have conceived almost immediately, because within a couple of weeks, I knew something about my body was different. Sure enough, the pregnancy test I took in the obstetrician's office was positive.

I managed to keep the secret until that night, when Jamie and I indulged in one of our favorite pastimes: bundling up—it was October—and lying on the beach behind the cottage. Each of us wrapped in a blanket, we lay close together like two cocoons, wool hats pulled over our heads, staring in contented wonderment at the autumn sky.

"There's one," Jamie said, pointing north. We were trying to distinguish satellites from the stars.

"Where?" I followed his finger to the only constellation I recognized—Pegasus.

"Look southeast of Pegasus," he said. "And watch it closely."

"You're right." I followed the slow drift of the light toward the north.

The sky behind our house was always full of stars, especially in the fall and winter when we had the dark northern end of the island nearly to ourselves. The sound of the waves was music in our ears. Suddenly, I felt nearly overcome with the miracle my life had become. I lived in one of the most beautiful places on earth, in a round house like something out of a fairy tale, with a man whose love for me was matched only by mine for him. I thought of the tiny collection of cells inside me that would become our baby, how soon the globe of sky above us would be mirrored by the globe of my belly. I thought of how our child—our *children*—and our children's children would someday lie on this beach and watch the same stars and hear the same waves. And suddenly the thoughts were too enormous for me to contain any longer. Overwhelmed, I started to cry.

"Hey." Jamie lifted his head. "What's the matter?"

"I'm happy."

He laughed. "Me, too."

I leaned even closer to my husband. "And I'm pregnant."

I could barely see him in the darkness, but I heard his sharp intake of breath. "Oh, Laurie." He opened his blanket and pulled my cocoon inside his, planting kisses all over my face until I giggled. "How do you feel?"

"Fantastic," I said. And I did.

He looked down at me, touching my cheek with the tenderness that I'd come to love in him. "Our whole world is going to change," he said.

He had no idea how right he was.

The next morning at ten o'clock, thirteen people including Jamie and myself, arrived at the Free Seekers Chapel for its first service.

Four were friends who had helped Jamie build it. Four others were acquaintances, and the last three were strangers, curious to see what was going on inside the five walls of the diminutive building. I was a bit curious myself. Jamie had said little about his plans for a service. I'd wanted to sew him a stole. I'd make it different than any other I'd seen, bright with blues pulled from the sea and sky.

"Thanks, Laurie," he'd said when I suggested it. "But I don't want a stole. I don't want anything that sets me apart that much, okay?"

I understood.

The small chapel smelled of new wood, a delicious smell I would always associate with the promise of my young marriage and the life I carried inside me, and I breathed in deeply as we moved into one of the pews.

We waited a few minutes, then Jamie stood up in his jeans and leather jacket. He cleared his throat, the only giveaway that he was nervous. When he spoke, his voice echoed off the walls and the pews.

"Let's talk about where we experienced God this week," he said.

No one spoke as he took his seat again. The sound of the sea was muted by the double glass of the windows. In the silence, I heard one of the strangers, a man wearing a thick red flannel jacket who was chewing tobacco, spit into the blue plastic cup he carried. We sat there quietly for what seemed like minutes.

The first time I'd heard Jamie describe God as an *experience* instead of as a *being,* it scared me. It felt somehow blasphemous. Yet, slowly I started to understand what he meant. Something awakened in me, pushed the big man in robes out of my consciousness and replaced it with a powerful feeling hard to put into words.

I remembered the night before, lying on the beach with Jamie. I stood up suddenly, surprising myself as much as him.

"Last night I was lying out on the beach watching the stars," I said. "The sky was beautiful and suddenly a...a happiness came over me." I looked down at where my hands clutched the back of the pew in front of me. "That's not the right word. Not a strong enough word." I chewed my lower lip, thinking. "I felt *overwhelmed* by the beauty of the world and I felt...a joy that wasn't just on the surface but deep inside me, and I knew I was feeling...*experiencing* something that was outside of me." I didn't think I was explaining myself well. Words were so inadequate at expressing what I'd felt the night before on the beach. "I felt something bigger than myself last night," I said. "Something sacred."

I sat down slowly. Jamie took my hand and pressed it between his palms. I glanced at him and saw the smile I loved seeing on his face. It was a small smile, one that said *everything is right in our world*.

Another moment passed and then the man chewing tobacco stood up. "So, we supposed to say when we felt God's hand in something?" he asked.

Jamie hesitated. "It's an open-ended question," he said. "You're free to interpret it however you like."

"Well, then, I'd say I experienced God when I laid eyes on this here church for the first time this morning," he said. "I hear about it over to the Ferry, hear how a crazy young fella thinks he's a preacher made a five-sided church outta concrete and clapboard. And when I got outta my car and started walking 'cross the sand and saw this—" he waved the hand holding the blue cup through the air, taking in the five walls and expanse of windows "—when I saw this out here...well I felt it. What you talkin' about, missy." He looked at me. "Something good and big come over me. It's a feelin' I wouldn't mind havin' again."

The man sat down. I heard Jamie swallow. I could always tell when Jamie was moved because he would swallow that way, as if he was swallowing tears.

Silence filled the little room. I wanted someone else to say something, but Jamie seemed unconcerned. Finally a woman got up. She was about my age—twenty-two—with very short blond hair.

"My name's Sara Weston," she said, "and I think I'm the only person who lives in North Carolina who doesn't go to church."

A few people chuckled at that.

"I moved down here because my husband's stationed at Camp Lejeune," she said, which explained her accent. I wasn't sure where she was from, but it wasn't North Carolina or anyplace else south of the Mason-Dixon Line. "Everyone's always asking, what church do you go to?" Sara continued. "And they look at me like I've got two heads when I say I don't go. To be honest, I don't like church. I don't like all the rituals and...I don't even know if I believe in God."

I heard Jamie whisper, "That's all right," though I was certain no one could hear him but me.

"Sorry." Sara let out a breath, giving away a touch of anxiety. "I'll try to keep this positive. Usually when people ask me what church I go to, I just say I haven't decided yet, but then they always want to take me to *their* church. Now, I'm going to tell them I go to the Free Seekers church."

She sat down, blushing, and the man in the flannel jacket set his cup down and gave her a short but hearty round of applause.

The next Sunday, there were seventeen people inside Free Seekers...but there were also seventeen people outside, and one of them was Reverend Bill from Drury Memorial. He was preaching through a bullhorn, saying that Free Seekers wasn't really a church and that

Jamie Lockwood was a heretic and blasphemer and his tiny congregation was full of atheists and agnostics.

Inside, Jamie said, calm as ever, "Let's share where we experienced our own personal God this week," and people began to stand and speak and it was as though no one could hear what was going on outside.

Finally Floyd, the man with the red flannel jacket and blue plastic cup, stood up. "I have a mind to go tell that man to shut his trap."

Jamie didn't budge from his seat. "Imagine how threatened he must feel that he'd come here and try to disturb our service," he said. "Let's treat him kindly."

Reverend Bill became Jamie's nemesis. He tried to shut Free Seekers down by attacking it on all fronts. It was in an area not zoned for a church, he argued. Jamie was a fraudulent minister. The building itself was a blight on the unspoiled landscape near the inlet. I stayed out of it, worried that Reverend Bill had several legal legs to stand on. I don't know how, but Jamie wriggled out of every possible attack. Perhaps the Lockwood name was enough to offset any wrongdoing. Where Reverend Bill *did* succeed was in turning his own small congregation against us. Jamie Lockwood and his followers were heathens. That bothered Jamie, whose intention was never to cause friction, never to force people to take sides. His vision was one of peace and tolerance. As he'd once said himself: pie in the sky.

I was four months' pregnant when Miss Emma and Daddy L kicked Marcus out of the house. He'd dropped out of college before he could flunk out, but he was working in construction and Jamie was upset by his parents' decision.

"I don't understand Mama and Daddy," he said to me one morning at breakfast. "Marcus already feels like the second-class son. Getting kicked out of the house is only going to make him feel worse."

I poured milk onto my granola. "Let's take him in," I said simply. "There's plenty of work for him on the island and we've got room. We can help him get on his feet."

Jamie stared at me, his spoon midway to his mouth. "You're utterly amazing, do you know that?"

I shrugged with a smile. "You're just rubbing off on me," I said.

"I thought of having him live with us for a while, but I was afraid to ask you." Jamie rested the spoon in his bowl. "I know he can be a pain. You already have to put up with a lunatic husband, and with the baby coming and everything..." His voice trailed off then, and he shook his head. "I've always been the golden child," he said. "I love my parents, but they've never treated Marcus the same way they treated me."

"He could never measure up to you."

"I'll feel better if he's with us and we can keep an eye on him." Jamie leaned across the table to kiss me. "Maybe we can straighten him out."

"Maybe we can," I agreed.

But that was not what happened.

Chapter Eleven

Laurel

THE SECURITY LINE AT THE WILMINGTON AIRPORT WAS
longer than I'd anticipated for six in the morning, and I was afraid
I hadn't allowed enough time to make our plane. Andy slumped
against me as we waited, and I could hardly blame him. We'd gotten up at 4:00 a.m. to make the six-thirty flight to New York, but
everything had taken longer than it should have. Getting Andy out
of bed took fifteen minutes alone. Changing his routine was always
dicey. I nearly had to brush his teeth for him and when I turned my
back, he'd crawled into bed again. The cab had to wait for us in the
driveway. I told myself we'd be fine. We were only going to be in
New York a couple of nights so we had no bags to check. Still, it was
nearly six by the time we reached the security line.

We were due at Rockefeller Plaza early the following morning
for our appearance on the *Today* show. I knew what I wanted to say
about FASD, and I'd done enough speaking on the subject over the
years that I knew I could get the information across quickly without seeming didactic or preachy. That was my goal. I also needed
to mention the Drury Memorial Family Fund. Dawn had asked if
I could get them to air the internet address for the fund so viewers
could make contributions. I promised I would try.

We were nearly to the security checkpoint. Finally. I nudged Andy, who was still leaning against me, his eyes closed.

"Come on, sweetie. Let's start taking our shoes off."

He bent over and untied his tennis shoes. "When did I go on a plane before, Mom?" he asked.

"When you were little." I kicked off my pumps and bent over to pick them up. "You were two or three. We flew to Florida to visit your grandmother who was spending the winter there."

"Grandma Emma, right?"

"That's right."

"I don't remember her."

"You were little when she passed away." We'd reached the conveyor belt and I slid him a plastic bin. "Put your shoes and your jacket in here."

He dumped his shoes in the bin. "Why do we have to take our shoes off?"

That was the sort of question I had to answer carefully. If I said anything about a bomb or terrorists, he'd fixate on the threat and the flight would be sheer misery.

I hoisted our carry-on bag onto the belt.

"They have to make sure we're only carrying safe things onboard," I said.

"I saw the sign."

"What sign?"

"That said don't carry guns, liquids and all those things."

"Right."

The conveyor belt swept the bins into the X-ray machine.

"Bye-bye shoes." Andy waved after them.

I smiled at the bored-looking security guard standing next to the metal detector as I handed him my driver's license and boarding pass.

"Hold your boarding pass so the security guard can see it," I told Andy.

I walked through the metal detector first, relieved I didn't set off the alarm.

"My turn?" Andy asked me.

"Hurry up, sweetie," I glanced at my watch. "We're running late."

Andy stretched his arms out to his sides as if for balance and walked toward the metal detector, a look of concentration on his face. I was afraid he was going to crash into the metal detector with his arms, but he dropped them to his sides just before stepping through.

The alarm pinged.

"Oh, great," I said, blowing out my breath and walking toward Andy. "It's his belt buckle," I said to the guard. "I should have thought of it."

"Step back, ma'am," the guard said to me. "You have a belt on?" he asked Andy.

Andy lifted his jersey to display his metal belt buckle. "It's not liquid or anything," he said.

"Are you trying to joke with me, boy?" the guard asked. "Take off your belt."

"He's not trying to joke," I said as Andy pulled off his belt. "He really thinks you're—"

"Ma'am, just let me do my job." The guard coiled the belt into a plastic bowl. "Walk through again," he said to Andy.

Andy stepped through the metal detector again.

Ping!

I was lost. What could he possibly be wearing that would set it off?

"I don't understand," I said. "He's not wearing a watch or—"

"Step over here." The guard motioned Andy to walk over to the other side of the conveyor belt, where a stocky, uniformed woman stood. She wielded a baton-shaped metal detector like a billy club.

"Hold your hands out to your sides," she instructed.

Andy looked at me as if for permission.

"Go ahead, Andy," I said. "It's all right. The guard just needs to figure out why you set the alarm off." I pulled our carry-on bag from the conveyor belt, then gathered our shoes, jackets and my pocketbook from the bins. My arms were shaking.

"We're very late for our flight," I said to the guard as she ran the wand over Andy's chest.

"Is that a microphone?" Andy asked. "We're going to be on TV and talk into microphones."

"We are." I hoped I could soften the woman up a little. "We're actually heading to New York to be on the—"

Dih-dih-dih-dih. The wand let out a staticky sound as it passed over Andy's left sock.

"Take off your sock," the woman commanded.

"His sock?" I was completely perplexed.

The guard ignored me.

"Go ahead, Andy," I said.

Andy pulled off his sock and something small and silver *plinked* to the floor.

"What's that?" I asked.

"My lighter," Andy said.

I leaned closer. "Your *lighter?*"

"Stand back, ma'am." The guard carefully picked up the object with her gloved fingers.

"Andy!" I was astonished. "Why do you have a cigarette lighter?"

Andy shrugged, splotches of red on his cheeks. He was in trouble with me and he knew it.

"Put your shoes on," the woman said, "and then I'll have to ask the two of you to come with me."

"Come with you?" I dropped one of the shoes from my over-laden arms, and dropped two more when I bent over to pick it up. "Where?" I scrabbled around on the floor trying to fit everything into my arms again.

"You can sit here to put your shoes on." The guard motioned to a row of chairs.

Giving in, I sat down and motioned to Andy to do the same. We put on our shoes, the guard watching our every move.

"Where do you want us to go?" I asked, getting to my feet. Our jackets and my pocketbook were over my arm and my free hand wheeled the carry-on.

"To the Public Safety Department for questioning," she said, turning on her heel. "Follow me."

Andy started to follow her. "Wait!" I said. "Our plane leaves in fifteen minutes. Can't you just confiscate the lighter and let us go?"

"No, ma'am." She rambled on in a monotone about federal regulations, all the while leading us down a corridor from which I feared we'd never escape.

She led us into a small office where a uniformed officer, his bald head gleaming in the overhead light, sat behind a desk. He looked up at our entry.

"Sir," the guard said, "this boy tried to get through security with a lighter concealed in his sock."

"I'm his mother, Officer," I said. The man had kind eyes beneath high, expressive eyebrows. "I'm so sorry this happened, but we're going to miss our plane if—"

"Sit down." He motioned to the two chairs in front of his desk.

"We have to go to New York to be on the *Today* show," Andy said as he sat down.

I remained standing. "Is there a chance you can have them hold the plane for us?" I asked.

He looked at me. "If you don't take this seriously, ma'am, how do you expect your son to respect the law?" So much for the kind eyes.

I sank into the chair next to Andy, wondering how long it was until the next plane to New York.

The man folded his arms on his desk and leaned forward. "How old are you, son?" he asked Andy.

"Fifteen."

"You're fifteen?" He looked like he didn't believe him.

"He is," I said.

"I'm small for my age," Andy said.

"Why did you have a lighter in your sock?" the officer asked.

"Because of the sign."

"And what sign is that?"

"The one that said don't carry guns and knives onboard. It said don't carry lighters, too."

"Oh, no," I said under my breath. "He took it literally," I said to the officer.

"Ma'am, I have to ask you to be quiet." Then to Andy, "If you knew the sign said not to bring lighters onboard, why did you have a lighter in your sock?"

I saw tears in Andy's eyes. "I put it in my sock so I wouldn't be carrying it," he said.

I reached over and rested my hand on his knee. "I can explain—"

"Ma'am." The officer gave me a warning look. Then he sat back in his chair, tapping a pen on his desk. "We have these regulations in place for your protection, son," he said, looking at Andy. "We don't take joking about them lightly."

"Please, Officer," I said. "He has a disability."

The man ignored me. "What were you planning to use the lighter for?" he asked.

Andy darted his gleaming eyes at me. "In case I wanted a cigarette."

"Do you know you can't smoke on the plane?"

"I wouldn't smoke on the plane."

"And where are your cigarettes?"

"I don't have any."

"But you had a lighter that was so important to you that you carried it on your person."

Andy had had it. "Mom?" He looked at me for help, one tear slipping over his lower lashes.

"Sir, Andy has Fetal Alcohol Spectrum Disorder," I spoke quickly. I wouldn't let the man stop me again. "He doesn't understand the fine point of what you're saying. If he sees a sign that says 'don't carry something,' he takes that literally to mean he shouldn't *carry* something. You carry things in your hands. I didn't know he had a lighter. I didn't even know he smoked." I darted my eyes at Andy with a look that said we would talk about *that* later. "But I can assure you, he had no idea he was doing anything wrong. We're flying to New York to be on the *Today* show tomorrow morning, because Andy saved some lives in a fire in Surf City."

The man's eyebrows shot halfway up his forehead. "You're *that* boy?" he asked.

"Yes, sir," Andy said in a small voice. "People followed me out the window."

The man pursed his lips. He picked up the lighter from the desk in front of him, flipped open the top and thumbed the wheel to produce a long slender flame. "Well," he said, snapping the lid closed. "Needless to say, we're confiscating this lighter. We have some paperwork to attend to. And—" he looked at the computer monitor on his desk, clicked a few keys on his keyboard "—there's another flight to LaGuardia at ten-ten."

"Three *hours* from now?" I was nearly whining. "That's the next one?"

"Yes, ma'am. There's room on it, though, so you're lucky."

It was nearly seven-thirty by the time we returned to the main part of the terminal. "Let's get something to eat," I said. "That'll kill some time."

We each got a muffin and a bottle of water, then found seats at the gate.

"Okay, Andy," I said, once we'd arranged our belongings on the seats around us. We were the only two people at the gate. "We need to have a talk. You promised me you'd never smoke."

Andy studied the toe of his well-examined sneaker as he chewed a mouthful of blueberry muffin.

"Andy?"

He swallowed. "I sometimes do," he said, "but I don't suck the smoke into my chest. Just my mouth."

"*Why?*"

"Because it's cool."

"Which of your friends smoke?" I asked.

He hesitated again. "Do I have to tell you?"

I thought about it. What difference did it make?

"No," I said, sighing. "You don't. But you *do* have to tell me where you got that lighter." It hadn't been a cheap little Zippo.

"I traded for it."

"What did you trade for it?"

"Mom, I don't want to talk about it!"

"You have to, Andy."

"I traded my pocketknife."

"*What* pocketknife?" I hadn't known he had one.

He rolled his eyes. "The one I've always had."

I sighed. "I know you want to fit in," I said. "I know you want to be...cool. But teenagers do some stupid things." As disturbed as I was about the lighter, I was more upset to realize there were parts of my son I didn't know. If he'd lied to me about not smoking, what else was he lying to me about? "What about drugs? You also promised me you wouldn't do drugs. How do I know you're not doing them, too?"

"I would *never* do drugs," he said with such vehemence I believed him. At least, I believed that he meant it at that moment in time.

"I'm tired," he said, slumping low in the seat.

"Me, too." I thought we'd had enough heavy discussion for one morning. I reached into my pocketbook for the novel I'd brought with me. "Why don't you close your eyes and take a nap?"

He leaned his head against my shoulder, my angelic little boy again. I let the book rest in my lap and shut my eyes.

How were we going to survive the rest of his adolescence? I wondered. I didn't like to think about what next year would be like without Maggie at home. She was a second set of eyes watching over him. Her own commitment to education—to excellence in everything she did—influenced him. She would be as surprised as I was to learn about the lighter.

We were both bleary-eyed by the time we filed into the small jet.

"Do you want to sit next to the window?" I asked, pointing to the two seats reserved for us.

"Yeah!" he said, sliding into the seat.

"Buckle your seat belt," I said as I buckled my own. He popped the buckle together and then I pulled it tight.

The flight attendant, an Asian woman with sad eyes and a bright smile, stood up and began going through her motions.

"Who is that lady?" Andy asked loudly.

"She's the flight attendant. She's explaining some things about the plane. Let's listen."

The attendant showed how to undo the seat belt and Andy obediently undid his.

"She's showing how for later," I said. "So buckle it back up now."

She demonstrated the use of the oxygen mask and Andy leaned forward, tongue pursed between his lips as he concentrated on her instructions.

He turned to me when the attendant had finished.

"Why did she say adults traveling with children should put their mask on first?" he asked.

"Because the adult can't take good care of the child unless she takes care of herself first," I said.

For some reason, that made him laugh.

"What's so funny?"

"You'd put mine on before yours," he said with certainty. "You always take care of me before anybody else."

Chapter Twelve

Maggie

LIGHTS WERE ON IN SOME OF THE HOUSES AS I DROVE TO THE Sea Tender. It was the first week in April, and people were starting to take vacations. In a couple of months, the island would be totally different. The everybody-knows-everybody-else feeling would morph into wall-to-wall strangers with new faces every week as they moved in and out of the rental houses and mobile homes. I dreaded it. There'd be people in the houses near The Sea Tender and they'd be snoopy and curious.

I didn't have to lie to Mom about where I was going tonight, since she and Andy were in New York. I hated lying, but that seemed like all I did anymore. It looked like my little brother had been doing some lying himself lately. Mom called from New York to tell me about the lighter. I had a feeling Andy smoked. I caught a telltale whiff on him sometimes, but when I came right out and asked him if he smoked, he said, "Of *course* not, Maggie!" I fell for it.

Andy's screwups scared me. So far, they'd been little things. As he grew up, the chance for him to make bigger mistakes would grow along with him.

Like I had room to talk.

I parked down the street and kept my flashlight off as I walked along the road. I turned up the little boardwalk between two of the front-row houses to where our old cottage sat on the beach.

I lugged the cinder block beneath the steps and climbed up to the front door. Inside the cottage, I didn't head for the rear deck like I did when trying to make contact with Daddy. I was there for a different reason tonight—a *worldly* reason, one that made lying absolutely necessary.

The bedroom that had been my parents' was smaller than the other two, but it was the only one with a view of the ocean. It was also the only room in the entire house without a broken or boarded-up window. I could see a couple of lights far out on the water. I watched them long enough to see that one was sailing north, the other south. Then I lit all six of the jasmine-scented candles on the little plastic table in the corner of the room. The full-size bed—just a saggy old mattress, box spring and rusty frame—was one of the pieces of furniture Mom left behind when we deserted The Sea Tender. I pulled back the covers on the bed and took out the sheets of fabric softener I'd left on the pillows. I never knew how long it would be before I came back, and I hated the smell of stale linen.

I just finished plumping up the pillows when I heard footsteps on the front deck, then the creak of the sticky old door.

"Anyone home?" Ben asked quietly.

I tore through the living room to get to him. He pulled me into his arms and I buried my face against his chest, suddenly crying.

"It's okay, angel," he said, stroking my hair. "It was too long this time. I know."

I couldn't stop blubbering. Total meltdown, like I'd been saving it all up for him—for the moment I could finally let it out. I always had to be the strong one in my family. With Ben, I could just be me. He held me till I stopped crying. He always knew what I needed.

"It's been torture," I managed to say.

We hadn't been together—not *this* way—since before the fire. We coached the Pirates together, acting like we hardly knew each other so no one would wonder about us and start gossiping. We talked and text-messaged and exchanged a few emails, but no way could that substitute for being alone together.

He leaned back from me and ran his hand over my cheek. A little candlelight spilled out of the bedroom and I could see his chocolatey-brown eyes and the gory new scar on his forehead.

"How is it?" I touched the scar lightly.

He winced and I pulled my hand away.

"Sorry! Sorry!" I hated that I'd hurt him.

"Just tender," he said. "Got the stitches out this morning." He touched the scar himself. "I'll always have a reminder of that night."

"You're safe, though," I said.

"Others weren't so lucky."

"I was so scared."

"Shh." He kissed me, then suddenly lifted me up, the way an old-fashioned groom carries a bride over the threshold. He carried me into the bedroom. The jasmine smell was so strong, I felt drunk. Ben put me down on the bed and started undressing me. My throat still felt clogged with tears. I didn't want to start crying again, though. I wouldn't. Ben needed a woman tonight. Not a little girl.

I wasn't one of those wide-eyed girls who believed in love at first sight, but the first minute I saw Ben, something happened to me. It was my seventeenth birthday, nearly a year ago, and I was in the lounge at the rec center waiting to meet the new coach of the older kids. Their old coach, Susan Crane, was moving to Richmond, so a new guy was taking her place. Susan was thirty-five, so I don't know why I expected the new guy to be my age, but I did.

Ben stood at the check-in counter, filling out paperwork and laughing with David Arowitz, one of the managers. I thought he was opening a membership at the center, and I took him in in one big gulp. He wore blue-and-green-striped jams, like he was checking in to use the pool, and a short-sleeve blue shirt and sandals. He was big. He'd probably been one of those boys who had to wear those "husky-size" clothes. His hair was short, dark and wavy. He had a straight nose, dimples—at least on the side of his face I could see—and long, heavy-duty eyelashes. I swear, I took in all those details in one instant and literally felt something happen to my heart, like someone squeezed it hard enough to send tingles down my arms.

I knew what he was like just by looking at him. He was kind, he loved animals, he'd rather play volleyball than golf, he believed in God but wasn't religious, he loved scary movies, he could talk about emotional things, he smoked marijuana but never cigarettes. I knew all of this in the time it took the tingling to run from my heart to my fingertips. I also knew he was way too old for me, but I didn't care. I was in love.

Suddenly David pointed in my direction. Ben said something to him, then started walking toward me. The one thing I hadn't figured out about him was that he was the new coach.

"Maggie?" He held out his hand. The dimple was only on one side of his mouth. "I'm Ben Trippett."

I wasn't all that used to shaking hands with people. When I shook his, I felt heat coming off his palm, like he ran a few degrees warmer than everyone else on the planet. I would learn that about him—his hands were *always* hot. Maybe it was the heat that did it to me. All I knew was that I was completely, totally lost.

He was all I could think about. I suddenly understood why my girlfriends developed tunnel vision when they were hung up on a guy. I couldn't wait for our twice-weekly swim team practice. Sometimes he and I would stop at McDonald's afterward. I'd get a soda; he'd get a milk shake. We'd talk about our swimmers—who was strong, who needed more work on a certain stroke. We'd set goals for our team. The whole time, I'd be thinking *I love you, I love you, I love you.*

He lived with Dawn Reynolds, but I tried not to think about that. I didn't know Dawn well; she'd only been on the island for about a year. I didn't believe in breaking anybody up, but I couldn't help what I felt for him. I made up reasons to see him. He worked at the Lowes in Hampstead, and sometimes after school I'd think of an excuse to go there. I bought paint for my room that I never got around to putting on the walls and a lamp I knew I didn't like and would have to return.

We started talking about other things when we went to McDonald's. Movies—we both loved scary ones, as I predicted. His divorce, which was "messy," and his seven-year-old daughter, Serena, who lived with his ex-wife in Charlotte. He missed her a lot. I could tell he was a good father. I loved that about him.

Then one night, he said he wanted to talk about Dawn.

"When I first moved here, I rented one of the mobile homes in Surf City," he told me. "I was in Jabeen's Java one day and started talking to her. She was about to tack a flyer on the bulletin board looking for a housemate. She'd gotten divorced around the time I did and she was going to lose her house on the beach if she didn't find someone to share expenses. So it was a no-brainer."

"So...you and Dawn are just housemates?"

When he nodded, I felt like I was sitting on a cloud instead of a molded plastic bench at McDonald's.

"Except it's a little more complicated than that," he said. "She'd just gotten divorced and I'd just gotten divorced and..." He looked straight at me with those chocolatey eyes. "Have you ever broken up with anyone?"

"Not really." I'd only had three dates in my life.

"Well then, it might be hard for you to understand, but when a marriage ends, especially if you tried hard to save it and you still care about the person, it leaves you really raw...and very lonely. Dawn and I were both in that place when I moved in." He took a sip of his milk shake. Then another. He wasn't looking at me. "She's a pretty woman," he said finally, "and I was attracted to her physically."

I cringed. "Am I gonna get TMI here?"

"TMI?"

"Too much information."

"Oh." He smiled. "Probably."

"Oh, no." I sat up straight and got ready to hear the worst. "Okay," I said. "Go ahead."

His cheeks had turned pink. I loved that he wanted to talk to me about something personal enough to make him blush. "Well, you've figured it out," he said. "I screwed up. We slept together the first week I moved in. By the second week, I knew it had been a mistake. She's a nice woman, but we were never going to be right for each other. I told her I just wanted to be friends and offered to move out. She was upset. In her mind, she thought—she still thinks—we're a good match and she didn't want me to leave. Not only that, but she needs the financial help. So that's why I'm there." He blew out his breath and poked down one of the little raised bumps on his milkshake lid. "And the reason I'm telling you this is because I have very strong feelings for you, Maggie."

Oh…my…God. "Me, too." I was amazed I got the words out. My mouth was so dry I thought they'd stick to my tongue.

"I know you do," he said. "There's such a connection between us. You might be seventeen chronologically, but you're no kid. No immature teenager. I don't really want to fight the feelings I have for you. But…you're seventeen."

"You already mentioned that."

"And I'm ten years older. I don't want to take advantage of you."

"Ben." I hated the table between us. "I love you. I've loved you for months. And you're right. I'm not an immature teenager. I hardly ever date because guys my age are such—" I shook my head "—total losers. The way I feel about you is different. It's like the way I love my brother and my—"

"What?" He laughed.

"I mean, it's really, really deep and…" I was afraid I was starting to *sound* like an immature teenager. It was hard to explain how I felt about him. "It's…pure," I said finally. "I don't know how else to describe it."

"Well—" his dimple was so cute when he smiled "—I like that description." He leaned back and sighed. "Whew," he said. "I've wanted to have this conversation with you for weeks. I wasn't afraid of what you'd say. I knew you felt the same way I did. But it changes things, and I don't know what to do next. You're just starting your senior year. Maybe we should try to keep it...you know, *platonic,* until you're out of high school."

I'd pictured lying in bed with him a thousand times. One of my arms would be across his chest, and one of his would circle my shoulders protectively. I didn't really care about having sex with him. I wanted something more than that. Something deeper that would last the rest of my life.

"I don't want to wait," I said. "The age of consent in North Carolina is sixteen. I'm seventeen and five months. You have my consent."

"We can't be out in the open," he said. "Your mother... God, your *uncle.* They'd kill me."

"I know." He was right about that. I was certain Mom had been a virgin on her wedding night, and Uncle Marcus was always giving me that "guys are out for one thing" lecture. Maybe guys *my* age were. Ben was totally different.

"And there's really no place we can be together," Ben said.

It was my turn to smile.

"Yes," I said, "there is."

Later, when I realized I could tell him anything at all—almost, anyway—I told him how I felt in the beginning. How I didn't think I wanted him sexually. He laughed and said, "Well, *that's* certainly changed." I guess it did, but my favorite part of being with Ben was still lying in his arms in the bedroom of The Sea Tender, telling him everything I thought and felt. I even told him two of my biggest secrets.

The first was that I threw the most important swim meet of the season when I was fourteen because I felt sorry for my competitor. That girl was so gangly, dorky and uncoordinated that her teammates groaned when it was her turn to swim. I couldn't make myself beat her. I pretended to get a cramp on my third lap.

Ben said I was sweet, but insane.

Second, I told him about feeling Daddy's spirit on the deck of The Sea Tender. That's when I found out I'd been wrong about one thing: Ben was religious after all. First, he just teased me about it, saying he hoped Daddy didn't show up when we were in bed together. When he realized I was serious, though, he got serious himself. He said the devil was playing tricks on me and I should be careful. I was disappointed that he believed in the devil. I wanted him to be my mirror image, with my thoughts and beliefs. I wanted him to be everything I needed—my confidant and best friend and lover. I realized then that no one person could be all those things to another. I was a little more careful about what I told him after that.

I would never even consider telling him my third secret.

After we made love, Ben got the marijuana from the kitchen while I crawled naked under the covers, breathing in jasmine and fabric softener. Ben got back in bed and I snuggled close to him while he lit a joint.

He took a hit, then passed it to me.

"God, this feels good, being here with you," he said. "It's been such a shitty week."

"I know."

"I have these...not nightmares, exactly. But when I go to bed, I start picturing Serena at a lock-in when she's a few years older. She gets scared a lot. Thunderstorms. Strangers. Dogs. You name it. She might have panicked if she'd been there. She could've been one of the kids who didn't make it."

"Don't think about that, Ben." *I* didn't want to think about it. I slipped the joint between his lips. "Think about that girl you saved. Uncle Marcus said she'd be dead if it hadn't been for you."

"I do think about her, believe me," he said. "She's still at New Hanover and I've visited her a couple times. She's going to be okay. Then I think about how close I came to leaving her there because my air was getting low and I was…" He shuddered. "I'll tell you, Maggie, I was sweatin' bullets."

"It must have been awful." I knew all about his claustrophobia, how he'd start to panic the moment he'd put the face piece on. I hated the rude things the other firefighters said about him right to his face, like he had no feelings. Once, I overheard one of them say to Uncle Marcus, "I don't know why you even bother to give him a pager. He's useless." It made me *furious.* He told me he was even thinking of leaving, going back to Charlotte, because he couldn't take it anymore. I freaked out when he said that. What would I do without him?

"How did you stand wearing the face piece?" I asked.

"I turned the emergency bypass valve on, just for a second," he said. "It gave me a little rush of air. A beautiful sound. It wasn't the air so much as just reminding myself that I had the bypass valve if I needed it."

"But when you got that low-air warning, you must've freaked."

"Yes, ma'am, I was as freaked as you can get. But I could also see that girl in the camera. I had to get her."

"I'm really proud of you. Have the other guys stopped giving you a hard time?"

He nodded. "I think they've finally accepted me," he said, letting the smoke pour from his lungs. "Even got a couple of apologies from some of the worst offenders. So that's my silver lining. The cost was too high, though."

Those big photographs from the memorial service popped into my mind, past the wall I'd built inside my head to try to keep them out. At the service, I felt sick to my stomach as Reverend Bill talked about each of them. I'd wanted to run out of the Assembly Building but was afraid of making a scene.

"Do you see why I have to believe there's an afterlife?" I asked Ben now. "Why I'm so sure Daddy visits me out here? I have to believe those three people—Jordy and Henderson and Mr. Eggles—that they're someplace better."

"I believe that," Ben said. "I just don't believe dead people can contact us."

He hadn't experienced what I had with Daddy, so he didn't understand.

We'd reached the end of the joint and Ben stubbed it out in a clamshell we kept on the floor next to the bed. I remembered that night in the E.R., how scared I was to see him there and how invisible I felt when Dawn practically knocked me over to get to him. People always thought he and Dawn were an item and although he never came right out and agreed with them, he also never bothered to set them straight. She was our cover, he said, which only bothered me when I saw her staring at him the way she did Saturday at the swim meet. I could see how much she loved him. It was all over her face. I felt sorry for her the way I'd felt sorry for the gangly fourteen-year-old girl I let beat me years ago. But I wasn't letting her have Ben.

"Dawn loves you so much," I said. "When she saw you at the E.R., she looked so relieved to see you were all right. It was like when I saw that Andy was okay. I feel like I'm hurting her by being with you."

"I haven't misled her. You know that."

"But she thinks you're unattached. That gives her hope."

"What can I do about it, Maggie?" He sounded a little pissed off. "I can't very well tell her about us."

"I know," I said quickly. I had never heard him sound annoyed with me before and it shook me up. "I feel sorry for her, that's all." What *did* I want him to do? I didn't know.

A breeze suddenly blew into the room from the living room, putting out all but two of the candles. I stood up and walked to the corner to relight them. When I turned to come back to bed, the candlelight must have landed on my hip.

Ben rose up on his elbows. "What's that on your hip?" he asked.

"A tattoo," I said.

"You're kidding." He sat up. "Is it new?"

"No. You just never noticed it before." I'd had it for over a year, placed low enough that my mother would never see it.

"I can't tell what it is from here," Ben said.

"Just a word." I stepped close enough for him to read it.

"*Empathy.*" He ran his fingers over the small calligraphied print. "Why?"

"To remind me to walk in other people's shoes," I said.

Ben laughed, pulling me down on the bed so that I straddled him. "You don't need any reminders of that, angel," he said, his superheated hands on my hips. "You wrote the book."

Chapter Thirteen

Andy

THEY PUT US ON A LITTLE COUCH THING. THERE WERE BIG cameras on stands and lots of men and ladies all over. One lady sat in a chair looking at us. I looked at the camera and smiled like you're supposed to do when you get your picture taken.

The lady in the chair said, "Andy, when we start talking, just look at me. Don't look at the camera. We'll pretend we're having a normal conversation, okay?"

"Okay." She was nice to look at. Pretty, with shiny hair like Mom's only blacker, and Chinesey eyes. Her voice was soft and reminded me of how Maggie talked sometimes.

Mom smiled at me and squeezed my hand like she always did. Her hand was cold as a Popsicle.

A man attached a teeny black microphone to my shirt and said not to worry about it. A lady wearing a headset held up three fingers, then two fingers, then one finger.

Then the lady started talking to us, and I looked right at her, like she said to do. I told myself, *don't look anywhere else except at the lady.* I didn't want to screw up.

"Tell us about the fire, Andy," she said to me. Her eyes had sparkles in them.

"I was at the lock-in with my friend Emily and all of a sudden there was fire everywhere," I said. "Some boys got on fire and I told them to stop, drop and roll!"

"You did?" the lady asked. "Where did you learn that?"

I couldn't remember exactly where. I wanted to look at Mom to ask her, but remembered I was only supposed to look at the lady. "I think school, but I'm not sure," I said.

"That's right," Mom said.

My knee was bouncing like it does sometimes and I thought Mom would put her hand on it to make it stop, but she didn't.

"And what happened then, Andy? People were trying to get out of the church, right? But they couldn't?"

"Because of the fire."

"I understand the front doors were blocked by the flames."

"And the back door, too."

"That must have been very scary."

"Emily was scared. She had her shirt on inside out."

The lady looked confused and turned to Mom.

"His friend Emily is a special-needs child who doesn't like to have the seam of her clothing touch her skin," Mom said.

"Ah, I see," the lady said. "So how *did* you get out of the fire, Andy?"

"I went to the boys' room and outside the window was the metal… the air-conditioner box thing and I climbed out onto it and helped Emily out. Then I went back in and got people to follow me out."

"Amazing," the lady said. When she turned her head a little, the sparkles in her eyes moved. "You saved a lot of lives."

I nodded. "I was a…" I remembered I wasn't supposed to talk about being a hero.

"He was a hero," Mom said, "but I've told him not to brag about it."

I accidentally looked at Mom for a minute. She had the sparkles in her eyes, too! Freaky.

"How do you feel about what you did, Andy?" the lady asked.

"Good," I said. "But some people died. I guess they didn't all hear me call to them. Your eyes are really pretty. They have sparkles in them."

The lady and Mom both laughed. "It's from the lights," the lady said. "But thank you for that compliment, Andy." She turned to Mom again. "Laurel, can you tell us a little about Andy and Fetal Alcohol Spectrum Disorder?"

"I can tell you about it," I said.

Mom did put her hand on my knee then, which meant *shut up.*

"Let's give your mother a chance to talk, Andy."

"Okay," I said, even though I've heard Mom talk about FASD so many times I could say it all myself. She talked about how she had a drinking problem when she was pregnant with me and that made me different than other kids. She went into rehab and hasn't had a drink since then. I was in a foster home and she got me back when I was one year old. She threw herself into making sure I got the best care and education possible. See? I could say it all myself.

"I'm on a swim team," I said. "And I always win."

Mom and the lady laughed again. Mom said I'm an excellent competitioner because of my startling reflex. And that I have an average IQ, which I know means I'm intelligent and can do things a lot better than I actually do if I'd just try harder.

"I'm as smart as most people," I said. "But my brain works different."

Mom said about the lighter and how we missed the plane, which I still don't really understand 'cause if you have a lighter in your sock you're not actually carrying it.

"There's a fund that's been created for the medical expenses of the children injured in the fire," the lady said to the camera. "If you'd like to help, the internet site is on your screen."

"Many of the children who were hurt at the lock-in are from families with limited funds," Mom said.

"She means they're poor," I said, proud that I understood.

"You have another child, too," the lady said to Mom. "Does she also have FASD?"

"Does she mean Maggie?" I asked Mom, though I kept my eyes on the lady.

"Yes, Maggie is my older daughter. I wasn't drinking when I was pregnant with her and she's fine."

"Maggie's the best sister," I said.

"She is?" the lady asked.

"She'd put my oxygen mask on first, too," I said.

Chapter Fourteen

Laurel
1989

"LOOK AT HER HAIR!" MISS EMMA SAID AS JAMIE SETTLED THE baby in her arms. "Your hair was exactly like this when you were born," she said to her son. "A thick head of beautiful black curls."

"Isn't she something?" Jamie sat down next to his mother on our sofa. He hadn't stopped grinning in the three days since we'd come home with the baby. "You have to see when she opens her eyes," he said. "She looks right at you."

"Are they brown like yours and Laurel's?" She ran a fingertip over the nearly translucent skin of the baby's forehead.

"They're kind of gray right now," Jamie said, "but the pediatrician said they'll most likely be brown."

Miss Emma looked at me where I sat in the rocker. "You must be in seventh heaven, darlin'," she said.

I was too tired to speak, so I smiled the same smile I'd been wearing for the past three days. I'd pasted it to my face shortly after the baby was born, and it was still in place. There was something wrong with me, and so far I'd managed to hide it from everyone else. I watched Jamie and Miss Emma sitting with the baby on the sofa and it was as if I was watching them in a dream. I felt apart from them, a strange sense of distance between us. If I tried to walk from the rocker to the sofa, it could take me days.

My pregnancy had been far easier than I'd anticipated. Except for some nausea early on and some puffy ankles toward the end, I'd felt very well. The baby was two weeks early, and although labor was harder than I'd anticipated, I made it through ten hours of agony without an epidural. I was nearly as concerned about Jamie as I was with myself. With his "gift," he looked as if he felt every single contraction. The baby was eight pounds, eight ounces and I was grateful she hadn't waited the two extra weeks to make her entrance.

I knew the moment when I changed from a woman in love with the baby she'd carried to a woman who no longer knew what love felt like. In the delivery room, I heard the baby cry for the first time, and I reached down toward my spread-apart legs, anxious to touch her. A nurse placed her on my chest. Jamie kissed my forehead as I lifted my head to look at her, but I felt like I was looking down a long, spiral rabbit hole. My world started to spin, faster, faster, and then it went black.

When I woke up, I was in the recovery room, Jamie at my side. I'd hemorrhaged, he'd said, but I was going to be fine. Maggie was perfect, and I'd be able to have more children.

I barely heard him. I was stuck on the word *Maggie*. Who was Maggie? I had a cramping pain low in my belly and thought I was still in labor. I was frightened by my confusion. It took Jamie several minutes to set me straight.

I didn't get to hold the baby until thirty-six hours after she was born. When she was placed in my arms, I felt absolutely nothing. No maternal tug of recognition that this was the familiar little presence

I'd been carrying inside me for nine months. No longing to explore her body. Nothing.

"Isn't she beautiful?" Jamie stood next to the bed, beaming, and that's when I pasted the smile on my face. Now at home, everyone seemed to think I'd returned from that rabbit hole. I was the only person who knew I was still stuck somewhere between the black abyss and the real world.

"Is she eating well?" Miss Emma asked.

Jamie looked to me to answer, which meant I was going to have to somehow force words out of my mouth.

"I'm—" I cleared my throat "—I'm having some trouble," I admitted. "She doesn't latch on well."

How I'd longed to nurse an infant! Working in the pediatrician's office, I'd watch with envy and anticipation as mothers slipped their babies inside their shirts for that secret, sacred bond. But my nipples were too flat for the baby to latch on easily. In the hospital, nurse after nurse tried to help me. A counselor from the La Leche League showed up in my room in the hours before I was discharged. Sometimes I was able to get the baby to suck, but more often she wailed in frustration. The woman from the La Leche League swore the baby was getting enough nourishment, but I was worried.

"Oh, switch to formula," Miss Emma said now, as though it was no big deal. "I bottle-fed both my boys and they turned out all right."

Jamie'd turned out great, I thought, but Marcus was questionable. He was *still* being bottle-fed. I felt tears fill my eyes, though, at receiving her permission. She was the first person who made it sound like no big deal to stop nursing.

"Well, it's important, Mama," Jamie said.

From where I sat, I could see the baby's face tighten into her pre-howling expression. A knot the size of a boulder filled my stomach.

"Oh-oh," Miss Emma said. "What's the matter, precious?" She raised the baby to her shoulder and rubbed her back, but the howling started anyway. "She wants her mama, bless her heart." Miss Emma handed the baby to Jamie—he already handled her with more assurance than I did—who walked with her toward my rocker.

"I'll try to feed her." It took all my strength to get to my feet. Jamie settled the baby in my arms and I walked toward the bedroom. I needed privacy, not out of a sense of modesty but because I didn't want witnesses to my failure.

In the bedroom, I sat on the bed with my back propped up against the pillows and started the battle to get the baby to latch on. She cried; I cried. Finally she started sucking, but not with the fervor I'd witnessed in other infants. Not with the contentment of being in her mother's arms. Her expression was one of resignation, as though she *had* to suck on my breast because it was her only option. She would rather be anywhere else but with me.

From the bedroom, I heard Marcus come home.

"Hey, Mama." I pictured him striding through the living room, leaning over to kiss Miss Emma's cheek. "When did you get here? Have you seen my little niece yet?"

"Lord have mercy, Marcus!" I heard Miss Emma say. "You smell like a barroom."

I couldn't hear the rest of the conversation, just the muffled sound of their voices—including that of a young woman—and I knew Marcus had brought home another of his girlfriends. He seemed to have one for every day of the week.

Closing my eyes, I listened to my own voice inside my head.

Your baby doesn't like you.

I know. I know.

You can't even give her enough milk.

I know.

The baby turned her head away from my breast, wrinkling her nose in what I could only interpret as distaste. I felt dizzy with tiredness.

"Jamie," I tried to call.

I heard laughter from the living room.

Gathering my strength, I called louder. "Jamie!"

In a moment, he opened the door to the bedroom and peered inside. "You doing okay in here?"

"Can you burp her, please?" I asked. "I need a nap."

"Sure, Laurie." He took the baby from me and, as I burrowed under the covers and gave in to the exhaustion, I felt the guilty freedom of not having to think about her for an hour or so.

Marcus had moved in with us during the sixth month of my pregnancy and he'd been a mixed blessing. Between Jamie's work at the real estate office, the fire department and the chapel, his hours were long and unpredictable and I liked having Marcus's company, even if I often had to share it with his girlfriend du jour and a few six-packs of beer. Jamie'd gotten him a construction job where he used to work. On the evenings Marcus wasn't working, though, he'd sometimes have dinner ready by the time I got home from my job at the pediatrician's office. He helped me turn the third bedroom into a nursery, painting it in greens and yellows and setting up the crib and dresser I'd bought. He'd long ago given up the electric piano, but he played the stereo in his room so loud that if I walked on the beach, as I did most mornings and evenings, I could hear it a quarter mile away. He'd turn it down if I asked him to. He did anything I asked, actually. The problem was not between Marcus and me but between Marcus and Jamie. They rubbed up against each other like sandpaper, and I soon realized it had been that way for most of their growing-up years. Jamie was a different person around Marcus. To say that Jamie tried to understand another person's feelings was putting it mildly. With Marcus though, he reacted before he thought. The music was too loud? He'd yell, "Marcus, turn that crap down!" If Marcus came home in the middle of the night, crashing into furniture and slamming doors after hours of partying, Jamie would get out of bed and I'd cover my head with the pillow to block out the fight.

I discovered it was impossible to intervene in the dance of anger between the brothers. It had been going on too long and my voice must have been a tiny, annoying buzz in their ears when I tried to make nice. Their parents had choreographed the rivalry many years ago with their deferential treatment of their older son. Marcus was no angel, to be sure, and he'd play dense when I tried to talk to him about the way he behaved with his brother. He drank way too much. Although he was only twenty, six-packs of beer appeared and disappeared and reappeared in the refrigerator with such rapidity that I lost track. We began to understand why his parents had planned to kick him out.

"You knew what he's like," I said to Jamie on one of our morning walks along the beach. It was a rare March day when the weather had turned so warm we were walking barefoot in the sand. My hands rested on my belly as we walked, cradling the baby I couldn't wait to meet. "You knew he drinks, he parties, he's rowdy."

"Lazy and irresponsible."

"He's not lazy at all," I countered, thinking of the help he'd given me with the nursery. I couldn't argue with "irresponsible," though. Several times, Marcus didn't show up for work, and the foreman called Jamie to complain. Having gotten Marcus the job, Jamie naturally felt responsible for his performance.

"Why did you want him to live with us?" I asked. "Did you think you could change him?"

Jamie ran his hands through his hair and looked out to sea. "I thought I could change *me,*" he said.

"What do you mean?"

"I always had problems with him when we were younger," he said. "But I feel good about myself. Good about the person I am now, so I thought I could learn to be more tolerant of him. But I swear, Laurie, he's a whiz-bang expert at pissing me off."

"I know." For all the help Marcus gave me, he did put Jamie to the test, like a rebellious teenager trying to see how far he could push his parents.

"Maybe it was a mistake letting him move in," Jamie said.

"We told him we'd try it for six months," I reminded him. "Can you tough it out that long?"

Jamie nodded. "If we don't kill each other first."

Jamie took three weeks off from real estate and the fire department after Maggie was born. It took me that long to begin thinking of her by her name. At her two-week checkup, the pediatrician I'd worked for confirmed what I already knew: she had colic. He took a finger-prick's worth of blood from me while I was there and told me I was still anemic, which accounted for my exhaustion and pallor.

"And I think you have a touch of the baby blues, Miss Laurel," he said, still referring to me the way he did when I worked there. He studied my face and I realized I'd forgotten to paste on my smile that morning. "Don't worry," he said. "Your hormones will sort themselves out in good time."

I told him about my struggle to breast-feed. Every couple of hours, Maggie and I were locked in a battle that left both of us drained and at least one of us in tears. He was hesitant about suggesting I stop, but something in my demeanor tipped him over the edge.

"The first two weeks were the most important," he said. "And if it's having a negative impact on how you feel about her and about yourself, I suggest you begin weaning her now."

I nodded, relieved. Things would be better, I thought. I wouldn't dread feeding time. I would start to love her.

But that didn't happen. She took to the bottle more easily than she had my breast, but she still seemed uncomfortable in my arms, fussing no matter how I held her. I could quiet her by slipping my finger in her mouth, but as soon as she realized there was no food coming from my fingertip, the crying started again.

She was undeniably different with Jamie. She'd sleep on his shoulder or in the crook of his arm. I was both envious of her comfort with him and relieved that *something* could put an end to her crying.

The night before Jamie returned to work, I begged him to take another week off.

We were lying in bed together, keeping our voices low so we didn't wake her even though she was a room away from us.

"I can't, Laurie," he said. "It's nearly high season and I've already taken too much time off."

"Please don't leave me alone with her!" I sounded desperate, which was exactly how I felt.

"She's your *daughter,* Laurie, not a rabid dog."

"You're so much better with her than I am," I said.

"I know you haven't felt well." He raised himself up on an elbow and smoothed my hair back from my face. "Just walk with her a little. I don't think you hold her enough. She wants to be held."

"She cries when I hold her."

"She picks up your tension. You just need to relax more with her."

"I used to be so good with babies," I said. I'd read nearly every book on babies ever written and suddenly seemed to know nothing at all. "Dr. Pearson always relied on me to help when a mother brought in her infant."

Jamie smiled. "And you'll be good with them again. You got off to a rough start with the hemorrhaging and everything. Don't be so hard on yourself."

So Jamie went back to work, and I didn't get better. I got worse. Having a baby had been a huge mistake, and only I seemed to know it. Sometimes I would look at Maggie—she could be screaming or sleeping, it didn't matter—and I'd have to remind myself she was my child. I felt detached from her. She could have been a wedge of cheese or a frying pan for all the emotion I felt looking at her. I began to feel the same way about Jamie. I'd look at him and wonder how I'd ended up living on this sparsely populated island with a man for whom I felt nothing.

The uncrowded quietness I'd relished living on the island suddenly felt like isolation. I realized I had very few friends nearby, and of those I did have, none were young mothers. I still had a few friends from college, but they lived in the city. The only one with a baby called to congratulate me on Maggie's birth, but her enthusiastic gushing over her own little boy only served to let me know I wasn't normal.

I apologized to Maggie repeatedly. "You deserve a better mommy," I'd say. "I'm sorry I'm so bad at this." Marcus still offered to cook a few evenings a week, but as long as he was sober, I'd hand Maggie over to him instead and make dinner myself. Even Marcus was better with Maggie than I was.

When Jamie came home from work, it was Maggie he rushed to see, not me, and that was fine. It gave me the chance to crawl back in bed with the covers over my head—my escape in the guise of a nap.

One day during that first week alone with my daughter, I put her in the infant seat on the kitchen counter while I heated her bottle in a pan of water on the stove. Maggie was screaming, her face red as a beet. I was keeping an eye on the water when I suddenly pictured myself standing above Maggie with a knife in my hand, plunging it through her little pink-and-white onesie into her tiny body.

I yelped, backing away from the stove, pressing myself against the pantry door. I saw the knife block on the counter and quickly grabbed the entire block, carrying it down the hall into Marcus's room, where I stashed it under his bed. Surely if I had to go to that much trouble to get a knife, I'd have time to talk myself out of harming Maggie with it.

Back in the kitchen, I trembled as I picked her up, took the bottle from the hot water, and settled down in the rocker to feed her. With the nipple in her mouth, she quieted down.

I thought of mothers who hurt their children. People who shook their babies so hard they caused brain damage. I was scared. Was I capable of doing that?

"I love you," I told her as I rocked, but the words sounded like a line uttered in a play by someone pretending to be someone else.

* * *

"I need to sleep," I muttered from bed the next morning when Jamie was getting dressed. We'd both been up half the night, taking turns walking with our colicky daughter.

"I'll take her to the office," Jamie said, surprising me. I didn't even wonder how he would manage having her at the real estate office with him. I rolled over and went back to sleep, my relief at the thought of a day without Maggie outweighing my guilt. Soon, he was taking Maggie with him every day while I slept. I vaguely wondered what his coworkers thought about the situation, but I didn't really care. Jamie would find a way to explain it.

I felt drugged half the time, as though someone was slipping narcotics into my drinking water. In my sleepy state, I fantasized about running away. I could go someplace where no one knew me and start over. When my chest hurt one afternoon, I hoped I was having a heart attack. A fatal heart attack would put an end to the numbness I felt inside. I wouldn't have to hear Maggie screaming any longer or do laundry or worry about what to make for dinner. And Jamie and Maggie would be better off without me. I was completely convinced of that.

"Do you remember Sara Weston?" Jamie asked me one Sunday afternoon.

It took me a minute to place the name. "The woman who came to the chapel a few times in the beginning?" I hadn't been to the chapel since Maggie was born, and the pentagonal building down the beach from our house seemed miles away.

"Right. She came back today with her husband, Steve. He's stationed at Camp Lejeune. Anyhow, the reason she hasn't been coming is because Steve wasn't interested but she finally talked him into it today."

"Did he like it?"

Jamie laughed. "I don't think it was his cup of tea, though he was a good sport about it. But anyway, what I'm getting at is that Sara asked about you and I said you could use some help with Maggie and she volunteered."

Oh no, I thought. "I don't want a stranger in the house, Jamie," I said.

"No, I know you're not up for that. But she can take Maggie when I'm tied up during the day."

"We hardly know her." I thought about the knives, which I'd had to bring back to the kitchen to avoid having to explain their whereabouts to Jamie and Marcus. Sara Weston could hardly be as dangerous as I was. "If you feel okay about her, then that's fine," I said.

I was still in bed the following Tuesday morning when Jamie knocked on the bedroom door.

"Laurel?" he said. "Sara Weston's here. Come out and say hi."

I shut my eyes, trying to draw energy from someplace inside me. "I'll be out in a minute," I said, too softly.

"What?" Jamie was right outside the bedroom door.

"In a minute." I spoke louder.

I got out of bed, pulling on the same clothes I'd worn the day before, and stumbled into the living room.

Sara looked as she had many months earlier, when I first saw her at the chapel. Only now, in summer shorts and peach-colored polo shirt, I could see that she was athletically built. She looked like a soccer mom. She sat on the sofa, holding Maggie on her lap.

"You have one gorgeous baby." She smiled at me.

"Thank you." I pasted on the smile as I sank into the rocker.

Jamie set a glass of sweet tea on the coffee table in front of her.

"And I love your house," she said. "So unique."

"Thanks."

"I wanted to meet you since I'll be helping out with Maggie," she said. "You know, to see if you have any special instructions or anything."

"Just—" I shrugged "—you know...don't kill her or anything."

She and Jamie stared at me, and I laughed.

"You know what I mean." I knew I sounded insane. I didn't care. I wanted to go back to bed in the worst way.

"Well, okay." She laughed, glancing at Jamie. "I think I can manage that."

I had my six-week postpartum checkup with my obstetrician in Hampstead. Once he was finished examining me, I sat up, crinkling the paper sheet around my thighs.

"I'm still so tired all the time," I said.

"The new mother's lament." He smiled, then scratched his balding head. "You're still slightly anemic. Are you taking your iron?"

I nodded.

"How are you sleeping?"

"Not great at night. I take care of the baby during the night because my husband takes her during the day."

"But you sleep in the daytime?"

I nodded again.

"How's your appetite?"

"I don't really have one."

"I think you've got some depression in addition to the anemia," he said.

I hated that catchall word "depression." I knew there was something wrong with me, but depression was too simplistic a term for it. "If I could just get caught up on my sleep, I think I'd be fine," I said.

"I'd like to start you on a trial of Prozac." He pulled a prescription pad from the pocket of his white coat. "Have you heard of it?"

The new miracle antidepressant. "I don't want an antidepressant," I said. "I don't feel *that* bad."

He hesitated. "Well," he said, "I want you to know it's available to you if you'd like to try it. And I can refer you to a therapist. It might be good to have someone to talk to about how you're feeling."

"I don't think so, thanks." How could I tell a stranger that I'd thought about killing my child or running away? He'd send me to the loony bin and throw away the key.

The doctor reached for the doorknob, then turned back to me. "Oh, and you and your husband can begin having sexual relations again," he said, and I masked my antipathy with a smile.

Over the phone that afternoon, I told Jamie the doctor had said I was still anemic.

"Did he say we could start making love again?"

"A couple more weeks." I winced inwardly at the lie. "He said I could have an antidepressant if I wanted one, but that I didn't really need it yet."

"You don't need drugs."

I could picture his scowl. "I know," I said.

"I think all you need is to be in better touch with God, Laurel," he said seriously. "You've lost that part of yourself. Where did you experience God this week?"

I wanted to punch him. If he'd been there with me instead of miles away in his office, I would have. "Nowhere," I said sharply. "I haven't experienced God in six long, miserable weeks."

Jamie was undaunted. "Well," he said, "I think we've identified the problem."

Sara stopped by a few weeks later. I was lying on the sofa in front of the TV watching an ancient rerun of *I Dream of Jeannie* when she knocked on the screen door.

"Let yourself in," I said.

She was carrying a pan of something as she shouldered her way through the doorway.

"I'm going to put a casserole in the fridge for you," she said, walking into the kitchen.

"Where's the baby?" I asked.

"I left her with Jamie. He's doing some paperwork at the chapel," she said. "I wanted to talk to you."

Oh no.

Sara pulled one of the dining room chairs over until it was next to the sofa. I looked at the TV screen instead of at her. It was the episode where Tony and Jeannie got married, not that I cared.

"How are you feeling?" Sara asked.

"Okay," I said.

She leaned forward. "Really, how are you feeling?"

I sighed, wishing she would leave.

"Tired," I said.

"What does your doctor say?"

"About what?"

"Your tiredness."

I didn't like her pushiness. "I'm anemic," I said, although I doubted I still was.

"Jamie told me your doctor offered you Prozac."

"That's really personal information."

"He told me because he's worried about you," she said. "Jamie's kind of old-fashioned about taking antidepressants, but I wanted to tell you that I have a friend in Michigan who takes Prozac and it's really helped her."

"I'm not that depressed, Sara," I said. "I'm *tired.* You'd be tired too if you were up all night with a screaming baby."

"Laurel, you're a *nurse*," she said. "I didn't even finish college and I can tell you're depressed. You want to sleep all the time. Jamie says you don't get excited about anything. Especially not about Maggie." She nearly whispered the last sentence as though someone might overhear her. "It's not normal to be so…uninterested in your baby."

I lifted my gaze to hers. "I want you to leave," I said.

"I'm sorry." She leaned back in the chair but made no move to get up. "I didn't mean to upset you, but I think you need help. It's not fair to Jamie to make him…" She made a clicking sound with her tongue and let out a sigh. "It's like he's a *single parent*," she said. "He's great with her, but that baby isn't even going to know who you are. Who her mother is."

I heard the screen door creak open again and looked up to see Marcus, home for lunch.

Sara finally got to her feet. "You must be Marcus," she said, reaching out a hand. "I'm Sara Weston."

Marcus shook her hand. I could smell booze on him from where I sat.

"You're the babysitter," Marcus said.

"Right. I just stopped over to—"

"To tell me I'm a basket case and a shitty mother," I said.

"Laurel!" Sara said. "That's not what I meant."

"I asked her to go but she won't leave," I said to Marcus, barely able to believe my own rudeness.

"You should go," Marcus said to her.

Sara raised her hands in surrender, as if trying to keep us calm. "I'm going," she said, heading for the door. She turned one more time before leaving. "The casserole goes in a three-hundred-fifty-degree oven for half an hour."

That night, Maggie started getting a cold. Her nose ran and her throat must have hurt because she screamed from nine o'clock until two in the morning. By that time, Jamie and I were both completely exhausted. I fell into a sleep so deep that when the phone rang, I thought it was the smoke alarm and I leaped out of bed and ran into the nursery—one very rare, small sign that I did indeed care about my baby girl.

I came back to the bedroom as Jamie was picking up the phone from the nightstand. I listened to his end of the conversation and knew it was Marcus.

"No, damn it, you can wait there until morning!" Jamie shouted before slamming the receiver into the cradle.

I sat down on the bed. "Marcus?"

"I've *had* it with him!" Jamie got out of bed and opened the dresser drawer, pulling out a T-shirt. "He got another DUI," he said. "He's at the jail in Jacksonville. Wants me to come bail him out."

"Are you going now?"

"Yes." He sounded tired. "I can't leave him there. But this is it, Laurel. This is the end. He's out of this house."

I knew Jamie was right. Kicking him out had seemed inevitable from the start.

"I've been thinking about it," Jamie said as he sat down on the bed to put on his sandals. "He's a big part of the problem."

"What problem?" I asked.

"With you. With your tiredness and everything. You have to worry about him as well as Maggie and me. You have to clean up after him. You can never predict what he'll do next, what woman he'll drag home with him. He wakes the baby up with his music. He's never sober. When's the last time you've seen him sober?"

I tried to think, but then realized Jamie wasn't really after an answer.

"He's keeping us from becoming a family. You, me and Maggie. And this is it. It's over. The great save-Marcus-from-himself experiment comes to an end tonight."

Marcus left The Sea Tender the following day. He packed up his stereo, his CDs, his clothes and his beer and moved into another of his father's many properties—Talos, the house next door to ours.

Chapter Fifteen

Marcus

FOR THE FIRST TIME SINCE THE FIRE, I TOOK MY KAYAK OUT on the sound at sunrise. Not a ripple in the water. The air full of marshland and salt. I was able to put the fire out of my mind for forty minutes while I paddled hard. Sometimes out there, I felt a bit of what Jamie called "experiencing God." I thought he was so full of it back then. I wished I could tell him I was wrong.

I lived in one of the old Operation Bumblebee towers that I'd converted into a house, and I made it home in time to catch Andy and Laurel's interview on the *Today* show. I was taping it just in case, but I got a kick out of seeing them live. Andy's knee jumped the whole time. He handled Ann Curry's questions like a pro. Laurel got her bit in, of course. Maggie'd already emailed me about the lighter fiasco, but I still got queasy hearing Laurel describe what happened. I'd have to have a talk with Andy about smoking. They both *looked* fantastic. Laurel had her hair down and she smiled a lot, which made me realize she doesn't smile much around me. And Andy was a good-looking kid. So young, though. More like twelve than fifteen.

Then it was back to reality at the fire station. I poured my first mug of coffee and was heading across the hall to my office when I collided—literally—with good ol' Reverend William Jesperson. Ordinarily, Reverend Bill and I went out of our way to avoid each other, but my shoulder connecting with his chest made that impossible.

"'Scuse me." I was glad I didn't spill on him. Wouldn't put it past him to sue my sorry Lockwood ass.

He looked down the hall toward Pete's office. "The chief in?" he asked.

"Just stepped out," I said. "Is this about the fire? Because if it is, it's me you should be talking to anyway."

He scowled. "Now come on, Lockwood. You know I'm not going to talk with you, so just tell Pete to call me."

Pete picked that moment to walk in the door carrying coffee and a pastry bag from Jabeen's. He stopped in the hall and looked from me to Reverend Bill and back again.

"Can I help you, Reverend?" he asked.

"You have any leads yet?" Reverend Bill asked him.

"You know we'll tell you soon's we know anything," Pete said.

"Oh, come on," Reverend Bill said. "You fellas know more than you're saying, and I think I have a right to know what your investigation's turned up so far, don't you?"

"It's ongoing, Reverend," I said. "Nothing solid yet." That was putting it mildly.

"Did you see his nephew on TV this morning?" Reverend Bill jerked his head in my direction.

"I missed it." Pete took a sip from his coffee. I knew he was itching to get at whatever he had in the bag.

"Well, it was quite informative," Reverend Bill said. "For example, did you know that Andy Lockwood got kicked off his flight to New York for concealing a cigarette lighter in his sock?"

Pete raised his eyebrows at me. "Andy?"

Son of a bitch. "He didn't get kicked off, Pete. You know what Andy's like. He saw the sign saying you couldn't carry a lighter onboard, so he stuck it in his sock."

"And they didn't let him board," Reverend Bill said.

"Security needed to talk to him, so he and Laurel *missed* their plane. They got on the next one."

Pete's jaw had dropped sometime during the back and forth.

"The boy carries a *lighter* around with him," Reverend Bill said. "And he turned out to be the big hero at the lock-in. Doesn't that seem a bit suspicious?"

"Andy's experimenting like every other fifteen-year-old," I said. "Didn't you try smoking when you were a kid?"

"Frankly, no. I thought it was disgusting then and I still think so now."

Bullshit. He grew up in tobacco country and never lit up?

"Look," I said, "we haven't ruled anyone out at this point."

"I'm really talking to Pete here, Mr. Lockwood." Reverend Bill cut his eyes at me.

"And I appreciate you bringing this to our attention," Pete said. "Like Marcus told you, we haven't ruled anyone out." He ushered Reverend Bill toward the door, his hand in a death grip on the pastry bag. "If you think of anything else, please don't hesitate to let us know."

Reverend Bill held his ground. "You know, it's easy for y'all to take this lightly," he said. "It wasn't *your* church that burned to the ground."

Now I was pissed. "Three people died," I said. "We didn't take the fire lightly when we were fighting it and you can bet we're not taking it lightly now." I turned and walked into my office, steam coming out of my ears.

As far as I was concerned, Reverend Bill looked like a mighty good suspect himself. He'd been bitchin' and moanin' about his raggedy old church for years, and his congregation was still a good bit shy of their fund-raising goal to build a new one. Why not set fire to his church, collect the insurance money for a new one and pass the guilt along to some innocent kid? Andy was a perfect target. Theory didn't hold water, though. Even Reverend Bill wasn't callous enough to burn the church with kids in it. Or stupid enough. Lawyers were already sniffing around for negligence. And the ATF agent said the good reverend was at a parishioner's house when the fire broke out, anyway. Airtight alibi, he said.

The forensic evidence was slight so far. We'd cut portions of the remaining clapboard and sent it to the lab. It looked like the accelerant was a mix of gasoline and diesel. That set off lightbulbs in all our heads: the same mixture had been used in a fire in Wilmington about six months ago. Old black church slated to be turned into a museum, so they'd figured that one for a hate crime. Plus, that building was abandoned. No one was hurt. This fire was definitely different.

From the burn pattern, it looked like the mixture had been poured all around the perimeter, as I'd figured out from my walk-around. The only place no accelerant had been spread was between the air-conditioning unit Andy'd climbed over and the building.

"Why's that fella hate your guts?" Pete walked into my office and sat down across from me. He pulled a blueberry muffin from the bag and took a bite. Pete'd come to the department a year ago from Atlanta. He didn't know much when it came to the island's history.

"He hated my brother, and I'm a relation." I didn't add that Reverend Bill, like a handful of the old-timers, also had me figured for a murderer.

"Your brother who had that Free Seekers Chapel?"

"Uh-huh. Ol' Bill didn't like the competition."

"Do you think there's anything to his concern?"

I looked at him over the rim of my mug. "About Andy?"

He nodded. "Does he smoke?"

"I didn't think so," I said. "He might just carry a lighter to be cool. To fit in. One thing for sure is that Andy'd never intentionally hurt anyone."

"Well, he did fight with that kid, Keith Weston." Pete wiped his fingers on a napkin. "Roughed *him* up a bit."

"Pete," I said with a laugh, "that dog don't hunt."

There were only two people from the lock-in we hadn't been able to interview: Keith Weston, still in a medicated coma, and Emily Carmichael. Emily'd been tight in the grip of post-traumatic stress and wouldn't even look at us, much less talk. But that afternoon, Robin Carmichael called, saying she thought her daughter was well enough to answer our questions now. We'd already spoken with Robin, who'd been a chaperone at the lock-in.

"Could you bring her in after school tomorrow?" I held the phone between my chin and shoulder as I poured a tube of peanuts into a bottle of Coke.

"She's not *in* school," Robin said. "She's got separation anxiety somethin' terrible. Won't leave my side. But you can talk to her here, if that suits you."

I changed into street clothes before picking up Flip Cates, the Surf City detective involved in the investigation. I figured it'd be easier on Emily if I wasn't wearing a uniform. Flip apparently had the same idea. So when we walked into the Carmichaels' Sneads Ferry living room, with its dark paneling and the cloudy mirror above the sofa, we looked like your average guys on the street.

"Emily, you remember Andy's Uncle Marcus," Robin said. "And this is Detective Cates."

"Hey, Emily," I said, as Flip and I sat down on the sofa.

Emily sat in an old threadbare wing chair, hands folded in her lap. She looked at me with her good eye. She had on a pink T-shirt, inside out, and white capris. No shoes or socks.

Every time I saw Emily, I felt for her and her parents. There was a prettiness behind the funny eyes and repaired cleft palate. Couldn't they operate on that eye? Give her a chance at a normal teenage life? Not much money in this house, though. And not much normal about Emily.

"Robin," I said, "can we try talking to Emily alone?"

"*No!*" Emily wailed.

Well, it had been worth a shot.

Robin shrugged her apology as she sat down on an ottoman near her daughter.

"Tell us everything you remember from the time you arrived at the lock-in, Emily," Flip asked.

Emily looked at her mother. "It got moved," she said.

"Right," Flip said. "Did you notice anything unusual when you got to the church?"

"We walked there."

"Right. From the youth building." Flip had a notepad open on his thigh, but so far, the page was blank. "Did you see anyone you didn't know hanging around the church?"

"I didn't know lots of kids. They came from all over."

"Did you see anyone pouring or spraying something around the outside of the church?"

She shook her head.

"When you got inside the church, what did you do?" Flip asked

"What do you mean?"

"Did you play games? Who did you hang around with?"

"Andy." She looked at me as if remembering my connection to Andy.

"Were you with Andy the whole time?" I asked.

"Right."

"Even when you left the youth building, was it Andy you walked with to the church?" Flip asked.

"Right—"

"No, honey…" Robin interrupted.

"Oh, no!" Emily corrected herself. "Actually—" she pronounced every syllable of the word "—I walked over with my mom."

Robin nodded. "That's right," she said to Flip and me.

I knew Robin thought she'd smelled gasoline as they walked toward the church. She'd told that to the police the night of the fire, but added that she couldn't be sure it wasn't from someone filling a car or boat nearby. "It was just in the air," she'd said.

"Andy liked a girl at the lock-in," Emily volunteered. "She was dancing with a boy, Keith. Do you know Keith?"

She looked at me, but Flip and I both nodded. We knew every detail of the fight between Andy and Keith. That was one thing most of the people we'd interviewed remembered.

"Andy got in a fight with him," Emily said. "I hate fights."

Flip looked at his notepad. "Emily, did you happen to notice anyone outside the church in the hour before the fire?"

"How could I?" she said. "I was inside the whole time."

"Right." Flip ran a hand over his brown buzz cut. "Did you notice anyone leave the church during the lock-in?"

"You mean besides Andy?"

Huh?

Flip and I both hesitated.

"Did Andy leave the church during the lock-in?" Flip asked after a moment.

Emily nodded. "I told him he wasn't supposed to, but sometimes Andy don't understand."

"Are you talking about when Andy left *during* the fire?" I asked. "You know, when he climbed out the bathroom window?"

Emily glanced at her mother.

"Is that what you mean, honey?" Robin asked. "Is that when Andy left the lock-in?"

"He left when people started dancing and I couldn't find him."

I looked at Flip. "That must be when he initially went to the men's room and noticed the air-conditioning unit outside," I said.

"No," Emily said. "That was a different time, because when he went to the boys' room, I went to the girls' room. But then he left again and I tried to find Mom to tell her but then he come back so I just said don't do that again."

Could I possibly not know Andy as well as I thought I did? Ridiculous. No way could Andy mix up a brew of gasoline and diesel, cart it to the church and spread it around. Any kid who would misinterpret a "do not carry lighters aboard the aircraft" sign could not possibly plan and carry out arson.

"Did you ask him where he was?" Flip asked.

"No, I just yelled at him."

"Emily," I said, "did Andy disappear before or after the fight with Keith?"

"I don't remember." She looked at her mother. "Do you remember, Mom?"

Robin shook her head. "This is the first I heard that Andy left the church at all," she said. "If he did." She nodded toward her daughter as if to say *take what she says with a grain of salt.*

"Don't even think what you're thinking," I said, when Flip and I got into my pickup after the interview.

"I don't like that bit about Andy disappearing during the lock-in," Flip said.

"Consider the source." I turned the key in the ignition. "No one else has said anything about Andy disappearing."

"It's possible no one else was paying attention to him," Flip said. "At least not until the fight."

"Look, Flip, Andy can't *plan* anything." I pictured Laurel's step-by-step charts on the corkboard wall of Andy's room. "He lives in the here and now."

"He figured out how to escape from the building when no one else could," Flip pointed out. "That took some planning, didn't it?"

Chapter Sixteen

Laurel

I WALKED INTO THE LOBBY OF SARA'S CHAPEL HILL HOTEL AND was relieved to find it spacious and nicely decorated, huge vases of flowers on every surface. I'd been worried about how she'd afford to stay in a hotel for so long in such an expensive area, but I guessed Keith's hospital had an agreement with this hotel and she'd been able to get a good rate. At least, I hoped so.

I decided the day before that I *had* to see Sara face-to-face. It had been nearly two weeks since the fire. Nearly two weeks since I'd seen her. I needed to know she was all right, as well as to lay to rest my new concern about her resentment over our financial differences. When I called to tell her I was planning to visit, she was quiet at first. I was relieved when she said she'd really like to see me. She asked if I could pick up some clothes and a few other things from her house. I was thrilled to be able to help her in some small way. I missed her so much.

I was to meet her in the hotel's coffee shop. I stood at the entrance to the restaurant, trying to see inside in case she'd gotten there ahead of me.

"Hi, stranger."

I turned to see her behind me and had to mask my shock. Sara was the type of woman who put on her makeup to run out to the mailbox, but she didn't have a speck of it on now. She was pale, the color washed from her face, which looked nearly skeletal. She'd lost a lot of weight in two weeks. Dark roots formed a line along the part of her hair, which was in need of a cut and, I feared, a shampoo.

I pulled her into my arms and hugged her hard. "I love you," I said, my tears surprising me. "I've missed you, and I've been so worried about you."

"I love you, too," she said. "You're so sweet to drive nearly three hours just for lunch."

I let go of her reluctantly.

She smiled at me. "I'm okay, Laurie," she said, smoothing a tear from my cheek. "I'm hanging in there."

The hostess led us to a table in the back of the coffee shop, as if sensing we needed the privacy.

Sara looked around as we sat down. "It's such a relief to be out of the burn center for a while," she said. "It's eighty-five degrees in his room. I'm so glad you came."

"I should have come sooner," I said. "How's Keith?"

She let out a tired breath. "A little better, so they say. It's hard for me to tell because they still have him in a drug-induced coma, but his vital signs and everything are better. They're pretty sure now that he's going to make it."

I reached across the table to wrap my hand over her wrist. "I'm so relieved."

She nodded. "The right side of his face is perfect," she said. "The left side was pretty badly burned, though. He'll have a scar, but right now, I just want him to *live*."

"Of course, sweetie," I said.

The waitress brought us glasses of water and menus.

"I wish I could *talk* to him," Sara said once the waitress left our table. "I miss him, Laurie."

"You *should* talk to him, Sara. He may be able to hear you."

"Oh, I do! Constantly. I tell him I love him and miss him and...I apologize for not doing such a great job with him."

"Oh, Sara. You're a terrific mom."

"Then why does he get in so much trouble?"

"It hasn't been all that much." I longed to reassure her. The truth was, you could be the best parent in the world and still have your kids screw up.

"Well, you're a single mother, too, Laurel," she said. "And look at Maggie. She's just a year older than Keith and at least five years more mature."

"She's a girl. And you and I both know it's Jamie who made her the way she is."

She looked down at the menu. "Give yourself some credit," she said. "Jamie died when Maggie was eight."

"Well, thanks," I said. "I just don't want you to doubt yourself, that's all."

"I know."

"Have you been in touch with Steve?"

She looked surprised, then shook her head.

"Don't you think he should know about Keith?" I asked.

"No. He's...you know the kind of father he's been."

I did. Steve and Sara divorced when Keith was barely a year old and Steve had never once been in touch with his son. Sometimes it took a tragedy like this one to wake people up, though. But it was Sara's decision to make. I wasn't sure what I would have done in her position.

The waitress returned to our table. Sara ordered soup. I ordered a green salad and a broiled, skinless chicken breast that was not on the menu and that I had to talk the waitress into writing on her little pad. Sara smiled. She understood why I ate obsessively well, ran every day, kept up with mammograms and Pap smears and flu shots. I was an orphan. My children had already lost one parent. I wasn't going to let them lose another if I could do anything to prevent it.

"I have zero appetite," she said after the waitress left.

"You've lost weight."

She smiled ruefully. "Well, there's the silver lining, huh?"

I'd been practicing my next words for days.

"Are things okay with you and me?" I asked.

"Of course. What do you mean?"

"Just...I guess it's just that we usually talk nearly every day and everything's changed since the fire. I feel distant from you."

"I'm totally focused on Keith right now, Laurie," she said. "I'm sorry if I—"

"No." I interrupted her. "It's me. I'm being paranoid. Maybe you don't even know this because you've been away, but Keith...at the dance, he called Andy a 'little rich boy' a few times. It got me worried that you might resent that my kids and I are so much more comfor—"

"Laurel." Sara smiled. "That has never ever been an issue between us, silly," she said. "I can't believe you've been worrying about that."

Right after lunch, Sara left the hotel to go to the hospital, and I waited until she was gone to approach the check-in counter. I hoped Sara was being straight with me about her lack of resentment, because I intended to pay her hotel bill.

I handed the young man behind the counter my credit card.

"I'd like you to use this to cover all of Sara Weston's hotel charges," I said. "She's in room four thirty-two."

He tapped his keyboard, eyes on the screen in front of him. "They've already been taken care of," he said.

"Well, you probably have her card number there," I said, "but I don't want her to have to pay for her room. I'd like to."

"It's taken care of, ma'am," he said with a smile. "Somebody beat you to it."

Chapter Seventeen

Laurel
1990

THE FIRST YEAR OF MAGGIE'S LIFE PASSED BY ME IN A HAZE.
We had a birthday party for her at The Sea Tender in May. I had forgotten the exact date of her birth, but Jamie had not. I planned the
festivities, inviting Sara and Steve, Marcus, who now lived next door
but who was around so much it was like he'd never left, and Miss
Emma. A few friends of Jamie's from his real estate job came, along
with their spouses, and they all seemed to know Maggie very well,
since Jamie still carted her with him most places. Daddy L had died
during the winter of a quick-moving pneumonia, and I recognized
in Miss Emma the mechanical movements of a grieving woman. She
reminded me of myself. We both wore smiles that didn't reach our
eyes. The only difference was that she had a right to the grief, while
I did not. Behind my back, I knew she called me lazy and I'm sure
she thought I was doing exactly what she'd pleaded with me not to
do: take advantage of her son's generous nature.

I went through the motions of mothering a toddler as if I were a
robot, a spiritless machine that clunked along at half speed, threatening to break down for good any moment. Maggie was already
walking, and I'd found the energy to baby-proof every cupboard
and drawer in the house, afraid that I might turn my back and she

would get into something that would kill her. I had no confidence in my ability to protect her. I'd shifted from occasionally wishing she would die to being terrified I would somehow cause her death. If she was home alone with me, which happened only when Jamie couldn't take her with him and Sara was tied up, I'd drag myself out of bed and try to attend to the little dark-eyed stranger who was my daughter. I followed her around the house like a shadow and checked on her repeatedly when she napped. It was hard for me to watch her for long, though; my own need for the escape of sleep was so great. The weariness I'd felt in the weeks after her birth had never abated, although I was no longer anemic. I began hiding my symptoms from my doctor. I didn't care if I got better; I was that far gone. I didn't care what happened to me. I sometimes still fantasized about leaving, though, about letting Jamie find a normal woman who could be a better mother to Maggie.

Sara had finally persuaded Jamie I needed "professional help," and for several months, they both badgered me about it. Jamie even made an appointment for me with a psychiatrist in Jacksonville and drove me there to make sure I kept it. But the man sat and stared at me and I stared back. I didn't cry. I'd moved beyond tears. The psychiatrist told Jamie he could force me into a psych unit for a couple of days, but Jamie didn't have the heart for that.

Maggie didn't like me. My early fears about that had come true, and who could blame her? She cried when I'd take her from Jamie's arms, sometimes screaming as if my hands were made of cold steel instead of flesh and blood.

"Dada!" she'd scream, reaching for him. "Dada!"

By her first birthday, she knew five words, recognizable to those close to her. *Dada. Bih,* which referred to her pacifier. *Missu,* which seemed to mean Miss Sara. *Nana,* which meant banana. And *wah,* which was water. She had no word for me.

Sara had become the closest thing I had to a friend, in spite of how I'd tried to push her away when Maggie was a baby. She'd bring us meals, occasionally do our grocery shopping and suggest ways I could deal with Maggie's developing personality. She had no children of her own, yet she knew better than I did how to mother my daughter.

One morning when Jamie had been called to the fire station and I was alone with Maggie, I had a sudden spurt of energy and decided to take her outside to the beach. It was September and the weather was warm and mild.

Maggie screamed the whole time I changed her into her ruffly pink bathing suit.

"We'll go out on the beach and make a sand castle!" I said. "We'll have such fun!" My hands shook as I slipped the straps over her shoulders. *What mother is nervous about dressing her sixteen-month-old child?* I chided myself.

She continued screaming while I doused her with sunscreen, but calmed down as we walked onto the deck. I picked up her pail and shovel, and she held my hand as we toddled down the steps to the beach. We sat in the damp sand close to the water and I built a little sand castle, trying to engage her, but she preferred running through the waves where they splashed against the shore.

I was adorning the sand castle with shell fragments when Maggie suddenly screamed. I looked up to see her crouched over, still as a statue.

"Dada!" she wailed.

I ran to her and saw blood trickling from her hand.

"What did you do, Maggie?" I grabbed her hand. "What happened?"

I spotted a narrow, splintery board stuck in the sand, water flowing over it. Picking it up with my free hand, I saw the rusty nail jutting from the surface.

"Dada!" Maggie screamed again, the blood running from her hand onto mine.

Scooping her into my arms, I ran with her to the cottage. She wailed in my ear as I opened the door and darted toward the kitchen sink.

I turned at the sound of footsteps on the deck and saw Marcus through the window. He'd been fired a few days earlier after showing up plastered at work and falling off a roof. At that moment, I was glad he'd lost his job and was home. I needed help.

He pushed open the door. "What happened?"

"She cut her hand on a rusty nail!" I said, turning on the water.

Marcus moved swiftly toward us. "Good thing her mom's a nurse," he said.

I was a nurse. I'd nearly forgotten. It seemed as though some other woman had gone through nursing school and worked in a pediatrician's office. Some happy, capable woman.

Maggie screamed, trying to squirm out of my arms, blood splattering everywhere.

"Hold her!" I said.

Marcus wrapped his arms around Maggie's little body, capturing her unharmed hand with his so she could no longer fight me off. "It's okay, Mags," he said.

I straightened Maggie's arm to hold it under the faucet as water flowed over the wound. It was deep and ragged across her palm. She'd need stitches. A tetanus shot.

Maggie's wails turned to earsplitting screams. I wanted to grab her hand *hard* and twist it clean off her wrist. I could imagine the cracking, grinding feeling of it. Letting go of her, I jumped back from the sink. "I can't do this!" I started to cry.

"Yes, you can." Marcus was so close I could feel his boozy breath against my ear. "You have a clean dish towel?"

I fumbled in the drawer near the stove, pulling out a dish towel. Still crying, I rinsed Maggie's hand again, then pressed the towel to her palm.

"She needs stitches, doesn't she?" Marcus asked.

"I can't do this, Marcus," I said again. My voice was a child's whine in my ears. I wasn't even sure what I was talking about. What couldn't I do? I hated myself.

"She'll be okay." Marcus misinterpreted my tears.

I nodded, sniffling. The dish towel, where I held it to Maggie's hand, was turning red.

"We've got to get her to urgent care," he said.

I nodded again.

"Come on," Marcus said. "I'll drive. You hold her and keep pressure on her hand."

He shoved Maggie into my arms, and I followed him outside to the driveway.

Together, we managed to buckle Maggie into her car seat. I sat next to her, trying to keep pressure on her hand while she screamed and screamed and called out for her daddy.

When we arrived at urgent care, I longed to hand Maggie over to the staff, but they wanted me to hold her as they cleaned and stitched her cut, erroneously thinking that, as her mother, I would be a comfort to her. I looked down at her dark curls as the doctor worked on her. Beautiful curls. Huge tears glistened on her jet-black eyelashes. Why didn't I feel anything for her? How could I be holding my own frightened, hurting child and feel nothing? I pictured my bed. How good it would feel to crawl under the covers! I could call Sara to come watch Maggie so I could sleep. I had it all planned out, my mind a million miles away as they worked on my baby, whose screams might have been made by a machine for all they touched me.

"It's okay, Mama." The young female doctor smiled at me as she finished bandaging Maggie's hand. "She's going to be fine. She'll just have an extra lifeline across her palm. Too bad we can't all be that lucky."

That night, Jamie sat on the edge of the bed as I burrowed beneath the covers.

"What would you have done if Marcus hadn't been here?" he asked.

I thought about the question. What *would* I have done? I remembered the image of twisting Maggie's hand from her arm and shook my head quickly to make it go away.

"Why are you shaking your head?" he asked.

"I don't know."

"You could have called me."

"Jamie." I wrapped my hand around his arm. "I want to leave."

He tilted his head to one side. "What do you mean, leave?"

"You and Maggie would be better off without me." It was not the first time I'd said those words in the past sixteen months, but it was the first time he didn't contradict me. Whatever Jamie and I'd once had together had disappeared. We rarely made love. We hardly spoke to each other. He'd stopped trying to understand me, to empathize with me, the way he'd stopped trying to empathize with Marcus. "I don't trust myself with her," I said. "With being able to take care of her."

Jamie looked down at my hand on his arm and covered it with his own. "Are you saying you want a separation?" he asked.

I nodded. The word itself brought me relief. "I'm not sure where I'd go, though." That uncertainty was the only thing that scared me.

"You'd stay here," he said, and I knew he'd already thought this through, that he'd been thinking of it for a while. Even planning it. "Sara and Steve have a spare room I can move into. I'll pay them a little rent. They can use the money."

I gasped. "Don't leave Maggie with me!"

Jamie shook his head. "She'd come with me," he said. "That's the whole point. You...I don't know what's wrong with you, Laurie, but whatever it is, it's interfered with you being able to be a good mother to Maggie. If I'm staying with the Westons, Sara would be right there to help with Maggie when I get called to the fire station or can't take her to work with me or whatever."

It seemed like a perfect solution and I was grateful he'd figured everything out and I didn't need to do a thing. I was a shitty mother. A shitty wife.

"Okay," I said, closing my eyes. "Thank you. That sounds good."

And I rolled onto my side to face the wall.

Chapter Eighteen

Maggie

MONDAY MORNING, I DROVE ANDY TO SCHOOL AND FAKED like I was going into the building with him, but once he was out of sight, I went back to my car and drove to Surf City. I hadn't slept all night. It had been more than two weeks since the fire, but those posters from the memorial service were still on the back of my eyelids every time I closed my eyes. Around two in the morning, I got up and drove to The Sea Tender. I sat on the deck and cried, because I couldn't quiet my mind enough to make contact with Daddy. It'd been so long since I felt him with me! Every time I tried to still my thoughts, those posters popped up again. I wanted to grab that blue-eyed Jordy and that scared-looking little boy, Henderson, and Mr. Eggles, who'd probably saved Andy from getting pulverized by Keith—I wanted to grab them and breathe life back into them. I kept saying, "Please Daddy, please Daddy, please Daddy," like he could somehow magically make things better. But he wasn't coming. I finally decided something, though, sitting out there in the dark. I'd cut school today and go to that accountant, Mr. Gebhart, to ask how I could help with the fund-raising. I had to do something besides give money. That was the easy way out.

Mr. Gebhart's office was on the mainland side of Surf City and it wasn't open yet. I sat in the parking lot, listening to music on my iPod and trying to read *The Good Earth.* I was so behind. It was one thing not to be valedictorian, totally something else to flunk out in my senior year. No way I'd let that happen. I *had* to graduate, because once I was in college, Ben and I could pretend to start dating. Publicly. Mom and Uncle Marcus would freak, but they'd just have to deal. Then maybe after a year, we could get married. I hoped Ben wouldn't want to wait until I got out of college. We'd never talked about it. I just knew I wouldn't be able to wait that long. I didn't care about a big wedding and all that, like Amber. She had it all planned out. The flowers and the music and the color of her bridesmaids' dresses, and I just wanted to say *grow up.* Ben and I could elope, for all I cared.

I'd fallen asleep when I heard the *tap, tap, tap* of stiletto heels walking past my car. I jerked awake and saw a woman unlocking Mr. Gebhart's office door.

I pulled out my earbuds, drank from my water bottle and followed her inside.

"Hey, honey." She was making coffee. "What can I do for you?"

"My name's Maggie Lockwood," I said, "and I—"

"You related to Andy?"

"Yes, ma'am. His sister."

She scooped coffee into the filter. "I bet you're real proud of him."

"Yes, ma'am."

"Unbelievable what that boy did. And wasn't he somethin' on the *Today* show?"

I smiled. "He was." No one with half a heart could have seen that interview and not fallen in love with my brother. He'd been too cute, all big brown eyes and jiggly knee and his simple view of the world that—as long as you weren't his teacher—couldn't help but suck you in. "I wanted to talk to Mr. Gebhart about helping with the fund-raising," I said.

"Oh, honey." She pushed the coffeemaker's On button, then sat down at her desk. "Mr. Gebhart only handles the money part of it. The donations. You need to talk to Dawn Reynolds. You know who she is?"

Oh, yeah. Unfortunately. "Yes, ma'am," I said. "I was hoping Mr. Gebhart could tell me what I could do, since I'm here right now."

"Well, he won't be in for another thirty minutes, and he's really not the one who knows what's going on," she said. "You go talk to Dawn, honey. You can find her at Jabeen's Java. She'll give you more work than you'll know what to do with."

I sat in my car across the street from Jabeen's for twenty minutes, trying to figure out what to do. Maybe there was some other way I could help. There were still six kids in the hospital—four at New Hanover and two at the burn unit at UNC in Chapel Hill. The elementary schoolkids had made cards for them and Amber and I'd volunteered to take them to the hospital in the next day or so, which I knew was going to really upset me but I had to do it. Still, that just wasn't enough.

I saw something move inside Jabeen's. Just a flash of white by the window. Someone's shirt or something. Suddenly, though, I spotted Uncle Marcus on the corner walking toward the café. I held my breath until he reached Jabeen's door and pulled it open. *Yes!* Instant courage. I wouldn't have to face Dawn alone.

I got out of my car and crossed the street.

"Hey, Uncle Marcus." I stopped behind him at the counter where Dawn was pouring coffee into a cardboard cup.

"Mags!" He grinned and gave me his usual one-armed hug. "What are you doing here?"

"I took off school this morning so I could talk to Dawn about volunteering."

Dawn looked up when she heard her name.

"You know—" I forced myself to look her in the eye "—for the Drury Memorial Family Fund."

Dawn snapped a plastic lid on the cup. "Well, bless your heart, Maggie," she said, handing the coffee to Uncle Marcus. "I can use all the help I can get."

I'd seen Dawn plenty of times, but not this close up. She was pretty, with reddish hair and freckled skin, but there were crow's-feet at the corners of her eyes and I realized I didn't know how old she was. A whole lot older than seventeen, that was for sure. The thought of Ben having sex with her made me feel nauseous.

"You know," she said, "I was hoping your high school would get involved in some kind of organized way, but so far, nothing."

"Maggie's gonna be valedictorian," Uncle Marcus bragged. "Maybe she could organize something at Douglas."

"I'm not going to be valedictorian, Uncle Marcus," I said, trying to get him to shut up.

"No?" He raised his eyebrows.

I shook my head. "I haven't told Mom yet, though, so—"

"My lips are sealed."

A woman next to me asked for a latte, and Dawn rang up the sale.

"Doesn't matter, sugar," Dawn said to me as she handed the woman her change. "You're going to graduate, right? That's what counts. But what d'ya think? Could you get something going at Douglas High?" She started working on the latte.

I liked the idea. I'd be doing something useful without having to actually work with Dawn. Douglas was great at car washes and pancake breakfasts, but maybe I could come up with something more original.

"Yeah, maybe," I said. "I'll talk to some of my friends and a couple of teachers and see what I can figure out."

"You're a doll!" Dawn said. "Call me in a few days and tell me what you've come up with."

Uncle Marcus's hand was on my shoulder. "Have a few minutes to sit?" he asked.

"Sure." I knew he was curious about the valedictorian thing. It was going to have to come out sooner or later.

We walked toward the table by the window, but before we got there, Reverend Bill came through the door and we had to do one of those move-to-the-left, move-to-the-right maneuvers as we tried to pass him. He didn't say anything and neither did we, and it felt really bizarre.

Uncle Marcus rolled his eyes at me as we sat down. "Reverend Personality," he whispered.

"Sara told Mom he orders some kind of giant fattening drink here every day," I whispered back.

"That must be all he has." Uncle Marcus looked down at his pager, then back at me. "So, Mags." He drew out my name. "You upset about not being valedictorian?"

I started to answer, but Reverend Bill suddenly walked up to our table and just stood there, skinny as a flagpole, not saying a word. We looked up at him.

"Reverend." Uncle Marcus nodded his head toward the third seat at our table. "You wanna join us?"

Reverend Bill hates my family, so I was totally shocked when he pulled out the chair and sat down. "I'm actually on my way to talk to Pete," he said to Uncle Marcus. "But I think you need to hear what I have to tell him."

Uncle Marcus looked like he was trying not to yawn, but he said, "And what's that?"

"Well." Reverend Bill lifted his cup and swirled the drink around a couple of times. "I went up to the hospital at UNC yesterday," he said. "As you know, one of my parishioners, Gracie Parry, is in the burn unit there, along with Keith Weston."

"Right," Uncle Marcus said. "How're they doing?"

"Gracie's being transferred to New Hanover tomorrow and she'll make a full recovery," he said, then added, "except she'll have some scarring on her—" he motioned toward his chest "—her torso."

"What about Keith?" I asked. I was afraid of what he would say. I loved Sara and although Keith could be a total asshole, I wanted him to get well.

"Keith Weston's improving, thank the Lord," he said.

"Glad to hear it," Uncle Marcus said.

"Yes, he's better." He sipped his drink. "But he's in a boatload of pain. That poor child was burnt mighty bad."

Uncle Marcus frowned. "Isn't he still in a coma?"

"They brought him out of it yesterday morning." Reverend Bill's lips curled up a little, like a twitch, then flattened out again. "He's able to talk now."

"Good," Uncle Marcus said. "I bet it was a comfort having you to talk to." He actually sounded like he meant it.

Reverend Bill looked at Marcus from beneath his bushy gray eyebrows. "I think it's the police he should be talking to."

I didn't like the way he said it, like he was saying *Nyah, nyah. I know something you don't know.*

"Well, we'll be interviewing him," Uncle Marcus said. "Did he give you some information about the fire?"

"Yes, he did," Reverend Bill said. "That's what I need to talk to Pete about."

"Spit it out, Reverend," Uncle Marcus almost snarled. I felt hot and sweaty all of a sudden.

"He told me about that fight he had with your nephew." He looked at me. "Your brother." Up till that moment, I wasn't sure he even realized who I was. "And he said that shortly prior to the fight, he happened to look out the window and saw Andy Lockwood walking around outside the church."

"He wouldn't have been outside," I said. "It was a lock-in."

"You haven't heard all I have to say, Miss Lockwood."

God. What a snotty freak this guy was.

"So, go on," Uncle Marcus said.

"That's a right sick boy in the hospital there," Reverend Bill said. "I don't see as he has much cause to be making things up."

"So what else did he say?" Uncle Marcus was getting impatient.

"Just that he didn't think anything of it at the time, since your nephew's known for doing strange things. But when the fire started, he couldn't help but wonder if Andy had something to do with it. Since it started outside and all."

"What's this about a window?" Uncle Marcus asked. "The windows in the church are stained glass. How'd he look out of them?"

"My job wasn't to interrogate the boy," Reverend Bill said. "It was to provide comfort. But since he volunteered that information, I thought it important the investigators have it. I'll leave a message for Pete and Flip Cates in case you choose not to tell them what I've told you."

Ouch. "Get off it, Rev," Uncle Marcus said. "I'll not only tell him, I'll make sure we talk to Keith ourselves today."

"Maybe you should stay out of it. You've got a bias, don't you think?"

"It'll be taken care of," Uncle Marcus said.

Reverend Bill scraped back his chair and stood up. "Good day." He nodded to me.

As soon as Reverend Bill was out the door, Uncle Marcus got to his feet.

"I've gotta run, babe." He bent over to kiss my cheek. "Don't worry about that whole Reverend Bill thing. I'm sure it's nothing." He headed for the door. "Love ya," he called over his shoulder.

"You, too." I stared after him, thinking about Keith. I knew his arms and half his face had been burned. What did that feel like? When I was a kid, I touched the handle of a hot frying pan. It was a small burn. Mom cut an aloe leaf from the plant she kept on the window-sill and rubbed the juice onto the burn, but it still hurt enough to make me cry. How could anyone tolerate pain like that on so much of his body? My eyes filled, thinking of Keith going through that. I didn't want to cry in public. Especially not in front of Dawn. I got up to leave, but even outside in the fresh air, Keith was still stuck in my mind.

Why would he lie about Andy being outside? And why would Andy be out there? I didn't believe it; he knew the whole point of a lock-in was to stay put. I was afraid, though, that Keith might screw things up by spreading lies about Andy...and even more afraid he could be telling the truth.

Chapter Nineteen

Marcus

DAMN, IT WAS HOT IN KEITH'S HOSPITAL ROOM.

I'd driven the three hours to Chapel Hill with my pickup windows down. Sucked in fresh air like I was storing it. I knew what it would be like at the burn center. Sure enough, the smell of bleach and ruined flesh nearly knocked me over when I walked into Keith's room. I'd forgotten, though, about the heat. Ninety degrees at least in there.

Keith was asleep. His arms and hands lay above the covers in massive bandages. Five surgical pins protruded from the bandage covering his left hand. Thick gauze padded the left side of his face, though the right side looked nearly untouched. Just like he'd sat out in the sun too long. An IV ran beneath the covers, probably to a port in his chest.

I pulled a chair close to his bed. Breathed through my mouth. Sat there without saying a word until I was sure I could speak without a catch in my voice.

I leaned forward. "Keith?"

Nothing. I was ready to say his name again when he made a humming sound and his right eyelid slowly opened. He turned his head toward me, flinching.

"*You,*" he said.

Me, what? What did I hear in that one word? Disgust? Disappointment? Or was I projecting my own feelings on him? How many times had I asked myself, *What if we'd gotten there one minute sooner? What if we'd had one more firefighter?* Would it have made a difference?

"How're you feeling?"

"Like shit." His words were slurred. "How's it look like I'm feeling?"

"I'm sorry," I said. "I know you're hurting bad, but I have to tell you, I'm glad to see you awake and talking."

He closed his eyes.

"Reverend Bill told me you remembered some things from the night of the fire. If you're up to it, I'd like to hear what you remember."

He groaned, shifting a little on the bed. "No, you wouldn't."

"Why do you say that?"

"Your nephew, is why," he said, his eye still shut. "He started the fire."

"What makes you think that?"

"He was...walk around church...just before it started."

"Keith?" I moved my chair until my knees were up against his bed. "Try to stay awake for a few more minutes, all right?" No response. I kept going. "My understanding is that you and he were in a fight just before the fire started, so that would place Andy inside right before the fire."

His eye fluttered open. "Place him?" It came out like *playsh um?* "Is that investigator talk?"

"I get that you're angry," I said. "You have every right to be angry at what happened."

Tears pooled in his eye. "Why *me?*" he asked. "Why the fuck *me?*"

I took a tissue from the box on the nightstand and blotted his cheek. "I know," I said. "It doesn't seem fair." How much did he know about the other kids at the fire? I wasn't going to be the one to say he was lucky to be alive.

"I saw Andy outside," he growled, "just before the fight, which started because he came onto Layla." He sniffled and started to lift his arm like he wanted to wipe his nose, till he remembered. "Shit," he said. "I can't do nothin' for myself."

I reached toward him with the tissue again, but he turned his head. "No," he said. "Don't."

"Where were *you* when you saw him outside?" I lowered the tissue to my thigh.

"Inside."

"What part of the church?"

"By the window."

"Which window, Keith?"

He hesitated. "In that office or whatever—" he winced, hunching his shoulders for a second "—back of the church. I looked out the window and there he was."

I remembered the small room at the back of the church. It was for brides to primp in. That sort of thing. It did have a clear-paned window or two. Or at least, it used to.

Snot was running toward his lips now, and when I reached with the tissue again, he let me take care of it.

"Why were you back there?" I asked.

"What's it matter?" He answered quickly, like he'd expected the question. "I was just hanging out."

I'd let it slide for now. "Were you alone?"

"Yes."

"And it was dark out, right?"

"Must of been a moon or something, 'cause it was light enough for me to tell it was Andy."

"What was he doing?"

Keith licked his lips. They looked dry, the skin cracked and flaking.

"Do you want a sip of water?" I asked.

He shook his head and shut his eye. I wasn't ready to let him fall back to sleep.

"Keith?" I prodded.

"He was walking by the side of the church," he said. "Looking at, like, where the ground and wall meet."

"You could see that?"

He opened his eye to cut me a look. "I'm not fucking making it up."

"Did he have anything in his hands?"

"Don't remember."

"Could it have been another boy who looked like Andy?"

He tried to laugh, but coughed instead. I held the plastic cup of water for him and he took a sip through the straw. "Only one Andy Lockwood," he said, shutting his eye again. "One's enough."

I'd let him sleep. Didn't want to hear more, anyway. I shouldn't have been there in the first place.

I called Flip Cates as soon as I got to the hospital lobby.

"Cates," he answered.

"It's Marcus, Flip," I said. "I'm taking myself off the investigation."

"I'm glad to hear it," Flip said. "Because I was about to take you off myself."

"You talked to Reverend Bill?"

"Yes."

"I don't believe Andy could be responsible for that fire," I said, "but as long as his name's getting tossed around, I figure I'd better—"

"There's something else," Flip interrupted.

"What?"

"A woman called the hotline last night. She said she was driving by the church the night of the fire on her way to Topsail Beach and saw a kid—a boy—walking alone outside the building."

"What time? Did she give a description?"

"She was vague on time. Between eight and nine. It was dark out, but she thought the boy had dark or brown hair and looked around thirteen. A young teenager or preteen, is what she said."

"Did you get her name? Why's she just calling now?"

"We got her name. She was renting a cottage the weekend of the fire and left that Sunday morning to go back to Winston-Salem. She didn't make the connection between what she saw and the fire until the hotline number was broadcast on her local news yesterday."

I rubbed the back of my neck. It felt like a noose was tightening around it.

"We're going to ask Laurel if we can search Andy's room," Flip said.

I don't know why I was surprised. If we had this kind of information on another kid, I'd expect the same action. But Andy? It seemed like overkill.

"Okay," I said, after a minute. "Keep me in the loop, all right?"

Chapter Twenty

Andy

I WAS MR. POPULARITY AT SCHOOL TODAY. THAT'S WHAT MISS Betts called me. They showed the *Today* show on the TV in all the classrooms. Everybody saw me. My friend Darcy said I was awesome. A boy I don't really know said, "Next, your ugly mug'll be on the cover of People magazine." He was the only one who said a mean thing, and I didn't mind. Could I really be on the cover of *People?*

Miss Betts had me tell what it was like to be on TV in front of everybody. *Don't brag,* I kept saying inside my head. *Remember, we don't brag.*

After school, I sat on the bench at the bus place when my friend Max showed up.

"Hey, Andy," he said. He was in the ninth grade but was way taller than me. "I heard about your lighter," he said. "That sucked."

"Yeah," I said. "If you go on a plane, don't put a lighter in your sock."

"I'll remember that," Max said. "You got any coffin nails on ya?"

"Sure." I took off my backpack and put it on the bench. I reached into the secret zipper place to find my cigarettes. I liked how Max called them "coffin nails." When you first had one, you coughed a lot. I didn't get the "nails" part, though.

I found my package of coffin nails and gave him one. I took one for me, too, and he lit them with a cool green lighter.

"You're in the market for a new lighter now, I guess, huh?" he asked.

I used to think "in the market" meant going to the store, but now I got it. "Yeah," I said. "You wanna trade me for that one?"

Me and Max were good traders. I got my old lighter from him. And one time a pen with water in it that had a girl in a bathing suit. You turned the pen upside down to make her bathing suit come off and then she was naked. I only had the pen for one day, because Max wanted it back. He traded me a whole package of cigarettes for it.

"You can have this lighter for five bucks," he said.

"I don't have five bucks," I said. "I'll trade the rest of my coffin nails for it."

"You only got four left, dorko. What else you got in that book bag?"

I took out my three books, my inhaler, my iPod. Two sticks of gum. A matchbox car.

"Why you carryin' around a retarded matchbox car?" he asked.

"I don't know," I said. I didn't. Matchbox cars were for little kids.

I saw something at the bottom of my book bag. "Look!" I pulled out a picture a girl named Angie sent me. I was sure Max wouldn't call the picture retarded.

"Oh, mama!" Max licked his lips. He looked like he wanted to *eat* Angie's picture.

"It's my favorite," I said. "I have four pictures."

"Who is she?" Max asked.

"My friend Angie."

"Your friend Angie's got some bodacious hooters."

Angie sat on a motorcycle in her picture with shorts and a shirt that let you see a lot of her hooters. Hooters are breasts. One day I said, "Emily's got almost no hooters," and Mom started yelling how we *never* call breasts hooters. But around Max, I still did.

"I'll trade you the lighter for this picture," Max said.

I had to think hard. I'd miss Angie's picture a whole lot. It was bent though. Kind of crinkly from being in my book bag. Max's lighter wasn't bent at all.

"Okay," I said. We traded fair and square. I'd have to hide the cool green lighter good, like in the secret zipper part of my book bag where I kept the coffin nails. I didn't like hiding things from Mom, but sometimes I had to.

The bus came and I got on it but Max didn't. He took a different bus than me. I waved to him, but he was staring at Angie's picture and didn't see me. I missed Angie's picture all of a sudden. I'd probably have more in the mail when I got home, though. Then maybe Mom or Maggie could take me to the store.

I wanted to see if my face was on the cover of *People*.

Chapter Twenty-One

Laurel

FROM THE PORCH OF OUR HOUSE, I COULD SEE THE LIGHTS ON the mainland across the sound. It was the first night warm enough to be outside without a sweater, and I welcomed the salty balm of the air as I sat on the old glider, my feet propped up against the railing. Maggie was studying at Amber Donnelly's and I'd finally gotten Andy settled down enough to fall asleep and could take a minute for myself.

I'd really had to rein Andy in today, his first day at school since being on the *Today* show. I had to remind him not to brag about his heroism or newly found celebrity status. I was beginning to wonder if appearing on TV had been a good idea. Today's mail brought dozens more cards and letters from around the country, and I knew he was being inundated with email. For a boy whom the world ordinarily treated with sympathy, curiosity or suspicion, such attention was heady stuff.

I heard a car door slam, the sound rippling across the water. Standing up, I peered around the corner of the house and saw the tail end of a pickup in my driveway. Marcus?

The doorbell rang as I walked back into the house. I pulled the door open to see him standing on the front porch.

"Is everything okay?" I asked. It was unusual for Marcus to show up like that, and I thought of Maggie, the only one of my small family not safe at home.

"Mostly okay." The porch light caught concern in his smile. "Just wanted to run a thing or two by you. Can I come in?"

"What does mostly okay mean?" I asked as he walked past me into the living room.

"Let's sit on the porch," he said. "It's a great night."

I led the way back through the family room to the porch. "Do you want some iced tea?" I asked.

"I don't need anything."

I sat on the glider once again, but without the sense of calm I'd had earlier. I couldn't recall the last time I'd been alone with Marcus. He visited Maggie and Andy frequently, because I decided long ago that whatever happened in the past, I wouldn't stand in the way of his relationship with them. I knew he loved them. My guidelines were simple: always let me know where you're taking them and when they'll be back, and no boats of any sort. So he visited them, but he didn't visit me. My arms automatically folded themselves across my chest, holding everything in. Holding me together.

"I wanted to let you know I'm not part of the fire investigation any longer," he said, sitting down on the old wicker rocker.

I wasn't sure why he'd make a special trip to tell me that. "Because Andy was there?" I asked.

"Because...there's some small...right now it's only hearsay and I'm sure it will stay only hearsay, but—"

I saw his discomfort, and it wasn't at being alone with me. It was something else.

"But what?" I prompted.

"We've had some reports that Andy was outside the church shortly before the fire."

I still wasn't getting it. "What do you mean?"

"Look, this is all confidential, okay?" he said. "I shouldn't even be telling you, but I don't want you to be blindsided by it."

"By *what*?"

"I went up to Chapel Hill today and talked to Keith Weston, and—"

"They've taken him out of the coma?" That sounded like good news.

"Yes. And Reverend Bill went to see him and Keith told him he saw Andy outside shortly before the fire. So I went to see him myself and he told me the same thing."

"Why would he be outside?" I asked.

"I don't know. But we also had a woman call the hotline to report seeing a boy with...a small stature outside the church that evening. And Emily Carmichael said that Andy disappeared for a while before the fire. Then there's that bit about him hiding a lighter in his sock."

"Oh, Marcus," I said. "You don't honestly think Andy had anything to do with the fire, do you?"

"No, I don't. But no one's reported seeing anyone *else* outside. So he has to be ruled out."

I was more annoyed than worried. "Okay, Marcus," I said. "So let's say it *was* Andy. Where did he get the gasoline or whatever was used? How did he get it to the church, huh?"

"I know it doesn't make sense," he said. "And I'm sorry he's being dragged into this. I just wanted you to hear it from me first, all right? We—they—have to explore every possibility."

Panic rose inside me, expanding in my chest. "I'm mad!" My fists curled around the edge of the seat cushion. "I'm mad you could...go along with this. That you could even *think* about it. You need to tell whoever's doing the investigation to leave Andy out of it."

Marcus didn't respond, and I continued. "Keith's a troublemaker," I said. "He smokes dope and he's done things you don't know about."

"I know."

"You *know*? You know about the truancy? Possession of marijuana?"

He nodded. "Sara talks to me sometimes."

I felt a kernel of jealousy that surprised me. Sara was my best friend. Why didn't I know that she'd confided in Marcus? Why didn't I know that Marcus cared enough to talk to her about Keith?

"Well, maybe *Keith* set the fire," I said. "Why else would he be trying to blame it on someone else? Someone who can't really defend himself?"

"He'll be questioned, but let's face it, why would he set a fire and get trapped by it?"

"Why would *Andy* set a fire and get trapped by it?" I snapped.

"Well, he didn't get trapped, did he?"

I stared at him. "It was just lucky he found his way out."

"Or he wanted to be seen as a hero, and he's the only one who seemed to know the safe way out of the building."

"Marcus!"

He held up his hands as if to ward off a blow. "Devil's advocate, Laurel," he said. "I'm just trying to think the way the investigators will."

"Of which you're one."

"Hi, Uncle Marcus."

I looked up quickly at the sound of Andy's voice. He stood in the doorway between the family room and the porch in his pajamas, his eyes squinty with sleep. I changed my expression from angry to benign.

"Hey, Andy." Marcus got up and pulled Andy into a hug.

Judas, I thought.

"Are you fighting with Mom?" Andy asked.

"We're having a noisy talk," Marcus said. I was glad he could find his voice. Mine was trapped somewhere behind my breastbone. "You ever have noisy talks with people?"

"Sometimes." Andy smiled.

"Go back to bed, sweetie," I managed to say.

"I'll take him." Marcus put his hand on Andy's shoulder. "Come on, Andy."

I thought of stopping him, concerned he would say something to Andy that would worry or confuse him, but I seemed to be frozen to the glider. And, anyway, Marcus wouldn't want Andy upset any more than I would.

I listened to their footsteps on the stairs inside the house.

I remembered the agent interviewing Andy at the hospital, how he'd needed me as a translator of sorts. If they talked to him again, I had to make sure I was present. I imagined him being questioned by interrogators not so much *smarter* than him, but more adept at thinking and reasoning. People with an agenda. I couldn't let that happen.

When he returned to the porch, Marcus surprised me by sitting next to me on the glider. He gave me a hug and for a moment, I was too stunned to pull away. But only for a moment.

"Marcus, please don't."

He let go, then leaned forward with a sigh, elbows on his knees.

"I know Andy's innocent, and that'll come out," he said quietly. "But there are a lot of people who don't know him. Who don't see what you and I see when we look at him. They see an uncool kid who wants desperately to be cool. To be a hero."

"It's…it's ridiculous." I still felt unsettled by the sudden hug. I'd forgotten how he smelled. It was a scent I would always associate with longing. With the sea. With deceit.

"I'll go," he said, standing up. "Stay here—I'll let myself out." But he didn't make a move toward the door. Instead, he put his hands in his pockets and looked toward the dark water of the sound and the lights on the mainland. He wanted to say something more to me; I could see the war inside him.

"What?" I asked.

He looked down at me, letting out a sigh. "They want to search Andy's room," he said. "Look into getting a lawyer, Laurel."

Chapter Twenty-Two

Marcus

WHEN I GOT HOME FROM LAUREL'S, I MADE A COKE-AND-peanuts cocktail, then climbed to the roof of my tower to think. There were a couple of old lounge chairs up there, but I liked sitting on the oceanside edge of the roof itself, my feet hanging over the side of the building. A couple of women I'd dated refused to sit on the edge with me. One was so afraid of heights that she wouldn't sit on the roof at all. *You're a fool if you don't install a railing up here,* she'd told me. Didn't bother calling her again.

Laurel and Jamie once sat up here with me. It was a hot summer night when I was still doing the renovations. I must have spoken to Jamie on the phone, telling him I was wiped. Next thing I knew, they'd gotten a babysitter and showed up with a bowl of gulf shrimp and a bottle of sparkling cider. We sat on the edge of the roof for an hour at least, talking and eating, dropping shrimp tails onto the patio below for me to clean up the next morning. Maybe Laurel had been uncomfortable sitting between Jamie and me, but she hadn't been at all afraid to sit on the edge of the roof.

I shook my head now, thinking of her. Man, I'd kicked a few holes in my ethical boundaries today. Taking it upon myself to talk to Keith before anyone else could. Telling Laurel about the search. But she had to know how serious this had become. I pictured her after I left, going into Andy's room, watching him sleep. He might have a little smile on his face. I'd seen him sleep like that a time or two.

In my mind's eye, Laurel reached out, pulling the covers over Andy's shoulders. I saw them both—two people who'd always have my heart—and I wished I could protect them from what I was afraid their future held.

Chapter Twenty-Three

Laurel
1990

I SLEPT NEARLY NONSTOP FOR DAYS AFTER JAMIE AND MAGGIE left. I can't say I was happy they were gone, because nothing made me happy, but with Jamie gone, I could sleep all day if I wanted to without feeling guilty. With Maggie gone, I didn't have to feel her disdain or listen to her cry or worry about plunging a knife into her heart or throwing her into the sea. I didn't have to feel Jamie's helplessness. So, while there may not have been happiness, there was at least relief in my solitude.

But after three or four days, I awakened to find Marcus standing near the end of my bed, silhouetted against the evening sky. His arms were folded across his chest. I was so dopey with sleep that I wasn't even startled to see him there.

"I'm supposed to check on you," he said. "Make sure you eat and all. Have you been out of this bed since they left?"

I had to think. "To use the bathroom," I said.

"How 'bout to eat?"

I knew I'd had water and apple juice, but I couldn't remember eating anything. "Not really."

Marcus shook my foot beneath the blanket. "Get up and come

next door. I picked up some shrimp, and I'll make grits. You'll feel better with some food in you."

"No, thanks." It was so much easier just to dig deeper under the covers.

"Do you know it stinks in this room?" he asked. "This whole house?"

I nearly laughed. "I bet you vacuum every day," I said. Marcus lived in Talos like the irresponsible, alcoholic, twenty-one-year-old bachelor he was.

"Yeah, well, my house doesn't stink."

I recalled the stench of stale beer and cigarettes from my last visit next door, but I was too tired to argue. "Go away, Marcus." I rolled on my side and put the pillow over my head.

The next thing I knew, he'd pulled the covers off me and was dragging me in my underpants and T-shirt toward the bathroom. "You've been sleeping in the same clothes for days, I bet," he said.

I didn't fight him as he pushed me, still dressed, into the shower and turned on the faucet. I screamed as the cold water spiked against my skin. He leaned against the shower door when I tried to push it open.

"I'm going to get pneumonia!" I shrieked.

"It'll warm up soon enough."

"Marcus, you bastard!" I backed into a corner of the shower to try to avoid the cold spray.

"You got shampoo in there? Soap?"

I looked at the bottles on the little ledge built into the tiled wall. "Yes," I said, giving in.

"Water warmin' up?"

It was. I ducked my head under the spray and felt it thrum against my scalp. "Yes."

"All right. Got any clean towels? The one out here's growing fungus or something."

"In the little closet."

The closet door squeaked open.

"I'll put this old one in the hamper, then I'll wait for you in the living room."

He was stripping the bed when I came out of the bathroom wrapped in a clean towel.

"These sheets are revolting," he said, bundling them into his arms.

"Oh, shut up." I clutched the towel tightly around me and leaned against the wall.

"I'll start a wash and then meet you at my house. If you're not there in twenty minutes, I'm comin' back for you."

I closed my eyes, waiting for him to leave. I heard him walk out the front door and clomp down the stairs to the laundry closet on the beach level. Resigned, I pulled the curtains closed against the darkening sea and began to dress.

I supposed having Marcus check up on me was Jamie's way of making his brother work for a living. Marcus had come over to the house one day, shortly before Jamie left with Maggie, and the two of them got into another of their heated battles.

"You need a job!" Jamie'd shouted at him. Marcus was the only person I'd ever heard him raise his voice to. I was in bed, and I pulled the pillow over my head but could still hear him. "All you do is surf, party, sleep, screw and drink!"

"I *don't* need a job," Marcus countered. "Neither do you. We're rich. Did you forget?"

"We weren't raised to be slugs," Jamie said.

"Let's face it, bro," Marcus said. "You were raised one way and I was raised another."

"You live off the income from family properties," Jamie said. "Don't you think you could manage a few hours a week on repairs and maintenance?"

"I suppose you'd expect me to be clean and sober while I worked?"

"Damn straight," Jamie said.

"Not interested," Marcus had answered.

Climbing the steps to the front door of Talos nearly did me in. I had no wind and my muscles felt flaccid and shaky. I opened the door without knocking and saw him standing at the stove, spatula in hand.

"Much better!" he said, appraising me. He wore the cute grin that had so captivated me when he was sixteen. "And you're almost smiling," he added.

Was I? I'd thought the muscles in my face had forgotten how.

The sharp smell of shrimp filled his kitchen. He pulled out a stool at the breakfast bar. "You better sit down before you keel over. What do you want to drink?" He was already well into a bottle of beer, and some empties littered the counter.

"Juice?" I lowered myself to the stool and put my elbows on the breakfast bar as Marcus opened his refrigerator.

"No juice. Beer?"

"Ugh. Have any wine?"

"No, but I do have these." He pulled out a wine cooler and set it on the counter. "I keep them around for the ladies."

I wrinkled my nose. "Just water," I said.

He opened the bottle. "Try it. You'll like it."

I took a sip. I could barely taste it. Although my sense of smell seemed overly developed, my sense of taste was shot, but the drink was cool and wet and I figured it would do.

Marcus set a plate of grits topped with shrimp and cheese in front of me. I liked shrimp and grits—at least, the old me did. The before-Maggie me. But I had no appetite at all anymore. My stomach was concave. When I woke up each morning, I could see the little mountains of my hipbones below the covers.

"It looks good, Marcus. I'm just not really hungry."

"Girl, you're wasting away." He circled my wrist with his hand. "Just eat as much as you can."

I'd been through all this with Jamie. With Sara. And I'd remained stubborn and unyielding with them. There was something about Marcus cooking for me, though. The second-best brother. I didn't want to hurt his feelings, so I slipped my fork into the grits and ate a bite. They might as well have been little bits of Styrofoam, but I managed to eat half of what was in my bowl. It was more than I'd eaten in months.

"Stay here for a while and we'll just veg," he said once we'd eaten. "I've got a couple of movies. Gotta get lonely over there by yourself."

I thought of telling him how much I liked the solitude, but it seemed cold and horrible to admit I liked being separated from my child and husband.

As soon as I stood up, I realized I had a bit of a buzz, and it was not at all unpleasant. I carried another wine cooler with me to the living room. Jamie and I rarely drank, and since Marcus moved out, there'd been no alcohol in the house at all.

Marcus knelt down in front of the VCR, two tapes in his hands. "Do you want to see *When Harry Met Sally* or *Born on the Fourth of July?*"

"I don't know anything about either of them," I said. "Put on whichever is lighter."

He inserted *When Harry Met Sally* into the VCR and sat on the opposite end of the sofa from me. We kicked off our shoes and put our feet up on his heavy wooden coffee table. I'd forgotten to put socks on and my feet were cold, so he loaned me a pair of his. They were too big and, as I wiggled my feet, the toes flopped back and forth.

I slid down on the sofa and lost myself in the movie. It made me giggle. When was the last time I'd giggled? Right after Meg Ryan faked an orgasm in the restaurant, Marcus said he was hungry again, so we stopped the movie while he made popcorn in the microwave.

"So what d'you think about the message in this movie, Laurel?" Marcus set the bowl of popcorn on the coffee table and handed me another wine cooler.

"There's a message?" I giggled again.

"Can men and women be friends without letting…you know… sex get in the way?"

"Of course!" I said. "You and I are friends."

"But you're my sister-in-law, so that's different."

"Well, I still think it's possible." I took a handful of popcorn. More Styrofoam, but it went down easy with the wine cooler. The image of Meg Ryan faking an orgasm in the restaurant slipped into my mind. "Speaking of orgasms," I said impulsively, "I had my first ever on the back of Jamie's bike."

Marcus's eyes widened. "That really happens? I thought it was a myth."

"Oh, it happens all right. There's something about fourth gear."

He laughed. "You're drunk."

"Am not." But I was and I knew it and I was grateful for it.

"Are, too." He grinned. "I like you drunk, though. Been a while since I've seen you look this happy."

I leaned forward for another handful of popcorn, but missed the bowl by inches. It swam in front of my eyes. I tried again, but moving my head made the room spin. Before *I'm going to be sick* was even a conscious thought, I threw up on Marcus's coffee table.

"Shit!" He sprang to his feet.

"Oh my God." Hands on either side of my head, I looked in disbelief at the pool of grits and masticated shrimp and wine cooler on his coffee table. "I'm so sorry."

Marcus darted for the kitchen. "My fault," he said. "I let you drink too much."

I was going to throw up again. I stood up, but fell against the side of the couch. Marcus came into my field of vision, a roll of paper towels in one hand, catching me by the arm with the other.

"To the bathroom," he said, half dragging me toward the hall.

I just made it to the toilet. He held my hair back as I got sick. When I was finally able to sit on the floor, my back against the shower door, he cleaned my face with a cool washcloth.

"I'm sorry," I murmured. "I made a mess in your living room."

"I'll clean it up. Stay right here."

I tried to say I'd help him, but the words wouldn't come out.

I must have fallen asleep—or passed out—because I woke up in a strange bed in a strange room. The door was closed, but I saw a line of light beneath it.

I sat up, my head pounding. "Marcus?"

In a moment the door opened and I winced against the light.

He walked into the room. "How d'ya feel?" he asked, sitting down on the bed.

"Did you have to carry me in here? Is this your bed?"

"Guest room. You know, the bedroom in the front of the house? And I only had to half carry you in here."

"What time is it?"

"Two in the morning."

"Why are you still up?"

He laughed. "I was afraid you were going to die on me. I told Jamie I'd get you to eat. He didn't say anything about getting you to drink, though." He patted my leg through the covers. "Can't hold your liquor, girl."

"I liked how I felt up until the time I threw up."

"Yeah, it was fun till then."

"What a mess. I'm really sorry." I giggled again, the sound surprising me, and Marcus smiled.

"C'mere, you," he said, gently lifting me into a hug. "You gotta promise me something, Laurel," he said.

"Mmm?"

"You'll try to work things out with Jamie. Because I want you to always be in my family. You're the only one who ever treated me like I was worth something."

"That's not true," I said into his shoulder. "Jamie treats you well."

"He kicked me out."

"You were a little shit."

Marcus was quiet for so long that I nearly fell asleep with my head on his shoulder.

"You're right," he finally said with a sigh. "We know our roles and we play them well. Jamie's the saint and I'm the sinner."

That night was the start of a new chapter in my life. Marcus and I ate dinner together at The Sea Tender or Talos most evenings, then watched TV or a movie, and I learned how many wine coolers I could drink so that I felt good without getting sick. Marcus usually cooked, but I shopped for any ingredients he needed, which felt like a huge step forward to me, since I hadn't grocery shopped in months. The outings to the store in Sneads Ferry wore me out and I usually napped when I came home, but I was no longer sleeping in my clothes or going for days without a shower. I looked forward to my evenings with him, although I worried at first that he felt the need to babysit me. I gradually realized he was choosing my company over that of his friends. We were proving *When Harry Met Sally* wrong, I thought. Men and women *could* be good friends and nothing more.

I started worrying about him. I felt scared when I'd see him out surfing alone, knowing he was probably wasted. I didn't want to lose him, not only because he was my brother-in-law and my friend, but also, frankly, because he was my drinking buddy.

The alcohol loosened my tongue, and I talked to Marcus in a way that I couldn't talk to Jamie or the therapist I'd seen or Sara. He was the only person I told about my fear of hurting Maggie.

"D'you miss her?" he asked me one night. We were curled up on opposite ends of the sofa at Talos.

I hugged my knees with my arms. "I miss..." There was no easy answer to his question. "I miss the woman I planned to be with her," I said. "The mother I expected to be. I thought I'd be such a great mother. Instead I'm the worst. I'm horrible."

"Don't say that."

"I'm actually *relieved* not to have her with me anymore." I plunked my forehead down on my arms. "I know that sounds terrible."

"You're too tired to take care of her," he said.

"That's not why I'm relieved." I looked him in the eye. "It's because I was afraid I was going to hurt her."

He laughed, but then realized I was serious. "You?" he asked. "You won't even go fishing because you think it's fish abuse."

"I know it sounds crazy, but I'd get frustrated with her and…I'd picture myself hurting her." I didn't want to tell him of the ways I'd imagined myself doing it. Those unwanted images that flew into my mind when I least expected them and made me feel both crazy and dangerous. I didn't want him to have to see them, too. "Just believe me," I said. "She's safer not being with me."

Once a week, Jamie would bring Maggie back to The Sea Tender. She was a beautiful child, with Jamie's large brown eyes and dark hair that already fell in silky waves over her delicate shoulders. I didn't see myself in her face at all. Maybe that's why she seemed more like a friend's child than my own. I wanted to feel love for her. When I'd see her get out of the car with Jamie, my heart would swell with a kind of longing, but it was as if the closer she came to me, the less I felt. I pretended, though.

"Hi, Maggie!" I'd say, in a voice that rang false to my own ears. "Would you like to play with your blocks? Or we could put together one of your puzzles?"

She'd cling to Jamie's leg, yet keep me in her field of vision. It would take all my energy and false cheer, but I could usually engage her in an activity if Jamie played along with us.

One day, Jamie gave me his usual hug when he arrived, then drew back with a quizzical look.

"Have you been drinking?" he asked.

My breath had given me away. "Just a wine cooler with lunch," I said.

"Be careful." He rested his big hand on Maggie's head. "You know alcohol's a depressant."

"Oh, I know." I brushed the comment aside. "You don't need to worry."

He smiled at me then. "You do seem a lot better these days," he said.

Alcohol might have been a depressant for most people, but it was having the opposite effect on me, I thought. It took away the ache inside me and let me feel a little bit like myself again.

The next time Jamie came over, I brushed my teeth and gargled with mouthwash. It sent a shiver up my spine to see my own deception. To realize I was drinking enough that I needed to hide it.

I was careful around Sara, too, in case Jamie told her to be on the lookout for my drinking. She'd occasionally bring lunch over, and I had the feeling she and Jamie had worked out some sort of schedule for their checking-up-on-Laurel visits.

One balmy November day, Sara suggested we go for a walk on the beach after lunch. "It's gorgeous out, Laurel," she said. "Do you feel up to it?"

My first thought was to plead exhaustion, but when I looked out the window, the sand sparkled and the sky and sea were the same rich shade of blue and I suddenly wanted to be walking in the sunshine.

"Sure," I said. "How chilly is it out?"

She was momentarily speechless at my response. "It's barefoot weather, believe it or not." She kicked off her tennis shoes and started tugging off her socks, leaning against the kitchen counter for support.

I took off my slippers and together we walked out on the back deck and down the steps to the beach. I felt a surge of happiness. How much was due to the splendor of the day or to the wine cooler I'd had before lunch, I couldn't say. I curled my toes deep into the cool sand as we started walking south on the beach.

"Bare feet in November!" Sara said. "I'm *never* going back to Michigan."

"Good," I said. "I'd hate for you to leave."

"Well, I'm not going anywhere, but things *are* about to change." She glanced at me, smiling. "I wanted to tell you before it became obvious." She rested her hand on her stomach.

"You're *pregnant?*"

She nodded. "Four months. Due in May."

"Congratulations!" I tried to get some oomph in my voice, but found myself suddenly consumed by envy. Sara would be a terrific mother—a mother filled with joy at the birth of her baby. "Is Steve excited?"

Sara laughed. "As excited as Steve gets. You know him. Always cool, calm and collected. That's why the military loves him, and he loves it."

Actually, I didn't know Steve very well. He was quiet and reserved and serious, and I sometimes had the feeling Sara liked it better when he was away on temporary duty, but maybe I was only projecting my own recent need to be apart from Jamie onto her.

I had a sudden thought. With a baby on the way, would Sara and Steve still want Jamie and Maggie living with them? I'd only been to their house once, and it was small. I was trying to formulate the question when Sara spoke again.

"You know that Jamie doesn't really want to be living with us, don't you? That he'd rather be here with you? He still loves you. He only left because you wanted him to."

"I know."

"Do you still love him?"

I blew out my breath and tipped my head back to search the sky for an answer. "I don't even love myself right now, Sara," I said finally, although an image of Marcus flickered in my mind. The warm gratitude I felt toward him was the closest feeling I had to love these days.

"I'm not sure it's the right thing for him not to live here. To separate you from your daughter."

I could read the writing on the wall and hated the way my heart sank. "Does he have to get out right away?" I asked. "You must need his room for the nursery."

"Actually, no," she said. "Maggie's in the third bedroom right now, but the baby will be in our room at least for a while, so it's not a problem. For the first week that we have the baby home, my mother will be coming from Michigan, so we'll need the room then, but other than that, Jamie and Maggie are welcome to stay as long as they want. Frankly, the rent helps. Plus, with Steve gone so much, Jamie comes in handy when the sink clogs up and the front door falls off its hinges and the toilet turns into Old Faithful."

I laughed, primarily with relief that my husband and child would not be coming home except for one week in May. "That all actually happened?" I asked.

"Last week," she said. "It was bizarre. Plus I'd miss Mags. She's such a delight."

I sidestepped a clump of seaweed. It jolted me, hearing her call Maggie "Mags," the way Jamie did. And it saddened me that Maggie was a delight around Sara and an uncomfortable little girl around me. How bonded had my daughter become to her? I didn't deserve any of the jealousy I felt.

"What happened, Laurel?" Sara asked. "I mean, you changed so much after Maggie was born, and here I am pregnant and I wonder if it could possibly happen to me."

I was glad of my sunglasses so she didn't see the way my eyes filled with tears.

"You'll be fine," I said. "I'm a freak of nature."

"Oh, no, Laurel. I think the baby blues got you and didn't let go."

"Well," I said, "I'm getting better." And I knew I would feel much, *much* better once I was back in The Sea Tender, a wine cooler in my hand.

Chapter Twenty-Four

Laurel

I BARELY SLEPT AT ALL THE NIGHT AFTER MARCUS TOLD ME that Andy was under suspicion for the arson. The words that kept running through my mind were *How absurd!* I wrote little speeches of indignation in my mind and nearly called Marcus in the wee hours of the morning because I needed to say the words out loud. *He is not capable of planning a crime, and he's certainly not capable of covering one up.*

I thought of the time he stole a candy bar while we stood in line at the grocery store when he was about five years old. I discovered it when I went to check his seat belt. I did what all good parents are supposed to do: I marched him back into the store and made him apologize to the manager, and I told him in no uncertain terms he was *never* to steal candy again. It was against the law.

A week later, though, I discovered he was carrying a toy water pistol when we got in the car after a trip to the pharmacy. He didn't even try to hide it.

"Where did you get that?" I asked him.

"In the store."

"I told you just last week it's against the law to steal!" I shouted.

"You said not to steal candy!" he shouted back at me.

Of course, he was no longer five years old. As frustrating as that experience had been, there was a cuteness about the story when I told it to friends. As he got older, his misunderstandings of the way the world worked were no longer quite so cute, as I'd discovered in the airport the week before. And people were not as quick to understand and forgive as the manager of the grocery store.

As soon as Maggie and Andy left for school, I went upstairs to Andy's room and stood in the doorway, trying to look at it through the eyes of a detective. On the surface, it looked quite neat. I'd drilled "everything in its place" into his head from the time he was little; otherwise his room would have been utter chaos. Even his bed was made. That was number one on his *Get Ready in the Morning* chart. It smelled a little stuffy, though. I opened the window that faced the sound and let in a tepid breeze.

I'd gotten him to pin some of the greeting cards and letters he'd received after the fire to his corkboard wall instead of strewing them around the room. There were about thirty on the board, and a large wicker basket on his dresser held the rest.

I went to his computer first. I had long ago installed parental monitoring software on both his and Maggie's computer, with their knowledge. I took the software off Maggie's a couple of years ago, at her reasonable request, deciding she was mature enough not to have her mother snooping through her life. She had a right to her privacy and was hardly the type to be taken in by a stranger in a chat room. It would probably be a long time before I could set Andy's computer free, though. I didn't like looking through his email or instant messages, because they were always a reminder of his immaturity and lack of friends. His emails were usually about swim team practice and meets, or from Marcus or Emily. I didn't read the emails from Marcus and only a couple from Emily, whose spelling was so atrocious I wondered how Andy made sense of them. He had instant messages, the majority of which were from Maggie about little things—*Have an awesome day tomorrow!* I knew her motivation behind sending them, because I shared it. She wanted him to receive some IMs, the way his classmates did. I steeled myself for a few nasty ones from kids, because I knew they would be there. Andy would occasionally IM some random kid from school, someone he considered one of his many "friends." The nicer kids would IM him back with a noncommittal response. But every once in a while, Andy would pick the wrong target. I read through them quickly with my new detective eyes.

Andy had received an IM from someone with the screen name *Purrpetual:* Thank U 4 saving my life! he or she had written.

Andy's response: Ur welcome. If I wasn't there U might of burned up.

I cringed. I'd forgotten to tell him to be modest in his emails and IMs. What would the police make of his self-aggrandizing?

There was an IM from BTrippett sent the day after the last swim meet: Andy, you rock!

Andy's reply, an appropriate: Thank U!!!!!

He'd sent an email to someone named *MuzikRuuls:* Do U want to skate Satrday?

MuzicRuuls replied: Not w U, loser.

That was enough. I didn't want to read any more.

I went through his desk drawers one by one, but found nothing out of the ordinary. I opened his top dresser drawer, bracing myself for the disorder I knew was inside. I allowed him one drawer he could keep however he liked. He tended toward disorder, and keeping things neat and folded was so hard for him. Letting him have one drawer where he could simply throw things was my way of giving him some release.

I could barely pull the drawer open, it was so full. It smelled rank. I found dirty socks, a balled-up T-shirt that smelled like salt and fish, probably from the last time he and Marcus fished off the pier. I tossed the dirty clothes onto the floor. I found his old Nintendo and a slew of probably dead batteries. A couple of old matchbox cars I hadn't seen since he was little. Acne cream, although he'd only had one or two pimples so far. A few empty and half-empty packages of gum and lots of crumpled tissues. In the very bottom of the drawer, I found a foil-wrapped condom and told myself not to overreact. It was a rite of passage for a teenaged boy to own a condom, wasn't it? I thought of removing it from the drawer, but left it there. It would make Andy seem like a normal kid for once.

There was a note dated the year before from one of his teachers, apparently brought home for my signature but which I'd never seen, stating that Andy was repeatedly tardy to class. And finally, a new, unopened CD of the Beatles. I didn't know he bought CDs, much less the Beatles, and I worried he might have stolen it. I felt the way I had when the lighter had been discovered in the airport. I didn't know all there was to know about my son. A familiar niggling fear crept into my chest. How would I guide him through the next decade as he entered adulthood? Could he ever hold a job? Live on his own? I doubted it. Right now, though, I had more pressing things to worry about.

I opened the next drawer where his T-shirts were folded, not particularly well, but they were stacked three across in piles. I was about to close the drawer when I noticed something white jutting from beneath the middle stack. I reached for it and my hand closed around a fistful of balled-up paper. Receipts. I pulled them out, flattened them on his bed. I was relieved to see one for the CD. One for gum and a Snickers bar. One for the pocketknife he'd "always had," that he'd traded for the lighter. One for cigarettes dated four months earlier. I lifted the stacks of shirts and found a crushed pack of Marlboros, three missing from it. I sniffed them. A little stale smelling, as if they'd been in his drawer for some time. My baby. Trying so hard to fit in.

I looked through his underwear drawer. Not very orderly, but nothing suspicious.

I opened the folding louvered doors of his closet and spotted the green-striped shirt and tan pants he'd worn the night of the fire. I'd washed them twice trying to salvage them, successfully, I'd thought, but when I pressed my nose to them, I could still smell the hint of smoke. Bending low, I picked out the sneakers he'd had on that night. They were dark brown with tan detailing, and we'd bought them the day before the fire. I held them to my nose. The odor was faint. Maybe the smell of the leather? I held them away from my face, took in a breath of fresh air, then sniffed again. Not leather. Definitely something with a chemical edge to it. The lighter in his sock! He'd worn these same shoes to New York. Some of the lighter fluid must have seeped onto his shoes. I'd have to explain to the police about the lighter in his sock in case they, too, caught a whiff of something they didn't think should be there.

Everything will be okay, I told myself. There was nothing here for the police to sink their teeth into.

And I was so, so certain I could explain away anything they might find.

Chapter Twenty-Five

Marcus

I LOADED MY KAYAK INTO THE BACK OF MY PICKUP AFTER MY later-than-usual trip through the sound and climbed into the cab. My shoulders ached in that good way they did after paddling for an hour. Checked my cell for messages. There was one.

"It's Sara, Marcus." Man, she sounded strung out. "Keith is able to speak now and I need to talk to you. It's important. I'm back in Surf City and I'll be at Jabeen's today."

Jabeen's was my next stop anyway. I was off duty and planned to nurse a coffee while I read the paper. I guessed Sara wanted to tell me what I already knew: Keith had seen Andy outside the night of the lock-in. Or maybe she was pissed I'd been to the hospital and hadn't tried to see her while I was there. Or maybe she was just annoyed I'd seen Keith and hadn't told her.

I was wrong on all counts.

She looked up as I walked into Jabeen's, giving me a nod as she made some fancy, steamy, overpriced drink for a woman at the counter. I hadn't seen Sara since before the fire. Only two and a half weeks had passed, but they'd been a crappy two and a half weeks and every minute of them showed on her face. Sara was one of those women with a year-round tan. Today, her face was actually pale. Pasty. Ever since I'd known her, she wore her blond hair short with bangs. Now it was swept to the side and tucked behind her ears, like she'd had no time to fix it.

"Large, Marcus?" She handed the drink to the woman ahead of me.

"That'll do it," I said.

"For here?" She had dark circles beneath her eyes.

I nodded. I really felt for her.

She ran the coffee from the machine into a white mug, her back to me. Tan capris hung loose around her hips. Even too skinny and too pale, she was a good-looking woman. A few years ago, I'd toyed with the idea of starting something up with her. But although she was pretty and smart and damn nice, I wasn't attracted to her the way I should have been. I didn't want to start something I was sure I couldn't finish. Living in a little town where we'd have to see each other all the time, I was careful about things like that. Besides, she wasn't Laurel.

She handed me the mug.

"You wanted to talk?" I asked.

An unfamiliar middle-aged man and woman walked into the café and I glanced at them. Tourists.

"I'm alone here this morning," Sara said. "Dawn's at the dentist, so I don't have a lot of time—" she smiled at the tourists "—but I *have* to tell you something."

"I'm gonna be here awhile." I nodded toward my favorite table by the window.

"Okay."

I sat by the window and opened my paper while she waited on the couple at the counter. Then she came over. Sat down across from me.

"Keith can speak now." She didn't look happy. "Did I say that in my message?"

"Yes. And I actually spoke with him myself yesterday. It's great he's doing better."

Her eyes flew open. "You did? At the burn center? What did he say?"

"He told me he saw Andy outside the church."

"Did he say anything else?" She was fishing for something.

"I wasn't there long," I said. "Sorry I didn't get to see you. They told me you went back to the hotel."

A couple of Realtors from the office down the block walked into the café.

"I'll be right with you," Sara said. Her hand shook as she brushed a wayward strand of hair off her forehead. She leaned toward me. "He found your old letter," she whispered.

"*What* old letter?" As soon as the words left my mouth, I knew. "You *kept* it?"

"Shh."

I lowered my voice. "Why the hell didn't you throw it away?"

"I filed it with my banking stuff when Keith was little. I never thought about it again. He went snooping through my files and found it."

What had I written, exactly? I couldn't remember the words, but the gist of what I'd said would be enough.

"What did he say?"

"He was furious. And very hurt. I told him he could never tell anyone about it, that it would hurt too many people."

"When did he find it?" I felt the impatient eyes of the Realtors on us. Or at least, on Sara.

"The day of the lock-in." She got to her feet. "I left a message for you, but then the fire happened and...I was just worried whether

Keith would live or die, not whether he'd tell anyone about the letter." She tapped her hand on the table. "Later." She walked behind the counter.

I vaguely remembered getting a message from her the afternoon before the fire, making a mental note to call her after I got off duty.

Maybe Keith started the fire, Laurel'd said. The letter gave him a motive—if being angry at the world counted as a motive. But, again, why would he set a fire and then get trapped by it?

Couldn't answer that one. Suddenly, though, I got why Keith called Andy a little rich boy that night. Keith would go home to his double-wide after the lock-in. Andy'd go home to a two-story stunner on the water.

I'd always felt that was an injustice, myself.

Chapter Twenty-Six

Laurel
1991

Talos had one thing The Sea Tender did not: a hot tub. When winter finally hit with those winds that felt positively arctic at the northern end of the island, Marcus and I got in the habit of stripping down to our underwear and sitting in the hot tub in the evening—with our bottles of booze, of course. Leaning my head back on the edge of the tub, studying the crisp white stars against a background of black velvet, reminded me of those nights Jamie and I would bundle up on the beach in the winter and search for satellites. Only a couple of years had passed since then, yet it seemed as though those nights had taken place in someone else's life, not mine.

One night late in March, we must have stayed in the tub too long, or the water had been too hot, or we'd had too much to drink. When I got into the house and quickly threw on my terry-cloth robe to stop the shivers, I suddenly felt woozy.

"Uh-oh." I closed my eyes as I leaned against the living room wall.

"You going to be sick?" Marcus asked as he threw a towel around his shoulders.

I opened my eyes. The room blurred but didn't spin. "I think I'm okay," I said.

"Want some coffee? Hot chocolate?"

"Ugh, no." I took one tentative step forward, then another. "I'm going to crash in your guest room."

"Party pooper," he said. Then hollered after me, "Call if you need me!"

In his guest room, which now felt like my home away from home, I slipped out of the robe, peeled off my wet underwear and crawled under the covers.

I don't know how long I slept. I only know that when I woke up, I was lying on my right side facing the wall and I slowly, very slowly, became aware that Marcus was lying behind me. I felt his arm around me, his finger lightly tracing the place where my breast met my rib cage, and the hard warmth of his erection pressed against my left buttock. I lay for minutes that way, neither asleep nor awake, sober nor drunk. Then I rolled over, and somewhere between facing the wall and facing him, I passed the point of no return.

Chapter Twenty-Seven

Andy

MISS BETTS LEANED BACK AGAINST HER DESK LIKE SHE DOES sometimes and asked, "What is some of the evidence of global warming?"

I raised my hand first out of everybody. She called on Brynn instead of me, even though I hadn't raised my hand in probably ten minutes. I was only supposed to raise my hand every third time I knew the answer. I was good at things like "the evidence of global warming" because it was facts. I could memorize facts. That part of my brain was excellent. I wasn't so good when we were supposed to debate things, like should we use the electric chair. Things like that. That part of my brain was weak. The electric chair killed people and it was wrong to kill people, so that was simple. But when we did the debate part, we weren't supposed to think in black and white, as Miss Betts said. That was harder. Mom was the one who told me I should only raise my hand every third time I knew the answer. She said I drove the teachers crazy raising it all the time. So that's what I tried to do, but sometimes I didn't get called on anyway.

Brynn gave the same answer I was going to give: melting glaciers. Then a lady from the office came into the room. I saw her look right at me as she walked toward Miss Betts. She whispered to her. Then Miss Betts looked right at me, too.

"Andy," she said, "gather your things and go with Mrs. Potter, please."

"Why?" I asked.

"Mrs. Potter will explain why to you."

I stuffed my books and notebook in my backpack, kind of mad because I didn't want to miss the rest of my class. Mrs. Potter was very, very old. She smiled when I walked toward her. She put her arm around me and we left the room.

When I got in the hallway, I saw a policeman standing there looking at me. He wasn't smiling. Everything I did that day ran through my mind really fast. Did I do something wrong? I couldn't think of anything.

In the hall, Mrs. Potter said, "Andy, this is Sergeant Wood. He'd like to talk with you for a few minutes."

He was big. I didn't want Mrs. Potter to leave me alone with him, but I could tell she was going to. My heart beat hard as I walked with him to the office. He had a gun! I saw it on his waist, like inches away from me. I'd never seen a real gun that close up. Mrs. Potter said, "Use the counselor's office," so we went in there. The policeman closed the door. I had trouble breathing all of a sudden. My inhaler was in my backpack on the floor. I didn't need it yet, but I liked that it was there in case.

"You can sit," he said to me.

I sat down in a chair by the tall file thing. He sat down in a chair by the window. The room was little. I didn't like being that close to his gun. He had a big badge on his chest with the word *sergeant* on it and above the badge was a skinny flag, like an American flag, but without enough stripes.

"Andy, you have the right to remain silent," he said. Then he said a bunch of other things really fast, but all I kept thinking about was that I had the right to remain silent. He rubbed his chin when he was finished talking. "Did you understand what I just said to you, Andy?" His eyes were really blue, like Uncle Marcus's. "About your right to remain silent?"

"Yes, sir."

"It means you don't have to talk to me right now. I'm going to ask you some questions, but it's your right not to answer them."

I nodded. It sounded stupid for him to ask me questions if I could be silent, but sometimes people don't make sense. I guessed this was just one of those times.

"You also have the right to have a parent present while I talk to you," he said. "Do you understand that?"

"Yes, sir," I said, even though I was very confused. Mom wasn't there, but he was talking to me anyway.

"I want to talk to you about the night of the fire," he said.

"Okay," I said.

"Did you go outside at all during the lock-in?" he asked.

I didn't know what to do. I could be silent. Even though he'd turned a little in the chair and I couldn't see his gun anymore, I knew it was still there. Any minute he could pull it out and shoot me. I thought I better answer him, but I was going to have to lie. What if he had one of those lie detector machines with him? My windpipe tightened up, but I was afraid to reach for my backpack. He might think I was reaching for a gun, too.

"Did you go outside at all during the lock-in?" he asked again.

"No, sir," I said.

"You didn't go outside during the lock-in?"

I shook my head. Why was he asking me another time? I leaned over to try to see under his chair to see if he had the lie detector machine hidden there. I only saw his feet.

"We had a few reports that you were seen outside the church during the lock-in," he said.

My shirt felt wet at my armpits. I'd forgotten to use the deodorant that morning. Mom added it as a new thing in pencil on the edge of my *Get Ready in the Morning* chart. I always missed it. "I didn't go out," I repeated.

"You were involved in a fight with Keith Weston at the lock-in, is that correct?"

Maybe that's what this was about. He was trying to figure out who started the fight first. "He called me a name," I said.

"And you were very angry with him."

"Yes, sir."

"Angry enough to start a fire."

"What?" He really confused me now.

"Did you start the fire, Andy?"

"No, I'm the one who *rescued* people," I said. He had me mixed up with someone else.

"Well, why don't you tell me how you rescued people?" he asked.

That was easy. I'd told the story so many times it came out of my mouth as easy as facts about global warming. I told him about climbing through the boys' room window and crawling over the air-conditioner box and everything.

"Okay, Andy." He stood up. The handle of the gun was right next to my eyes! "You can go back to your classroom now. Thanks for your help."

"You're welcome."

I left him and went back to Miss Betts's room. The class was over and she had to help me figure out where I was supposed to go next. Once my day gets out of order, it's confusing. She told me I should go down the hall to my art class, and then she said, "How did your talk with the policeman go?"

"Good." I tried to sound happy. Then I walked to art class. On my way, I thought about the policeman's questions and my answers, and I decided it would have been smarter to remain silent. Even if he did have a gun.

Chapter Twenty-Eight

Laurel

BONNIE BETTS POKED HER HEAD INTO MY OFFICE WHERE I WAS taking a fourth-grader's temperature. "When you have a minute," she said, then ducked back into the hallway.

I took the thermometer from the girl's mouth. "Normal, sweetheart," I said. "I think it's allergies."

She twisted her mouth into a grimace. "My nose don't clear no matter how much I blow it," she said.

"That can be pretty frustrating," I said as I dropped the plastic sheath from the thermometer into the trash can. "Ask your mom to get some saltwater spray at the store. It'll help."

She stood up like she had a sack of potatoes on her shoulders and left my office.

I called Bonnie in. The elementary school where I worked shared a campus with the middle school, as well as the high school where Bonnie taught, but it was unusual to see her in my building in the middle of the day.

"How are you, Bonnie?" I asked. "You want to have a seat?" I motioned toward the small chair the fourth-grader had vacated.

Bonnie stood in the doorway. "No, I'm fine, thanks, but I thought you'd want to know that Mrs. Potter took Andy out of my class to talk with a police officer last period. He seemed just fine when he came back, but I thought you should know."

"They talked to him without telling me?" I wasn't sure if that was even legal.

Bonnie shrugged. "I didn't think to question it." She looked at her watch. "I'd better get back, but wanted to let you know."

I thanked her, then sat at my desk, wondering if I should pull Andy out of his next class to find out what had happened. I'd really mess up his day then, but I'm sure he was already befuddled from talking to the police. Before I could decide, Flip Cates called on my cell phone.

"I just heard that one of your guys talked to Andy," I said. I'd known Flip for years and knew he'd be straight with me.

"That was Sergeant Wood," he said. I didn't recognize the name. "We needed to ask him some more questions about the fire."

"Shouldn't I have been there?"

"It's mandatory for a parent to be present when questioning a minor under fourteen," Flip said. "Sergeant Wood told Andy he had a right to have a parent present, but he didn't seem to have a problem with it."

"He was probably confused, Flip!" I stood up and shut my office door. "Someone should have contacted me."

"I think he did fine, Laurel," Flip said. "And I'm sorry to lay this on you right now, but we'd like to search Andy's room. We'll need you to sign a consent-to-search form, and we'd like to do it this afternoon. Can you take some time off work?"

"You want to search his *room*?" I thought I'd better sound shocked. Most likely Marcus had been out of line when he tipped me off.

"Yes. It won't take long."

I could say I wouldn't sign. That consent-to-search form wasn't the same as a warrant. But what would they find in Andy's room that I hadn't already found? The shoes, I thought. I should have simply thrown the shoes away. *Stupid.* Why didn't I toss them? I'd just have to tell them about the lighter fluid.

"I can be there in about forty-five minutes," I said. I'd let them search the room and clear his name, putting an end to the rumors. Then they could get on with the business of looking for the real criminal.

"Great," Flip said. "We'll meet you at your house at noon."

Even though I arrived home at eleven forty-five, a police car was already parked at the end of the street by the water, and I waved at the two figures inside as I pulled into my driveway. I wondered if they were intentionally early because they thought I might try to go through Andy's room before their arrival. Surely that would be a typical parent's response.

I met them on the front porch. Flip smiled and shook my hand. "Laurel, this is Sergeant Wood," he said.

"Ma'am." Sergeant Wood nodded to me but didn't offer his hand. He was prematurely gray with bright blue eyes, and he would have been handsome if he'd allowed anything approaching a smile to cross his lips. I didn't like picturing Andy being questioned by him.

Flip handed me a clipboard and pen. "Here's the consent-to-search form," he said.

I looked at the form as if I were actually reading it, but the words ran together in front of my eyes. "You just need to look at Andy's room, right?" I asked as I signed. "You don't need to see the whole house?"

"Correct," Flip answered. I thought I saw an apology in his eyes.

"It's no problem." I led them inside. "I know you have to follow up every lead and I want Andy's name to be cleared."

They followed me upstairs to Andy's room. The sergeant carried a large canvas bag and I wondered if he planned to take items away with him. How would I explain *that* to Andy?

In the doorway to the bedroom, both men stopped and put on latex gloves.

"Can I stay while you look?" I asked.

"Yes, ma'am," Flip said, as if forgetting how long we'd known each other.

I took a seat on the very corner of Andy's bed, folding my damp hands in my lap, trying to stay out of the way as they started opening drawers and reading the cards on the corkboard wall. "When you spoke to Andy today, Sergeant Wood, did he say anything that made you want to search his room?" I asked.

"No, ma'am," Flip answered for the sergeant. "We'd already planned to ask your consent."

"What did you talk to him about?"

"You keep parental monitoring software on this computer, ma'am?" Sergeant Wood asked as if I hadn't spoken.

"Yes, I do. He's not much of an internet surfer. He likes games, mostly."

Sergeant Wood sat down in Andy's desk chair and popped a CD into the writable drive. I thought of the nasty IM from *MuzicRuuls* and wondered what other hurtful messages he would come across.

While Sergeant Wood clicked mouse buttons and studied the computer screen, Flip started pulling out desk drawers. I knew what he was seeing in them and relaxed a bit. He asked me to stand up, then ran his arm beneath the mattress and box spring and peered under the bed.

"What exactly are you looking for?" I asked as I sat down again.

"We're particularly looking for lighter fluid. Matches. Arson instructions he might have looked up on the internet. That sort of thing," Flip said. "I know this must be hard to watch."

"Well, Andy's not the kind of person who could or would set a fire, so I'm not concerned," I said. "You know that, too, Flip," I added, trying to remind him of our friendship.

He was into the messy drawer now, his back to me. I knew when he found the condom, because he asked me if Andy was sexually active.

"Not hardly," I said with a laugh.

I heard the front door slam shut.

"Mom?" Maggie called, and I suddenly remembered today was a half day for the seniors.

"I'm up here," I said.

"Why's a police car here?" she called from the stairs. She nearly flew into the room. "What's going on?"

"Hi, Maggie," Flip said.

"Are you—" she looked from me to Flip to the sergeant "—are you searching Andy's *room*?"

"Yes, they are," I answered.

"*Why?*" Maggie looked at me. "Shouldn't you...can they just do this?"

I nodded. "It's only Andy's room," I reassured her in case she was afraid of her own privacy being invaded. "Not the whole house."

"But it's ridiculous!" she said.

"I know, sweetie." I patted the bed next to me. "Sit down."

"Is this because of what Keith said?" She directed the question to me and I shrugged.

"Probably."

Sergeant Wood stood up from the computer, popped out the disk and dropped it in a small plastic bag he took from the canvas carry-all. Then he pulled out a stack of paper bags. "We'd like to take the clothes Andy had on the night of the fire," he said.

"Sure, but I've washed them." I stood up, pulling open the lou-vered closet doors. "A couple of times, actually, to get rid of the smoke smell."

"We'd still like to have them," the sergeant said.

I reached into the closet for the green-striped shirt, but my hands, as if they had a mind of their own, moved to his solid sage-colored shirt instead.

"No, Mom," Maggie said, "he had on—"

I looked at her sharply enough to cut her off. She understood.

"Oh, I forgot," she said. "I thought he wore that other shirt, but he had that on during the day, didn't he?"

I nodded, afraid she would say too much, embellish the lie to the point of it being obvious. I handed the shirt to the sergeant, who put it into one of the paper bags. Then I reached for his pants. Thank God, he had several pairs of tan pants. My hands passed over the ones he'd worn and handed some khaki ones to Maggie, who gave them to Sergeant Wood.

Flip looked up from the basket of cards he was filing through. "Don't forget shoes and socks," he said.

"I'm not sure which socks he wore," I said. I leaned over to pick up the shoes, but Maggie beat me to it, pulling out a different pair of sneakers than the new ones he'd had on that night. She avoided my eyes as she handed them to the sergeant, who put each shoe in a separate paper bag. We were in it together now, Maggie and I. I cringed at the realization that I'd made her a party to tampering with evidence.

"We appreciate your cooperation," Sergeant Wood said, as he added the last paper bag to his canvas carryall.

"Thanks, Laurel." Flip took one last look around the room. "We'll let ourselves out," he said.

Maggie and I didn't look at each other as the men went downstairs, even after we heard the front door close. We listened to the sound of their car doors slamming shut and the crunch of their tires on the gravelly end of the road where they'd parked. I wondered if Maggie felt as stiff with guilt as I did. I couldn't believe I'd dragged her into my lie.

I put my arm around her shoulders. "I'm sorry," I whispered.

"I would've done the same thing if I'd thought of it first," she said.

"But why?" I asked her. "Why did we do it? If we're one hundred percent sure of his innocence, why did we…why did we just tamper with evidence?"

She shook her head slowly. "To protect him. We don't know what they'd find on the clothes he wore that night," she said. "I mean, maybe he accidentally stepped in a puddle of gasoline or something and then they'd really go after him. This way, we know they won't find a thing."

My gaze drifted to the shoes he wore the night of the lock-in, and I thought I could still smell the scent of something caustic, something *flammable,* on them even from where I sat. I wouldn't tell Maggie. I didn't want to make her doubt him.

"I was afraid maybe his lighter leaked onto his shoes," I said.

I let go of her to reach for Andy's pillow, which lay on the side of the bed where Flip had tossed it after searching beneath the mattress. I hugged it to my chest. Andy's scent was on it, still more the scent of a little boy than a man. Even if he could have figured out how to get fuel to the church and how to set it on fire in a way that would make him appear heroic, he never would have done it.

I knew my son. I knew his heart. He would never hurt a soul.

Chapter Twenty-Nine

Laurel
1991

SARA'S BABY ARRIVED THREE WEEKS EARLY. SHE AND STEVE named him Keith, and he had a mild heart condition that might require surgery when he got a little older. I felt terrible for Sara. She deserved the perfect baby I'd had.

Sara and Keith spent two nights in the hospital in Jacksonville. The second night, Steve called to tell me that Jamie was in the emergency room. While visiting with them in Sara's room, Jamie had suddenly doubled over with chest pains.

I tried calling Marcus, but he was out, so I had to drive myself to Jacksonville. I'd had an accident the week before. I'd been parked in front of the grocery store, and when I backed out of the space, I somehow smashed into a light post. I got out of the car to check for damage and tripped over my own feet, cutting my cheek on the side mirror. A few people rushed to help me, but I scrambled back into my car, waving them away with a smile as though my cheek didn't hurt a bit and the parking lot wasn't spinning around me. I didn't want them close enough to know I was three sheets to the wind. When I got home, I discovered the long, deep crease in the fender of my car and hoped Jamie would never notice it.

As I drove to the hospital in Jacksonville, though, I wasn't drunk.

Still, I'd had enough to drink that I knew I had no business being on the road. I drove slowly, my eyes wide open and fixed to the white line. There were few other cars on the road that late, but I worried about running into a ditch or smashing into a deer. I wasn't worried about Jamie, though. I was quite sure what was wrong with him.

Sure enough, the E.R. doctors could find no problem with Jamie's heart, but they kept him overnight for observation. I sat by his bedside, woodenly holding his hand. In his eyes, I saw that he, too, knew what was wrong, something he wouldn't try to explain to the doctors: Sara and Steve's pale little baby had triggered Jamie's empathy gene. His gift. His curse.

Jamie and Maggie moved back into The Sea Tender while Sara's mother stayed with the Westons for a week. The first night, Maggie had trouble going to sleep in the crib she hadn't slept in for nearly a year, and I listened to Jamie getting up with her from his bed in our guest room. I was relieved he hadn't expected to sleep with me.

I felt awkward with him in the house, especially the second evening when Marcus stopped by to greet his brother and niece. Marcus and I had made love only that once. In a sober, remorseful moment the following day, we'd made a pact never to let it happen again and we'd stuck to it in the month since that night. But we were close, emotionally bonded in a way I no longer was with Jamie, and I felt shaky and awkward when both brothers were around.

"Listen, bro," Marcus said as he played with Maggie on the floor. "I'd like to help out with the...you know, the property management. The maintenance you talked about a while back."

I caught Jamie's look of surprise. His smile. He probably thought Marcus was finally growing up or that his bout of chest pains had scared him. I knew the reason behind Marcus's offer though: good, old-fashioned guilt. In my sober moments, I had plenty of it myself. Whatever the reason, the sudden ease between the brothers helped settle my nerves.

The plan was for Jamie to stay home from work the first couple of days to help Maggie adapt to being back at The Sea Tender, but on the second day, he got a call from the fire department and had to leave. He'd just put Maggie down for her nap, so we were both hopeful he'd return before she woke up. With Jamie out of the house, my first thought was to get one of the wine coolers from the refrigerator, but I knew I wouldn't be able to stop at one. I wanted to be alert in case Maggie woke up. Instead, I took a nap to keep myself from drinking, leaving my door open so I'd hear her if she needed me.

I woke up to the sound of a distant chant coming from the nursery.

"Dad-dy. Dad-dy. Dad-dy."

I got up and walked into the nursery to see her standing in her crib, holding onto the railing, midchant.

"Dad—"

She saw me and her eyes widened.

"Hi, sweetie!" I worked at sounding cheerful.

Maggie let out a scream, flopping facefirst onto her mattress. "Dad-dy!" she wailed. "Dad-dy!"

"Daddy had to go to the fire station, but he'll be home soon." I rubbed her back, but she twitched away from me with another wail.

My hands shook as I reached into the crib and lifted her out. She writhed in my arms, pushing me away, and I set her down on the floor.

"Daddy!" She ran out of the room, diaper drooping, clearly on the hunt for Jamie. I watched her helplessly, following her from room to room to be sure she didn't hurt herself. I held the front door shut as she reached up to jiggle the knob.

"Come on, sweetie," I said, "I need to change your diaper."

"Nooooo!" She flopped onto the living room floor as she had on her mattress and let out one scream after another, punctuated occasionally by the word *daddy*. I stared down at her, uncertain what to do.

Finally, I sat next to her on the floor. I didn't touch her, but spoke quietly to her, telling her Daddy would be home soon. I doubt she even heard me. I tried singing "Itsy Bitsy Spider," but the screaming didn't cease. Was this the terrible twos? She was only twenty-three months old. I got up and moved to the toy box, where I took out the toys one by one, talking about each of them. "I *love* this puzzle," I said. "I wish Maggie would help me put it together."

She ignored me. I read from one of her books, while she continued screaming.

She hates me, I thought. *She truly hates me.*

I took a wine cooler from the refrigerator and drank the entire bottle in one long, sweet pull.

From the bookshelf in the living room, I pulled down the book on one-year-olds that I'd studied so long and hard during my pregnancy. *"Tantrums wear themselves out,"* it said. I turned on *One Life to Live* and watched it through my tears. My daughter hated me, and who could blame her? I was an atrocious mother.

The tantrum lasted forty-five minutes. I heard her voice dribble off into nothing as she finally fell asleep on the floor. I got up, lifted her into my arms and carried her back to the sofa. She smelled of poop and urine, but I didn't want to risk changing her and waking her up again. Having her sleep now would probably wreck Jamie's schedule for her, but she was so quiet and limp in my arms. I rocked her gently, her hair soft against my cheek.

"I love you," I whispered, although the feeling behind the words still escaped me. "I'm sorry," I said. That, I knew, was the truth.

She awakened and the cycle started again. I had another wine cooler; I had to. Maggie was still screaming for Jamie when he came home. I heard his car door slam and cringed, certain he could hear her screams from the driveway.

As soon as he opened the door, she ran to him and he scooped her up. "What's the matter, Mags?" He looked at me where I stood leaning against the side of the couch, knotting my hands together. "How long's this been going on?" he asked.

I hesitated, humiliated by the truth. "She was upset when she first woke up. Then she settled down for a while, but I didn't want to change her because…"

"She's soaked. You're soaked, Maggie-doodle." He walked past me into the nursery. I heard her protest a bit when he changed her; I never would have managed. I brushed my teeth and rinsed with mouthwash as he tended to her.

"Why didn't you change her?" he asked as he walked back into the living room, Maggie toddling at his side, sniffling, holding his index finger with her little hand.

"She was screaming for you," I said. "Jamie, she doesn't like me."

"Shh," he chided. "She understands more than you think. Of course she likes you. We just upset her routine, that's all."

Over the course of the week, things between Maggie and me improved a bit. I threw out the remaining wine coolers—except for three, which I stashed in the bedroom closet just in case. I lasted through two full days without one, proving to myself that I was *not* an alcoholic. I made an effort to play with Maggie. I'd read to her any time she'd let me, which grew more frequent. She never really warmed up to me, though, as if she could see behind my mask, and I might have been babysitting for a friend's child, for all the warmth I felt toward her in spite of my longing to fall in love with her. Yet, I pretended. I'd gotten very good at pretending.

Marcus's work on the Lockwood properties lasted exactly three days. The first day, he power washed decks. The second, he repaired a roof. Jamie was so pleased that the third day, he asked Marcus to replace a couple of windows in one of the Surf City cottages. Marcus removed the old windows and enlarged the openings for the new ones, but he made them too big and too crooked because he was, quite simply, too drunk.

He came to The Sea Tender that evening to admit his mistake.

Jamie handed Maggie to me and told me to take her into the bedroom. I did so gladly, not wanting to witness the fireworks. I sat on the bed with Maggie in my arms. The fireworks, though, pierced the thin bedroom door.

"Did you *measure?*" Jamie shouted.

"Of course I measured!"

"Daddy!" Maggie scrambled out of my arms toward the edge of the bed. I held on to the back of her shirt to stop her progress.

"Well, then how did this happen?"

"I don't know!" Marcus said. "It just did. It's not like it's the end of the world, Jamie."

"Daddy!"

I closed my eyes. *Please stop.* I couldn't take the yelling.

"Sloppy work, Marcus," Jamie shouted. "It's going to cost an arm and a leg to fix."

"We can get bigger windows."

"*We're* not doing anything! I'm not letting you near those windows again!"

"You've just been waiting for me to screw up!"

Maggie sprang free of my grasp.

"That's the *last* thing I wanted," Jamie said. "I was hoping you'd finally gotten your act together. It's about time. You're twenty-two years old! You're a damn *drunk,* Marcus. You need help. And you're fired."

I reached for Maggie, but she toppled headfirst off the bed. I picked her up and saw that she was fine, but her face was quietly twisting into that I'm-getting-ready-to-let-out-a-bloodcurdling-scream expression.

"*No,* sweetie." I bounced her on my lap. "Shh."

Marcus was laughing. "Fired from *what?*" he shouted. "It's not like I'm getting paid. And I don't need the hassle, man. It's all yours."

The front door slammed, and Maggie let out the scream I'd known was coming.

I walked out of the bedroom and held her toward Jamie, who was staring red faced at the front door, hands on his hips.

"I need a nap," I said, handing Maggie over to him before he could protest. Back in the bedroom, I locked the door, took the third and last wine cooler from the bedroom closet, and drank it warm.

The following night—the night before Jamie and Maggie were to return to the Weston's—Jamie got another call from the fire station. Maggie was already asleep, thank goodness, and by the time Jamie returned, I was in bed. He knocked on the door.

"Can we talk for a minute?" he asked, opening the door a crack.

I wasn't yet asleep. "Uh-huh," I said. I sat up against the headboard, tucking the covers across my chest because I had nothing on.

Jamie's anger at Marcus had blown over sometime during the day—or at least he'd known better than to dump it on me. Now, he sat on the edge of the bed, the light from the hallway pooling on his cheeks, catching in his eyes. I'd so loved those big brown eyes! I wished I could feel love for them—for *him*—again. And for my daughter, who deserved so much better than I was giving her.

"It's been good being here with you this week," he said.

I nodded, although I was anxious for them to leave. I wanted my easy sleeping-and-drinking life back. "At least Maggie doesn't scream when you leave her with me now," I said.

He didn't smile. "You made a big effort with her. I know you still aren't your old self, and I just want you to know that I appreciate how you tried to…to be a mom to her this week."

Tears welled up in my eyes.

He moved closer, taking my hand and holding it between those big teddy-bear paws of his. "What is it?" he asked. "Why the tears?"

"I just wish I could *feel* something for her." I swallowed. "For *you*. Like a normal mother and normal woman."

He leaned forward, surprising me with a kiss. "You will," he said, his hand on my cheek. Then he kissed me again. His lips against mine felt familiar, tugging at a place deep inside me—a place I wanted to get to again but couldn't seem to reach.

His fingers curled beneath the sheet where it lay across my chest. He started to lower it, and I let him, because I couldn't shut him out of whatever was left of my heart. He fumbled in the nightstand for a condom, tore it open and put it on.

I feigned desire for him, a gift I wanted to give him, but my body felt nothing as I opened it up to him. For the first time, I faked my orgasm.

When we were finished and he pulled out of me, he swore.

"Damn!" he said. "Well, that's a first."

"What's a first?" I asked, worried he was referring to my poor acting job.

"It broke," he said, and I realized he was talking about the condom. "It must have been old." He lay down next to me, his hand on my stomach. "Where are you in your cycle?" he asked.

I thought back to the last time I'd had my period, well over a month ago. *Well over a month ago.* I remembered feeling woozy for a few days the week before, a light-headedness I'd attributed to drinking too much. My heart gave a great, breath-stealing leap in my chest. I wanted to jump out of bed and run to the kitchen calendar, count off the days, hoping I was wrong. But I didn't budge, trying to stay calm.

"I'm not sure," I managed to say.

"That's the last thing you need now," he said. "Another pregnancy."

It may have been the last thing I needed, but I knew it was what I had.

Chapter Thirty

Marcus

COKE WITH PEANUTS WAS MY COMFORT FOOD, BUT IT WASN'T working for me that morning. I sat on the back deck of my tower, watching the waves make chop suey of the beach. The surf was high and rough, spraying my face and the Wilmington newspaper on my lap. I waved at a couple of beachcombers. Watched their yellow Lab fetch a ball from the water. Tried to pretend it was an ordinary day, which almost worked till I lifted the paper again.

Could Fire Hero Be Villain? the headline read.

The last couple of days, the rumors had started flying. The police had a press conference the night before to try to squelch some of them. It backfired. Too many questions asked. Too few answers given.

Even CNN had people there. That's what happened with exposure on the *Today* show. Suddenly a small-town fire was big news.

"Is it true several witnesses saw Andy Lockwood outside the church during the lock-in?" a reporter had asked.

How did this information get out? I'd wondered. Did it float through the air and settle in people's heads?

"As I said," the police chief repeated for the third or fourth time, "the investigation is ongoing and we're still conducting interviews and collecting evidence."

"Would you call him a person of interest?" someone asked.

"Everyone with a connection to the church that night is a person of interest," the chief said.

"We've heard reports of Andy Lockwood's temper," a reporter said. "Can you verify that he's lost his temper in public before?"

"That's not something I personally have ever witnessed," the chief said.

I remembered a time Laurel went out of town to give an FASD speech. The school called me, since I was Andy's second backup emergency contact. The first was Sara, of course, but they couldn't reach her. Andy'd been suspended for the day. He'd hit a girl who called him a jerk-off. There were other incidents Laurel had dealt with over the years, though not an infinite number. Andy could be unpredictable—calm and cuddly one minute, furious the next. I could see him beating up Keith at the lock-in. His temper was a flare, though. Impulsive. Never premeditated.

It didn't matter that nothing incriminating had been said about Andy at the press conference; the seed was planted by the questions themselves.

"Hey, Uncle Marcus."

Maggie walked across the sand near the corner of my house. I turned the paper upside down on the off chance she hadn't already seen it.

"Hey, Mags," I said.

"I knocked, but I figured you were back here when you didn't answer." She climbed the steps to the deck.

"Don't you ever go to school anymore?" I teased.

"I *had* to see you." She stood in front of me, her hair blowing in long wavy strands around her head. "You have to tell me what's going *on*." She pulled an elastic band from her pants pocket and tied her hair back as she spoke. "That press conference last night was flippin' unbelievable, and I just don't get what's *happening!*" She grabbed the long ponytail and raked her fingers through it.

"Sit down, Mags."

She plunked down in one of the deck chairs. "I am so *totally* pissed off," she said.

"Can I get you a Coke?" I asked, although caffeine would probably be a mistake for her at the moment.

"No, you can tell me what's *really* going on in the investigation."

I watched the Lab get flipped by a wave. He shook himself off and ran in the water for more.

"Uncle Marcus! *Tell* me."

"You know I'm not on the team any longer," I said.

"They searched Andy's room yesterday."

I nodded. "Did they find anything?"

"A condom and some cigarettes." She shrugged. "They took the clothes he was wearing that night. Like they'd actually find something on them."

"A condom, huh?" Did Laurel ask Andy where he got it? Did he tell her? She'd kill me, but he was fifteen and I didn't know how much she'd talked to him about sex. *Someone* had to do it.

"It was so...*invasive,*" she said. "Yuck." She sounded like a real teenager. Most of the time, she seemed much older. I usually had to remind myself she was only seventeen.

"Is your mom okay?"

"*No,* she's not okay. Everybody's suddenly saying Andy's an arsonist. How could she be okay? It's insane." She looked at me. Her face was crimson. "First of all, the guy at the press conference didn't even *call* it arson. Couldn't it have been some kind of accident?"

"They won't officially call it arson until the investigation is over, but a burn pattern like that doesn't happen by accident."

"Couldn't it have something to do with the electricity going out in the youth building, though?"

"That still wouldn't explain the burn pattern."

"Tell me what evidence they have," she demanded. "Do they have something on Andy I don't know about?"

"They know the type of fuel," I said. "A gasoline and diesel mix."

She snorted. "Like Andy carried gasoline and diesel to the lock-in. I drove him there. I think I would have noticed."

"I know, babe."

She looked toward the beach. "I feel like they're only looking at Andy as a suspect now. Not even trying to figure out what really happened."

"Andy just makes a colorful rumor, that's all. The truth will come out eventually."

"Didn't a church burn down in Wilmington this year? Could it be, like, a serial arsonist?"

"Pretty good, Mags." I was impressed. "I'm going to suggest the investigators hire you."

"Seriously?"

I laughed. "No, not seriously. If *I* can't be on the team, they sure won't take Andy's sister. But that was a good catch about the church in Wilmington. The big difference is, that church was empty."

"But they'll still consider the possibility, won't they?"

"Of course," I said. "Has your mom talked to a lawyer yet?"

"I don't think so."

"What's she waiting for?" I said. "She's in denial."

"I don't know. All I know is that Andy's so confused. He cried in bed last night. He kept saying, 'But I'm the *hero*.'" Her voice cracked. "I didn't want him to go to school today. Kids are going to be so mean to him."

"Maybe he should stay home for a day or two," I thought out loud.

"I'm starting to plan this fund-raiser at school for sometime in May," Maggie said. "A big makeover event with the beauty college coming in and a silent auction and everything. Now I don't even feel like doing it."

Couldn't keep that niece of mine down. Who cared if she was valedictorian or not? "Well, just remember it's for the victims," I said. "Don't punish them because people are spreading rumors about Andy."

She screwed up her face. "You're right," she said. She looked at her watch. Sighed. "I'd better go back to school."

"Listen, Mags," I said as she got to her feet. "The best thing you can do—and I can do—is be there for Andy. Be his support right now, all right? Don't let this get you down."

"Okay." She still looked glum as she leaned over to kiss my cheek.

I watched her walk down the steps. Once she'd disappeared around the corner of the house, I turned the newspaper over. Stared at the headline again. Could Fire Hero Be Villain?

I felt suspicion closing in on Andy, the way it had closed in on me years earlier. I knew how destructive it could be. How unstoppable. Like the waves ripping the sand away from my beach.

Chapter Thirty-One

Laurel

I WAS SUMMONED TO THE PRINCIPAL'S OFFICE LIKE A WAYWARD little kid. That's how I felt, sitting on one of the small, armless wooden chairs outside Ms. Terrell's office in my white nurse's jacket, waiting to be invited inside. From where I sat, I could see one end of the high school through the office windows. How was Andy faring over there today? Maybe I should have kept him home. I told him that if anyone called him names or said anything upsetting to him, to use it as an opportunity to practice self-control. He said he would do that and I knew he meant it at the time, but even I had little faith in his ability to tune out ugly words from his classmates.

Certainly, this visit to Ms. Terrell's office had something to do with Andy. I knew a few parents had called the high school principal, angry that he was still attending classes. They were worried that, like some other kids who didn't fit in, he might bring a gun to school and slaughter his classmates. I imagined his principal calling Ms. Terrell, asking her to persuade me to withdraw him for the rest of the year.

"Mrs. Lockwood?" Ms. Terrell had opened her office door and stood smiling at me.

I followed her inside. At my modest five feet, five inches, I towered over her.

This was Ms. Terrell's first year at my school, and I didn't know her well personally, although I did know quite a bit about her. She was fortyish with a doctorate degree in education, a petite African-American woman who'd grown up on the streets of Baltimore and who, despite her tiny size, the string of pearls she always wore, and the heels you could hear clicking through the halls, was tough as nails with the kids. They both feared and respected her. I found, sitting across the desk from her, that I had the same reaction.

"How are you holding up?" she asked.

"I'm managing." I smiled, trying not to look as wary as I felt.

"I wanted to touch base with you, given the situation with your son," she said, folding her hands neatly on her desk. "I thought you might want to take some time off while you're coping with this."

I hesitated, trying to read her face. There were frown lines on her forehead and what I read as concern in her eyes.

"Are...have parents complained that I'm here?" I asked.

"No," she said. "I *do* know that some parents over at the high school have complained that *Andy's* still attending school, but I've had no formal complaints about you at all. I simply—"

"You've had informal complaints?"

She sighed. "*Complaints* is too strong a word," she said. "Certainly there's no problem with your work here. The children adore you." She unfolded her hands and dropped them to her lap. "But people talk. You know how that goes."

"They have no right to speculate about my life or my son," I said sharply. Then I pressed my hands together in front of me as if in prayer. "I'm sorry," I said. "I'm not usually so defensive. I just...I know Andy's innocent and it's hard to...he's misunderstood enough as it is. This is the icing on the cake."

"I hear you," she said. She looked out the window toward the high school and I wondered what she was thinking. "I have a son, myself," she said finally.

I was surprised. "You do?" I didn't think she'd ever been married.

"I had him when I was fifteen years old. He's now twenty-five and in medical school at UNC."

"Oh my God," I said. She must have been a determined little dynamo right from the start to get where she was today. "How did you ever manage to..." I waved my hands through the air as if taking in her office and the diplomas on the wall. "You've accomplished so much."

"I had plans for my education even back then," she said, "and I would've had an abortion, if I hadn't been scared and waited too long, but of course I have no regrets." She smiled, looking at a framed picture on her desk. I couldn't see the picture, but I imagined it was a photograph of her son. "I was very lucky," she said. "My mother and grandmother helped raise him so I could keep up with school. When he got into his teens, the area we lived in...well, it was no good for an African-American male. He wasn't a Goody Two-shoes, but he also wasn't a misogynist hip-hoppin' junkie, like a lot of the other boys his age. The cops didn't know that, though. They saw this black teenaged boy and lumped him together with the others. I was making enough money teaching by then that I could get him out of the city. As I said, I was lucky." She folded her hands on her desk once again and leaned toward me. "I'm telling you this to let you know that *I* know about being young and doing irresponsible things like getting pregnant at fifteen, or—" she nodded toward me "—like drinking while you're pregnant, and I know about ostracism and about motherhood. So, I'll understand if you need to take some time off while this is going on."

I stared at her for a moment, taking it all in. "Thank you," I said finally. "Maybe I could take a few days while I try to find a lawyer."

"You don't have one yet?" She seemed surprised.

I told her I'd called the attorney I used for my will and other documents, and he gave me the name of a woman in Hampstead who, as it turned out, had a nephew injured in the fire. She refused to take the case and didn't bother to offer me other names. I was ready to turn to the yellow pages.

Ms. Terrell wrote a name on the back of one of her cards. She tapped a few keys on her computer keyboard, then jotted a number beneath the name.

"I don't know this man well," she said, handing the card to me. "But I do know he's handled criminal cases. His name's Dennis Shartell and I met him through a friend of a friend. He's all the way in Wilmington, though, but he might at least be a starting point for you."

I stood up. "Thanks again," I said.

Walking back through the hallway, I clutched the card in my hand. I'd call this man, this Dennis Shartell. By the time I reached my office, my hopes were pinned on him. He'd be the one to stem the tide of suspicion that was rising against my son. I'd made mistakes in my life. Failing Andy a second time would not be one of them.

Chapter Thirty-Two

Laurel
1991–1992

WITH THE REALIZATION OF MY PREGNANCY CAME THE SUCKING, sticky grip of a depression that made the black mood I'd experienced since Maggie's birth seem like little more than a rainy afternoon. A voice in my head repeated incessantly *You're a liar, an adulterer, a hideous mother.* I hated myself. I withdrew from everyone, including Marcus, never going to Talos, although he still came to The Sea Tender a few nights a week to drink and watch TV. He probably attributed the change in me to my desire to avoid the hot tub and a repeat of that night in his guest room.

I missed him. He was my best friend. My only real friend. I was afraid, though, that spending too much time with Marcus would lead me to tell him what I didn't want him to know.

I knew I couldn't have this baby, the child of my husband's brother, another child I would ruin with my lack of maternal instinct. A child I certainly didn't deserve and who didn't deserve to be born with me as his or her mother. But getting an abortion required picking up the phone, making an appointment, driving myself alone to the clinic in Wilmington as well as back home again, and every time I thought of all I needed to do to make the abortion happen, I crawled into bed and cried until I fell asleep.

I was lying in bed one afternoon when I felt the flutter of bird wings between my navel and my hipbone. Just a quick little ripple, but it scared me. Could I possibly be that far along? The sensation finally motivated me to get out of bed and call the women's clinic.

"When was your last period?" the woman asked me on the phone.

I glanced at the calendar on the wall of the kitchen. It was still turned to the page for May, although I knew we had to be well into June.

"I don't know," I admitted. "Probably two, or maybe three, months ago."

She gave me an appointment for the following day.

There were protestors, maybe twelve or thirteen of them, on the sidewalk in front of the clinic. They carried signs I avoided reading as I parked my car. *I have to do this,* I told myself.

I felt the hungry eyes of the protestors on me as they waited for me to get out of my car. I opened the door, shut it quietly behind me and started walking in the direction of the clinic door.

"Don't kill your baby!" they chanted as I passed them. "Don't kill your baby!"

One woman thrust her sign in front of my head so that I had to dart to the left to avoid running into it.

A young woman greeted me on the walkway to the clinic. "I'm your escort." She smiled, and I let her take my arm and guide me inside. I walked into a waiting room, where a receptionist sat behind a glassed-in desk. I wondered if the glass was bulletproof. Maybe today would be the day the clinic was bombed. The idea didn't distress me. I wouldn't mind, as long as I was the only person killed. Spare the greeter and the staff and the other patients, I thought. Just take me.

The receptionist gave me a clipboard covered with brochures to read and forms to fill out. I took a seat and set to work on them. Once I'd filled out the forms, I let my attention wander to the people sitting around me. Who was here for birth control? Who was here for an abortion? One teenager caught me looking at her and gave me a snarly, scary look that made me study my hands. I didn't lift my gaze again until a nurse brought me a paper cup and pointed to the water cooler in the corner of the waiting room.

"You need to drink water for the sonogram."

I stood up. "A sonogram?" I whispered to her. "I'm here for an abortion."

"We need to know how far along you are so you can have the correct procedure," she said.

I drank the water, cup after cup, until I was certain my bladder would burst. Finally, I was led into a dressing room where I changed into a thin yellow gown, gritting my teeth against the need to urinate. Once I was on the examining table, I became aware for the first time that my belly was round—a smooth, gently sloping hillock above the rest of my body. I felt the flutter of wings again.

"Hey, there." The technician, a woman with short, spiky dark hair, swept into the room carrying the clipboard and my forms. "How are you today?"

"Okay," I said.

She wasted no time, reaching for the tube of gel, smearing it across my stomach. The sonogram screen was turned toward her as she pressed the transducer on my belly.

"Hmm," she said. "About eighteen weeks. Do you want to see?"

"Eighteen *weeks?*" I asked in disbelief. Could it possibly have been that long since that night with Marcus? "What date is it now?"

Her gaze darted from the screen to me. "What do you mean?" she asked.

"Today. What date is today."

"Oh. July twenty-first. Would you like to see the sonogram?" she asked again.

I shook my head. No. I was still stuck on the fact that we were well into July when I thought we were still in June. I pressed my hand to my forehead, rubbing hard, as if I could stuff the cotton back into my brain. "I'm so confused," I said, unaware that I was speaking out loud.

"Well—" the technician turned off the ultrasound machine and wiped the gel from my stomach with tissues "—pregnancy *can* be pretty confusing sometimes. That's why we have counselors to help you think things through." She offered me a hand to help me sit up. "You can empty your bladder in the bathroom across the hall. Then get dressed and go to the first room on the left and the counselor will talk to you about the abortion. It's a two-day procedure at eighteen weeks. And you will absolutely have to have a support person with you to drive you home each day."

In the bathroom, I sobbed as I urinated. I felt completely alone. I knew a second-trimester abortion was a two-day procedure. I was a nurse; I knew what it entailed. In my alcohol-and-depression-fogged brain, I'd hoped I wasn't that far along, that an abortion would be easy. But it wasn't the complexity of the abortion or my inability to supply a "support person" that upset me. It was that I could remember Maggie's eighteen-week sonogram with perfect clarity. She'd sucked her thumb. Rolled a somersault. Waved at Jamie and me. The technician that day had told us she was probably a girl. She'd been so real. So perfect. A tender little bundle of potential, into which we'd poured our hopes and dreams and love.

In the counseling office, I sat across from a woman with short-cropped gray hair, thick white eyebrows and a deep leathery tan.

"Are you cold?" She looked at me with real worry and I realized my entire body was shaking.

"Just nervous," I said. I clenched my teeth to keep them from chattering.

She pulled her chair close to mine until our knees were almost touching.

"The technician doing your sonogram said you seemed surprised to learn how far along you were," she said.

I nodded. "I'm not going to have the abortion," I said, "so I guess I really don't need to talk to you."

"It's your decision," she said. "What made you change your mind?"

I knotted my hands together in my lap. "Because I remember my daughter's sonogram at that...at eighteen weeks, and I can't...it would feel wrong to me, with the baby being this developed."

"Ah," she said. "I understand. You must have very conflicted feelings about this pregnancy to have waited so long."

I nodded, thinking of the little market I'd passed on my way into Wilmington. I could stop there to get a wine cooler on my way home.

"Do you have some support at home?" She glanced at my ring finger. "Your husband? Did he want you to have the abortion?"

"He doesn't know I'm pregnant," I admitted.

"Is it his?" she asked gently.

None of your business, I thought, but I shook my head.

"What do you want to do?"

"I don't know," I whispered.

She looked at the clipboard on her lap, flipping through the forms. "You live on Topsail Island? I can refer you to a therapist in Hampstead," she said. "You have some hard decisions to make and I think you'll need some help."

I nodded again, although I knew I wouldn't go. I was still afraid of seeing a therapist, afraid I might end up in a psych ward if I opened up too much.

The counselor checked a Rolodex file, then wrote a name and number on a card and handed it to me.

"If you're sure you don't want an abortion, please see an obstetrician right away to get started with prenatal care," she said.

"I will."

"And one other thing." She leaned forward, studying me from beneath her white eyebrows. "The escort told me she thought you'd been drinking this morning."

I opened my mouth to protest, but didn't have the strength. I looked down at my hands where they clutched the card she'd given me.

"Alcohol is toxic for your baby," she said.

"I only drink wine coolers."

"They have as much alcoholic content as a beer."

I shook my head. "No, they don't," I said. "The label on the beer says you shouldn't drink it while you're pregnant, but the wine cooler label says nothing about it."

"It should. Right now the law doesn't require that they do, but trust me, they contain the same amount of alcohol as a beer."

I thought she was wrong, or maybe making it up to scare me. Probably, I thought, the brand of wine coolers I liked simply didn't have enough alcohol in them to merit the warning.

"Okay," I said to stop the lecture.

"Would you like me to find an AA meeting near your home?" she offered.

"I don't need an AA meeting." I felt my cheeks flush.

I was shaken by her words, though. Shaken enough to drive the hour home without stopping for a wine cooler, and once at The Sea Tender, I found the remainder of the prenatal vitamins I'd taken while pregnant with Maggie and popped one in my mouth. When I opened the refrigerator door to look for something to wash it down with, though, my choice was between the three-week-old carton of orange juice and the six-pack of wine coolers I'd purchased the day before, which was really like having no choice at all.

For another two weeks, I sat with my secret. I tried and failed to cut back on the wine coolers, but I forced myself to eat better and take the vitamins. I didn't see a doctor. I asked Jamie not to bring Maggie over, telling him I didn't feel well, which was certainly the truth.

Sara was so wrapped up with baby Keith that she rarely stopped by anymore, and that was a relief. Marcus still came over, and I wore loose beach dresses and was boring company, my dilemma the only thing occupying my mind. I knew I'd give birth to this baby, but I wondered if I should keep it. Maybe I could go away someplace where I could have the baby and place it for adoption with no one any the wiser.

One evening in my twenty-first week, Marcus was over and we drank too much and ate pizza as we watched *Seinfeld*. He carried our empty plates into the kitchen and I followed a moment later with our empty bottles.

"You look like you're pregnant in that dress," he teased me.

I was too taken by surprise to speak, and our eyes suddenly locked.

He reached over to touch my belly, then jerked his hand away. "Jesus!"

"It's Jamie's," I said quickly.

"*Jamie's?*" he asked, as though shocked I'd slept with Jamie during our separation.

"It was the week he and Maggie stayed here," I said. "Remember? When Sara had her baby."

"Does he know?"

I shook my head. "I haven't decided what to do."

"Looks like you've already decided to me. Why didn't you have an abortion?"

I rubbed my eyes, suddenly very tired. "Don't ask hard questions," I said as I walked back into the living room and sat down again on the sofa.

He followed me into the room. "What's hard about it?"

"I lost track of time and I waited too long," I said. "Now I have to decide if I should go away someplace, have the baby, and let someone adopt it."

He shook his head. "You need to tell Jamie."

I let out my breath, dropping my head against the back of the sofa in resignation. "I know." I'd known all along, deep in my heart, I would not go away, not because I felt any special bond to the baby I was carrying, but because I didn't have the energy to figure out where to go.

He sat down at the other end of the sofa. "How do you know it's Jamie's and not mine?" he asked.

"Because," I said, lifting my head to look at him again, "that's the one thing I *have* decided."

* * *

Jamie and Maggie moved back into The Sea Tender when I was nearly seven months pregnant. Jamie was furious with himself for the broken condom, as though it was his fault. He should have checked the date, he said, and he shouldn't have made love to me when I was still so depressed. He wanted to take care of me, and he was upset that I hadn't felt able to tell him about the pregnancy from the start. I was nervous about being two weeks farther along than I said I was. I hoped the baby came two weeks late and would then seem like it was right on time.

Maggie was two and a half and talking a blue streak, but I couldn't understand most of what she said and Jamie needed to serve as her interpreter. I tried hard to understand her, struggling to make sense of the words.

"I'm sorry, honey," I'd say over and over. "Can you say that again, please?" And when she'd repeat her statement and I still didn't get it, she'd wail in frustration. Jamie, on the other hand, could listen to her nonsensical-sounding words and know their meaning almost every time. It was uncanny, as though the two of them shared a secret language I could not be part of.

He seemed to know better than to leave me alone with her, and he hired a nanny to babysit during his work hours at the real estate office and on Sunday mornings when he was in the chapel. He gave up the volunteer fire department altogether so he wouldn't be called away unexpectedly.

Although I was fully in favor of having the nanny take care of Maggie, I disliked being in the house when the middle-aged woman was there. I felt her judging me. I was certain my strained relationship with my child was obvious to her. Jamie had told her my doctor wanted me to rest during the last couple of months of my pregnancy, so that my withdrawal and constant napping wouldn't seem odd to her, but I felt in the way in my own home. So I spent most of my days at Talos. I napped on Marcus's sofa, watched TV, and drank the wine coolers that were forbidden to me at home. I needed them more than ever, with a craving that I knew had become more physical than emotional.

That's why I was drunk when I went into labor, three weeks early, a full five weeks before the fictional due date I'd told Jamie. And that's why I called Marcus to take me to the hospital, not wanting Jamie to see me until I was sober.

Andy was only ten hours old when the social worker came into my room at the hospital. Jamie was in the chair next to the bed, telling me he wanted to name the baby Andrew after his father, and I rolled the name around in my mouth even though I was thinking, *I don't care what we name him.* What I really wanted was to go back to sleep.

The social worker, whose name I instantly forgot, was about thirty, five years older than me. She wore an expression that I read as ten percent pity and ninety percent condescension as she sat in a chair near my bed and asked me questions I didn't bother to answer. I didn't care what she thought of me. I closed my eyes so I didn't have to see Jamie's frown as I ignored her.

"Your baby was premature, but even considering his gestational age of about thirty-seven weeks, he's smaller than he should be," she said. "He didn't grow well inside you."

My eyes still shut, I tried to figure out if anything she'd said could make Jamie doubt his paternity, but the words and the weeks clotted together in my brain and I couldn't sort them out.

"The staff called me in because of that, and because you were in-ebriated when you arrived."

"I still can't believe it," Jamie said. He'd already chewed me out for it and I hoped he wasn't going to start up again.

"You have what we call a dual diagnosis," the social worker said.

"What does that mean?" Jamie asked.

"First, you have a substance-abuse problem."

I opened my eyes, but only to roll them at her.

"Your blood alcohol level was .09 when you were brought in," the social worker said. "The man who brought you...your brother-in-law? He told the staff you'd been drinking throughout your pregnancy."

I was angry with Marcus. What right did he have to tell anyone anything about me?

"Well, I think she *was* drinking early on," Jamie said naively. "We were separated. But the last couple of months, I've been home and she hasn't had anything except I guess last night—" I saw the light dawn in his eyes. "Have you been drinking over at Marcus's during the day?" he asked.

"Just wine coolers," I said.

"Oh, Laurel."

I wasn't sure if it was disappointment or disgust I heard in his voice.

"The second part of the diagnosis is postpartum depression," the social worker continued as if I'd said nothing. "I spoke with the nurse who talked with you, Mr. Lockwood—" she nodded at Jamie "—and it seems like that's been a problem for your wife since the birth of your last child."

Jamie looked at me. "*Finally,* Laurel," he said. "Finally we know what's been wrong with you all this time."

I knew about postpartum depression, but whatever was wrong with me was so much worse than that. I'd imagined running a knife through my child's heart. Wasn't that more than depression?

The social worker gave us a tutorial about hormones and brain chemistry. She said, "I think you must have felt pretty isolated living on Topsail Island after your daughter was born."

In a flash, I relived the weeks after Maggie's birth when she cried constantly and I felt as though I had no one to turn to. I started to answer, but the words couldn't get past the knot in my throat.

"Your brother-in-law said that you barely drank at all before then," the social worker said. "I think you felt so bad after your daughter was born that you started to medicate yourself with alcohol to take away the pain."

I wanted a wine cooler right then, more than anything.

"The pediatricians in the neonatal intensive care unit believe your baby may have problems caused by your drinking."

I was suddenly alert. "What kind of problems?"

"His small size is probably related to your alcohol consumption," she said. "His Apgar scores were low. Fortunately, he doesn't have the facial deformities we often see in babies with fetal alcohol problems, but he did have some respiratory distress that was more than they'd expect in a preemie of his gestational age. There's often central nervous system involvement. Possibly intellectual or cognitive impairment. It's too soon to know how severely he might be affected or even if he *will* be affected that way at all."

I froze inside. What had I done? I felt the way I had the day I'd pulled into the street and cut off Jamie's motorcycle. I'd hurt another human being through my actions. I'd hurt my own baby.

"Jamie, I'm sorry," I said. "I'm so sorry."

He turned his face away from mine, and I knew that he would not be quick to forgive me this time. I didn't blame him.

"Is he…" I tried to picture the baby I'd seen only briefly in the delivery room. "Is he suffering?" I asked.

"It's hard to know how much neonates feel," she said. "What you need to know at this point, though, is that Andrew's now in the custody of Protective Services. When he's ready to leave the hospital, he'll go to a foster home until we can evaluate your home situation."

"What?" Jamie asked. "We can take perfectly good care of him." He didn't look at me. "At least *I* can."

"Protective Services will make that evaluation," she said. "You've had a nanny helping with your other child, is that right?"

Jamie nodded.

"She contacted Protective Services when Laurel went into labor. She was worried that your home isn't a safe environment for an infant."

"That woman hates me," I said. I couldn't even remember the nanny's name.

"So her report," the social worker continued, "on top of a substance-abuse problem and Andrew's fragile health means we have to do what's best for him, and that's to place him in foster care once he's released from the hospital and the home is evaluated."

"How do we get him back?" Jamie asked.

"The best chance of getting your baby back is for Laurel to go into a rehab program. There's one in Wilmington that's specifically designed for people like you with dual diagnosis. It's expensive, though, so—"

"The money doesn't matter," Jamie interrupted her.

I was frightened. "Jamie, please don't let them lock me up!"

"It's completely voluntary, Laurel," the social worker said. "But I highly recommend you go if you want a chance to regain custody of your baby."

"Please go into rehab." Sara leaned forward from the chair next to my hospital bed that evening. She'd come into my room and told Jamie to take a break. When she sat down next to me, that was the first thing she said. "Please do it for your family, if not for yourself."

"I wish y'all would just leave me alone," I said. Jamie'd been pleading with me about the rehab program for the last few hours and my nerves were brittle. Ready to snap.

Sara sat back in the chair, while I turned my head to look out the window at a darkening winter sky. She was quiet for so long, I thought she'd given up. I heard her shift in the chair and imagined she was getting ready to go, but she was only leaning forward again.

"I remember this woman," she said slowly. "I saw her a few years ago in a little chapel her husband built. Her husband got up and spoke to the people who were there, and this woman…well, she looked up at him like he'd hung the moon. I remember watching her with envy, thinking *I wish I could feel love like that*."

I wanted to tell her to shut up, but my mouth wouldn't open. I stared through the window at a distant water tower as she continued.

"The man asked people where they'd felt God that week, and when no one answered, that woman got to her feet because she loved her husband so much she didn't want to see him fail. And she said how she felt God when she was under the stars the night before. She said she was overwhelmed by the beauty of the world."

I turned to her then. "You still remember that?"

"Oh, yes," Sara said. "I admired that woman. Admired her and envied her."

"Where—" my voice was tight, a whisper "—where did she go?"

"She drowned in a bottle of booze," Sara said bluntly. "Her husband wants her back. And her children need her back."

"Maggie doesn't care," I said. "She hates me."

"She's not even three years old!" Sara's voice rose. "She's not capable of hate, Laurie. She just doesn't *know* you. She doesn't trust you."

I shook my head. "All I want right now is a drink," I said.

Sara suddenly grabbed my wrist. I gasped in surprise, trying to wrench my arm free, but she held it fast. "You've become a selfish, self-absorbed bitch." She looked hard into my eyes and I couldn't seem to turn away from her gaze. "I understand that your hormones got screwed up," she said. "I understand you can't help the depression. But you can *fix* it, Laurel. You're the only one who can."

It was Sara's anger more than Jamie's pleading that propelled me into rehab. I didn't go to get my baby back—I was certain he'd be better off without me. But Sara had made me remember the happy, contented, honorable woman I used to be. If there was a chance I could reclaim that woman—the woman who'd drowned—I had to take it.

The rehab facility was in a peaceful, bucolic setting that belied the intensity of the work taking place inside its four buildings. In the beginning, I hated everything about it: the forced structure, the food, the exercise, the group sessions, my assigned individual therapist. I was surrounded by addicts and crazy people with whom I had nothing in common. They allowed no one to visit me, not even Jamie. They gave me the Prozac I'd resisted a couple of years earlier. I was there a full month before I began to feel a change come over me. I broke down during therapy, crying a river of tears that had been locked inside me, perhaps since the deaths of my parents so many years earlier. I remembered Jamie telling me, so long ago, *If you don't deal with loss, it could come back to bite you later.* Was that what had happened to me?

One memorable day, I laughed at a commercial on television and it was like hearing the voice of a stranger in my ears. I couldn't remember the last time I'd laughed.

And one morning, almost two months into the program, I woke up caring. I cared how Maggie and Jamie were doing. I cared about my newborn son whose face I'd barely noticed and wished now I could see and touch. I had a picture of him that Jamie had taken at the hospital and I kept it in my pocket during the day and on my night table at night. A palm-size, dark-haired baby, he lay in an incubator, his head turned away from the camera, hooked up to more wires and tubes than I could count. I knew he was now in a foster home, and I prayed he was with people who were holding him and loving him. It felt extraordinary to care about him and Maggie and Jamie. It felt extraordinary to care about *myself.*

By then, I knew the names of the addicts and crazy people and I knew they were not all that different from me. Some of them had lost their children for good. I wouldn't let that happen. I was going to fight to get well and then I would fight to get my baby back. And once I had him in my arms again, I would never, ever, let him go.

Chapter Thirty-Three

Maggie

BEN LEANED UP ON HIS ELBOW AND STRUCK A MATCH TO LIGHT the joint he held between his lips. In that quick flash of light, I saw the smooth, dark hair on his chest. I put my hand on his belly and rested my cheek against that hair. Sometimes I couldn't get close enough to him. Even when he was inside me, it wasn't really quite enough. What was wrong with me? He gave me so much and I still wanted more… though I wasn't sure what it was, exactly, that I wanted more of.

He held the joint to my lips and I pulled the smoke into my lungs, holding it there as long as I could before letting my breath out across his chest.

"I'm worried about Andy," he said suddenly.

"Me, too." I knew Mom was still upset we'd given the cops the wrong clothes, but I was glad. I wished I could tell Ben. I wanted to tell *someone* about that split-second decision Mom and I had made. That weird, sudden connection between us. That no-turning-back moment. I couldn't lay that on him, though. There were so many things I wanted to tell him but couldn't. "Everyone's turned against him all of a sudden."

"Well, you haven't. And I haven't. And I'm sure as hell your mom hasn't."

"True."

Ben took another hit on the joint. "Your mother's made Andy her life's work," he said when he finally exhaled. "I figured that out the first time I met her at the pool, when she gave me written instructions on the best way to deal with him." He laughed. My head bounced on his chest.

"That's my mom," I said.

"She doesn't mother *you* much, though, does she?"

"Well, I'm seventeen."

"But has she ever?" he asked. "Has she ever taken care of you the way she takes care of Andy?"

I felt a hurt inside me that I didn't want to feel. "I never needed taking care of the way Andy does," I said.

"Everybody needs to be taken care of."

"That's why I've got you," I said.

He didn't say anything, and the hurt expanded inside my chest. He held the joint to my lips again, but I shook my head. I felt a little sick from it now. I tried to think of a different subject we could talk about. His daughter. He loved talking about her. I could ask him when he'd see her again. I opened my mouth to speak, but the alert tones suddenly rang out from his fire department pager, which was buried somewhere in the pile of clothes on the floor.

Ben jumped to his feet, as I knew he would.

"Are you getting up?" He pulled his T-shirt over his head.

I stretched beneath the covers. "I'm going to stay here awhile." The long window in front of the bed was full of stars. I could sit outside and try to make contact with Daddy's spirit. It had been so long since I'd been able to reach him, and all that talk about needing to be taken care of really got to me.

"I don't like you being here alone at night." He had no idea how often I came to The Sea Tender alone.

"I'll be okay," I said.

I listened to him walk through the living room and close the front door. I heard the *thump* as he jumped from the steps to the sand. I tried to hear his van start, but he must have parked too far away.

He'd handed me the joint before he left. I held it between my lips without inhaling as I pulled on my shorts and top. I blew out the candles, then walked outside to sit in my favorite spot on the edge of the deck. I dropped the rest of the joint to the sand below. *Wasteful,* Ben would say.

Closing my eyes, I took in a deep, salty breath as I tried to still my mind.

At least the fire had been good for Ben, I thought. He was happy in the department now. He wouldn't leave.

Stop thinking!

I took in another deep breath, and my mind was on the brink of clearing up when those damned posters from the memorial service popped into it again.

I groaned. "Daddy," I whispered in frustration. *"Please come."* What if he was just as frustrated as I was? Maybe he was waiting on the other side for me to quiet my mind long enough for him to break through. Maybe I was failing him like I was failing everybody else.

I thought I heard a sound from inside the house. I turned to listen through the screened door, but all I could hear was the ocean.

A flash of light bobbed on the railing next to me. I jumped to my feet.

"Maggie?"

A woman's voice. I felt so busted and was glad I'd dropped the joint.

I tried to block the beam of the flashlight with my hand to see who was aiming it at me, but it was impossible. I was dizzy from standing up too quickly. I grabbed the deck railing. "Who are you?" I called.

"Oh my God, I don't believe this!"

Dawn. She pushed open the screened door. Her flashlight blinded me.

"What are you doing here?" I asked as I backed against the railing, shielding my eyes with my arm.

"I could ask you the same question."

What did she know? The light was trapping me. I had to get away from it. I pushed past her and into the house. She followed me inside.

"This is the cottage where I lived when I was little." My voice shook. "I visit it sometimes. I was just going to leave."

Dawn scanned the living room and kitchen with her flashlight. I could just make out that her hair was in a ponytail and she had frown lines like stripes across her forehead. She sat down on the arm of the sofa and put the flashlight on the floor, aiming it toward the corner of the room. She was too quiet. I wanted to get my pocketbook out of the bedroom so I could escape, but what if she followed me in there and saw the unmade bed? Did she have a clue what was going on? Why was she *here?*

I picked up my bottle of water from the breakfast bar and started talking to fill the silence.

"I'm sorry I didn't call you about the fund-raising yet," I said. "I was waiting till I worked out details, but we're going to have this massive makeover event at the high school, with—"

"Why was Ben here?" she asked.

Shit. Shit. Shit. "Ben?" I asked. "What makes you think he was here?"

"Don't play dumb," she said. "D'you think I just happened to show up here tonight? I followed him. I wanted to know where he disappeared to so many nights without explanation. When I saw him leave this cottage, I decided to see what was so...so *alluring* to him about it. Now I get it."

I opened the water bottle and took a sip to give me time to think. "We meet here sometimes to talk about the swim team," I tried.

"You can do better than that," she said.

"Dawn, it's really not like—"

"Don't give me that crap." She sounded harsh, not like the Dawn I thought I knew. "How long's this been going on?"

I sighed. Gave in. I felt my shoulders sag. "A while," I said.

"I can't believe he's cheating on me with a *teenager*. A *kid*. It's sick."

"He's *not* cheating on you!"

"What do you call it?"

"You're just friends."

"Oh, cut me a break," she said. "Did he tell you that?"

I was afraid of getting Ben in more trouble by saying the wrong thing, but I was so nervous I couldn't think straight. "I know when he first moved in, he...the two of you...you slept together, and I know you hoped you'd be more than just friends, but—"

"That goddamned son of a bitch." She rubbed her neck. "I thought he was different, but turns out he's like all the rest. He wants the thrill of doing something forbidden, behind closed doors. With a tight little body." She motioned toward me, toward my body.

"Ben's so not like that."

"Don't tell me what Ben's 'so not' like!" she snapped. "I *live* with him, sugar. I know him better than you ever will."

I twisted the cap of the bottle back and forth, afraid of her anger and what she might do. Who she might tell.

"Does your mama know about this?" She was a mind reader. "She can get him for statutory rape."

"The age of consent is sixteen."

She let out a nasty laugh. "You've figured this all out, I see," she said. "Even if it's not illegal, it's *immoral* for a twenty-eight-year-old man to sleep with a seventeen-year-old girl."

"Age is just a number." I wrinkled my nose as the cliché popped out of my idiotic mouth.

"And it's immoral to sleep with two women at once and lie to them about it."

"It's not at once. You are so *yesterday* to him!" I felt like a bitch, but she deserved it. "You think he's your boyfriend, but he's not."

She stared at me, then started laughing again. "Lord have mercy," she said, "I'm going to give that bastard one hell of a talking-to." She tilted her head to the side. "Was he your first?"

"None of your business."

"I just bet he was. Men love that, don't they? Popping the cherry."

"Don't talk that way about him!" I said. "Don't lump him together with all the losers you've been—"

"Does your mama know you're smoking weed?"

"*What?*"

"Don't play innocent with me, Maggie. It reeks in here."

Oh God. Now she had two things on me. My hand twisted the bottle cap back and forth. Back and forth.

Suddenly, she stood up. When she spoke again, her voice was totally different. She growled like a tiger. "Lay off my man, girl," she said. She picked up the flashlight and walked to the door. "If you don't, I'll have to tell your mama what you're up to, and she's got enough to worry about right now. You sure don't want to add to that now, do you, sugar?"

I threw the bottle hard—*really* hard—before I knew what I was doing. It caught her on the side of her neck and she screeched, dropping the flashlight.

"Bitch!" she said.

"I'm sorry!" I pressed my hands to my face. "I didn't mean to do that, Dawn! Honest!"

She picked up the flashlight and I thought she was going to come after me with it, but she opened the door and ran onto the front deck. I listened to the creak of the stairs and heard her jump to the sand.

I slammed the door shut and turned the lock. Then I pulled my phone from my pocket and hit the speed dial for Ben's cell. No answer.

As fast as I could, I typed a text message into the keypad.

D knows.

Chapter Thirty-Four

Laurel

"Have a seat, please." Dennis Shartell led me into his office and gestured toward one of the leather chairs in front of a massive mahogany desk.

"I appreciate you seeing me so quickly," I said as I sat down. I'd only received his name from Ms. Terrell the day before, but the attorney's receptionist said he'd be able to squeeze me in.

"I can imagine what you're going through," he said as he sat down on the other side of the desk. "I've heard the rumors."

"You've heard them here? In Wilmington?"

"The fire was big news," he said, "and although the officials aren't calling it arson, everyone knows it's arson—or in legal terminology, the 'burning of a church.' People love a good twist to a story. What better twist than the hero turns out to be the villain?"

"He's not, though."

He nodded, the overhead light glinting off his glasses. He was a slender man, but soft looking, as though he didn't have to work hard at keeping the weight off. His face was long beneath thinning dark hair, and he wore a smile that was equal parts kind and self-confident. I liked him. I was practically in *love* with him. He would help me make sense of this ridiculous mess.

as if she had to think about her answer. "Doesn't Maggie keep you informed?" she asked.

It took me a moment to realize that my children would see Ben at swim practices. "Oh, of course," I said, "I guess if he were having any problems, Maggie or Andy would have let me know." Actually, I wasn't sure either of them would think to tell me. "He *is* all right, isn't he?"

"He's fine," she said quickly. Then she chuckled, and I imagined she was thinking of a private moment between them, because when she spoke again, it wasn't about anything funny. "Listen, sugar." She leaned forward, resting her elbows on her knees. "I know there's all this talk about Andy, and it must be driving you 'round the bend."

"It is," I acknowledged.

"Well, I just want to say that, even if Andy *did* have something to do with the fire, I'm sure he'll be able to get off because he couldn't possibly understand the seriousness of what he was doing."

I stared at her, momentarily speechless. I knew she was trying to comfort me, but it certainly wasn't working.

"Andy didn't do anything wrong," I said.

"I'm just saying, even if he did."

I let out a long sigh. "All right." I gave up. People were going to believe what they wanted to and there wasn't much I could do about it. "Thanks for the coffee. And if you talk to Sara before I do, please tell her I was asking about her and Keith."

As I drove home, I wondered if Sara hadn't returned my calls because she, too, believed Andy was responsible for the fire. Ludicrous. Sara knew Andy nearly as well as I did. I'd try calling her again as soon as I got home.

"Tell me what you know," he said, clicking his ballpoint pen above a yellow legal pad. "What evidence do they have so far?"

"As far as I know, they just have the word of a few people that Andy was outside during the lock-in. I don't believe it, though. Even if it's true, so what? But my son is a very concrete thinker. If the rules say, 'this is a lock-in and you stay inside,' he'd stay inside."

"What do you mean, he's a concrete thinker?"

I explained FASD to him. Maybe it would have been better to find an attorney already familiar with the disorder. But Dennis took notes and appeared to be listening carefully.

"All right," he said when I had finished talking. "Who are the witnesses who claim they saw Andy outside during the lock-in?"

"One is a boy named Keith Weston." I told him about Andy's fight with Keith during the lock-in and about their long-ago history as childhood friends. "Another was a woman who was just passing by the church that night. Of course, she couldn't identify Andy by name, but she described seeing a boy who may have resembled him. Then his friend Emily—who's also a special needs child—said he disappeared during the lock-in."

He looked at me as if waiting for more. "That's it?" he asked finally.

"That's all I know of. They searched his room."

"They had a warrant?"

"No. I signed a consent-to-search form."

"Did they remove anything?"

"They took the clothes he had on the night of the lock-in. And I think some information from his computer."

Dennis tapped the pen against his jaw. "Andy seemed to be the only person who knew a safe way out of the building, is that correct?"

"Yes. But that's not a crime."

"Hardly." He chuckled. "From what I've read, your son is viewed as an outsider. Not very popular. Do you agree with that description of him?"

I nodded. "Yes," I said. "He doesn't fit in very well, but that doesn't mean he'd set a fire to make himself look like a big man on campus."

"Well." Dennis rested his pen on the legal pad and sat back in his chair. "Unless there's more to this picture than meets the eye, it would seem that all they have now is circumstantial evidence. Nothing they can use to pin a felony on your son, that's for sure. How did he get to the lock-in?"

"My daughter—his sister, Maggie—drove him."

"And I assume Maggie knows he wasn't carrying a couple of gallons of flammable liquid, right?"

I smiled. I was beginning to relax about this whole thing. It was, as I'd thought all along, absurd. "Right," I said.

"As long as his clothes don't come back from the lab with traces of accelerant on them, I'd say he's home free."

"That won't happen," I said. I knew that for a fact.

I was so relieved after speaking to Dennis that I sang along with the radio in my car. I opened the windows, letting my hair blow around my head in the warm spring air as I sang oldies-but-goodies at the top of my lungs all the way to the swing bridge.

I turned right after crossing the bridge and headed for Jabeen's. Maybe Sara was still in Surf City and would have some time to catch up. Once again, I felt out of touch with her. I'd called twice in the past few days, but she hadn't called back.

Dawn was cleaning the counter when I walked into the empty café. She looked up and gave me a halfhearted wave.

"Hi, Dawn," I said. "Is Sara in today?"

"She's back at the hospital." She barely glanced at me as she sprayed a spot on the counter, but I could see that her eyes were bloodshot and I was immediately worried.

"Is Keith okay?" I asked.

"He's actually doing better." She put down the cloth and spray bottle and picked up a paper cup, holding it under the spigot of one of the coffeemakers. "But those burn treatments don't sound like fun."

"I know," I said. "I had a couple of burn patients when I was in nurse's training." Scrubbing scorched skin raw had been, without a doubt, one of the most disturbing parts of my training. "Poor Keith. It's got to be so hard for Sara to watch him go through that."

Dawn snapped a lid on the cup of coffee I hadn't ordered and handed it to me.

"Thanks," I said, taking a sip.

"She makes out like she's doing all right with it," Dawn said, "but you know she must be wrung out." Dawn looked wrung out herself. There were puffy bags under her eyes.

"How about you?" I didn't want to pry, but something was clearly wrong. "Are you all right?" I asked.

She nodded. "Just tired." She sat down on the stool behind the cash register, her feet propped up on the rung, and rubbed her palms on her lean, denim-covered thighs. "You wouldn't believe how the money's been rolling in since the *Today* show," she said with a little more pep in her voice. "Thanks for your help with that."

"You're the one doing all the work." I took another sip of the coffee. "Is Ben's head healed?"

She ran her fingers through her pretty red hair, taking her time,

* * *

There was a police car in front of the house when I pulled in my driveway, and the sight of it wiped Sara from my mind. I hurried into the house and found Maggie standing in the entryway with Sergeant Wood.

"They think we gave them the wrong clothes," she said quickly.

I looked from her to the sergeant.

"Sorry to disturb you again, ma'am," he said. "But we have some pictures from the lock-in that kids took with their cell phone cameras. The clothing and shoes you gave us are not what Andy has on in those pictures."

"You're kidding." I didn't look at Maggie. I never should have dragged her into this.

"I'd like to take another look in his room for the right articles of clothing."

I hesitated, maybe a moment too long. "Sure," I said. "Go ahead."

We followed Sergeant Wood upstairs, Maggie gnawing her lip. I wished she didn't look so guilty.

In Andy's room, I watched the sergeant pull the correct pair of sneakers from his closet. "These look more like it," he said. He withdrew a photograph from his shirt pocket and studied it, then handed it to me.

My hand was damp with sweat as I took the photograph from him. The picture was of two boys I didn't know, posing like bodybuilders, flexing their arms to show off their small adolescent biceps. Andy and Emily stood off to one side of the boys, vacant looks on their faces, clearly incidental to the main subjects of the photograph.

"I was sure he was wearing those others," I said, afraid the sergeant would lift the shoes to his nose and smell what I had smelled on them, but he simply dropped them into two separate bags. I looked at the picture again. "And I could have sworn he'd had on that sage-colored shirt."

"Me, too," Maggie added. "He had it on earlier that day, so I guess we got mixed up."

I wanted her to be quiet, afraid she'd give us away—if we were not already given away.

"Uh-huh," Sergeant Wood said. I didn't think he believed a word we were saying, but apparently he wasn't going to call us on it. At least not yet.

He finished his collection of clothing and we followed him downstairs again.

"Good day, ma'am. Miss." He nodded to us, then let himself out.

As soon as the door shut behind him, Maggie grabbed my arm.

"Why didn't you throw them away?" she asked. "The shoes and his clothes?"

"I didn't think of it," I said. "I never thought of pictures. But I should have given them the right clothes from the start. That was really stupid of me. I'm sorry, Maggie."

We fell quiet, neither of us moving away from the front door.

"What should it matter?" I asked. "He's innocent, so the clothes won't have anything flammable on them, right?"

"Oh God, I hope not."

"Maggie, you can't possibly think—"

"What if his cigarette lighter leaked, like you said?"

"Then we'll explain about the lighter," I said calmly. "I met with the lawyer this morning, and he said everything's circumstantial evidence so far. So as long as the clothes come back clean, Andy's in the clear."

She looked at me with worry in her eyes.

"Nothing will be on them, Maggie." I hugged her to me and she melted in my arms, unusual for my independent daughter. "We have nothing at all to worry about."

Chapter Thirty-Five

Maggie

I DIDN'T HEAR ANYTHING FROM BEN THE DAY AFTER DAWN busted me, even though I left six messages for him. Between the cop coming back for Andy's clothes and me waiting for Mom to say, *I had a call from Dawn Reynolds today, Maggie,* I was ready to slit my wrists. And I had the tiniest—just the teeny tiniest—bit of doubt about Ben. That was the worst part of all.

He finally called on my cell that night. "I'll call you right back!" I said. Then I went out to our pier; I couldn't take the chance Mom would overhear me.

I speed-dialed him as soon as I was far enough from the house to talk. "I've been freaking out!" I said when he picked up. "What did Dawn say?"

"Everything's cool," Ben said. "At least for now. She was rabid when I got home last night, though."

"What did you tell her?"

"I calmed her down. That took a while." He laughed a little. "I told her...you know...how she thought we...her and me...have something that we don't."

I relaxed. I used to feel sorry for Dawn, but after last night when she was such a bitch, that was over. "Was she really upset?"

"Yeah. Sure. I think she got it, though."

"Do you think she'll tell?" I'd reached the end of the pier and sat down on one of the posts. "I thought for sure she'd call my mother today."

"Well, that could still be a problem, Maggie. She thinks it's wrong for us to see each other. That I'm robbing the cradle."

"That's *our* business!" I heard my voice carry over the dark water and wondered if the pier was such a good idea after all.

"Well, I just don't want her to make it *her* business, if you get what I'm saying."

"What do you mean?"

"I think you and I need to lay low for a while. Just till Dawn settles down."

"What do you mean, lay low?"

"Not see each other. Definitely not at The Sea Tender. We can talk and email, but I don't think we should get together."

How could he even say the words? "Ben!" I said. "I *have* to see you! I'll go crazy if I can't see you!"

"I know," he said. "Me, too. But we can't risk pissing Dawn off. You're going to be eighteen soon and out of high school. Then it won't matter so much. So let's just—"

"Couldn't we... We have swim practice Saturday. Wouldn't it seem normal to get together afterward like we used to? You know, to talk about the team? Dawn couldn't make a federal case about that."

He waited a second, then said, "Dawn's coming to practice Saturday."

"What?" I stood up. *"Why?"*

"She said she misses watching the kids, but I'm sure it's to keep an eye on us. So we have to act cool, Maggie, all right?"

"Why didn't you tell her she can't come?"

"Because I'm trying to *protect* us." I thought he sounded a little fed up with me. "Not only could she tell your mother, but Marcus or the rec center staff or the parents of the kids we work with. Let me deal with her, okay? I know her better than you do. We just need to keep our noses clean for a while. Till you graduate."

"That's over a month away!"

"It'll fly by, angel."

"How can you sound so *calm?*"

"I'm not. It's just that I've had twenty-four hours to think of the best thing to do. It's fresh news to you."

I lowered myself to the pier and lay down on my back. It was too cloudy to see the stars. My eyes were full of tears, anyway. The thing was, I knew he was right. I sucked at being patient, but I could wait another month to have a lifetime with him.

"Maggie? You still there?"

"I think..." A plan was taking shape in my mind. "I think I won't live on campus next year," I said. "I'll commute. Maybe I could find a roommate here on the island and not have to live at home."

"What are you talking about? You've always planned to live on campus."

"I don't want to be that far from you."

"It's only forty-five minutes."

"That's too far." I wiped tears off my cheeks with my fingers.

"I think you should live on campus. It'd be a good experience for you."

"Don't you want me to be closer?"

"Of course. But I'll visit you there all the time, if you're not too embarrassed to be seen with an ol' man."

I smiled. "No way." I loved the idea of finally being able to show him off in public.

"Don't decide now, Maggie," he said. "I think it'd be good for you, though. You know. Get that whole college experience."

If it was *him* going away to college with me staying on Topsail, I wouldn't want him to live on campus. How could he just let me go that easily? I thought how it felt to rest my head on his chest. How content I felt when he wrapped his arms around me.

"Ben?"

"I'm here."

"Can we…maybe in a week…can we find someplace to be together. Just for a while? The beach at night or someplace? No one will know. Please?"

He was quiet and I tightened every muscle in my body, waiting for his answer.

"All right," he said. "I'd better get off now."

"I love you."

"Love you, too."

I clicked off my phone, and lay there on the pier until I fell asleep, hanging on to his "love you, too" by my fingertips.

Chapter Thirty-Six

Laurel

I HUNG UP THE PHONE, THEN RACED ACROSS CAMPUS FROM the elementary school to the high school. I was breathless and perspiring by the time I arrived in the main office.

"In there." The secretary nodded toward the room used for meetings. The door was slightly ajar and I pushed it open without knocking. Flip Cates sat at the long table, and although Flip was not a large man, he dwarfed Andy sitting across from him. Andy leaped up from his chair and ran into my arms, sobbing.

"It's okay, sweetie." I rocked him back and forth like I did when he was little. "Don't be scared. It's going to be all right." Was it? Could Andy feel how my own body trembled beneath his arms?

Flip had left a message on my cell that they had a petition requesting Andy be taken into custody. Now I looked at him over Andy's head. *"Why?"* I asked.

"His pants and shoes had traces of accelerant on them," he said. "I'm sorry, Laurel."

The lighter. "Maybe he spilled lighter fluid when he—"

Flip shook his head. "It's gasoline and diesel."

Was that what I'd smelled on his shoes? It couldn't have been. "That can't *be*, Flip!" Andy had settled into my arms as if he planned to stay there forever. "It's got to be a mistake. A conspiracy or something." I grasped at straws as my heart lost its rhythm behind my breastbone. "This is completely impossible!"

"I know you're upset, Laur—"

"Flip! You *know* this child." I hugged Andy even closer to my body. Tears slid down my cheeks that I didn't want him to see. "You've known him nearly all his life! Please! At least tell me you think this is some kind of crazy mistake!"

I supposed there was some sympathy in Flip's eyes, but I was blind to it at that moment.

"I'm sorry," he said, "but I need to take him to the juvenile detention center in Castle Hayne. You can follow in your car or ride with him in mine."

"With *him*," I said. "I'm not letting him out of my sight."

I called Marcus's cell from the back of Flip's cruiser.

"Already on my way," Marcus said. "I just heard."

"I don't know what's going on, Marcus." I tried to keep my voice even for Andy's sake. I'd scared him with my hysterics at the high school. Now he shivered next to me, his body close to mine. I hadn't seen him this frightened since he was a little boy.

"Call his lawyer," Marcus said. "I'll see you there."

"Is he going to shoot us?" Andy whispered to me when I shut my phone.

"Who?" I asked. "*Flip?* No, of course not. No one's going to shoot us."

At the detention center, the thirty-something, balding intake officer had me fill out a form while he talked to Flip in legalese. Then he fingerprinted Andy, because of "the serious nature of the crime."

Marcus arrived just as another uniformed officer handed Andy a navy-blue jumpsuit and said to follow him. I suddenly understood that they meant to keep him there.

"He can't *stay* here!" I said to the intake officer as Marcus came to stand at my side. "I'll put up bail. Just tell me how much and—"

"There is no bond in juvenile cases, ma'am," the man said.

Marcus reached across the man's desk to shake his hand, and I was glad he was in uniform. "I'm Marcus Lockwood," he said. "The boy's uncle."

"You the fire marshal in Surf City?"

Marcus nodded.

"What do you mean, no bond?" I asked.

"He'll have a secure custody hearing within five days and the judge will decide if he waits here until his trial or if he can be released to home. Given the serious nature of the crime, though, I imagine he'll be staying here."

"Five days!" I said. "I won't let him stay here a single night!" I grabbed Marcus's arm, knowing I was digging my nails into his flesh but unable to stop myself.

"Andy has special needs," Marcus said. "He won't do well in detention."

"Mrs. Lockwood here's explained about his special needs," the officer said.

"I didn't realize you expected him to actually *stay* here when I told you, though!" I said.

"What did you think the word 'detention' means, ma'am?" he asked.

"She didn't know it meant overnight," Marcus said with more calm than I felt. "He's never stayed away from home overnight."

"I'll recommend a hearing be scheduled as quick as possible," the officer said.

"Today," I said. "Please. It needs to be today."

"Ma'am, it's already three o'clock. This is not considered an emergency case. However, one thing you may not have thought of is that when this gets out, the community is going to be mighty angry. It may be best your boy remain here for his own safety, and the judge will take that into account."

"There's no way it would be best for him to stay here!"

"She's right," Marcus said to the officer. "Aim for tomorrow."

Andy returned to the room in a navy jumpsuit that was too big on him and blue flip-flops. The skin around his eyes was puffy and red, but he no longer looked terrified. More like defeated. I drew choppy breaths through my mouth, trying to keep from crying. That would only scare him more.

Marcus hugged him, and I wanted to pull him into my arms again, but knew I'd fall apart if I did. Andy didn't say a word. It wasn't like him to be so quiet and I worried about what the other officer might have said—or worse, *done*—to him.

"Andy," I managed to say, "please don't worry, sweetie. We're going to get this all straightened out."

"Y'all can sit down again," the intake officer said, although he remained standing himself. "I need to make a copy of the petition. We'll be sending it along to your attorney, ma'am."

We sat down on the hard wooden chairs as he left the room.

"The man said I have to stay here." Andy looked at Marcus.

"For a couple days," Marcus said. "It'll be all right. Your mom has an attorney...a lawyer. He'll come talk to you."

"His name's Mr. Shartell, Andy." My voice sounded remarkably calm given how hysterically I was screaming inside. "He's on *your side,* sweetie, so you don't have to be afraid to tell him the truth when he comes, all right?"

"I don't want to stay here." He hadn't heard a word I'd said. I was sure of it. I wondered if Marcus caught the tremor in his chin.

"I know," I said. "I know you don't. And we'll get you out as soon as we can." Over Andy's head, I mouthed the words to Marcus, *I can't leave him here!*

Marcus reached across the back of Andy's chair to squeeze my shoulder.

Andy looked at Marcus again. "I don't understand, Uncle Marcus," he said. "I didn't do anything wrong."

Marcus moved his hand from my shoulder to Andy's, a small smile of encouragement on his lips. "I know, son," he said.

I stared at Marcus. I'd never heard him call Andy "son" before. Never. That was the way I'd always wanted it. But now, I wanted to hear him say that word again and again and again.

Chapter Thirty-Seven

Marcus
1992

JAMIE DIDN'T LET ME SEE LAUREL TILL SHE'D BEEN IN REHAB three months. Not that I didn't try to visit her before that. Got turned away by the sentry at the front desk. "Only her husband and people he authorizes can visit her," I was told. Apparently, I wasn't one of those people. Jamie said I'd "enabled" her drinking. Give me a break. Laurel was no alcoholic and I didn't believe there was a damn thing wrong with her baby. Jamie and the hospital and Protective Services had made a fuss about nothing.

"You can see her," Jamie finally told me one afternoon at The Sea Tender. "She's strong enough now."

"She's got to be 'strong' to see me?" I was pissed.

"Yeah, exactly. She does."

"Go fuck yourself," I said.

Jamie closed his eyes the way he did when he was angry and trying to control it, like he was silently counting to ten. I hated when he did that. Hated his self-control.

"You know." He opened his eyes again. "I have a two-year-old daughter in the next room. Maybe she's napping, but maybe not, and I don't appreciate you using that language in her presence."

"You self-righteous—"

"Do you want to see her or not?" he interrupted me. "Because I can still tell them not to let you in."

"Yes, I want to see her!"

"Then shut up. And when you go there, go sober."

I hardly recognized her as she walked toward me in the rehab lobby. She filled out her jeans again—I hadn't realized how much weight she'd lost the past couple of years—and she wore a red V-neck sweater, a blast of color beneath her dark hair. She smiled at me as she came closer. I hugged her hard, not wanting to let go, because she'd see the tears in my eyes. I'd forgotten what the real Laurel looked like. Forgotten the smile. The light in her eyes.

I finally released her. "You look unbelievable," I said.

She knew it. Knew she gave off a glow. "It's good to see you, Marcus," she said. "Come on. Let's go to the lounge where we can talk." Taking my arm, she guided me through a maze of hallways until we reached a small room filled with armchairs. We were the only people there. We sat in a couple of chairs by the windows.

Kicking off her shoes, she lifted her feet onto the chair and hugged her knees.

"How are you?" she asked.

"I'm okay," I answered. "But I want to know about *you*. What's it been like to be locked up in here?"

She smiled again. A secret smile. It reminded me of Jamie when he talked about his "relationship with God," like it was something only he could understand and someone as low on the food chain as myself could never get it. I wasn't so crazy about the secret in her smile.

"It was bad at first," she said. "And I hated this place. But they've helped me so much."

"They convince you you had a drinking problem?" I asked.

That frickin' smile again. "I'm an alcoholic." She sounded like a parrot, repeating what she'd been told.

I leaned forward. "You drank little pink girly things."

"I had withdrawal symptoms getting off those little pink girly things," she said. "That's how bad it was. I'm an alcoholic, Marcus. And so are you."

I rapped the side of her head with my knuckles. "Hello? Is my favorite sister-in-law still in there?"

She rested her chin on her knees, her eyes pinning me to the back of my chair. "I hurt my baby," she said. "I was depressed after I had Maggie. That part I couldn't help, except that I should have taken antidepressants when my doctor told me to. I'm sorry I've been a crappy mother to her, but I have to forgive myself for that and move on. I won't be a crappy mother to my little boy when I get him back. My Andy."

I'd lost her. It wasn't like I wanted her to be a bad mother to her kids, but I still wanted her to be my friend. She'd been my *best* friend. More than that. The night in my guest room—a night I knew she regretted but I couldn't—would always be in my memory. That Laurel was gone now. I'd never get her back.

"What have they done to you?" I asked.

"What do you mean?"

"They've turned you into a Stepford wife or something."

"I'm sober, Marcus," she said. "And I'm happy and starting to feel good about myself again."

I looked out the window. Acres and acres of rolling pasture, bordered by dense forest. I supposed the setting would seem peaceful to most people, but I was suffocating, looking at it. I needed the ocean. Didn't she?

"When are you coming home?" I asked.

"I'm nowhere near ready to leave here," she said. "I feel safe here. Safe from alcohol." She pinned me again with her eyes. "Safe from you."

I wanted to say *Bullshit,* but stopped myself. Because I suddenly got it. I may have loved her. I may have been the closest thing she had to a friend for a couple of years. But I hadn't been good for her.

She pulled a picture from her shirt pocket and handed it to me. The baby. I'd seen him after he was born, hooked up to monitors in the intensive-care unit. He'd looked barely alive, his puny little chest struggling to rise and fall above ribs like bird bones. I hadn't been able to look at him for long. I felt sorry for her that this flimsy piece of paper was all she had of her baby.

"He was completely vulnerable," she said. "Completely dependent on me to take care of him." She pressed her fingers to her mouth as her eyes filled. "I don't care how hard this is, being here. I'd climb Mount Everest for him. I'll gladly give up alcohol to have him back. To be a true mother to him."

I stared at the baby, and something snapped inside me. I saw bruises where this tube or that entered his body. Saw veins under his skin. He was so defenseless. Fragile. Damaged. If they said it was alcohol that hurt him, then maybe it was. And I'd done my part to make his mother a drunk. For the second time in an hour, my eyes burned.

"Marcus," Laurel said. "Please get sober. If you don't, then I don't want you coming over to The Sea Tender once I'm home. Understand?"

"No," I said. "I don't understand."

"If you don't get sober, I'll have to avoid you." Her voice broke. What she was saying cost her something.

"You'd cut me out of your life? Out of Maggie and—" I lifted the picture in my hand "—this little guy's lives?"

She nodded. "Get sober, Marcus," she pleaded. "I love you, and you're a good man, deep inside. I know you are."

No, I wasn't. There'd been something off about me, right from the start. I always managed to push away the people I cared about. The people who cared about me.

I tried to give the picture back to her, but she cupped her hands around my hand, forcing my fingers to tighten around the photograph.

"Keep it," she said. "It's *yours*."

I stared at her, the moment so charged it stole my voice. *What's mine?* I wanted to ask. *The picture? Or the baby?*

But the moment passed. She looked away from me, quickly. So quickly, that she told me all I needed to know.

I drank half a bottle of whiskey that night, staring at the baby's picture. The booze didn't taste as good as it usually did. After a while, in a moment of monumental strength, I poured every damn ounce of alcohol I had in the house down the kitchen drain. I called AA's twenty-four-hour number. There was a meeting in Wilmington the next morning at seven.

I couldn't sleep that night, afraid I'd miss my alarm. I left the house at five-thirty and drove through a pink dawn to Wilmington. Found the church building where the meeting would be held. Forced myself to walk into the room and was bowled over to see Flip Cates inside the doorway. He was a rookie cop in Surf City, a year or two older than me, and he'd made that same hour drive I'd just made to get there. He gave me a surprised smile. An arm around my shoulders as he led me into the room.

"Glad to see you, Marcus," he said.

"This your first meeting, too?" I asked.

He laughed. "More like my hundred and first," he said, and I thought, *If he could do it, maybe I can, too.*

I hit meetings every night, piling the miles on my pickup. Flip got me a construction job with a boss who'd let me take off for a meeting on days when I knew I was sinking. I doubt I would have made it through without Flip, because eighty percent of me wasn't sold on sobriety. Eighty percent of me craved a beer. But that other twenty percent was stubborn as hell. It hung on to the image of a baby chained to tubes and wires. Of a woman who'd said the words "I love you" to me, even if she'd only said them as a sister-in-law to a brother-in-law. That part of me was stronger than I'd ever known.

I kept my sobriety to myself. I didn't want to hear Jamie say he was proud of me, when I'd wanted him to be proud of me all along. I didn't want to feel him watching me, waiting for me to screw up. And I didn't want to feel the burning guilt that seared me every time I remembered that I'd slept with my brother's wife.

I got jumpy as Laurel's release day neared. I wanted to see her, sure, but living near her again? A mistake—for both of us. I didn't want to be her brother-in-law. I wanted more than that. Not being able to have it, yet living next door to her, would be torture. The last thing I needed with only two months of sobriety under my belt was torture.

I had an AA buddy from Asheville. I decided to move there—

a good six-hour drive from Topsail—the week before Laurel came home. Jamie was shocked, but pleased.

"Good for you, Marcus!" he said. "It'll be good for you to really get out on your own. Maybe get yourself straight."

Fuck you, bro.

After Laurel's return, my mother wrote to tell me it was like having the "old Laurel" back. I remembered the old Laurel. Very cool woman. I was glad for her.

Several months later, Mama told me that one-year-old Andy had been returned to Jamie and Laurel. I wanted to visit. Wanted to see Laurel and the boy I was sure was my son. I didn't go. I stayed in Asheville, joining the fire department—first as a volunteer, later as paid staff—and making a life for myself four hundred miles from my family. I was never going back, because seeing Laurel again would be like taking a sip of booze: I would only want more.

Chapter Thirty-Eight

Andy

I HAD MY OWN ROOM LIKE AT HOME, BUT IT WAS A BAD ROOM. I didn't have any windows except in the big metal door, and the bathroom was right next to my bed. When I went to the bathroom, I worried someone would look in the window in the door. I got nervous when I had to go and by the end of the first day, my stomach hurt.

I was a lot littler than the other boys. Everybody wore dark blue jump things and flip-flops. The man who gave me mine said it was the littlest size they had. At dinner, it was like the cafeteria at school with long tables and everyone being there except there were no girls. I said hello and smiled at everyone. It was hard because I was scared. And nobody smiled back. I asked everybody, when can I go home? Some of the boys said maybe never.

I couldn't sleep good last night. I was scared someone would come in the metal door and hurt me. I watched the door all night. Maybe I slept a little though, because I had a dream I was fishing on the pier with Uncle Marcus.

A bad thing happened at breakfast this morning. I said hi to a boy and smiled at him. He started laughing and said to the other boys, "We got us a little pansy," and the boys laughed too and started saying things. One of them nearly pushed my tray off the table and said, "We don't allow no faggots at our table." I knew what that word meant

and I ran around the table and started punching him. Then they all
started punching *me*. I don't know all what happened then except I
ended up in the nurse's office. The nurse, who was a man but he said
he really honestly was a nurse, put burning stuff on my cuts. It hurt
and I was scared and wanted Mom. I said, when can I go home? The
nurse said a bunch of words I didn't understand about a "pearance." I
asked him to explain and he said, "You dumb as a bag o' hammers or
you jes' playin' like it?" I sat on my hands to keep from hitting him.
He said to me to "buck up." I didn't know what that meant except I
thought it was swearing.

They said I could have meals in my room then, and even though
my room wasn't nice, I was glad. That way, the boys wouldn't get
to see me cry.

Chapter Thirty-Nine

Laurel

I WAS WORRIED ABOUT DENNIS SHARTELL. I COULDN'T BELIEVE I'd had such confidence in him in the beginning. He thought Andy was guilty. He didn't say as much, but I could tell. Before the secure custody hearing, he told me he thought Andy would be safer if he stayed in detention until his trial because, as the intake officer had predicted, people were angry.

"Absolutely not!" I said. "Get him out of there."

He shrugged as if to say *It's your funeral.*

The judge, a very young-looking woman who reminded me of Sara, was compassionate, and I knew we'd lucked out in getting her. She seemed to take the innocent-until-proven-guilty statute to heart. In the end, she reluctantly allowed Andy to leave detention.

"Mrs. Lockwood," she said, "I would suggest Andrew not go to school during this period. If he were to stay in detention, we could guarantee his safety. In the community, we cannot."

I nodded, already thinking about tutors and home schooling and other ways he could keep up. It seemed unjust, but I had to face reality. Somehow, the accelerant had gotten on his clothes. I believed that now. Marcus had managed to talk me out of conspiracy theories and lab errors. But he and I were both in agreement that Andy lacked the capacity to plan and carry out arson. I was afraid, though, that Andy's attorney was not so sure.

"Andrew," the judge addressed him. "Will you and Mr. Shartell please stand."

Andy and Dennis got to their feet.

"Andrew, you're being charged with the burning of a church, three counts of first-degree murder, and forty-two counts of attempted murder. Do you understand these charges?"

Although I already knew the charges being brought against Andy, hearing them spoken from the mouth of the judge gave them an un-bearable credibility. I thought I might faint, and I was sitting down. I could only imagine what Andy was feeling.

Dennis whispered something to him.

"Yes, ma'am," Andy said, though I wondered if he knew what he was agreeing to.

"Your probable cause hearing will be scheduled within fifteen days," she said. "At that time, it will be decided if you'll be bound over to the superior court for trial."

"Bound over?" I whispered to Marcus.

He didn't look at me. He stared straight ahead but licked his dry lips, and a muscle twitched in his jaw.

"Adult court," he whispered. "They'll decide if they should try him as an adult."

Then, for the first time in my life, I actually did faint.

I had a long talk with Dennis on the phone later that afternoon. He explained that, "given the serious nature of the charges," a phrase I was quickly coming to hate, it was likely Andy *would* be bound over to the adult system at the probable cause hearing. He might—or might not—have a bond. I told Dennis if he did have one, I would pay it; I didn't care how much it was.

"*If* he has one, it could be in the millions," Dennis said. "But you need to prepare yourself, Laurel. Given the serious nature of the crime, they may see him as a danger to others and not let him post bail." He blathered on. "Murder committed in the perpetration of arson is considered murder in the first degree. If he's charged as an adult, he can enter a plea of guilty to the burning and maybe get the murder charges dropped."

"But what if he's *not* guilty of the burning?" I asked.

Dennis hesitated so long I wondered if we'd lost our connection. "We'll have time to talk about all that."

"Did you hear what I said, though, Dennis? I want you to *fight* this! You need to fight him being bound over." If they tried him as an adult and found him guilty, he was doomed. "What's the chance he can stay in the juvenile system?"

"I'd say there's still a small chance of that," he said. "They don't like to bind over juveniles. If no more evidence is found and no more witnesses come forward with incriminating testimony, we've got a shot at it."

Maggie, Marcus and I did our best to celebrate getting him home that evening. We ignored the camera crews outside the house, and I turned the ringers off on all the phones except my cell. We had a pizza delivered and Marcus picked up an ice-cream cake. We ate in the family room—although only Andy seemed to have an appetite. I'd felt dizzy ever since my fainting episode, and Maggie'd gone absolutely white when I explained to her about the upcoming probable cause hearing.

"They could try him in *adult court?*" she asked, wide-eyed. We were in my bedroom and she waved her arms around in outrage. "He's only fifteen!" she shouted. "This whole thing has ballooned into something insane! Is his lawyer totally brain dead? I don't know how gasoline got on Andy's pants, but he *could not have done it!*"

"It won't happen," I said quickly, taken aback by her outburst. "I'm sure his lawyer can make a good case to keep him in the juvenile system, so please don't worry about it."

I regretted giving her so much information. Maggie was suddenly more fragile than I'd ever guessed she could be. I'd caught her crying a couple of times the last few days. When I'd ask her what was wrong, I'd get the usual "nothing" in reply, but I knew she was frantic about Andy, as we all were. I decided right then to keep the gory details between myself and Marcus. She didn't need to know.

Sitting in the family room, nibbling on the edges of our pizza slices, we talked about everything other than Andy's experiences in detention or what had happened in court that morning or what lay ahead of us. For the moment, I felt safe.

Marcus's cell phone rang as I started cutting the cake I knew only one of us would be able to eat. He walked outside to answer it.

"This is like my birthday," Andy said as I handed him the first slice.

"Right, Panda." Maggie's eyes were red again, and I wondered when she'd found a private moment to cry. She was trying so hard to be upbeat for her brother, and it touched me. "So now we don't have to celebrate on your real birthday," she teased him.

"Yes, you still do," Andy said.

Marcus appeared in the doorway and motioned me to join him in the kitchen. I handed the cake knife to Maggie.

"What is it?" I asked once we were out of earshot of the kids.

"They found a couple of plastic gasoline containers in the land-fill this morning," he said. "Might be the ones used to lay the fire, because they each contain a bit of a gasoline and diesel mixture."

I drew in a breath. "Are there fingerprints on them?" I hoped the real arsonist had been sloppy enough to leave his prints behind.

"They've sent them for testing." He nearly smiled. "Pretty mi-raculous they found them. If there are some good prints on them, Andy could be out of the woods."

Chapter Forty

JAMIE HUNG UP THE PHONE, HIS SMILE BORDERING ON INCREDulous. "He's coming," he said with relief. "He's driving down tomorrow."

I put my arms around him. "Good," I said, as though my feelings about Marcus's arrival weren't mixed. Miss Emma had died the day before after a long battle with cancer, and it was right that he come, yet I hadn't seen him or even spoken to him in the four years since he moved to Asheville. We knew little about his life there except that he had become a firefighter and was supposedly sober. He emailed Jamie occasionally and sent birthday cards and Christmas gifts to the kids, but other than that, he'd cut himself off from his family and I'd been frankly glad of it. Jamie'd been afraid Marcus wouldn't come for the service. He thought his brother had stayed away all these years because of his animosity toward his mother and possibly toward Jamie himself. He never guessed it could have anything to do with me.

Marcus arrived at The Sea Tender the next afternoon. The last four years had put muscle on his slender frame, chiseled his face with maturity and brightened the blue of his eyes. I knew instantly that the change in him was more than superficial. It was a confident man who drew Jamie into an embrace. The brothers held on to each other for a full minute before letting go, eyes glistening.

"I've missed you, bro," Marcus said. Then his gaze fell on me. Smiling, he reached for me and I hugged him, both of us pulling away after only a few seconds. How different he smelled! Shampoo and soap. Not a trace of booze or tobacco. "I've missed y'all," he said.

"We've missed you, too," I said with stiff formality. I couldn't look him squarely in the eyes without feeling a tug I hadn't expected— and certainly hadn't wanted—to feel.

Marcus leaned over until he was eye to eye with seven-year-old Maggie. "Do you remember me, Mags?" he asked.

"Uh-uh." She shook her head.

Marcus laughed. "That's good." He straightened again. "I wasn't the best uncle when you were little. And where's Andy?" He looked at me. "I've never even *met* him."

I was afraid to have Marcus meet Andy. To me, the resemblance was as strong as a positive DNA test.

"He's napping," I said, wrapping my arm around Jamie's waist to ground myself in him. In our marriage. I'd fought hard for the peace of the past four years. I didn't want it disrupted now.

My six months in rehab had profoundly changed me. I'd cried my lifetime allotment of tears during those months, tears of guilt and remorse, along with fierce tears of determination. When I got home, I embarked on the adventure of getting to know my three-year-old daughter, the child I'd been so unable to mother. Maggie clung to her daddy at first, cutting her eyes shyly at me. I was a stranger to her. I looked different and I'm sure I smelled different from the woman she'd known as Mommy. I imagined she connected the scent of alcohol to me the way some children connected their mothers with the scent of perfume.

The first night I was home, Jamie and I'd sat with her between us on her bed as we read to her. She leaned against Jamie, and I found my voice breaking when it was my turn to read. I felt her curious gaze on me instead of on the pictures in the book. Jamie rested his chin on the top of her head as I read. Sometimes love is nearly palpable, and the love between my husband and my daughter was like that—a presence I could feel in the room. I was not a part of it, and although my relationship with Maggie grew over the years, I knew I would never have the closeness to her that Jamie had earned.

Although I adored my little girl, my love for her so new and rich, I was preparing for the return of my son. I learned all I could about children with fetal alcohol syndrome. There was precious little information available, but I searched it out. I became an evangelist for healthy, alcohol-free pregnancies the way reformed smokers became intolerant of cigarette smoke.

Sara coached me in what to expect from a year-old boy. She and Steve had recently divorced and she was raising Keith alone. I felt sorry that she was losing her husband just as I was getting mine back. We drew her into our fold, and I delighted in discovering that I had enough energy and love inside me to extend to her and Keith as well as to my own family.

Now that Marcus was back for Miss Emma's funeral, I couldn't deny that I was attracted to him. But although that attraction made me feel awkward around him, I wasn't afraid of my feelings. I'd grown up. In my four years of sobriety, I'd learned how strong I could be. I had a husband spun from pure gold—how many men would stick by the sick, self-destructive, cold woman I'd been in the years after Maggie's birth? I had two amazing children I was devoted to. And every time I saw Sara, now living in one of the many old mobile homes in Surf City, I was reminded of how precious my marriage was and how far I would go to hold it together.

Jamie couldn't stop smiling in those first few days after Marcus's arrival. He lit up around his brother, and the kinship between the two of them was fun to watch. Certainly he was sad over his mother's death, but his joy in rediscovering his now sober, respectful and thriving brother tempered his sorrow over the loss of Miss Emma.

Both children fell in love with Marcus. He played with them on the beach, tossing a beach ball, letting them bury him up to his chin in sand, roughhousing with Andy in a way that made me nervous but that put a smile on Jamie's face. Jamie wasn't the roughhousing sort, but I could see that he admired his brother's playful rapport with the children.

"He needs to have some kids," Jamie said to me one night in bed. "He's great with them."

"He needs a wife first," I said.

"Yeah," Jamie said. "Sounds like he hasn't had much luck in that department. He told me he's had a few relationships, but nothing serious."

"He's only twenty-eight," I said. "He's got plenty of time."

Jamie sighed. "I only wish Mom had gotten to see him this way."

"I know." I thought of Miss Emma, how her love for her sons had hinged on their achievements, with Marcus never able to measure up to Jamie in her eyes. I kept the thought to myself; it wasn't the time to criticize Miss Emma.

"I'm going to try to persuade him to move back here," Jamie said.

I stiffened at the thought of watching Andy grow into Marcus's image right before our eyes. I wasn't one hundred percent certain that Marcus knew Andy was his, but how could he not? How could anyone look at the two of them and doubt their relationship?

"Do you think he would?" I asked. "Would it be okay for him? I mean, this is where he got so screwed up drinking."

"I don't know. Topsail might make him remember some bad times, but it's obvious how much he's changed. I can hardly remember what he used to be like. It won't hurt to ask him, anyway. Wouldn't it be great for the kids to have an uncle here?"

"Yes," I said. It would be. And it would be great for Jamie to have his brother back.

Jamie talked to Marcus the next night over dinner. We were on the deck eating grilled catfish, macaroni salad and hush puppies, and the sun was beginning to set on the other side of The Sea Tender. In a couple of weeks, the mosquitoes would make it impossible to eat outside, but that night was one of those magical June evenings. It was warm but not hot, and the sea was calm—a pale opaque blue— swaying like gelatin. I thought, how can he possibly resist?

Marcus took a long swallow of iced tea, as if mulling over the question. "I don't know," he said, setting the glass down on the picnic table. "I do miss it. Being back here...it's part of me, you know?" He looked at his brother. "I love the mountains, but it's not the same as living on the water, and it'd be great to see y'all all the time." He smiled at Maggie and Andy, who was pulling apart catfish with his fingers. "It's very tempting."

"So what's holding you back?" Jamie asked. "There's an opening coming up at the Hampstead fire station."

"Move here! Move here!" Maggie jumped up and down on the bench and I put a hand on her shoulder.

"You're rockin' the boat, sweetie." I smiled at her enthusiasm.

"I'll think about it, Mags," Marcus promised.

Jamie got the kids ready for bed later that evening, while I cleaned the kitchen. Marcus came in and began to wipe the counters with a sponge. He'd been with us five days, but this was the first time I'd been alone with him.

"How would you feel about me moving back here?" he asked quietly as he wiped the breakfast bar.

I kept my eyes on the soapsuds in the sink. "Jamie really wants you here," I said. "And the kids are crazy about you."

"But how do *you* feel, Laurel? Would you be okay with it?" He lowered his voice. "Comfortable with it?"

"I'd like you to be part of the family again," I said as though I'd never felt anything other than friendship for him.

"It's important to me you're all right with it," he said.

I didn't want him to say another word. I was afraid he'd say something about Andy. I looked at him then as though I had no idea why he was so concerned. As though I didn't share those concerns. "It will be fine," I said.

"I'm not proud of—"

I put my fingers to his lips, then dropped my hand as quickly as I'd raised it. "Let the past stay in the past," I whispered. "Please, Marcus."

He stared at me a moment, long enough for me to turn away.

"Okay," he said. "You don't need to worry."

Marcus became a fixture in our lives and on the island. He moved into the most unlikely of the properties he and Jamie had inherited from their father: one of the Operation Bumblebee towers. He added on to the three-story tower, remodeling it with amazing speed, painting the exterior a sea-foam green with white trim.

He was respected at the fire department, and he and Jamie loved working shoulder to shoulder. I respected him as well. I knew how difficult it had been for me to get sober in a structured rehab environment. The fact that he'd gotten straight with only the help of AA earned my admiration.

As for me, I felt as though I had my cake and was eating it, too. I loved my husband, but I also loved being around Marcus once it was clear he'd keep his promise not to bring up the past. I loved his spirit and sense of fun, and any attraction I felt for him I filed neatly under *i* for *in-law*.

With Andy in preschool, I took a part-time job in a dermatologist's office. The rest of my energy went into fetal alcohol projects—developing a website, writing a newsletter and speaking occasionally at a medical or education conference. Maggie and Andy loved it when I went out of town on a speaking engagement because Marcus would stay at the house, and he and Jamie would take them to the movies and play games with them and feed them pizza and other junk food that was forbidden when I was around.

About a year after Marcus moved back to Topsail Island, he picked me up at the Wilmington airport when I returned from an out-of-town conference.

"Where's Jamie?" I asked, surprised to see him waiting for me in the terminal.

"He and the kids wanted to sleep in, so I volunteered to come get you." He took my rolling carry-on and pulled it behind him as we walked toward the exit.

"Did y'all have a good weekend?" I asked.

"Great." We were walking across the parking lot toward his pickup. "Only I deserted everybody yesterday to buy a new boat."

"A new boat?" I laughed as I got into the passenger seat. I rolled down the window to let in some of the sticky June air. I'd flown in from New York. It had to be fifteen degrees hotter in Wilmington. "What was wrong with your old one?"

"It was old, that's what."

We pulled out of the parking lot, and he told me about the movie they'd watched the night before and how many times they let Andy win at CandyLand.

"Maggie's such a little honey-bunch," he said, looking over his shoulder to change lanes. "She'd let Andy win every time if she could."

"I know," I said. "I worry about her that way."

"Well, I don't think you have to *worry* about her."

"I think she has Jamie's…you know…his *empathy* thing."

"Oh." He understood. "I hope not."

I was thinking about his statement—that he hoped Maggie didn't have Jamie's overdeveloped capacity for empathy—when I realized he'd fallen silent.

"Thinking about your boat?" I asked him. "Have you named her yet?"

He licked his lips, flexing his hands on the steering wheel. "I have to ask you something," he said as if he hadn't heard my question.

Oh, no. Was this why he'd wanted to pick me up at the airport? I'd finally relaxed about the subject of Andy's parentage; Marcus never seemed to concern himself with it. Finally, though, the question was coming, and I braced myself.

I watched his Adam's apple bob in his tanned throat. "I thought it would be okay when I moved here," he said.

"Thought what would be okay?" I asked cautiously.

"I thought I had my feelings for you under control."

That was not what I'd expected. "What are you talking—"

"Stop." He glanced at me. "Don't say anything. Just let me talk for a minute, okay?"

"No," I said. "I—"

"Every time I see you, my feelings get stronger," he said. "It doesn't have anything to do with the past, all right? It has to do with the here and now. Not with the people we used to be. We were both sick then. Now we're healthy and...I admire you, Laurel. The way you deal with Andy. The way you've taken on the whole FASD cause, and—"

"Marcus, please don't," I said. "I mean, thank you. For the compliment. I admire you, too. We both turned our lives around. Let's not do anything that could screw that up again."

"I'm in love with you."

"Please don't say that." I looked out the side window, not wanting to see whatever had been laid bare in his face.

"I've been fighting it all year," he said, "and I'm tired of fighting it. I need to know if there's a chance. That's all I'm asking. You tell me there isn't and I'll shut up and never mention it again. But I need to know if you'd ever consider—" He shook his head. "I'm not talking about an affair. I wouldn't do that again. I'm talking about you and me, out in the open. With you divorced from Jamie." Although my gaze was riveted to the side of the road, I felt him looking at me. "I love my brother," he said, "and I hate the thought of hurting him, but I don't know how to keep my feelings for you hidden any longer. Every woman I go out with...I keep wishing she was you."

"Marcus, please stop!" I said, turning to face him. "I won't ever divorce Jamie. He stood by me through so much. He——"

"Are you saying you have feelings for me?" he interrupted. "That if it weren't for Jamie, you'd——"

"I love you like a brother-in-law," I said.

"I don't think I believe you."

"Why not?"

"I catch the way you look at me sometimes."

Had I been that transparent?

"I love Jamie, Marcus," I said evenly. "He and I have a family together. Please support that. Don't..." I let out my breath in frustration. "This year's been so much fun with you here. Please don't mess it up."

He was quiet for a moment. "You're right," he said then. "Absolutely right. I'm sorry, Laurel. I had to ask."

"Now you know."

"Now I know."

An awkward silence fell between us. Finally I spoke.

"You need to find yourself a woman who's free and who'll love the dickens out of you," I said, wondering how it would feel to see him touching, loving another woman.

"You're right," he said grimly. "I'll do that."

The next day was Monday and both Marcus and Jamie had time off from work. The sun had just broken over the horizon, sending a pink glow into our bedroom, when the phone rang. Jamie answered it from his side of the bed. I listened to his groggy end of the conversation.

"Yeah," he said after a few minutes. "I'd like that." He set the phone back on the night table.

"Was that the fire station?" I asked. No one else would call that early.

"No. It was Marcus." He sat up and swung his legs over the side of the bed. "I'm gonna meet him at the pier and check out his new boat."

"Now?" I asked. "It's your only day to sleep in."

"Yeah, but look outside." He motioned toward the sunrise and I could understand his desire to be on the water. He leaned over to kiss me. "You go back to sleep. I won't wake the kids."

A few hours later, Marcus called me from the police station in Surf City. He was sobbing, and I could barely understand him. There'd been an accident on the boat, he said. A whale had lifted it into the air, tossing him and Jamie out. Marcus had searched the water, trying to find his brother, but had to finally give up.

I hung up the phone, trembling and nauseated. The kids were right there, and I did my best not to show the terror I felt. I called Sara to come stay with them, although she was nearly as upset as I was. She blew into the house with six-year-old Keith and hugged me, crying, while the three children anxiously tried to figure out what was wrong.

I sped to the police station and when I looked into Marcus's eyes, the eyes of the man who only the day before had asked me if I'd leave my husband for him, I realized exactly how well I knew him—well enough to know that the story he was telling was a lie.

Chapter Forty-One

Laurel

THE PROBABLE CAUSE HEARING WAS SCHEDULED FOR WEDNES-day, two short days away and too soon for my comfort. I knew that the hearing could literally mean the end of Andy's freedom forever, "given the seriousness of the charges." Dennis sounded more and more certain that Andy would be bound over to adult court, and less and less certain that he would get any sort of reasonable bail. That meant he would stay in prison until his trial, which could be months, if not years, away. His sentence could be life without parole.

"He can't get the death penalty, though," Dennis said, "so don't worry about that."

What an asshole! I only needed to worry about my FASD son getting life in prison. I should have gotten a new lawyer when I first started having doubts about Dennis.

I thought he should make a case at the probable cause hearing that Andy shouldn't be bound over to the adult system because of his FASD, and I tried again to educate the lawyer about the disorder, but it was like trying to educate Andy himself. It was as though Dennis's brain shut down when I talked about it now.

"It's a very weak argument," he said. "It used to hold water as a defense, but now every Tom, Dick and Harry claims their mothers drank before they were born. Andy's IQ is in the normal range, he's not insane, and he knows right from wrong, and that's what the judge will be looking at."

"Whose side are you *on?*" I was losing it with this man. Every time I spoke with him, I felt panic bubble up in my chest. "You're not hearing me! First of all, I'm not talking about his *defense*. I'm talking about why he shouldn't be tried as an adult. He may be a teenager and he may have an IQ in the normal range—the *low* normal range—but he *thinks* like a child. I'm an expert in FASD. I speak to groups about—"

"You're his mother," Dennis interrupted me. "Your expertise doesn't count."

One night a few years earlier, I woke up and saw Jamie sitting on the edge of my bed. I was probably dreaming—it had happened a few times before—but it felt so real. He sat there in jeans and a blue T-shirt, his empathy tattoo as big as life. I wasn't afraid. I was happy to see him. He spoke to me, although his lips didn't move. He said, *You're a fighter, Laurie. You're the champ.*

I had thought about that dream—or whatever it was—often since that night. Every time I faced a challenge, I thought of his words. Words he'd never said to me when he was alive, but that I could imagine him saying. I'd had more than my share of challenges, that was for sure. Now, though, I was facing the biggest challenge of my life, and I was going to fight with all my power to keep Andy out of jail.

So if *my* expertise didn't count, I would find someone whose expertise did. I was fired up. I'd find someone with experience testifying in court cases for people with FASD. I went online and, through my network of FASD parents around the country, found the name of a neurologist in Raleigh. I called his office and set up an appointment to meet with him the next day. He suggested that at this point,

I come alone but bring Andy's medical and psychological records with me. If the case actually went to trial, then he would do a thorough evaluation of Andy. For now, he would give me ammunition to share with Dennis that might prevent Andy from being bound over to the adult system. I cried with relief when I got off the phone. He was optimistic, and his optimism gave me hope.

I made arrangements for Andy to spend the next day with the mother of one of his swim team members. Ben had convinced me that Andy should stay on the team, and I appreciated his willingness to deal with whatever repercussions arose from that decision. Andy didn't understand why he wasn't going to school; taking him away from the swim team he loved would leave him more confused than he already was.

I tucked him into bed that night and told him about the plans for the next day.

"I have to go out of town tomorrow," I said, "so you'll—"

"To make a fetal alcohol speech?"

"No." I smiled. "Not this time. I'm just going to Raleigh for the day. So you'll stay at Tyler's house with his mom, and—"

"Will Tyler be there?"

"He'll be at school, so you'll take your books with you and—"

"Can I take my iPod?"

"Yes, but I want you to do some reading and that math we talked about, okay? I marked it in your book. And I'll tell Tyler's mother so she'll be watching to be sure you do it."

"Can I have lunch?"

"Tyler's mom will make you lunch. Then after school, she'll take you and Tyler to swim team practice and Maggie will pick you up afterward."

"Tyler's not a good swimmer."

"No?"

"Even though Ben explains things good."

"Well," I said. "Ben explains things well."

"Ben said if I work hard, I can be a top swimmer."

"I think you already *are* a top swimmer."

"No, Mom. Not just a top Pirate swimmer. A top swimmer of all time. A champion."

I ran my hand over his curly hair. "What a wonderful aspiration," I said.

Andy yawned. "What's a 'aspration'?" He rubbed the back of his hand over his eyes. My sleepy boy.

"A goal. You know, how we have your goal chart?"

"Uh-huh." He shut his eyes.

"I love you," I said.

"Mmm." He was already breathing steadily, a tiny smile on his lips.

I watched him for a few minutes, biting back tears. Then I leaned over, whispered in his ear, "You're a fighter, sweetie," I said. "You're already a champ."

Chapter Forty-Two

Marcus

The boat is too small for such a rough day on the ocean. I realize that as soon as we pass through the inlet into open water. A monster yellow boat the size and shape of a school bus passes us. We rise high on its wake, then plunge down in the gully, water pouring over us. For a moment, I'm afraid, but when Jamie starts to laugh, peeling his wet T-shirt over his head, I relax and laugh with him. I open the throttle, and the nose of my boat rises as we speed across the water.

"Look!" Jamie's eyes are wide and he's pointing to the east. I turn my head to see a pod of jet-black whales, all in a row, all spouting at the same time. Like a drawing in a children's book.

"God's swimming with us!" Jamie says.

I WOKE UP FROM THE DREAM GASPING FOR BREATH, LIKE I always did, even though I'd managed to wake up before the bad part. My heart hammered in my chest. For nearly ten years, that dream had dogged me. I got out of bed to shake it off. Was I going to have that damn dream for the rest of my life? I doubted my heart could take it.

In the bathroom, I splashed water on my face. If I went right back to bed, the dream would turn into the nightmare. No way I was letting that happen.

I got on the computer and started playing Freecell, but my mind was muddy. I stared at the cards until they blended together. Closed my eyes.

I could have changed the outcome that day. I could have suggested we take the boat into the sound instead of the ocean. Go in the afternoon instead of the morning. I could have bought the boat the week before or the week after. It wasn't the first time I'd made myself crazy thinking about the what-ifs.

The day before the accident, I'd picked up Laurel at the airport and asked her the question that had been in my mind for months: was there a chance for us? She'd given me her answer and I was determined to live with it. I had to. I dropped her off at The Sea Tender, but Jamie came out before I pulled away.

"Hey." He got in on the passenger side. His hair was wet from a shower or a swim. "Do you have time to hang out later today?" he asked. "Just with me, I mean."

Weird request, but that didn't register. All I could think about was that I didn't want to spend time with him right then. Not after the conversation I'd just had with Laurel.

"How about tomorrow?" I asked. "You have the day off, right?"

"Okay," he said. "I'll call you in the morning."

"You can help me christen the new boat," I suggested.

"Whatever." He looked toward The Sea Tender, then got out of the pickup.

When I called at sunrise the next day, I expected him to balk at the early hour. He liked sleeping in on his days off. But he sounded like he couldn't wait to go out on the new boat. That should have tipped me off right there.

We met at the boat docks and I could tell something was up.

Forced smile. Kept his hands in his shorts pockets as he admired the boat. He asked me questions about her, but I knew he wasn't listening to my answers. Just the early hour, I told myself. He wasn't awake yet.

I jumped into the boat with a thermos of coffee and a couple of foam cups, and he followed. "I wanted something small enough to maneuver well, but large enough to fit all of us," I said. In my imagination, I'd pictured Laurel and the kids with me in the boat while Jamie worked. I was one hell of a brother.

I sank into the cushy seat at the helm. "Coffee?" I held the thermos out to him as he sat down in the front passenger seat. He shook his head, still smiling that not-quite-real smile.

"You okay?" I asked him.

He shrugged. "A little preoccupied," he admitted. "So!" He motioned to the boat. "Show me what she's got."

"You game for the ocean?" I asked as we pulled away from the pier. I'd already cruised the sound and the Intracoastal Waterway. I wanted to see how she handled in the open water.

"Sure." He adjusted his sunglasses. "Got a name for her yet?"

I'd thought about naming her *Laurel*. Seriously. I was such a fool.

"Maybe *Maggie*," I said.

"Cool," said Jamie. "She'd love having a boat named after her."

In a few minutes, we were cruising through the inlet. I felt a thrill, as I always did, when I saw the open sea in front of us. So wide, I swore I could see the curvature of the earth. How I'd survived four years in the mountains, I didn't know.

As we sailed into the ocean from the inlet, a massive ship appeared out of nowhere. Materialized from thin air. Steamed past us with a killer blast from its horn. I tightened my hands on the wheel as we headed straight into its wake.

"Holy shit!" I said, as we climbed the first swell.

"Hang on!" Jamie shouted. Like he needed to tell me.

We crested the wave, dropping like a stone on the other side of it, and the next wave was on us before we recovered. It tore off my sunglasses, blinding me with a wall of water and nearly swamping the boat. I hung on to the wheel. Jamie let out a *whoop* like he was riding a bucking bull.

Two more waves, and then finally, the worst was over. I turned to see Jamie laugh as he peeled off his sopping wet T-shirt. He took off his sunglasses, looking around, I guessed, for something to dry them with. "I couldn't see a damn thing," he said.

"No shit," I said, able to laugh now myself. "And I lost my frickin' sunglasses."

He propped his own sunglasses on top of his head. Wrung his T-shirt out over the side of the boat. "Well, your boat handled well," he said.

"Thought I might lose her there for a minute."

We sailed into the sea, and I opened the throttle wide. After a while, Jamie cleaned his sunglasses with his damp T-shirt. Slipped them back on his face. Then he pointed south.

"Is that a *whale?*" He had to shout for me to hear him over the roar of the engine.

"Where?" The surface of the water was calm.

"He's gone under."

"Can't be a whale!" I shouted. "Not the season."

"You're right," he said. "Sure looked like one, though."

We soared across the water. "Is this baby smooth or what?" I shouted.

"She's great!"

She was *dynamite*. We were flying.

"There he is again!" Jamie pointed. "We're practically on top of him."

I saw him this time. Couldn't miss him. He breached just south of us, a thirty- or forty-thousand-ton mountain shooting straight up from the sea, then slipping back into the water.

"Holy…" I slowed the boat, and we scanned the water to find him again. "I don't believe it. It's *June!*" You'd see humpbacks in December or January as they headed south, and in the spring as they returned north. But late June?

I heard the *pop* of the whale's blow spout and turned to see a fountain of water spray into the air not twenty yards away. Then the massive tail rose in the air like a great bird, wings spread above the water. The tail thwacked the surface as he dove under again. I throttled back the engine until we were simply drifting.

"Is he alone, do you think?" Jamie nearly whispered.

"I have no idea," I said. "Should've brought my camera. No one's going to believe this."

The whale suddenly breached a second time, rocketing toward the sky in front of us.

"Is that the same one?" Jamie asked.

"I don't know, but damn! That's one big Mama Jama!" And too damn close for comfort. I'd seen whales up close before. Close enough to scratch their backs with a net from a fishing charter. This was different. This guy dwarfed us. Dwarfed my boat. I could imagine Jonah setting up house in his belly.

"How can anyone see this and not feel God's presence?" Jamie asked.

I didn't answer. I'd found my own higher power through AA, but Jamie's God and mine were not the same.

The whale slipped underwater again. We waited a few more minutes, swiveling our heads left and right for the next sign of him. He was gone.

I reached for the throttle.

"Wait," Jamie said. "Let's sit here a while longer."

"I think he's gone."

"Yeah, I know," he said. "I want to talk to you, though."

I let go of the throttle. Shit. Had Laurel told him about our conversation?

"I'll take some of that coffee now," he said.

I handed him the thermos and a cup. Watched him pour. His hand had a tremor, but so did mine after our close encounter with Moby Dick.

He took a sip of the coffee, then blew out his breath. "Damn, bro," he said, "this is hard to say."

I wiped my sweaty palms on my shorts. "What's going on?"

"I've made a hard decision." His sunglasses masked his eyes, but I knew he was looking right at me. "It's selfish. Really selfish. And I'm gonna need your help, bro."

I relaxed. No way this was about Laurel and me. "Anything, Jamie," I said.

He looked toward where we'd last seen the whale. "I'm going to ask Laurel for a divorce," he said.

The muscles around my heart squeezed so tight that I rubbed my hand across my chest. "What are you talking about?"

"I know it's a shocker," Jamie said. "You probably think I'm crazy. Like I have the best marriage going and why would I screw it up?"

"Exactly," I said. "You're...I don't know anyone more into his family than you."

He reached beneath his sunglasses with his thumb and forefinger. Maybe rubbing tears away. I couldn't tell. "I love her, but it's like loving a friend," he said. "It's been that way for a long time. When she was in rehab, I started feeling different about her. It's not fair, I know. What happened wasn't her fault, and I kept hoping the old feelings would come back, but—" He shook his head.

"How can you not love her?" He was crazy. How could he want to leave her? And wasn't that what I'd wanted only twenty-four hours ago? No. It wasn't. I'd wanted Laurel to ask *him* for a divorce. I wanted *her* to be the one calling the shots. Not the one getting hurt.

"I'm not sure how to tell her," Jamie said. "I don't want to hurt her more than I have to."

"Is that a question?" I asked. "Because if it is, the answer is, there's no way you won't be killing her." I wanted to tell him how she'd turned me down out of her devotion to him. I wanted to rub his face in it.

"I know," Jamie said. "And I'm sorry to lay this on you. I wanted you to hear it from me first, though, because they're going to need you. You care so much about her and the kids. They'll need to lean on you for a while."

A couple of gulls flew overhead. I watched one of them dart to the surface of the water, then glide into the air again with a small fish in its mouth like it took no effort at all.

"This is unbelievable," I said. "I mean, so you tell her and then what? You move away? Go to California to start a new life or what?"

"You're pissed," he said.

"Just...I don't get it."

"Yeah, I don't blame you." He blew out his breath again. His jugular pounded beneath the damp skin of his throat. "Look," he said, "here's the truth, all right? I'm in love with someone else."

I wished I could see his eyes behind the dark lenses. "You've been cheating on Laurel?"

"That's an ugly word."

I laughed. "You got a better one?"

"It's not like that."

"Well, why don't you tell me what it's like then." I folded my arms across my chest, suddenly the nobler of the two sons of bitches in my boat.

"I shouldn't have told you."

I didn't want him to stop talking. I needed to know everything. "You can't blame me for being pissed," I said. "You're not Jamie anymore. You're somebody else."

"It's Sara," he said.

His words hung in the air for a few seconds before they sank in. "Oh, nice," I said. "You pick your wife's best friend."

"It wasn't...that isn't how it happened." He lifted his damp T-shirt from the bottom of the boat and wiped his forehead with it. "I lived with Sara and Steve back when Maggie was little, remember? I fell for her then. We clicked. Laurel was such a mess and Sara was... Her marriage wasn't so great and Steve was gone a lot. We needed each other."

"That was a long time ago," I said. "This has been going on all these years?"

"No. At least not physically. Once Laurel got pregnant with Andy and I moved back into The Sea Tender, it was over with Sara as far as I was concerned. But it's one thing to say something's over and another to feel it." He rubbed his chin. "Sara's been great." A smile curled his lips. I wanted to smack it off his face. "She always told me it's up to me what happens. During the last few months, I realized I've been living a lie, pretending I love Laurel, telling her I love her when I don't. Living a lie isn't fair to anyone."

"You son of a bitch. You're just going to walk out on your kids?"

"I'd never do that," Jamie said quickly. "That's why we'll stay here. Either on the island or maybe inland. We're thinking of Hampstead. That way I can still be a part of Andy and Maggie's lives but Laurel won't be tripping over me at the grocery store. I'll always provide for them," he added. "For Laurel, too."

I really wanted to hit him. When we were kids, I'd try to beat him up and he always won. He had the brawn and the years on me. Now, though, I had the anger. I could take him down if I tried.

"Marcus." He spoke in the quiet, calm voice that echoed in his chapel on Sunday mornings. "Look at me."

I did, my lips pressed together so tightly they hurt.

"I have another child to provide for," he said. "To be there for."

"What are you talk…" I pictured Keith. Six years old now. Handsome kid. Big brown eyes. Dark wavy hair. Slowly, I shook my head.

"Keith," Jamie said, as if I hadn't figured it out. "I've been giving Sara money for him since he was born. She deserves more from me than just a few hundred bucks every month."

"I feel like I don't know you," I said, staring at the stranger in my boat. "You encouraged Sara to help Laurel. You practically forced them to be friends. Your wife and your…mistress. How many times have you had your wife and your mistress in your house at the same time?"

"Shut up, Marcus."

He was getting angry with me and I was loving it. *Damn.* I hated his self-control. His calmness.

"And your bastard kid," I said. "Do you expect him and Maggie and Andy to be playmates? All one big happy family, except without Laurel?"

"Look in the fucking mirror, Marcus." Jamie crushed the empty cup in his hand and tossed it over the side of the boat. "You screwed my wife."

I must have shaken my head, because he leaned toward me.

"Don't try to deny it! You think I was born yesterday? You screwed her and you got her pregnant and hooked on booze. Andy is the way he is because of you."

I dove for him. Punched him hard on the side of his jaw. His head whipped to one side, but he recovered quickly, grabbing my arm and wrestling me to the bottom of the boat. I fought him with strength I didn't know I had. I bent my legs, put my bare feet on his chest, and sent him flying across the boat. He grunted as he crashed into the back of one of the seats.

I was dizzy in the bottom of the boat. The sky twirled above me. Scrambling to my knees, I felt like I was rising into the air. Jamie started toward me, but then he felt it, too. The shifting of the boat.

"What the—" He tried to steady himself, his legs wide apart, arms out at his sides.

I looked around for a boat that might have created a freak wave. Then I saw it—the huge tail over the gunwale. Before I could grab hold of one of the seats, I flew into the air.

Jamie shouted as we were tossed from the boat. He flew upside down, and I heard a *thud* as his head hit the bow. Then I was deep under water, unsure which way was up, unsure if the dark shadow above me was my boat or the whale.

I found the surface of the water. Gulped air. My eyes stung from the salt. The boat was already yards away from me, and my anger at Jamie turned into a fight to survive. I swam to the boat, grabbing onto the short ladder at the stern as I scanned the water for my brother.

"Jamie!" I shouted, listening hard for his voice. A few seagulls cawed from the air overhead, but that was the only sound. I climbed into the boat for a better view of the water. *"Jamie!"* I shouted again and again. The sound of that *thud* replayed in my head. I dove into the water once more, opening my eyes in the murk as I searched for him. I swam underwater until my muscles gave out, and still I stayed in the water, crying hard, gagging on each watery intake of breath.

Climbing into the boat again, I scanned the water once more from that height. He couldn't be gone. He *couldn't* be. I expected him to rise out of the water any minute. Laughing. Getting me back for being asshole enough to try to fight him. I couldn't leave. Leaving would mean giving up on him.

"Jamie!" I called, until finally, I was only whispering the word. I wanted my brother.

Even as I sailed back through the inlet, crying openly, I thought he might greet me at the pier. He'd say I deserved his cruel hoax and chew me out for being such a hypocrite.

But of course, he wasn't there, and my real nightmare began when I told the police what happened: a whale lifted the boat and tossed us out. In *June,* when the humpbacks should be somewhere north of New England. Ludicrous. Sometimes I wondered if I'd imagined the great thwacking tail. I told no one about our fight, no one about our conversation, but I had scratches on my shoulder. Bruises on my neck. Was it any wonder I failed the polygraph I'd stupidly agreed to take?

People who'd known our family for many years remembered the old rivalry between Jamie and myself. Did we fight on the boat, they wanted to know? They remembered my drinking. Had I been drinking out there? In the end, they had no evidence against me and had to let me go. The firefighters, whose love and admiration for me was nearly as strong as it had been for Jamie, stuck by me, but Laurel didn't believe a word I said. And she was the only one who mattered.

Chapter Forty-Three

Maggie

"YOU'RE REALLY BRAVE TO VISIT KEITH," AMBER SAID. SHE was slumped in the passenger seat of my car with her bare feet flat against the dashboard. I'd warned her that if we crashed and the air bag burst open she'd end up with two broken legs and her knees would smash her nose, but she told me I worried too much. I *did* worry too much. I couldn't help it. The fire showed me how quickly things could go wrong. You think you have control over your life, and then bam! Major wake-up call.

"What's so brave about it?" I asked.

"I've heard burn units are beyond gross." Amber had always been a wimp. When we took the elementary schoolkids' handmade cards to New Hanover Hospital, she stayed in the lobby while I went to the patients' rooms. Most of them were there for smoke inhalation and minor burns, so it wasn't that bad. It seemed like my duty, taking the cards to those kids. I was one hundred percent healthy. It was the least I could do. I even got out of school legitimately today, since my counselor said a visit to Keith counted as "community service," just like planning the makeover event. I'd been working my butt off on that thing, but no way was I talking to Dawn about it again. I'd send her a big fat check when the event was over. I was never talking to Dawn again about anything.

"I feel bad that I haven't gone before now," I said to Amber. "I've been carrying the cards for him around for a week."

Amber had interviews in the business department at UNC in Chapel Hill, where she'd be going in the fall. I'd said I'd drive her there, and her parents would pick her up later in the week. I wanted to see Keith, and not just to give him the cards. Keith was the one person who swore he saw Andy walking around outside just before the fire. No way did that make sense. I wanted to know exactly what Keith was telling the police so I could figure out how to poke his story full of holes. Mom had found the world's lamest lawyer, so it was up to me to get Andy out of this mess. While I was in Chapel Hill, Mom would go to Raleigh to talk to a neurologist who specialized in FASD. The probable cause hearing was tomorrow, and although Mom said everything would turn out fine, I could tell she was nervous about the whole thing.

"Travis's parents had a meltdown when they found out I'd be going to Carolina," Amber said with a laugh. Travis's parents thought he and Amber were getting too serious too soon.

"Not much they can do about it," I said. "Travis is a big boy."

"Exactly."

I didn't care about the ongoing saga of Amber and Travis, but there I was, stuck for two-and-a-half hours listening to every stupid detail about their relationship from the girl who used to be my best friend, while I couldn't tell her a single thing about Ben. She'd never understand. She'd probably write about it on her Facebook page. Amber had no idea what it was like to have *real* problems.

God, I was so *jealous* that Amber got to be with Travis, out in the open, hanging all over each other. It was so unfair. I missed Ben! We talked on the phone, but I wanted to *be* with him. We planned to meet Friday night on the beach at the very north end of the Island, where what was left of Daddy's old chapel stood. I hoped it didn't rain, but even if it did, I was going. Every time I thought about being with him again, my heart sped up.

Amber hugged herself through her UNC sweatshirt. "I'm glad I'll be inland tonight," she said as we got on the Beltline.

"Why?"

"Where've you been?" She brushed a speck of something off her pink toenail. "There's like a major nor'easter coming. Supposed to blow hard on the coast. I mean, I guess I'll see some of it at UNC, but not like you'll get on the island."

Was that why it seemed so dark? I took off my sunglasses and saw that the clouds looked like clumps of ashes. Maybe the storm could screw up the hearing tomorrow. A really good storm might make them close the courthouse for the day. Maybe the hearing would have to be postponed and we could find a better lawyer or something.

I dropped Amber off on the UNC campus, and then spent forty-five minutes trying to find the hospital and parking lot for the burn center. I forgot the blue gift bag of cards on the backseat of my car and was almost to the elevator when I remembered. It was already starting to rain a little when I went to my car for them. I didn't want to have to drive in a nor'easter, thank you. I'd have to rush.

I found the burn center. There was a big desk with a bunch of nurses, and I asked them for directions to Keith's room.

One of the nurses—overweight, blond and about Mom's age— looked up from a computer keyboard. "It's not visiting hours, sugar," she said.

I cringed at the word *sugar*. I didn't need any reminders of Dawn.

"I looked the hospital up on the internet and it said visiting hours were from six to ten," I insisted.

"The burn center has its own hours," she said, but she stood up. "Who're you here to see? Keith Weston, did you say?"

I nodded. "I drove all the way from Topsail Island."

"Bless your heart," she said. "Oh, you go ahead. His mama's not here today and he can probably use the company." She pointed down the hallway. "Second door on the right."

I stood in Keith's doorway, suddenly scared to walk inside. I could see him in the bed closest to the door, watching a TV suspended from the ceiling. I thought he had two long, thick tubes of white fabric lying at his sides until I realized they were his arms and hands, completely covered with bandages. This is what the fire did, I thought. This is only a *tiny part* of what the fire did. My knees went soft and I leaned against the door frame. Amber was wrong. I wasn't brave. I wanted to run back down the hallway and out of the hospital.

But I had to do this. I made my mushy knees walk into the room.

"Hey, Keith," I said. I'd known Keith his whole life. We had a picture of me when I was three holding him on my lap. For years, I thought it was Andy in that picture, until Mom told me Andy didn't live with us until he was a year old. I was eleven when she told me about drinking too much while she was pregnant with him and that's what made him the way he was. I was so angry with her that I tried to hit her when she told me. She caught my hand, and in typical Mom fashion told me she understood my anger, that she felt angry at *herself* for what she'd done, but she'd tried to forgive herself and she hoped I could, too. I still wasn't sure I had.

Keith turned to look at me and I saw the bandages covering one whole side of his face. I felt like crying. He seemed sort of spaced out, staring at me like he didn't know who I was.

"It's Maggie." I moved right up against his bed.

"I know who you are," he said. "What are you doing here? Slumming?"

Slumming? What was he talking about? I held up the blue gift bag. "The kids at Douglas Elementary made a bunch of cards and pictures for you," I said.

Obviously, he couldn't reach for the bag. I looked at his arms and noticed skinny metal rods sticking out from the bandages around his left hand. I thought I might get sick. There was a chair next to his bed and I sat down.

"Would you like me to read the cards to you?" I asked.

"Does this ease your conscience or something?" he asked. "The rich girl visiting the poor boy in the hospital?"

His attitude shook me up. What was his problem? I knew he'd called Andy a rich kid or something at the lock-in and now he was doing the same thing to me.

"What are you talking about?" I asked. "Why are you suddenly calling Andy and me rich?"

"Because you *are,* aren't you? Especially compared to me and my mom. Rich and lucky."

I figured he meant that Andy had escaped from the fire with minor injuries, while he was lying there covered with bandages. "I know we're lucky," I said. I glanced at the TV and saw a weather map on the screen before looking at him again. "Keith, tell me what you told the investigators about seeing Andy outside before the fire."

He either coughed or laughed, I wasn't sure which. It took a minute for him to catch his breath. "So that's it," he said finally. "You're not here to visit poor Keith. To bring poor Keith some crap made by second-graders. You're here to convince him that your precious, lame-o baby brother is innocent."

"Not true," I said. "I just wanted to know what you think you saw."

"I've got a news flash for you, Maggie," he said. "He's not just *your* brother."

"What do you mean?"

"He's *my* brother, too."

Maybe the pain drugs were messing with his head. "Did you really see him outside the church, Keith?"

"Did you hear me?" He looked like he was trying to sit up but couldn't manage it. I didn't know if I should help him or not. "Andy's my brother," he said. "And *you're* my sister."

I stood up. "I'll ask one of the nurses to come check on you," I said.

"Why? You think I'm talking crazy? Full of shit?"

"I don't know what you're talk—"

"Your father fucked my mother," he said.

"What?"

"You heard me. He fucked my mother and nine months later I was born. That makes me your half brother. The side of the family that lives in a trailer and eats ramen noodles while you and Andy-the-hero eat steak."

"I don't believe you," I said.

"Go ask your uncle," he said. "He knows all about it."

I took a step backward, my knees mush again. "You're full of it," I said. "My father would never do something like that."

He croaked out that half laugh, half cough sound again. "Looks like you didn't know him very well, big sister."

"I knew him better than anyone!" I pictured myself as a little girl sitting next to Daddy on the deck, running my fingers over the tattoo on his arm. "You're just trying to piss me off."

"You don't look pissed," Keith said. "You look like someone just kicked you in the gut. What's the matter? Don't you want another brother?"

I stared at him and suddenly felt like I was looking in a mirror. The dark wavy hair. The enormous brown eye. Lashes thick and black. The room felt as long as a tunnel, its dark walls closing in on me. I took another step backward and my hand grasped the doorjamb.

"Go ask your uncle," Keith said again. "He can fill you in on all the juicy, sicko details."

I turned and flew out of the room, nearly tripping over my rubbery legs in my rush to escape, but his voice followed me all the way to the elevator:

"Bring me some of your money next time, sis!" he shouted, and I pushed the elevator button with my elbow, my hands pressed tightly over my ears.

Chapter Forty-Four

Maggie

I DIALED MY CELL WHILE DRIVING SEVENTY-FIVE MILES AN hour through the rain.

"That you, Mags?" Uncle Marcus answered.

"I need to talk to you." I heard radio static in the background. "Are you at the station?"

"I am. You at school?"

"I'm driving back from Chapel Hill." I had to slow down because the car in front of me was practically crawling. "I talked to Keith."

Total silence.

"Oh my *God!*" I wailed. "Don't tell me it's true!"

"Listen, Maggie. Calm down. How close are you? When can I see you?"

"I'm like still two hours away! You need to tell me now."

"Uh-uh. Not over the phone. It's nearly two. Call me when you get closer and I'll try to get away, okay?"

"Is Keith my half brother?"

"Maggie. I'm *not* talking about this now. Turn on your radio or a CD or whatever and put this out of your mind. Is it raining where you are?"

My wipers slapped back and forth. "Yes," I said.

"Concentrate on your driving, babe, all right? I love you. Call when you get closer."

I tossed my phone onto the passenger seat. Then I screamed out loud. Just screamed until I was hoarse.

The turtle in front of me was actually slowing down even more. I had to pass it or I knew I'd snap. I checked my mirror. No cars behind me. As soon as I started to steer to the left, though, someone laid on his horn and I jerked back into my lane and saw a black Saab in my mirror. Where'd *he* come from? I pressed my brakes to slow down to the turtle's speed. Adrenaline raced down my arms to the tips of my fingers. I had to be more careful. I could have died right there, and if I died, who would help my brother?

I picked up my cell again and tried to call Ben to tell him about the whole Keith thing, but I got his voice mail. "This is Ben Trippett. If that's who you're trying to call, please leave a message." I didn't know what to say that wouldn't worry him, but I loved hearing his voice. I kept hitting redial over and over again to listen to it. I didn't want to repeat what Keith had told me anyway without knowing the truth, but I knew there was something to it for Uncle Marcus to go quiet like that.

I passed the turtle when I was sure it was safe. I turned on the radio like Uncle Marcus suggested. I couldn't get my regular station that far from Surf City, so I hit scan and listened to snippets of country music and Bible talk for the next hour, not even noticing that I was getting the stations only in ten-second bursts.

"Daddy," I whispered to the only perfect person I'd ever known. "Please don't let it be true."

Uncle Marcus said he'd meet me at Sears Landing. I got there first and sat in the far corner of the restaurant. I wanted to be as far from the door and the kitchen as possible because I knew I was going to cry. I watched the rain beating down on Topsail Sound outside the window. It came down at an angle to the water, the wind already kicking up. The sky was so heavy and low, the clouds almost touched the water.

Uncle Marcus showed up looking wet and old. My phone call had gotten to him. I didn't have the energy to stand up for a hug, so he bent over and kissed my cheek.

"How're you holding up?" he asked.

"Awesome," I said sarcastically.

"Yeah." He sat down kitty-corner from me. "I can imagine." He rested his forearms on the table. "So, tell me what Keith said."

"That he's my half brother. Andy's and mine. He said Daddy and Sara…you know." I could not—absolutely could not—think about it. "I thought maybe he was just trying to piss me off. He's so angry about getting burned. Not that I blame him."

Uncle Marcus played with the saltshaker on the table, moving it back and forth with his fingertips. I tried to be patient, but he was getting on my nerves. And then the waitress, a girl named Georgia Ann who graduated from my high school a few years earlier, showed up at our table.

"Hey, Marcus. Maggie," she said, opening her little notepad. "You must be fixin' to graduate, huh, Maggie?"

"Soon." I knew coming to a restaurant had been a bad idea, but it was too rainy to meet on the beach and Uncle Marcus didn't want to talk at the station.

"I'll have a beach dog and onion rings and iced tea." Uncle Marcus got right to the point with her, although I didn't see how his appetite could be all that great. "How about you, Maggie?" he asked.

"I'm not hungry," I said.

"Bring her a sweet tea," Uncle Marcus told Georgia Ann.

"Sure will," she said, and I was relieved when she walked away.

Uncle Marcus started working on the saltshaker again. "I've decided to tell you everything," he said, "because if I start...leaving parts out, I..." He leaned back in the chair and looked at the ceiling. "The thing is, your mother should hear all this first."

"She doesn't *know?*"

He shook his head. "And I was going to wait at least until after the hearing tomorrow, because she has enough on her mind. Is she in Raleigh?"

I nodded. "She might be on her way home by now."

"Where's Andy?"

"His team has a special practice today and he was getting a ride there. I'll pick him up later." I was getting antsy. "You can't leave me hanging until after you tell Mom," I said.

"Right. I know." He gave the saltshaker a few more back-and-forth taps. "Well, it's true," he said simply. "I'm the only one who knows everything that happened, Mags. I never wanted Keith to find out. I sure never wanted you to find out."

"How can Keith know, but nobody else?"

Georgia Ann brought our teas and tossed a couple of straws on the table. "Food'll be up in a jiffy," she said.

Uncle Marcus waited until she walked away again. "Well, he doesn't know everything." He unwrapped his straw and dropped it into his tea. I didn't touch mine. "You know how your Dad died, right?"

"The whale."

"Yes. And I know you've probably heard old-timers' suspicions that I had something to do with it."

I shook my head. No way.

"Well, some people thought that."

"Is that why Reverend Bill is so weird about you?"

"Partially, yeah. And he didn't like Jamie because Jamie's brand of religion didn't fit with his."

"I don't get why anyone would think you had something to do with Daddy dying, though."

He poked his straw up and down in the tea. "Well, first of all, it wasn't the right season for whales to be off the coast," he said. "Plus Jamie and I didn't always get along when we were young, so some people thought maybe I...that I killed him."

"That's totally ridiculous," I said.

"You're right. It is. We *did* have a fight on the boat, though, and that's the part nobody knows about. Not Keith. Not anyone, except you and me."

Georgia Ann showed up with his beach dog and onion rings. The smell of them turned my stomach.

"Y'all need anything else?" she asked.

"We're fine," Uncle Marcus said.

"You holler if you do now, hear?"

Uncle Marcus sipped his tea as she walked away. "While Jamie and I were on the boat," he said, "he told me he was in love with Sara and wanted to divorce your mom so he could marry her."

"No *way*," I said.

"I'm sorry, Mags. He did. And he told me he was Keith's father." He took a bite of an onion ring, the onion pulling from the batter. I tried to be patient while he chewed it.

"I never told anybody about that conversation, because I figured the secret would die with Jamie," he said once he'd swallowed. "He'd been giving Sara money for child support, and once he died, that stopped, of course. I wished that he'd never told me, but he did, and I couldn't sit back and watch Keith who was only what...six at the time? I couldn't watch him grow up with nothing when I knew he was Jamie's son, as well as my nephew. So, what I did was start a trust fund for him with forty thousand dollars of my own money."

"Get out!"

"I wrote a letter about it to Sara and gave it to her with a check. Wrote something like, 'This is Keith's college fund. I know Jamie loved you and wanted to provide for you and Keith.' I wanted to let her know that I knew. That I got that she was grieving, too, but wasn't allowed to show it. I felt sorry for her."

"What about for *Mom?*"

"I felt sorry for your mom, too," he said, "but the thing was, she didn't know the truth. As far as she was concerned, Jamie died her loving husband. Sara, on the other hand, had lost someone she had to pretend she was only friends with."

"How can you sound so sympathetic about her?" I nearly shouted. "She's Mom's best friend, and she was..." I couldn't even say it.

"I know it's hard to understand, Mags. I was angry at first, too. Angry enough to fight with your father. People make mistakes, though. And their feelings change over time."

I thought of Ben, trying to imagine my feelings for him changing. Impossible.

I took the wrapper off my straw so I'd have something to play with. I wadded the thin paper into a tiny ball and squeezed it between my fingertips. "So, I still don't get why Keith is talking about this all of a sudden," I said.

"Sara kept my letter," Uncle Marcus said. "She stuck it with the account information someplace where Keith stumbled onto it. He found it the morning of the lock-in, which explains why he was so mean to Andy that night."

"He said things about me being rich when I saw him at the hospital."

"Well, you *are* rich. You live on a tidy inheritance from Jamie, plus his life insurance kept you and Andy and your mom going for quite a few years. Sara and Keith had very little, and even though I was thoroughly pissed at your father for what he did, I couldn't let his son end up with nothing."

I looked out the window at the sound. The rain had stopped, at least for now. "I always thought Daddy was perfect," I said. "I don't understand how he could do something like that. Cheat on Mom and his family that way."

"You know, Mags, he was a great man in a lot of ways. A really good father. He had high standards for himself. I almost never heard him curse, not as an adult anyway. He stuck by your mom when she got pregnant with Andy even though she wasn't much fun to be around. Neither was I," he added quickly. "We were both drunks. I lived next door at the time and your mom and I drank together and were pretty bad for each other."

I nodded. I knew Uncle Marcus was a recovering alcoholic like my mother, but I'd never imagined him and my mother getting drunk together. It was totally impossible to picture either of them drinking at all. Together? No way. My mother was such a cold fish around him. Suddenly, though, things started to make sense.

"Did Mom think...was she one of the people who thought you might have killed Daddy?" I whispered.

He nodded. "I..." He hesitated. "I really liked your mom and she knew it. She thought that was motivation for me to...get rid of your father."

"Oh, Uncle Marcus, that's insane!"

"Damn straight." He took a bite of his hot dog, washing it down with a swallow of tea. "So I guess the moral of the story is, we're all fallible," he said. "We all screw up at least once in our lives."

Some of us were more fallible than others, I thought.

"Do you know about your Mom's depression?" Uncle Marcus asked.

"Just that she says she medicated herself with alcohol."

"Right," Marcus said. "After you were born, your mom fell into what's called a postpartum depression. Hormones out of whack, which sometimes happens to women after they have a baby. Anyway, we thought she was upset at being a mother or whatever. Your dad tried to help her, but she wouldn't see a counselor or anything, and she wanted...they decided to separate for a while."

"They separated? I didn't know any of this."

"He moved in with Sara and the man she was married to at the time, Steve. Steve was gone a lot in the service, and I guess your dad and Sara...comforted each other."

"Oh, ick." I cringed.

"Mags." He covered my hand with his on the table. "Please, babe. Be an adult about this."

I rolled my eyes. "I'm sorry," I said. "I'll try. Where was I while he was living with Sara?"

"You were with him. Your mother could hardly take care of herself. Sara helped him with you. Even though I was angry with him at first, I think they really needed each other."

"He was going to *leave* us, though," I said. "Leave Andy and me." I felt a tear roll down my cheek before I even knew I was crying.

"No, he planned to be there for *all* his children." He covered my hand again. "You were his baby girl, Maggie. The person he was closest to. He adored you. He was both father and mother to you for your first three years."

That explained so much. "I still feel so attached to him," I admitted. "I think about him a lot. I remember him so well from when I was little, but I hardly remember Mom at all. Like she wasn't there."

"She wasn't, really, but don't blame her either, okay? She became a very good mother to you and Andy once she got sober, so there's no use blaming her or Sara or your dad for any of this now. It's in the past and everyone's tried to move on."

"If Keith told *me*," I said, "he might tell *Mom*." She wouldn't be able to take it. I thought my father had been perfect, but Mom thought he walked on water. "You said she has no idea."

"I know, and I'm going to tell her, but not yet. Not with the hearing tomorrow. So keep this between us for now."

"What if Keith calls her?"

"I don't think he can manage a phone right now."

I remembered his bandaged arms, the metal rods sticking out of his fingers.

Uncle Marcus's pager suddenly went off, and he was on his feet in an instant, wrapping his food in a napkin. "Gotta run, babe," he said, dropping a ten dollar bill on the table. "You okay for now?"

I nodded, and watched him head for the door. Then I stood up to leave myself. I didn't want to have to talk to Georgia Ann again.

My phone jangled on my hip when I got outside. A text message from Ben.

Had fite w/ D. She's on rampage. Keep ur cool. ILU, B.

Chapter Forty-Five

Laurel

THE RAIN WAS COMING DOWN IN BUCKETS BY THE TIME I LEFT
Raleigh and I knew I had a miserable drive ahead of me. It was after
four, and I'd just hung up on Dennis. I couldn't remember another
time when I hung up on someone, but I was furious. I was starting
to hate him, and that's a bad way to feel about the man who holds
your son's life in his hands. First, it took him two hours to return
my phone call when he knew I was trying to find someone to help
us tomorrow at the bind over hearing. Second, even after I told him
about my nearly two hour long meeting with the neurologist in Raleigh, he still didn't think it was worth talking to the man himself.

"I told you, it's an overused defense, Mrs. Lockwood," he said.
"It's lost its punch."

"Well, it hasn't been overused in Andy's case!" I shouted into my
cell phone. "You're not using it at all?"

"Once the case reaches the trial level, then the neurologist's testimony could be helpful in negating intent."

"But he'll be in adult court by then!" That's when I hung up. I
knew I was going to start crying or cussing or both. Shartell didn't
seem to get it. Andy wouldn't survive in jail. He simply wouldn't.

I was still crying twenty minutes later when my cell phone rang.

I hoped it was Shartell, having reconsidered, although I knew that was unlikely. I answered my phone.

"Hold on," I said quickly into the mouthpiece. I put the phone on my lap and drove through the spiking rain to the shoulder of I-40. I picked up the phone again as I came to a stop.

"Hello?" I hoped it wasn't obvious that I'd been crying.

"Laurel, this is Dawn." Her voice sounded strange. Tight. Scaring me. I was afraid Keith had taken a turn for the worse and she was making the calls for Sara. The rain thrummed on my roof and I turned the volume up on the phone.

"Is everything okay?" I asked.

"That depends on your definition of okay," she said. "Where are you? What's that noise?"

"It's rain. I'm driving back from Raleigh. What's going on?"

"I'm calling because I think you need to know what your daughter's up to."

"Maggie?" I asked, as though I had more than one daughter.

"She's having an affair with Ben. He's been cheating on me with her."

"Maggie?" I repeated.

"It's been going on since they started coaching together."

"Dawn, what makes you think—"

"Ben told me everything. He says he's trying to end it with her, but he's taking his sweet time about it."

"Maggie doesn't even date," I said.

Dawn laughed. "They're doing a lot more than dating, Laurel."

I was quiet, thinking of the time I watched Maggie comfort Ben in the emergency room. "He's...how old is he?"

"Twenty-eight. A mere eleven-year difference."

"Did he start it?" I felt a rare emotion—an overwhelming need to protect my daughter. All my protectiveness had gone toward Andy; I'd had none left over for her. Quickly replacing that need, though, was rage. How dare he!

"Does it matter who started it?" Dawn asked. "Lord have mercy, Laurel! My boyfriend's banging your teenaged daughter. Not only that, but she smokes dope with him."

"I don't believe that." Maggie knew—I'd made sure both my kids knew—that substance abuse was *out* in our family. I had zero tolerance for it.

"Then you're hiding your head in the sand."

"I've got to get off the phone, Dawn. Sorry." My hands shook as I clicked off that call and then speed-dialed Maggie's cell phone.

"Did you have any luck?" she asked when she picked up.

"That's not why I'm calling." I ran my free hand around my steering wheel. "I just had a call from Dawn."

Maggie's silence told me all I needed to know.

"Oh, Maggie." Disappointment welled up in my chest. "It's true?"

"Mom, let me explain. It probably didn't come out sounding too good from Dawn."

"No, it sure didn't. You've been lying to me all year. 'Oh, I don't want to date, Mom. I want to concentrate on studying, Mom.' How could you lie to my face like that?"

"Because if I told you the truth, you wouldn't let me see him."

"Damn straight I wouldn't! He's twenty-eight and living with his girlfriend."

"She's not his girlfriend. And why does his age matter?"

"Because there's a huge difference between seventeen and twenty-eight."

"You always say how mature I am, so I don't get what's so shocking and terrible. I love him. He's the best thing that ever happened to me."

"You're smarter than that," I said. "Don't you realize he's taking advantage of you? He's living with Dawn and has you on the side. Where's the future in that?"

"He and Dawn are just housemates."

"She seems to think they're more than housemates."

"Well, she's wrong!"

"Everyone knows they're a couple, for heaven's sake."

"He doesn't love her. She's just our cover."

"Maggie!" I was shocked. "How dare you! If that's true…how can you use someone like that?"

"They are *not* a couple!"

"Maggie—"

"I'm not going to let you ruin this for me!"

"Ruin *what?* Do you think he's going to leave Dawn for you?"

"How many times do I have to tell you, he's not *with* Dawn!"

"What kind of future do you expect to have with him?"

"A *long* one!" she yelled.

"I wouldn't count on it. If he's cheating on Dawn, he'll cheat on you, too."

"You're not *listening* to me! If Dawn thinks he's her boyfriend, she's living in a fantasy world."

"I'm afraid you're the one living in a fantasy world, Maggie. She said he wants to end it with you."

"She's so full of it! I'm hanging up."

"Don't you dare."

"We can talk about it later."

"No, now!" I said. "We can talk about it *now,* because I want you to call him up and tell him it's over."

She laughed. "All of a sudden you want to be involved in my life after ignoring me for seventeen years?"

"Maggie!" One of my heartstrings broke. *She's upset,* I told myself. *She's just trying to hurt you.* "Never mind," I said. "I'll call him myself."

"No!"

"He's probably had any number of lovers," I thought out loud. "Do you realize that? He could have a venereal disease, for all you know. You could get pregnant."

"Mother, give me some credit. I'm not stupid."

"Yes, that's *exactly* what you are!" The rain was so loud that I had to plug my free ear with my finger. "You're being incredibly stupid. How could you trust a man who'd have a secret affair with a girl half his age?"

"Because I'm not like *you!*" Maggie snapped. "I *trust* people. You don't trust anyone. You don't even trust Uncle Marcus. You're going to end up alone forever and I don't want that to happen to me."

"I do so trust people," I said, grabbing her bait. "I trusted your father completely."

"Well, guess what, Mom. Turns out that was pretty stupid of *you.*"

"Maggie! Why would you say that?"

"Because he was cheating on you, that's why."

"That's ridiculous," I said. "Don't try to turn this into something about me," I said.

"It *is* about you," she said. "You think Ben's so untrustworthy and you talk about Daddy like he was a saint. Well, guess what? He wasn't. He was in love with Sara."

"*Sara?*" Where in God's name was this coming from? "Sara helped him a lot when you were little. Is that what you're remembering?"

"Keith is Daddy's son!"

I nearly laughed, it was so ludicrous. "Maggie, where are you? You're scaring me." I'd never heard her sound so vicious and desperate before. "I'm going to ask Marcus to come stay with you."

"Mother! It's Uncle Marcus who told me everything. Daddy confessed it all to him when they were on that boat the day he drowned. He was going to leave you for Sara and Keith."

My mind spun as her words sank in. *Impossible.* "Even if this is the truth, why would Marcus tell you?"

"Because Keith knows and Keith told me."

"*What?*"

"Uncle Marcus never wanted you to know. You play ice queen with him because you think he had something to do with Daddy's death, but all this time he's just been trying to keep you from finding out. He set up a college fund for Keith after Daddy died and Keith found the papers or something, so now he knows the truth. Uncle Marcus was going to wait until after the hearing to tell you."

My car closed in on me, the rain sheeting down my windows like a second layer of glass. I felt the blade of a knife slip into my heart, then twist.

Maggie was crying.

"I'm sorry, Mom," she said. "I didn't mean it to come out that way. I know this is a bad time, but you pushed me about Ben. Please, please, just accept that he and I are together. Dawn's jealous, that's all. It's not like he's cheating on her. He told her he just wanted to be friends a long time ago. She's angry that—"

"Maggie—" I wasn't really listening to her "—I'm on my way home. It's been a terrible day."

"Why? What did the neurologist say?"

"We can talk about it in a few hours when I get home. It's raining here and the wind's blowing and I want to miss the worst part of the storm if I can." I sounded remarkably calm to myself even though the knife was turning and twisting and cutting me deeper.

"Mom, just tell me you understand," she pleaded. "That you believe Ben and I are together for the right reasons. I love him."

"We'll talk when I get home," I said. "And don't forget to pick Andy up from swim practice."

"Have I ever once forgotten him?" Maggie snapped, and then the line went dead.

I flipped the phone closed, pressing my forehead to the steering wheel. Jamie had always been mine, I thought. Solid and supportive and loving. We had a few good years after I got sober. All those *I love you*'s. Tender moments with the children. With each other. They were excellent years, weren't they? Had they been my imagination? Were those *I love you*'s meant for Sara, not me?

Sara?

Why *wouldn't* Jamie have fallen for Sara? She was pretty, sweet and his helpmate. Her husband had been frequently absent and emotionally distant even when he was around, while for years I'd been drunk, slovenly and very, very hard to love.

And Marcus. Had he really been keeping the truth from me all these years, while I froze him out? I wanted to call him, to separate what was true from my angry daughter's manipulation of things he'd told her. But I needed to get home and I couldn't possibly drive in the pouring rain and talk on the phone at the same time. Not today. Not about this.

I turned the key in the ignition and pulled back onto I-40.

Chapter Forty-Six

Maggie

ANDY RAN TOWARD ME THROUGH THE RAIN AS I GOT OUT OF my car in front of the rec center.

"I'm getting good at butterflying!" he shouted to me in greeting.

"Good, Andy," I said, opening my umbrella. "Wait in the car, okay? I need to talk to Ben. I'll just be a minute."

I ran into the building and downstairs to the pool. Ben was talking to the parents of one of his team members. He demonstrated a stroke, his arm arcing through the air. He was so amazing. *Oh, God, please don't let this be the end.* I sat down on the lowest bench of the bleachers to wait for him. He spotted me and excused himself from the parents.

"Dawn told my mother," I said when he was close enough to hear me.

"Damn." He sat next to me. "I'm sorry. I was afraid she would. Your mother had a fit, I bet."

"Yes, but there's so much else going on," I said. I'd tried to call Uncle Marcus to tell him I'd blown it with Mom, but he hadn't picked up. I thought of texting him, but he was totally lame at text messages. Besides, I was afraid to tell him what I'd done. I'd been so mean to my mother. Part of me felt guilty about it, but another part loved every second of hurting her. I'd had the empathy of a rattlesnake. "You won't believe it all." I looked up to see another mother walking toward us. "I have to talk to you. Can you call me later?"

He stood up, turning his back to the woman who waited a few feet away. "I'll try," he said.

"Ben..." I got to my feet. "My mother said that Dawn told her you want to break up with me."

He shook his head. "You know Dawn," he said. "She's just trying to make trouble for us. We'll talk later, okay?"

Outside, a gust of wind nearly blew me off my feet. I put up my umbrella, hanging on to it while the wind tried to tear it out of my hands. I was soaked by the time I got to the car.

"You look like you fell in the pool," Andy said.

"I feel like it, too." I shivered as I turned the key.

"Did you bring my iPod?"

"I forgot it. Sorry."

"The thing with the butterfly is you have to get the breathing right," he said, as I pulled into the street.

"Just like everything else in swimming." I knew I sounded snippy, but he didn't seem to notice.

"I want to be the champion."

"Andy, you don't need to be the best at everything all the time."

"Yes, I do."

"Why?"

"So I'll be happy."

I had to laugh. "Your life is pretty simple, isn't it?" I asked.

"Yes."

Did he know about the hearing tomorrow? He sure didn't sound worried about it. "It's good that you try hard," I said, "but part of growing up is learning how to lose gracefully."

"What does that mean?"

"You know when Ben tells you to congratulate the winner on the other team?" I liked hearing myself say Ben's name.

"I hate that."

"That's losing gracefully."

"It's still better to win, though, right?"

"I guess so." I sighed. I couldn't focus on the conversation any longer. "I'm in charge of dinner tonight because Mom won't be home till later." Oh, I dreaded seeing her! "What do you feel like eating?"

"Pizza!"

"I think there's one in the freezer. I'll make it while you get changed."

I was sliding the pizza into the oven when the phone rang. I checked the caller ID. Uncle Marcus. He was going to kill me.

"Hey, Maggie," he said when I answered. "Is your mom home yet?"

"No, and I blew it," I said. "She called and I got mad at her about something and I told her." I bit my lip, waiting for his reaction.

"*Why*, Maggie?" He sounded more shocked than angry.

"She was giving me grief, and then she said how Daddy was the only trustworthy man she ever knew or something like that and it just came out. I know I shouldn't have. I couldn't help myself."

He was quiet, and I scrunched up my face, waiting for him to yell at me.

"Do you know how she made out with the neurologist?" he asked finally. "She left me a message, but I think her phone's off."

"I don't know. She said it was a terrible day."

"Damn."

"It'll be okay, though, won't it? Tomorrow, I mean?"

"Not if Andy's bound over to adult court, it won't be."

"But—" I was confused "—Mom said that probably wouldn't happen."

"She said that *today?*"

I tried to remember my phone conversation with her. "No. She told me the day Andy came home from jail. I was going off about it and she said not to worry. That it wouldn't happen."

Uncle Marcus was quiet again.

"Could it happen?" I asked.

"I think your mother was just trying to keep you from getting upset, Mags," he said. "If she said it was a terrible day, it sounds like she either didn't have any luck with the neurologist or else with the lawyer. And if that's the case, then there's a really good chance Andy will end up in adult court."

"So…" What did that mean exactly? "When would he have a trial? He could stay home while he's waiting for it, right?"

Andy came downstairs. I watched him walk into the family room and turn on the TV.

"No, Mags. Look, I know your mom doesn't want to worry you, but here's the deal. If he gets bound over, they'll lock him up right away and—"

"What do you *mean,* lock him up right away?" I whispered, turning my back to the family room.

"I mean, after the hearing tomorrow, they'd take him back to jail. And it's very doubtful he could get bail, so he'd have to stay in jail until his trial. And sometimes it can take a year or even longer for a case to go to trial. Then if he's found guilty, he could end up in prison for the rest of his life."

I couldn't speak. This couldn't be happening.

"So that's why your mom's been knocking herself out to find the right expert and why she's been so worried and why you really were...you were cruel to her today, Maggie. She didn't need that on top of everything else."

"I can't believe it," I said.

"What part of it?"

"Any of it." I looked into the family room. I could see the back of Andy's head where he sat on the sofa. He had no idea how his world might change tomorrow. *I'd* had no idea. "I'm so sorry," I said to Uncle Marcus. "I didn't realize...I knew it was serious, but I didn't get how bad it was."

"It's worse. That's what I was calling to talk to your mother about."

"How could it possibly be worse?"

"Here's how," he said. "Those empty containers from the landfill? One of them has Andy's prints on it."

Chapter Forty-Seven

Laurel

I HAD TO STOP ONCE MORE ON THE DRIVE HOME FROM Raleigh, this time because of the blinding rain. Mine wasn't the only car to pull over with its emergency blinkers flashing, but I bet none of the other drivers were in the sort of turmoil—the sort of emotional pain—I was in. I'd failed to get the necessary help for my son, and my daughter had been lying to me for the past year, turning into a girl I didn't know. I thought of all the times Ben Trippett had talked to me about Andy's swimming, all the while chortling to himself about the wool he was pulling over my eyes.

And then there was that knife beneath my breastbone, the most visceral pain of them all. My beloved Jamie had led a double life. My best friend had deceived me. I'd been blind to it. Why did I always *lose* people? My parents. My aunt and uncle. Jamie. And now even Jamie's memory would be lost to me. And Sara! How could she? Even Marcus had betrayed me in the guise of protecting me—an act of nobility I could barely fathom, given the wrath with which I'd blamed him for Jamie's death. Nothing was as it seemed. The only person in my life I felt sure about was Andy, and tomorrow, he could be ripped from my arms for being too naive, too defenseless against a world he didn't completely understand. I started to cry. To sob so hard that, even as the rain let up and the other cars took off, I stayed on the side of the road trying to get a grip on myself.

By the time I got home, the nor'easter was in full swing. The sky was eerily dark for so early in the evening, and the thunder made a ripping, growling sound that reminded me of when the church roof caved in during the fire. The slender trees in my yard bowed toward the sound. I caught them in my headlights, and that's when I realized that my headlights were the only lights near the house. The power must have gone out.

The garage door opener worked, though, and as I pulled inside, I noticed that Maggie's Jetta wasn't there. I let myself into the house, feeling even more unsettled. Something wasn't right.

"Maggie? Andy?"

The wind rattled the windowpanes, but even so, I could hear the refrigerator's loud hum. The power *was* on. I flipped the kitchen switch and the room filled with light. An uneaten pizza rested on a cookie sheet on the granite counter. Where were they?

I walked through the house, calling for them, afraid the police might have taken Andy away again. Why, though? And where was Maggie?

I sat on the family room sofa and dialed her cell phone, but she didn't answer. She was probably afraid to talk to me after our conversation earlier. I tried Andy's phone but, as with Maggie's, I was dumped to his voice mail.

"Hi! This is Andy. Leave...leave me a message when the tone rings." It had taken us an hour to get that message properly recorded.

"Andy, this is Mom," I said. "Call me right away!" I tried Maggie's phone again, this time leaving a message. "Where are you and Andy? I'm home and very worried!"

Then I dialed Marcus's cell.

"Do you know where Maggie and Andy are?" I asked when he picked up.

"I spoke to Maggie about an hour or so ago," he said. "She was home with Andy. She said they were making pizza."

"Well, I just got home and the house is dark and empty and a whole pizza is on the counter. Her car's not here. She was mad at me. We had a fight on the phone." I ran my hand over the green fabric on the arm of the sofa, unsure how much to say about that conversation.

"Then you don't know about the containers?"

"What containers?"

"The ones found in the landfill." He hesitated. "At least one of them has Andy's fingerprints on it, Laurel."

"No!" I stood up. "Oh, Marcus, that's impossible! It's just impossible. I don't understand what's happening."

"I'm coming over."

"Could the police have picked him up?"

"I doubt it. I think they have other things to worry about with this storm, but I'll call them on my way to your house to make sure."

"Please do." I hung up. I tried to make a pot of coffee, but forgot to add the grounds and ended up with a carafe full of murky-looking water. Sobs shook my shoulders as I tried again. I remembered the grounds this time, but the power died as the first dark drops poured into the carafe.

Fumbling in the darkness, I found my hurricane lanterns and flashlights. I lit the lanterns, setting them on the tables and fireplace mantel in the family room.

If the police had Andy, could Marcus somehow get him out again? Or was this it, now that they had his prints on those containers?

Would Andy be locked up tonight, then sent to jail after the hearing tomorrow, never to get out again?

It was nine o'clock when Marcus arrived. I heard the slamming of his pickup door and I raced to my front door, anxious to talk to him. He literally blew into the house, the wind lifting him off his feet.

"Damn!" he said, knocking into the small table in the foyer. "My pickup hydroplaned half the way here." He helped me close the door against the wind. "We need to go out there again," he said. "We need to get your patio furniture in the garage."

I was usually a clear thinker in a storm. Tonight, though, I could barely picture the furniture he was talking about.

"Do the police have him?" I asked.

"No. I'm worried about tomorrow, though, Laurel. I mean, I thought maybe we had a chance till these containers turned up."

"I don't understand!" I said for the hundredth time.

"Let's get things secured outside and then figure out what to do."

"I don't care about the patio furniture!" I said. "I don't care if the house falls down. I just want to know where my children are!"

"You stay here, then. I'll do it."

I knew he was right. A nor'easter last year had sent someone's trash can through my front window. I followed him outside and together we managed to get the chairs and patio table into the garage. My trash can was already gone, blown away who knew where. I cried in the windy darkness, letting myself break down unheard. I just managed to pull myself together before we went into the house again.

"Let's think," he said, as I relit one of the lanterns that had gone out. "How could Andy's prints have possibly gotten on the container?"

"Someone set him up," I said. "That's the only possibility. Maybe Keith, since he was angry that..." I stopped, pressing my hands to my temples as all that Maggie had told me rushed back. "Marcus." My voice cracked as I leaned against the stone of the fireplace. "I know about Keith. Maggie told me. Is it true about Jamie and Sara?"

He lowered himself to the sofa. "I'm sorry Maggie told you the way she did," he said. "I wanted to wait until a better time."

I shook my head, sinking into the chair behind me. I had no time to wallow, I told myself. Right now, I just needed to focus on Andy. "We should go out and look for them," I said.

"We wouldn't be able to see two feet in front of my pickup."

Again, he was right. I rubbed my arms with my hands, watching the hurricane lantern flicker on the mantel. "What do you think?" I asked. "Could Keith have set Andy up?"

"But then we come back to the question of why he'd get trapped by the fire if he set it himself."

"Ben!" I said suddenly, getting to my feet and grabbing the wireless phone from the coffee table. "Maggie and Andy might be with Ben!"

"With *Ben*? Why?"

"Well, here's the other piece of terrific news I got today," I said. "Dawn called to tell me that Ben and Maggie have been seeing each other for nearly a year."

"Seeing each other?" Marcus's eyes grew wide. "You mean...intimately?"

"That's exactly what I mean. That's why Maggie got mad at me. I talked to her about it and I was furious. She——"

"Ben?" Marcus was incredulous. "I saw him with Dawn the other day, all lovey-dovey. And he's pushing thirty, for God's sake."

"I know it. I'm going to strangle him."

"I'll beat you to it."

I sat down again, glad to have something to do. Some action to take. "Do you know his phone number?" I hit the talk button on my phone, but there was no dial tone. Of course. "The power," I said, holding the dead phone in the air.

Marcus pulled his cell phone from his belt. "Cells are iffy tonight," he said, frowning at the display. "I only have one bar."

I watched as he dialed. He listened, shaking his head. "Voice mail," he said to me. Into the phone, he said, "Ben, it's Marcus. Call me."

I leaned back against the chair, feeling defeated. "It's my fault, Marcus," I said. "Maggie and Ben. I've been a terrible mother to her. An absent mother. I made her parent Andy with me without giving much thought to *her* needs. Jamie raised her until he died and then I let her be. I expected her to take care of herself."

"She seemed really good at it."

"How could I not have known she was seeing Ben? And for so *long?*"

"Man!" Marcus got to his feet, pacing toward the stairs and back again. "I'm going to flatten him!"

"Could they be over there?" I wondered. "At Ben's?"

"Since it's actually *Dawn's* house, not likely."

I massaged my forehead. A headache was starting, or maybe I'd had it for hours and hadn't noticed. "This thing about the containers," I said. "It makes no sense." I rubbed my temples harder. "But if Maggie had a secret life, maybe Andy did, too." There was no other way to explain it all. "I think about the mothers of those kids who shoot up schools. I'm sure they never suspected their child could do such a thing." I dropped my hands to the arms of the chair. "Marcus, I *knew* there was something on his shoes," I admitted. "I hoped it was fluid from his lighter. You know, how he put it in his sock when we were at the airport? With all the time and attention I gave Andy, did I still screw up with him? Is there a side to him he's managed to keep hidden from me?" Just then, I felt as though everyone in my life had deceived me.

"Don't *you* start doubting him, all right?" Marcus stopped pacing. "You're the one person who can't afford to ever doubt him."

"But how do you explain it?" I raised my hands in the air, palms up. "He needed to feel powerful and looked up to. He loved being a hero. Maybe he—"

"How can you even think that?" he asked.

I looked across the room at the man I'd mistrusted for the last fifteen years. "Because," I said, "today I learned that I don't know a thing about the people that I love."

Chapter Forty-Eight

Maggie

THE UNIVERSE WOULD HAVE TO PICK THIS NIGHT FOR A STORM. I parked on a side street at the northern end of the island. The rain sounded like nails hitting the roof of my car. The houses were dark: people must have gotten the word about the weather and stayed away from the beach. That was totally fine with me. The darker and emptier, the better.

"Where are we?" Andy asked when I made no move to get out of the car.

"We're near The Sea Tender. *You* know. We've driven past it a couple of times."

"The circle house where I lived when I was a baby?"

"When you were little, yes. That's the house. We're going to stay there tonight. It'll be fun."

"Cool," Andy said. He peered into the dark rain. "Where is it?"

"Just a short walk away." It didn't seem as though it would stop raining anytime soon, so I grabbed the flashlight and a trash bag I'd filled with clothes for each of us, along with Andy's iPod. "We're going to have to get wet." I opened the door, hanging on to the handle to keep the wind from tearing it from my hands. The ocean roared in my ears as if I'd parked right on the beach. "Be careful getting out!" I shouted, too late. The wind grabbed Andy's door and he went sprawling onto the sandy side of the road. He got up, laughing. He was clueless. About tonight. About tomorrow.

I was practically blinded by the rain as I walked around the car to help him shut the door. The wind was like a living being, pushing the door toward us. It spooked me, like we weren't alone out there. Everything I was doing spooked me, but I had to do it. This wouldn't be the first crazy thing I'd done. I wished Mom had told me how bad things were! I would have done something sooner. Made a better plan. *Something.* Tomorrow, Andy was supposed to sit through a hearing he could never understand that could lead to him being locked up and the key thrown away. I would *not* let that happen. I hadn't thought things through past tomorrow, but if they couldn't find Andy for the hearing, they couldn't lock him up. That was all that mattered.

"Can you carry the food?" I shouted, handing him a brown paper bag I'd filled with bread and peanut butter and fruit. There was nearly a case of bottled water in the cottage. That would last us through tonight and tomorrow. "Hold the top closed so everything doesn't get soaked," I said as he took the bag from my hand. I swung the garbage bag over my shoulder and we started walking toward The Sea Tender.

"I can't see *anything!*" Andy said.

"We're almost there." I could hardly make out one house from another. I squeezed my eyes nearly closed to keep out the wind.

We walked right past the narrow boardwalk that led to the house and had to backtrack.

"Come on," I said, turning onto the boardwalk. "Stay close to me."

We reached the puny dune in front of the house. Even in the darkness, I could see the waves crashing into each other as they raced toward the beach. I shone the flashlight toward the sand below The Sea Tender. Something was different, and it took me a moment to realize that the silvery glow in the beam of my flashlight was not sand at all but swirling water. The ocean churned around the pilings of the cottage, tossing foam and spray up to the deck. I'd never seen the water so high on this beach. I didn't want to let Andy know how it freaked me out.

"The rain is biting me!" Andy shouted.

"It's the sand blowing." The sand stung my face and hands. "Come on," I said, jumping down the sharp angle of the dune.

"This bag's—" The wind cut off whatever Andy said, and I didn't ask him to repeat it. I was too busy reminding myself that the cottage had survived dozens of hurricanes and plenty of nor'easters. It would survive this one, too.

I found the cinder block and moved it into place beneath the front stairs. "I'll go up first, then I'll help you up," I shouted. It took me three tries to throw the heavy trash bag onto the little front deck. Then I climbed on the block and hoisted myself onto the steps.

"I can do that," Andy shouted. "I don't need help."

"Okay, hand me the bag of food."

He lifted it toward me, and I grabbed the top edge of the bag. It was soggy and before I could get a better grip, the wind ripped it from my hands, spilling everything onto the wet beach.

"I'll get it all, don't worry, Maggie!" He scrambled around on the sand, the wind tossing the loaf of bread in the air like it was made out of feathers.

"I'll be down in a sec, Panda!" I shouted. I unlocked the door and tossed the trash bag into the house. Then I jumped off the deck, and together we picked up as much of the food as we could find.

Once we were both up on the deck, Andy made me shine my flashlight on the sign.

"Condem-ned," he read.

"Condemned," I shouted. "When we were kids, Hurricane Fran demolished a lot of the island."

"I know that," Andy yelled back at me. "I learned it. And *condemned* means *keep out,* but we're not going to keep out."

"You've got it," I said. I pushed the door open again and ducked under the sign.

"Are we doing a bad thing?" Andy asked as he walked into the living room. His tennis shoes squeaked on the floor, and I knew he was twisting his feet to make them squeak louder.

I picked up a second flashlight from the kitchen counter. "Here's one for you." I handed it to him. "About this being a bad thing, some people will think so, but I don't."

"Will Mom?" Andy turned the flashlight on and off, shining it in my face.

"Stop that." I pushed it away. "You're blinding me."

"Sorry. Will Mom think this is bad?"

"There's a bunch of candles all around this room. Let's light them and then I'll answer your question." I handed him a box of matches.

"Can I use my lighter?" He reached into his pocket and I shone my flashlight on the green lighter in his hand.

"You still have that thing? I thought the security people at the airport took it away from you."

"This is a different one."

My baby brother had some rebel in him after all. "Why?" I asked. "Are you still smoking?" I thought I'd smelled smoke on him a few days ago, but since the night of the fire, the whole world smelled like smoke to me.

"Don't tell Mom," he said.

"I won't. But it's so bad for you, Panda Bear. I wish you wouldn't."

"I lied to Mom," he admitted.

"Yeah," I said. "I've done some of that myself."

"I told her I didn't suck smoke into my chest, but I do."

"Great for your asthma." I lit one of the candles on the counter.

"I like to make it come out of my nose."

I tried to picture him smoking. "Where do you smoke?" I asked. He was always supervised, really. We'd smell it if he smoked at home and he sure couldn't do it at school.

"I do it when I'm hanging in with my friends on the days I don't ride home with you."

"Hanging out," I corrected him. I pictured him waiting for the bus with other kids from school, kids he thought of as his friends but who probably bummed cigarettes off him and called him names behind his back.

"If a fire started in this house, I could jump out this window onto those boards out there." He shone his flashlight through one of the living room windows onto the back deck.

"Right," I said. "And there's a door in the kitchen we could use to get out on the deck, too."

"Deck, I mean. Not boards."

He sounded embarrassed by his mistake. "It's okay," I said. "I knew what you meant. And decks are made out of boards, so you were technically correct."

"We have a big deck at home."

"Yes, we do."

"When do we go home?"

I set out the food on the kitchen counter. "We'll stay here tonight, and then decide what to do tomorrow." I opened the bag of bread.

"You want some bread and peanut butter?" I asked. I should have figured out a way to bring the pizza with us. What would Mom think when she saw the whole pizza on the counter?

"Okay."

In the candlelight, he watched me spread peanut butter on two slices of bread. I handed one to him.

We sat on the couch together facing the dark window, eating the bread and peanut butter and drinking from bottles of water. "The ocean's out there," I said. It was so dark and we were up so high that I couldn't see the white froth of the waves.

"I know that. I'm not an imbecile."

"Good word, Panda," I said.

We munched our bread in silence for a while. I kept imagining how Mom would feel when she walked into the house to discover Andy wasn't there. I'd dumped all the stuff about Daddy on her when her day had been crap to begin with. Then she had to drive home in the wind and rain worrying about tomorrow and then discover that her children had disappeared. There were two voices in my head, one telling me to let her know we were okay, the other telling me to keep quiet. My tattoo burned into my hip every time I thought of her worrying.

"I'm going to call Mom and let her know we're okay," I said when I'd finished eating. I got his iPod out of the trash bag and handed it to him. Then I checked my phone. No bars at all. Weird. I could usually get reception in the cottage. The storm, probably. I wondered if Ben had been trying to call me. I didn't want to think about Ben. That would totally mess me up right now.

Andy's phone was on the counter, but he had no reception either. I pictured Mom growing more frantic by the minute. Why why why had I told her about Daddy? I had such a mean side to me. I'd wanted to turn the tables on her. Get her off my back about Ben.

"Andy, I'm going out on the deck because I can't get a phone signal inside."

"Okay." He didn't look up from his iPod.

On the deck, I had to grab the railing to keep my balance in the wind. Even if I could get a signal—which I couldn't—I'd never be able to hear her. I'd have to call from my car.

In the kitchen again, I tore a hole for my head in the trash bag and put it on like a poncho.

"Be back in a few minutes, Andy," I said, glancing at the candles scattered around the room to make sure they were burning safely. Just what we needed was my brother in another fire.

I made it to the car, but still had no signal, so I started driving. There was water on the road and I drove very slowly, afraid of skidding into the sand. Getting stuck. What if something happened to me and Andy was left alone at The Sea Tender? *Oh God,* I told myself. *Stop thinking that way!*

I didn't see a single light in any of the houses and knew the power was out. I was all the way to the huge condominium building, Villa Capriani, before I got a signal. I had three messages from Mom. She sounded scared to death, her voice shaking, and I knew I was making the right decision to call her. I pulled into Villa Capriani's nearly deserted parking lot and dialed my mother's cell number.

"Maggie! Where *are* you?" She sounded so bad. I knew she'd been crying. I should have called earlier or at least left her a note.

"I'm just calling to let you know Andy and I are fine," I said. "We're perfectly safe."

"Where are you, Maggie? What are you doing?"

"I can't tell you. I just wanted you to know that we're fine."

"She won't say," Mom said to someone.

"Who's there?" I was afraid it was the police.

"Maggie?" It was Uncle Marcus on the phone now. "What's going on? Are you with Ben?"

"*No*," I said. Oh God. So now Uncle Marcus knew about Ben and me, too. "He doesn't know anything about this, so leave him out of it. I just wanted to let Mom know that Andy and I are fine."

"Why are you doing this?" he asked. "Come home. You're only going to make things worse, babe."

"How could they get any worse?" I asked. "Can you picture Andy in a jail cell without bail? Waiting a year for a trial, like you said? Getting picked on and maybe beaten up and maybe raped by the other prisoners? And not really getting it?" My voice broke as the images ran through my mind. "Not understanding what's going on?"

"I know, Mags," he said. "But try to calm down, all right? Maybe the judge will see reason tomorrow and not lock him up. Maybe he'll even let him stay in the juvenile system."

"Oh, sure," I said. "That's not what you said a couple of hours ago. Especially now that they have his fingerprints on that container."

"If he doesn't show, it'll be worse for him," Uncle Marcus said.

"I'm hanging up." I turned my phone's power off so I wouldn't have to hear it ring when they tried to call me back. I wondered if, by now, even Mom and Uncle Marcus believed Andy had done it. Was I the only one who knew he was innocent?

I was scared driving back to the cottage. I drove faster and faster, thinking again about the candles. I was so relieved when I saw that The Sea Tender was still standing. I parked the car on New River Inlet Road this time and ran as fast as I could back to the cottage.

Inside, Andy had his earbuds in and barely seemed to notice when I burst into the living room.

I talked him into playing a game of Concentration with the sticky old deck of cards from one of the kitchen drawers. We spread them out between us on the sofa, and my hands shook when it was my turn to turn over a pair. Now that we were here, with my brother fed, my mother called and nothing more that needed to be done, I was starting to freak out. What was I doing? What had I done?

"I win!" Andy shouted, when we counted our pairs. For once, I envied his ability to see life so simply.

We played a few more hands. Then I blew out the candle on the windowsill and we watched the rain and salt water tap against the glass in front of us. The cottage vibrated, I guessed from the water swirling around the pilings. My nerves were going to snap any minute.

Andy had kicked off his shoes and now he put his feet on the windowsill. "I wish we could see the ocean," he said.

I leaned forward to see if the white water was visible.

"Do you mind getting wet again?"

"Are we going back to the car?"

"No," I said. "It's not raining that hard right now. Let's sit out on the deck and watch the ocean."

He followed me out the kitchen door onto the deck. It may not have been raining hard, but the wind made balloons out of our shirts and whooshed in our ears. I sat down where I always did, on the edge of the wet deck with my legs dangling over the side, my arms on the lower rung of the railing. The vibration was much stronger out here. The deck shook as if someone was running across it.

I patted the boards next to me and Andy sat down, too.

"Now we can see the ocean." I could tell from the frothy white water that the waves were very high, crashing crazily into each other. The darkness scared me, though, because I couldn't get a good sense of how high up the beach the waves were coming. I felt the spray on my bare feet as the water swirled around the pilings.

"We could fish from here," Andy said. "If we run out of food, we can catch fish."

Right, I thought. Like *that's* in my plans.

"Yes, we could," I said.

I put my arm around Andy's shoulders. A different fifteen-year-old boy probably would have knocked my arm away, but Andy didn't seem to mind. What I really wanted to do was wrap both my arms around him. Hold him tight. I'd resented my mother for pouring one hundred percent of her love and attention into Andy, giving him the fifty percent that should have been mine. But I'd never resented Andy. It wasn't his fault she loved him more.

"Do you remember Daddy at all?" I asked him.

"I rode on his shoulders," Andy said. In his room, he had a framed picture of Daddy holding him on his shoulders when he was about two. I was sure his memory wasn't of Daddy, but of the picture.

"Sometimes," I said, "when I sit out here, I feel his spirit."

"Like a ghost?" Andy asked.

"No, not exactly. It's hard to explain. You remember Piddie?" Piddie had been his goldfish. We'd found him belly-up in his bowl a few months ago.

"Yes. He was pretty."

"Do you ever, sort of, feel him around? Like, you know perfectly well he's not there, but you feel like he is."

"No. He's dead."

"Well, okay. I'm trying to explain what I mean by Daddy's spirit, but I don't think you can understand it." I lowered my arm from his shoulders and leaned on the railing again. "I just feel like he's here with me sometimes."

"He's *dead!*" Andy sounded so upset that I laughed.

"I know, Panda Bear. Don't worry about it."

Between the wind and the light rain, it was chilly on the deck but I didn't want to go inside. I thought I should keep an eye on the ocean, although I was sure we were okay. If the deck started to actually sway, though, maybe we'd have to leave the house.

"My friends think I'm going to go to jail," Andy said suddenly.

"You won't go to jail."

"I'm scared I'll have to because I lied to the policemen. I lied to everyone."

I was confused. "What do you mean, Andy? When did you lie?"

"I said I didn't go outside while the lock-in was there, but I did."

"You *did?* Why?"

"To see if the bugs were dying. To see if the bug spray worked, but it was too dark."

I shut my eyes. I knew what he was talking about. I knew everything.

"I promise you, Andy," I said, "I will not let you go to jail."

"Cross your heart and hope to die?"

"Cross my heart and hope to die." I felt a chill up my spine, saying those words.

"How can you stop the police from putting me in jail?" he asked.

"I can stop them."

"But how?"

I put my arm around him again. "By telling them what really happened that night."

Chapter Forty-Nine

Laurel

IT WAS NOT DAMP IN MY HOUSE SO MUCH AS RAW, AS THOUGH the weather had crept in through the windows. I huddled on the sofa beneath an afghan, while Marcus tended the fire he'd built.

"At least you know Maggie's got him someplace where he's safe." Marcus sat down on the sofa near my feet. "Do you think you should call Shartell?"

"I don't want to." I realized that whatever insanity had made Maggie spirit Andy away tonight, part of me shared it. As long as he was with her, he wouldn't be afraid and he wouldn't be in jail. "But I don't know what I'll do in the morning when we're supposed to show up for the hearing."

"I guess we'll deal with it then," Marcus said.

I lifted my head to look at him. "Thank you for saying *we*," I said. "You've always tried to be…a *we* when it came to Andy. I'm sorry I made that hard."

"I understood." He shifted on the sofa. "I don't know how much Maggie told you, but Jamie and I had a colossal fight on the boat. I was angry with him about the whole Sara thing, and when I got on his case about it, he turned on me, saying I didn't have much room to talk. He'd figured out that Andy was mine, and—"

"He *did?* I was never even sure that you knew." Relief washed over me now that it was out in the open. It should have been for years.

The light from the hurricane lantern caught his smile. "I was pretty sure about that right from the start. From when you told me you were pregnant. Jamie probably was, too. We just let it be the elephant in the room. But that elephant didn't fit on my boat with us."

I remembered the bruises on Marcus's body that had caused the police to suspect foul play. "Do you mean you had a *fistfight?*" I couldn't picture the brothers physically fighting.

"Most definitely. That's why I was scratched up, but I only told the cops about the whale. I couldn't tell them the rest of it without getting into what led to the fight and all that."

"Was there really a whale, Marcus?"

He nodded. "We watched it for a while, and then it disappeared. While we were…having at it, the boat suddenly shot up in the air and we were tossed out. Jamie hit his head on the bow. All of that part is true."

"You should have told the truth," I chided. "If I'd known the truth, it would have made me more open to you. You had to know that."

"At what cost?" he asked. "I didn't want to hurt you or your memory of Jamie. I didn't think it would ever have to come out."

"Keith is really Jamie's son?" I whispered.

"Jamie told me he was. And once he said it, I could see Jamie in him. Do you see it?"

I thought about Keith's dark hair, the body that was already growing thick and brawny. I rubbed my breastbone. "My heart hurts," I said. "Ever since Maggie told me. It just hurts so much."

"I know." Marcus rested his hand on my foot through the afghan. "I'm sorry."

I drew in a long breath and blew it out. "Maggie said you set up a college fund for him."

"I did," he said. "That's how Keith found out. It just seemed so wrong that Jamie's other kids had so much when Keith had so little."

"Oh!" I suddenly remembered the day I tried to pay Sara's hotel bill. "You're paying for Sara's hotel room!"

He nodded.

I dropped my head back against the sofa. "I'm so humiliated," I said. "Sara...I thought she was my best friend."

"She *is* your best friend."

I shook my head. "How could she have done that to me, though?"

Marcus squeezed my foot through the afghan. "How could you and I have done it to Jamie?" he asked.

I don't know how I managed to fall asleep. Marcus shook my shoulder and I jerked awake, flinching at a pain in my neck from the cramped position I'd slept in on the sofa.

"Did they come home?" I sat up and looked toward the stairs.

"No." He shook his head. "It's a little after five and the weather's settled down. I'm going to try driving over to Ben and Dawn's. I can't just sit here any longer, and maybe Ben'll have a clue where they are."

I tossed the afghan onto the back of the sofa and stood up, my legs wobbly beneath me. "I'm going with you," I said.

I felt as though I was riding in a boat rather than a pickup as we turned onto New River Inlet Road from my street. Marcus's headlights illuminated the water on the road, but it was impossible to know how deep it was. Tall wings of it rose up on either side of the pickup, although Marcus drove slowly. The wind had let up and it was no longer raining, but aside from our headlights, the island was in complete, disconcerting darkness that my eyes couldn't pierce. The sky felt as though it was mere inches from the roof of the cab.

"I don't think I've ever seen a night this dark," Marcus said as he drove. He sat upright, close to the steering wheel, and I knew he felt as tense as I did.

Although there wasn't another vehicle on the road, it took us half an hour to drive the seven miles to Surf City. Marcus got out of the pickup a few times to shine his flashlight on the road ahead of us, making sure the water wasn't too deep or too swift to drive through. Finally, we turned onto the beach road near Dawn's cottage, and Marcus inched along as we tried to make out one dark building from another.

"I think that's it." I pointed to the barely visible cottage.

"Isn't that Dawn's car on the street in front?" Marcus asked.

I followed the beam of his headlights to the car and saw that it was parked in front of Ben's van.

"Why are they on the street?" I asked.

Marcus pulled into the driveway, his headlights answering my question: the parking area beneath the cottage was under at least a couple of feet of water.

"Oh boy." Marcus turned off the engine. "I bet this storm did a number on the beaches."

We got out of the pickup, each of us carrying a flashlight, and Marcus put his hand on my back as we walked toward the cottage. At the top of the front steps, he banged on the door with the side of his fist.

We waited thirty seconds, then Marcus tried the door.

"Locked." He banged again, relentlessly this time. "Ben!" he shouted.

I saw a flicker of light inside one of the windows, and a second later Ben opened the door, a flashlight in his hand.

"Is there a fire?" he asked. Then he noticed me. "What's wrong?"

"Let us in." Marcus pushed past him and I followed.

"Do you know where Maggie and Andy are?" I asked.

"Aren't they home?" Ben wore a pair of tan shorts, unbuttoned at the waist, and nothing more. I didn't want to think about Maggie touching him, touching that bare chest.

"No, they're not home," Marcus said. "Maggie took him away, hoping to keep him from the hearing tomorrow."

"Shit." Ben ran a hand through his hair. I suddenly hated him.

"How dare you take advantage of her!" I smacked his bare shoulder with my flashlight, creepily aware of his manliness. My assault barely made him flinch. "She's in high school!"

I felt Marcus's hand against my back again. "Time for that later," he said. "Did Maggie tell you anything about her plans?"

"Who's here, Benny?" Dawn came into the room, tying a short robe closed over her legs and carrying a lantern. She stopped short when she saw us.

"Maggie and Andy are missing," I said.

"Missing?" she asked. "What do you mean? Like kidnapped?"

"Maggie took Andy somewhere to keep him from the hearing in the morning," I said.

Dawn looked at Ben. "Do you know anything about this?" she asked.

Ben shook his head. "Nothing." He was avoiding my gaze.

"I bet I know where they are," Dawn said. She looked at Ben. "You do, too."

"Where?" Ben said, then shut his eyes. "Oh, no. The Sea Tender."

"*The Sea Tender?*" Marcus and I spoke in unison.

"But it's condemned," I said.

"That's where Ben was meeting Maggie," Dawn said with disgust.

That was too much reality for Marcus. "You son of a bitch!" He threw a punch at Ben's jaw, snapping his head back and knocking him halfway to the floor.

I grabbed his arm before he could lash out again. Now that I knew where my children were, I wanted to get to them. Hold them in my arms. "Let's go," I said.

"I cared about her!" Ben held his hand to his jaw as he regained his balance. "It's not like I didn't have any feel—"

"Shut up, Ben!" Dawn said.

Marcus flexed the fingers of the hand he'd struck Ben with. "I'm not done with you, Trippett," he growled to Ben as he flung open the front door. "I'll catch up with you later."

"The Sea Tender," I said as we drove through the darkness. I wanted Marcus to drive faster, but knew he didn't dare. "How would Maggie even think of that?"

"That place is dangerous," Marcus said. "It was condemned for a reason. It should have been torn down long ago."

"I thought Maggie had a good head on her shoulders," I said, knotting my hands in my lap. "I thought she didn't need my guidance. My *mothering.* I don't know her, Marcus."

"Yes, you do." Marcus let go of the steering wheel to hunt for my hand in the darkness. He found it, squeezed it. "You know she'd do anything for Andy," he said. "Same as you."

Chapter Fifty

Andy

I OPENED MY EYES, BUT COULDN'T SEE ANYTHING. I BLINKED and blinked to be sure my eyes were really open. I thought I was going to barf. My brain was rolling around inside my head. The only other time I felt that way was on a boat. I could go in a boat on the sound, but not in the ocean. Last time I went on a boat in the ocean was with Emily and my brain rolled around inside my head the whole trip. I threw up three times and one almost time. Mom said I never had to go on a boat in the ocean again. Mom didn't like boats, anyway.

I knew I wasn't on a boat, though. I was in the house where I was a baby. I was on the couch. It was dark but I could see some things and it was kind of cold. And loud. Under me and over me I heard popping noises and screeching noises and creaking noises. I was afraid if I sat up, I'd throw up. But finally I did and there was no glass in the window. The sky was pink by the ocean. I couldn't see Maggie, but I heard her call my name.

All of a sudden I fell off the couch and my brain rolled and rolled and I couldn't remember where the bathroom was to run to throw up. Maggie said the bathroom didn't work anyway. I could hardly stand up. I had to hold on to a wood thing. And then I saw that I wasn't in the cottage anymore. I was on a kind of boat and big chunks of wood and things floated around me. Water went over my feet. The beach was far away. I forgot about throwing up. I started thinking about how to save our lives, because I knew we were in trouble and it wasn't like the fire where I could climb out a window.

"Maggie!" I hollered, and I ran across the floor trying to find her, as it bounced and broke apart beneath my feet.

Chapter Fifty-One

Laurel

THE PREDAWN LIGHT HAD CHANGED FROM COAL TO PALE GRAY by the time we turned off Sea Gull Lane onto the continuation of New River Inlet Road. Marcus's pickup rolled forward slowly in a foot of water. Between the oceanfront cottages, I could see the wash of pink above the horizon. Then I spotted the first of the condemned cottages behind those lining the street and heard Marcus suck in his breath.

"What?" I asked.

He shook his head.

I rolled down my window and saw what had caused his reaction. I knew where the second condemned house should be, but a pile of rubble stood in its place. The sliver of sun resting on the horizon glinted off shards of glass and metal.

"Oh, no." My heart kicked into gear.

"Is that Maggie's car?" Marcus braked the pickup so quickly, I flew forward a couple of inches before my seat belt caught. Parked on the opposite side of the street was the only other vehicle in sight—Maggie's white Jetta.

"Maybe they're in the car!" I jumped out of the pickup into water up to my knees and sloshed across the street. I shone my flashlight through the car windows. Empty.

"Anything?" Marcus called through his open window.

"No." I waded back to his pickup. "But Dawn must be right. Why else would Maggie park here, a block from The Sea Tender?"

We inched forward, passing another of the old condemned cottages that had been reduced to a pile of rubble. Had The Sea Tender—had my *children*—stood a chance?

"Let me out!" I said, pulling open the door. "I can't stand it!"

"Laurel—"

I didn't hear the rest of his sentence as I lost my footing and fell into the water. I got quickly to my feet, not bothering to close the pickup's door as I waded toward the space between two of the front row of houses. I needed to get to the beach. *Please, God, let my babies be okay.*

I was barely aware of Marcus catching up to me as we slogged through the water between the houses.

"Where's the little dune?" I searched the gray light ahead of me, thoroughly disoriented. The water was only up to our ankles here but I couldn't see the little rise of sand that marked the boundary between the front row of houses and those on the beach.

"I think it's gone," Marcus said.

We ran forward now that the water wasn't holding us back, and what I saw turned my knees to jelly. "Oh God, Marcus!" I grabbed the back of his shirt to keep myself from keeling over.

"Ah, no," Marcus said with such quiet resignation that I wanted to shake him.

In front of us, the beach looked like a war zone. None of the condemned houses were still standing; they'd been reduced to mountains of debris covering acres of sand, although many of the pilings still poked from the rubble, like totem poles against the lightening sky.

The Sea Tender had been the last house in the row and I needed to get to it. Although I felt weak and nauseated, I started running north.

"Be careful!" Marcus called from somewhere near me. "There's glass everywhere."

It was hard to tell one demolished house from another and when we reached the final pile of rubble, panic gripped me. "I'm turned around!" I said, searching the strange, unrecognizable beach for something familiar. The explosion of boards and glass and metal in front of me simply couldn't be The Sea Tender.

"Maggie!" Marcus called into the massive pile of debris as he circled it. "Andy!"

I stood frozen, my hands covering my face, afraid of seeing a lifeless arm or leg poking from the rubble. I peeked between my fingers to the deceptively calm ocean, littered with the remains of the cottages, and my eyes were suddenly drawn to the splashes of peach and purple above the horizon.

"Marcus, look!" I pointed toward the sunrise.

"Where?" He straightened up from the ruins. "What are you looking at?"

"There!" I kicked off my sodden shoes and started to run into the chilly water.

"Laurel, don't go out there!" He caught up to me, grabbing my arm. Then he saw what I'd seen. On a floating piece of debris, far in the distance, were two tiny silhouettes.

My children.

Chapter Fifty-Two

Maggie

AT FIRST I THOUGHT WE COULD SWIM, BUT AS WE PSYCHED ourselves up to jump from the floating wreckage, I caught Andy around his waist.

"We're too far, Andy," I said. The current was pulling us away from the beach more quickly than I'd realized, sucking us toward a blinding orange sun. The beach, lit up like pink gold, looked very far away. "We won't make it."

We lost our balance for the fourth or fifth time, dropping to our knees. I stared again at the beach. What choice did we have but to swim?

I had to think. I wasn't sure what part of the house we were kneeling on. It had been a bigger surface at first, but it had morphed into a Huck Finn–type raft, with a chunk of built-in bookshelf jutting up from one side of it. The floor of the living room, maybe. It didn't matter. Whatever it was, it kept breaking apart, leaving us with a smaller and smaller barrier between life and death. It wouldn't float forever.

"We can swim," Andy said. "We can pretend it's laps."

"But it's not," I said. "It's much colder than the pool, and a pool doesn't have a riptide. See how we're being pulled out to sea? That's what would happen to us if we tried to swim."

I was so scared. What if instead of saving my baby brother, I was killing him?

Another piece of our creaky raft broke away and Andy yelped as I pulled him tight against me. I watched the part of the flooring with the bookcase float away from us, then buckle and slip underwater. I was watching our fate.

"Are we going to drown?" Andy asked.

The pink beach seemed farther away than only a few seconds earlier. I grabbed Andy's shoulders and looked him in the eyes.

"Listen to me," I said. "We'll have to try to swim, but we have to stay together as much as we can. Don't lose sight of me and I won't lose sight of you. And listen! We can't swim straight toward the beach! Okay? Swim *parallel* to the beach."

"What's 'parell'?" He looked scared. He was picking up my own fear.

I let out a sob, surprising both of us. I brushed tears away with the back of my hand. "It means we'll swim in this direction." I pointed north.

"How will we get to the beach then?" His voice was so tiny.

What have I done? "Panda." I hugged him quickly. "I promise. We swim in that direction for a little bit and then we'll be able to swim to the beach. But you have to stay calm. Don't panic."

"You're not calm." His lower lip trembled.

"You know how you're supposed to pace yourself during a race?" I asked.

He nodded, even though I'd never once seen him pace himself.

"You've *got* to pace yourself this time, Andy." My voice cracked. "Please, Panda. Don't swim all-out, okay? Slow and steady, in that direction—" I pointed again "—and we can do it."

Andy's gaze had drifted from my face, and I suddenly saw the whole of the sun reflected in his brown eyes.

"Look!" He pointed behind me.

I turned in time to see a wall of water headed for us, rising out of a sea that was totally calm. I clutched Andy's arm, letting out a scream as the wave bore down on us. It tore us from our flimsy deck and ripped my brother from my hands.

I tumbled underwater like a gymnast through the air. I held my breath, my eyes open, searching the frothy, swirling water for Andy as the wave turned me in corkscrews. I couldn't see him. Panicking, I batted at the water as if I could clear it away from my face like a curtain.

"Andy!" I shouted into the ocean, water filling my mouth, my lungs.

I rose in slow motion to the crest of the wave. It felt like someone was lifting me up, carrying me. My lungs hurt as they sucked in the amazing pink air, and when I plummeted into the water again, I gave in. Gave up. Gave myself over to the sea.

Chapter Fifty-Three

Laurel

"I can't see them anymore!" I shouted to Marcus. I couldn't see him, either, but I knew he was searching the yards of the front row of houses for a boat or raft.

"What?" He appeared suddenly, running toward the water with a surfboard.

I pointed toward where we'd last seen Maggie and Andy. "They've disappeared!"

He stopped running to look toward the horizon.

"I don't know what happened!" I said. "I blinked and they were gone."

He headed for the water again, dropping the surfboard on the surface and starting to paddle.

"Let me go, too!"

"Stay here and keep trying the phone!" he shouted.

We'd been trying to get a signal with both of our phones ever since we got there. I lifted my phone to punch in 9-1-1 again with my cold, shaking fingers, but something caught my eye on the beach a good distance north of where I stood. People? A small figure, pink lit in the shallow water, nearly to the inlet. It couldn't possibly be one of my children. There was no way either of them could have swum to shore that quickly under the best of circumstances.

But whoever it was had dark hair and was very slight.

"Marcus, come back!" I shouted as I started running. The wet sand was like concrete beneath my bare feet. I tried to make sense of the tiny image on the beach. What was he or she doing? Not standing, that much was clear, and I ran faster. The sandpipers and gulls dashed out of my way. I'd never run so fast in all my life.

"Be careful, Laurel!" Marcus shouted from behind me. I heard his own thudding footsteps on the sand. I knew he was warning me about the debris scattered along the beach in front of me, but I wasn't going to slow down for shards of glass or rusty nails. I knew he wouldn't either.

Andy was getting to his feet in the wet sand, gentle waves lapping at his legs.

"Andy!" I waved my arms. He was alive! "Andy!"

He tugged at something in the water and it wasn't until I was nearly on him that I realized it was Maggie.

"Oh my God!" I ran into the chilly knee-high water, splashing it behind me.

"Mommy!" Andy lost his footing and sat down again. When I reached him, Maggie's head was in his lap.

"Maggie!" I dropped to my knees next to my children.

Andy was wheezing, his breath whistling above the soft murmur of the waves and his chest expanding and contracting like an accordion.

"Baby!" I grabbed his neck and kissed his forehead, but quickly turned my attention to Maggie.

"Is she all right?" Marcus dropped to the water next to us as Maggie started coughing. Her eyes were closed, her skin an icy blue, but she was alive.

She gasped, choking on salt water, and I rolled her head from Andy's lap to mine, turning her onto her side.

"Maggie, sweetie, it's Mom. You're okay, baby."

She hacked and coughed, but I wasn't sure she was conscious. She was a deadweight on my lap and an incoming wave washed over her face.

"Let's get her out of the water," I said.

"Is she breathing okay?" Marcus asked as we carried her a few feet higher on the beach, turning her onto her stomach.

Andy knelt next to her face. "Maggie!" he shouted. "Are you okay, Maggie?"

I saw blood on Andy's legs. "Andy, you're bleeding! Where are you hurt?"

Andy looked down at his legs. The blood appeared to be pouring from his knee.

"It's Maggie!" Marcus rolled her onto her back, and I saw what I had missed when we'd been sitting in the water: a deep cut on her neck, gushing blood onto the sand. Marcus lifted his T-shirt over his head and pressed it to the wound.

Maggie coughed, and we started to roll her over again, but she seemed to get her breathing under control.

"Maggie, sweetie, can you hear me?"

She mouthed something I couldn't understand.

"What, honey?" I leaned closer.

"Did you swim all the way from out there?" Marcus asked Andy incredulously.

"We didn't have to swim," Andy said. "A big wave came and lifted us way up." He reached his arms toward the sky.

Maggie whispered something again, her mouth moving soundlessly.

I leaned my ear against her lips, "What, Maggie?" I asked.

She mouthed the words silently, then cleared her throat. "It was Daddy," she said.

Chapter Fifty-Four

Maggie

SOMEONE HELD MY HAND. I THOUGHT IT MIGHT BE DADDY. My lungs burned when I breathed in. Everything hurt, especially my neck, and I wanted to reach up and touch the place that ached, but my arms were too heavy, and anyway, I didn't really care. My head seemed disconnected from the pain somehow. If heaven existed, did it feel like this? Floating above the pain, holding Daddy's hand? I thought it probably did.

"She's smiling," a man's voice said.

Uncle Marcus? I tried to open my eyes, but my eyelids were as heavy as my arms.

"Maggie?" *Mom.* It was Mom's hand holding mine.

I remembered the wave. I remembered losing Andy.

"Andy?" My eyelids flew open and I tried to sit up.

"Whoa." Uncle Marcus put his hands on my shoulders and lowered me down again.

"Not so fast, sweetie," Mom said.

I was in a strange white room. Mom was on my right, still holding my hand; Uncle Marcus was on my left, running his hand over my hair.

"I lost Andy," I said. My voice was raspy, not like my voice at all.

"Andy's fine," Mom said.

"I'm sorry!" I started to cry. "I lost him in the wave!"

"He's fine, Mags," Uncle Marcus said. "Don't cry. He'll come see you later."

My neck hurt. The pain cut through the floaty feeling in my head. I felt sick to my stomach and swallowed once. Twice. I was definitely not in heaven.

"You're in Cape Fear Hospital," Mom said. "You have a cut on your neck. It probably hurts a lot."

I nodded, my eyes shut. Andy was safe? Would they lie to me about something like that?

"Does it hurt to breathe?" Mom asked.

"Yes," I whispered.

"You're going to be fine," she said. "You and Andy were incredibly lucky."

"Is Ben here?" I opened my eyes again, squinting from the bright light in the room. I didn't care who knew about Ben now. I wanted him with me.

"No, Mags," Uncle Marcus said. "Just your mom and me."

"You said something about Daddy saving you," Mom said. "Helping you. What did you mean, sweetie?"

I closed my eyes again. I remembered the sense of calm I'd felt as the wave lifted me high in the air, but I was awake enough to know how crazy that would sound to Mom. How crazy it sounded even to me. I'd keep it to myself. "I don't know what you're talking about," I said.

Mom hesitated, and I thought she wasn't going to give up. "Okay," she said finally.

I suddenly remembered the whole reason I was there. "The hearing!" I said, trying to sit up again. "Is it—"

"Postponed." Mom held me down. "Don't think about that now."

I remembered Andy in The Sea Tender, telling me he'd gone outside to check for bugs during the lock-in.

"I need to talk to someone," I said.

"What you need is rest." Uncle Marcus rubbed my shoulder.

"No. *No.* I need to talk to Andy's lawyer. No! To the *police.* Right now."

"You have a lot of pain medication in you," Mom said. "It's not the time."

"Yes, it's time!" I insisted. "*Yesterday* was the time. Last *week* was the time. Last *month* was the time."

"Mags, what are you talking about?" Uncle Marcus asked.

I couldn't tell them. They might stop me from doing what I needed to do. What I should have done weeks ago.

"I'm awake," I said. "I'm not out of it, and I need to talk to the police now." I looked from my mother's face to Uncle Marcus's and saw their confusion. "*Now,*" I said again. "You've got to let me. Before I chicken out. I need to tell them what really happened."

"What do you mean, 'what really happened'?" Mom asked. She looked a thousand years old. "Did Andy tell you something?"

She was scared. Was she afraid I'd reveal something that would send Andy to prison for certain? I wondered if the same fear would be there if she knew that *I* was the one who was going to be locked up for good.

"You really should have a lawyer here," Uncle Marcus said for at least the tenth time, when Flip Cates finished reading me the Miranda Warning. I knew he'd asked Flip to come instead of that weird Sergeant Wood and I was glad. But no way was I waiting for a lawyer. I'd already waited an hour for Flip.

I shook my head—a mistake. The doctor had told me not to move my head or I might open the cut on my neck again. I touched the bandage lightly with my fingers. The cut burned and my whole body ached, but I refused to take any more pain medication until after I talked to Flip. I didn't want anyone to say that I wasn't in my right mind when I spoke to the police.

Mom stood up from her chair to check my bandage. "It's not bleeding," she said. "I wish you'd reconsider, Maggie. Maybe Mr. Shartell could just talk to you on the phone before you say anything."

"I can wait, Maggie," Flip said. He was sitting where Uncle Marcus had been earlier, and he'd put a tape recorder on the rolling table. Uncle Marcus stood at the end of my bed.

"I don't *want* to talk to him," I said again. Mom and Uncle Marcus had been badgering me about a lawyer ever since I said I wanted to talk to the police. "He'll spin things around until I don't understand what I'm saying myself. I want to tell what really happened the night of the fire."

My mother twisted her old wedding ring on her finger. "You can't cover for Andy, sweetie," she said.

I was surprised. "I'm not," I said. "He didn't know it, but he's been covering for *me* all this time." I looked at Flip. "Can we get started now?"

"Sure, Maggie," Flip said. "Do you want me to question you or would you rather just talk?"

"I'll just talk," I said.

"Okay, then." He did something with the tape recorder, moved it a little closer to me on the table. "Go ahead," he said.

I took a deep breath and began.

Chapter Fifty-Five

Maggie

WHEN YOU REALLY LOVE SOMEONE, WHEN THEIR JOY FEELS like your joy and their hurt like your hurt, it's both a wonderful and a terrible thing. That's how it was with Ben and me. I was like a living, breathing clump of empathy around him. I thought he was so amazing, inside and out. Always patient with the kids on the swim team. Always encouraging my baby brother. Believing in Andy the way I did. I loved Ben for that, and for his tenderness with me, and for the way he adored his daughter. For the way he kept trying to do well in the fire department when it was so hard and scary for him.

"When I was a little kid," he told me one night when we were in bed at The Sea Tender, "my father would punish me by locking me in a cupboard under our stairs. I felt like I was suffocating. I'd panic. I'd pound on the cupboard door, but no one would come."

I rubbed his arm as he spoke. I couldn't imagine a parent being that cruel.

"I didn't have any more problems with claustrophobia, though, until the first time I had to put on SCBA gear during my fire training," he said. "It was like I was five years old again and trapped in the cupboard. That's the way it is every time I put on the face piece. I can't seem to get past it. I've mastered everything else. Your uncle says to give it time, but I think it's getting worse instead of better."

I was amazed he'd tell me something so personal. He trusted me with a secret. It made me feel like I could trust him back. With *anything*.

A couple of weeks later, I was in Jabeen's with Amber and some other girls, back when I could still stand hanging around with them. We sat in a booth, and the next booth over had some of the volunteers from the fire department. Two men and a woman.

I looked up from my latte to see Ben walk in the door. He nodded to me and I nodded back. We were good at acting cool around each other, like we were the coaches of the swim team and nothing more.

"Hey," Ben said to the volunteers as he walked up to the counter where Sara was working.

"Hey," the volunteers said back to him.

He ordered a coffee to go. Amber was blathering on about Travis, but it was like a white noise in my ears because I was so focused on Ben, while trying not to *act* like I was focused on him.

As soon as Ben left Jabeen's, the volunteers burst out laughing. It took me a second to realize they were laughing at *Ben*. One of the guys cackled like a chicken.

"Chickenshit," he said.

"What a pussy," the other guy said.

My cheeks grew hot, and my heart broke. Just cracked apart inside my chest.

"I told Marcus, no way I'm going in with that FNG again," the woman said. "He ditched on me in that warehouse last week. Hyperventilatin' like a fool."

FNG. *Fucking new guy.* I knew more firehouse slang than was good for me.

"And Travis said if he ever, *ever* saw Marty touch me again, he'd castrate him," Amber was saying.

"If he can't hang," one of the guy volunteers said, "he needs to just keep his butt on the truck."

"Damn straight," said the other guy. "I'm not lettin' him screw with me in a fire."

"Shh!" The woman lowered her voice. "His girlfriend works here."

"Dawn? She ain't here now."

His girlfriend's sitting right behind you, you dork, I thought.

Ben had told me the other volunteers teased him because of his problem with the SCBA gear, but this was more than teasing. This was just plain vicious.

I'd never tell Ben what they said. Some girls might have thought less of their boyfriend, hearing stuff like that. It just made me want to help him more. To be a comfort to him.

He'd told me he was working hard on the claustrophobia problem. He had some workout equipment at home, and when he'd exercise, he'd sometimes put on the SCBA gear so he'd get more comfortable with it. He went to Washington, D.C., to take a special class in using SCBA. He did exercises to slow down his breathing: five seconds breathing in, five seconds breathing out. I wished those volunteers who were making fun of him could see how dedicated he was.

"I'm so ready," Ben told me one night when we were lying out on the beach. It was one of those strange warm nights that could pop up for no reason in winter. We'd made love on the beach, and now we were cuddling together, wrapped in a quilt. "I told Marcus I can do it now," he said. "Not sure he believes me, though. I just need a chance to prove myself."

A few weeks went by without a fire where he'd need the SCBA gear. Then a couple more. I knew the other volunteers were being cold to him. Freezing him out. Ben was torn up about it, and I started hating some of them.

One day in March, he called me upset because someone had stolen his pager while he was in the shower. Whoever it was left a note in its place, saying something like, *we're taking your pager out of self-defense.*

"I'm thinking of leaving," Ben said to me on the phone.

"What do you mean?" I was afraid I knew. I was in my car coming up to the only stoplight in Surf City, and I turned left, sailing right through the red. Didn't even realize it until a few seconds after I turned.

"I could go back to Charlotte," he said. "Be closer to my daughter. Join the fire department there where I could start fresh. I love the beach, but this abuse is getting to me."

"Please don't go!" I was having my own sort of panic attack. I stepped on the brake and pulled to the side of the road so I could concentrate on talking. I'd die if he left.

"I know," he said. "I'd hate leaving you. You're the best thing about being here."

"Then don't leave!" I wondered if I could still get into UNC-Charlotte for the fall. It was too far away, though. Too far from Andy.

"I won't make a decision for a week or two," he said, sighing. He sounded really tired. "I'll have to see how this mess plays out. I just wanted to let you know what I'm thinking."

So, I came up with a way to make the "mess play out." Drury Memorial was going to be demolished and rebuilt in a couple of years, so what would be the big deal if it burned down? In the back of my mind, I knew it was a crime. No one would be hurt, though. If anything, I'd be helping ol' Reverend Bill get his new church faster. And I'd be giving Ben a chance to shine.

Ben had told me about a church that burned down in Wilmington, and I remembered he said the arsonist used a mixture of gasoline and diesel and hadn't been caught yet. I figured if I used the same mix, the investigators would think it was the same arsonist.

I wasn't sure how much fuel I'd need or how to get it without attracting attention. I got a couple of those big plastic gas containers at Lowes. Then, a few nights before I planned to burn the church, I drove to two different gas stations outside of Wilmington where no one would recognize me. I got the gas at one station and the diesel at the other. No one said a word to me. I kept the containers in my trunk.

I waited for the right time. That Saturday night, I knew Ben was going to Daddy Mac's for dinner with a couple of guys, so he'd be right near the station. When the call went out, he could get there fast and be on the first truck. I was all set. I had to time it right, though. I had to wait until it was dark enough that no one would see me pouring the fuel, but not so late that Ben had gone home already. I thought I could pull it off. I felt pretty calm about the whole thing.

Then Mom asked me to give Andy a ride to the lock-in that night.

"I'm going over to Amber's to study," I said as I loaded the dishwasher. I *did* plan to go to Amber's as soon as I'd set the fire. That way, I'd have an alibi if I ever needed one.

"Well, you can drop Andy off on your way," Mom said. "I need to work on a speech."

"It's not exactly on my way," I said. To be honest, I'd totally forgotten about the lock-in, even though I was the one to talk Mom into letting Andy go to it. Did I really want to burn down a church less than a block from the youth building where a bunch of kids would be hanging out? I wasn't worried about the youth building catching on fire. It was far enough away. I just didn't want to freak out the kids—especially not Andy. But I already had everything planned so perfectly. And who knew how fast Ben was going to make his decision about moving back to Charlotte?

"I'll take him," I said.

That sudden change in my plans, though, made my nerves start to act up.

Around seven-fifteen, I called Ben on his cell.

"Hey." I tried to sound normal. I could hear restaurant noise in the background. Talking. Glasses clinking.

"Hey," he said. "What's up?"

"You still at Daddy Mac's?"

"Uh-huh. Where are you?"

"Home. I'm going over to Amber's to study. You gonna be able to talk later?"

"I expect so. I'll call you?"

I was trying to figure out how to casually ask him how much longer he'd be at Daddy Mac's. I couldn't think of a way other than just blurting it out.

"What time are you leaving there?" I asked.

"Oh, we'll probably be another forty minutes. Maybe an hour. Why?"

"Just making conversation." That didn't give me much time to work. "I'll let you get back to dinner. Later?"

"Later."

I got off the phone with my mind ready to explode. This wasn't going to work. The lock-in didn't start till eight. Ben would probably be gone by the time I set the church on fire. I'd just have to drop Andy off early at the lock-in. That was the only way.

When Andy and I pulled up in front of the youth building, it was so early that none of the other kids were there yet.

"You can't drop me off without other kids being here!" Andy shouted when I told him to get out.

"I can see an adult inside," I said, giving him a nudge. Through the youth building window, I saw Mr. Eggles with his back to us. I recognized him by his ponytail. "Go ahead. You'll be fine."

"I'm not going until kids are here and that's that." Andy folded his arms across his chest and wouldn't budge.

I didn't have time to argue with him. I'd just have to pour the gasoline mixture with Andy in the car. I made up my story as I drove down the block.

"I have to do something at the church," I said. "So you can wait in the car and then I'll take you back to the lock-in." I was really jumpy now. How was I going to make this work? I couldn't *light* the fire with Andy in the car, so I'd pour the gasoline, drive him back to the lock-in, then go back and toss a match on the fuel. I just hoped Ben stayed as long as he said at Daddy Mac's. If he wasn't on the first truck, the fire could be out by the time he got there.

I pulled up around the corner from the church and turned off my car.

"You stay here," I said. "I have to pour some insecticide around the church. They have a bad bug problem and they asked me to—"

"What kind of bugs?"

"I don't know, Andy." I reached for the door handle. "Just stay here."

"Is it ants? Or bees? Or those crepe paper wasps like we had by the deck?"

"Paper," I said.

"What?"

"Just paper wasps. Not crepe paper wasps."

"Is it cockroaches?"

"It's all kinds of bugs!" I said.

"I'll help you." He started to get out of the car.

"No!" Perspiration was dripping down my back beneath my T-shirt and jacket. "Just stay here. And listen." I grabbed his shoulder and turned him to face me. "This is a secret. The person who asked me to pour the insecticide told me never to tell anyone about it because the people who go to the church would freak out if they knew there were bugs."

"But bugs are *interesting*," Andy said. He opened the car door and hopped out before I could stop him. "I want to help."

It would be quicker to let him help than to argue with him about it. I opened my trunk and got out the two containers. My hands shook so hard I could hear the gasoline sloshing around. I'd brought latex gloves with me to keep my fingerprints off the containers, but only one pair. I gave Andy some tissues to use to hold the second container with.

"Be very careful not to touch the container without the tissues," I whispered, even though there was no one anywhere around. "The insecticide could hurt you if you get it on yourself."

"Right," he said. "Even though I'm not a bug."

"Right."

We started walking toward the church. I had on flip-flops because I planned to just throw them away after in case I left footprints. I didn't think about Andy's shoes. I just wasn't thinking, period. "You pour on this side, right where the ground and the building come together, okay? Make sure to get every single inch. I'll pour on the other side."

"Every single inch," he repeated.

"And remember, don't touch the bottle. And be careful not to splash any on you."

Now my entire body was shaking. I started pouring. It was dark, but I could tell I was pouring on top of crisp pine straw. It would catch right away when I lit it. The smell was so strong. I turned my head away to inhale, then held my breath as long as I could while I poured. Then I turned away for fresh air again and worked my way down the side of the church like that. I hoped Andy wasn't passing out on his side.

The air-conditioning unit was right up against the building, so close that I couldn't pour the fuel behind it. No problem. With all that pine straw, a few feet without gasoline wouldn't matter.

Andy walked around to my side of the church just as I finished up. "I ran out," he said.

"Me, too."

We walked back to the car. Thank God that part was over! I put the containers in a big trash bag I'd brought with me. Stuck my flip-flops in there, too, then put the bag back in my trunk. I'd brought sandals to change into and I slipped them on before getting into the car.

Andy was already back in the passenger seat.

"Okay!" I tried to sound cheerful. "You ready for your very first lock-in?"

"If the other kids are there," he said.

"I think they will be by now." At least the early birds. "Remember what I told you about the insecticide," I said as I pulled away from the curb.

"What?"

"What did I say about telling anyone?"

"It's a secret. Because the people would freak out."

"Excellent!" I said.

There were other kids in the youth building now. Andy spotted Emily Carmichael, which made him forget he'd felt shy a few minutes earlier. He ran out of the car without even saying goodbye.

I drove down the block to the church again, but just sat in my car with the box of matches on my lap. *It's okay to do this,* I told myself. *They're going to demolish it soon anyway.* I thought of the old houses the fire department sometimes burned down to train the firefighters. How was this any different?

I decided I'd better drive over to Daddy Mac's, though, to make sure Ben's van was still in the parking lot. I was stalling, but I convinced myself I had to make sure as I drove to the restaurant.

Ben's white van was parked right smack in front of the entrance. I felt disappointed. I didn't realize until that second that I'd wanted the van to be gone to save me from my crazy plan. But it was still there, and I could see it all playing out in my imagination. The fire starting. Someone calling the department. Ben reaching for his pager. Ben racing down the street to the fire station, climbing on the truck. He'd be so excited. A little scared, but ready to show the other guys that he was one of them now. That he could be trusted.

It was like a movie in my mind as I drove toward the church. I decided to park over by Jabeen's, which closed at six. That way, I could walk to the church, set the fire, and run down the block in the dark with nobody noticing me.

I got out of my car and tossed the bag with the containers and flip-flops into the Dumpster behind Jabeen's. Then I realized if anyone found the containers, they'd also have my flip-flops, so I reached into the Dumpster, got the bag and just tossed the containers back in. My flip-flops I threw in the trash can out front along with the wadded-up bag.

I started walking to the church, but I suddenly saw a ton of kids around the youth building, which was completely dark. What was going on? I stuck the box of matches in my jacket pocket and headed toward the youth building. The kids were starting to walk in my direction and I was totally flustered. I found Andy and pulled him aside.

"What's going on?" I asked.

"The lights went out," he said. "We're going to the church instead."

I couldn't believe my relief! I felt it from the top of my head to my toes. I didn't have to do it! Now I *couldn't* do it, even if I wanted to. It was like some crazy girl had planned the whole thing and expected me to pull it off for her. I was free!

I ran back to my car and started driving toward Amber's, but I suddenly felt sick to my stomach. I pulled into the driveway of a deserted house, opened my car door, and threw up in the sand.

Then I knew where I wanted to go. It was Daddy I needed, not Amber.

I headed for The Sea Tender.

Chapter Fifty-Six

Laurel

I COULD BARELY BREATHE FOR THE TEARS. AS MAGGIE SPOKE, I wanted to leave so she wouldn't see me fall apart. At the same time, I wanted to gather her in my arms and tell her everything would be all right. I chose to stay because the thought that ran through my mind as she told her story was, *Where was this girl's mother?*

How had I missed all the signs? How could I not have known that she was sneaking out of the house in the middle of the night? That she rarely was where she told me she would be? That she was not only in harm's way, but capable of *doing* harm? Where had I *been?*

I knew the answer, of course: I was with Andy. Letting Maggie fend for herself, as I had since her birth. I wiped my cheeks with my hand.

"Are you saying you felt like two different people?" Marcus asked Maggie, when she seemed to be finished speaking. "The crazy girl and you?"

"You mean like a split personality?" Maggie crossed her arms, tucking her hands beneath them as if they were cold. "No," she said. "It was all me."

Flip, Marcus and I exchanged looks. I knew what we were all thinking, and Flip finally put it into words. "But you ultimately *did* light the fire, Maggie, correct?" he asked.

"No!" Maggie started to shake her head, then seemed to remember the wound on her neck. "That's what I'm trying to explain," she said, touching the bandage. "When I realized the kids were going to be there, I just forgot about it. I would never set fire to a building with people in it!"

Flip didn't believe her. His expression didn't change, but the flat look in his eyes betrayed him.

I reached for Maggie's hand, prying it from beneath her arm. Her hand *was* cold and I held it between both of mine to warm it. I remembered how Maggie had held my hand as we rode together to the hospital after the fire. How she didn't want to let go of me. And I remembered her shock—her *genuine* shock—when I called to tell her the church was on fire.

"So, after you spoke with Andy, you drove directly to The Sea Tender?" Flip asked.

"Yes. And I called Mom to tell her the lock-in was moved to the church."

Flip looked at me.

"She did," I said. "But you were at Amber's then, weren't you?"

"You thought I was, but I wasn't."

"Do you recall hearing anything in the background when Maggie called?" Flip asked me.

"No." I'd been working on a speech for a meeting with a teachers' organization and remembered little of the call other than that the lock-in had been moved. That had worried me—that the change might be confusing for Andy.

"What did you do at The Sea Tender?" Marcus asked Maggie.

"I..." Maggie looked toward the end of the bed, where the covers bulged a little over a bandaged toe—her only other real injury.

With her free hand, she brushed a nonexistent lock of hair from her forehead. I had the feeling she was stalling. "I sat on the deck for a while," she said. "I was…I felt like I'd dodged a bullet or something."

"Did anyone see you there?"

"It was…you know. Still March. No one was in the houses."

Flip shifted in his chair, folding his arms across his chest. "So how *did* the fire start?" he asked.

"I don't know." Tears filled her eyes. "Honest, I don't. All I know is that I didn't start it. And neither did Andy."

"Let's take a break," Marcus said, and I was relieved. Maggie had been stoic and brave throughout the past hour. Now, though, she was beginning to crumble. I wasn't doing too well, myself.

Flip clicked off the tape recorder and stood up. "Good idea," he said. "I could use a cup of coffee."

"I'll join you." Marcus got to his feet as well. "You all right, Maggie?" he asked.

She gave a little nod, not looking at him. Not looking at any of us.

"Coming with us, Laurel?" Marcus asked. I supposed he and Flip wanted me to join them so we could discuss all we'd heard, but I wasn't leaving.

I shook my head, still holding Maggie's hand. "I'll stay here," I said.

Once the men left the room, Maggie began crying for real.

"I'm sorry, Mom!" she said, gripping my hand. "I'm so sorry for everything."

"Shh," I said. "I know."

"I'm so relieved, though!" she said. "I'm so…I should have told the truth as soon as people started thinking Andy did it."

Yes, she should have. But she didn't. "You've told us now," I said. "That's the important thing."

"There's more," she said. "I mean, not so big. It's big, but not like that. Like the fire. And it'll only matter to you. It's about The Sea Tender."

"I know you've been meeting Ben there."

She shook her head. "Not just that," she said. "I've been going there ever since I got my driver's license. My permit, actually. Alone, I mean. Not with…a boy or anything."

"*Why?*" I asked. I remembered Dawn telling me she smoked marijuana. Did she go there to do drugs?

"You're going to think I'm crazy. Or crazier than you already think I am."

"I don't think you're crazy."

"I felt close to Daddy there. Sometimes I'd sit on the deck at night and I'd close my eyes and suddenly feel like he was there. His spirit or something."

I felt a chill. I could almost feel Jamie in the room with us.

"Do you think I'm deranged?"

"If you are, insanity must run in the family, because I've dreamed he's…visited me at night sometimes, too."

Her pretty brown eyes opened wide. "Honest? Do you really think it's him?"

"I have no idea, Maggie. I just think he left a mark on both of us—in different ways, of course—and we must both have a need to stay attached to him."

She suddenly stopped crying, looking right at me. "I'm sorry about how I laid that whole Daddy and Sara thing on you. That was so mean."

"It hurt, finding that out," I acknowledged. That pain already seemed weeks old instead of hours, usurped by a more immediate heartache. "It helps me understand how you must be feeling about Ben right now, though."

She turned her head toward the window. In her eyes, I saw the rectangular reflection of sunlight.

"If he cared about me, he'd be here with me," she said. "At the hospital. Wouldn't he?"

I thought that even if Ben *did* care about her, he was wise to stay away from Marcus and me right now.

"I think he would be," I said.

"Do you think Ben was really…you know, *with* Dawn the same time he was with me?"

"Yes, sweetie, I do." I remembered Dawn at her house the night before, wrapping her satiny little robe over those long legs as she swept into the living room. *Who's here, Benny?*

"I trusted him totally. I loved him so much. I still do."

"I know it hurts."

She turned back to me. "Aren't you totally *furious* with Sara?"

I sighed. I *was* furious. That was something I'd have to deal with on my own, though. "It was so long ago, Maggie," I said. "And there are things I did that I regret from long ago, too."

"Drinking."

"That's for sure. Other things, as well. I guess most people do things when they're young that they come to regret. Sara and I have been friends for so long. I hope we can find a way to put it behind us." I thought of Keith's injuries. How could Sara ever forgive my daughter? In her place, I wasn't sure I could.

"Mom, I just hurt so much!" she said. "I want to erase everything. The fire. Ben. Everything!"

"I'd love it if you could wipe all of that from your memory," I said. "But you know what your father said to me one time?"

"What?"

"You know that my parents died when I was little, and then my aunt and uncle cut me out of their lives, right?"

"Yeah."

"I tried, especially with my parents, not to think about them. To just keep going on with my life. Moving forward. Never looking back. And when I told your daddy that, he said that if you don't think about your losses, they'd come back to bite you."

"Bite you?" Maggie smiled. "That's his exact words?"

"Yes, because I've never forgotten them, even if I haven't always followed his advice. He meant that sometimes you just have to go through the pain."

"So did you try to think about them?" she asked. "Your parents?"

"Not until I was in rehab. I cried buckets about them then. But the thing I learned was that you don't just get over one loss and then you're home free. Life keeps tossing them at you, and you have to learn how to handle them. How to keep going. Ben won't be your last heartbreak, honey. But there'll be wonderful experiences to make up for the hard times."

My own eyes teared up at the thought of the hard times ahead of her. She read my mind.

"Will Andy still have a hearing?"

"I don't know how that works, but he won't be going to jail."

"But I will be, won't I." It was a statement, not a question.

"I'm going to find an excellent lawyer for you. And I'll be by your side the whole time, Maggie. I will." I'd been so strong for her brother for fifteen years. I wanted to be strong for her, now. Finally.

"I'm sorry for not being a better mother for you. You were so independent and Andy so dependent, that I sometimes forgot you needed me as much as he did."

"I didn't, though," she said. "But I think I really do need you now." She licked her lips and looked squarely into my eyes. "I know it looks like I set the fire, Mom," she said. "I could tell Flip totally didn't believe me."

"No, I don't think he does. But I believe you."

"You do?"

I smiled. "Absolutely, sweetheart."

There was so much I didn't know about my daughter. At this point, I barely felt certain she wouldn't burn a church with children inside. But one thing I did know with absolute certainty: she would never burn a church with *Andy* in it.

Chapter Fifty-Seven

Marcus

ONE MORE TIME, I WAS IN A HOSPITAL ROOM, THIS ONE HOT-ter than blazes. I'd driven to Chapel Hill to tell Sara about Maggie's confession; it was the kind of thing I didn't want to say on the phone. I wasn't sure about telling her with Keith there, but decided he had a right to know. Maybe a bigger right than any of us. I just didn't want to be there when his rage hit. He'd been pissed off enough when he thought it was Andy who started the fire. When he found out it was Maggie, who had no mental handicap to use as an excuse…well, I wanted to be anyplace else.

But there I was, standing at the end of the bed while Sara adjusted the bulky bandage on the left side of Keith's face.

"Maggie was having a relationship with Ben Trippett," I began.

"No," Sara argued, as though I had no idea what I was talking about. "Ben was with Dawn."

"It looks like he was involved with both of them," I said.

"Oh, no." She sat down in the chair next to Keith's bed. "Poor Dawn."

"Maggie didn't realize he was still seeing Dawn, though." I came to my niece's defense. I had the feeling I'd be doing a lot of that in the coming days. "He told her they'd broken up."

Sara frowned. "That's horrible," she said. "And I thought Ben was so nice."

"Why are we talking about Maggie's pathetic love life?" Keith muttered. His right eye was squinched shut and he looked like he was in pain. Lines on his forehead. A deep crease in the peeling red skin between his eyebrows.

I went on to tell them how Ben was getting ragged on by the other firefighters for his claustrophobia. How Maggie had wanted to help him and how she'd been afraid he'd leave town if she didn't. I said it all without emotion because my whole body felt like it'd gotten a massive shot of Novocain. I was numb all over. I couldn't even get my lungs working right. It was hard to pull air in and out. I *still* couldn't wrap my mind around Maggie doing it.

Neither could Sara, apparently. She wasn't getting it.

"What does this have to do with the fire?" she asked.

I shifted from one numb foot to the other. Folded my arms across my chest. "Ben thought he finally had the claustrophobia thing under control," I said, "but he needed a fire to prove himself. So—"

"You're not saying *Maggie* set the fire?" Sara asked.

I nodded. "She confessed to it. But she didn't mean for the kids to be there," I added quickly. "Remember, the lock-in wasn't—"

"I just don't believe it!" Sara interrupted me. "Maggie wouldn't do something like that. Could she be protecting Ben? Maybe he set it and she's taking the fall?"

"Maggie wanted to help him," I repeated. "She was so...hooked on him. So nuts about him. She wasn't thinking straight."

Sara's face went white. She clasped a hand over her mouth like she was holding in a scream.

"She poured fuel around the church," I said. "Andy helped her because…it's a long story, but he didn't know what he was doing. That's how his prints got on the gas container."

"Oh my God," Sara nearly whispered. "I just can't picture it. Little Miss Perfect. How could she hurt so many people?"

I couldn't picture it either, and yet everything about Maggie's story fit into place like the pieces of a jigsaw puzzle. All except her denial that she didn't light the fire. It was like she looked up the law on the internet and learned the charges against her wouldn't be as bad if she didn't actually burn the building down. I talked to her till I was blue in the face, trying to get her to own up to it, but she wouldn't. I believed her because she was Maggie. And I didn't believe her, because that part of her story just plain didn't hold together.

"I don't think she meant to hurt anyone," I said.

"How can you *say* that? She burned down the church!" Sara had found her voice and, with it, her anger. The pallor in her face was gone now. Her cheeks were splotched with red, and I knew that, in a split second, she'd gone from loving Maggie to despising her. "She *killed* people!" she shouted.

"She swears she didn't ignite the fuel," I said. "She said once she saw the lock-in was moved to the church, she gave up the whole plan."

"Oh, right," Sara snapped. "Spontaneous combustion."

"I know," I said. "I don't know what to make of it either."

Keith had gone quiet in the last minute or so, and when I glanced at him, I saw tears running down his unbandaged cheek.

"Oh, baby!" Sara leaned forward, mopping his face with a tissue. "Oh, honey."

"I thought it was all *my* fault." Keith was just about sobbing. "I thought *I* did it."

"What do you mean?" Sara asked. "How on earth could it have been your fault?"

It took a few seconds for him to catch his breath. "I was on the back porch of the church, getting ready to have a smoke," he said. "I lit my cigarette, and when I threw the match on the ground, flames shot up. *Massive* flames. They blocked the back steps, so I ran back inside and then I was stuck in the fire, like everybody else. I thought it was my fault."

"Oh, Keith." Sara tried to hug his quivering shoulders. With the gigantic stiff bandages on his arms and hands, it must have felt like holding a block of wood. She pressed her face against his and I watched their tears mix together. "My poor baby," she said. "All this time you were thinking you did it? It wasn't your fault, honey. Not at all."

I stood there watching, letting Keith's words sink in. Sometimes relief feels like a trickle from a faucet. Other times, it's a tidal wave. *This* was a tidal wave. My eyes burned. I could suddenly feel my arms. My legs. My lungs moved air in and out. My heartbeat was rock steady.

Maggie'd been telling the truth! There wasn't much to celebrate about the whole damn mess, but just then, I felt like shouting for joy.

I called Flip from my pickup and told him to get someone up to Chapel Hill to take Keith's statement. Then I stepped on the gas. I wanted to get back to Cape Fear. To the hospital and Laurel and Maggie. I wanted to see Andy. To see where we went from here.

People asked me why I'd never settled down. Never started a family. "Not my thing," I'd say. Or "Just haven't met the right woman." I'd dated a fair amount. Lots of one-night stands. A few three-month-long relationships. Some six months. A couple lasted a year. But there was one good reason why I'd never settled down. Never started a family. I already had one.

Epilogue

Six months later
Andy

I SIT ON THE BENCH AT THE POOL WAITING FOR MY TURN. I don't like swimming as much as I used to. I don't win as much now that my startling reflex is gone, but Mom says I have to swim until Christmas. Then I can quit. Our new coach, KiKi, is a girl. Ben went to live with his wife in Charlotte. I cried at first because I missed him, but now I don't remember what he looked like. Mom said I got so upset because he left right after Maggie did. It was like losing two people at once, she said.

I like a new girl on my swim team, so I watch her swim the butterfly that she does better than anyone. Uncle Marcus says I have to be extra careful about personal space now that I'm getting older. He's not careful about it at all, though. Right now he's sitting on the bleachers with his arm around Mom. Sometimes they kiss. The first time I saw them kiss I said, "Yuck! What are you *doing?*" Mom said I better get used to it, that there would be a lot more kissing from now on. But she meant her and Uncle Marcus. Not me. I'm not supposed to kiss anybody that's not family.

I get to see Maggie every month. I like seeing her but not at the prison because the people are scary. Like the lady with the spider tattoos on her neck. Maggie shouldn't be with them. She's the best person and I won't ever get why she has to be there. At least, I don't get why me and my friend Keith aren't there with her. Me and Maggie put the bug spray which was really car gas around the church. Keith threw a match and made it burn. If me and Maggie and Keith all had something to do with the fire, I don't know why only Maggie is in jail, but that is what happened.

At night sometimes I think about how I can sneak her out. I told her about that the last time I went there and she laughed. "Oh, Panda, you're a goofball!" She got real serious then and told me she belongs where she is. "I'll get a second chance at life, but the three people who died in the fire only got one," is what she said.

I have a big calendar on my corkboard wall, and every day I cross off is one day closer to having her home.

Then she can start her second chance.

Laurel

They took my daughter from me the week before her eighteenth birthday. They convicted her of attempted arson and obstruction of justice, and her lawyer was able to get involuntary manslaughter charges dropped. She was incredibly brave.

She'd done something terrible. Insane. I thought she needed counseling instead of incarceration, but it was not my opinion that mattered. I worry what she'll be like at the end of twelve months in prison. How will she be different? The only thing I'm sure of is that I will be a very different sort of mother. I plan to smother her with love. She'll be nineteen, but she'll still be my beautiful little girl. And once I have her back in my arms, I'll never, ever, let her go.

Acknowledgments

ON MY FIRST RESEARCH TRIP TO TOPSAIL ISLAND, I STUMBLED into a realty office to ask directions. When Realtor Lottie Koenig heard my name, she told me she loved my books and gave me a hug. That was my introduction to the friendly people who call Topsail Island home. Lottie gave me a tour of the island and hooked me up with another valuable resource, fellow Realtor and longtime Topsail Island resident Patsy Jordan. In turn, Patsy introduced me to Anna Scott, one of the few teens on the island. Anna gave me a wealth of information about what life would be like for the teenagers in *Before the Storm*. I'm grateful to these three women for their help and enthusiasm.

Thank you to special friends Elizabeth and Dave Samuels and Susan Rouse for generously allowing me to use their Topsail Island homes as I did my research.

I could not have written this story without the help of Ken Bogan, Fire Marshal of the Town of Surf City's fire department. Ken went out of his way to give me an understanding of my firefighting characters, instruct me in arson investigation and much, much more. Ken and his wife, Angie, also introduced me to Sears Landing Grill, where I arrived armed with a list of forty-five questions for them to answer over dinner. They answered them all and would have answered another forty-five had I asked.

Thank you, Ken and Angie! Thanks also to these other Surf City firefighters: Tim Fisher, Kevin "Butterbean" Head and Bill Lindsey.

I found several excellent resources on Fetal Alcohol Spectrum

Disorder, but none better than Jodee Kulp, an FASD activist, author and mother of a daughter with FASD. The Best That I Can Be, a book Jodee wrote with her daughter, Liz, was a huge help to me in understanding Andy. Jodee not only answered my questions, but read Andy's first chapter to make sure I was on target with his character.

For helping me understand the legal and juvenile justice system, I'm indebted to attorneys Barrett Temple and Evonne Hopkins, as well as to Gerry McCoy.

I kept Ray McAllister's book, Topsail Island: Mayberry by the Sea, close at hand as I wrote. It's an excellent, lovingly written treat for anyone wanting to read further about the Island.

In a raffle sponsored by the North Carolina Writers' Network, Jabeen Akhtar won the right to have her name mentioned in Before the Storm. I hope she's happy I named a coffee shop after her!

Although some of the places mentioned in Before the Storm do exist, Jabeen's Java, Drury Memorial Church and The Sea Tender are, like the characters themselves, figments of my imagination.

I'm also grateful to the following people for their various contributions:

Sheree Alderman, Trina Allen, Brenda Burke-Cremeans, BJ Cothran, Valerie Harris, Christa Hogan, Pam "bless your heart" Lloyd, Margaret Maron, Lynn Mercer, Marge Petesch, Glenn Pierce, Emilie Richards, Sarah Shaber, Meg Skaggs, David Stallman, MJ Vieweg, Brittany Walls, Brenda Witchger, Ann Woodman and my friends at ASA.

Thanks to the readers of my blog, especially Margo Petrus, for inspiring this book's title.

Finally, I often hear that agents and editors are so busy that they can't take the time to help their authors create the best books possible. That certainly is not true in my case. Thank you to my agent, Susan Ginsburg, and my editor, Miranda Stecyk, for their skill, wisdom, commitment and passion. You two are the best!

READER DISCUSSION QUESTIONS

1. Empathy is a theme that runs throughout the book. Jamie's mother talked about him having the "gift" of extreme empathy, being able to feel what others were feeling. Do you believe that some people have this gift and, if so, do you believe that Jamie had it? Maggie? Why or why not?

2. Discuss Maggie's feeling that she could connect to her father's spirit. Do you think she believed he was coming to her from "the other side"? How did her connection to him influence her actions? How did it influence her relationships with Laurel, Ben and Marcus?

3. Even though Andy was clearly the favored child, Maggie seemed to love him unconditionally and without resentment. Why do you think this was?

4. Maggie was an honors student with college plans and a bright future. What in her upbringing and personality allowed her to achieve so much? What in her upbringing and personality contributed to her falling so far?

5. Speculate as to why Jamie and Marcus were treated differently by their parents and the impact that treatment had on them and their relationship.

6. Were you able to remain sympathetic to Laurel during her post-partum depression and alcoholism? What other emotions did you feel toward her?

7. Do you think Laurel ever doubted Andy's innocence? What do you think played into her assumptions and emotions? Could you relate to her desire to tamper with evidence to protect him? What would you have done in her place? Did you have doubts about his innocence yourself? Why or why not?

8. After learning that Keith had called Andy a "little rich boy," Laurel worried that Sara might resent her wealth. Do you think Sara was resentful of Laurel? Discuss the dynamics in their friendship and how they changed—or didn't change—over the years.

9. Which characters garnered the most sympathy from you? How did your feelings about Andy, Maggie, Laurel and Marcus change throughout the story?

10. In your opinion, should Andy be told about his relationship to Keith? What are your feelings about family secrets?